HASIDISM AS MYSTICISM

RIVKA SCHATZ UFFENHEIMER

HASIDISM AS MYSTICISM

Quietistic Elements in Eighteenth Century Hasidic Thought

Translated from the Hebrew by Jonathan Chipman

PRINCETON UNIVERSITY PRESS, PRINCETON, NEW JERSEY
THE MAGNES PRESS, THE HEBREW UNIVERSITY, JERUSALEM

Published with the assistance of
The Louis and Minna Epstein Fund
of the American Academy for Jewish Research

First Published in the U.S.A. by
PRINCETON UNIVERSITY PRESS,
41 William Street
Princeton, N.J. 08540–5237

And in the United Kingdom, by Princeton University Press, Chichester, West Sussex

Princeton University Press books are printed on acid-free paper, and meet the guidelines for permanence and durability of the Committee on Production Guidelines for Book Longevity of the Council on Library Resources.

Printed in Israel
Typesetting: Keterpress Enterprises, Jerusalem
Printing: Graph-Chen Press, Jerusalem

Library of Congress Cataloging-in-Publication Data

Schatz Uffenheimer, Rivka.
[Ḥasidut ke-mistiḳah. English]
Hasidism as mysticism: quietistic elements in eighteenth century hasidic thought/Rivka Schatz Uffenheimer: translated from the Hebrew by Jonathan Chipman.
p. cm.
Includes bibliographical references and indices.
ISBN 0-691-03223-8
1. Hasidism–History–20th century. 2. Quietism. 3. Cabala. 4. Dov Baer, of Mezhirech, d. 1772.
5. Mysticism–Judaism.
I. Title.
BM198.S29713 1993 — 92-31378
296.8′332—dc20 — CIP

To my beloved husband Binyamin

Contents

Foreword

The present work is an attempt to examine a number of spiritual problems involved in the eighteenth century Hasidic movement. Numerous historical studies, monographs and memoirs have been written concerning this movement, which originated towards the end of the first half of the eighteenth century, but hardly anything has been written concerning the phenomenology of Hasidism from a philological-historical viewpoint. No accounting on a theoretical level has been rendered to date of this highly significant movement in our history.

The Hasidic movement was borne upon the successive waves of crises involving Sabbatianism, Frankism, Enlightenment, Zionism, and the confrontation with external challenges, each one of which was a unique chapter unto itself. While some dim light has been shed upon these chapters, our knowledge of the internal history of Hasidism of its first hundred and fifty years, both from a social and from a theological viewpoint, is extremely fragmentary.

It is no longer possible to accept the approach of "erecting monuments to the memory of Hasidism" as one answering the needs of the present. The emotionalist element underlying this kind of writing, whether deliberate or unintentional, destroys the capacity for understanding and evaluation, and often obscures problems rather than illumines them. It may be that the historical distance and social changes occurring in our own generation will contribute to the balancing of our judgment and raising the standards suitable for such an evaluation.

There are a number of objective difficulties standing in the way of the contemporary scholar in this field, with regard to the literary-historical aspect. First, the sources are written as homilies, thus constituting a problem in their own right. Second, one confronts here the problem of the unique Hasidic terminology, composed of all the various layers of Jewish culture, including that of Kabbalah. In order to distinguish the terminological innovation of Hasidism, one needs to discern how it differed from that which came before it: there is at present no existing lexicon which can serve as a guide for those wishing to study this subject. The only Hasidic source which has appeared in a critical, explicated edition is this author's edition of the Maggid of Mezhirech's *Maggid Devarav le-Ya*ᶜ*aqov*, published by Magnes Press in 1976 (second, enlarged edition, 1990), which contains at the end a lexicon with entries built in the above manner.

In the present work, I propose to examine one of the most interesting features of Hasidic thought — the quietistic elements within Hasidism. To analyze these questions requires that one trace the most deeply concealed elements in its religious life, dealing here as we are with problems that are on the borderline of organized religion. Because of its tendency to spurn dogmas and conventions, quietism presents a problem to all religions: it alarmed the official institutions that may undermine its orthodox foundations and upset the existing religious order, and predispose its followers to a "change of values" dangerous to the accepted norms of that particular religion. The quietistic element goes even beyond the spiritual, in that it tends to emphasize the principle of passivity as the main goal to be striven for in religious life. In so doing, it tends to exclude from its universe both religious *praxis* as well as emotional and intellectual activism.

In this book, I note the outstanding parallels in Christian religion, indicating that the same inner logic prevails in Christian quietism as in Hasidism. These parallels bring out the fact that we are dealing with manifestations of essentially the same religious phenomena, sharing a common doctrinal starting-point with regard to such conceptions as pantheism or the theology of immanence, and using similar methods of religious argument in their striving for self-expression. On the other hand, I conclude that conservative factors within Hasidism set limits to the quietistic tendency, as Hasidism had no desire to detach itself from the main body of Judaism or to become an antinomian sect. Thus, while one cannot speak of Hasidism as a form of quietism, one can nevertheless clearly discern the border lines where Hasidism's quietistic yearnings came into collision with its historical conscience and sense of responsibility, and these may be investigated in terms of their quietistic aspects.

This book deals primarily with Hasidism until the end of the 18th century, the golden age of Hasidic creativity. The main emphasis is upon the teachings of the Maggid of Mezhirech and upon the various trends that emerged in the thought of his disciples in relation to this quietistic strain. One can discern here certain extremist tendencies in which I see authentic interpretations of the Maggid's doctrine, as well as more moderate tendencies which also seek support in his utterances.

The clarification of these problems demands a careful philological analysis of the sources. I attempt to carry this out to the best of my ability, in light of the great transformations undergone by many concepts between the time when they were given currency by the Kabbalists until their adoption by Hasidism. From this study of the migration of concepts, there emerges the fact that we cannot expect to understand the conceptual universe of the Hasidic *derashah* (homiletical discourse), nor to appreciate what happened to the concepts as they moved from the Kabbalistic into the Hasidic universe without first possessing an exact analysis thereof in Kabbalah itself.

The book is divided into fifteen chapters and an appendix, each one of which is devoted to a particular aspect of the subject, particularly in relation to quietism. The discussion is linked throughout to an analysis of the texts. It was first published in Hebrew in book form in 1968. I wrote a new and expanded introduction for the English edition, including a description of the status of Hasidism until modern times, and further sections presenting the approaches of scholars of Hasidism in the nineteenth and twentieth centuries. I have discussed in detail the debate in the early 1960's (in which I also participated) between the two great modern interpreters of Hasidism: Martin Buber and Gershom Scholem. Thus, the controversy concerning the manner in which Hasidism ought to be understood has continued literally to the present day, and I have related critically to each of the stances presented.

It goes without saying that I have updated all of the chapters in the body of the book in terms of the new bibliography relevant to the subjects treated in the book. Chapters 12 and 13 were added to the English text of the book, introducing new aspects of the significance of quietism within Hasidism — each from a different point of departure. I have likewise added an appendix, the Hebrew version of which appeared in the third edition of the Hebrew book, containing the Ba^{c}al Shem Tov's *Commentary to Psalm 107*. This document is a literary gem of great poetic power, but its language is strewn with Kabbalistic references rendering it unintelligible to those unacquainted with this vocabulary. An analysis of this literary unit, to which hardly any attention has been paid by Hasidic scholarship, reveals a ritual framework belonging to the first generation of Hasidism, as well as the development of a myth — the essential features of which are to be found in 16th century Lurianic Kabbalah — bearing Hasidic nuances handed down from the circle of the Besht.

* * *

Chapter 1 contains a brief exposition of the basic propositions of classical quietism.

Chapter 2 treats the concept of *annihilatio* — the reduction of all things to "nothing" — and the relation of this idea to the extinction of the individual will. I show that this problem occupied an important place in the thought of the Maggid of Mezhirech and in that of several of his disciples.

Chapter 3 deals with indifference to human existence and the "suffering of the world," which is a prerequisite for submission to the discipline of quietism. The chapter also stresses the principle of acquiescence in God's judgment and "casting one's burden on the Lord," and the renunciation of any reward whatsoever either in this world or the next, as these elements manifest themselves in Christianity — to the displeasure of the Church which cried out in protest against this "renunciation" of "divine mercy." In each of these chapters I have noted the similarities between the arguments of the Jewish opponents of Hasidism (the *Mitnaggedim*) and those used by the Church (as an institution) against Christian quietists.

Chapter 4 treats the concepts of despair, dejection and regret, and their meaning and role in Hasidic quietism. I likewise discuss in this context Hasidism's deviation from the traditional view of the concept of "transgression," using this as a point of departure for understanding the general change of values in the Hasidic world.

Chapter 5 is concerned with the significance of the *miẓvot* in the struggle over the spiritual character of Hasidism. A study of the relevant texts brings out with particular clarity the border lines between the revolutionary and conservative elements within Hasidism. I show that Hasidism was quite aware of the logical consequences of its assumptions and the points at which it needed to set boundaries to their development. In other words: spiritualism has its limits fixed from the start by certain premises in the sphere of action.

Chapter 6 is devoted to the altered status of prayer, in the literal sense of supplicatory or petitional prayer, as a result of the ascendance of the mystical prayer of *devequt*. I describe the conflict between these two types of prayer, and consider the meaning of the formula frequently appearing in Hasidic sources, "Let him pray only for the Shekhinah," which was intended to disqualify personal petitionary prayer.

Chapter 7 turns to contemplative prayer, the stages of its development and its ultimate aim — the extinction of the personality. I show that its chief concern is the activation of the divine element at the time the personality is extinguished. The theoretical basis for this view of the divine as the active principle within man is the immanentist conception of the divine. The analysis of these ideas brings out the interesting transformation undergone by basic theosophic concepts of the Kabbalah, which acquired a psychological significance in Hasidism. I conclude the chapter with a discussion of mental as against verbal prayer, and refer to the halakhic conflicts arising from the preference shown to mental prayer.

Chapter 8 deals with the immanentist idea from another aspect — as contributing to such psychological phenomena such as prophesying. I discuss here the quietistic formula, "the Shekhinah speaks from their throats."

Chapter 9 analyzes the concepts, "World of Speech" and "World of Thought," which are, in my opinion, metapsychological formulae carrying significance for the issue of quietism.

Chapter 10 concerns the struggle over the place of the Lurianic doctrine of *kavvanot* (mystical intentions in prayer). I show that this issue caused much agitation in the school of the Maggid of Mezhirech, as this religious practice was by its very nature incompatible with the doctrine of *devequt* that replaced it. In other words, the general rejection of Lurianic doctrine by Hasidism was brought about by cultural tendencies related to quietism.

Chapter 11 discusses manifestations of anarchism in Hasidic life. Social anarchism of a particular kind was one of the charges brought by the Church against the quietistic trends within it; similar accusations were brought by the opponents of Hasidic doctrine. I bring several examples testifying to this characteristic and its significance in the Hasidic world: for instance, the practice of "racing through" the prayers, the indifference to public opinion, the dualistic approach to values ("inner" and "outer"), and the recognition of the autonomy and exclusive dominion of the "law of the spirit," based upon the premise that man is first of all a creature of the "upper world."

Chapter 12 deals with Ḥabad Hasidism, one of the more radical departures from the spiritualistic approach of the Maggid. This stream was characterized by the transfer of the problem of the service of God in the "world" — which was characteristic of classical Hasidism — to the psychological problem of the suppression of the Evil Urge. This fact signifies a quietistic stand of withdrawal from the struggle in the classical mundane realm.

Chapter 13 suggests that one accept the agnostic position of "I know not," as a kind of intellectual quietism, which tends to stress the element of paradox in the Hasidic ethos. The author of the manuscript discussed here, R. Israel Dov of Stepan, sees the quest for understanding and significance, both of the fact that evil is a structural emanation of the divine good, and of the indifference of God towards human suffering, as illegitimate. Both are unintelligible, hence unworthy of human effort: an understanding of their enigma is only possible in an eschatological world.

Chapter 14 discusses the problem of Torah study and the debate with the *Mitnaggedim* concerning this matter. The central question is whether it is possible to engage in study and at the same time to be in a state of *devequt* (mystical attachment to God). By analysis of the sources, I demonstrate that, whereas the Maggid of Mezhirech answered this question with an unequivocal "no," the topic disappears in later Hasidic sources, or at any rate is reduced to a purely sociological argument over whether or not Hasidim do in fact study Torah. Thus, the revolutionary attitude attributed to the Hasidim in this matter comes up for discussion in the sources, but is afterwards consigned to oblivion by the conformist tendencies adopted by Hasidism in the realm of practice.

In Chapter 15 Hasidism's passive attitude towards history is examined; it was this attitude which reduced the urgency of the Messianic idea. I note the tendency to allegorize the idea of "exile" and "redemption" as spiritual and social values which eclipse the historical interest. The *consciousness* of exile tends to be obliterated by the intense religious communal life of the Hasidim, and is replaced by an expansion of the consciousness of the "I" as individual salvation which displaces national redemption. It is likewise striking in this connection how the path of the exiled Shekhinah is transformed into the mystic foundation of individual redemption.

* * *

I am indebted for many of my best insights and understanding to my late revered teacher, Prof. Gershom Scholem, in whose presence I studied for many years. I cherish the memory of my old and dear friend, the late Prof. Joseph Weiss, from whose approach towards the internal reading of Hasidic texts I learned a great deal. My appreciation is likewise due to my friend and colleague, Prof. R. J. Zvi Werblowsky, from whom I have learned much concerning Christian quietism. With the passing of the years, I have gained much benefit from my students, who have written books and articulated their own feelings in these matters.

I cannot conclude without expressing my deep sense of gratitude to the translator of this book, Rabbi Jonathan Chipman, who devoted meticulous attention to the conveying the exact meaning of the numerous Hasidic texts cited in this book, as well as checking the sources and citations found within them and double-checking bibliographical references. My thanks, too, to Ms. Rebecca Toueg, who edited the completed text of the book. Finally, my thanks to the J. L. Magnes Press of the Hebrew University and to its director, Mr. Dan Benowitz, who worked tirelessly to bring this work to press in a suitable form.

Jerusalem
Hanukkah 5752 (December 1991)
Rivka Schatz-Uffenheimer

Introduction

I. Modern Attitudes to Hasidism

Judaic scholarship of the nineteenth century (Wissenschaft des Judentums) did not look upon Hasidism with a sympathetic eye; even those scholars who dedicated themselves to gathering the Kabbalistic writings scattered throughout the libraries of the world did not turn their attention towards the subject of Hasidism. Heinrich Graetz (1817–1891) stigmatized Hasidism by his passionately scathing criticism;[1] the same mood was continued by David Kahana (1838–1915)[2] and, in a slightly less aggressive mode, in the version of Simon Dubnow (1860–1941).[3] While Graetz's remarks are primarily directed against the "obscurantism" which he found present in Hasidic teachings *per se*, Dubnow is more interested in the "social injustice" to be found therein. The common denominator of both these views is their ignoring of the inner values of Hasidism, in the name of which it first appeared in the world.

One can no longer discuss Hasidism while ignoring its theological focus. On the one hand, the tendency of the 19th century Eastern European *Maskilim* to silence the more balanced view of Eliezer Zweifel (1815–1888)[4] and, on the other hand, the fact that the "return to Judaism" among certain Western European Maskilim of that same period did not bring even the most Orthodox among them to Hasidism, left their impression upon the study of this movement. Everyone spoke of Hasidism in negative terms; the arguments put forward by Samuel Abba Horodetzky (1871–1957)[5] in the attempt to "correct the injustice" did not carry sufficient inner conviction to confront the true problematics of Hasidism. One does not understand what all the fuss was about, and one certainly does not find adequate justification for the note of sentimental kindheartedness towards Hasidism which appears within the pages of his books. In the final analysis, it is insufficient for us merely to know that the power of Hasidism was not based upon

1 Heinrich Graetz, *History of the Jews* (Philadelphia, 1956), Vol. V: 374–394; for the original German, see *Geschichte der Jüden* (Leipzig, 1900), Vol. X: 93–115.

2 David Kahana, *Toldot ha-Mequbalim ha-Shabbetaʾim veha-Ḥasidim* (Odessa, 1913–14).

3 Simon Dubnow, *Toldot ha-Ḥasidut ʿal yesod Meqorot rishonim*, 3rd. ed. (Tel-Aviv, 1967). Originally published in Berlin, 1930–32.

4 E. Z. Zweifel, *Shalom ʿal Yisraʾel* (Zhitomir, 1868).

5 S. A. Horodetzky, *Ha-Ḥasidim veha-Ḥasidut* (Tel-Aviv, 1951), 4 v. in 2.

the charlatanism of its leaders! His "arguments in defense" are rather weak. Micha Josef Berdyczewski (Bin-Gorion, 1865–1921) likewise had a highly changeable attitude toward Hasidism, going from an enthusiastic identification with Hasidism and its values to a harsh criticism and disappointment with the attitude of Hasidism towards the Enlightenment.[6]

Raphael Mahler (1899–1977), a Marxist scholar who valued the folk culture of Hasidic society, seemed more interested in repeatedly emphasizing his opposition to the Haskalah authors, who collaborated with the Austrian absolutist rulers, than he was in penetrating the inner world of Hasidism.[7] By contrast, Ben-Zion Dinur (1884–1969)[8] gave serious treatment to the subject of Hasidism, and his book is filled with interesting material. But even he did not attempt to understand, in principle, the phenomenon in other than social terms, nor did he reflect upon the inner theoretical structure of Hasidism in a comprehensive manner.

Unique among the students of Hasidism and Kabbalah was Hillel Zeitlin (1871–1942), who went to his death in Treblinka holding a copy of *Sefer ha-Zohar* in his arms. From the moment of his religious conversion, he ceaselessly attacked scientific positivism, Darwinism, and materialism. He did not even refrain from criticizing William James, author of *The Varieties of Religious Experience*, although he respected him more than any of the others. Possibly in wake of his example, he tried to assemble an anthology of religious experience based upon Hasidic sources: the writings of the Maggid of Mezhirech, *Me᾿or ᶜEinayim* of R. Naḥum of Chernobyl, *Qedushat Levi* of R. Levi Yitzḥak of Berdichev, R. Shnuer Zalman of Lyady, and others. He saw in this material both a revelation of the Divine and an expression of human truth, which is the unique vehicle of the "divine potential":

> Intuition is the inner sense which is ready to receive all influences and all phenomena, exactly like all the physical senses ... It is based upon the recognition of this spiritual ability, with its power of apprehension and absorption ... so much so that the inner enlightenment takes place unmediated, drawing upon the highest source of divine knowledge and participating in its service with the energy of the omnipotent Godhead, by means of which man becomes visionary and knowledgable in the secrets.[9]

6 See on this Samuel Verses, "Hasidism in the World of Berdychewski" (Heb.), *Molad* 1, no. 24 (1968), 465–475.

7 Raphael Mahler, *Hasidism and the Jewish Enlightenment* (Philadelphia, 1985); originally published in Yiddish and in Hebrew. Cf. my review of this book: R. Schatz, "Professor Raphael Mahler, Militant Historian" (Heb.), *Kivvunim* 33 (1986), pp. 197–199.

8 Ben-Zion Dinur, "The Beginnings of Hasidism, Its Societal and Messianic Foundations" (Heb.), in his *Be-mifneh ha-dorot* (Jerusalem, 1955), pp. 83–227.

9 H. Zeitlin, *ᶜAl gevul shenei ᶜOlamot* (Tel-Aviv, 1976), pp. 46–47.

On the other hand, protested Zeitlin, "In Darwinism one senses the stale odor of petty people, the odor of want and poverty." To use the Nietzschian terminology so beloved of him, Zeitlin projected all of his *Sturm und Drang* onto the interpretation of Jewish mysticism. He particularly identified with "the religious over-man," as he understood R. Naḥman of Bratslav to be — a kind of Nietzschian Jew in uniquely modern garb, who insisted upon the existence of God "outside of the contradiction." In the very depths of his soul, Zeitlin was a Bratslav ḥasid, even though his family background was from Habad.* Zeitlin sought two things in Hasidism: a sense of man's consciousness of his status in the world, and of his obligation towards God. It seems to me that, in the portrayal of these two elements, he came closer to the authentic meaning of Hasidism than did Buber during those very same years. For Zeitlin, the essential claim of Hasidism that man is first and foremost "a denizen of the higher world" (to use the definition given by the Maggid of Mezhirech), and that life with God is the main thing, represents its power of attraction. Buber, by contrast, tended to interpret the Hasidic ethos and its ethical teaching in terms of man's meeting with the world as dialogue. For Zeitlin, the consciousness that the soul is a princess, a spark of the divine, determines the "eros" tension towards the world. This consciousness, and not the free dialogue with the world and with nature, guides life and sustains it on an ethical level of obligation. There were certainly not only ideological differences, but also biographical and spiritual differences between these two thinkers.[10]

* Bratslav was a more emotional school of Hasidism, rooted in the Ukraine, whereas Ḥabad was a more sober, rational approach, whose origins were in Lithuania.

10 See Zeitlin's remarks on Hasidism in *Be-Pardes ha-Ḥasidut veha-Qabbalah* (Tel-Aviv, 1965), and *ᶜAl gevul shenei ᶜOlamot* (Tel-Aviv, 1976). Cf. my article: R. Schatz, "Hillel Zeitlin's Path to Jewish Mysticism" (Heb.), *Kivvunim* 3 (1979), pp. 81–91.

It might be worthwhile on this occasion to cite Gershom Scholem's remarks about Hillel Zeitlin, which he addressed to me in a personal letter dated 10 Av (3 August) 1979, after receiving a reprint of my above-cited article: "... I was happy to read your remarks about Hillel Zeitlin, whom you attempted to understand in a manner true to his spirit. Zeitlin was among the first authors whom I read about Hasidism, already during the early years of the First World War, and they made an impression upon me. In 1916, I also translated his article in his *Collected Writings*, 'The Shekhinah.' This German translation was not published at the time due to my misgivings concerning this matter, even though Buber, whom I told about this, encouraged me to submit it to his monthly, *Der Jüde*, and it is still in my possession. However, I did not find his remarks about the Kabbalah, published in *ha-Tequfah* [a journal of thought], to be suitable, due to the lack of any historical feeling which predominated therein. I was sorry that his long series of articles about Lurianic Kabbalah (based upon *Sefer ᶜEmeq ha- Melekh*), printed in the 1930's in Warsaw, was never published in book form. One of the remnant of the survivors of the Warsaw Ghetto who came to Israel told me that Zeitlin had spoken with him at length concerning my essay, "Redemption Through Sin" [in *The Messianic Idea*

In his writings on the subject, Martin Buber (1878–1965) confronted the essential teachings of Hasidism.[11] While influenced by Berdyczewski, Buber's thesis was far more profound. His earliest works on Hasidism are written in the spirit of mysticism, while in his existentialist teachings, which he especially developed and consolidated during the 1930's and 1940's, Buber utilized the principle of dialogue as a criterion for understanding the essence of Hasidism, which he saw as giving support to the direct, active and creative encounter between man and the world surrounding him. According to Buber's mature work, the reality of God is revealed in the dialogue of encounter: the cosmos is potentially holy, while the encounter with man makes it holy in actuality. Buber sought to locate the origin of this fundamental concept, which he called pan-sacramentalism, in the Hasidic doctrine of the worship of God through the corporeal and worldly dimensions of man's being (*ᶜavodah be-gashmiyut*), through which he attempted to view that aspect of the revival of Judaism that found expression in Hasidism, as opposed to the halakhah. The Hasidic renascence was seen by Buber as a fresh and living religious phenomenon, as well as a process of social and communal consolidation of unique educational importance. He believed that the *ẓaddiqim* gave expression to this new educational and religious meaning, for every *ẓaddiq* represented a special experience acquired as a result of the encounter through a dialogue. Particularly emphasizing the concrete and historical import of Hasidism, Buber placed little value on the abstract ideas of Hasidism or the intellectual "games" of the Kabbalah, and its millenarian hopes and expectations, being convinced that Hasidism had liberated itself from these elements and constructed a realistic experience of life. He understood the Hasidic imperative, "Know Him in all thy ways," as transcending the bounds of the *miẓvot*, calling for religious experience over and above the halakhah. Buber's interpretation shall be discussed at greater length below.

The studies of Gershom Scholem (1897–1982) in the various disciplines of Jewish mysticism — Kabbalah and Sabbatianism — raised the discussion of the

in Judaism and Other Essays on Jewish Spirituality (New York, 1971), pp. 78–141], which appeared at the time in *Kenesset* [a literary yearbook; 2 (1937), pp. 347–392], and which left a deep impression on him. I think that the two personalities — Hillel Zeitlin and Rav Kook — shared something in common; it is a shame that Providence did not place him next to Rav Kook rather than the *Nazir* [i.e., Rabbi David Cohen]."

11 Buber's work on Hasidism includes the translation and reworking of traditional Hasidic legends: *Die Geschichten des Rabbi Nachman* (Frankfort am Main, 1906); English, *Tales of Rabbi Nachman* (New York, 1962); *Die Legende des Baalschem* (Frankfort am Main, 1908); *The Legend of the Baal-Shem* (New York, 1955); *Die Erzälungen die Chassidim* (Zúrich, 1949); English: *Tales of the Hasidism*, 2 vol. (New York, 1947–48). His theoretical essays are collected in: *Be-Pardes ha-Ḥasidut* (Tel Aviv, 1945); *The Origin and Meaning of Hasidism* (New York, 1960); *Hasidism and Modern Man* (New York, 1958); and elsewhere.

theological factor to new levels. As a historian of the Jewish spirit, Scholem protested against the approach of the classical school of Judaic studies founded by Zunz and Steinschneider, particularly what he labelled as their "antiquarian" approach.

While the antiquarian approach contributed much to drawing attention towards the sources of Judaism, it was an attention which was possibly melancholy-romantic, possibly dismissive or "liquidatory," as Scholem calls it.[12] Scholem himself sought to regain the creative view of any given work, and that honest meeting with the past which is prepared to confront, and not to weep over the ruins, which knows how to look beyond what is written to the "hidden life" within. In brief: he sought the authentic pulse of religious life. In Scholem's writings, Judaic scholarship ceased to serve external interests, whether theoretical or social, and began to serve the interests of reflection of Judaism upon itself in terms of its immanent values: this is no mere "mood of the soul," but a mature, rational mastery of a spiritual world which had troubled Judaism throughout its generations, because it did not know how to render account of it. The "yard-stick" called Jewish mysticism rose and fell without anyone being able to identify the forces which moved it. Scholem explained the nature of this law in Jewish spiritual life, by virtue of which one ought to be able to understand various basic questions in Hasidic thought.

One also ought to mention here the special place occupied in the study of Hasidism by Joseph Weiss (1918–1969). Weiss attempted to comprehend the fine distinctions among the different nuances within Hasidism itself, rather than, as was customary among most scholars, to obscure the differences and exemplify only that which was common to all.[13]

For an example of interesting new directions in the study of Hasidism, see Louis Jacobs book, *Hasidic Prayer* (London, 1972). Jacobs developed an understanding of Hasidic liturgy on the basis of mystical and literary sociology. Likewise deserving of special notice is the contribution of Arthur Green, in his book, *Devotion and Commandment; The Faith of Abraham in the Hasidic Imagination* (Cincinnatti, 1989). Green surveys the history of the status of the *mizvot* during the pre-Christian period and the period preceding the polemic with Christianity, via the Talmudic literature, medieval literature, and the metamorphoses it underwent in accordance with the intellectual system of the time. The position of

12 See Scholem's essay, "The Science of Judaism — Then and Now," in *The Messianic Idea in Judaism*, pp. 304–313; originally published in German: "Wissenschaft vom Judentum einst und jetzt," *Judaica I* (Frankfurt am Main, 1963), pp. 147–164.

13 His major essays on Hasidism were collected posthumously in *Studies in Eastern European Jewish Mysticism*, ed., D. Goldstein (London, 1985). His studies on Bratslav Hasidism appear in *Meḥqarim be-Ḥasidut Braslav* (Jerusalem, 1974).

Hasidism regarding the question of spiritualization seems to be, in his view, a conservative one; Green demonstrates that the primary confrontation with the value of the *mizvah* had already taken place prior to the emergence of Hasidism.

Both books relate in particular to Ḥabad: Jacobs' book contains an inspiring analysis of *Kuntres ha-Hitbonnenut* by R. Dov Baer Schnersohn of Lubavitch;[14] in Green, there is an emphasis upon the return of Habad to Lurianic Kabbalah. Regarding the ideational models in the Ḥabad school, one ought to mention the important book by Rachel Elior, *Torat ha-Elohut ba-dor ha-sheni shel Ḥasidut Ḥabad* (Jerusalem, 1982).

Before discussing Buber and Scholem's interpretations of Hasidism in greater depth, it is worth examining the earlier history of scholarship on the subject for an overall picture of the history of the debates over Hasidism through modern times.

II. The Attitude Towards Hasidism Until Modern Times

From the beginning, the Hasidic movement has attracted the attention of both supporters and opponents in each succeeding generation.[15] Anti-hasidic polemics appeared in print even before the publication of the movement's own earliest writings. Although complaints were primarily voiced against the eccentric practices of the sect, the accusations also included matters of principle which were destined to figure prominently on both sides in the modern debate over Hasidism.

The earliest opponents of Hasidism, such as Moses b. Jacob of Satanov, author of *Mishmeret ha-Qodesh* (Zolkiew, 1746), charged the Hasidim with avarice, boorishness, and contempt for the halakhah. During the 1770's, more militant criticism began to be voiced[16]; among the more important of these testimonies are the works of Israel Loebel, ᵓ*Ozer Yisrael* (Shklov, 1786) and *Sefer ha-Vikuaḥ* (Warsaw, 1798). Loebel accused the Hasidim of changing the liturgical conventions from the Ashkenazic to the Sephardic rite; of following Isaac Luria's doctrine of *kavvanot* in prayer; of exaggerated joy during prayer, whereas proper devotion demands tears and repentance; and of praying with wild abandon accompanied by bodily movements. Solomon of Dubna, a follower of Moses

14 Cf. Jacob's biography of this figure: *Seeker of Unity* (New York, 1966); and his translation of R. Dov Baer's *Kuntres ha- Hitpaᶜalut*, under the title: *Tract on Ecstasy* (London, 1963).

15 Portions of this section and of Section V of the Introduction are based upon my entry, "Hasidism," *Encyclopaedia Judaica* (Jerusalem, 1971), Vol. VII: Col. 1416–1420, 1407–1413.

16 For the fullest history and collection of documents to date pertaining to the polemic between Hasidim and Mitnaggedim, see Mordecai Wilensky, *Ḥasidim u-Mitnaggedim; le-toldot ha-pulmus she-beineihem be-shanim tql"b-tqᶜ"h [1772–1815]*, 2 vol. (Jerusalem, 1970).

Mendelssohn, reproached the Hasidim for their pride, high-handedness, and a propensity to drunkenness.

A more inclusive attack, embracing a wide range of accusations concerned mainly with the Hasidim's changes in traditional Jewish ways and practices, was made by Mendelssohn's teacher, Israel of Zamosc, author of *Nezed ha-Dema*[c] (Dyhrenfurth, 1773). Inveighing against both the spiritualism of their religious demands and the "moral corruption" of *ẓaddiq* and *ḥasid* alike, he pointed towards practices suggesting the movement's tendency towards sectarian separatism, such as the wearing of white garments and the adoption of blue-colored fringes (*ẓiẓit tekhelet*) worn outside of one's garments. Among the ritual and spiritual claims of the Hasidim which he denounced were: the pretension to a profound religiosity; the practice of ritual immersion prior to morning and evening prayers in order to become worthy of the Divine Spirit; abstinence and fasting; spiritual arrogance; the claim to be "visionary" seers; violation of the "fences of the Torah"; the doctrine of "uplifting the sparks" (*niẓoẓot*) by the act of eating, according to the doctrine of *tiqqun*; and the introduction of a "new liturgy of raucousness." Among their immoral practices he counted cupidity, hypocrisy and abomination, gluttony and inebriation.

Israel of Zamosc did not assemble his charges into an ordered exposition of the nature of Hasidism; they nevertheless served as the basis for an interpretation of Hasidism which was expressed in the writings of the most profound, systematic and recondite of its opponents — R. Ḥayyim of Volozhin, the leading disciple of Rabbi Elijah b. Solomon Zalman, the Gaon of Vilna. His book *Nefesh ha-Ḥayyim* (Vilna, 1824), in which the term *ḥasid* is discretely omitted, adumbrated for the first time the principles of an interpretation of Hasidism as a novel religious phenomenon. R. Ḥayyim presented Hasidism as a spiritual movement which ignores a cardinal principle of Judaism — namely, that where the very nature of a *miẓvah*, as well as its fulfillment, is jeopardized by an idea, the latter should be set aside. Equally, where new values — lofty though they may be — threaten to come into conflict with tradition, the latter must be upheld. He rarely voiced an objection to specific hasidic practices, but objected on theoretical grounds to various matters of fundamental belief in Hasidism which appeared to him as dangerous. In so doing, he managed to detach his polemic from its historical context. R. Ḥayyim of Volozhin saw the spiritual uniqueness of Hasidism as follows:

1) Hasidic teachings imparted a new significance to the concept of "Torah for its own sake" (*Torah li-shemah*), an idea understood by Hasidism as "Torah for the sake of *devequt*" ("communion") with God. According to R. Ḥayyim, the study of the Torah for itself alone (and not for the sake of *devequt*) possesses a value transcending the fulfillment of the *miẓvot* themselves. 2) R. Ḥayyim objected to

Hasidism's emphasis on "purity of thought," as in his opinion the essence of Torah and *mizvot* do not necessarily lie in their being performed with "great *kavvanah* and true *devequt.*" Here, R. Ḥayyim of Volozhin observed the opposition between mysticism and the halakhah, emphasizing the dialectic process by which the performance of a *mizvah* with excessive *kavvanah* actually leads to the abrogation of the *mizvah.* The fundamental principle is the very act of fulfilling the *mizvah,* and not the *kavvanah* accompanying its performance. He therefore challenged Hasidism on a matter of basic principle: performing *mizvot* for the sake of heaven, he stated, is not a value in itself; 3) He regarded the Hasidic attempt to throw off the yoke of communal authority as social amoralism; 4) He objected to the practice of praying outside the fixed times set for prayer, and the consequent creation of a new pattern of life.

By the 1770's, Hasidism had already come under the fire of the Jewish Enlightenment *(Haskalah).* In Warsaw, Jacques Kalmansohn published a scathing criticism of the social nature of Hasidism, as did Judah Leib Mises in his *Qinʾat ha-ʾEmet* (Vienna, 1828). But the author who displayed the most striking talent for caricature and pointed sarcasm was Joseph Perl of Tarnopol, who portrayed the material and spiritual conditions of the Hasidim in the lowest terms,[17] in order to exert pressure on the Austrian authorities to force all the Hasidim to receive a compulsory education within the state-run school system. Perl's major contention was that as a socio-religious phenomenon Hasidism was an anti-progressive factor, owing to its spiritual insularity and its social separatism: it was idle and passive in spirit and as a social group it was unproductive.

A more ambivalent view of Hasidism appears in the memoirs of Abraham Baer Gottlober[18] who, when he later adopted the principles of the Haskalah, became convinced that it was Hasidism which had facilitated the spread of the Haskalah movement, in that it constituted a critical stage in the life of Judaism. According to Gottlober, Hasidism threw off the yoke of rabbinical authority, and in so doing opened the gates for the advance of the Haskalah. He also believed that Hasidism lay at the root of the crisis involving the *Shulḥan ʿArukh.* It displaced Sabbatianism and the Frankist movement, and tarnished the glory of "rabbinism." Gottlober evinced a particular admiration for Habad Hasidism because of its affinity to the Haskalah. However, he regarded Hasidism itself as a social movement which was in its very essence disintegrative, because its criticism was inwardly directed.

Toward the end of the 1860's and the beginning of the 1870's, selections of the writings of Eliezer Zeʾev Zweifel began to appear in print under the title *Shalom*

17 In his pamphlet, *Ueber des Wesen der Sekte Chassidim aus ihren eigenen Schriften gezogen im Jahre 1816*, Jerusalem– National Library, MS. Var. 293.

18 *Abraham Baer Gottlober un Zayn Epokhe*, (Vilna, 1828).

ʿal Yisraʾel — a work which came to the defense of Hasidism, attempting to interpret its teachings on the basis of Hasidism's own authentic sources. In his balanced and well-informed argument, the author undertook an analysis of fundamental Hasidic homilies and teachings, noting their significance and underlining their uniqueness in comparison with Kabbalah. As a *maskil*, he had of course certain reservations both about the "popular" elements of Hasidism and a number of its social aspects. Among those *maskilim* most influenced by *Shalom ʿal Yisraʾel* was Micha Josef Berdyczewski, whose interpretation of Hasidism in his book *Nishmat Ḥasidim* (1899) was couched in romantic terms. Viewing the movement as a Jewish renascence, an attempt to break down the barriers between man and the world, he saw in Hasidism "joy and inner happiness" and the opportunity to worship the Lord in many different ways.

Early in the 20th century, the Zionist *maskil* Samuel Joseph (Shay) Ish-Horowitz published a series of articles, which later appeared in booklet form under the title, *Ha-Ḥasidut veha-Haskalah* (Berlin, 1909), containing a scathing attack against the "modern" Hasidism of Berdyczewski and Buber. In this work, Beshtian Hasidism is depicted as a wild, undisciplined movement, while the Baal Shem Tov himself is seen as a charlatan influenced by his rustic surroundings and by the Haidamak movement.* According to Ish-Horowitz, Hasidism contributed no new truths or ways of looking at the world; it appropriated to itself the vocabulary of the Kabbalah without fully understanding its implications, coloring it with quasi-philosophical notions of the "petit-bourgeois mentality and the chronic psychology of the ghetto." Modern or neo-Hasidim (specifically that of Berdyczewski and Buber) attempted to discover ethical values and a positive popular force in Hasidism, particularly in its emphasis on "joy," which they interpreted as a protest against the dejection produced by the conditions of the Diaspora. For Ish-Horowitz, however, the Sabbatian movement was to be preferred to Hasidism, taking as it did a straightforward and honest stand of calling to break the bonds of the Diaspora and the ghetto. Ish-Horowitz dismissed as little more than arrant nonsense the claims that Hasidism was a movement of revival and revolt; far from rebelling against the rabbinate, Hasidism observed the *miẓvot*, minor as well as major. He contended that the neo-Hasidic reinterpretation of Hasidism in secular terms was a self-deceiving distortion of history in the spirit of a new humanism. He believed that Hasidism represented continuity rather than revolt and that, by viewing it as a revolutionary movement in Jewish history, the neo-Hasidim did violence to its true nature.

* Haidamaks — paramilitary bands of peasants that disrupted life in the Polish Ukraine during the 17th century, culminating in the Cossack uprising led by Chmielnicki in 1648.

III. Existentialist and Idealist Interpretations of Hasidism: Martin Buber and Gershom Scholem

The most profound and serious confrontation with the meaning of Hasidism in our generation seems to me to have been that of Gershom Scholem and Martin Buber, which for that reason deserves our special attention. The debate between the two was one between an idealist and an existentialist, each of whom gave different meanings to the Hasidic material.[19]

Gershom Scholem defined 18th century Hasidism as "practical mysticism at its best." "Practical mysticism" — because in his opinion Hasidic thought at its best, unlike Kabbalah, is not concerned with speculative mystical theories; "at its best" — even though Scholem himself does not read out of it those magical elements and mystical extravagance which are not always to the taste of contemporary researchers. Scholem did both justice and kindness with Hasidism. With his overall vision and perceptiveness, he was able to give a phenomenological expression of Hasidism which emphasized its ideal contours and "its place on life" in Hasidic society — something which, despite the voluminous writings on the history of Hasidism, had hardly been done prior to himself. With the exception of Zweifel's interesting attempt during the previous century to understand the motivations of Hasidism, no attempt had been made at a phenomenological description thereof, so that Scholem did a kindness in that he was tempted neither to praise it nor to denigrate it when he was unable to find some common ground between his own system of values and theirs.

One cannot however claim that the study of Hasidism was performed in the last generation in a disinterested manner. Horodetzki, Buber and Scholem all attempted to chart for themselves new paths, and presented positions both *ad initium* and *post facto*, as did Ben-Zion Dinur and Raphael Mahler. The common denominator of all these scholars was the attempt to draw an affinity between Hasidism and the movement of national rebirth. As Scholem understands Ahad Ha-Am:

> They soon perceived that the writings of the Hasidim contained more fruitful and original ideas than those of their rationalistic opponents . . . Even so restrained a critic as Ahad Haam wrote around 1900: "there, rather than in the literature of the

19 The following is a somewhat revised version of a lecture delivered at a memorial meeting held by the Israel National Academy of Sciences and Humanities marking the *sheloshim* of Scholem's death in 1982, which appeared in Hebrew in a pamphlet dedicated to his memory: R. Schatz, "The Interpretation of Hasidism as an Expression of Scholem's Idealistic Outlook" (Heb.), in *Gershom Scholem: ᶜal ha-ʾIsh u-Foᶜolo* (Jerusalem, 1983), pp. 48–62. The Academy intends to publish an English translation of the entire pamphlet at a future date.

> *Haskalah*, one occasionally encounters ... true profundity of thought which bears the mark of the original Jewish genius."[20]

In truth, it is difficult not to feel the definitive rebuttal given by all of the figures of the Hebrew renascence to such historians of the Haskalah as Graetz, or to territorialists such as Dubnow, who criticized it even through their so-called "praise" thereof. But as a result of the enthusiastic defense of Hasidism in the last generation, there have also come about certain historical distortions, such as the loss of a proper perspective on the connection between traditional Jewish culture, via the crisis of the Haskalah, to the Jewish national rebirth. If Hasidism was in fact a phenomenon of Jewish rebirth or renascence, should it not be possible to portray it as the direct bridge thereto, in the sense of being the "mark of the original Jewish genius" which carried the "genes" of the renascence? We have seen that Ish-Horowitz did not refrain from the argument that, if one is to speak of any past movement as being a forerunner to Zionism, it is preferable to seek such a continuity in Sabbatianism, rather than to glorify a movement whose tendency was Exilic and which lacked the revolutionary impulse found in a messianic movement. Ish-Horowitz described Sabbatianism as:

> ... a human nationalist movement, [marked by] its awakening to leave enslavement for redemption, the dark ghetto for the Jewish state. How much glory and splendor and human greatness it had, in order to excite the longing and expectant hearts, whose power of waiting had failed to sustain the Exile [*Galut*] and its material and ethical straits ... The consciousness of the Sabbatian movement was in principle the same as that of today's Zionist movement ... It was a human longing, a beautiful and exalted movement, the awakening of a feeling within man which lay [dormant] within the Hebrew heart after the long years of slumber of the Galut. Sabbatai Zevi, like Herzl in our generation, was "the king [leading] the regiment, crowned with the crown of the Almighty on his head among those who dwell in darkness." It was he who opened new vistas to those "weeping for the festivals," so that those who were weary from troubles, the tired ones of the Galut, as human beings, might find rest.[21]

It is clear that a Herzlian Zionist — then as today — would find more of interest in Sabbatianism than in Hasidism, feeling greater affinity to the former historical phenomenon than to the latter. In practice, all those who sought to establish some kind of relationship between Hasidism and Zionism — whether themselves religious or secularists — were forced to interpret it sociologically as an internal, anti-establishment Jewish revolution stirring up great creativity and vitality, which then became a kind of archetype for the pioneering society in the Land of Israel.

20 Gershom Scholem, *Major Trends in Jewish Mysticism* (New York, 1945), pp. 326.

21 S. J. Ish Horowitz, *ha-Ḥasidut veha-Haskalah — Maḥshavot ᶜal devar ha-Ḥasidut ha-Yeshanah (ha-Beshtit) veha-Ḥadashah* (Berlin, 1911), p. 12.

In the circles of the Mizrachi (Religious Zionists), a quasi-scholarly style developed wherein all of the great rabbis were so-to-speak transformed into good Zionists.[22]

The only thinker who internalized the Hasidic system of values and attempted to use it as a model for Zionist social and ideological education — a task requiring multi-dimensional interpretive powers — was Martin Buber. Buber removed Hasidism from its historical context and viewed it as a phenomenon in its own right, acquiring a dimension of value at the cost of historicity, in this manner hoping to convey it as a message to the new Jewish society in Eretz-Yisrael. In practice, I know of no interpretation of Hasidism, apart from Buber's, which confronts the spirit of the Jewish rebirth. Even Gershom Scholem, who quoted Ahad Ha-Am, refrained from drawing any far-reaching implications of the profundities of Hasidism for the renewed national life. On the contrary, the more Scholem delved into Buber's theories, the more he fled his "gospel," seeking instead the historical and theoretical authenticity of Hasidism. Under Buber's influence, Scholem sought a modern translation of the intellectual mood of Hasidism — a translation which would not harm the exactitude of its sources and their inner tendencies.

From the point at which he became intellectually mature, Scholem always sought the Archimedean point from which to view every historical phenomenon — known in Hebrew by the *terminus technicus* "the point of depth" (*ᶜamqut*) — which he found among such Eastern European scholars as Buber and Zalman Shazar. These figures gave him a reliable perspective, both because they seemed to him very learned in Jewish matters, and because they possessed a prophetic breadth of vision and spoke in Western language. Thus, Shazar influenced him in the direction of Sabbatianism and was the first to interest him in its study, whereas Buber interested him in the study of Hasidism — so much so that, until the end of his life, Scholem continually returned to the problem of his discussion with Buber. One can see from Scholem's remarks that there was no one who fascinated him so much as Buber, whom he called

> ... a deep and penetrating thinker [and master of inituition] ... He has that rare combination of a probing spirit and literary elegance which makes for a great writer ... In one sense or another we are all his disciples. In fact most of us, when we speak about Hasidism, probably think primarily through the terms that have become familiar through Buber's philosophical interpretation.[23]

22 See Simon Federbush, ed., *Ha-Ḥasidut ve-Ẓion* (Jerusalem, New York, 1963).

23 See G. Scholem, "Martin Buber's Interpretation of Hasidism," in *The Messianic Idea in Judaism*, pp. 227–250; the quotation cited here appears on pp. 229–230. The essay first appeared in *Commentary* 32 (1961), pp. 305–316; cf. Buber's reply, "Interpreting Hasidism," appeared in *Commentary* 36 (1963), pp. 218–225.

In Scholem's view, Buber began as a devotee of Jewish mysticism, who saw in Hasidism a living mystical kernel — as indeed, Scholem himself continued to define Hasidism as "mysticism at its best"! But it was not the neo-romanticism of Buber's interpretation of the legends of the Besht or the tales of Rabbi Nahman of Bratslav which was, in due time, to draw Scholem's criticism, as it was the existentialist turn in Buber's interpretations, following the publication of *I and Thou* in the early 1920's. While Buber's primary slogan, that Hasidism was the crowning glory of Jewish mysticism as "Kabbalah made ethos" continued to occupy a central place in Scholem's evaluation of Hasidism, the existentialist axioms underlying this saying brought Scholem to a parting of the ways with Buber. The existentialist interpretation not only moved this formula in the direction of the de-gnostification of Hasidism — as if gnosis were the exclusive prerogative of Kabbalah — but wove an Hasidic ethos which spoke with the world as it is.[24]

Scholem perceived the radicalism of Hasidism in the fact that it taught that the entire world is "filled" with God. By this statement it also declared, in his opinion, that whatever is seemingly secular also has a religious value. But the radical mood of "In all your ways know Him" [Prov. 3:6] — the formula around which the Besht developed his teaching — does not mean that the service of God "in corporeality" sanctifies corporeality as such or, as Buber called it, "the here and now." Scholem took exception to such formulations of Buber as "life as it is," "the concrete as such," and similar formulae, which contained more than a small element of extravagance and flirtation with this world — elements which Scholem did not find present in the Hasidic writings. This was an expression of Buber's "modernity," which had its own intoxication with the concrete. Scholem did not like this intoxication: not only because Hasidism is itself idealistic and not existentialist on this point, lifting its eyes upwards to the supernal world; not only because Scholem correctly perceived that Hasidism speaks of the purification of life in order to achieve life with God, and did not abdicate the inwardly suffering eros of every classical ethos; but because Scholem is himself an idealist in his own world-view. This idealistic outlook is expressed in his article, "Reflections on Jewish Theology,"[25] where he again dissents from Buber's existentialist views and their effect upon what he sees as the contemporary distortion of Jewish theology.

24 Regarding Buber's interpretation of Hasidism, see R. Schatz, "Man Facing God and the World in Buber's Interpretation of Hasidism" (Heb.), *Molad* 18, nos. 149–150 (1960), pp. 596–609. English: "Man's Relation to God and World in Buber's Rendering of Hasidic Teaching," in *The Philosophy of Martin Buber* (London, 1967), pp. 403–434.

25 G. Scholem, "Reflections on Jewish Theology," in his *On Jews and Judaism in Crisis; Selected Essays* (New York, 1976), pp. 261–297. Originally published in *Devarim be-go* (Tel-Aviv, 1976), pp. 557–590.

Scholem believes that Buber's interpretation of Hasidism stems from this same stance, which introduces existentialism in inauthentic ways as an element neutralizing historical Jewish concepts, such as the fear of God and the belief in the validity of other primary concepts, which are not subject to new "interpretations" coinciding with Buber's view. Scholem was not seduced by Buber's "beauty" and modernity, and was not prepared to sacrifice basic elements of Hasidism or to summarize all of its problematics in one simple formula. Scholem allowed for the problematics of Hasidism, which Buber eliminated by giving one answer, the formulation of which has its own shortcomings. In his phenomenological description, Scholem allowed room for nuances, while Buber pressed the "message," always holding before his mind's eye the "messengers" carrying the new teaching. Scholem did not like this message, nor was he enthusiastic about Buber's "this-worldly" humanism, and he certainly did not believe that it represented Hasidism. His ear was attuned to the internalized rhythm of the hasidic ethos, and he valued more highly the elements of withdrawal from the world that he found in Hasidism than he did the tidings of a "positive meeting with the world." He saw the "bringing down of God into the soul of man," to quote his remarks about Buber, as a radically secular tendency with which he never identified.[26]

Scholem generally did not like any form of radicalism. He was even uneasy with those radical aspects whose existence he acknowledged in Hasidism and which he considered, perhaps, as the heritage of Sabbatianism. He was particularly sensitive to certain trends in modern Religious Zionist thought, such as that of Rabbi Abraham Isaac ha-Kohen Kook, whose explanations of the *saeculum* in light of the holy were seen by Scholem as a continuation of the process of levelling of values, a confusion of the clear chasm between sacred and profane in the world of Judaism and, in the final analysis, a Sabbatian logic.

Despite the fact that Scholem devoted his best efforts and research to the study of Sabbatianism, he was also attentive to the unique nuances of Hasidism. His primary attention was turned towards clarifying the meaning of those concepts which are wide-spread in its writings, in order to paint a phenomenological portrait of it through their precise understanding. Thus, by clarifying the term *ᶜavodah be-gashmiyut* in his polemic with Buber, Scholem arrived at the conclusion that, in the final analysis, the message of Hasidism centered upon the "casting off of corporeality"; Scholem likewise rejected the meaning given by Buber to the concept of "uplifting of sparks" — a term that entered Hasidism via Lurianic

26 See R. Schatz, "'Freedom on the Stones' — Theology under the Sign of a Crisis of Authority" (Heb.), *Yediᶜot Aḥaronot*, December 3 1977, Supplement Dedicated to G. Scholem's Eightieth Birthday.

Kabbalah, which meant that the fallen sparks from the Divine sphere scattered in the material world ought to be restored to their primordial state.

Scholem rejected Buber's attempt to nullify the gap between God and the world or, to be more precise, between life with God and "life in the world." This is in fact a variation on the polemic concerning *ᶜavodah be-gashmiyut*, only it introduces the eschatological-messianic element into the discussion, thereby stressing the contours of the polemic. What is revealed in the process of uplifting the "sparks" is not concrete reality — says Scholem — but the messianic reality in which everything returns to its place in a purified manner. Buber's formulae blur this essential difference.[27]

This being so, the argument is not only about the "here," but also the "now." For Buber, action itself is redemptive action, while Scholem understands that Hasidism did not renege on the eschatological dimension, and that its idealism continued to raise the sparks to the "true place" to which they belong, to their divine source. It is also clear that this indicates that Hasidism continued to be connected to the "gnosis" of Kabbalah from which Buber "liberated" it.

The divergent directions contained in the respective interpretations of Buber and Scholem are therefore clear; however, their justifications for the striking transformation in Hasidism in the service of God "in all your ways," and the "exaggerated" legitimation of divine service in corporeality and the lifting of sparks from the corporeal realm to a status of equality with the classical forms of Divine worship — all these require further study. Had Buber been asked to define the nature of this turn, he would have said that a change had taken place in the respective valuation of "above" and "below," the "below" now receiving a status of its own and by virtue of itself. Scholem answered this indirectly; he basically sees in this change a compensation for the loss of faith in the possibility of actual messianism, saying the following:

> ... the Hasidim laid great stress on the teaching that human activity is not able to really bring about or reveal the messianic world ... they were left, in their view, only with prescribing ways or means for the individual to use the concrete as a vehicle to the abstract, and thereby to the ultimate source of all being ... Though couched in the language of very personal religion, this may be conventional theology and not nearly as exciting as the new interpretation which Buber has read into it.[28]

I will not deny the fact that I am not excited by the assumption that *ᶜavodah be-gashmiyut* ("worship in corporeality") was, so to speak, a substitute for the feeling of eschatological helplessness. I agree with Scholem that Hasidism is not

27 See Scholem, "Martin Buber's Interpretation of Hasidism," p. 243.
28 Ibid., p. 244.

to be defined as a messianic movement,[29] but I do not share the idea that it was forced to be so for external reasons. Scholem's statement here strengthens the claims of his opponents regarding this question, who think that it incorporated a concealed messianic element. I do not believe that movements build themselves on the basis of militant slogans concerning one subject, when in fact they have in mind quite another one: Hasidism struggled on behalf of *ᶜavodah be-gashmiyut*, and not for messianism. But if Scholem had in mind the negative connection between these two elements, one may find phenomenological justification for this statement; that is, it is possible to assume that a movement which did not have an acute messianic interest would be open to the interiorization of religious life and to a-historical answers to its problems. Thus, the concept of "service through corporeality" as a form of quietism with regard to history makes sense.

Moreover, on the basis of the writings of Hasidic thinkers, it is very difficult to determine the dominant tone used regarding *ᶜavodah be-gashmiyut*: at times it is spoken about in very serious tones, as something essential, and at other in an apologetic tone, implying that it is "also" available as an optional form of Divine worship. During the generation of the Besht, one feels more strongly the encouraging tone of mission accompanying this matter, particularly as part of a social rebellion which directed all "theology" downwards. On the other hand, during the generation of the disciples of the Maggid of Mezhirech, one detects a clear attempt to halt the peripheral boundaries of *ᶜavodah be-gashmiyut*; on the contrary, they attempt to confer upon it elitist characteristics, as something demanding special care and a special level on the part of the individual performing it. There is a conscious flight from the fear of vulgarization, and perhaps also from "the concrete as it is."

Buber and Scholem both shared an understanding of the extraordinary impact of the social element upon Hasidic religious life; where they parted company was in evaluating its significance. The everyday life and social behavior of the Besht and his colleagues were rightly understood by Buber as testifying to a broadening of the scope of hallowing the concrete or worship in corporeality, denoted by Buber as "pan-sacramentalism." Hasidic sources, however, bear evidence to restrictions upon this "pan-sacramentalism"; indeed, Scholem argued that there are a priori limitations to the extension of the holy over the profane, or of the sacred over the secular. Secondly, he contended that the Kabbalistic element, or what Buber called the Gnostic element, still prevailed in Hasidism. On the other hand, I would also challenge Scholem's view, contending that he was unaware of the far-reaching, radical extent to which the Besht was willing to go in exercising his socio-religious ideas. Scholem gives too conservative a picture of the Besht's behavior toward the

29 See Chap. 14 of this book, "History and National Redemption."

concrete, while Buber presents too adventurous an understanding of the Besht's apparent abandonment of the upper world. In my opinion, Scholem understood that the dialectical principle immanent in Hasidism saved it from any sort of anarchism, while Buber attacked metaphysics as such through Hasidism.

Scholem also opposed Buber's approach because it removed Hasidism from the traditional world of laws and *mizvot*. In overly stressing the "how" and not the "what," Buber emphasized the anarchistic aspect of its approach towards tradition. Scholem criticizes him for this, in that he did not attribute the concept of holiness to the commands of the actions themselves, but removed the question to another framework, as if Hasidism were only concerned with one's moral responsibility towards the manner of performance, and not towards the action itself and its contents. This is expressive of a kind of anarchism to which Scholem — who also declared himself an anarchist — was not party. Scholem's anarchism expressed itself rather in the area of authority[30] and not in the realm of values; he respects internalized values and is suspicious of their becoming established, his moderation is shown in his loyalty to their original meaning.

Maurice Friedman has recently written an article defending Buber's thought against Scholem's critique.[31] Friedman claims that Scholem attempted to discredit Buber in the eyes of the public in order to usurp his position and to upset the credence given to Buber's portrayal of Hasidism.[32] It is Friedman's intention here to balance the controversy, or at least to present its proper parameters. He attempts to summarize Buber's position as teaching that man is unable to reach God while bypassing the human — a message which Buber found in Hasidism. He likewise attacks the present author's article on Buber,[33] which still — according to his view — presents Hasidism within the context of Kabbalah, interpreted as *gnosis* rather than as *devotio*. Friedman incorrectly thinks that the distinction between the theoretical and legendary literature of Hasidism gave legitimation to Buber's interpretation of the principles of Hasidism, leaving scholarship the equal right to interpret the theoretical literature by its own standards. But the truth of the matter is that it is impossible to read the Hasidic story while ignoring or bypassing the prism of the theoretical teachings of Hasidism, so that a distinction of the sort proposed by Friedman would not serve to protect "ethos" from "gnosis."

Friedman states that (p. 453), "Unlike Scholem, Schatz did not entirely deny the validity of Buber's interpretation of Hasidism." He slants my words inexactly, as if I had said that it were solely a question of proportion: more like legendary

30 See R. Schatz, "Freedom on the Stones," op cit.

31 Maurice Friedman, "Interpreting Hasidism: The Buber-Scholem Controversy," *Yearbook of the Leo Baeck Institute* 33 (1988), pp. 449–467.

32 Concerning Scholem's article, "Martin Buber's Interpretation of Hasidism" (op cit., n. 23).

33 See above, note 24.

narrative rather than theoretical literature. Had he properly understood my position, he would have realized that I do not criticize Buber's selectivity merely as a question of proportion, but as a position in principle. Buber takes advantage of the fact that there are no limitations placed upon the interpretation of the Hasidic story by unequivocal theories, while I would claim that the theories found outside of the Hasidic narrative place limits upon our reading of that narrative itself.

The second point on which Buber, according to Friedman, differs from Scholem and myself is in his insistence that there are, in point of fact, two kinds of Hasidism: that of the Baal Shem Tov, which teaches the "hallowing" of mundane life, and that of the Maggid of Mezhirech, which insists upon the gnostic spiritualization of existence. Buber of course preferred the approach of the Besht — according to Friedman.

Such "distinctions" — while I do not deny the differences between these two personalities — are intended to bolster the central thesis of the article: namely, that Buber's approach is equally legitimate to that of Scholem and of myself, and that it cannot be claimed that one constitutes "objective" truth and the other "subjective" understanding. Friedman thereby wishes to do justice to Buber and to refute the demand for objectivity, brought especially in Scholem's article. Friedman takes a further step when, speaking about the superiority of Buber's approach to that of the historical-critical approach, he states that he takes into account what is important for the future, and not for the past! Such a statement of course implies a protest against the cultural importance of scholarship and its role in conveying the values of the tradition to future generations. Buber himself in fact spoke of two different ways in which one may preserve culture from the ravages of time for succeeding generations — that of historical learning and that of passing on the vitality and power of faith. The latter helps to renew the connection with the absolute, which had been severed (p. 459). In order to achieve the latter goal — according to Buber — one should present, not all the historical data, but a partial selection thereof, guided, not by objective learning, but by presumably subjective criteria.

While Buber in fact mocks "theory" and values instead of the "event" within cultural life, hence explaining his abstention from discussing the theoretical writings of Hasidism, it is clearly difficult not to be carried along by an anarchistic sentence which prefers "life" over "theory"! Buber repeatedly distinguished between the "original" teaching of the Besht (i.e., life) as opposed to the gnostic-spiritualistic doctrine of his disciple, the Maggid (theory).

Buber's response to the arguments brought against him was essentially the following: 1) that the theoretical and legendary levels within Hasidism do indeed contradict one another; 2) that the teachings of the Besht and those of the Maggid contradict one another, making it impossible to choose both. Hence, Buber is free to prefer one or the other, as he quite legitimately did, just as it would be legitimate to choose the other path; it is thus improper to confront him with claims of "objectivity."

There is no need to state that I cannot accept the dichotomy proposed in Friedman's article, as a reply intended to reinstate Buber's status within the "community of scholars," without the "stain" of mistrust concerning his use of sources, as Friedman believes happened to him. It seems to me that such a defense of Buber, by reorganizing anew the cultural criteria, is entirely superfluous and does not succeed in rebutting Scholem's criticism. Buber's place of honor remains unshaked, even in the eyes of Scholem — as I have shown by my above remarks — as well as in the eyes of his readers. Buber would certainly have preferred to continue to shed influence in his own nonchalant manner rather than via the kind of methodical "defense" presented by Friedman.

I have expanded upon the polemic between Scholem and Buber at some length, because Buber was the main, if not the only, catalyst for the fruitfulness of Scholem's thought in this area. Scholem would certainly define Buber's approach "the price of existentialism in research."

IV. Scholem's Interpretation of Hasidism: Mysticism and Ethos, Continuity and Change

Scholem's own perception of Hasidism was focused upon two main areas: one, upon the image of the *ẓaddiqim* and their own direct religious experiences, and the second, in stressing the creativity of the thinkers of the movement. Scholem was cautious about attributing to Hasidism an originality which it did not possess, and always attempted to be honest with himself and meticulous in understanding those things which it in fact innovated.

> The truth is that it is not always possible to distinguish between the revolutionary and the conservative elements of Hasidism ... No less surprising, however, is the fact that this burst of mystical energy was unproductive of new religious *ideas*, to say nothing of new theories of mystical knowledge .... The new element must therefore not be sought on the theoretical or literary plane, but rather in the experience of an inner revival, in the spontaneity of feeling generated in sensitive minds ... [34]

For Scholem, the center therefore lay in the fact that "Kabbalistic concepts passed

34 Scholem, *Major Trends*, p. 338.

through the refining fire of new mystical thinking." In the final analysis, there is also an element of novelty in the fact that Hasidism was a popular movement, and not only a stream in Jewish thought, and that the creative element within it did not avoid confronting this fact in the realm of ideas as well.

In two major articles which are important in principal for understanding Hasidism, Scholem drew a line leading from religious renascence to religious organization on a mystical basis. In the course of analyzing basic concepts in Hasidic thought, he sketched the contributions of two central figures in Hasidism — the Baᶜal Shem Tov (also known as the Besht: R. Israel ben Eliezer, c. 1700–1760), and his disciple, R. Dov Baer, the Maggid of Mezhirech (d. 1792). I refer to the two articles: "The Historical Image of Rabbi Israel Baᶜal Shem Tov,"[35] and "Devekut, or Communion with God."[36]

Although so much has been written about the figure of the Besht, the *zaddiq* from the Carpathian mountains, some scholars conceived of him as a purely legendary figure. Thus, Scholem needed to prove his very existence by gathering sources from the 1740's testifying to the existence of his opponents: if he had contemporary opponents, this surely means that he must have existed.[37] The border between history and legend is not always clear in Hasidic sources about the Besht, and there is no doubt that Scholem took the correct path in reaching the conclusion that *Sefer Shivhei ha-Besht*,[38] first published at the beginning of the 19th century, is a combination of legend and realia deserving of serious consideration. Through close reading of *Shivhei ha-Besht*, Scholem arrived at the conclusion that the story of the Besht's participation in the debate against the Frankists was not circulated by his own followers. This is one example of the way in which this book confirms the results of historical criticism.[39]

Scholem was the first one who dared to relate seriously to the charismatic power of a figure like the Besht, whom he described as "a magician and charismatic figure,

35 G. Scholem, "The Historical Image of R. Israel Baᶜal-Shem-Tov" (Heb.), in *Devarim be-go*, pp. 287–324.

36 G. Scholem, "Devekut, or Communion with God," in *The Messianic Idea in Judaism*, pp. 203–227; originally published in *Review of Religion* 14 (1949–50), pp. 115–39.

37 See Aaron Zeʾev Aescoly-Weintraub, *Le Hassidisme* (Paris, 1928), pp. 39–40. Aescoly argues, in the absence of any authoritative historical testimony to the contrary, that the Besht as founder of the movement existed only in folk legend created by the Hasidim themselves. He likewise strongly criticises the works of Horodetzki and Dubnow for being insufficiently critical.

38 *Sefer Shivhei ha-Besht* is an hagiographical collection of tales relating to the life of the Baal Shem Tov. First published in Capost, 1815; the standard edition today is that of S. A. Horodetzki (Tel-Aviv, 1947), with introduction and notes.

39 Meir Balaban has already rejected the claim that the Besht participated in this polemic, and has suggested the originator of this version. See his *Toldot ha-Tenuᶜah ha-Franqit* (Tel-Aviv, 1934), pp. 68–69.

who knew how to make his words penetrate the heart of the folk." Even Buber, who shaped a very positive educational image of the Besht, was "forced" to play down the magical interpretation of the Besht's activity, as the Hasidim of the second and third generations had themselves done, by rationalizing the Besht's ability to see the future and his use of folk remedies. The emphasis upon the less "acceptable" elements of Hasidism, which were still beyond of the *bon ton* of Hasidic research during those years, neutralized the unease felt in light of the popular phenomenon in general, and perhaps assisted us to clarify the rules of the game which were in fact used in the militant books of R. Jacob Joseph of Polonnoye, disciple of the Besht, from whom most of the traditions about the Besht came down to us.

In my opinion, Scholem nevertheless gave greater emphasis to the sublime element in the Besht's trend of thinking, and diminished that of vulgar mysticism — if one may use such a term — whether in terms of the involvement of the instincts in Divine worship or of the social anarchism expressed by his personality and the doctrine which he taught. Both his demonstrative behavior — as related in *Shivḥei ha-Besht* (the hagiography of his wondrous deeds) — of going places where Talmudic scholars were generally not wont to be, as well as his going into solitude in the forests, are not signs of ordinary asceticism. A story which I found in one of the later traditions of the school of Rizhin indicates the clearheadedness with which the Hasidim themselves saw the image of the Besht. A disciple of R. Israel of Rizhin, who was known to live luxuriously, asked him to explain why the Besht was accustomed to live modestly and dwelt in the forests, while he lived in a palace and sat on a golden throne. The Rizhiner answered: "in the time of the Besht the thieves lived in the forests, so he also dwelt there; today, the thieves live in palaces, and therefore I am also here."

The ethical tension in the Besht is too greatly involved with the demand for the right to the "forbidden area" — i.e., that forbidden by the Torah — for us not to perceive its problematics. This is so, even if we accept the assumption that the interpretation which emphasizes the value of the "concrete" does not serve as its justification. On second thought, one may, of course, ask whether this "concreteness" in itself is the central problem of Hasidism, or whether the true question is in fact that of defining the borders of the periphery that must be taken into account as the "space for Divine service" — that is, the space within which confrontation is permissible. While this formula is no less problematical, it involves another conceptual area.

The saying, brought by Scholem in the name of the Besht, that "man must long for the things of this world,"[40] from which he arrives at true Divine service, is a

40 Scholem, "The Historical Image" (op. cit.), p. 321.

major part of the new ethos which champions "involvement" and "experience," without which things are not done. The Besht's remarks, cited by Scholem in the name of R. Pinḥas of Korets in *Pe'er Yesharim*, are an additional layer in this structure:

> Is it possible for a person to correct the world, while the evil continues to cling to him. The Besht revealed this thing [to Menahem Mendel of Bar]: that one must descend to Gehinnom on behalf of God, may He be blessed. And this is alluded to in the *gemara* [Talmudic aphorism], "Greater is a sin for its own sake [than a mitzvah not for its own sake — Horayot 10b; Nazir 23b]."

Scholem did not believe that this teaching of "descent for the sake of ascent"[41] — with all the complexity involved — was the authentic teaching of the Besht, but rather tended to attribute it to the Maggid of Mezhirech. He did not draw any conclusion from the abundant information on this score found in the writings of R. Jacob Joseph — a point which in itself I find puzzling. He similarly refused to derive the obvious conclusions from the above-cited saying of R. Pinḥas of Korets. It seems to me that Scholem denied that degree of mystical extravagance which was present within the Besht. In my humble opinion, Scholem entirely overlooked another kind of mystical extravagance, which pertained more to the social realm, depicted in the same small story in *Shivḥei ha-Besht* cited by Scholem in his article. The story relates that:

> The Besht was unable to speak with people because of his *devequt*, but would speak "outside of the system." And his renowned [legendary] teacher [i.e., Ahiyah the Shilonite] taught him to recite daily the psalm, "Happy are they of the upright way" [Psalm 119] . . . and he showed him a wise trick, by means of which he began to speak with people without abandoning his *devequt*.[42]

Although Scholem protests that, "they [i.e., the scholars] specifically ignored these testimonies," it does not seem to me that this story suggests that the Besht did not have "the gift of speech," in Scholem's words. What is implied here is rather the difficulty entailed in learning the technique of remaining in *devequt* while at the same time being involved with and speaking to other people! The "wisdom" of how to be constantly in a state of *devequt* while simultanously fulfilling one's social obligations was one which the Besht learned from his prominent "teacher," so that this knowledge belongs to Hasidic praxis from its very beginning.

Indeed, the sources indicate that the teachings of "constant *devequt*" and of "turning towards people" were of equal importance; more than once the Besht

41 For a comprehensive treatment of this problem, see the Appendix to the present volume, "The Besht's Commentary to Psalm 107 — Myth and Ritual."

42 Scholem, "The Historical Image," p. 311.

taught that, if a person addresses one in the middle of prayer, one should leave one's *devequt* to God in order to answer him! There is more than a little social extravagance in this. At times, Scholem defended the Besht against the claims of Haskalah historians, who read the theory of "partnership" between the masses and the elite as a sinister exploitation of the masses. But he himself shares their criticism in saying that, "the entire catastrophic doctrine of Zaddikism is herein concealed." But for some reason he is apologetic towards the Besht who, in his opinion, "did not exploit his charisma for personal interests." In any event, Scholem was no less charitable towards the image of the Besht than were the latter's own disciples, who stressed his unique ethos. As Zweifel rightly saw: "It is astonishing that all of his holy disciples hardly related in their books anything of his miracles and wonders of healing and charms, but rather extolled his piety and holiness, his *devequt* and ardor (*hitlahavut*)."[43]

Nevertheless, in stressing the seemingly classical ethical elements in the Besht's teaching, Scholem taught an important lesson — namely, that the true nature of ethical realization is dictated by its historical circumstances. The real object of study is not the fact that everything seems to be "as it was in olden days," but the manner in which the system of values was activated and the considerations which determined their role. Thus, for example, Scholem analyzes the concept of *devequt*, not as a static concept, but as a revolution wrought by circumstance. "The history of religion abounds in examples of such different evaluations of the same tenet under different historical conditions."[44] Long before Hasidism the concept of *devequt* enjoyed a privileged place even above that of study, according to Scholem, but this change in the scale of values did not bring about a revolution, and was certainly not subject to "persecution," so long as the social conditions which changed it into a dominant revolutionary force were not present. With the emergence of Hasidism as a revolutionary movement, its "views" became dominant and gave an ideological push to the shaping of the revolution. I would add to this interpretation the pantheistic slogan, "no place is empty of Him," which was among the factors leading to the Gaon of Vilna's joining the anti-Hasidic forces. Yet was not this "Zoharic" concept omnipresent in the literature prior to Hasidism? Only after pantheism became a decisive factor in the change wrought by Hasidism in religious life did the Gaon became fearful of the potential vulgarization of its interpretation.[45] Indeed, Scholem stressed the duality present in any concept once it becomes dominant and living; wherever one finds the

43 Zweifel, *Shalom ᶜal Yisraᵓel*, p. 22a.

44 Scholem, "Devekut," p. 208.

45 On this problem, see Yosef Ben-Shlomo, "Gershom Scholem's Study of Pantheism in Kabbalah" (Heb.), in *Gershom Scholem; ᶜal ha-ᵓIsh u-foᶜolo*, pp. 17–31.

spiritual radicalism of "innovators," one also finds its converse — the vulgarity which springs up as a result of the very experience. Scholem points out that:

> Once the radical slogan, "Judaism without *devekut* is idolatry" was accepted, its very radicalism already contained the germ of decay, a dialectic typical of radical and spiritualist movements.[46]

Drinking liquor and smoking the *lulki* became means of attaining *devequt* exactly like contemplation of the letters of prayer.

But Scholem did not pay attention to the criticism of Hasidism's spiritual radicalism on the part of the conservative intelligentsia such as R. Ḥayyim of Volozhin, whose book *Nefesh ha-Ḥayyim* presents a severely critical analysis of Hasidism, based upon authentic understanding of its inner dialectic moving in the direction of spirituality. In the eyes of R. Ḥayyim, spirituality became the enemy of the normative Jewish system.[47] The interpretation of *Torah li-shemah* (Torah for-its-own-sake) as meaning "without self-interests" is considered in this tract as one of the signs of the mystical elite, which allows itself such a strict definition that any deviation therefrom removes one from the classification of *ḥasid*. This is indeed the authentic Hasidic interpretation, in the spirit of the Besht's remarks:

> "Lest you turn aside and serve other gods" [Deut. 11:16], meaning, once a man turns aside from *devekut* and the fixation of his thought on God, he is considered as one who serves other gods.[48]

R. Ḥayyim stresses the tension among the Hasidim regarding the relation between study and *devequt*, opposing the entire ritual of "purification of thoughts" because, "the essence of Torah and *mizvot* does not necessarily depend upon their performance with tremendous *kavvanah* and true *devequt*." He feared mystical realization, lest the fulfillment of the mitzvah with excessive *kavvanah* be its downfall! The commandment is that which is given in the halakhah, in the form in which it is given. "For the sake of heaven" is not a value in itself, while *devequt* is defined by him as rational "study with pure thought."

Scholem rightly stressed that one does not find the same longing for mystical annihilation in the Besht, "that level of unprecedented surrender to the emotions"

46 Scholem, "Devekut," p. 209.

47 Opinions differ concerning R. Ḥayyim of Volozhin's position. The tendency is to ignore his frontal attack on Hasidism in his book, *Nefesh ha-Ḥayyim*, which to my mind is the definitive anti- Hasidic manifesto, in which he understood the deeper implications of the spiritualist-social tendencies of Hasidism. Emanuel Etkes, who wrote on R. Ḥayyim, did not to my mind display sensitivity to this text. See his *R. Yisra᾿el Salanter ve-reshitah shel Tenuᶜat ha-Musar* (Jerusalem, 1984), pp. 41–45, and at greater length in *PAAJS* 38–39 (1972), pp. 1–45.

48 In Scholem's formulation; "Devekut," p. 209.

— as he defines it — which people call the mystical intoxication of the abandonment of self. But there is tremendous religious fervor present in him, and every prayer performed to the accompaniment of movements of the entire body is, in the Besht's words, like one who is drowning who performs motions to save himself, grabbing onto every straw for this purpose: "I must give thanks to the Holy One, blessed be He, that I remain alive after every prayer." It is true that from here there arises a cry, rather than that same *unio mystica*. As against that, the goal longed-for by the Maggid of Mezhirech approximates such union. To quote Scholem: "He is the ascetic whose gaze is fixed on, or, I might rather say, lost in God. He is a mystic of unbridled radicalism and singularity of purpose."[49]

Scholem was concerned in a number of different ways with two primary questions related to the phenomenon of Hasidism. The former relates to the relationship of Hasidism to earlier Jewish mysticism — that is, the nature of its connection, both conscious and unconscious, to the literature which preceded it. The second question relates to the manifestations of the unique spiritual energy with which Hasidism was graced, in two different areas — the mystical and the social. I will begin with the first of these issues.

It is not my intention here to write an essay concerning the relationship of Hasidism to Kabbalah, even though this is a desideratum. A discussion of Hasidism's conscious relation to Kabbalah would require an analysis of that Hasidic material which deals explicitly with the role of Kabbalah in the Jewish world generally, and in Hasidism in particular. This subject entails several aspects: there were those Hasidim who rejected the study of Kabbalah by the masses, even though (and perhaps because) they believed in its Divine authority, while there were others who stressed the inner continuity of the mystical tradition, together with emphasizing the innovation brought about by Hasidism. In both cases, one frequently finds a formulation referring to R. Simeon bar Yoḥai, R. Isaac Luria, and the Baᶜal Shem Tov as constituting a central chain of mystical teachers; one which, so far as I know, none of the Hasidim attempted to challenge. It is true that acknowledgment of such a continuity is likely to be a mere facade concealing the essential divergence between the two positions. Hasidism was able to claim the right to regard itself as a continuation of the Kabbalistic tradition, while on the other hand continuing to expand the discipline of Kabbalah *per se*, and simultaneously representing the spiritual realm introduced by the Besht, not as a new discipline, but as a new form of religious life.

In effect, Gershom Scholem presented the theoretical question concerning the relationship of Hasidism to Kabbalah; however, it seems to me that the two examples which he cited in explanation of this problem do not necessarily support

49 Ibid., p. 226.

the conclusions which he reached regarding this question. These conclusions were in fact "snatched" by Buber and interpreted in his own way,[50] as I shall explain below.

Scholem cited the remarks of R. Shlomo of Lutsk concerning the position of his teacher, the Maggid of Mezhirech, on the relationship between Kabbalah and Hasidism, from which he concluded that the supposedly decisive claim of Hasidism was that, in effect, nothing had changed with the appearance of Hasidism, and that the latter was no more than a natural continuation of Kabbalah. It seems to me that, from the remarks of R. Shlomo of Lutsk, the claim of conscious continuity was joined to that of innovation, and that both seemed to prevail in the field of theoretical and speculative doctrine, and not only as ethos. I will cite R. Shlomo's words:

> Behold, in our great sins, the generations have gradually declined, and the hearts have diminished and this wisdom [of Lurianic Kabbalah] is nearly forgotten, [being preserved] only among a few unique individuals. Even among those who drink thirstily the words of the Ari *z"l*, they only [understand] the simple [meaning of] things, and in small measure, like the measure of a handsbreadth, in order to moisten that handsbreath [wordplay on *maṭpiaḥ/ṭefaḥ*] and to ascend, by his view, to the knowledge of the Most High — but he does not understand the substance of the things. As in the saying in *Sefer Yeẓirah*, "Ten sefirot of *Beli mah* [double entendre, that may be read "without substance" — i.e., of transcendent spirituality — or "without anything"]" — that is, they are only like divine vitality, for they have thrust behind their backs the books of the early ones. Until, with God's mercies upon us, there appeared to us the light of Israel, the divine and holy rabbi, R. Israel Baal Shem Tov and his holy disciples, who sat in the dust at his feet to drink with thirst his words, the words of the living God. For he revealed this precious source, this glory of wisdom, with mountains of [knowledge of] the ways of the supernal world upon every jot and tittle, and of its unification in the lower world, with his every motion and step and word and action. As they [the Sages] said about Enoch, that he sewed shoes, and with every stitch he would say, "For the unity of the Holy One, blessed be He," as will be explained inside this book [i.e., *Maggid Devarav le-Yaᶜaqov*], with God's help, as were many of his words brought to the home of Joseph [an allusion to the *Toldot*, which had been published just one year earlier] . . . And in truth I feared to approach the holy place within, to place upon the altar of the press the holy words of our master and teacher, the Divine and holy R. Dob Baer, the author, *z"l*. For they are words which are upon the heights of the world, and words which are uttered upon the supreme side, that not every mind can comprehend. And in his holy words there are alluded the interpretation of several chapters of [R. Ḥayyim Vital's] *ᶜEẓ Ḥayyim*, and

50 See Buber's response to my article (op cit., n. 19), "Antwort zum Darstellung des Chassidismus," in *Martin Buber* [Philosophen des 20. Jahrhunderts (Stuttgart, 1963)], pp. 626–635.

> of the *kavvanot* of the Ari, *z"l*, and of the *Zohar*, as is known to whomever among the great ones of the world hears his hundreds and thousands of pleasant sayings. And his words entered into their hearts like a burning fire, and their hearts were ardent for the service of the Creator; for this book is only like a drop in the ocean of his great wisdom, of which he utters speech every day like a spring of living waters, with holiness and purity and separation from his wife for several years ... And at times he would speak and talk of the praises of his primary teacher, our master R. Yitzhak [i.e., Luria] ...[51]

Thus, R. Shlomo of Lutsk understood Hasidism as a particular interpretation of Lurianic Kabbalah. Concerning the Besht, he states that he innovated a certain matter, and that this reflects "the paths of the supernal world [according to Lurianic Kabbalah] and its unification in the lower world, with every motion and step and word and action." Scholem clearly understood R. Shlomo's remarks as an acknowledgment that this is not considered an additional ideological layer, but an application of the teachings of Luria to the questions of everyday behavior: "the paths of the supernal world and its unification in the lower world," etc. He arrived at this conclusion, not only from the remarks of R. Shlomo himself, but also from the example brought from the Maggid of Kosnetz. Scholem argued, with considerable justice, that the writings of the Kosnetzer Maggid do not integrate Hasidic doctrine and Kabbalistic teaching, even though he places Hasidism above all his other concerns. From the fact that Hasidism does not so-to-speak confront the Kabbalah in the realm of the latter, Scholem wished to infer that Hasidism is not interested in such a confrontation, as it does not at all understand itself as a strictly theoretical movement, but as an ethos which arose alongside Kabbalah.[52]

There is no doubt that Scholem noted a significant phenomenon. Moreover, he pointed to an important problem which may serve as a test of authenticity. However, in examining this question it is impossible to ignore another fact: namely, that the strictly Hasidic sources are not only filled with Kabbalistic terminology; they also engage in actual confrontation with it. That is to say: one finds there exegesis and discussion between strictly Kabbalistic, theosophic questions, and Hasidic Torah novellae, such that it is impossible to reflect upon the consciousness of continuity in Hasidism without relating to the factor of Hasidic thought. While it is true that not all theoretical Hasidic novellae draw their inspiration from the Kabbalah — and I am prepared to assume that Kabbalistic Musar literature did play an important role in creating the bulk of the ethos of

51 See his Introduction to Dov Baer of Mezhirech, *Maggid Devarav le-Ya^caqov*, critical edition, with Introduction, Commentary, Notes and Index by Rivka Schatz Uffenheimer, 2nd ed. (Jerusalem, 1990), p. 2.

52 Scholem, *Major Trends*, p. 339.

Hasidism — it was intellectually rooted in Kabbalah in several respects, and its novellae in Torah are made within its context.

The intellectual innovation of Hasidism is not to be measured in terms of the addition of a new speculative layer to the complex gnostic structure of Lurianic Kabbalah, as the latter did with respect to the schools of Kabbalah which preceded it; however, it presented both mystical and social problems with regard to the assumption that these problems cannot be understood except by knowledge of the Lurianic Kabbalistic world. Even in all of the "turn-abouts" that Hasidism made as a result of its greater interest in man than in theosophy — as Scholem felt — it was built and supported primarily by means of central principles of Kabbalah. Scholem does not argue for the de- gnostification of Hasidism, as Buber attempted to do:[53] he does not deny the presence of Kabbalah within Hasidism, but rather — to the best of my understanding — represents Hasidism as a popularization of the Kabbalistic elements, without any real theoretical innovations in the realm of Kabbalistic thought. While this conclusion seems to me factually correct, one ought not to exaggerate its importance regarding the question as to whether or not Hasidism may — and in fact did see itself — as a direct continuation of Kabbalah. So long as we are dealing with a cultural climate of Kabbalah — and not only with its use as terminology — even if it turns to new spiritual interests and displays a turn of multiple significance (as Hasidism indeed did), it remains a spiritual intellectual creation within this realm.

According to Scholem, the vital force within Hasidism is the ethical-religious element, as opposed to the theosophic, in which one also recognizes the social expressions of the mystical element. This is a statement of the greatest importance for the historian who wishes to trace the path of the tremendous flow of mystical energy stored in Hasidism, whose Kabbalistic source and popular character are both noted by Scholem. Scholem identifies the revolutionary element in Hasidism in terms of an ethical-social revolt against the society within which it grew, laying particularly stress upon the reasons for its success as rooted in the ethical authority of the *ẓaddiq*, who gave confidence in the validity of this change. In other words, he stresses the spiritual-social climate which constituted a decisive factor in the conquests of Hasidism. It is true that the persistence of Hasidism depended upon the personality rather than upon the doctrine — as Scholem formulated these fine distinctions — but its power of growth is not sufficiently explained by these circumstances. Did not anything occur by virtue of its power of autonomous mystical self-renewal? The creators of Hasidic literature wrote with the feeling of discovering a new world of ideas and, even though they did not tend towards theorizing, they did explain themselves on a certain theoretical basis which they borrowed from Kabbalah and Musar literature. The past was confronted anew by the very act of selection from this literature, and at the same time they were aware that they were innovating from a purely spiritual aspect. It may be that the revolutionary power of the Hasidim is rooted elsewhere than that of the authors of Hasidic teachings, but at the same time it is impossible to ignore the revolutionary power immanent in the Hasidic idea as such. In the final analysis, the Hasidim were not merely interested in doing the same thing as their non-Hasidic colleagues, only in a different manner; nor did they only protest against the petrified approach to tradition and to the *mizvah*, being interested in their performance as a religious experience and not merely as mechanical, routine acts. They brought with them a message of renewal — and not only of the renewal of religious life. This renewal was rooted in the very process of questioning the inner value of action, and in the attempt to anchor its significance in metaphysical and psychological speculations. Action as such was openly confronted by the objective values of the spirit, and was weighed on the basis of its criteria.[54] We are not dealing here with the question of the historical status of action and of the *mizvah* or with an attempt to explain their force in temporal terms, as was the case regarding this same question in Sabbatianism; we are concerned with a value-oriented speculation, in whose discussion no temporal ideologies are involved. The challenge posed to Hasidism by religious action was therefore different from that which it posed to Jewish mysticism in general, in that it aroused a conflict between values. Action appears therein as a value which needs to struggle for its place in terms of significance — albeit not in terms of its being questioned as a basic framework or "starting point" — beyond which the true problems of religion begin.

Hasidism was the first mystical movement in Judaism to create a true conflict with action. Sabbatianism did not require action as a point of departure for its internal discussion, having ruled that the *mizvah* is no longer necessary in the messianic age, and being ready to sacrifice it as a sign of that age: the abolition of religious action was merely an external sign of the historical crisis. Hasidism did not do away with action (including practical mitzvot), which it saw as the permanent background for religous confrontation; the conflict with action is of the very essence of Hasidism, the pulse of its religious life and the area which enjoys the most vigorous defense — but it is enacted on a problematic front.

I do not intend in the course of the present discussion to relate to the concept of action in the limited religious sense; my discussion of this problem occupies one of the chapters in the body of the book.[55] However, I do need to give a certain explanation of the broader concept of "action" in Hasidism, as Hasidism also expanded the framework of its discussion to the area of the concrete in general.

53 See "Antwort," op cit.

54 On the status of action in Hasidism, see below, Section V.

55 See Chapter 5, below, "The Status of the *Mizvot.*"

A contemporary critique of Scholem's approach to the study of Jewish mysticism and Hasidism is featured in a recent book by Moshe Idel.[56] As the title of the book indicates, its author has taken upon himself the task of presenting Jewish mysticism, including Hasidism, from a new perspective. Idel proposes a radical departure from accepted methods of research; to this end, he challenges the conventional reliance upon textual research, as well as the historical-philological approach, which he holds accountable for the limitations of research and of the prestige of the discipline. He seeks a way to understand Jewish mysticism as mysticism — something which, in his opinion, was slurred over due to the pressure of the intellectual interests of rationalistic scholars, who prevented this material from being available. In other words: he seeks a phenomenology which will stress the understanding of mysticism as such, as experience rather than as theory, as experiential testimony rather than as a source for textual analysis. At times, he even engages in outbursts against the accepted discipline of Kabbalah of the school of Gershom Scholem, which he denotes as "ideology of textology," while the scholars who engage in its study are "textologists."

In Idel's opinion, the Kabbalists themselves thought that their primary message was embodied in praxis; even though Idel admits that the written and printed records of Kabbalah deal predominantly with theory, according to his opinion the hidden, unpublished testimonies speak more of the experience. Had Idel illustrated in a practical manner how he proposes to study Jewish mysticism, including Hasidism, using this hypothetical method, basing himself upon evidence which is, so to speak, recorded somewhere but not published, or were he to present us with a serious prospect for discovering this experiential spiritual archive — one might be able to accept this. But instead, he plays with such ideas as if such records were already a reality, depending only upon the diligence of the scholar in seeking them out. Moreover, one senses in Idel a certain feeling of revolutionary drama concerning the future of research, as if these new, anticipated data already existed in reality. He creates expectations for which there is no real backing to the extent that he thinks, anchoring his expectation in two different realms: first, in the testimony of Jewish mysticism, so to speak, and second in the psychological study of the religious experience among mystics of other religions.

In Idel's view, the main bases of mysticism are inspiration, *unio mystica* and mystical revelations — elements which the mystics themselves censored and refused to print. One cannot ignore the fact that there are elements of Jewish mysticism which were considered by the Kabbalists to be more profoundly hidden, just as there were elements that it was less desirable to make known in public for

56 M. Idel, *Kabbalah: New Perspectives* (New Haven–London, 1988).

one reason or another — and not necessarily because of their spiritual depth.[57] However, there is a great gap between this and the conclusion that, in order to engage in authentic research, one must change the medium studied — a distance which a cautious and experienced researcher ought not to easily bridge. Furthermore, Idel does not demonstrate how one is to go about this. His own analysis is strictly textual, based upon the "old" — indeed, at times antiquated — method.

Another problem bearing methodological implications for the study of Jewish mysticism is the phenomenological distinction drawn by Idel between normative and ecstatic mysticism. According to him, the former is fundamentally theosophic and conservative, expanding the mysticism of the Talmudic Sages by interpreting the *mizvot* in a mystical manner. He does not explain whether this "conservatism" consists primarily in distancing oneself from ideational heresy, or in the strict conservatism imbedded in the attention shown to the praxis of the *mizvot*. It seems to me that, from the very beginning, the exegetical element in Jewish mysticism was linked with the insistence upon the right of "alternative exegesis" — that is, to serve the right to mysticism[58] — or, if you prefer, the right to revolutionary change. Even in the classical Rabbinic sources, mystical exegesis does not appear as a conceptual super-structure of the halakhah. Secondly, one must ask whether Hasidism in fact belongs to the genre of ecstatic mysticism when, according to Idel's definition, all of its writings are exegetical-conservative. I support the

57 See, for example, the critical stance taken by Ashkenazic Hasidism toward the Kabbalist Abraham Abulafia and his prophetic Kabbalah in the testimony of R. Naphtali Treves, in R. Schatz, "The Influence of Gnostic Literature on R. Shlomo Molcho's *Sefer ha-Mefo'ar*" (Heb.), *ha-Mistiqah ha-Yehudit ha-Qedumah*, ed. J. Dan [*Mehqerei Yerushalayim be-Mahshevet Yisra'el* 6, nos. 1–2] (Jerusalem, 1987), p. 263, n. 77. See also the criticism of Abulafia by R. Joseph Solomon Delmedigo of Candia (*Yashar*) because of his contemplative-prophetic approach, in his book *Mazref la-Hokhmah* (Jerusalem, n.d.), p. 31b.

See also my remarks concerning R. Shlomo of Lutsk and his refusal to record the teachings he had heard from the Maggid of Mezhirech because it does not reflect the inner level of the Hasidic praxis, in the "Introduction" to *Maggid Devarav le-Ya'aqov*, ed. Schatz, pp. xx–xxi.

See likewise the testimony of R. Israel Dov of Stepan in the present book (Ch. 13), that there were Hasidim who wrote for "the drawer," because their thought was too personal to "represent" accepted exegetical writing. Perhaps R. Shneur Zalman of Lyady's work, *Tanya*, ought to be seen as deviating from that same sort of writing, which led to the polemic surrounding concerning its author (see the chapter on Habad in this book). See below also my comments on the book of R. Yitzhak of Radzivilow, one of the five sons of the Maggid R. Michal of Zloczow, whose book remained unpublished, and was even censored by one of the copiests of his manuscipt, because of the visionary phenomena described there. The examples which I have brought here represent different types of censorship.

58 See my article: "Kabbalah — Tradition or Innovation (An Historical Perspective)" (Heb.), in the forthcoming Memorial Volume for Ephraim Gottleib, ed. Amos Goldreich and Michal Oron.

position which grants the text the right to reflect all systems in a hermeneutical manner, and do not perceive the exegetical medium as a limiting or limited one, if it is in fact the mystic's intention to use it to describe ecstatic elements, or for that matter any other elements, such as the magical or prophetic.

Despite the fact that Idel is greatly influenced by the positions of scholars of religion and anthropology, or by the proponents of one or another hermeneutic school whose positions differ from those of Scholem, and who naturally extend the field of comparison in the discipline of religious studies, he states that, "I prefer a solid textological study to a bad comparative one" (p. 23). Nevertheless, I find the central issue raised by Idel's book to be that of the ethical issue of textual study, rather than what this study contributes to the extension of comparative research.

It seems to me incorrect to characterize textual study as limiting the study of mysticism *ab initio*: Idel himself only anticipates the "revolution" that will take place as a result of the discovery of new manuscripts. I would understand from this that these "revelations" will provide us with the keys to a new method of research, which has thus far been impossible because of their unavailability. This statement contradicts common sense. Idel himself acknowledges that even an important scholar such as Mircea Eliade arrived at his phenomenology without any basis in texts. He does not advocate the mechanical adoption of Eliade's methods or those of the Jungians, agreeing on this point with the stance of Gershom Scholem, albeit the latter does not let down the critical side of the balance — namely, the historical-philological method. This does not mean that Scholem's scholarship became an "arid ... conceptual approach." On the other hand, a purely phenomenological, comparative approach requires that one ignore the historical life and texture of the writings upon which we base ourselves. Idel's work in this book seems to me to present a striking example of the loss of social-historical contours and, in my opinion, of the lack of intellectual precision — the latter being an imperative of the highest order.

There is a troubling tone of complaint in Idel's book, a complaint that Jewish mysticism has not received the place of honor enjoyed by other mysticisms, and that, "because of scholars' restraint in regard to utilizing current concepts and notions of comparative and phenomenological studies of religion, they have rarely succeeded in integrating the study of Kabbalah into the larger discussion of mysticism .... Moreover, the structure of Kabbalistic thought has been only poorly elucidated in a conceptual manner, which could fructify the modern research of religion in general and mysticism in particular" (p. 24). I wish to assure those readers who may be upset by these words that the failure of Gershom Scholem and his school is not nearly so total as is represented here, and that the future of Kabbalah research does not depend upon the slim thread held out by Idel.

Idel blames the established school of Kabbalah research for the fact that it has not admitted the presence of *unio mystica* in Jewish thought. It is true that Scholem was very cautious about this question — and rightly so, for he wished to be precise both in his understanding of the message of the mystical testimony, and to ascertain the mystics' degree of awareness of the theological significance of this testimony. He behaved in a similar manner regarding other basic concepts in religious thought, such as pantheism.[59] Nevertheless, I do not believe that he was shocked when I discussed with him the dominant role played by *unio mystica* among some Hasidic thinkers, most notably the Maggid of Mezhirech — a conclusion which follows naturally from careful textual reading. Indeed, the present work, whose first version appeared in Hebrew over two decades ago, portrays *unio mystica* as an important phenomenon in Hasidic mysticism, even though for some reason Idel writes that nobody has noted this until now! It is also a pity that Idel completely ignored the struggle of two major figures, Buber and Scholem, to formulate their positions vis a vis both mysticism and the place of the text in the study of Hasidism — a subject which I discuss in the present introduction. Another serious lack, which is likewise a cause for regret in what presents itself as a panoramic survey of contemporary research in Jewish mysticism, is the absence of reference to the classical studies of Isaiah Tishby and their implications for the study of Jewish mysticism, not to mention those of a whole series of other scholars, Idel's contemporaries in the various universities throughout the country and abroad, who have played an important part in the shaping of new tendencies and their establishment, even while maintaining a certain element of respect for the historical-philological approach. I would also differ with Idel's formulation: "A scholar who approaches Kabbalistic literature only textologically (almost the single main perspective in present research) is unable to be sensitive to vital aspects of Kabbalistic phenomena" (p. 24). The reader no doubt anticipates a great deal following such declarations, yet it requires great effort to find in Idel's book those same "vital aspects" of Kabbalistic phenomena whose roots the "textologists" were unable to plumb due to the sin of textology.

We know the attention that has been given to the psychological aspects of mystical experience from the beginning of this century, since the appearance of William James' *Varieties of Religious Experience*, and rightly so. In his pioneering work of that time, James symbolized pragmatism, pluralism and empiricism, reflecting the influence of the natural sciences. His aim was psycho-technical, and in many of his motifs Idel returns to this research. However, James engaged in extensive field work as a psychologist of religion, rather than as a historian of religion; in his phenomenological description, the latter must take into account the

59 See Ben-Shlomo's analysis in, "Gershom Scholem's Research on Pantheism" (op. cit., n. 45).

social, historical and cultural circumstances involved in the influence of religion, and not only the experiential, spiritual processes of the individuum. That which is appropriate to a method which isolates the individual from his surroundings in order to understand his individual experience — or for any other pragmatic purpose — is not relevant as a way of understanding religious phenomena, or even "purely" mystical phenomena. It is true that pragmatism is based upon experience rather than upon ideas, while the study of the history of ideas, as in the school of Gershom Scholem, is indeed "ideational." However, the experimentalistic image that Idel would like to give to his research does not seem to transcend an emphasis upon certain technical elements, which indeed appear in a more striking manner among certain Kabbalists than among their fellows. What we have here is not a "new dimension" of Kabbalah, the uncovering of which would serve to introduce a new perspective — as Idel's book itself indicates. One is hard put to find in his approach and his analysis even one innovation concerning the understanding of mystical phenomena which has not already been raised by scholarship — and certainly not in the chapters pertaining to Hasidism.

Scholem himself took great care to avoid falling prey to psychological theories. Indeed, in those places where he gave free rein to the understanding of psychological phenomenon — such as in his description of the motivations of the Sabbatian movement — we do find a certain breakdown of the intellectual integration which he sought. He was himself aware of the fact that the psychological framework cannot explain the other frameworks, be these religious or social, of movements or of individuals. Positivistic psychological understandings dictate ideological principles to no less a degree than do other systems, and Idel fails to define, beyond the technical description of experience, what he means by his experiential emphasis. Hence, I am not at all certain that he speaks here in a consistent way of any substantive change in the rules of the scientific game.

There may also be certain specific limitations to the phenomenon of Jewish mysticism, which is far more textual and exegetical than other mysticisms. I see no reason why it needs to be uprooted from its natural locus in order to bring about a forced parallel to the method of research of other mystical schools of different makeups. In any event, I see no place for the severe accusation made by Idel against the alleged exaggerated intellectualism of the scholarly method which supposedly, unconsciously and at times consciously, hid the experiential element in Jewish mysticism — as if modern scholarship were a partner to the historical self-censorship by which one of the important elements in religion was concealed. Idel's assumption that the revelation of visions and the emphasis upon praxis in Abraham Abulafia indicates that the philological-historical method of research has missed the mark because it deviates from what the Kabbalists thought about themselves — namely, that they were first and foremost men of praxis — is greatly exaggerated.

There is no little danger of academic anarchism when one alters one's method of research on the basis of the testimony of an involved party. A good example of this is Idel's argument, against Scholem, that one ought to accept the testimony of the Kabbalists that their tradition is a continuation rather than a revolution![60] This is not only discredited logic methodologically, but also doubtful intellectual ethics, as the basis of all scholarly discourse is distance and the drawing of distinctions among the various testimonies on the basis of objective criteria of judgment determining the limits and applicability of each document, while taking into account the apologetic intent of one or another statement. In this case, Scholem argues that Kabbalah is an innovation, an "explosion" in the heart of Judaism, whereas Idel argues that it represents a certain continuity. Each one is entitled to argue as they wish, provided that their predetermined assumptions do not lead them to draw far-reaching conclusions as if they were historical proofs. Idel assumes that the Kabbalah represents an ancient tradition whose roots are found in Midrash and Talmud, where one can find there the hidden growth of Jewish esotericism. He states, "I assume that Kabbalah has probably preserved some ancient conceptual structures that supply a more unified view of the otherwise unrelated and sometimes unintelligible motifs and texts" (p. 33). But these are all essentially hypothetical statements which, if they are to be understood as new methodological statements, return us to the harmonistic approach, as opposed to that of historical-philological research. I have my doubts as to whether the true meaning of mysticism is to be found in the realm beyond academic research — not that I identify the two, but that I appreciate the seriousness of the system which Idel wishes to dethrone, to be replaced by hypothetical methodological truths which supposedly represent new perspectives. They are not such. The attempt to reduce the distance beteen Kabbalah and the Talmudic sages and to argue — in the name of the Kabbalists and in the name of the truth — that, wherever one finds ambiguity in their words, the Kabbalah is indeed meant to be the authentic interpretation of the Sages, is not only anachronistic if presented as an alternative approach, but also anarchistic as research generally. Idel's positions are spontaneous "brainstorms"; even if his chapter on methodology contains important polemics with several principles of Kabbalistic thought (such as the connection between Kabbalah and philosophy), his approach does not allow any true *Lebensraum* for the historical philological method. He rejects the approach in order to save a half-baked assumption opposed to a supposedly exaggerated "rationalism." All this is true even if the substantive question itself remains open

60 See Idel, Chapter 7, pp. 156–172.

to discussion: namely, to what extent is the understanding of Kabbalah as a revolution in the world of Judaism correct?

Idel's remark that, "there seems to be a great gap in the estimation of the Kabbalah between its popular understanding as an ancient authentic esoteric Jewish lore and the scholarly disenchantment with this phenomenon as an intrusion of Gnosticism and Neoplatonism under the misleading guise of esoteric Judaism" (p. 34), seems to me to be a total misreading of Gershom Scholem's understanding of the place of Kabbalah in Judaism. Scholem did not describe Kabbalah as a deception within Jewish culture; on the contrary, he described Jewish mysticism as a vibrant and even central element of creativity, and at the same time as catalyzing the greatest crises in the homogenous wholeness of this culture. The question of the function fulfilled by the Kabbalah, and the historical question as to whether its gnostic character originated in an external Gnosis or from an inner Jewish one, are totally unrelated. Scholem simply did not wish to sacrifice his own critical distance. His respect for the distinction between historical conjecture and the exegetical forcing of the texts in consequence, on the one hand, and the philological caution needed to reconstruct the cultural contours of these texts, on the other, is deserving of our appreciation. These are the basic tools of any philological research. Philology is not the enemy of phenomenology, as one might think from Idel's study, nor does it constrict the boundaries of consciousness or experience — and certainly not those of historical or social science.

What does Idel have to say about the study of Hasidism?

Idel presents himself as one who has pioneered the understanding of Hasidism as mysticism generally, and the phenomenon of *unio mystica* in particular. It is true that he stresses the interesting fact that *unio* already existed among the Kabbalists prior to Hasidism. However, this is far from being an attempt at an alternative methodological reading of the Hasidic text. One does not see the traces of this methodological revolution in his repeated descriptions of the school of the Maggid of Mezhirech, which closely follow the general outlines sketched in the present study. Indeed, the principles of the descriptions of the mystical aspects of Hasidic personalities, the choice of literature, and at times even the very quotations cited in this book, constitute the focus for Idel's interest as well.[61] It is superfluous to add that one could have chosen an entirely different set of texts from among those found in Hasidic literature, and that we would have benefitted had Idel's remarks contained some new analysis of them. The opposite, however, is the case: Idel takes a "stance," so to speak, from which he attacks certain unnamed opponents, but does not describe any new experiential circumstances nor any new mystical ideas, such as one might have expected from the new methodology that he proposes.

61 See Idel, Ch. 4, esp. pp. 65–73.

In conclusion, I would like to mention certain substantial problems in the study of Hasidism which still require analysis, whether it be "rationalistic" or "experimental-experiential": e.g., the relationship of mysticism to the overall social framework; to the ritual framework; clarification of the literary sources and the differences among them as regards the function which they fulfilled in Hasidism; the teaching of the Besht and his circle, which has not yet been adequately studied — despite the substantial studies of Heschel and of Joseph G. Weiss; Lurianic Kabbalah and the influence of its ritual upon Hasidism; and the like. In my opinion, under the influence of his pretense to a new method, Idel lost sight of what research has already accomplished in the location of those problems which remain outstanding between mysticism and other frameworks, while his alleged new perspective has not added to the understanding of mysticism itself.

V. The Teachings of Hasidism

The teachings of Hasidism are notable both for their striking content as well as for the colorful literary form in which they are cast. Their sources, however, are readily traced to Kabbalistic literature and to the Kabbalistic–Musar literature of Safed which derived from it. The first generation of Hasidic teachers generally embodied their teachings in terse aphorisms, which likewise reflect the influence of the aforementioned literature. The earliest evidence of the spread of Hasidic teaching dates from the 1750's, and comes from the anti-hasidic polemical writings of their implacable opponents, the Mitnaggedim. Authentic Hasidic teachings appeared in print only at the beginning of the 1780's, and make no reference to the doctrines ascribed to them by their Mitnageddic opponents. Two possible explanations suggest themselves for this curious fact. Either the Mitnaggedim were guilty of exaggeration and distortion in their hostile description of Hasidic doctrine, or a process of internal criticism had moderated the original Hasidic teachings during the decades preceding their publication. It seems likely that both factors were at work. This does not mean to imply, however, that the teachings of the Baᶜal Shem Tov recorded by his disciples are to be regarded as having been censored, thus casting doubt on their authenticity, but only that the antinomian and anarchistic doctrines taught by certain circles were not incorporated into classical Hasidism. While no evidence of the specific character of such teachings is available, there can be no doubt of the existence of such groups.

The teachings of the earliest circles of Hasidim were transmitted in the name of Israel Baᶜal Shem Tov, Judah Leib Piestanyer, Naḥman of Kosov, Naḥman of Horodenka, and others. This was a group of decided spiritual (i.e., pneumatic) cast, which fashioned for itself a specific communal life-style built, not around family units, but rather on meetings organized around prayer circles. As a matter of principle, this pattern served as the basis for the development of the classic Hasidic community.

One may say that, for the first time in the history of Jewish mysticism, Hasidic thought reflects certain social concerns. One finds a confrontation with distinctly societal phenomena and their transformation into legitimate problems within mysticism as such. This is expressed, not by the establishment of specific liturgical norms or formulas devised for the convenience of the congregation, but in such doctrines as the worship of God through every material act and the "uplifting of the sparks" (*niẓoẓot*). In the teachings of the Besht and his circle, these doctrines involved a sense of social mission.

One of the most widespread teachings of Hasidism from the very outset of the movement is that calling for man's worship of God by means of corporeal acts (*ᶜavodah be-gashmiyut*); that is to say, the physical dimension of man is regarded as an area capable of religious behavior and value. A variety of religious tendencies follow from this assumption. To be especially noted is the extraordinary emphasis placed on the value of such worship and the subsequent attempt to limit it to a devotional practice suitable only for spiritually superior individuals. This doctrine developed in uncontrolled fashion in the teachings of the Besht, culminating in the tenet that man must worship God with both the good and the evil in his nature.

The ideological background of worshipping God through such physical acts as eating, drinking, and sexual relations was suggested by the verse, "In all thy ways shalt thou know Him" [Prov. 3:6]. If it is incumbent upon man to worship God with all his natural impulses by transforming them into the good, then the realization of such an idea demands involvement in that very area in which these impulses are made manifest — the concrete, material world. In addition, the revolutionary views concealed within the interstices of the teachings of the Besht make it clear that corporeal worship saves man from the dangers of an overwrought spiritualism and retreat from the real world. This is expressed by Jacob Joseph of Polonnoye, a disciple of the Baᶜal Shem Tov, in the name of his teacher:

> I have heard from my teacher that the soul, having been hewn from its holy quarry, ought ever after to long for its place of origin; and lest its reality be extinguished as a result of its yearning, it has been surrounded with matter, so that it may also perform material acts such as eating, drinking, conduct of business and the like, in order that it [the soul] may not be perpetually inflamed by the worship of the Holy One blessed be He, through the principle of the perfection (*tiqqun*) and maintenance of body and soul.[62]

62 R. Jacob Joseph of Polonnoye, *Toldot Yaᶜaqov Yosef* (Jerusalem, 1966 [photo edition of Korets, 1780]), *Parashat Tazriᶜa*, p. 83c.

The point made here in advocacy of corporeal worship is largely psychological and not theological.

The theological concept designed to reinforce the affirmation of corporeal worship is grounded in the dialectical relationship between matter and spirit. Man must pass through the material stage in order to reach the spiritual goal, as the spiritual is only a higher level of the material. The Ba^{c}al Shem Tov's parables of the "lost son" point to the theological function served by the concept of "corporeal worship." The son, in foreign captivity, enters the local tavern with his captors, all the while guarding within him a hidden secret which is the key to his redemption. While his captors drink only for the sake of drinking, he drinks in order to disguise his true happiness which consists, not in drinking, but rather in his "father's letter" — his secret — informing him of his impending release from captivity. In other words, there is no way to be liberated from the captivity of matter except by ostensibly cooperating with it. This ambivalent relation to reality is a supreme religious imperative.[63]

The dialectic tension between matter and spirit or matter and form — the conventional formulation in Hasidism — acquires social significance, and the polarities come to denote the relationship between the *ẓaddiq* and his flock. In this context, the opposition between spirit and matter is conceived so as to create a seeming tension between the inner content of the mystical act and the forms of social activity. However, it is within the community that mystical activity should be performed — though of course in hidden fashion. Those who surround the *ẓaddiq* are incapable of discerning individually the moment at which the transformation of the secular into the holy occurs, which can only be experienced communally. Thus, the community of Hasidim becomes a necessary condition for the individual's realization of the mystical experience. It became the imperative of Hasidism to live both within society and beyond its bounds at one and the same time. The social and psychological conditions necessary for fulfillment of "corporeal worship" are rooted, not only in the disparity between form and matter — i.e., between the *ẓaddiq* and the folk — but rather in the inner spiritual connection between the two. Only the presence of a common denominator facilitates the emergence of a mystical personality which grows dialectically out of otherwise disparate elements. The *ẓaddiq* represents the "particular amid the general." The absence of such integration precludes the consequent growth of the spiritual element.

Relatively little stress is placed within the teachings of the Ba^{c}al Shem Tov on those aspects of Lurianic Kabbalah which center upon the "uplifting of sparks." Nevertheless, these theories later served as the justification for *^{c}avodah*

63 The concept of *^{c}avodah be-gashmiyut* is developed at greater depth below, in the Introduction.

be-gashmiyut. Lurianic theory, as interpreted by the Ḥasidim, maintains that, by means of contact with the concrete material world through *devequt* ("communion" with God) and *kavvanah* ("devotional intent"), man uplifts the sparks imprisoned in matter. Within this context, the concept of *ᶜavodah be-gashmiyut* carries a distinctly polemical note, as it is asserted that its validity has particular application to the sphere of social life.[64] Thus, a major religious transvaluation finds expression in the creation of a new system of social relations. This is exemplified in the instructions given by the Besht permitting one to desist from *devequt* during prayer in order to respond to some social need. He indicates that, should a person be approached during a period of *devequt* by another wishing to talk to him or seeking his assistance, he is permitted to cease praying because, in the latter action (i.e. the redirecting of ones attention from prayer to his fellow), "God is present." Here, the temporary abandonment of the study of Torah (*biṭṭul Torah*) and of *devequt* is justified by the fact that this encounter too constitutes part of the spiritual experience of the "spiritually perfect man." As a result, the meaning of religious "perfection" is determined by a new system of values.

These motifs disappear in the teachings of the Baᶜal Shem Tov's disciple, Dov Baer, the Maggid of Mezhirech, whose thinking takes a completely typical spiritualistic direction. *ᶜAvodah be-gashmiyut* is conceived of as an indispensable necessity, although it is covertly questioned whether everybody is allowed to engage therein. A pupil of one of the Maggid's disciples, Meshullam Feibush of Zbarazh, specifically states that it was not the Maggid's intention to proclaim *ᶜavodah be-gashmiyut* as a general practice, but rather as one intended for an elite immune to the danger of the concept's vulgarization. One of the most important disciples of the Maggid, Shneur Zalman of Lyady, mentions the practice with a touch of derision.[65] It nevertheless came to occupy a central place in the literature of Hasidism. The meaning and limits of the concept served as the focal point for an ongoing controversy among the movement's proponents.

Everyone praised the "wisdom" of Hasidism for its affirmation of "service in corporeality" (*ᶜavodah be-gashmiyut*), with the knowing wink of those who understand the way of the world, imagining that therein lay the secret of its success in society. There would seem to be no easier way to serve God than that of Enoch, "who sewed shoes, and with every stitch united the Holy One blessed be He and his Shekhinah": i.e., to fulfill one's religious obligations easily and to enjoy the acknowledgment of the social elite at one and the same time.

But two important questions arise at this point in our discussion: First, what is

64 See the Appendix to the present volume, "The Besht's Commentary to Psalm 107 — Myth and Ritual."

65 See Chapter 12 below, "Anti-Spiritualism in Hasidism."

the nature of this "worship" and how does it acquire its religious legitimacy? Second, does one find within the Hasidic writings a call to the masses to choose it as an easy path, and as one by which they may join the Hasidic movement? In other words: was there a sociological distinction in the religious formula of "service through corporeality" from the outset?

It is a known fact that the earliest circle of Hasidim, which both speaks in praise of *ᶜavodah be-gashmiyut* and deals with social questions — and even attempts to classify society in terms of "men of matter" and "men of form" (as does R. Jacob Joseph of Polonnoye, for example) — makes no attempt to call upon people to join Hasidic society on the basis of ideological arguments connected with this concept. On the contrary: the religious practice of *ᶜavodah be-gashmiyut* (whose meaning will be explained below), which in principle acknowledges every act as a form of religious action under certain circumstances, does not relate at all to the "men of matter." It would follow from this that the earliest theoreticians of Hasidism did not draw any connection between the social stratum of an individual and the form of religious worship which was, so to speak, appropriate to them. If, in the primary sources, they spoke in an encouraging way of the masses of the populace or "men of matter," this was not intended to be connected with a dialectical ideology, which so to speak says that the simple person should worship "in matter" and the educated person "in spirit." The fact that the founders of Hasidism were not conscious of such a distinction teaches us that the problem of religious action is not resolved in terms of social interests, but through a totally different spiritual outlook.

A second fact which strengthens this observation is connected with the *Hanhagot* (Regimens Vitae) literature, which Hasidism disseminated as propaganda to the masses. Study of this literature reveals how surprisingly strict Hasidism was regarding the dissemination of its ideas, and that it refrained from any attempt to win over the masses at the price of a distorted interpretation of *ᶜavodah be-gashmiyut*. It preached its innovations in their full spiritual stature, and did not attempt to compensate anybody for the loss of worldly pleasures. On the contrary, it taught that only an attitude of indifference towards the things of this world will turn him into a true servant of God! This idea is not particularly powerful as propoganda for winning over souls: if Hasidism in fact intended to missionize (which I believe was its intention!), it did not do so at the price of vulgarization of its ideas. I reject from the outset the idea of the "popularization" of Hasidism as an intellectual system.

Another point which cannot be ignored is the tone used by the earliest sources — particularly the teaching of the Maggid — in referring to the question of *ᶜavodah be-gashmiyut*. One does not feel here any sense that the burden of the spirit has been eased through means of *ᶜavodah be-gashmiyut* but that, to the contrary, man is required to serve in corporeality even though it is a difficult area to master! The Maggid of Mezhirech comforts man, "that he should not feel sorry if he serves in corporeality," as there is no escape from this necessary standing before God. This can also hardly be considered as a "popular" propaganda point.

But our main concern is with understanding the second question: the significance of *ᶜavodah be-gashmiyut*. An explanation of this problem, however brief, will clarify the stance and nature of Hasidic activism, which is of vital importance for understanding the relation between activist and quietist elements in Hasidic religious thought.

ᶜAvodah be-gashmiyut is interpreted in Hasidism as an expansion of the scope of "holy service" (*ᶜavodat ha-qodesh*). Instead of viewing certain specific times and acts as suitable for this "service," the boundaries of action and time are expanded and themselves become legitimate givens. This changes the criterion for the concept of "holiness" in itself, as it no longer recognizes in principle the sanctifying or sanctified "acts" in themselves, but rather the manner of their performance as sanctifying the action; we are no longer dealing with the execution of a sacrament, but with man's overall meaningful experience with the world of the spirit. The horizon of action broadens to include all of man's actions — even the most elementary — such as eating, drinking and sexual relations, and all forms of work and business.

Hasidism unequivocally prohibited flight from the world or self-mortification as a religious experience. From now on, the sphere of religious problematics was confined to the activist obligation, on the assumption that the flight from contact with concrete reality was forbidden. Suddenly, the realm of the concrete appears before man in a personal way to demand of him its redemption; it seeks contact with him, to which he must respond. The myth of cosmic redemption comes to life here again in a new and interesting fashion: it is not man who seeks to redeem the Godhead in order to restore its full stature and thereby bring the messiah — as in Lurianic Kabbalah — but the "divine sparks" present in reality which approach man to seek their redemption and to be restored to their source. Man is unable to ignore the "cry" of the sparks imprisoned within matter; therefore, his ignoring of the realm of the concrete which is on the periphery of his life is considered as an insult to the longings of the concrete to be redeemed.[66]

The active power is present within human thought, and only through its means is the transformation from the concrete to the abstract possible — i.e., to the Divine "Nothing" by which the things are again "equal" to one another. This means that the negation of concrete existence is its redemption, and it yearns towards this eternal redemption, in the sense that its own negation is its redemption.

66 See below, "Myth and Ritual."

This is the classical explanation of the "uplifting of sparks" (*ha*[c]*alat ha-niẓoẓot*) — in great brevity, of course — and a positive connection exists between this matter and [c]*avodah be-gashmiyut*. Man is expected to respond. The call for [c]*avodah be-gashmiyut* is therefore one which makes greater, rather than lesser, demands upon the individual; flight and insulation from concrete reality, and the sense of contempt towards "corporeal" phenomena, are thus a sin and a closing of one's ears to the mission to which man is called. The expansion of the realm of "holy service" thus presents us with the basic problem: is not one's attitude towards concrete reality as such also changed as a result of the expansion of the realm of divine service?

I stated previously that the problematics begins only within the framework of inner obligation towards the concrete; indeed, the true gap between man and reality only opened up from the moment that [c]*avodah be-gashmiyut* became seen as obligatory. This gap is a necessary one, making the redemption of the "spark" conditional and assuring that man will not be drawn into the concrete itself. Hasidism worked hard to explain itself through saying that contact which is seemingly necessary is not true spiritual contact! It stressed the schizophrenic element within [c]*avodah be-gashmiyut*, explaining that the full service within "corporeality" is only that which man performs as a given action, while his spirit is focused elsewhere. It explicitly warned against "corporeal happiness," for which reason it attempted to limit this "service" to unique individuals alone! Indeed, even those who argued that "one who does not serve in corporeality does not serve in the spiritual realm either," did not intend to change its meaning or to soften this concept. Everyone knew that there was an inherent danger of vulgarization of this idea, yet nevertheless did not hesitate to preach it. In any event, none of the Hasidic thinkers advocated an interpretation which would encourage "the sanctified profane," as Buber put it, and no one claimed that one is required to rejoice in the concrete as such, which is sanctified by contact with man. One cannot imagine Hasidism coming up with a secular formula such as that which Buber ascribed to it, according to which the very act of dialogic contact with reality is its sanctification. While we are dealing here with a positive activism on the part of Hasidism, this is a very paradoxical activism, which strives to negate and to be negated within the divine reality. Man is asked "to attach himself" to the concrete in order to nullify it as such; in practice, Hasidism created a severe crisis in relation to the concrete, for it did not seek to reach out and to apprehend it — as in Buber's opinion — but, without passing it over, sought to reach beyond time and place. At most, it was a paradoxical motivation for the true strivings of Hasidism.

It is true that the great enthusiasm attached to the Beshtian formula, "In all your ways know Him," primarily evokes the positive emotional feeling of Hasidism towards [c]*avodah be-gashmiyut*, and that this slogan is everywhere accompanied by the joy of elevation — at times an intoxicated joy towards receiving the great truth which has been revealed. This joy doubtless carries an enormous emotional weight, both in the life of society and in ecstatic prayer. However, this tone is immanently connected with the inner style of Hasidism, which thrusts itself with all its power to meet any situation and any idea which it advocates, and does not need to delude the reader with the theoretical meaning by which Hasidism explains itself. The self-analysis emerging from its own propaganda is transparent and unequivocal, and its principles are clearly known to itself through the very fire with which they are expressed. Even those passages describing situations which are extremely passive from a spiritual viewpoint are expressed with an ardent tone, which leaves a very activistic impression; even there the minor key does not penetrate, so that all the talk of human and cosmic "nothingness" (*ʾayin* and *ʾefes*) are imbued with both pathos and nonchalance. Hasidism knew how to live with the paradoxes within itself, with simultaneous feelings of intense mission and a tendency to negation and non-activity, so that the boundaries between things is not always clear. It knew how to wage battle for the purity of its ideas and how to distort its values when historically necessary; it was simply too rich in the realm of the spirit and too successful in the social-historical realm to confine itself to loyalty to a well-defined, "clean" ideological line. It is impossible to decribe it in monovalent terms, albeit the present work is an attempt directed towards that impossible goal. The phenomenon always incorporates more than the sum of the lines used to describe it analytically, a point which must ultimately be taken into account whenever we speak of any living historical phenomenon. Nevertheless, we cannot excuse ourselves from making some effort at understanding. We are attempting to understand one group of ideas which stands out within an entire system of teaching — that is, in which one can recognize the signs of an inter-weaving bearing a certain logic, making one idea subordinate to another. When such a system becomes transparent to the eye of the reader, he must isolate and analyse it, understand its arguments and weigh it in terms of the historical-religious factors out of which it emerged.

From the moment that the formula *yeridah le-ẓorekh ʿaliyyah* ("the descent in behalf of the ascent") became established in the context of the emphasis placed upon it by the Baʿal Shem Tov, a certain perturbation of the traditional system of ethical values in Judaism was imminent. Although the precise limits of the descent into the region of evil were still open to debate, the acceptance in principle of man's mandate to "transform" evil into good, through an actual confrontation of evil in its own domain, was an idea definitely unwelcome in any institutionalized religion. The classical example of dealing with this problem propounded in the teachings of the Baʿal Shem Tov was that of the encounter with evil in the sphere of human impulses: "A man should desire a woman to so great an extent that he refines away his material existence, in virtue of the strength of his desire." The significance of this statement lies in its granting a warrant to exhaust the primordial desires without actually realizing them; it is not a dispensation for the release of bodily desires through their physical actualization, but through their transformation. This concept is of great importance for an understanding of the significance of confronting evil, as it points to the peculiar inner logic implicit in the idea of *ᶜavodah be-gashmiyut* as expressed in the ethical sphere.

Within the framework of the concept of "descent" (*yeridah*) — a concept over which Hasidism wavered a great deal — one may include the idea of the "descent" of the *ẓaddiq* to the sinner in order to uplift him. This "descent" carries with it bold ethical implications, in that it justifies the "descent" into the sphere of evil and demands the consequent "ascent" from the domain of sin. There is of course an implicit moral danger that a person may "descend" and thereafter find himself unable to achieve the consequent ascent. Here again, the very act of confronting evil requires an independent valuation, admitting of no previous criticism or censorship, although such confrontation was regarded as the special prerogative of men of "spirit" — i.e., the *ẓaddiqim*. Thus, a primary imperative to turn toward material reality and the worldly inferior sphere arose from the teachings of the Baᶜal Shem Tov. If only in moral terms, this demand grew from a basic ethic-religious claim that man is not at liberty to abstain from the task of transfiguring the material world through good.

The teachings of the Maggid of Mezhirech reveal a more restrained doctrine, on the one hand, and an interiorization of spiritual problems, on the other, evidenced by the greater degree of introspection and inwardness characteristic of the mystic. One can discern in the Maggid a tendency toward increasing spiritualization, accompanied by greater moral restraint. Among the followers of the Maggid, however, developments took a number of rather different directions. In the courts of some *ẓaddiqim*, the influence of the thinking of the Baᶜal Shem Tov was apparent in their doctrines, propagating social responsibility and a communal mysticism. Centers of this teaching developed primarily in Galicia, the Ukraine, as well as at the court of the Rabbi of Lublin in Poland. This latter school reached a crisis point during the period of its heirs in Przysucha, Kotsk, and Izbica, when it began to cast doubt on the large bulk of accepted Hasidic doctrines, especially on their moral significance. At the same time, Ḥabad Hasidism in Belorussia developed in the direction of a rationalized religious life by preserving pre-Hasidic moral biases and shunning the mystical adventurism of the Baᶜal Shem Tov and even of the Maggid of Mezhirech. The latter, in his attempt to spiritualize reality, declared the necessity of confrontation with evil and laid down the conditions for this conflict, seeing the great mission of Hasidism in the "uplifting of the sparks."

Nevertheless, in the person of Dov Baer, son of Shneur Zalman of Lyady, the founder of Ḥabad Hasidism, one can discern a thinker with a tendency toward a pure and aristocratic mysticism, which establishes his affinity to the views of the Maggid of Mezhirech, albeit this is true only in terms of this aristocratic bent. In terms of "ethical mentality," as it were, Dov Baer is a representative of his father's line of thought.

In the second and third generation of Hasidism, some Hasidim testified to the fact that, in their view, the major innovation of the Baᶜal Shem Tov lay in his introducing a fundamentally new significance to prayer, as well as new modes of praying. R. Kalonymus Kalman Epstein of Cracow, disciple of R. Elimelech of Lyzhansk and author of the book *Maᵓor va-Shemesh*, writes, "Ever since the time of the holy Baᶜal Shem Tov, of blessed and sanctified memory, the light of the exertion of the holiness of prayer has looked out and shone down upon the world, and into everybody who desires to approach the Lord, blessed be He . . ." This can be understood to mean that the Hasidim saw two things in the doctrine of the Baᶜal Shem Tov, which are essentially one: the radiance (of the light of holiness) and new hope, and the revived exertion (involved in the holiness of prayer). These dual motifs began to function as guidelines for Hasidic prayer, in the following senses:

1) The origins of prayer lie in the conflict with the external world, known as "evil thoughts." Prayer requires a great effort of concentration if man is to overcome the tendency for his consciousness to be permeated by the plentitude of exterior reality. This perfectly natural permeation to which man instinctively responds is considered in Hasidism as the "straying" of thought, and as such is the very opposite of its concentration, which requires negation of the world and turning away from it, and is based on man's ability to achieve pure introspection devoid of all content. The function of this introspection is to achieve the utter voiding ("annihilation") of human thought and to uplift the element of divinity latent in man's soul. The transformation of this element from a latent to an active state is understood as true union with God, marking the climax of *devequt* ("attachment to" or "communion with God"). Prayer, then, is regarded as the most accessible foundation for the technique of *devequt*. The spiritual effort involved in prayer was considered so strenuous as to give rise to the Hasidic dictum, "I give thanks to God that I remain alive after praying."

2) The two stages described as constituting the process of prayer are *dibbur* ("speech") and *maḥshavah* ("thought"). In passing through the first of these stages, man contemplates the words of the prayer by visualizing their letters. Concentrated attention on the objects before his eyes gradually depletes the letters of their contours and voids thought of content, and the verbal recitation of prayer becomes automatic. Man continues to recite the prayers until an awesome stillness descends upon him, and his thought ceases to function in particulars; he establishes

a connection with the divine "World of Thought," which functions simultaneously on transcendent and immanent perceptible levels. This immanent activity is identical with the revelation of the "apex," the inner "I." In the word-play of the Hasidim: "the I (*ʾani*) becomes Nought (*ʾayin*)"; a condition of utter annulment is established in the "flash of an eye," tantamount to the state of nothingness sought by the mystic.

3) For Hasidism, the significance of prayer lies neither in beseeching the Creator and supplicating Him, nor in focusing attention on the contents of prayer. Rather, prayer is primarily a ladder by means of which man can ascend to *devequt* and union with the Divinity. Hasidism did not embrace the Lurianic doctrine of *kavvanot*, as it failed to accord with the primary intent of *devequt*. However, in spite of all the individualistic tendencies inherent in prayer through *devequt*, the Hasidim did not belittle the importance of communal worship, nor did they demand that the *ḥasid* achieve *devequt* outside the bounds of the community and the halakhic framework of prayer. When problems arose concerning prayer through *devequt* within the framework of the time sequence conventionally set for prayer, there were those Hasidim who chose to dispense with that framework, and even allowed a man to worship outside of the time limits set for prayer, provided that he infused his prayer with *devequt*. However, as a result, the Hasidim rapidly felt themselves in danger of jeopardizing the framework of the halakhah and, for the most part, recanted and accepted the authority of the existing frameworks.

4) *Devequt*, which was the banner under which Hasidism went forth to revitalize religious life and modify the traditional hierarchy of values in Judaism, quickly led to a confrontation with the daily pattern of existence of the *ḥasid*. Not only was traditional worship and its significance confronted with new problems, but the same held true for Torah study. The reason for this lay, not in a fundamental revolt against the study of the Torah as such, but in the fact that *devequt* laid claim to the greater part of man's day and left little time for learning. *Devequt* gained the ascendency in this confrontation, although one can detect in Hasidic sources a tendency to strike a balance with the problematic nature of prayer in order to prevent the study of Torah being swallowed up in mysticism. During the 19th century, a distinct reaction took place in certain Hasidic "courts" in the direction of scholarship at the expense of *devequt*.

The performance of the *miẓvot*, too, and all of man's attendant actions, was overshadowed by *devequt*, as the fulfilling of the *miẓvot* was assessed in terms of the *devequt* achieved by man. The *miẓvah* itself became no more than one of several means of achieving *devequt* in the hierarchy of values. The widespread Hasidic slogan, "Performance of the *miẓvah* without *devequt* is meaningless," bears supreme testimony to the fact that the new mystical morality came to terms with traditional Jewish patterns on a new plane.

Man's existential status was conceived anew in Hasidism, and an attitude of resignation toward the world was emphasized. The *ḥasid* was asked to rejoice in order to obviate any possibility of self-oriented introspection which might lead him to substitute personal satisfaction for the worship of God, as his initial goal. The Hasidim went to great lengths to crystallize the primary awareness that they were first and foremost "sons of the higher world."

VI. Activism and Quietism

There can be no doubt that, in terms of the scope of material discussed in Hasidism, there is far more which pertains to our understanding of its activist teachings than to its passive aspects. Nevertheless, in attempting to isolate these two factors from each other, I chose to deal specifically with the passive-quietistic elements therein, in view of the scope of my project. The reason for this is rooted, first of all, in the fact that the activist side is treated far more extensively in the existing descriptions of Hasidism in the scholarly literature, although there is still need for a comprehensive study of this aspect as well. Such problems as "the raising up of the sparks," the redemption of "alien thoughts" during prayer, *ᶜavodah be-gashmiyut*, and the doctrine of the "descent" or "fall" of the *ẓaddiq* — all of which are discussed at length in Hasidic sources — have enjoyed scholarly attention, even if they have not been examined in terms of their internal role within the overall context of the Hasidic system of ideas. It has not yet been clarified what religious interests underlie these theories, which of them are the result of renewed religious awakening, which of them dominate the world of Hasidism as a result of certain social developments which Ḥasidism underwent, and what transformations each of these ideas had undergone in the course of history. All of these questions need to be considered in a substantive analysis of Hasidic activism.

However, the main reason for my decision to portray the quietistic elements within Hasidism is not only the fact that this question has not yet been discussed thus far, but its own intrinsic importance. Had Hasidism shut itself off from the beginning within the narrow limits of contemplation, we might have found ourselves dealing with a phenomenon typologically more similar to the quietistic streams in other religions; the refusal to ignore the challenge of reality determined the difference and uniqueness of Hasidism, and made it far more complex, so that the balance of forces between quietism and activism is a question to which there is no unequivocal answer. Hasidism's choice of the path of paradox — which is not at all typical of quietistic movements — according to which one arrives at the most passive form of contemplation through confrontation with concrete reality, and not by bypassing it, was one which blinded scholarly study of Hasidism, which had been taken in by external appearances. Reality as a moving force does indeed constitute an important subject in Hasidism, combining within itself several central themes, but it also reflects the problem concerning the boundary between activism and quietism, this being no longer a motive for an eschatological tendency, as it was in the Kabbalah, but bearing a specifically mystic tendency. This change in values seems to me to bear an internal connection to quietistic concerns.

On the activist plane of "lifting up the sparks" or "lifting up alien thoughts," emphasis is placed upon the Lurianic picture of reality, as an abyss filled with divine light; man's active relation to reality, according to Hasidism, is required in order to separate the passive element of the *qelippah* (shell), which is never able to connect with holiness, and thereby prevents the integration of the spirit — for the spirit is united in all things, so that man returns this "exiled" element to its root by means of the pneumatic element within it. Likewise, the social-mystic sphere enjoys a similar enlightenment on the part of Hasidism, in which the affirmation implied in the "descent" or "fall" of the *ẓaddiq* into the realm of sin and impurity coalesces within a new ethical doctrine, which states — again according to the same logic — that external factors are relevant to the question of the wholeness of the spirit. Even the "abyss" within which the sinner finds himself is permeated with divine being, so that one is obligated to confront it. But this activism is also cautious, and does not tend to stress its paradoxical insights save on rare occasions. It is interesting that the activist plane remains in the shadow of the Lurianic doctrine of the "sparks" — albeit given a mystical exegetical twist, rather than a strictly eschatological one as in Lurianic Kabbalah — while those teachings which deal with pure contemplation and its meaning repeat the immanentist formula that "the whole world is filled with His glory." True, one also finds in Hasidism the attempt to identify these two doctrines concerning the "sparks" dwelling within the world with the doctrine of divine immanence. However, not only is there no historical identity between the two, but there is no similarity of content between the two approaches; generally speaking, one can recognize that the use of the immanentist doctrine and its emphasis is more common when the subject is one of contemplation and the explanation of the metapsychological elements in the human soul — i.e., questions which lead towards quietistic mysticism. I have already noted in the body of this work that the same holds true with regard to the theoretical basis of quietism outside of Hasidism.

But we must not be misled by the spirit of that activism which rejoices over realization. Since it is based in Hasidism upon an acosmic world-view, it is unable to have a fully "realistic" tendency: while it does require concretization, it simultaneously uproots its independent basis. The "real" is an illusion which, although demanding attention, is nevertheless the means through which one arrives, not at the existential, but at the ideal.

I will not enlarge any further upon the nature of these quietistic elements in the introduction, as the body of this work is concerned with its explanation and comparison with similar phenomena in the Christian world.

Several charges related to this subject are already alluded to in the anti-Hasidic polemics of the Mitnaggedim. Even though the problem is not articulated there in an explicit or precise manner, one can sense between the lines that there are complaints there concerning the "strangeness" to Judaism of the quietistic element, and the dangers inherent in both spiritual and social anarchism and in the tendency to cast off the burden of the law. Even the Maskilim who wrote against the Hasidic movement at the end of the 19th century did not overlook the "anti-quietistic" claims (if one can call them such) in their portrayals thereof as a threat to communal peace and social progress. However, their main concern was to stress several innovations in the social realm which, in their opinion, indicated the peculiar apathy of the Hasidim towards the values of classical Jewish civilization. Although they no longer identified with that tradition as their own — or at least not in the form in which it was to be found at that time — they feared that the "anarchistic" tendency of Hasidism hurt the interests of the Haskalah, and justifiably pinned greater hopes upon the rationalistic and well-organized society of non-Hasidic Jewry. A movement which sustained itself upon the inner values of the spirit and not those of external authority, and which in the course of doing so knew how to take measure of the relative value of the external world, was not an appropriate vehicle for the growth of the Haskalah.

The substance of the Mitnaggedic claims against Hasidism are brought in the course of this work, in which I also clarify the issues in terms of its overall context and meaning as a religious phenomenon. I have intended to clarify certain problems in Hasidism, the logic of whose presence within the context of organic, quietistic growth finds strikingly exact parallels in the writings of the Christian quietists and the arguments lodged against them by the Catholic Church.

However, my primary concern in this work is not to point to the resemblance between ideational "systems," except insofar as these are inherent in the very reading of the problems within the homiletic sources of Hasidism itself: the deliberate call within the sermonic material considered as a religious document — in which are contained the longings and the true conflicts of religious life. Both the nature of Hasidic quietism and its boundaries will be discovered by the reader within the work itself.

Chapter One

The Basic Argument of Quietism

In the history of religion, quietism is known as the path towards God via the abandonment of the self, the primary goal of which is the destruction of the natural forces in order to facilitate the action of the Divine within man. Miguel de Molinos (1640–1697), one of the greatest Christian quietist thinkers, said that "natural activity is the enemy of Divine grace."[1] So long as man continues to act, be it only in the realm of thought, God cannot act. True religious life implies total and utter identification with the activity of God, which is His will — a state of identification or unity that can only be attained by complete suppression of the human will. The first conclusion drawn from this identification of the human will with God is that the action of the perfect man is equivalent to the action of God Himself.[2]

It is clear that no established religion could oppose the principle, "Negate your own will before His will" [Avot 2:4] *per se*, as all religious precepts are ultimately given in order to realize God's will upon earth. The theological heresy discerned by the opponents of quietism throughout history was rather in the *reductio ad absurdum* whereby the Divine will becomes the only actor manifested in the world. According to this view, all that man needs to do to facilitate God's manifestation of His will is to erase the personal element; the more successful man is in refraining from voluntary activity, the closer he comes to realizing God's will on earth. The hidden core of quietistic faith is revealed in man's very readiness to serve as a vessel for Divine action. It follows from this that the best action a religious man may perform is to detach his self — i.e., as an active will and presence — before God, as such a presence is considered the most arrogant possible presentation of human will against Divine will; nothing is more strikingly opposed to true faith — in the eyes of the quietists — than the consciousness of self.

These theological assumptions might not have alarmed the opponents of quietism in themselves. What made it a persecuted and undesirable sect in the eyes of official Christianity was the accompanying transformation in the psychological

1 See P. Pourrat, "Quietisme," in *Dictionnaire de théologie catholique* (Paris, 1899–1950), Vol. XIII: col. 1537–1581, esp. col. 1572; the 4th Clause of the Bull issued by Pope Innocent XI against Molinos, in J. B. Bossuet, *Ouvrages sur le quiétisme* [Oeuvres Completes. 10 (Besoncan, 1863)], p. 153.

2 Pourrat, ibid., sec. 10.

means of attaining true contemplation, the loss of consciousness of self, and the anti-eucharistic conclusions which followed from the development of this new scale of values. Molinos, as an extreme quietist, was described as "the personification of the quietistic heresy."[3]

The central axiom of quietistic thought is the pantheistic idea that all that remains following the erasure of the self is God: God is present in man only in a passive way, which becomes able to act once the various garments or *potentia* of the soul and the intellect cease to act. The only human act which may be identified with the Divine will is that of total self- annihilation. Therefore, one can no longer speak of a voluntaristic outlook within the quietistic framework: God does not desire any particular thing from man — neither good nor evil, neither the performance of certain actions nor the refraining from others. On God's part, there is only the pure will which acts within us. It is clear that such a religious outlook is one of extreme quietism. But one may also speak of quietistic "tendencies" or "moods" without requiring such a strict definition of the exclusive will of God. Such a "tendency" may be expressed in an attitude of human indifference towards the world, society and the self, which yet allows room for a Divine voluntarism that is not indifferent towards His commandments. This is certainly a "respectable" way out, avoiding the outburst of anarchistic forces within religious society by recognizing the many legitimate means of realizing the Divine will.

The teachings of Hasidism, in which quietistic tendencies were prominently represented, exemplify the manner in which such phenomena were expressed in practice.

3 Ibid., col. 1572.

Chapter Two

The Concept of "Annihilation" (*ʾAyin*) and the Extinction of Human Will

At first blush, it seems strange that a broad social movement known primarily for its optimistic mood towards the world and its encouragement of everyday joy should serve as a source for understanding the phenomenon known as quietism. I wish to make it clear from the outset that it is not my intention to describe Hasidism *per se* as a quietistic movement; such a statement would clearly be a distortion of the truth. There is not yet much of a quietistic note during the earliest stages of the movement's growth, in the ideological formulations of the Baᶜal Shem Tov, considered to be the founder of the movement.[1] There is again, in the third and fourth generations of the movement, a decrease in the quietistic tension. Even within the school of the Besht's leading disciple, the Maggid of Mezhirech, there were some among his disciples who stressed this note, while others presented a less problematic form of Hasidism. There were in fact some disciples of the Maggid who outdid him in their radical quietism. The vacillation between quietism as a predominant stream and its retreat to the margins of religious life certainly gives room for thought. This study attempts to portray quietistic elements which were dominant within Hasidism, and to explain the factors which made for its flowering and decline, both in terms of immanent factors and external social reasons.

As we have seen, Christian quietism based the religious force of self annihilation, or *annihilatio*, on the negation of the individual will as the pre-condition for the activity of the Divine will. Quietism claimed that spiritual experience can only begin after the soul has already surrendered to God.[2] But this act of surrender is not based upon submission to Divine justice, but rather upon the negation of the powers of the soul. It is an inner "clearing of space," rather than the acceptance

1 J. G. Weiss, "*Via passiva* in early Hasidism," *Journal of Jewish Studies* 40, nos. 3–4 (1960), p. 145. Weiss alludes there to the absence of such motifs on the Baᶜal Shem Tov; however, one cannot speak of them as being entirely absent, as analysis of the sources cited below reveals that, while such elements are mostly found in the teaching of the Maggid of Mezhirech, aspects of this are not entirely absent in the teachings of the Baal Shem.

2 Ronald A. Knox, *Enthusiasm; A Chapter in the History of Religion* (Oxford, 1951), p. 239.

of the Divine yoke in the classical sense. The major quietistic features within Hasidism connected with the concept of annihilation (ʾ*iyun*) appear in the teachings of the Maggid, who was the leading theoretician of Hasidism. The tendency and theoretical context of his writings will be discussed in later chapters. However, before beginning the discussion of quietism in Hasidism *per se*, I would like to state an important axiom, which will be clearly seen throughout this work:

The predetermined boundaries of Hasidic quietism are clearly reflected through its very precepts. Whenever one attempts to sense the quietistic element within Hasidism which, particularly in the teachings of the Maggid and of his disciples, is quite powerful, one finds it engaged in a covert internal polemic with activist values, which Hasidism never refuted. Wherever one finds the aspect of the supreme value of the annihilation of individual will, one finds alongside it the problematic role of an activism which attempts to justify its existence by the claim that it also reflects the Divine will. It is as if God found pleasure in the simultaneous "stripping off of corporeality," as well as in the most elementary corporealization of physical life (even if this latter element entailed a strong spiritual direction!).

Quantitatively, the approach which attempts to portray the Divine will in relation to the "obligations of the limbs" is greater than that which sees it as demanding absolute self-abnegation. But statistics are not the decisive factor in the portrayal of inner tendencies. It is clearly not easy to distinguish between these two tendencies in all the sources from the school of the Maggid, but neither is it impossible. At times, the claim on behalf of the active life is made in an apologetic tone, while at others it is asserted in its own right. In both cases, the same formulations are used, so that only the general atmosphere and nuance enable one to define the tendency of the particular statement. Yet again, one's attention is drawn by formulations which speak in praise of total *annihilatio* as the primary longing of the *ḥasid*, understood as the willed identification of man and of God along lines similar to those of quietistic thought.

Formulae which speak explicitly of annihilation as an expression of the "Will" are not very common — as we have already said — but neither are they totally absent. In the small collection entitled *Kitvei Qodesh*, composed entirely of the teachings of the Maggid of Mezhirech,[3] we read:

3 On the title page it states that this is a collection "from four prominent people," imitating the title-pages of other works, such as *Liqqutei Yeqarim* and others (Lemberg, 1865; first published, 1796). This collection is extremely important for understanding the thought of the Maggid, and contains many formulations which do not appear in the other collections. All this was preserved in manuscript form by the Koznitzer Maggid for many years, and was only printed much later. A formula similar to the one found here appears in MS. Jerusalem–National Library 3282, which was in the possession of R. Ḥayyim Ḥaykl of Amdur, one of the important disciples of the Maggid. This

> In the name of R. Baer, may he live long, [concerning] the matter of the changes in the Creator: he and his changes are one,[4] for the Master receives his kingship from the opposites [act of] changing, for kingship is used [in reference to] the servants, to the fact that they do the opposite of their own will in order to do the will of the King. For if it were their will to do this thing, from whence would we know that they are doing this in order to receive the kingdom? ...[5]

These brief remarks imply that the true kingdom of the Divine is to be perceived in that situation in which man elevates his own will to the Divine "nothing," to the world of reconciliation of opposites in which "He and his opposite are one." The "servants" transform their personal will by its negation in the Divine will, thereby expressing their true acceptance of the kingship of God. This perception of the world of opposition as being situated within the Divine "nothing" is again mentioned in another sermon in the same source:

> ... for those who gaze at the Creator, blessed be He, bringing everything to nothingness... When they bring everything to nothingness, to the primordial matter, then everything is transformed — and this is called "war," and this is the world of transformation and of opposition,[6] and thereby one is victorious in all wars.[7]

An expansion of this Maggidic source concerning the changing of the individual will to the Divine will appears in certain remarks of R. Ḥayyim Ḥaykl of Amdur (d. 1787). He also accepted the axiom, important to our subject, that the

manuscript consists primarily of the Maggid's teachings as these were recorded by R. Levi Yitzhak of Berdichev; see the Introduction to my critical edition of *Maggid Devarav le-Yaᶜaqov* [below: Schatz, "Introduction"], p. xiv ff. It would seem that both the Maggid of Koznitz and R. Ḥayyim Ḥaykl preserved copies from the same source. The manuscripts also contain other teachings, which are evidently those of R. Ḥayyim Ḥaykl himself, and to which there are parallels in his book, *Ḥayyim va-Ḥesed* (Jerusalem, 1953).

4 Should read, *u-temurato*. This is a formula from the "Prayer of R. Neḥunyah ben ha-Kanah" composed by the circle of *Sefer ha-ᶜIyyun*, as G. Scholem informed me.

5 *Kitvei Qodesh me-Ḥakhmei ᵓEmet* (Warsaw, 1884), 26c. This work is a collection of writings of the Besht, the Maggid of Mezhirech, R. Levi Yitzhhak, and the Maggid of Kosnitz.

6 Which, according to the Kabbalah, is the world of the "Other Side" (*sitra ᵓaḥra*). It is however clear here that we are speaking of a world in which all the contradictions within reality are nullified.

7 *Kitvei Qodesh*, p. 8c. The identity of the concepts of nullity and will appears also in the MS. of R. Ḥayyim Ḥaykl of Amdur mentioned above, f. 155a: "'Even with wisdom He established the earth' [Prov. 3:19]. That Wisdom contracts itself [out of its great shame], and draws itself down into nothingness for his great shame, and as the primal love is called the simple Will, there it is just love, and there it is simple goodness, and all the miracles in the world come from that place; and he may correct the matter, even though it was a very long time, he may advance the good in a miraculous way when he brings the thing about to simple will, and there is no time there, as said above, but only simple goodness..." The idea that the "negation of the intellect" brings about the connection to the supernal will also appears in R. Ḥayyim Ḥaykl of Amdur's *Ḥayyim va-Ḥesed*, p. 54.

transformation of the human will to the Divine will is tested at the time of annihilation, and that only thereby can man bring the things towards the Divine nothingness. Instead of the "I" being transformed into "nothing" (*ʾani* to *ʾayin* — a widely-used Hasidic word-play), the human will becomes Divine.[8] He writes as follows:

> It is known that the Holy One, blessed be He, created in us a distinct [i.e., autonomous] will, so that we might subject our will to His, from which He has pleasure — and such would not be the case if we did not have a distinct will. And when we negate our own existence, we are united with the hidden [i.e., with the nothing], and this is alluded to in [the verse], "And it (*hu*) and its substitute shall be sacred . . . [Lev. 27:33]" — that is, when he is united with "He" (*hu*),[9] which is hidden, then his "substitute" — i.e., even the will within us which is counterposed to the Holy One, blessed be He — "will be holy" — then all of his words will be for the sake of heaven.[10]

One might add that the sequel to these remarks of R. Ḥayyim Ḥaykl is quite illuminating, explaining not only the command of *annihilatio*, but also the dialectic existing between the Divine and the human will, which is also part of the innate law of the Divine will. That is to say: God, who reveals his will through speech (i.e., in a limited form), reveals the dual law of His will simultaneously in its pure form and in its specific contents. Man is therefore required to determine the point of departure of the fulfillment of the Divine will through the act, which reflects the manifestation of the Divine will, and therefrom to arrive at the pure will, from which every human desire has been removed. Only in the supreme place of the nothing does he become aware of the dialectical truth of "a thing and its opposite." This point is important, not only for understanding the theory of the doctrine of will, but also for the hidden purpose alluded to in these things — namely, that one's point of departure must be rather that we have been commanded by the Divine word. This approach is more harmonistic than that of classical quietism, which

8 It is interesting to compare here the quietistic claim (as cited by their opponents) that "they no longer have any will, as they are united with the Divine, and have reached negation with regard to themselves" — Pourrat, "Quietisme." The accusations came in wake of the quietistic conclusions regarding the cessation of all activity, and not because of their theories *per se*.

9 A term used for the hidden *Sefirah*, identified with the Divine "Nothing" (*ʾayin*).

10 *Ḥayyim va-Ḥesed* (Jerusalem, 1953), p. 155. In this edition, the book is arranged in a different sequence, based upon the sequence of verses in the Torah, specifically opposed to what is stated in the Introduction by the author's grandson in the first edition, Warsaw, 1891. This sentence is omitted from the Introduction to the 1953 Jerusalem edition; in the teachings themselves, I have not found any variant readings.

would deny entirely the importance of the active life,[11] whereas in Hasidism the struggle for the passive life exists in constant tension with the requirements of the active life.

R. Ḥayyim Ḥaykl's remarks continue:

> For servants are submissive to their king because of his word,[12] for the will of the king himself is not able to touch them, but only the word alone, for the will is revealed through the word. Certainly, were they able to comprehend his will, they would obey it, and the king does not reveal his will through speech, unless he knows that they obey him. For behold, the servants must negate their will before that of the king, [because] in the will of the king is revealed also the will of the servants.[13] For behold, the will of the king is very broad, and when he wishes to receive pleasure from it . . . he always sees that they should go into the act, and bring him pleasure from it, and this is called, "reflected light."[14] . . . But when we raise up our acts to their source . . . the will of the king becomes as it was in his will, and the will remains expanded as it was,[15] and afterwards he may draw down new life. And this is [what is said], that the righteous changes the attribute of judgment into the attribute of compassion, for they lift the act to its source, and for this reason the will of the king comes in expansion, and we are thereby able to draw down new life and compassion into the world. And this is [the aspect of] the king standing up. Meaning, when does the king stand? When the princes prostrate themselves, when they are bent to his will, and he lifts the acts up to their source.[16]

In R. Ḥayyim Ḥaykl's words, we find a reflection of all of the severity of

11 See, for example, *Early Fathers from the Philokalia*, selected and translated from the Russian Text *Dobrotolubiye* by E. Kadloubovsky and G. E. H. Palmer (London, 1954) [below: *Philokalia*], a collection of writings of the Eastern Church fathers and the hesachysts, at the beginning of the chapter on Symeon the New Theologian, pp. 98 ff.

12 The "word" here refers to the specific, delimited commandment, which reflects the non-"expanded" Divine will.

13 In the latter sense, of the will in the world of changes.

14 It is interesting to note here the use of the Kabbalistic concept of "reflected light" (*ʾor ḥozer*), in the context of the return of the "deed."

15 Before it was revealed in speech.

16 *Ḥayyim va-Ḥesed*, pp. 157–158. The inner dialectic between the "expanded" true will of God and the will apprehended by "slaves" is expressed sharply in the manuscript of R. Ḥayyim Ḥaykl, MS. Jerusalem,–National Library 4088, f. 6b. I cannot explain here the interesting connection between the concept of "contraction" (*ẓimẓum*) and "will" (*raẓon*), expressed in the same innate dialectical principle itself (ibid., f. 2b). Both *ẓimẓum* and the revelation of the Divine will are "worthless in his eyes." However, he surrendered to his inner longings in order to enter into the "deed," and therefore (according to one version there, fol. 1b), "The Holy One, blessed be He, gazed at the souls of the righteous and created the world." Read: not within the framework of the primeval Torah, but in terms of the spiritual ability of the mystics!

quietism, which finds it necessary to warn against any attempt to "separate oneself from the body" for eudaemonistic ends, even if this "separation" is motivated by the pursuit of spiritual pleasure and intoxication. It is difficult to know whether his warnings referred to any specific historical tendency, or whether they were merely intended to explicate the quietistic doctrine of annihilation, which sees itself as thereby fulfilling the Divine command and Divine will.[17] This may also be intended as a response to the external criticism of the Hasidim, which accused them of being preoccupied with "casting off materiality" between themselves and their Creator, and noted the nonchalant and anarchistic element in such preoccupation. He writes:

> There are people who separate themselves from the body because they wish to be free and not because of the will of the Creator, and this is also called a path — but it is false. And it is called a path on which I walk, as in, "a false path remove from me" [Ps. 119:29].[18] I beseech you that the path not be false, as above, [but] have mercy on me, that my removing of myself from the body be only because of Your will and Your Torah.[19]

There are two aspects to the repeated demands in Hasidism that a person become "as one who is non-existent" or "that he reach nothingness": namely, the metaphysical and the ethical. The metaphysical aspect is itself based upon two assumptions: the former associates *annihilatio* — the emptying out or negation of the individual — with the apprehension of the level of the divine "nothing," while the second assumption is based upon its acosmic philosophy. Already in the teaching of the Maggid of Mezhirech, we find a certain ideological complexity surrounding the concept of the "nothing." This concept, which originated in the early Kabbalah[20] as a purely theological concept defining the highest level of the divine hypostasis, acquired new theoretical contents in Hasidic thought. This was determined by the very fact that man is able to attain the Divine "nothing," and at that very moment to himself become transformed into "nothing." The application of theological terminology to the psychological life of man, which is a general characteristic of the Hasidic spirit, is in this case based upon more than mere similarity of terminology. The abnegation of the human "form" of man — that is, his existence as a human being — is the attainment of his true ideal form:

17 Concerning a possible historical source for this, see below, near the end of Ch. 12.

18 Based upon Ps. 119:29: "A false way remove from me, and by your Torah have mercy on me."

19 *Ḥayyim va-Ḥesed*, p. 119.

20 See G. Scholem, *Origins of the Kabbalah*, trans. A. Arkush (Philadelphia–Princeton, 1987), p. 414ff. [from the German: *Ursprung und Anfänge der Kabbala* (Berlin, 1962), p. 366ff.]; and *Reshit ha-Qabbalah, 1150–1250* (Jerusalem, 1948), p. 104.

read, the Divine "nothingness" which is simultaneously the truest and innermost essence of the Godhead. The Maggid says:

> "Make for yourself two trumpets (*ḥaẓoẓrot*) of silver" [Num. 10:2] — that is, two half forms (*ḥaẓi ẓurot*), as in, "And on the throne there was an image like the appearance of a man upon it from above" [Ezek. 1:26], for man is only *dalet mem* [i.e., *dam*, "blood" — the last two letters of the word ᵓ*Adam*], and speech inhers in him. But when he cleaves to the Holy One, blessed be He, who is the Master of the World [ᵓ*Alufo shel* ᶜ*Olam*, i.e., the ᵓ*Aleph* of the world], he becomes man (ᵓ*adam*) . . . and a man must separate himself from all corporeality, so that he ascends via all the worlds and unites with the Holy One, blessed be He, until he himself ceases to exist entirely, and then he is called ᵓ*Adam*. This is alluded to in [the verse], "upon the image of the throne" [ibid.] upon which He, may He be blessed, is covered, in the manner of "and cloud and fire turning within it" [ibid., v. 4] . . .[21]

While the two different usages of the term ᵓ*ayin* are not mentioned in the above passage, elsewhere in the Maggid's teaching the concept of "negation from existence" [*biṭṭul mi-meẓi*ᵓ*ut*] overlaps the state of "nothingness."[22] R. Ḥayyim Ḥaykl of Amdur makes some explicit comments about this:

> ". . . Long suffering" [Ex. 34:6] For among the thirteen qualities [of God's mercy] is the quality of long sufferingness [ᵓ*erekh* ᵓ*appayim*], meaning that we are below time while He, may He be blessed, transcends time; and this is [alluded to in the word] ᵓ*appayim* — two faces. And the Holy One, blessed be He, wished us to apprehend His face; therefore, he drew His light down via length, which is below time. This is [the hermeneutical principle known as] "a major principle [*binyan* ᵓ*av*] derived from two verses" — that is, the major principle [*binyan shel* ᵓ*av*, lit., "the structure of the father"] is drawn down by changes [*shinuyim*, a word play on "two (*shenei*) verses"].

Further on in the same sermon, he continues:

> This is [the meaning of] "A Song of Degrees, I lift up my eyes unto the mountains, from whence cometh my help" [Ps. 121:1]. The Patriarchs are called mountains, for they are the roof tops [*gagot* — also the initials of *Gedulah*, *Gevurah*, *Tif*ᵓ*eret*, the three *Sefirot* to which they correspond] from which one may gaze afar. And King David is the attribute of *Malkhut*, and he wished to gaze afar, and he said that "He

21 *Maggid Devarav le-Ya*ᶜ*aqov*, §24, pp. 38–39, and in ᵓ*Or ha-*ᵓ*Emet* (Brooklyn, 1942: photo ed. of Hosiatin, 1899), 10b, and elsewhere.

22 See, for example, *Shemu*ᶜ*ah Ṭovah* (Warsaw, 1938), in which the teaching of the Maggid is given, edited by R. Levi Yitzḥak of Berdichev, where, on p. 70b, it states: "and to strip off initially the vitality coming from the material thoughts and from the existence of ourselves, that is, that we may be able to enter into the gate of the nothing."

> [God] cannot be my help unless I connect myself to the Nothing." And this is "From whence [*me-ʾayin*, lit, from Nothing] cometh my help ..."[23]

The Maggid went so far as to utilize the *terminus technicus* of *ʾayin*, which appears in the older Kabbalah exclusively for God, as a synonym for the human soul.

> The Master[24] also said, "How is man the attribute of *ʾayin*? Only if man does nothing but that which pertains to his soul is he in the attribute of *ʾayin*, for the soul is something which nobody can apprehend."[25]

The divine Nothing is defined in identical terms in Kabbalistic literature: "that there is no one who apprehends it."[26] This axiom of *annihilatio*, although of great importance for understanding the mystical character of Hasidism generally, does not *per se* render it quietistic. The second assumption mentioned, that of acosmism, is more essential to the quietistic consciousness of the Hasidim. The concept of *ʾayin* — namely, the axiom that the world itself has no real existence, and that everything would be reduced to nothingness were it not for the fact that God sustains it at every moment — was used in its literal sense in the doctrine of acosmism. The *ʾayin* is the negation of all being, and also functions grammatically as a word of negation. It would be unnecessary to emphasize this point were it not for the fact that it serves as the background for the consciousness of man's nullity in Hasidic teaching. Man is not spoken of here as "nothing" in the sense of a positive being which disappears, whose metaphysical source is God and who is able to achieve "complete unity" with Him, but in terms of the self-understanding of man as a creature among others, entirely without independent existence. These are the Maggid's words:

> The *kavvanah* of [the word] "one" in the unification of the Recitation of *Shemaʿ* is to meditate that there is nothing in the entire world but the Holy One, blessed be He, for the whole world is full of His glory. And the main *kavvanah* is that man see himself as nought and nothing, and that his essence is only the soul that is within him, which is a portion of God above. Thus, there is naught in the entire world save the Holy One blessed be He, who is One, and the main intention of [the word] "One" is to

23. *Ḥayyim va-Ḥesed*, sec. *Ki Tisaʾ*, p. 47.

24 The publisher notes in parentheses, following the word "the Master" (*ha-Rav*), that this refers to the Baʿal Shem Tov. This seems to me to be incorrect, as in all of the works of the disciples of the Maggid the term, "the *Rav*" refers to the Maggid. See *Shemuʿah Ṭovah*, also edited by R. Levi Yitzḥak of Berditchev, as in the book *ʾOr ha-ʾEmet*, where the Baʿal Shem Tov is referred to throughout as "the famous Hasid" (*he-ḥasid ha-mefursam*), while the Maggid is called "the *Rav*."

25 *ʾOr ha-ʾEmet*.

26 See Scholem, *Reshit ha-Qabbalah*, op cit.: "what the thought cannot comprehend." However, Scholem explains this as only indirectly referring to human thought,

> reflect that the whole world is full of His glory, and there is no place empty of Him, may He be blessed.[27]

One of the most interesting commentators upon the Maggid's teaching, R. Meshullam Feibush Heller of Zbarazh, strongly emphasized this acosmic point. While homilies expressing this point of view already appear in the Ba^cal Shem Tov,[28] the Maggid's doctrine incorporated the acosmic assumption within his own ethical teaching: that is, the assumption of nothingness and nihility were converted into the *consciousness* of nothingness and nihility. Meshullam Feibush, who generally interprets the Maggid's teaching authoritatively and in depth, says concerning this question:

> The important thing regarding *devequt* is that God, blessed be He, thereby receives pleasure from us, [even] as we have said, that by pushing away the evil we cling to the good; that is, we fulfill what is said, "I have always placed God before me" [Ps. 16:8]. And we must accustom ourselves to the attribute of faith, to believe at every moment that the Holy One, blessed be He, fills the entire world with His glory and that there is no place empty of him, for [the presence of] a physical thing does not prevent place being left for a spiritual entity, as is known from our senses. And from this there devolves upon us the fear of God, may He be blessed, each one according to his own measure and time and place, and by that means this fear is great, to acknowledge the assumption, [each one] to be as nothing compared with the power of God, may He be blessed. For it is known what is written in *Shenei Luḥhot ha-Berit* [handbook of Kabbalistic ethics by R. Isaiah Horowitz (1565?–1630)] concerning [the verse], "And you shall know this day and reflect in your heart... that He is God, there is no other" [Deut. 4:39]. He wrote there that this does not mean that there is no other God, for it is superfluous to even state this, but that there is no other reality in the world apart from His existence,[29] for all things which exist were *in potentia* with Him prior to the Creation, and He emanated their *potentia* and created spiritual and physical garments for them, and His powers enliven all of them, and without it — that is, were they to return to their source, as [they were] before the Creation — the spiritual and physical garments would have no existence whatever ... Therefore, no other thing in the world exists apart from Him and His powers, which are one; and without Him there is no existence, and even though it seem that there are other

27 *Liqqutei Yeqarim* (Lemberg, 1865), 12b [no pagination]. About this compilation, see Schatz, "Introduction," p. xvii ff.

28 G. Scholem notes the origin of this idea in Hasidism already in the Ba^cal Shem Tov. See his article, "Devekut"; cf. the Besht's Commentary to Psalm 107 in the Appendix to the present volume.

29 One can speak at greater length concerning his interpretation of the Maggid's teaching, but here I will simply note that he summarizes its basic principles with the aim of demonstrating that they are not directed towards "every person." He feared the vulgarization of the understanding of the Maggid's teaching, and preferred to prevent those who wished to follow this form of *devequt*.

entities, it is all [in reality] His existence and powers. And read what it says there in *She"lah, Masekhet Shavu^cot*, and understand it.[30]

... We find that, if we merit this clinging (*devequt*), we will think of ourselves that we are nothing without God, may He be blessed, who sustains us, and who is the one that exists, and without Him there is no other... And perhaps at times, when the spirit of God begins to move upon us [cf. Judges 13:25], we can understand this to a fine measure, as a thin needle. Therefore, when we understand in truth that we are as nothing, and it seems to us as that there is nothing in the world but God, may He be blessed, as there was before the Creation, then God so-to-speak receives from us the true pleasure for which he hopes.[31]

... We thus find that, if a man wishes to become a new creature, not physical and material to lust after the material, but only for God, may He be blessed, he must bring his thought insofar as possible to the level of fear which leads to modesty, [in order] to come to the quality of nothingness.[32]

The expression, "to go to the quality of nothingness," bears here an ethical meaning associated with the acosmic assumption, implying total resignation from everything connected with the world, which is filled with naught and nothingness. The two fundamental ethical touchstones of Hasidism are the fear and awe which fill man's heart in wake of his sense of the Divine "fulness" which surrounds him, and the sense of modesty and humility which he feels in light of the consciousness of his own nothingness against the only true existence and reality. As we have said, total self-abnegation is the precondition for ethical life in the presence of God. By denying the world and its goodness, as well as his own individual existence, man opens the door for life with God. This denial, which is the passage-way into the ethical "quality of nothingness," is likewise the precondition for entering the divine "nothingness."

And this is because the end desired[33] is that prior to prayer he must cast off corporeality, which is characterized by finitude and limit, and enter into the aspect of nothingness, which is without end. For man must direct all the wishes of his heart toward the Creator alone, and not do any thing or [even] half a thing from his own

30 *Shenei Luḥot ha-Berit, Masekhet Shavu^cot* (Amsterdam, 1695), p. 189b. Indeed, this is the author's original meaning.

31 *Liqqutei Yeqarim*, p. 18b–c.

32 Ibid., 18d, and also in *Shemu^cah Ṭovah*, 29a, for stress upon the motif of the feeling of human nothingness.

33 G. Scholem pointed out to me that the formula, "the end desired" [*mevuqash ha-takhlit*] is a formula which comes from the editing of R. Levi Yitzḥak of Berditchev. However, everything contained in this quotation appears word for word in many other places as the Maggid's teaching regarding this verse. I have more recently come to the conclusion that R. Levi Yitzḥak of Berdichev was the disciple who preserved nearly all of the extant teachings of the Maggid; see Schatz, "Introduction," p. xvi ff.

> self; and this is impossible unless he enter into the attribute of Nothingness, that is, [to know] that he does not exist at all, and then he will not turn to any thing of the world at all, seeing as how he does not exist at all. But let man beseech his Maker for God's sake alone... And this is perhaps what was meant by the early authorities [who stated] that prior to the *ᶜAmidah* Prayer one must recite the verse, "O Lord, open my lips, that my mouth may recite Thy praises," [Ps. 51:17]. The meaning of this is that we beseech Him, may He be blessed, that "my lips" (*sefatai*), which comes from the language of border and edge, as in "the banks of the river" (*sefat ha-nahar*), which symbolizes corporeality, "shall be opened" — that is, that You will open the bonds and fetters of corporeality, to cast them off and to cling to the nothing (*ᵓayin*).[34]

A shorter version of the same idea is brought in the name of the Maggid:

> "From whence (*me-ᵓayin*) shall wisdom be found" [Job 28:12] — that is, one who makes himself as nothing cleaves to the Nothing (*ᵓayin*), and the Nothing overflows [into] being, which is Wisdom. In the name of the Divine R. Baer.[35]

Similar formulations appear among such Christian quietists as Callistus, the disciple of Gregory of Sinai, who also combined the sense of the nothingness of the self with the ethical standing before God. Callistus said that man must consider himself as nothing, for if his thoughts depart from the Creator for a moment he becomes filled with pride and is no longer a fitting vessel for the Divine.[36]

The presence of the cosmic element in Hasidic thought enhanced the force of the spiritual effort towards God. Even if man as such[37] lost his own self in the context of the general "annihilation," he was still left with the path by which to live with God, a path which is only open to man, in which lies his superiority over the beast. Thus, R. Ḥayyim Ḥaykl of Amdur could say, "There you shall isolate yourself with your Creator, as if you had already died(!) to the world, and there is no one there but you and the Creator, may He be blessed."[38] A man who has "died to the world" sees himself as if "he is not," to use the Maggid's formula — as one whose existential reality no longer exists. He is disinterested in the world

34 *Shemuᶜah Ṭovah*, 79b–80a. Concerning this edition of the Maggid's teachings, see Schatz, "Introduction," p. xix ff.

35 MS. Jerusalem 3282, f. 75b.

36 *Philokalia*, chapter on Callistus, pp. 162–270.

37 See also Meister Eckhart, *An Introduction to the Study of his Works with an Anthology of his Sermons*, selected and translated by J. M. Clark (London, 1957), p. 173. "All creatures are a mere nothing. I do not say that they are insignificant or something; they are a mere nothing. What has no being does not exist. All creatures have no being, because their being depends on the presence of God. If God turned away for one moment from all creatures, they would be annihilated."

38 From the letters of R. Ḥayyim Ḥaykl of Amdur at the beginning of *Ḥayyim va-Ḥesed*, p. 18. In the Jerusalem edition, the letters are brought at the beginning of the book and not at its end, as in Ed. Warsaw 1891.

and in the question of its redemption; even "alien thoughts" no longer approach him or seek their redemption through him. His dominant social characteristic is the quality of equanimity. That is to say: he does not care at all about his social status or his spiritual accomplishments in this framework. For the one who seeks to escape it, the world is [as if] already closed off. This closedness is necessary for one who wishes to hear the voice of God alone.

> Let him make himself as if he does not exist, as in the saying of the Talmud (Soṭah 21b) concerning the verse "From whence (*me-ʾayin*) shall wisdom be found" [Job 28:12], the intention being that he shall consider himself as if he is not in this world, so what benefit can there be if I am considered important in the eyes of other people.[39]

> "If I am not for myself, who shall be for me?" [Avot 1:14] In prayer, one must be as if one is removed from corporeality, and does not feel his own existence in this world. That is, when I reach the level that I do not know or feel at all whether I am for myself in this world or not, then I certainly have no fear of alien thoughts, for alien thoughts do not then approach me at all, because I am removed from this world.[40]

> "But when I am [only] for myself, what am I?" [Avot, ibid.] That is, when I know of myself, then here are numerous alien thoughts. Even the statement, "If I am here, then everything is here" [said by Hillel regarding his own presence in the festivities at the Temple on festival days], is to be interpreted in this like manner.[41]

According to this school of thought, if one is aware of self, then the world again enters in, blocking the way to God.

A comprehensive expression of this human negation appears in the words of another disciple of the Maggid, R. Menaḥem Mendel of Vitebsk (d. 1788):

> The sum of the thing is that one should oneself be as if one does not [exist], to completely disown one's own body and soul, [that it may be] obliterated for the sanctification of the Name from this world and the next, in whatever way [possible]. And wherever he may be, he does not long for or turn in any direction save to Him, may His Name be great, he is [only] occupied with the greatness of the Creator, may His name be praised, as Jonah said, "from the belly of Sheol I cried out . . ." [Jon. 2:3] Even from the Netherworld of Gehinnom and Sheol he turns toward God, for why should he relate to himself at all, how he is and in what manner he is, or whether he had never been created, or whether he had been created but was already lost like the animals who are silent? For he has already abnegated himself completely, because of his meditation upon the greatness of the Creator, blessed be He, and his entire wish and longing is but to magnify and sanctify His Name, may He be blessed and His Divinity uplifted.[42]

39 *Ẓavaʾat ha-Riva"sh* (Jerusalem, 1948), p. 13.

40 Ibid., p. 15.

41 Ibid., p. 26.

42 R. Menahem Mendel of Vitebsk, *Peri ha-ʾAreẓ ᶜim ᶜEẓ Peri* (Jerusalem, 1953), p. 76.

An interesting parallel to this mood of total self-forgetfulness appears in Symeon the New Theologian, the noted quietist thinker:

> Our mind is pure and simple, so when it is stripped of every alien thought, it enters the pure, simple, Divine light . . . It finds there nothing to move it to thought of aught else, but abides within it . . . [this] is followed by a quietude which contemplates all.
> The mobile mind becomes motionless and unthinking . . . at the same time remaining in conscious contemplation and apprehension ... The mind enters therein after relinquishing everything visible and mental, and moves and turns motionlessly among those incomprehensible things, living a life more than life, being a light while yet in the light, though no light when in itself. Then it sees not itself but Him Who is above it and, being inwardly transformed by the glory surrounding it, loses all knowledge of itself.
> A man who has attained the highest level of perfection is dead and yet not dead, but infinitely more alive in God with Whom he lives, for he no longer lives by himself . . . he sees not with his natural eyes, for he is above all natural vision, receiving new eyes ... and through these he looks above nature. He is inactive and at rest, as one who has come to the end of all action of his own. He is without thought, since he has become one with Him Who is above all thought, and has come to rest where movement of mind can have no place ... He can neither know nor understand the incomprehensible and the miraculous, yet he finds perfect rest therein through this blessed stillness of the senses . . .[43]

A person "who makes himself as if he does not exist," and who sees himself through the prism of his own cessation-of-being, is no longer a loyal participant in the world, but rules over it by the superiority of the disinterested spirit within himself as the source of pleasure and benefit. The quietistic ideal is that of the totally disinterested person, as expressed in the saying of R. Ḥayyim Ḥaykl of Amdur: "If anything is still important to you apart from the Holy One, blessed be He, you are not [yet] cleaving to God, for the connection is not whole."[44] A person cannot simultaneously cleave to God and be in the world.

43 *Philokalia*, pp. 132–133. Despite the great similarity of spiritual moods in the descriptions of the extinction of the "I," the Hasidic sources do not speak at such length about peace as the blessed aim. The "nothing" itself appears among the quietists in such descriptions as these as filled with contentment, unlike Hasidism. See Pourrat, "Quietisme," sec. 3: "on arrivait par cette méditation au sentiment calme et universel du néant!"
Generally speaking, in Hasidism the nostalgia for submission to annihilation is not depicted in such personal terms as in Christian mysticism. For a notable exception to this, see the selections from R. Moshe Leib of Sassov, below, at the end of Ch. 3.

44 *Ḥayyim va-Ḥesed*, p. 51.

Chapter Three

The Standing of Existential Problems in Hasidism

Generally speaking, Hasidism responded to man's existential questions with a resounding no, its theoretical assumptions leaving no room for the importance of existential pain. This-worldly existence, itself so doubtful, does not receive any attention or recognition on the part of Hasidic thinkers. The questions concerning it do not demand the right to an answer from God; in the perspective of the absolute, they seem insignificant, arousing a condescending smile in light of the eternal truths. In the eyes of the Maggid of Mezhirech, who knows something of the unity of the two sides of life, the existential aspect is like a house of cards that has fallen: from the viewpoint of the child who built it, it seems like a great tragedy, but from the perspective of his royal father, who intends to give him magnificent palaces in the future, this "tragedy" is little more than a joke. Throughout his life, the Maggid depicted God sitting and playing with man's creations, saying much in this connection.[1] Concerning our subject, the Maggid said:

> Regarding the reason why the righteous person has no satisfaction in this world, and at times, even when he prays concerning worldly matters, he is not answered and his prayer is ignored: the truth is that, because of the great love and fondness that He [God] has for the righteous man, for this reason he is not answered concerning matters of this world. This is compared to the king's small son, who made for himself a small house out of matchsticks as children do in their play, and a certain person came and broke the house that the king's son had made, and the son came to his father the king with a great complaint, and screamed and cried before his father concerning the great harm done him by that person. Upon hearing this, even though he loved him very much, the father also laughed, for in his eyes that house was as naught compared to the good things ready for him to receive from his father the king. The king also had in mind to build for his son a great and glorious palace and court, but this lowly and poor building was considered by his father as nothing, that he should take vengeance

1 This "playing" has two aspects in the Maggid's teaching, reflecting the internal dialectic in the relation of God to the world: God enjoys the "small" acts of human beings and desires them but, from the point of view of the eternal, their insignificance or nullity is self-evident. This tension in the valuation of things appears in all the Maggid's teachings. It is interesting that this concept, with all of its ambivalence, also appears in Eckhardt; see *Sermons*, Clark ed., pp. 185–186.

> against that same person who destroyed it; even though his son had great pain from it, he nevertheless paid no attention to it, for it is [only] a pain to the mind of the child, but [not] to his father, who knows that he is destined for greater things, because of all the good things that he is to receive from him. And the parable is clear: because of the great love and fondness which the Holy One, blessed be He, has for the righteous, because of this love he will cause them to inherit all of the hidden good which the eye has not seen in the World to Come. Therefore the Holy One, blessed be He, takes no heed of the pain which the righteous suffers in this world, for he knows that all of the good of the World to Come is double and doubled again, for all of the goodness of this world is as nothing against the great and strong love, for which he will receive the goodly reward in the World to Come.[2]

Superficially, this appears like a traditional Jewish perspective on reward in the World to Come, which sees a just recompense for every human pain. But in truth, Hasidism abnegated far more of the world than did traditional Judaism. It forbade its adherents to even think of demanding recompense, while its major thinkers even waived the need to justify God's ways with man. They did not believe that one was entitled at all to demand such a form of justice. A number of Hasidic sayings which correspond to the quietistic mentality elicit the deep feeling that Hasidim, together with their non-Jewish quietistic counterparts, plumbed the depths of the religious absurd by rejecting the option of bringing before God the good deeds of human beings who are suffering from troubles and seek compassion in times of illness:

> "He thinks evil on his couch" [Ps. 36:15]. That is to say, in this too he [the Evil Urge] deceives him — that when he falls upon his sick-bed he prays to God, may He be blessed, to heal him from his illness by virtue of the Torah and mitzvot which he has performed; and he does not know that he mentions his sins, for it is all the temptation of the Evil Urge (i.e., which makes it seem to him as if he had performed a *miẓvah*, while in truth the *miẓvah* was barren, without *devequt*).[3]

The supreme and exclusive value attached to *devequt* in Hasidism, together with the feelings of human nullity, demanded that man completely abandon and forego any hopes and expectations, requiring a stance of apathy and equanimity towards psychological needs and unawareness of their absence. "For thus they [human beings] must abandon themselves and forget their troubles, so that they may come

2 *Liqqutei Yeqarim*, p. 12b, and *ʾOr ha-ʾEmet*, 77b.

3 *Ẓavaʾat ha-Rivaʺsh*, p. 17. See the formulation of the same idea in Eckhardt who says that, if one is ill he prays to God for health, he is no longer your God — *Sermons*, p. 139. It is interesting to note the resemblance between this approach and that of Bahya ibn Paquda, who mentions among the distinguishing signs of "people of level" those who chose sickness rather than health, for the same quietistic reasons. See *Ḥovot ha-Levavot* (Leipzig, 1846), *Shaʿar ha-Biṭaḥon*, Ch. 4, p. 120a.

to the world of thought, where everything is equal."[4] Only one who no longer feels the need or lack of anything whatsoever has achieved the desired end; for so long as we are aware of the troubles of the world, we cannot be free for the service of God. The Maggid's disciple, R. Zeᵓev Wolf of Zhitomir (d. 1800), said:

> The rule seems to be that, before a wise man enters into [study of] true wisdom [i.e., Kabbalah], he must not feel his own pain at all. If it happens that the Holy One, blessed be He, brings before him an incident which is not good, heaven forbid, such that he walks in darkness and not light, he should take counsel with his soul, that this is certainly of the ways of the good God, be He blessed, to perform good to his creatures. Therefore, why has this not-good thing happened to him? And as he troubles himself that this aspect of pain applies specifically to him, he will know for certain that he has evidently not prepared his heart to seek God with all his soul and all his strength, for certainly it is not the path of a scholar to [feel] so, as I explained at length above. For such is the purpose of man's service, to perfect his soul and his spirit so that he not feel his own physical suffering. And for this [reason] he should take to heart that which befell him of temporal accidents and occurrences, that all [takes place] through individual Providence from Him, may He be blessed. And this is also from His goodness and mercy, may He be blessed, who wishes to show man how to correct his affairs, to know that that which he has injured in the upper worlds [is visited upon him] attribute for attribute; therefore He has sent him such a thing, that he may feel from this a supernal lack, and that he may set his heart and soul to pray for the supernal *tiqqun*. For the main thing is to sweeten the judgments in their supreme source, but not to suffer his own physical pains, for in truth, temporal accidents and occurrences are without limit, from the day that he first becomes conscious until the [termination of] his life's vitality. And if a person wishes to separate himself from His *devequt* and service because of them, then when shall he do the Torah and the service for which he was created? ...[5]

The most profound formulation of the indifference with which man ought to behave towards his personal affairs was that given by R. Jacob Joseph, the Maggid of Ostrog (1738–1791):

> This is what is written in Scripture, "And God said, 'let there be light,' and there was light" [Gen. 1:3]. That is, when a person has faith in God, blessed be He, like that of Nahum of Gimzo, to say that [the divine name] *ᵓElohim*, which is [the attribute of] *Din* [i.e., rigor, judgment], itself "was light" — [that is,] was mercy and

4 *Maggid Devarav le-Yaᶜaqov*, §110, p. 186.

5 *ᵓOr ha-Meᵓir* (New York, 1954), p. 7d and p. 10d, "And he does not feel anything of the suffering itself." On p. 8a: "He should take to heart so that he feel nothing of his own needs." And in R. Ḥayyim Ḥaykl: "... We therefore need to strengthen ourselves and to uproot our needs from our hearts, so that we may forget ourselves completely through our clinging to Him, may He be praised, and all this explanation depends upon 'the Ancient One' (*ba-ᶜatiqa talya*)" — *Ḥayyim va-Ḥesed*, p. 9.

> compassion, and that so was it done. "And there was" (*va-yehi*) — which signifies suffering — "light." And he does not distinguish between the suffering, which is darkness, and the light. But whoever has not this faith, to believe that ᵓ*Elohim* Himself "was light," but that rather, "God (ᵓ*Elohim*) saw the light, that it was good" [ibid., v. 4] — that is, that a person perceives it as *Din*, called ᵓ*Elohim*, and it is a source of suffering for him, and he does not believe that it is itself good; but he sees the light, which is compassion (*Raḥamim*), "that it is good" — then, truly, judgment and darkness is with him, and there is a distinction between himself and the light. This is [the meaning of] "And God (ᵓ*Elohim*) separated between the light and the darkness" [v. 5]. And why is this so? Because "And God called" (*va-yiqra* ᵓ*Elohim*; lit., "and he called God") — that is, that man called this suffering by the name ᵓ*Elohim*, which is judgment. Therefore, [he called] "to the light, day" and "to the darkness" — therefore it is darkness, because of "night." But in truth, "and there was evening" — for he who does not believe, the suffering is evening and darkness; "and there was morning" — for he who does believe, the suffering is for him as morning. And it is all "one day" [ibid.], for everything that He did was done for the good — and contemplate this."[6]

To the believing *ḥasid*, the distinctions between judgment and mercy are blurred, and it does not matter with what attribute God acts, for there is no difference between "darkness" (the attribute of *Din*) and "light," or between "night" and "morning" (the attribute of *Raḥamim*), all of these being subjective valuations determined by the feelings of man. A person does not know what is good for himself, but he knows that the events of his life are guided by one who directs them towards his good. The Maggid said:

> A great rule: "Commit thy works unto the Lord, and thy thoughts shall be established" [Prov. 16:3]. In whatever happens [to one], one should think that it is from Him, may He be blessed, and he should ask God, may He be blessed, that He always prepare for him that thing which God, may He be blessed, knows is for his good, and not that which seems so to human beings, according to their own intellect. For it may be that that which is good in his own eyes is bad for him, but one should only cast all of his affairs and his needs upon Him, may He be blessed.[7]
>
> In everything that befalls him, he should say, "Is this not from Him, may He be blessed, and if it is good in His eyes,"... his entire intention being for the sake of heaven; but in terms of his own self, it makes no difference — and this is a very great level.[8]

6. Jacob Joseph of Ostrog, *Sefer Rav Yeivi* (New York, 1954), *Bereshit*, p. 2b.
7 *Ẓavaᵓat ha-Riva"sh* (Jerusalem, 1948), p. 4.
8 Ibid., p. 1. Cf. the somewhat expanded text in MS. Jerusalem 3282, p. 175a: "And he does not [make] any distinction between one thing and another, whether the thing is done according to his will or not according to his will, everything is the same to him, as everything is from the Creator blessed be He, and he knows that it is thus good for him, that it is not done according to his will."

The enlightened Jews of the period (*Maskilim*) mocked the Hasidim concerning this "thrusting of one's yoke upon God" [cf. Ps. 55:23], which seemed to them extremely irrational. Even those who wished to see the "light" in Hasidism could not tolerate this passive mood, which to their mind expressed a "love of laziness and an irresponsible attitude towards the future."[9]

It is a fact in the history of religions that such ideas as "the thrusting of one's yoke upon God" have a great impact upon the external form of religious life as well. The implication here was total freedom from worries concerning man's destiny. This applied not only to eternal questions, to which we shall return, but also to concrete worries about the future. The *ḥasid* claims that worries not only distract man from essentials and prevent him from serving God, but that there is no inherent justification for them, as in any event all things are determined by God alone and not by ourselves. Both good and evil come to man from God so that, for the person who believes that God desires for us only the good, there is no difference between them. The *ḥasid* does not dwell extensively upon the problem of existential evil and the way in which the divine good is reflected in it, and he does not argue with his Creator like the "Job" type. The quietist is not interested in knowing how to understand God's ways, nor has he any motivation to explain the problems of theodicy. He is interested in acquiring the attributes of wholeness, peace and trust, and of indifference towards the question itself.[10] Meister Eckhardt says in one of his speeches:

> Perhaps you may ask: how do I know whether it is God's will or not? You must know that if it were not God's will, it would not happen at all. You have neither sadness nor anything else unless God wills it. And as you know that it is God's will, you ought to have so much joy and satisfaction that you would not regard any pain as pain, even if it come to be the very worst of all pains ... You should accept it from God as the best, because it must needs be the best for you ... Hence I should will it also, nor should anything else please me better.[11]

The common denominator of all quietistic approaches is the assumption that God does that which is good for man, which has various manifestations which do

9 See Zweifel, *Shalom ᶜal Yisraᵓel*, Pt. III: p. 30, citing the opinion of Isador Busch in *Jahrbuch für Israeliten* (Wien, 1847).

10 Molinos states: "After we have consigned everything into God's hands, we must also thrust upon Him the thought and worry of everything which pertains to us, and allow Him to act within us without our involvement, according to His divine will" — *Dict.*, sec. 13. And in sec. 17: "After we have placed our will in God's hands, and our worries are removed from our hearts, there is no longer any room to be unquiet because of the 'trials' which overtake us..."

11 Eckhardt, *Sermons*, p. 170–171. Pourrat also cites the opinion of the Stoics, who are in this respect close to the idea of the quietists, that "the perfect man would choose illness if he knew that it were desired by destiny" — "Quietisme," sec. 3.

not always correspond to the existential feeling of the good. Other quietists, more extreme than Eckhardt and less careful than Falconi, explicitly stated that a person need not wish anything, either good or bad — thereby eliminating the small comfort that may have remained in the knowledge that God wishes only that which is good for man.[12] As we said, Hasidism generally took a stand which recognized that both suffering and pain are intended for man's good from the viewpoint of God, such as:

> "The brutish man knoweth not, nor does the fool understand this" [Ps. 92:7] — that even in tribulation he must serve Him, may He be blessed, with this attribute, according to the attribute and aspect in which He appears to him now, that the Creator, blessed be He, knows how to correct your affairs better than [you do] yourself. He therefore seems to you, in dividing actions according to reasons known to Him, as His wisdom ordained. He therefore sends to man the aspect of suffering due to temporal accidents for man's own good, to bring him benefit in the end.[13]

From this point-of-view, in which man does not know what is good for him, the Hasidic thinkers did not refrain from stating that there is no sense in praying that a certain Divine edict or trouble not come, but only that it come for one's good, according to God's will. Thus, in his *Sefer Reb Yeivi*, the Maggid of Ostrog said of David [i.e., in II Sam. 24:10ff.], "that he did not wish to pray that the trouble not come at all, but rather that He, blessed be He, save him within the trouble when it does come upon him."[14]

"Thrusting one's burden upon God" was not only a theoretical principle advocated by Hasidism, based on the needs of theodicy. It was an overall mood shaping the consciousness of the *ḥasid*, which was passive with regard to everything pertaining to contact with the world — a philosophy of "distracting one's mind" from reality. It was against this background that the attitude of *biṭaḥon* ("confidence" or "trust"), for which Hasidism was renowned, grew. The concept of *biṭaḥon* implied the silencing both of man's outer and inner reality, and the negation of the value of the external challenge in order to immerse oneself in the service of God. An extreme example of this appears in the following remark of R. Jacob of Ostrog:

> Our rabbis stated in *Pereq Ḥeleq*: "Three things come about unintentionally, namely: the Messiah, a lost article, and a scorpion" [Sanhedrin 97a]. And this applies to every

12 Pourrat, col. 1559.

13 *ᵓOr ha-Meᵓir*, p. 8b.

14 *Sefer R. Yeivi*, p. 29c. Compare: "Therefore a person must ask to pray before God, that He give to him as God, may He be blessed, knows, whether it be for his good that God should give him, or if not for his good, not to give him" — p. 31b.

> person: even when an individual encounters difficulty, and is thereafter redeemed from it, it is as if the Messiah had come for him, and this is because he was not expecting this ... Therefore [David] said, "I lay down" [Ps. 3:6] — that is, when I lie down before my enemies who pursue me, and I am unable to ascend and to overwhelm them, then "and I sleep" — I turn my mind away from it, like a person whose mind is removed from the things which he needs while sleeping. Then, while I turn my mind away, I am redeemed from the trouble, and it is as if the Messiah has come for me, because I am redeemed from my trouble, and this is "and I awoke." The reason why redemption comes at a time of forgetfulness, is that when a person is conscious, he thinks of [various] actions by which he may be saved from his trouble, and he has not complete trust in God, may He be blessed. Therefore, he does not receive assistance from God, for God says, "as you wish to save yourself by means of your actions, I do not wish to save you, and I will see how you are able to help yourself." But when a person removes his attention from his troubles, and says, "Why do I need to perform any actions?" then God, may He be blessed, will do what he wishes, and then God, may He be blessed, will help him — and this is, "for God has been my support" [ibid.].[15]

There is no doubt that the concept of *biṭaḥon* underwent numerous transformations, which expanded its use in the school of the Maggid. In the thought of the Maggid himself, we still find the "elitist" use of this concept, if one may use such an expression, where it was based entirely upon an attitude of apathy and indifference towards the results of God's acts upon man. *Biṭaḥon* is involved there, less with the assumption that God indeed fulfills one's wishes, than with abandonment and abnegation of the self. The more "popular" version of this concept was formulated primarily by some disciples of the Maggid, such as the passages quoted above from "Rav Yeivi" or R. Shlomo of Lutsk. The latter discussed the idea of *biṭaḥon* within the context of everyday problems such as earning a living.[16] In practice, this latter nuance, in which the question of *biṭaḥon* was associated with matters of livelihood, became a characteristic one in Hasidism. The practical aspect of the concept of *biṭaḥon* necessarily emerged from the fact

15 *Sefer R. Yeivi*, p. 29c. R. Ḥayyim Ḥaykl of Amdur wrote in his *Hanhagot*: "Man: Every day you will encounter a new trial, curses and [verbal] abuses, or monetary loss; and see that you are prepared for this in advance [sic], so then you can receive it with joy, and you will not bolt against chastisements, but you will stand up to all the sufferings and damages, Heaven forbid." — *Ḥayyim va-Ḥesed*, p. x. It is interesting, on the other hand, to see the sharp comment of Meshullam Feibush of Zbarazh against the component of masochistic "enjoyment" in the quietistic approach: "That he not say that these are chastisements of love, because this is the wisdom of the unfortunate one" — see *Yosher Divrei ᵓEmet* (Munkacz, 1905), p. 7d.

16 See Shlomo of Lutsk, *Dibrat Shlomoh* (Jerusalem, 1955), Pt. II: 50b; Pt. I: 27b. On this author and his role as a disciple of the Maggid in publishing the latter's teaching, see Schatz, "Introduction," p. xx ff.

that a person who was a *ḥasid* abandoned "temporal life" in order to devote himelf to "eternal life." Upon what might he rely for his livelihood, if not upon the attribute of *biṭaḥon*? The Hasidic motto that was not to worry about tomorrow was based upon this, and had a decisive influence upon tendencies within Hasidic society. It must be stated here that this understanding of the attribute of *biṭaḥon*, according to which God will see to a person's livelihood without man undertaking any deliberate directed effort does not entail the same degree of resignation towards action and its results as the "elitist" understanding thereof, for even if the *ḥasid* knows that he is exempt from thinking about them, he does not renege on their performance and is not apathetic to their accomplishment.[17] The truth is that Hasidism also related to this problem when it attempted to prohibit the feelings of disappointment and frustration resultant from the failure to fulfill human hopes and expectations.[18] This pain, mingled with frustration, was viewed as a kind of protest against God, and as such was seen as an insult to the Divine mercies. Hasidism did not in practice require the total negation of human will, but merely protested against man's insistence upon the fulfillment of his own will. But even such Maggidic formulations as, "that it make no difference to him whether it is done according to his will or not by his will," do not appear too frequently in Hasidism. Hasidim, including the Maggid, did not speak of destroying the human will as a psychological reality — something toward which some extreme quietists yearned — and therefore did not advocate any special technique for achieving this goal. But the quietistic frame of mind may also be detected in the protest against those who demand their heart's wish from God. The Maggid of Mezhirech wanted people to entirely forget their own longings, while his disciples were satisfied that they overcome their tendency to feel frustrated when their personal wishes were not realized.

The longing and expectation that the human will be realized by God, and the turning of one's attention to this petty consideration, were considered forbidden:

> For by man's great faith and trust he is connected to and cleaves with all his thought and vitality to the good of the Creator, blessed be He, for which a person hopes and anticipates, and by this means [his wish] is quickly performed, without interruption and without obstacle. And this is not the case if, Heaven forbid, there is not faith and

17 On the history of the term *biṭaḥon* and its significance in the history of Jewish thought up to and including Beshtian Hasidism, see R. J. Zwi Werblowsky, "Faith, Hope and Trust; a Study in the Concept of Bittahon," *Papers of the Institute of Jewish Studies, London* (Jerusalem, 1964), pp. 95–139.

18 For example, *Darkhei Ẓedeq* (Lemberg, 1865): "He should not feel pain if his wish is also not done."

great trust, and he introduces within his thought doubts as to whether or not it will be — this in itself is a delaying or obstructing [factor], heaven forfend.[19]

One can clearly see from these latter remarks the anticipation of the fulfillment of human will, and the struggle with scepticism lest it not be fulfilled. This was in practice the authentic tone associated with the concept of *biṭaḥon* in Hasidism generally; in the writings of this school, the Maggidic approach of equanimity gradually disappeared.[20]

It is worth mentioning here an additional stage in the understanding of *biṭaḥon*, encompassing the limits of the possible in the non-rational understanding of this concept. R. Levi Yitzḥak of Berdichev (d. 1809) writes:

> "Praised, I cry, is the Lord, and I am saved from mine enemies" [Ps. 18:4]. King David, of blessed memory, because of his great trust in the Holy One, blessed be He, would recite songs [of praise] in all the troubles which befell him, even before the salvation [came], as he trusted in Him, may He be blessed, that he would surely save him . . . Likewise at the Red Sea, when Israel, because of their great trust that the Holy One, blessed be He, would surely split the sea for them, as in the saying of our rabbis and of Rashi's commentary on the verse [Ps. 114:2], "Judah was his holy one" — that because of their great trust, Nahshon went down into the sea before it was split. And because their trust was so great, then certainly He, may He be blessed, would perform salvation for them. And as in Rashi's commentary on the verse, "Why do you cry unto me?" [Ex. 14:15], that the faith with which they believed in Me was sufficient [to split the sea for them.] For they believed that God would certainly perform salvation for them; it therefore immediately entered their hearts that they ought to recite song prior to the salvation. For he who is attached to God and trusts that He shall surely save him, recites the song for the salvation prior to the salvation, like King David . . .[21]

19 *Dibrat Shlomoh*, Pt. II: 578b.

20 In R. Ḥayyim Ḥaykl of Amdur, the more extreme reason is still preserved: "A human being should not say, I have trust in God, may He be blessed, that He will do this thing... He should only say, I am confident that he will help me to fulfill His mitzvot. And in worldly matters let a person's trust be in this manner: that he trust in the source of all mercies and grace that He will certainly recompense him with His great grace and mercy, even if He will not do this thing which I beseech but will act with me according to the attribute of sternness, this [too] comes from His grace and mercy, for He knows that it is good for him that this thing that I beseech not be done. But [just] that the trust be with a full heart, without any thoughts... and when a person is confident in this, that he not think after Him [i.e. question or doubt His acts], even though his request is not granted certainly. And this is the fulfillment of the verse, "And God will be His trust" [Jer. 17:6] — that God, may He be blessed, will guarantee [*baṭaḥ*, word play on *baṭaḥ* in the sense of "trust"], that he not doubt Him! — *Ḥayyim va-Ḥesed*, "*Hanhagot*", p. 7.

21 *Qedushat Levi ha-Shalem* (Jerusalem, 1958), pp. 117–118. This stance of placing God in trial is not acceptable to the quietistic spirit. See on this *Ḥovot ha-Levavot, Shaᶜar ha-Biṭaḥon*, Ch. 4, p. 109a. R. Levi Yitzḥak of Berdichev, in all of his quietistic teachings, tends to "sweeten" the pill in order to bring every man close to the Hasidic path. He also "allows" man to begin his service with the

The quietistic motif is completely obliterated here, as an activism rooted in the attribute of trust is able to accomplish even the impossible — to perform miracles. The attribute of *biṭaḥon* is thus transformed here into a power forcing the laws of nature to submit to human will. This "aggressive" and anti-quietistic understanding of R. Levi Yitzḥak of Berdichev is not an isolated motif within the overall context of his thought — a point to which we shall return elsewhere. For us, this fact is interesting in its own right, as certain linguistic usages, which were originally coined as the result of certain specific moods, did not necessarily preserve their original meaning throughout the history of Hasidism.

R. Moshe Leib of Sasov (1745–1807) made some interesting critical comments, within the context of Hasidism itself, opposing the non-radical approach of these Hasidim to the "attribute of trust." He complains that the Hasidim pay too much attention to matters of livelihood and that their hearts are filled with anxieties about the future. Like other Hasidic doctrines, this doctrine provoked internal criticism because of its failure to be fulfilled in its entirety. He states that:

> Because of our great sins, we pray to God, may He be blessed, to provide us with sustenance, and afterwards on the very same day, each one of us under various pretexts turns to his own way and abandons the study of Torah. At times we perform the truth and at times its opposite, and we do not believe in our hearts what we said with our mouths that very day. This is like a person who inquires with his mouth how much a certain object costs, and in his heart does not wish to buy it [at all], and this is considered fraudulent [behavior] ...[22]

The *Hanhagot* (Regimen Vitae) of R. Moshe Leib of Sasov[23] are imbued with a quietistic spirit, mixed with a joy and ecstasy originating in the feeling of abnegation and liberation from the life of this world. These few pages are marked by a kind of intoxication stemming from transcendence of this world and the negation of worries concerning it. The feeling of nullity and unreality of this world brings about a sense of calmness and tranquil joy to the soul which seeks to serve God, removing all anxiety and burden and taking away the dark bitterness, the imaginary world being a source of sorrow and disappointment. The solemn sense of the "coronation of God" over human life, contained in these *Hanhagot*, is

assumption that he is not thereby "forfeiting" this world and its rewards. In any event, during the early stages this is explicitly permitted. On the contrary: R. Levi Yitzḥak thinks it better that a person to be honest with himself and believe that he "deserves" a given thing, and thereby be freed of the Evil Urge which [otherwise] distracts him from *devequt*. See, e.g., *Qedushat Levi ha-Shalem*, Pt. I: p. 59b.

22 Moses Leib of Sasov, *Liqqutei Rama"l* (Lemberg, 1865), [no pagination], p. 3.

23 Printed at the end of *Liqqutei Rama"l*, and bearing his unique and inspired style, in contrast to the *Hanhagot* of others.

unequaled in all of Hasidic literature. A poetic nostalgia for total peace in the bosom of God, and a mocking of death and suffering, combine with an optimistic sense of "trust" and resignation to fate. I will quote a few brief passages from the *Hanhagot*:[24]

> If you conclude in your mind that this world was only created so that by its means your soul might arrive at eternal rest, then from whence shall the black depression evolve? (4) If you decide within yourself that you are the servant of a great king to whom silence is praise, how greatly ought you to rejoice. (5) Death is a very great and bitter evil to the wicked person, but how precious it is to God in seeing the death of his pious ones [cf. Ps. 118:15], for by its means they reach eternal peace. (6) A man ought not to be vain concerning his own affairs, and if heaven forbid any troubles befall you, do not give up, for this world has no reality, for it is not thus. (8) A certain holy person was once [greatly] angered against a [certain] person whose son died, and he did not shed for him even a single tear. (10)[25]
>
> Accept evil and good with equanimity, for you are a stranger in the land. (3)[26] Why should you worry about a world which is not yours? (5) Remember well the words of the divine man, "And what are we?" [Ex. 16:7,8][27] and the words of Scripture, "And all the inhabitants of the earth [are considered as nought]" [Daniel 4:23] (8) Go every morning and evening to the House of Study, and pour out your supplication before God, and correct your deeds, and He shall do that which He knows to be good for you. (23) If you believe and decide in your mind that evil and good are both from God, and that nothing is done without Him, it is impossible that you will have worry of the soul or vain thoughts concerning that which is not done according to your will. (39–40) Remove yourself from this world, and let your eyes be enlightened by the words of the Sages, like nails well fastened in their sayings [after Eccles. 12:11]. (4)[28]

24 *Liqqutei Rama"l, Hanhagot ha-Simḥah ba-ᶜAvodah.*

25 This sentence is problematic, as it *prima facie* seems intended as a protest against the person who wanted to weep for the death of his son, as "a holy man was angered with him" because of this. Earlier, he wrote, "Search your deeds and remove your heart from ill so that God will have mercy"(9), so it would appear that the "holy man" was angry with him because he thought that the death of a person's son was punishment for his evil deeds. This inappropriate apathy on the part of the father seemed too "quietistic" to this "holy man," as I am not certain that R. Moshe Leib does not support the man who did not shed any tears in this case as well. What is more interesting in this context is a testimony which I found in R. Yitzḥak of Radzivilov, who testifies as to the great joy felt by R. Moses Leib of Sasov when he thought that he was going to die in a disaster at sea. See *ᵓOr Yiẓḥaq* (Jerusalem, 1861), p. 131b.

26 A new series, without a heading, begins here.

27 A famous saying in the name of the Maggid of Mezhirech, cited in a number of sources in the name of the Maggid of Zloczow. I refer to the saying, "we are like a breath." This matter is likewise mentioned in the ethical instructions of R. Nahman of Kosov, quoted in *Toldot Yaᶜaqov Yosef, Ḥayyei Sarah*, p. 18c.

28 *Mavoᵓ ha-ᵓEmunah.*

In summarizing our discussion of the question of the problem of existential suffering and the "thrusting of one's yoke upon God," I would like to again emphasize that this tendency within Hasidism, which is marked by a strongly quietistic tone, originates with and is exemplified by the Maggid of Mezhirech and a few of his disciples. It is true that in the Ba^cal Shem Tov we already find the preliminary assumptions concerning the imaginary nature of pain in a world which is entirely imaginary, but in his teaching one does not yet find a "psychological mood" marked by quietistic tension. As in all his teachings, here too the doctrine of the existence or presence of God in everything, i.e., even within existential pain, is stressed in principle. The Ba^{c}al Shem Tov's response is thus ultimately the traditional answer that human suffering is to be understood as a kind of trial on the part of God, albeit this traditional outlook was embodied within the Hasidic dress of the multi-faceted revelation of God in the spiritual and the physical, and even in sin itself. The common denominator of the doctrine of the Besht and of quietism lies in their acceptence of the judgment without questioning God's justice, while their teaching differs from his in the latter's emphasis upon the element of indifference towards the question itself. That is, the teaching of the Maggid is not concerned with a certain theory, but with an existential "removing of one's mind" from the problem itself. The second important point is that, in the Ba^{c}al Shem Tov, human suffering is still understood in the traditional manner as involving the idea of sin, a perspective which does not square with the mood of the Maggid's doctrine.[29] The following are the words of the Besht, as transmitted by R. Jacob Joseph of Polonoyye (d. ca. 1782):

> "And unto thee is its desire, but you may rule over it" [Gen. 4:7]. I heard a parable concerning this: that there was once a king who [ruled] over several countries, near and far, who after many days wished to examine the situation of the inhabitants of that country, whether they served him in truth, so he sent one of his servants, who changed his clothing and his speech as though he were [another] king who wished to wage war against this king. And there were those who stood up to do battle against him, and there were those who said, "Why should we fight, if so-and-so is the king, we are his servants, etc." Finally, he came to a certain country where there were very wise men who examined this matter [and said:] "How could it be that this thing is as it appears? For a number of reasons, it must be that this person is a messenger of the king, [sent] to test whether the people will rebel against him." Therefore, they came forth to meet him and said these things, and it was good in his eyes because of their wisdom, and he went on his way. And the meaning is clear, for this is what is stated in the *Zohar* [*Terumah* II: 163a] that the Evil Urge is compared to a wanton

29 The Maggid intends here to shift attention away from the awareness of sin itself, as we shall explain in subsequent chapters.

> woman who was ordered by the king to seduce his son ... And this also refers to an inner matter, as I heard from my teacher concerning the matter of the [Yom Kippur] Confession [beginning] ʾ*Ashamnu*: that the king himself changed his garments and his language, and came to seduce the queen, and this is sufficient for one who understands.[30] And it is a great thing, as I received from my master, that in every human pain, in physical or spiritual [matters], if he turn his heart towards the fact that God Himself, may He be blessed, [is present] in this pain, only by way of garments. And when this is known to him, the garment is removed and the pain is extinguished, as are all evil decrees. And he expounded this at length ...[31]

We may therefore state that the Maggid's motto, "do not worry about tomorrow's trouble,"[32] left an impression upon his school, whether this was understood in terms of the "elitist" stance which was close to extreme quietism, or in terms of a more popular interpretation.

Thus far, we have not yet posed Hasidism against the decisive test which it was to later face when its quietistic teachings confronted the basic principles of Jewish tradition.

30 The implication is that the Evil Urge is itself the Holy One, blessed be He, in another guise, come to test man; such knowledge is in itself sufficient to nullify the suffering. The Maggid wanted to negate suffering as an "irrelevant" phenomenon in the Service of God, interfering with *devequt* and the casting off of corporeality (*hitpashṭut ha-gashmiyut*, drawing as it does man's attention to himself and his personal destiny, rather than to God. The Besht's explanation here has nothing to do with the true problem of the religious person, according to Maggidic Hasidism, which does not explain the phenomenon of "suffering" in terms of the viewpoint of man, but rather in terms of the doctrine, typical of the Besht in all of his teachings, that "the whole world is filled with His glory." The formula, *kesut ve-lashon shinah* ("he changed raiment and language"), used in reference to the Evil Urge, is also used by R. Naḥman of Kosov, in the sense of the temptation to perform a *miẓvah* which comes from this Urge! Abraham J. Heschel, "Rabbi Nahman of Kosow: Companion of the Baal Shem" (Heb.), *Sefer ha-Yovel li-khevod Ẓevi Wolfson*, ed. S. Lieberman (New York, 1965), pp. 113–141, cites this in the name of the *Toldot*, ibid., p. 131 [English: in his *The Circle of the Baal Shem Tov: Studies in Hasidism*, ed. Samuel H. Dresner (Chicago–London, 1985), pp. 113–151]. I thank my late teacher, Gershom Scholem, for drawing my attention to this article after the Hebrew version of the book was nearly completed.

31 *Toldot Yaᶜaqov Yosef, Va-yaqhel*, p. 67c-d, and see also *Va-yeḥi*, p. 35d.

32 *Ẓavaʾat ha-Riva"sh*, p. 11.

Chapter Four

Despair, Sadness, Regret, and Their Connection with Sin

Three thought-provoking imperatives were intertwined in Hasidism from its very beginning: never to despair, to be sad, or to be regretful.[1] All three bear a certain quietistic stamp. Not to despair did not mean that one continued to hope that God would fulfill one's wishes or reward one with the life of the World to Come or some other recompense; it meant, rather, that a person should not fall into despair because he is unable to worship God with full, disinterested *devequt* in accordance with the authentic demands of Hasidism. Similarly, not to be sad meant that a person should not feel sad upon comparing his actual religious accomplishments with his own potential for perfection. Perfection is well and good as a stimulus prior to performing Divine service, but it is not desirable as a test after the fact. A person's reflection upon his degree of success, even if this concerns matters of religious import, is considered by Hasidism to be improper; for the same reason, Hasidism opposed a person feeling regret over sins which he performed or *mizvot* he failed to perform. The examination of ones deeds committed by mistake, or even the regret over them, does not in itself constitute an element of worship for the sake of heaven. Reckoning of the past is ultimately an accounting of individual attainments, in which a person enumerates what he has accomplished. "Quietistic" Hasidism is not interested — indeed, rejects — the gathering of past deeds into an account which man "presents" to God, as being transparently in order to receive reward. The pondering of the sinful deed — although the aspect of sin within that deed has not expired, from the legal point of view — was regarded an obstacle to Divine service, as it does not assist man in performing any positive religious acts. The new criteria of Hasidic value did not alter the halakhic status of one or another deed, to claim that it was not at all a sin; however, the Hasidim argued that there are certain basic, fundamental values, the most important of which is to constantly serve God. In light of this new positive command, the severity of past sins is measured against the fundamental sin of "interrupting" one's service. Hasidism

1 The term *ye'ush* (despair) primarily appears in practice in Hasidic folk stories. The use of the verb *lo' yid'ag* ("he should not worry") frequently serves all three of these meanings.

responded to this conflict unequivocally, stating that the new values of Hasidism rightly minimized the importance of inadvertent sins from the religious point of view. This admittedly did not alter the halakhic weight of the transgression — which everyone agreed was a sin — but did change its religious status, in that it's gravity was weakened, if not completely obliterated. Due to this fear of "interruption of service," in the words of the Maggid of Mezhirech, Hasidism was willing to push aside the heart's desire of every Jew — namely, the World to Come. This does not mean that Hasidism denied belief in the World to Come, but that it was more interested in removing the "landmark" of a fixed and permanent goal for the sake of which the religious effort was made. Hasidism is not interested in the question of whether or not there is an Afterlife because, if such a concept is found in the Jewish tradition, it presumably does exist (even though this subject is itself given spiritualistic interpretations and explanations which removed its literal meaning). As we said, its main concern was with uprooting it from the heart.[2] Ḥayyim Ḥaykl of Amdur formulated this as follows:

> "For your generations" (*le-dorotekhem*; Num. 9:10). That one serves God, may He be blessed, for the sake of the dwelling (*dirah*) which he will have in the World to Come. In this too the soul is polluted, even if he does not serve [God] for the sake of the body.[3]

Similarly, R. Zechariah Mendel of Jaroslaw said:

2 This subject appears in the Christian quietists, such as the Hesychast thinker Callistus, who speaks of freedom from all worry, including for one's own salvation, as the condition for true faith (see *Philokalia*, chapter on Callistus, pp. 271–76); in Eckhardt, who is apathetic towards Sanctification and is even prepared to relinquish the kingdom of Heaven (see Pourrat, "Quietisme," col. 1551); and in Molinos, who says that, "The soul need not meditate either on recompense or punishment, neither on Paradise nor on Hell, not on life nor on eternity" (see ibid., Sects. 7 and 12, "Molinos," col. 1564). Dudon speaks with a certain note of anger concerning Molinos' teaching of apathy towards Divine grace, and his belief that the transformation anticipated by the holy ones in the next world is already present for contemplatives in this life — see P. Dudon, *Molinos* (Paris, 1921), p. 202. Knox mentions apathy and the attitude towards salvation among the main features of quietism: see *Enthusiasm*, p. 254–55. He cites the extreme statement of Brother Lawrence, who stated that he never in his life gave any thought to the question of Heaven and Hell, and that these things had nothing to do with his love of God. It was his practice to conceal his pious deeds from God, in order not to receive a reward from Him — an approach called by Knox, "une amoureuse folie." Angela of Folignio wrote in a similar vein, and Knox states that Bossuet (the 17th century French theologian who persecuted the quietists) would prevent these things from being publicized; ibid., p. 285. It is clear that unlike Christianity, in which "waiting for salvation" was an arch- principal of faith, in Judaism such great bitterness could not have possibly arisen about the position of Hasidism concerning this specific question. In Christianity, unlike the case in Judaism, this attitude carries the meaning of an attack on a dogmatic issue.

3 *Ḥayyim va-Ḥesed, Parashat Be-haᶜalotkha*, p. 56.

> He should not serve for any reward or level, even for the World to Come and Paradise or to be saved from punishment in Gehinnom, but He should only worship Him for the love of the Creator, in truth and simplicity, as it is fitting to worship Him, for he is one, single and unique, the Creator of All.[4]

The innermost spiritual meaning of the attribute of trust (*biṭaḥon*) is expressed in the conquest of sadness and despair which signifies, not only the faith in man's ability to free himself of his own self-interest in the reward for Divine worship, but his overcoming that reflective thought which periodically reminds him of his failures in the service of God. Sadness and despair are the conscious psychological manifestation of lack of faith and confidence in man's spiritual ability. Hasidism, as the bearer of explicitly spiritualist tendencies, necessarily saw the greatest sin in the sayings of despair — "I am not able now" — or of sadness — "I did not do enough," or "how much have I done?" Surrender to despair means surrender to the Evil Urge; in the Maggid's teaching, this Urge took the specific form of deceiving and leading man to misunderstanding of the true nature of Divine service. The confrontation within Hasidism among the various values of Judaism — such as that between the fulfillment of a *miẓvah* with *devequt* and a "shade of transgression," or the neglect of Torah study which were occasionally performed because of the primary goal — led to the motif of "deceiving" the Evil Urge. The usual approach to this problem in non-Hasidic Judaism was seen by them as a kind of submission to the Evil Urge. Sadness, weeping, and self-afflictions, which were fundamental aspects of pious practice during the generations preceding Beshtian Hasidism, seemed to them to be temptations of the Evil Urge, distracting man from his true goal of disinterested worship of God. In principle, weeping and despair focus man's attention upon himself rather than upon God. Despair is the result of rendering of account, and as such is the reverse side of worry and anxiety. Hasidism wished to avoid this, and thereby created an air of quietism.[5] The following are the remarks of the Maggid:

4 *Darkhei Ẓedeq*, at the end of the *Hanhagot* (no pagination). Cf. the warning of the Maggid of Ostrog that repentance is worthless if intended to save the person from punishments in Hell — *Sefer Rav Yeivi*, p. 32d. The idea of forfeiting all hope of reward is also mentioned in *Ḥovot ha-Levavot, Shaᶜar ha-Biṭṭaḥon*, Ch. 4, p. 119a.

5 While Hasidism originally held an ambivalent attitude towards self-afflictions, it is worth noting that even when Hasidim did take upon themselves such afflictions, albeit with reservations, they gave them a different twist. That is: a person does not afflict himself in order to mollify his sins and to acquire atonement for them, but to share in the pain of the Shekhinah, which seeks its own *tiqqun*. "For there is nought for man to seek, but that in His great mercies he see my affliction, to ease pain for his Shekhinah, and remove the shells from us, by means of my affliction. And I cause all the *qelippot* above to save the Shekhinah, that she become purified and unified with her husband" (*Ẓavaᵓat ha-Riva"sh*, p. 10). It is interesting to observe here how the religious value of afflictions squares with the fear of extraneous motivations when man in fact fulfills it. These issues were viewed

> I trust in Him that He created all the worlds with His word out of nothingness, and that all is as nothing compared to Him, and He oversees them to give them abundance and life; and moreover that He is able to bring power down to them, and that in His mercies He also looks over me and saves me so that the Evil Urge not prevent me from performing any of the afflictions [that I have undertaken: i.e., as a voluntary penance for sins], saying to me that I am weak and that I am in danger [i.e., because of my afflictions], and various other temptations ... So today also He will help me and save me from all the things which hinder me [from worship], and which on His part should not be considered as afflictions, for everything is from Him, may He be blessed. But for my part I would be unable to afflict myself at all, and I turn myself over to He who created all the worlds with His speech, to suffer all the afflictions and humiliations for the sake of His unity. And I wish to fulfill [the commandment], "And you shall be holy" [Lev. 20:7], and I trust in His mercies that He will give me strength so that I may be able to serve Him in truth.[6]

The fear of being unable to withstand trials and the withdrawal from positive acts are seen as a kind of temptation of the Evil Urge: i.e., to succumb to one's own spiritual inability. In this matter, which is connected with Divine service, Hasidim explicitly took the path of "haughtiness" (*gavhut*), for which they were criticized by the Mitnaggedim in their writings.[7] "Haughtiness" is the belief in man's spiritual power — whether the power to overcome one's own weaknesses[8] or the ability to act in the supernal worlds. As the Maggid said:

so seriously in Hasidism that, for this very reason, the Maggid himself wished to counter the religious value of fasting; see *Maggid Devarav le-Yaᶜaqov*, §150, p. 250. A later and interesting testimony concerning the Maggid's behavior regarding fasting appears in a manuscript of *Perush la-Torah* by R. Yaakov Yoles, a prolific Hasidic author (the manuscript is found at the Hebrew University Library), in which he relates: "... I heard in the name of the Holy Rabbi Reb Baer Maggid Mesharim of the holy community of Rovno [the Maggid of Mezhirech was formerly Maggid of Rovno] that it was his custom, after fasting from Sabbath to Sabbath, to go out on Shabbat morning after the prayer and stand at the place where the women left the synagogue. If they were then in his eyes completely like white geese [an allusion to the story about R. Joḥanan in Berakhot 20a], he knew that he no longer needed to fast or to torture his body at all, for he had already completely purified himself. But if he felt [their presence] somewhat, according to his measure, [so that] he was greatly agitated [based on Ps. 50:3], [he knew] this was not the case; he then continued to fast more, and knew that he needed to purify himself further. And this is, 'and the polluted mouths' — through this a person can determine whether he is still 'impure until the evening' [Lev. 15:16 and passim] — that is, so long as he feels in his soul a certain sweetness in corporeal things, he is not yet completely pure, and his intellect must even more dominate over his soul and purify it further — Ibid., fo. 201b, *Shemini*. It is difficult to know whether this testimony is in fact historically reliable.

6 *Ẓavaᵓat ha-Riva"sh*, pp. 10–11.

7 For an extensive discussion of this topic, see the beginning of *Derekh ᵓEmet*, by R. Meshullam Feibush of Zbarazh.

8 It is interesting to note that the idea of despair and fear of one's inability to stand up to trial appears also in Callistus, who says that a person ought not to fear that he will be unable to stand up to difficult

> Every person must have great faith that whatever he does, be it some *mizvah* or study of Torah or prayer, will arouse pleasure above. And he must not say in his heart, "How is it possible for me to do such a thing, that I so to speak cause pleasure above." Of this it is said, "a whisperer separateth the familiar friends (*ᵓaluf*; Prov. 16:28), for His [i.e., God's, called "the *ᵓAlef* of the world" — a pun on *'aluf* in the above verse] Glory, blessed be He, is called "faith, the craft of a craftsman" (*ᵓemunah ᵓemunat ᵓomen*) [after Isa. 25:1]. And in all the commandments he should think that he causes great pleasure up above, that brings all things into the World of Pleasure, where the [cosmic] rupture [i.e. *shevirat ha-kelim*] did not take place ... But if a person should say in his heart that he is very great, and come from this to great pride; concerning this it is said, "I cause thee to increase, even as the growth of the field ... and thou came ... yet you were naked and bare" [Ezek. 16:7]. Who gave you this power? "I, even I, am He" [Deut. 32:39].[9]

The two contrasting aspects of the Maggid's teaching — of "greatness" (*gadlut*) and of "humility" (*shiflut*) — constitute the psychological dialectic of his spirituality, a characteristic feature of a number of quietists.[10] This position, which makes no concessions to man's actual spiritual ability, seems at first blush to be extremely activistic; however, it is followed by an explicitly quietist comment, shedding light on its activist side: "'Yet you were naked and bare.' Who gave you this power? 'I, even I, am He.'" This is not a metaphorical expression, but a fundamental theme in the Maggid's teaching, meaning that man only apparently acts, but the true actor standing behind this superficial appearance is God Himself. We shall return to our discussion of this point further on. What is important here is that despair of man's ability to act is ultimately seen as an insult to God's power. This position returns us to that same remarkable approach, which sounds almost aggressive, in which Hasidism calls to achieve *devequt* in prayer by forcibly

tests, because God will not test him beyond his ability (see *Philokalia*, chapter on Callistus). In *Zavaᵓat ha-Riva"sh* as well, the above-quoted section ends with words of consolation: "I do not fear the weakness resulting from the fast, for even without that there are many people who are ill, and furthermore the Shekhinah provides for the ill person ... 'Trust in God and do good' [Ps. 37:3] — one is allowed to rely upon the *mizvot* ..." (Ibid., p. 11). Knox refers to the subject of despair as it appears among the quietists in the following words: "... If a thought (say) of *despair* comes to them while they are praying, they must break off at once and make an act of confidence in God to dispel the *blasphemous intruder*" — *Enthusiasm*, p. 282.

9 *Maggid Devarav le-Yaᶜaqov*, §161, p. 258, and also *ᵓOr Torah* (Jerusalem, 1956), p. 49a. Concerning the Maggid's *ᵓOr Torah*, see Schatz, "Introduction," p. x and xix.

10 I have thus far alluded to only one side of quietism, primarily that related to the feeling of "humility." In practice, the unrestrained attack of the church on Molinos accusing him of "contemplatio aquisita" points at maintaining the same view. They saw in him a certain "arrogance towards Heaven" and haughtiness; one may note a certain similarity in principle betweeen this and the phenomenon of Hasidic faith.

breaking through the veils of this world which prevent and disturb us from doing so. This "breakthrough" is understood in terms of the struggle against that despair which attacks a person when he realizes that he is unable to pray properly when, even though he knows that the King of the Universe is close to him, he is unable to find his way to Him through the corporeality surrounding himself.

> If at times he is unable to pray, he should not think that today he will certainly not pray [with *devequt*], but he should strengthen himself even more, and greater and greater fear will descend upon him, for this is like a king who went out to war and surrounded himself ... But he is unable to approach the king because of the great protection which surrounds the king; therefore he must strengthen himself with fear and with great strength, with extra *kavvanah*, so that he will be able to draw close and to pray before Him, may He be blessed. Then he will be able to pray with great *kavvanah*.[11]

One can see from this passage that resignation and inactivity due to doubt concerning the success of an action is unacceptable to Hasidism. Man is required to forgo everything only concerning his own pleasure, about which he is expected to be humble; but with regard to the service of God, pride and an uplifted spirit are more appropriate. Despair and lack of faith are the opposite of this, in that they lead man to sadness. The quietistic motif is placed here within the context of an internal paradox which states that "a person should not reflect upon his worship"[12] — meaning that he ought not to ponder as to whether or not he has in fact attained his goal, and that "he should not think whether [or not] the king loves him, so that he may love Him."[13] This indifference towards the results of the religious act — concerning which Hasidism does not counsel inaction or passivity --is very far-reaching: man is not even to reflect upon the "place" or *Sefirah* in the Divine world to which his thought has ascended. There is no room in Hasidism for the constant localizing of man's spiritual attainments in which classical Kabbalah

11 *Ẓavaʾat ha-Riva"sh*, p. 17. In a slightly different formulation on p. 21: "A person should not say, 'When I am able to pray with *hitlahavut* (enthusiasm) I will pray, and if not I will force myself to pray [i.e., even without *devequt*].' For to the contrary, as in the simile of the king ... he should therefore strengthen himself even more, for is not the king here, and they hid Him from his face?"

12 *ʾOr ha-ʾEmet*, p. 3a: "He need not reflect upon his service, in order not to come to external motivations, for 'and she had no eyes'" ... [expounding the Zoharic passage concerning the 'beautiful maiden who had no eyes' in *Saba de-Mishpaṭim*, reading *ʿeinin* (eyes) as if it were *ʿiyyun* (reflection)].

13 *Maggid Devarav le-Yaʿaqov*, §21, p. 34: "For his service [that of Moses] was like a throne with one leg, that he served Him with all his essence. Just as one who sits before the king is greatly embarassed before him, so that he does not think at all whether the king loves him so as to love him, but thinks only of his greatness, so that he may be ashamed before him." See also *Kitvei Qodesh*, p. 10a, "that he should not intend that the Creator come to the attribute of love!"

engages. Hasidism barely discusses the possible boundaries of the human spirit — i.e., whether he has reached this *Sefirah* or another — as it is not really concerned with these issues. On the contrary, most formulations of this question in Hasidic teaching indicate a bypassing — perhaps deliberate — of the realm of the *Sefirot*, and also suggest a direct connection to *Ḥokhmah* or *ʾEin Sof* (i.e., the very highest *Sefirot*, understood as hypostases of the Godhead itself).[14] This is certainly not accidental, as Hasidism is only interested in the moment of meeting and *devequt* between man and God: that is, in the negation of corporeality and the divesting of matter in order to encounter the spirit in its purity. I do not mean to say by this that the world of *Sefirot* plays no role in Hasidism, but only that it lost one of the central functions which it had in the consciousness of the Kabbalists.[15] This fact derives from the shifting of the primary interest of Hasidism to the question of *devequt* itself and its significance, rather than with the "topographical" stations to which man ascends in his *devequt*. There is one destination defined in Hasidism, namely, the "Nothing" (*ʾAyin*). The reader can clearly see that Hasidism chose this *Sefirah* as its destination due to its symbolic value, which allows for rich and multi-faceted interpretation.[16]

We may therefore state that the decline of interest in the doctrine of the *Sefirot* shown by Hasidism derives to a large extent from the quietistic element, which requires that one turn one's attention away from clearly defined "accomplishments." There is an interesting passage in *Ẓavaʾat ha-Riva"sh* which relates to this change:

> "And he shall set it one cubit (*ʾamah*) from the top." [Gen. 6:16] — that is, fear (*ʾeimah* — i.e. of God). Or one may say that, after the word has left his mouth, there is no need [thereafter] to mention it. Below, [we state that] he may not see that it goes to a supernal place, [in the same manner as] one is unable to gaze at the sun. And this is "set it above" — and do so. Likewise, "Go, you and all [your body] into the ark" (*teivah*; also "letter").[17]

14 For details of this theory, see the chapter on prayer below.

15 See G. Scholem, *The Origins of the Kabbalah*, pp. 209–210, 216 [Hebrew: *Reshit ha-Qabbalah (1150–1250)*, pp. 74, 96], where the discussion revolves around the "place" to which human thought goes, and to what *Sefirah* one prays.

16 They attributed the *ʾayin*, not to the *Sefirah* of *Keter*, as is generally done in Kabbalistic teaching, but to *Ḥokhmah*. This also allowed for the multi-faceted nature of the interpretations concerning *ʾayin*: it is both the darkness and the Divine depth in which "everything is equal," and at the same time the divine wisdom; it is both the fulness of the Divine attributes, and the absolute lack of definite contents. There is more than historical accident here in the history of religious symbolism.

17 *Ẓavaʾat ha-Riva"sh*, p. 18. After a person has recited the word with utter *devequt*, "when he comes into the ark / letter" [play on Gen. 7:1], as befitting a true mystic, he no longer need turn his attention to the place where his word ascends or "goes." The word itself ascends "to a high place" through its

Similar things are said in the treatise *Darkhei Ẓedeq*:

> If a person looks after the prayer, to examine whether any impression was left on one of his characteristics (*middot*) more than there was prior to the prayer, then he has not prayed as he should.[18]

The same embodiment of quietistic ideas within an activistic spirit seen in the *Ẓava*ʾ*ah* appear here as well. In this spirit, the *ḥasid* is commanded not to postpone prayer because of doubts or considerations relating to the wholeness of the prayer, but he is also told after the fact not to regret its imperfections. The flight from consideration and reflection upon the success of the religious act, both before and after, indicate the extent to which Hasidism wished to prevent or avoid the joy of victory and accomplishment; these are in effect but two sides of the same coin. In the *ḥasid*'s eye, both these psychological manifestations detract from the religious value of *biṭaḥon* (trust). Refraining from action — due to considerations which in themselves may be relevant — when, according to the *Shulḥan* ᶜ*Arukh*, one is required to act, is considered a sin, not so much because of the non-performance of a *miẓvah*, but because of the violation of the Hasidic religious value known as "the attribute of trust."

> A person should not say, "I am now [caught] in sadness and alien thoughts, [therefore] I will not pray or study [Torah]." For perhaps afterwards he will not be free, and thus nullify them entirely — and likewise regarding all the *miẓvot*. For when they wish to punish a person, they deprive him of the attribute of trust. It is therefore seemly that one strengthen [oneself] and pray before God, may He be blessed, so as not to lose the attribute of trust.[19]

While the decision that one ought not to postpone prayer until a time of "inspiration"[20] may have been influenced by consciously conservative motivations, based upon the fear that otherwise the prayer might be completely nullified (in this case as well, they did not cite the reason that they would thereby

own spiritual power, but a person must not "remember" it. He has already fulfilled his task by spiritualizing it and thereby "completing" it; from here onward, it is of no interest to him. His task is to enter into the "letter" just as it ascends upwards. After releasing it from his mouth, his own task is completed.

18 *Darkhei Ẓedeq, Hanhagot*, 31.

19 Ibid., 15, 16.

20 Ibid., 58: "He must take trouble in preparation for prayer, and not despair because disturbances and alien thoughts come to him, to consider this an aspect of descent, Heaven forbid." Here too, one can clearly see the tendency encouraging man to "trouble himself" and to "prepare" for prayer, the primary warning being against despair and fear of failure. Such fear is a religious transgression, as it damages the trust man has in God that He will help him, and indicates that he has a self-interest outside of the prayer itself.

transgress the proper time for prayer), one should nevertheless not ignore the official reason given here, in which such "postponement" is seen as harmful to one's full faith in God, by which a person can in fact overcome the obstacles, external and internal, which hinder prayer. This argument corresponds to the above-mentioned passage from the *Ẓavaʾah*, in which man is called upon to actively break through the circle which closes in upon him. Surprisingly, this activist command is characterized by a quietistic spirit which thrusts all of one's burden upon God, and refuses to rely upon human ability.[21] Were Hasidic doctrine less conservative than it is in fact, these quietistic tendencies might have taken a totally different direction; i.e., it might have argued that man is required to wait to pray until he indeed feels that God has come to his aid, and only then may he begin his prayer without feeling any obstacles. Such a position would have subjected Hasidic quietism, and its conception of trust, to a much sharper test — but, as we said, this path was too daring for Hasidism.[22] Hasidism never reached the stage of untrammeled confrontation between quietistic tendencies and the traditional values of the Jewish tradition. Regarding its quietistic demands of the other kind — i.e., not to pay attention to accomplishments of any kind whatsoever — Hasidism took a longer route. Here, it hardly came into confrontation with the tradition, but only with such beliefs as reward and punishment and the Afterlife (which we have already discussed above), and not with the concrete way of life based upon strict observance of the *miẓvot*.

Despite the conservative restrictions placed by Hasidism upon its own path, it gave broad scope for confrontation with accepted values in Jewish thought. One could hardly expect it to protest against prohibitions which were viewed strictly

21 But against this there is the claim of the *Mitnaggedim* that the Hasidim do in fact wait for a time of "inspiration." See R. Ḥayyim of Volozhin, *Nefesh ha-Ḥayyim*, Part IV, Ch. 4, p. 36b.

22 R. Meshullam Feibush of Zbarazh made some explicit statements regarding those *ẓaddiqim* who go to extremes in thinking that they do not do enough in prayer, Torah and good deeds. These thoughts bring them to "improper modesty... until bit by bit they come to neglect all good deeds. All of this because of their improper modesty, and that he waits until he reaches the highest level to worship God in truth. But so long as he does not feel the truth within himself, because of the [Evil] Urge which deceives him, he does not do anything: he does not study Torah, he does not fast, he does not repent, and he does not pray. And he makes himself simple, because he finds faults in all these things [that is, in his incomplete deeds!]. And all this is the doing of the Urge, to cause him to cease his acts completely and to make him empty, and thereafter to tempt him regarding other matters, until he Heaven forbid pulls him down into the deep pit ... and for this [reason] it is good that he hold on somewhat to greatness ..." — *Yosher Divrei ʾEmet*, p. 38a-b. The opinion is quoted in the name of the Baʿal Shem Tov that, if he is unable to free himself of alien thoughts when he starts to pray, he should not wait: "Let him not say, 'When I will be free ...'" [paraphrase of Avot 2:4] — *Toldot Yaʿaqov Yosef, Va-yishlaḥ*, p. 27c.

by the halakhah, but there is no want of levity on the part of a number of Hasidic thinkers with regard to the seriousness of sin. There was one transgression which was thought to weigh more heavily than any other in terms of its religious consequences: the expression, "worry over sins," became a term of opprobrium in Hasidism, implying that a person paid attention to the past out of anxiety to save his own soul, thereby preventing him from engaging in the service of God. Sadness is a great sin in Hasidism; indeed, it is the very embodiment of Sin. Not even the gravest explicit sins are considered as serious as it,[23] and even those spiritual accomplishments to which Hasidism gave the highest value are not to be acquired at its cost. Such an extreme and radically spiritualist thinker such as R. Ḥayyim Ḥaykl of Amdur says, "he should not be sorrowful if he does not worship God with wholeness of mind."[24] One might state that the primary religious value established by Hasidism was the attitude of a person towards the deed. Actions themselves lost their static, fixed position and came to be measured in Hasidism on the basis of a new criterion. If Hasidism sought to create the spiritual tension characteristic of the transcendent human being who knows how to "ascend" "above time" and above everyday life in general, it also established the opposite rule — namely, that a person ought not to feel badly if he falls short of this.[25] While the *ḥasid* is asked to observe all the commandments strictly according to the Law, it also told him that if he failed to do so he need not worry or feel sorrow or remorse.[26] There is no conflict between these two seemingly contradictory positions. Just as a person ought not to note his accomplishments in the one case, he ought not to pay heed to his failures in the other. What determines the Hasidic nature of the following sayings is their disinterested stance: a person is not to regret "the loss of his vessels," as R. Zechariah Mendel of Jaroslaw says. In a more general sense, Hasidism dared to break more than a few of man's "vessels," so that he might not hold on to them as things of value in their own right. Traces of this nonchalant spirit already exist in the teaching of the Baᶜal Shem Tov himself, according to Hasidic tradition. His lenient position concerning seminal emissions — which was considered by the *Zohar* and the subsequent mystical tradition as The Cardinal

23 "He should take very great care against sadness, even that concerning worry over his sins" — *Darkhei Ẓedeq* (end).

24 *Ḥayyim va-Ḥesed*, 200, 201. This sermon also seems to carry a certain polemic sting against the advocates of an "intellective" path among the Hasidim — i.e., R. Shneur Zalman of Lyady of Ḥabad: "... to exclude one who thinks in his thought alone. Then the intellect does not enter the heart, and this is only arrogance, that he wishes to be among those who serve God with the intellect."

25 *Darkhei Ẓedeq, Hanhagot* 63.

26 See MS Jerusalem 3282, fo. 175b: "even if he stumbles into sin, he should not be overly sad."

Sin — is particularly well known.[27] It was perhaps for this reason that the Besht saw fit to warn against sadness resulting from the Great Sin, because this happening, which is outside of the individual's control,[28] is liable to disturb the smooth continuity of his basic service of God. In the Besht's view, it was preferable to minimize the severity of this sin rather than to be guilty of the true sin of sadness and remorse. R. Ḥayyim Ḥaykl of Amdur accepted this assumption, and went on to explain that it was possible to overcome the consequences of sin merely by being oblivious to it:

> "Those who sow in tears shall reap in joy" [Ps. 126:5]. Thus, what is the correction (*tiqqun*) for one who spills his seed in vain? "In tears, in joy." What shall be his guarantee (*ᶜarevo*)? [a pun on *ᶜarev*, "pleasant" — i.e., that his *tiqqun* takes place through pleasantness and joy] That is, that he should always walk in the streets in the joy of Torah and *miẓvot*. "Shall reap" — he shall thereby reap the shells [*qelippot* — i.e., the non-Divine negative forces in the cosmos]. But he should not walk in sadness at all, Heaven forbid, for because of this, Heaven forbid, they will pursue him, to pollute him with emissions.[29]

True, this approach was criticized within the Hasidic camp itself by R. Jeḥiel Michel of Zloczow (ca. 1731–1786), who continued to emphatically preach the need to take cautions against seminal pollutions.[30] However, it is clear that he took

27 See, for example, *ᵓOr Torah*, p. 65b: "R. Israel Baᶜal Shem said that a person should not be anxious concerning an impure accident, that he unwittingly had *qeri* (a seminal emission); but only for the impure thought, and not for the *qeri*, for the evil went out of him, for had it not [done so] he would die."

28 Regarding seminal emissions, he drew a distinction between thought and deed. See *Maggid Devarav le-Yaᶜaqov*, §160, pp. 256–257, and also MS Jerusalem 3282, fo. 159b. It is interesting to compare R. Nahum of Chernobyl's tradition that the Maggid required one to weep over *qeri*, "for penitence is a positive commandment of the Torah, and therefore he must perform it joyously; but for this sin it is not appropriate to be joyous, but only to be sad and to weep, so he therefore cannot come to repentance ..." — *Meᵓor ᶜEynayim* (Jerusalem, 1960), p. 217b. It is clear that to the members of that generation, particularly those who were influenced by Kabbalah, not necessarily in the Hasidic camp, this sin was considered a very serious one. See, for example, R. Abraham Heller, *Zerizuta de-Avraham* (New York, 1952), pp. 8b, 17c, 36d, 37d. An interesting testimony by the author of *Mishmeret ha-Qodesh*, one of the opponents of the early circles of Hasidism, denounces them as being among those who spill their seed in vain. Perhaps the Besht's opinion already reflects a certain reservation concerning this matter, which is tolerant only with regard to involuntary emissions. See on this G. Scholem 's article, "The Two Earliest Testimonies Concerning the Circle of Hasidim and the Besht" (Heb.), *Sefer ha-Yovel le-R. Naḥum Epstein* (Jerusalem, 1950), p. 232.

29 *Ḥayyim va-Ḥesed* on Ps. 126; p. 120.

30 See *Mayim Rabbim* (Jerusalem, 1964). The commentary on this work, *Migdanot Natan*, cites the following remarks of the author of *Ẓemaḥ David*, son of R. Ẓevi Elimelekh of Dynow: "'Remember not against us the former sins; May your compassions speedily come to meet me, for we are brought very low' [Ps. 79:8]. [This] was the renowned event which took place in the days of the holy R.

exception only regarding this specific matter: one cannot conclude from this any general objection to the characteristic mood of the *ḥasid* who, in R. Ḥayyim Ḥaykl's words, no longer worries "if he is good or bad."[31]

As we have said, pain and regret over one's failures and transgressions became the archetypal religious sin in Hasidism,[32] signifying that sin was measured in

Menaḥem Mendel of Rymanow, *z"l* [abbreviation for *zikhrono li-verakhah* — i.e., "may his memory be blessed"], when the souls of Israel came to him from the upper worlds with the complaint that the holy rabbi, the Maggid of Zloczow, *z"l*, was the Head of the Court in the upper world, and was very strict concerning the sin of emissions, heaven forbid, because he was holy and pure during his lifetime, and he never tasted of this sin. And their request was heeded, and another was named in his stead, and they returned to him to thank him for this, because he lightened [their burden]. For the sin is in accordance with the generation..." On p. 44b, it cites an interpretation from *No^cam Megaddim* in the name of R. Michel on the verse, "the firstborn of your sons give to me" [Ex. 22:28]. The same interpretation is offered by *Ṭurrei Zahav*, 31a and 108d, in the name of R. Menaḥem Mendel of Przemyślany. As against this, R. Pinḥas of Korets enthusiastically supports the formula of the Ba^cal Shem Tov — see MS. Jerusalem 3759, fo. 100a: "Concerning the rabbi [R. Pinḥas of Korets] before whom he [i.e., R. Raphael of Bershad] complained about one who sees *qeri*, Heaven forbid, that he had replied that he should not be afraid. And he [R. Raphael] said, 'How is it possible to hit a man over his head with a beam, and for him not to be afraid!' And he explained [this appears to refer to R. Raphael himself, who explained it in the name of R. Pinḥas] at length that a person sees [*qeri*] so that he not be proud when he engages in much divine service, for they show him, 'Who are you?' ..." [and when he admits to himself that he is lowly and contemptible he has nothing to fear!]. Elsewhere in the same manuscript, p. 195a: "Of the Rabbi who answered concerning one who sees *qeri* that the *miqveh* (ritual bath) atones, and that he need not have fear. Likewise, concerning one who complained to him that it is impossible to sanctify oneself properly during the time [of intercourse] ... he replied that the *miqveh* atones ..."

I find it surprising that Heschel (in "R. Nahman of Kosov," pp. 133 and 139) did not stress this point regarding R. Pinḥas of Korets (for these things were certainly recorded in the MS. he possessed concerning R. Pinḥas), when he tried to "purify" R. Nahman of Kosow of the matter of seminal emissions, relating to *Shivḥei ha-Besht*.

31 "'I have always placed (*shiviti*) God before me' [Ps. 16:8]. This means that a person never has any opportunity to look at himself, whether he is good or bad, because God is always present to him." — *Ḥayyim va-Ḥesed*, p. 96. This interpretation is in the spirit of the Maggid's teaching. The phrase *shivayon* ("to place," literally, "equal"), used here in the sense of "indifference," entered use in Hasidism primarily in the teaching of the Maggid of Mezhirech (in the Besht *shiviti* generally does not mean "equanimity of soul"). This usage is taken from *Ḥovot ha-Levavot, Sha^car Yiḥud ha-Ma^caseh*, Ch. 5, p. 137b.

32 R. Yitzḥak of Radzivilow also speaks of regret as a temptation of the Evil Urge (see *^ɔOr Yiẓḥaq*, p. 156b), and of the need to uproot the feeling of sin (ibid., 195b). The distinction between the positive value of regret and its negative value is expressed in the allegory brought by Reuben ha-Levi Horowitz, as follows; "One person stood by the king and spoke evil of the king, and did not take notice at all that he was standing by the king. And afterwards he regretted it, and said to the king, 'Your majesty the king, I am very regretful. But it is not because of fear of punishment or lack of reward that I regret it at all, but I only regret that I did not notice at all that I was standing by the king, for by rights I should have noticed that I was standing by the king, that the fear of his royalty should

terms of a new criterion — namely, the psychological state of man. "Repentance" as a religious value continued to play a dominant role in Hasidic thought, but it was no longer based upon remorse or regret over past deeds, but upon the consciousness that man intends to sin no more and that he does not make light of sin as defined by the *halakhah*. The person who repents is simply required to decide that he no longer intends to perform the acts of sin.[33] If a *ḥasid* starts to beat his breast, he is guilty of a grave sin of immanent religious power, even if not considered as such by the *Shulḥan ᶜArukh*. The Maggid of Mezhirech said the following:

> At times the Evil Urge deceives a person, telling him that he has committed a great transgression, even if it is only a [Rabbinic] stringency or not a sin at all. Its intention is [to lead] that person to a state of sadness, so that by reason of his sadness he will be distracted from the service of the Creator. But a person must understand this deception, and tell the Evil Urge, "I do not pay heed to this stringency which you say, for it is your intention to cause me not to perform His service, may He be blessed, and you speak falsehood. And even if it is a little bit of a sin, it is more pleasing to my Creator that I not pay heed to this stringency which you tell me, to cause me sadness in His service, but that, to the contrary, I serve Him with joy. For this is a basic rule, that it is not my intention in His service [that it be] for my own needs, but only to be pleasing to Him. Therefore, even if I do not pay heed to the stringency which you mentioned, the Creator will not be strict with me, for the reason why I am not strict is in order not to nullify His service. For how can I nullify His service for even one moment?" And this is a great rule in the service of the Creator, that he take care against sadness in so far as he is able.[34]

The "deception" of the Evil Urge here means an uneven and unbalanced

have been upon me, and this is my main regret.' ... And thus shall be the repentance for the like, that he forgot and removed the fear of the king from his face. And this is the meaning of, 'Indeed, there is God in this place' — that I did the sin — 'and I did not know it' [Gen. 26:16]; this is my regret. And understand this very well, for this is the essence of the service of the Creator" — *Dudaʾim ba-Sadeh* (Ereẓ Yisraʾel, n.d.), p. 14a.

33 The Mitnaggedim in fact criticized the Hasidim because they viewed sadness as heresy and their hearts were not broken in regret, and because they are not punctilious about the details of the *miẓvot*. See Zweifel, *Shalom ᶜal Yisraʾel*, Pt. II, pp. 50–52.

34 *Ẓavaʾat ha-Riva"sh*, pp. 11–12. A similar formulation appears in MS. Jerusalem 3282, in possession of R. Ḥayyim Ḥaykl of Amdur, f. 175b (these pages belong to the *Ẓavaʾah*, and are taken from it nearly verbatim): "And sadness is the greatest obstacle to the service of God, as is known, and even if he falls into transgression, Heaven forbid, he should not be greatly sad and cease from [performing] service." In the eyes of the quietist Molinos, it is also Satan who moves man to an uneasy conscience, in order to keep him from the true inner path. See Dudon, *Molinos*, p. 198; on the source of this idea in the Hasidic literature of Safed, see the article by E. Shohat, "On Joy in Hasidism" (Heb.), *Ẓion* 16 (1951), p. 34.

evaluation of the fixed values of tradition, as against the new Hasidic criterion, which introduced man's religious stature as the decisive factor. "That which brings greatest pleasure to the Creator" is not a halakhic consideration *per se*, but rather a religious consideration of the highest order. This preference in no small measure determined the image of Hasidism as a movement of religious renewal. Although this tendency was not a radical one destroying existing frameworks, as was the case among extreme quietist Christians, it was sufficient to give room for thought regarding these questions, or even to establish new patterns of religious life in practice.[35]

But if it was not a true breakdown, there were "cracks" detectable in the hasidic way of life and social ethic: the moment that Hasidism brought down from his pedestal the Jew who fulfilled all of the six-hundred thirteen *mizvot* in every detail and nicety, all of whose deeds were dedicated to self-examination lest he had violated some negative commandment, it was able to state with confidence and solemnity that it is strictly forbidden for a person to regard himself as wicked simply because his neighbor is stricter in his observances than he is, or because the *zaddiq* had reached a higher "level" than himself.[36] Hasidism likewise prohibited the exacting of feelings of regret, due to the element of masochism involved therein:

> I heard from my teacher that, when a person is aroused to repentance because of his great remorse, he at times curses himself and awakens against himself judgments and sufferings and wishes that it [i.e., death] come upon him because of his sin. A person ought not to do so, but he should ask God to strengthen his heart to repent, and not to awaken judgment. This is the temptation of the Evil Urge, which wishes to make him lost without proper repentance, that he may die before his time. And once there was a certain *talmid* who did so, and he was criticized by our master in principle.[37]

35 R. Ḥayyim of Volozhin, who was the only one among the Mitnaggedim to plumb to the depths of the Hasidic religious phenomenon and to comprehend its religious significance, writes: "Moreover, this too he will try in disguise, telling you that sin and transgression are also considered as a *mizvah* if it is [done] for the sake of heaven, to repair (*tiqqun*) some matter, for God desires the heart, and 'great is a gratuitous transgression.'" See *Nefesh ha-Ḥayyim*, Pt. IV, Ch. 7 (p. 37b).

36 "At times the Evil Urge brings down sadness upon a person, day and night, [saying] that he is an evil person, and does not allow him to rejoice in the commandments of God, but shows him the gap between himself and the great *zaddiqim* and their good deeds..." — *Darkhei Zedeq: Hanhagot la-ᶜAvodat ha-Borei Yitbarakh shemo.*

37 Ibid., *Hanhagot*, 50. Particularly interesting are the remarks of R. Dov Baer b. R. Shneur Zalman of Lyady on the difference between Hasidim and Mitnaggedim concerning the matter of remorse: "He used to say: What is the difference between the Hasidim and the sect of the Mitnaggedim, as the intentions of both are for the sake of Heaven? But the difference is the following: The Mitnagged certainly learns Torah for-its-own-sake [sic! — reflecting the conciliatory mood of the Habad movement], and performs *mizvot* with love and awe, and if he performs a transgression, Heaven

The quietistic mood of leniency towards sin and lack of remorse is consistent with the expressions of passivity which we have already observed. We find the same attitude toward remorse among such Christian quietists as Molinos and Falconi, as we found among the Hasidim; their attitude is appropriate to the conceptual system and overall attitude of the passive outlook. Molinos formulates this idea quite succinctly: "It is a divine gift that the soul not think about its sins." He thought that the soul need not know whether it is following the path desired by God so long as it is inspired with a sense of harmony with the Divine will. Neither does it need to know its own status or "nothingness"; all it need do is to remain as a body without life. He thereby seeks to eliminate all reflection upon our human acts and our sins.[38]

Notwithstanding the similarity between Molinos' quietistic stance and that of Hasidism, one must note an extremely important difference between the two. Molinos went so far as not to recognize the reality of sin; he believed that a person who had attained mystical unity with God is no longer able to sin, and that what appears to human beings as sin is in fact an act of the limbs alone, sent by Satan to test the man engrossed in contemplation. Such an act, in which there is neither the will nor the intention to sin, is completely without any inner significance.[39] Such an approach was problematic for Hasidism, with its conservative bent. The

forbid, he does not move from there until he has repented fully, with weeping and crying out and fasting and afflictions to repair what he has harmed, and his soul is very bitter within him, so that he is unable to open his mouth in joy. But the *ḥasid* studies Torah for its own sake, performs *mizvot* and good deeds with love and awe, and if he commits a sin, Heaven forbid, does not move from there until he repents with regret and bitterness and a pained heart; nevertheless, the moment he comes to study Torah or to pray or to perform *mizvot* and good deeds, he does so with great joy and completely forgets that he has done a sin at all, for all the ways of his service are to do the will of the Creator and to cause pleasure to Him, with love and longing and desire, and not out of any motivation — neither fear of sin nor for a reward in Paradise and the World to Come. Therefore, even when he performs a sin and stumbles in it, Heaven forbid, he regrets it from the depths of his heart, but the sin does not extinguish the *mizvot* and good deeds, preventing him from doing them with joy and goodness of heart out of abundance of everything. For he says in his heart, 'I do not worry about myself, whether I will be in Gehinnom; as there is now before me some thing by which I may do the will of my Creator, I will do it with joy and righteousness, and give pleasure to the Creator of all the worlds.'" — cited in *Seder ha-Dorot*, p. 39.

38 The author of the article makes the following remarks on the words of Falconi: "Quand nous péchions, nous ne dévions point nous troubler, mais dire seulement que nous faisons ce que nous pouvions ..." — Pourrat, "Quietisme," col. 1559.

39 See Dudon, p. 202, who states that according to Molinos people of the spirit are liable to sin according to the law, but in practice they only sin in the vulgar eyes of the masses, who think that they sin against the laws of the Church. This problem arises in Hasidism as well, in connection with the special "merits" of the *zaddiq*, particularly in light of the claim that sins are in his eyes only apparent (*Ma*ʾ*or va-Shemesh*). However, there it has a slightly different meaning, which I will discuss elsewhere.

concept of "apparent" sin was suitable to the Sabbatian outlook[40] within Judaism, but could hardly find a place for itself in Hasidism. Molinism reached its extreme when it argued that one ought not to respond to the challenge of evil coming from without; in his eyes, the body which had already submitted to the spirit was subject to the law of the spirit, which differed from the general, external laws, and was therefore no longer required to reject foreign desires and thoughts.[41]

But despite Hasidism's different position in principle concerning sin and its evaluation thereof within the framework of its religious values, one cannot say that it was untouched by the consciousness of the problematics inherent here. One might say that it was saved from taking the final step in this direction thanks to its ideology of uplifting sparks. In what way?

When Hasidism wished to explain its position of non-withdrawal from the world and affirming positive confrontation therewith, it made use of an important idea of Lurianic Kabbalah, which describes the principal task of the Jew in the world as raising up the fallen sparks of Divinity scattered throughout the entire cosmos. This messianic ideology of the Kabbalah, which was given a more neutral, mystical interpretation in Hasidism, was used to justify the idea of *ᶜavodah be-gashmiyut*, by means of which a person is able to uplift the sparks. By means of this affirmation, the balance was swung in favor of the idea of struggling in order to elevate alien thoughts up to holiness, and the option of flight and withdrawal was rejected.[42] This activist approach, which prevented one from escaping the field of struggle and activity, thus placed a barrier against extreme quietistic tendencies. The inner affirmations of Hasidic mysticism stopped short at the threshold of Hasidic ideology, which understood the problem of action in far more conservative terms.[43] But while this was generally speaking the case, it was not altogether

40 See, for example, G. Scholem, *Sabbatai Ṣevi; The Mystical Messiah, 1626–1676*, trans., R. J. Z. Werblowsky [Bollingen Series. 93. (Princeton, 1973)], pp. 163–164 [Hebrew: *Shabbetai Ẓevi* (Tel-Aviv, 1957), p. 131], and the subject index in the Hebrew edition, s. v. *maᶜasim zarim*.

41 See Pourrat, "Quietisme," col. 1551; and Dudon, p. 72: "L'intérieur de chacun est sujet à d'autres lois que les lois communes." He cites the formula of Molinos, who says: "Quand l'entendement parvient à un degré d'élévation qui attache l'âme incessamment à Dieu ... quelques *désordres* ... qui se passent dans les sens ... on ne doit plus les regarder comme des péchés, mais tout au plus commes des tentations et des efforts inutiles du démon ..." — p. 172.

42 These two views were commonly held at the beginning of Hasidism, and it is clear that there is competition between them. It is perhaps worth noting that among the Eastern quietists we also find an approach which rejects alien thoughts. See, for example, the chapter from Gregory of Sinai's writings in *Philokalia*, pp. 35–96.

43 I will not enter here into the question, interesting in itself, of the assimilation of this ideology and its place in Hasidic thought. But see my comments about Scholem's interpretation of Hasidism in the Introduction to this volume, sects. iii, iv.

unproblematical, when cautiously plumbed to its depths. I refer to the profound understanding of the Maggid's teaching by R. Meshullam Feibush of Zbarazh, who struggles openly on behalf of an aristocratic interpretation of Hasidic teaching, which he wishes to restrict to those who understand such things. As an example of the proper understanding of the Maggid's teaching, he invokes the incident of Ulla (Shabbat 13a) who "would kiss his sisters upon their breasts." He explains that:

> If a person is removed from corporeality, he is then divided within himself. Within himself he is attached to the Creator with great longing, while externally, within the world, he performs all physical actions, such as eating and sexual union. Within himself he is like an angel separated from corporeality, while externally he seems like an animal to those who see him. But if, Heaven forbid, this is not the case, then he is one with his animal appetites, and is not separated or divided from them at all... Why did he [Ulla] do this? Because he was divided within himself: that is, his spirituality was separated from his physicality; for if not, how could he do such a thing?[44]

This is not the place for a comprehensive discussion of R. Meshullam Feibush's interpretation of "service through corporeality" (*ᶜavodah be-gashmiyut*) in general. With regard to our subject, it is important to understand that even the ideology of lifting up of the sparks, which is inextricably connected with the mystical conception of *devequt*, must inevitably bring one to the conclusion of a division within man, who is "divided within himself," in the words of the Talmud there. In the "unimportant" area of action, he is even allowed to kiss his sisters on their breasts, because in this ideal situation of the split personality, he is no longer responsible for the actions of his limbs, which are no longer of any importance in themselves.

Such things were certainly not written in Hasidism very often, but it is enough that they were written at all, for them to be regarded as a faithful representation of the basic principles of the Maggid's teaching.[45] One ought not to conclude from my remarks that Hasidism taught a Molinistic doctrine and completely scoffed at the significance of sin.[46] It does not preach this at all, although when it completely plumbed its own teaching, it encountered anew all of those problems which

44 Meshullam Feibush Heller of Zbarazh, *Derekh ᵓEmet* (Jerusalem, n.d.), p. 19a.

45 The idea of the spiritual "split" at the time of *devequt* is attributed to the Besht by his disciple, R. Jacob Joseph of Polonnoye; see *Toldot Yaᶜaqov Yosef, Parshat Va-yishlaḥ*, p. 26b.

46 A claim such as that lodged against Meister Eckhardt blaming him for holding that a person need not regret a sin for the reason that this thing was permitted by God, has no place in Hasidism. See Pourat, "Quietisme," sec. 13, col. 1551.

constitute an inner paradox, one which pertains to the quietistic question of the relation to sin.

Dudon's remarks — whether or not they are correct in principle — explain Molinism in terms of its relation to sin in a manner which is not too far removed from that proposed by R. Meshullam Feibush; that is, that sin provides an opportunity for the transformation of impurity into holiness. This is precisely the concept of elevation of sparks.[47] I have already said that Hasidism was saved by virtue of the ideology of the uplifting of sparks — albeit not by its underlying conception of the divided personality, but by virtue of the activity, encounter and confrontation which this demands. As we shall see elsewhere, this imperative required the activistic line of Hasidism, unlike the case in classical quietism. The body was not a framework for the arbitrary activity of Satan from which one needed to flee, as in the doctrine of Molinos,[48] but the site of a positive struggle of the divine sparks which seek redemption from their shells by means of man, and for which man is responsible. Of course, one cannot imagine in Hasidism the more radical approach of certain quietists, who said that, "The greatest sacrifice it is possible to make on behalf of God is to perform that sin of which one is most afraid."[49]

In conclusion, it must be said that, with regard to certain values in Judaism, the three central Hasidic imperatives of abjuring despair, worry and regret are symptomatic of a spirit of resignation. This resignation is characteristic of the quietistic spirit, although in Hasidism it was accompanied at times by activistic imperatives, which in practice restricted the domination of passivity. This very struggle, which reveals the bursting forth of the longing for the eradication of self-interest, and the reservations regarding this very thing for conservative reasons, can likewise be inferred from the stance of Hasidism with regard to the *mizvot* and to prayer, to which we shall now turn.

47 "Quelle mystique que celle la qui prétendait faire trouver aux âmes, dans les bas fonds du plus abject sensualisme, le vrai lieu d'une transformation divine!" — Dudon, p. 199.

48 "Les actes éxterieurs ... se produisent sans que le tenté soit responsable aucunement d'un désordre dont son corps est le théâtre, mais où son âme n'a aucune part." — Dudon, p. 195. See also Knox, *Enthusiasm*, p. 281 and p. 310, concerning his principle of non-resistance to temptation. Knox says on p. 314 regarding the teaching of Molinos: "its most intolerable feature evidently was the view that externally sinful acts can be inculpable if the director sees them to proceed from the violent interference of the devil."

49 The author says that this was the conclusion reached by Lacomb and Madame Guyon from the teaching of Molinos. See Pourrat, "Quietisme," col. 1575; this may simply be a barb concerning a biographical matter between them. See the introduction by N. Hoffmann to the German translation of Madam Guyon's book, *Zwölf geistliche Gesprache* (Jena, 1911).

Chapter Five

The Status of the *Mizvot*

At the beginning of the above discussion, I stated that Hasidism fixed the limits of this problematic when it took upon itself *ab initio* the punctilious observance of all the *mizvot.* The attitude toward sin discussed in the previous chapter only applies retroactively; with regard to any point in the future, the *mizvot* remain an obligatory, closed system. It is worth noting here an interesting point: Hasidism paid less attention to the meaning of the *mizvot* than it did to any other realm, most of its discussions in this area being focused upon one of two extremes — i.e., prayer, and "service in corporeality." In its struggle to mend the gap between spirit and flesh, explanations of *ṭa^camei ha-mizvot* occupied a secondary place. Spiritual life found expression in contemplative prayer, for which reason prayer was largely interpreted in terms of its significance as a point of departure for inner contemplation. On the other hand, the ideology of "service through corporeality" (*^cavodah be-gashmiyut*), which was the primary heritage of the Ba'al Shem Tov, was given profound spiritual meaning by the Maggid of Mezhirech and his circle.[1] Relatively little attention was given to the *mizvot* as the natural meeting point of thought and deed, or spirit and matter. Were one to take a rough cross-section of Hasidic thinkers regarding this question, we would find that this problem was given short shrift as a result of the theological structure of Hasidism and its centers of gravity. By this, I refer to a point easily recognizable in reading Hasidic sources: one ideological focus, which is fundamentally spiritualistic, saw as its primary aim the life of contemplation, and therefore naturally concentrated upon the question of contemplative prayer, from which it was easy to turn to that which was "beyond time." A second focus, widely-discussed in Hasidic writings, was concerned with the crucial question of the value of service in corporeality in the most literal sense: namely, eating, drinking, sexual union, and the other mundane activities. This affirmation, which is also one of the central messages of Hasidism, led to an extremely interesting inner conflict, and thereby served as one of the major focii for many of its internal discussions. Those *mizvot* which lay between these two

1 The nature of the tension between these two poles will be discussed elsewhere. See, *inter alia*, my discussion of Scholem's interpretation of Hasidism in the Introduction to the present volume, Sect. III–IV.

extremes were of only secondary interest in Hasidism. Paradoxically, it was those thinkers who followed the radical spiritualistic tendency for whom the system of the *miẓvot* formed a separate subject of interest. I will elaborate upon this point below.

In discussing the attitude toward *miẓvot* in Hasidic thought, it is worth turning our attention to another interesting phenomenon: that Hasidism rarely discusses the mystical significance of the *miẓvot* in the precise Kabbalistic sense of the term. This subject, which was the focus of interest for generations of Kabbalists and which they tirelessly reexamined, did not find a sympathetic ear among the Hasidim. They had little interest in discussions of which of the lower seven *Sefirot* corresponds to the various aspects of the *lulav,* or what facets of the World of Emanation are alluded to by the *ṭallit* and *tefillin.* They were no longer enthusiastic about the intellectual manipulations through which Kabbalists attempted to direct the divine realm by means of acts of *miẓvot* on this world, just as they were not in principle interested in the complexities of *kavvanot* in prayer; Hasidic mysticism was more of the a-meditative type.

One should not conclude from this that Hasidism was content with simple performance of the *miẓvot*; on the contrary, the Maggid of Mezhirech opposed this view, on the basis of his overall approach that action is of no independent value unless accompanied by *kavvanah* leading to *devequt.* Even an act that is seemingly holy in itself, which Jews are commanded to perform, is insufficient to fulfill one's obligation. The only religious obligation acknowledged in Hasidism is one that leads to *devequt,* and it was by no means self-evident that the performance of *miẓvot* was presumed to be holy *per se.* Thus, the Maggid did not even exclude from the obligation of ongoing sanctification those things that were agreed and accepted as being holy. The dynamic of the Maggid's system sought to transform even the realm of the sanctified into holy in actuality. It is in light of this that we can understand the following remark of the Maggid:

> Do not say that, because I engage in God's Torah and in His *miẓvot,* which are pure holiness, that [their performance] is holy even without *kavvanah.* Do not say this for, to the contrary, [it is] precisely in holy things one must make your intentions acceptable and your thoughts pure and your speech whole, for "they are life to them that find them" [Prov. 4:22] ...[2]

This insight, which is consistent with the Maggid's overall approach, is essentially based upon the placing of religious commands at the service of spiritual attainments. From this point of view, there is no difference in principle between

---

2 *Liqqutei Yeqarim,* p. 8b, and *Biʾur Torah,* Chap. 8, p. 4.

the performance of the *mizvot* and "service in corporeality" (albeit prayer nevertheless enjoys a special status).

In the Maggid's approach, we can already sense the overshadowing of the commandments themselves by the quest for significance. In this respect, he paves the way for the deeper investigation of this question by his disciples, R. Ḥayyim Ḥaykl of Amdur and, particularly, by R. Menaḥem Mendel of Vitebsk. This was expressed in two primary assumptions: 1) the understanding of the need to perform the *mizvot* as the fulfillment of a Divine command; 2) the acknowledgment of the principle that the observance of the *mizvot* is in itself neither an exclusive nor necessary path for the attainment of *devequt*.

In the following remarks, R. Levi Yitzḥak of Berdichev cites the opinion of the Maggid on this point, given in the latter's book *Shemuᶜah Ṭovah*:

> The world was only created for the enjoyment of the Holy One, blessed be He, and His pleasure, as it were, is in the act of the *mizvot*, and that He speaks and His will is done. That is, His main pleasure is that a person desires and is enthusiastic to fulfill His will; this causes Him contentment. But this is not the main thing,[3] for at times a person may study because of his natural desire to study, just as [another] person may engage in trade because he desires to do so. What, then, is the difference between them, if it [the learning] is only done to fulfill his own wishes? For the primary service of God is in the ardor (*hitlahavut*), but ardor alone does not constitute a vessel in which to clothe itself, and must be clothed in deeds.[4]

R. Ḥayyim Ḥaykl of Amdur concurred in this assumption when he argued that the *mizvah* connects us with the divine will,[5] and that there would be no point in performing it without the knowledge that God desires it. In this view, the performance of the *mizvah* carries a certain drawback: a person feels a certain satisfaction and pride in every active deed that he performs as a *mizvah*, in that he has fulfilled his own role as one who is commanded. This self-satisfaction, which is a natural psychological reaction, seemed to the Hasidim to be the greatest obstacle in the way of one who wishes to serve God with all his heart. This understanding of the "service of God," whose basic premise is the erasure of the "I," came into confrontation with the formal religious imperative of fulfilling the *mizvah*. The Hasidic reply that one ought to fulfill the *mizvah* because thus it was decreed by the Divine will is of course non-immanentist. This type of conflict

3 The question is of course how to read this sentence: 1) that the acts themselves are not the essential thing; 2) that the essential thing is not Israel, who perform the acts, but that they are performed for the sake of His pleasure. The text itself supports both possible interpretations, while its sequel favors the latter interpretation.

4 *Shemuᶜah Ṭovah* (Warsaw, 1938), p. 63a–b.

5 See *Ḥayyim va-Ḥesed*, p. 127 (section on Proverbs), and a similar formulation in *Shemuᶜah Ṭovah*, p. 63.

reveals the inner religious interest of Hasidism in eliminating the activist aspects of the cult, which are in themselves meaningless. The Maggid's answer thus became the classical answer of Hasidism, which was never challenged in any serious way.

The second above-mentioned principle, according to which it is possible to achieve the religious goal of *devequt* by other forms of action, and not only, or necessarily, through the performance of the six-hundred thirteen *mizvot*,[6] was justified, not by the immanent discussion of the value of the *mizvot*, but by historical example. The use of Rabbinic homilies concerning historical figures who lived prior to the Revelation of the Torah, and who clearly "fulfilled the entire Torah," in the words of the Midrash, are not merely chance occurrences in Hasidism, as these homilies are not used in a naive way. Their approach is not guided by the original intention of these Rabbinic *midrashim* --namely, that these figures fulfilled the *mizvot* by means of knowledge attained through the Holy Spirit. In the new Hasidic spirit, the intention of these texts is seen as saying that, even if they did not literally fulfill these *mizvot* in practice, they fulfilled them in the sense that they performed actions which were aimed at *devequt*, such as the digging of the "wells" by Isaac or the use of the "sticks" by Jacob:

> The patriarchs performed with the wells and the sticks the same deeds as are performed through *tefillin*. While the patriarchs were performing the deeds, their primary connection was in the World of Thought ...[7]

This homily is far more daring than the original: while it is not the intention here to say that it is possible to forgo the wearing *tefillin* (as we live subsequent to the Giving of the Torah!), there is a definite sense in which there is no substantive difference between the results accomplished by the "wells" and "sticks" and that brought about by the explicit performance of the *mizvot*. Even the aspect of "hiding behind" the "patriarchs," which seems intended to exclude from this doctrine the actions of any person living at present, is not stressed in the Maggid's teaching as much as in that of his interpreters.[8] The "historical," non-contemporary spirit of the homily seems to convey a clearly eschatological interest, the concern with the distant past being none other than a projection of longings concerning the future, in which things will again be as they were in the past. But in analyzing the

6 R. Naḥum of Chernobyl carried this matter quite far, vigorously advocating "service in corporeality" without any limits. See, for example, *Me᾿or ᶜEynayim* (Jerusalem, 1960), p. 28a, where he states that there ought to be no distinction between eating and drinking and the *mizvot* of *zizit* or *tefillin*.

7 *Maggid Devarav le-Yaᶜaqov*, §77, pp. 132–133; *᾿Or Torah* (Jerusalem, 1956), p. 140a.

8 See *Derekh ᾿Emet*, p. 23. R. Ḥayyim of Volozhin strongly felt the spiritual danger in the use of the above-mentioned midrash. See *Nefesh ha-Ḥayyim*, IV: 7.

ideological mood, such spiritualistic landmarks also need to be considered in their contemporary context, in which the historical-eschatological framework comes only in order to prevent an actual revolution, which is the conscious fear of all religions. The conflict between "pure," conscious truth and present needs creates the inner paradox found in the written theories. This was the case in the teachings of R. Menaḥem Mendel of Vitebsk, who sought to continue the path established by his master, the Maggid of Mezhirech. The authentic value in R. Menaḥem Mendel's teaching is sustained by his extreme spiritualistic position, which sought to eliminate the practical element insofar as possible; the question here was not only one of giving preference to the spirit, but of the sense of sinfulness within "corporealization." The problem is brought to absurdity by its very formulation: how is it possible for God to command a person to perform *miẓvot* connnected with physical actions? In the eyes of a spiritualist, such a thing is utterly absurd! The only possible escape from such a formulation lies in the above-noted paradox: to perform the *miẓvot* despite their apparent absurdity, to bring about their spiritualization as if they were in fact totally concerned with spiritual spheres, and to ignore the element of coercion entailed in their physicality.

The nostalgia for the historical past, in which Adam was able "to cling to Him" merely by performing one *miẓvah*, or in which "Abraham our father, of blessed memory, was able to fulfill the entire Torah, including ᶜ*Eruv Tavshilin* [a Rabbinic edict enabling one to prepare for the Sabbath when a Festival Day falls on Friday by means of a certain legal fiction], by means of one attribute, namely, that of love,"[9] well suits the eschatological motif present in the teaching of R. Menaḥem Mendel, who sees the complete spiritualization of all the *miẓvot*:

> ... until he reaches the root of all of the Torah and the *miẓvot*, namely, "I am the Lord your God" — a perfect unity and Infinite. And when he stands there, all the wings [i.e. offshots thereof], the *miẓvot* and laws, are weakened and nullified, for this is the negation of the Evil Urge, to stand above and prior to the beginning of Creation ...[10]

It would seem that all of divine service must be purely spiritual, and the reason for fulfilling *miẓvot* in the corporeal world is:

> ... There is awe of the *miẓvah* when a person contemplates that the act of the *miẓvah* is a matter of the Godhead, as is known. And when he begins to perform it with his physical limbs, and the articles [used in] the *miẓvah* are also physical, he is confused and his spirit is agitated: how can he corporealize a Divine matter, for is God physical, heaven forbid?! But after his agitation for a certain time, he is nevertheless

---

9 *Peri ha-ʾAreẓ*, p. 16 (based upon Yoma 28b).
10 Ibid., p. 16.

> strengthened in his faith that the *mizvah* is the connection with the word of the living God, from the supernal Will, that spoke and His will was done.[11]

We find here a clear echo of the spiritual problematic which is limited from the very outset by the "divine will," as it were, which requires the activism of performing *mizvot.* The author is disturbed by the very idea of "corporealization," but on the other hand accepts the concrete command; his subtlest spiritual longings are therefore directed towards the Eschaton.

In one homily, R. Menaḥem Mendel of Vitebsk gives two "historical" examples of fundamentally mistaken attempts at Divine service: one which attempts to ignore the spiritual aspect, and the other which attempts to entirely bypass the realm of "action." The former originates in an authentic inner need of his own path in Hasidism, while the latter is invoked to determine the outer limits of spiritualization. He writes:

> And this is what is said thereafter, "And Noah the man of the soil began (*va-yaḥel*), and he planted a vineyard" [Gen. 9:20] — that is, when Noah became profaned (*ḥullin*), as Rashi explains [there]. "He became a man of the soil" — that is, he became corporeal — "and he planted a vineyard" — that is, the act of *mizvah*, as in the saying, "'My own vineyard I have not guarded' [Songs 1:6]: that the *mizvot* also became corporeal." And this is, "And Ham the son of Canaan saw the nakedness of his father" [op cit., v. 22] — that is, the shame of his Father in Heaven, in being a corporealized God ... And this is, "And Japheth and Shem took the garment" [v. 23] — which was the garment of all — "and their faces were backwards" [ibid.] that is, humility and fear, which retreats, fearing to come close to Him; thereby, "the nakedness of their father they saw not" [ibid.]. In sum, the connection of lowly man with the Supreme Will is by means of humility and fear, from which he arrives at contemplation and intellectual reflection upon the [divine] wisdom, bringing them into every *mizvah* in which he engages. But without contemplation and apprehension, the *mizvah* is also physical; on the contrary, without the *mizvah* and the corporeal involvement, man cannot be connected by contemplation and apprehension alone with the Creator. And the proof of this is King Solomon of blessed memory, of whom it is said, "He was wiser than any man" [I Kings 5:11]: because he wished to be wise without the *mizvah*, [he violated] the prohibition, "he shall not multiply his horses" and "he shall not take many wives" [Deut. 17:16, 17]. He said , "I will multiply them and not be led astray" [Sanhedrin 21b], but he nevertheless stumbled! This is what the Sages expounded: "'Happy is the man' [Ps. 1:1] — this is Noah; 'who has not walked in the advice of the wicked' [ibid.] — this is the generation of the flood" [Gen. R. 26:1]. That is, to use only the intellect without involvement in the *mizvot*, for the increase of apprehension is called a flood ...[12]

11 Ibid., p. 5.
12 Ibid., p. 8.

R. Menaḥem Mendel of Vitebsk was one of the few figures in the Hasidic camp to stress strongly the paradoxical nature of the existence of man, who finds himself commanded within a series of antinomies which cannot be bridged without profound faith, for whose sake he seeks divine assistance. He declares the bankruptcy of the rational faculty, which is unable to cross the bridge to recognition of this paradox and seeks a faith free of "explanations" or "reasons."[13] According to R. Menaḥem Mendel, even the most sublime commandments appear to us as "paradoxical,"[14] and one must make a supreme spiritual effort in order to overcome human understanding. In his opinion, this is the most difficult trial confronting man, similar to that faced by the patriarch Abraham, which was more difficult and "more bitter than death and sacrifices."[15] The obligation to perform *miẓvot* in the physical world belongs to the incomprehensible realm within the divine command, and draws upon this power. The Vitebsker disagrees here with Maimonides, who attempted to provide rational explanations of the *miẓvot* and to make them "reasonable" in themselves. The explanation of the *miẓvot* within the framework of natural law affronts the mystic from Vitebsk, who sees *devequt* in terms of the unification with God beyond nature and beyond the laws of rational "connection" rooted in a theory of human character; he objects to that approach which is satisfied with finding "beauty" and "value" in the *miẓvah*. In his opinion, the manifestations of truth within the *miẓvah* can only be explained in terms of an irrational faith totally beyond both the laws of "connection" found within nature and the laws of cause and effect and of "value." The following are his remarks concerning this subject:

> Maimonides wrote [in *Guide* III: 49] that the reason for the commandment of circumcision is to weaken the power of the [sexual] appetite. And the truth is that his holy mouth uttered true things concerning the profoundest matters, although he himself did not intend them. For like the intention and rationale of the cutting of the foreskin, so is that of the commandments of the "uncircumcised" vineyard, and of the commandment of bringing the first-fruits (*bikkurim*). And it is as in the verse, "like the first-fruits before the summer" [Isa. 28:4], etc. For the first one and the beginning are precious things, and they are only dear because of their being first, for it is the way of all first things to be precious and beloved, for they are the joy and connection between one world and another: from the first to the one after it, and from that to the one thereafter is called the first — and so on forever. But the essence of service and connection with Him is to attain that *devequt* which is beyond all

13 Ibid., p. 12.

14 This is the sense of the Hebrew *mehupakhim*, used here as a *terminus technicus* (ibid., p. 13).

15 Ibid., p. 14. On the problem of the rationale for observance of the *miẓvot* on the part of the Patriarchs, see Arthur Green, *Devotion and Commandment: The Faith of Abraham in the Hasidic Imagination* (Cincinnatti, 1990), esp. pp. 9–24.

> apprehension, for connection is not apprehension of Him, as He is beyond all created things and beyond all endearment and love and beyond the nature of that connection, for He is the Creator of all. But *devequt* to Him is through faith alone, without reason of love or preciousness or desire. And of this it is written, "to weaken the power of the appetite": for the commandment of circumcision by which we are sealed in the organ of procreation and of bringing forth souls, which is *devequt*, must be [intended] to weaken the power of the appetite, that [it be] rather by the power of faith alone.[16]

The so-called rational realm, to which the laws of nature apply, is in the eyes of Menaḥem Mendel of Vitebsk precisely the most hidden realm of all; the inner logic of its own rules is itself an irresolvable inner paradox and antinomy. The surety for the possibility of "understanding" the laws belongs to a realm beyond these laws — a dialectical dilemma which R. Menaḥem Mendel thinks it might be possible to resolve (at least theoretically) in the messianic future. Relying upon the Midrash concerning the red heifer — which in Jewish tradition became the symbol of those *miẓvot* for which one cannot find a rationale — which draws the distinction between *ḥuqqah* and *miẓvah* (edict and commandment), he transforms these two concepts into fundamental concepts, in which *ḥuqqah* symbolizes the realm of the edict closed to human understanding, while *miẓvah* symbolizes trans-paradoxical understanding. In the eschatological age, *ḥuqqim* will be transformed into *miẓvot*, while today's *miẓvot* will lose their "educational" value, as they will no longer be needed to rein in the Evil Urge, as man will be able to devote himself to contemplation as an end in itself. He states:

> All the roots and branches, general rules and details, which have a root above, bear fruit below in the act of the *miẓvah* — and this is our holy Torah, with all its *miẓvot* and teachings. For our Rabbis said [Yoma 28b], "'Because Abraham hearkened to my voice and performed my watch' [Gen. 26:5] — this teaches that Abraham our father performed the entire Torah, even *ᶜEruv Tavshilin*." This is seemingly illogical, for from whence did he know them? And even if we say that he apprehended those *miẓvot* and laws required by the intellect, it is nevertheless difficult [to know] how he apprehended the *ḥuqqim*, which do not have a reason necessitated by the intellect, such as the red heifer and the other *ḥuqqim*. But from our words, one may understand the words of the Sages [in Numbers Rabba 19:4], that He said to Moses, "To you I reveal the secret of the red heifer, but to others it is a *ḥuqqah*." For all the *ḥuqqim* have a rationale and root in the order of Creation, for the Creation was based upon the Torah, although not every mind can comprehend this; therefore, "to others it was a *ḥuqqah*." But the Torah did not address itself to great ones such as Moses and Abraham our father, for there is nothing which stands in their way that it need be

16 Ibid., p. 10. The sense being, "not for any ethical reason as such," which was clearly not Maimonides' intention! On a similar criticism of Maimonides' reasons for the *miẓvot*, see R. Schatz, "Maharal's Conception of Law; Antithesis to Natural Law Theory," *Jewish Law Annual* 6 (1988), pp. 109–125.

> a *huqqah*, for all the *huqqim* are to them as if *mizvot*, regarding their knowledge and the apprehension of their rationales and roots. But it is impossible that the *huqqim* be changed to *mizvot* for him, unless it be by the nullification of the *mizvot* for him, that they not be practiced by him,[17] like the prohibitions such as, "Do not murder, do not commit adultery, do not steal" [Ex. 20:13]. For just as these prohibitions are not perceived by him in terms of breaking of the appetite with all of its corporeal qualities — for he does not use them for his own needs at all, but only for God himself — so are all performances of his bodily needs abhorrent to him, like the filth of dirt and offal, concerning [the avoidance of which] one need not warn any person, for he will in any event do so out of disgust. And in this way King David, *z"l*, said, "My heart is empty within me" [Ps. 109:22]. For a person such as this, to whom the *mizvot* are not applicable, the rationales of the *huqqim* are revealed, and the *huqqim* are for him as the *mizvot* [are for others]. And regarding this our rabbis said [Niddah 61b] that the *mizvot* will be nullified in the times of the Messiah, for the world shall be filled with knowledge of God, that they shall have another Torah: for the *huqqim* shall be *mizvot*. And when he ascends from strength to strength, and he is only above, until he reaches the root of all Torah and *mizvot*, which is "I the Lord am your God," an absolute and perfect unity and Infinite: when he stands there, all the parts of the *mizvot* and *huqqim* will be weakened, and they shall all be negated, for it is the negation of the Evil Urge to be standing above and prior to the beginning of Creation; and the Evil Urge from whence . . .[18]

The closest position to the quietistic approach concerning this question is implied in the discussion of R. Hayyim Haykl of Amdur. He sees external activism which prevents the performance of the act for its own sake as evil:

> Whoever performs an act [does so] out of self-aggrandizement, for because he wishes to aggrandize himself he performs the act, while nobody knows when it stays within his thoughts [alone]; we thus find that the act comes about because of self-aggrandizement.[19]

He claims that the act itself constitutes a bias and reveals the person's personal interest. For this reason, in which indifference becomes the highest value (as expressed in his other views as well), he theoretically disqualifies every action

17 The sense here is that they no longer treat it as a commandment, but as a self-evident way of behavior.

18 *Peri ha-ʾArez*, p. 16. A homily on the same midrash, in the spirit of negating the need to receive reward for the *mizvah* in the messianic Future when the *huqqim* will also become *mizvot* (in the sense of rational, comprehensible *mizvot*), is brought by the editor of *ʾOr ha-ʾEmet* in the name of his grandfather, R. Joseph of Yampol, who in turn relates that this homily was revealed to him in a dream by his teacher, R. Hayyim of Krasnoye. But despite the use of the same midrash, one cannot compare the nature of the spiritual message and problematics found in the two cases (see the editor's introduction there).

19 *Hayyim va-Hesed* on Ps. 119, p. 118.

whatsoever, including the performance of the practical *mizvot*. The Maggid's reason for negating the value of the *mizvah* in its literal sense was primarily spiritual; in addition to this, R. Ḥayyim Ḥaykl adds a dimension of strictness regarding the quietistic moment. Further along, he invokes the classical Hasidic reason:

> And not like some people who only perform the act as it is, and do not lift [the act] up to the Creator; for this path is not pure, but is called evil . . .[20]

Here, the performance of the *mizvah* is itself viewed with severity, being called evil, in the sense of being performed as an external act without inner spiritual justification.

R. Ḥayyim Ḥaykl's attitude reminds us of Molinos' extreme remark: "Velle operari active est Deum offendere" — that is, the very will to act and "to perform acts" is evil. But R. Ḥayyim Ḥaykl's conclusions are not as far reaching as those of Molinos, who was consistent in his view that there is a great virtue in the absolute avoidance of action, including spiritual activity.[21] It is nevertheless important to note that even in Menaḥem Mendel of Vitebsk and R. Ḥayyim Ḥaykl of Amdur one does not find the same enthusiasm for "service in corporeality" as found, for example, in R. Ze'ev Wolf of Zhitomir's *'Or ha-Me'ir* or, more sharply, in R. Naḥum of Chernobyl's *Me'or ᶜEynayim*, even though they do not offer any different interpretations of the concept of *ᶜavodah be-gashmiyut* per se.

We would be delinquent in our task if we did not explicitly state that Hasidism was concerned as much with establishing its activist ideology as it was with holding back from the value of action in itself. The Maggid of Mezhirech even adopted the Lurianic ideas of *shevirah* and *tiqqun* as a basis for Hasidic activism; Lurianic Kabbalah established the active role of man in the process of *tiqqun* in retrospect, only after the *shevirah*, whose reason is unknown and not sufficiently clear, had taken place. The Maggid was the author of the interesting idea that the *shevirah* was a deliberate act of God, intended to facilitate human activity!

> The act of the breaking (*shevirah*) was needed by the world, for if each thing and attribute were attached to its source and were as "nothing" in its own eyes, then all the worlds could not exist. For example, were the World of Action (*ᶜasiyyah*) to be perpetually attached to the Creator without any forgetting, its own existence would be negated, and they [the "Worlds"] would attach themselves to their root in the

20 *Ḥayyim va-Ḥesed*, p. 118; there may be an echo here of the dispute between the Maggid and R. Pinhas of Korets; see on this below, Ch. 10, near n. 45.

21 See Evelyn Underhill, *Mysticism; A Study in the Nature and Development of Man's Spiritual Consciousness* (New York, 1955), p. 324.

> Nothing; nor would they do anything, for they would think that they were Nothing.[22] And because of the great fear and shame of the Root, they would all be as if non-existent, and they would all attach themselves to the Root, to the Nothing — and so forth in all the worlds. It was therefore necessary that there be the *shevirah*, for by this means forgetfulness occurs in the Root, and each one can lift up his hand to perform an act. And afterwards they attach themselves to the Root, to the Nothing, in prayer and in worship, in the manner of "and what (*mah*) are we?" [Ex. 16:7], and they thereby elevate the sparks of the World of Action ...[23]

One again sees clearly that Kabbalistic ideology served as a basis for the activist doctrine within Hasidism, as we have already seen elsewhere. This ideology was intended to explain the need to act and to perform external deeds in order to redeem the external world by its spiritualization. It is not difficult to guess which of the two doctrines — the activist or the quietistic — was the dominant one; for our purposes, it is important to note the internal confrontation which took place within Hasidism itself when it stressed its activist nature. But under no circumstance was this activism free of ambivalence, as some of those who discussed the nature of Hasidism would have it.

I stated earlier that Hasidism did not seek a specific rationale for each individual *mizvah*, but was primarily interested only in the relationship between action and intention (*kavvanah*) in general. The *mizvot* were therefore understood as one unit, and were discussed as such. Any attempt to favor the performance of one *mizvah* over another was therefore rejected out of hand, as one which would harm the very axiom of indifference. On the basis of this line of reasoning, we can well understand the demand of the Maggid that one be as strict with a light *mizvah* as with a serious one, for otherwise considerations of profitability and of the recompense to be anticipated would be reintroduced. Even more paradoxically, it was the quietistic spirit which specifically fostered the sense of strictness in fulfilling "light as severe."

> "Take care with a light *mizvah* as with a serious one, for" then "you will not know the reward of the *mizvot*" [Avot 2:1] — [that is, only then, when you do not pay attention to whether a given *mizvah* is light or weighty, do you ignore the anticipated

22 This sentence has a double meaning: 1) that the worlds will eventually be attached to the Nothing; 2) that you see yourselves as unable to act out of humbleness. A similar homily appears in R. Ḥayyim Ḥaykl of Amdur, who explains in greater depth that the "breaking" (*shevirah*) was necessary in order for man to "forget" and to distance himself from his root, so that he might return to remember and even to attain "that which he had previously attained" (that is, before the "breaking") — namely: the Godhead itself. See *Ḥayyim va-Ḥesed* on Daniel 12, s.v. *ve-hamaskilim yazhiru*, p. 153.

23 *Maggid Devarav le-Yaᶜaqov*, §73, pp. 126–127; *ᵓOr ha-ᵓEmet*, p. 36a.

reward]; but perform them so as to cause pleasure to the Creator, without any reward or recompense, rather than to receive aggrandizement.[24]

In this context, "to receive aggrandizement" means to enjoy one's own praise or that of other people. Such a formulation fits in well with the opinion articulated by R. Ḥayyim Ḥaykl of Amdur concerning the pleasure which a person necessarily receives from the "act" itself or from the very performance of the *miẓvah*, a fact that was dipleasing to Hasidism.

From all that has been said, it is clear that the extra punctiliousness in *miẓvot* in Hasidism was intended to eliminate from their observance the element of personal interest and satisfaction. Joy in the *miẓvot*, and joy *per se*, for which Hasidism has been widely praised, is contrary to the intention of Hasidism itself; while there was indeed joy, this was an impersonal joy, expressing the fulfillment of the will of God, which brings satisfaction to Him, and to Him alone. The added care over "both light and severe [*miẓvot*]" is intended to deliberately blur the notion of the immanent "importance" of this or another *miẓvah*, which the quietistic spirit sees as invalid.

The problem has thus far been described in terms of the confrontation between the spiritualistic and quietistic tendencies within Hasidism and the obligation to fulfill the explicitly binding *miẓvot* of the Torah — a confrontation in which there was no doubt that the activist position enjoyed the upper hand. But the difficulties within Hasidism are also apparent in a second area, in which the wish to fulfill the *miẓvot* competes with the quietistic value in which all personal interests are negated. Wherever one is clearly obligated to perform a given *miẓvah*, there is no doubt about the matter; but as soon as one wishes to perform the *miẓvah* over and above the letter of the law, or even according to the letter of the law, Hasidism poses a serious question mark.

Even those who affirmed *miẓvot* in the latter case, such as the Maggid himself, needed to indulge in mental acrobatics in order to justify them on the same quietistic grounds as were used to explain the opposite position. The very raising of such a problem, which sees the human desire to act as itself a sign of self-interest, demands explanation and indicates one of the weak points in quietism. Molinos

---

24 *Or ha-ʾEmet*, p. 22b. In MS. Jerusalem 3282, which was in the possession of R. Ḥayyim Ḥaykl, f. 76b, we find the same homily quoted in the name of the Maggid, albeit slightly expanded. In the sequel to the above passage, it states: "If you wish to receive aggrandizement, you will be punctilious in *miẓvot*, [to reckon] if they are of light consequence: for if they are strict [ones] you will receive aggrandizement, and if they are easy you will not perform it! But if so, you do not know (the reward of the *miẓvot*)" (!); see also in *Kitvei Qodesh*, 24b. On this compendium, see Schatz, "Introduction," pp. xvi–xvii. One frequently finds as well the formula: "not to be meticulous to do it properly, which is the temptation of the Evil Urge" (see, for example, MS. Jerusalem, op. cit, fo. 17b).

made some penetrating comments on this subject: "It does not seem right to these souls (i.e., the perfect ones) to perform acts out of their free will and choice even if they are good, for otherwise they do not die."[25] In his view, "a dead soul" is one which is bereft of all self-interest whatsoever — a definition likewise appropriate to a number of remarks of the Hasidim. I have already stated that the Maggid answered in the affirmative regarding the question of the observance of the *miẓvot* out of will and personal initiative; in this respect, he was consistent in his conservative tendency. Hasidism as a whole generally followed his path in its tendency to raise religious problems which exposed its spiritual "weaknesses" and hidden tendencies, and at the same time its conservative decisions. The following are the Maggid's remarks in *Ẓavaʾat ha-Riva"sh*:

> "It is time to act for God, they have negated your Torah" [Ps. 119:126]. If at times there is a *miẓvah* in which there is a hint of sin, he should pay no heed to the Evil Urge, which only wishes to prevent him from doing that *miẓvah*. And he should say to the Urge, "it is not my intention in this *miẓvah* [to anger my Creator],[26] but only to bring pleasure to the Creator by that *miẓvah*" ... But in any event, he must determine in his mind if he will do this *miẓvah* or not.[27]

Elsewhere, he writes:

> If he desires to perform a *miẓvah*, he should see and attempt to do it, and not allow the Evil Urge to prevent him from it by saying that it is great and he may thereby come to pride, but he must nevertheless not negate it ... And he should perform as many *miẓvot* as he can, and the Holy One, blessed be He, will help him, so that everything may be without [extraneous] interests, but he may strengthen himself as much as he can [that it be without interest].[28]

From both formulations of this problem which I have given, one can see how difficult this decision was. It is clear that, in terms of practical "behavior," the Maggid affirmed action; we are interested in the factors which weighed in his balancing, and in the fact of the balancing itself.

The Hasidic thinkers knew quite well that there is satisfaction gained from the

25 See Pourrat, "Quietisme," col. 1567.

26 I have placed the text of the *Ẓavaʾah* within square brackets, as it appears in R. Ḥayyim of Amdur; see *Ḥayyim va-Ḥesed*, p. 2. The sense is that it is not the intention in performing the *miẓvot* to anger the Creator by surrendering to the Urge to do *miẓvot*, for it may be that its performance stems from personal interest and is for the sake of personal benefit. His position was that radical!!

27 *Ẓavaʾat ha-Riva"sh*, p. 12. This implies that, if it is clear to a person that there is a personal interest in this will of his, he may at times feel it necessary to forego the performance of the *miẓvah*. This is the interpretation given here to the verse, "it is time to act for God, they have nullified your Torah" [Ps. 119:126].

28 Ibid., p. 13, and in *Liqqutei Yeqarim*, p. 2c.

very performance of the *mizvah* in itself. As R. Moshe Leib of Sasow put it: "for in truth a person has pleasure in himself when he performs a *mizvah* as instituted, or when he prays or studies with love and fear [of God]."[29] But he wished to minimalize this pleasure as far as possible,[30] and particularly to prevent the decision on behalf of religious action being made on the basis of prior considerations of interest and aggrandizement. While the *Zavaʾah* contains a cautious formula of the Maggid's position on this subject, this is stated in *Liqqutei Yeqarim* and *Maggid Devarav le-Yaᶜaqov* without any hesitation. Moreover, in *Maggid Devarav le-Yaᶜaqov*, he states:

> This is a great rule: when a certain *mizvah* comes to a person in his thought, he should not refrain from performing it because [he fears] pride or any other consideration, for certainly through performing it not-for-its-own-sake, he will come to do it for-its-own-sake; for a good deed also activates a goodly vessel above, and the inwardness of the vessel is formed by thought. For first the choice needs to be good, and thereafter his mouth and heart must be at one, that he believe with perfect faith without any interest that the whole world is full of His glory, and that His [divine] life is present in every thing. Therefore, all love and fear and all other traits are from Him, even in the evil things of the world. He is therefore not allowed to love or to fear, nor boast or be victorious or any other trait, except through Him ... For is not everything from Him, may He be blessed? ...[31]

This formulation of the Maggid's teaching carries an extreme activist tone, in which the status of action as such is enhanced on the basis of pantheistic tendencies. In other words: 1) it rejects the doubt which had existed regarding the very possibility of action for its own sake ("from doing it not-for-its-own-sake, he will come to do it for-its-own-sake"); 2) action or "the good choice" is valued as a condition of metaphysical significance even without *kavvanah*; 3) human action enjoys metaphysical justification even when, as during the earlier stages of one's divine service, it entails a certain self-interest. This justification involves a new claim, namely: that in any event, the individual is not entirely free in the choice of his path of service, and God, of whom "the whole earth is full of His glory," guides his decision. If a person is initially unable to serve God without self-interest, this is evidently what has been decreed — i.e., that he should come to Him via his Evil Urge — and there is therefore no need for concern. The rationale invoked here thus implies total reconciliation with the "half-perfection" of the ideal Divine

29 *Liqquetei Rama"l*; *Va-yeshev u-derush le-Ḥanukah*, p. 2.

30 It is clear that the anti-spiritualists and anti-quietists among the Maggid's disciples completely rejected even the possibility of refraining from the thought of receiving a reward for the *mizvah*, "for it is impossible to banish it." See *Meʾor ᶜEynayim*, p. 92b.

31 *Maggid Devarav le-Yaᶜaqov*, §146, pp. 246–247.

worship; the unambiguous imperative to fulfill those *miẓvot* which stem from personal will follows from this, even if this clearly entails extraneous self-interest. The remarks cited in the *Ẓavaʾah* and in *Liqqutei Yeqarim* reflect a different line of thinking from that of *Maggid Devarav le-Yaʿaqov*. In the former two books, the individual is called to action on the ground that, if he does not do so, he has surrendered to the Evil Urge which attempts to dissuade him by telling him that there is an element of pride in his desire to perform the *miẓvot* (even if in fact there is!). The Evil Urge is, so to speak, identified with the quietistic argument which confronts the activistic imperative to act. But action is in fact not forbidden, and this too on the basis of a fundamentally quietistic reason: namely, the unlimited trust, resulting from placing one's burden upon God, that He will indeed act in such a way that man will be able to act without self-interest.

Such speculations surrounding the question of the *miẓvot* demanded an explicit statement in support of their performance. The same is true of the teaching of R. Menaḥem Mendel of Vitebsk, which combined radical spiritualization with the advocacy of everyday performance of *miẓvot*. In light of this approach, it is not difficult to understand why the Maggid found it necessary to interpret the Mishnah, "whatever Torah is not combined with labor will in the end be nullified" [Avot 2:2], as specifically referring to the performance of *miẓvot*![32]

While R. Menaḥem Mendel of Vitebsk struggled with the radical spiritual interpretation of the *miẓvot*, albeit affirming their practical performance in present actuality, one can sense the continuation of the Maggidic theory in the thought of R. Ḥayyim Ḥaykl of Amdur, who stresses the problematic of the "will" and "desire" to fulfill the *miẓvah*. This profound Hasidic thinker, who is continually suspicious of any element of self-pleasure even in the realm of the spirit, finds himself forced to argue, regarding the fulfillment of *miẓvot* out of "desire" and "appetite," that the hand of Divine will, which requires the performance of the *miẓvah* even under such psychological conditions, is presumably present here:

> When he turns all his thoughts over to the Creator, that He will send him in his thoughts what he needs to do, as is written, "Thrust upon the Lord your burden" [Ps. 55:23], and he wishes and desires and longs for some act of piety — then he presumably needs that thing, and God will send him that thought.[33]

One can clearly observe here the tendency to "justify" action, as if someone had

---

32 See MS. Jerusalem 3282, fo. 76a: "In the name of the Holy R. Baer, *z"l*, 'Any Torah which is not accompanied by labor, will in the end be abnegated' [Avot 2:2] — meaning, that if he does not add labor to the study of Torah or *miẓvot* to the study of Torah — this is, 'it will in the end be abnegated' — and note."

33 Ibid., fo. 166a.

presented a contrary argument; indeed, quietistic logic daringly challenged accepted religious conventions. To whom were such warnings as the following addressed? "And he should not perform *mizvot* in bunches, for if he performs *mizvot* as bunches, he will be unable to perform them joyfully ..."[34] Such "devouring" of *mizvot* is contrary to Hasidic reasoning, as it destroys the opportunity given man to cling to the Creator during the time of performance; the "storing up" of *mizvot* in order to merit the World to Come lost its significance in light of the joy of *devequt*. According to Hasidism, the *mizvah* is the objective opportunity given man by the Divine will above; as such it is holy, and a person ought not to pursue new, artificial "opportunities." The spiritualistic position sought to understand how to "exploit" this objective opportunity for purposes of *devequt*; the semi-quietistic position (so called because its conclusions are not quietistic!) was primarily interested in the individual's personal attitude to the *mizvah*, while negating any self-interest or involvement which must of necessity accompany the action. This is quietistic logic, with the additional complication that it affirms action in the form of *mizvah*.

The struggle surrounding the performance of *mizvot* through free "will" (i.e., in the case of performance over and above the requirements of the Law) is expressed in a striking story concerning R. Meshullam Feibush of Zbarazh, quoted in the book *Qevuzat Yaᶜaqov*:

> I heard from his [i.e., Meshullam Feibush's] holy mouth that he said: There once entered into my heart a great desire to pray the Afternoon Service wearing *tallit* and *tefillin* [i.e., not ordinarily worn for this service]. And you know that I am not quick or impulsive to perform [any] actions until I have examined them seven times over: perhaps my [Evil] Urge is attempting[35] to take a prime share in this matter. And I waited some time until my thoughts became settled concerning this matter, until it seemed to me that I was free of all self-interest concerning this, and I prepared myself to don my *tefillin*. And as I started to take the *tefillin* in order to don them, my heart began to burn within me with greater desire than that felt for donning *tefillin* in the

34 Ibid, fo. 169a. Also in R. Yitzḥak of Radzivilow, *ʾOr Yiẓḥaq*, fo. 190d (based upon the Talmud, Sotah 8a). The *Tifʾeret ᶜUziel* gives a totally different reason, in the name of R. Levi Yitzḥak of Berdichev — namely, that he should not perform the *mizvot* "in bunches," in order not to share them with the Other Side (*Siṭra ʾAḥra*), and not as stated against the increase in the quantity of *mizvot* per se. See ibid., 78b. R. Shmelke of Nikolsburg even advocates the performance of the *mizvot* in bunches; see *Divrei Shmuʾel* (Jerusalem, n.d.), *Parashat Noaḥ* (stated in the name of the Maggid!). This book, which gives oral testimony concerning the Maggid's teaching, miraculously overlooked all of the major teachings of the Maggid concerning explicitly Hasidic doctrines.

35 According to the advice of the Maggid in the *Ẓavaʾah*; see above, near the beginning of Ch. 4, concerning the danger that the desire to perform a *mizvah* may originate in the Evil Urge, for the sake of self-interest.

morning for the Morning Service [which is mandatory] — and I immediately withdrew my hand and did not take them. For I said to myself: There is a reason [to suspect] that this is an unfit thing, for the desire for *tefillin* in the Morning Service should be greater than in the Afternoon Service. Certainly, the Evil Urge has stolen into this![36]

What conclusion is to be drawn from this peculiar story? In the case of supererogatory religious performances, the argument, "I will do it, and God will see to it that it is clean of self-interests!" is no longer applicable. Rather, in those situations where one is free to decide whether or not there is any trace of interest in the action through one's own understanding, it is better to refrain from doing it; but where an obligatory *mizvah* is involved, one has no option but to perform it, and to beseech the mercies of one's Creator! Furthermore, the desire and enthusiasm for the performance of the *mizvah* must be associated with the actual command concerning the *mizvah*, and not with any other performance which is not commanded, even if it is on the same plane of action, as in this story. The conservative tendency here clearly reveals the weak point of that position, which blocks the way against possible spiritual antinomianism: namely, that the performance in and of itself is meaningless in both cases — i.e., whether he wears *tefillin* in the Morning or Afternoon Prayers. The act can be transformed into a meaningful one if the person arrives at *devequt* as a result thereof, and from an "objective" point of view he is equally able to attain *devequt* in both cases! But at this point there enters the confrontation between the "*mizvah*" and that moment which is neutral from the point-of-view of the Divine command, and it is here that the theoretical guidelines of Hasidism are determined by its conservative traditionalism.

The argument of the "will" on behalf of performing a particular *mizvah* is drowned out by the fear of self-interest — unlike the case when there is an obligation to perform the *mizvah*. R. Meshullam Feibush is an extreme critic of action performed in and of itself, discovering the primary religious interest in the negative injunctions of the Torah, and particularly in the subjugation of the appetite and in the rejection of worldliness and of honor. In his view, the eradication of the Evil Urge from one's heart is a positive precept of great

36 *Yosher Divrei ᵓEmet*, p. 38c. The matter of wearing *tefillin* at the Afternoon Prayer is also mentioned in the MS. of R. Pinḥas of Korets as an individual merit, the reason for which is unclear to me. There is also an apologetic note to this, without any explanation of the theoretical basis for these hesitations: "He said: When I began to wear *tefillin* at Minhah, I had no fear that another person would do likewise, *zol nokh tun* ("will imitate me"), because I did it in sincerity. For if a person does a certain thing, and does not do so sincerely, then the thing comes down into the world on a lower level, *in ein niederigein olam*, and another person acts likewise thereafter" — Jerusalem MS. 3759, fo. 31b.

importance — one so strictly regarded that he interprets one of the sections of the *Hanhagot* (*Regimen Vitae*) of his teacher, R. Menaḥem Mendel of Przemyślany, as declaring war against exaggerated activism.

> This is the intention of the Midrash: "'This is the thing which God has commanded to do it' [Lev. 9:6]. Remove the Evil Urge from your hearts [. . .] just as He is unique in His world, so shall your service be unique in your hearts before Him" [*Torat Kohanim*; *Shemini*]. Not as those fools think, that there is no service of God but to learn all day long and to pray with force and to fulfill pious precepts [sic!], while the fear of God is forgotten from their hearts, only wishing to serve through the positive precepts, to be a righteous and pious one (*ẓaddiq* and *hasid*), as explained above at length. [In such a way] your service is not unique before Him, for at times one also needs to cease from Torah and prayer, if this is truly the will of the Creator, in order to guard oneself against the sin [i.e., of arrogance!?]; then is your service unique before Him . . .[37]

37 *Yosher Divrei ᵓEmet*, p. 38b. It is worth mentioning in this connection another position of R. Ḥayyim of Krasnoye, who attempted to play on the paradox inherent in this passive approach in order to argue on behalf of activism; he points towards the vicious circle brought about through "negotiation" with the Evil Urge, and decides in favor of action even if one is initially guided therein by the Evil Urge. He states as follows: ". . . And from this one ought to learn not to hold oneself back from the good deed and *miẓvah* which comes about because of the counsel of the Evil Urge. For the ways of the Evil Urge are known, for he is a king who rules over every person, and he comes to every person with tricks in his ways and paths. For example, [in the case of] a proper (*kosher*) person who rises from his sleep prior to the morning light, and wishes to get up in order to learn and study and the like, there immediately comes to him the Tempter and Deceiver, saying to him, 'Why do you rise and weaken your strength?' And he casts upon him great laziness, which overcomes him so that he does not get up to learn. But to he who is truly God-fearing and who feels that these things are the counsel of the Evil Urge, and has already taken upon himself not to listen to his counsel, he will not come with such a counsel, but will be more clever in his wiles, and will say to him, 'Stand on your feet, and gird your loins like a man to rise and to study, for it is not fit that a pious man such as yourself, who is renowned for his fear-of-God, sleep after midnight. And what will people say when they do not see candles burning in your house, but that you are like an ordinary person who does not serve his Creator!' And he confuses his thoughts by these words, [to think] that he does these things with improper thoughts of self-interest or greatness, Heaven forbid. And in truth, now too the anger of the Urge is not content to leave him be, for in a moment he will come to him and say: 'Have you known, my son, that all this is the counsel of the Evil Urge, who comes to confuse you with self-interest and [thoughts of] greatness, and wishes that through your study and prayer you will give power to the Other Side. Therefore hearken to my counsel, and sleep in your bed, and then he will not give you any self-interest or unfit thoughts. And what does it matter to you if you are not renowned as a *ẓaddiq*, so long as your intentions are acceptable to God, who probes hearts and knows that your intention is for the sake of heaven, that you not be proud, heaven forbid!' But from that story [i.e. the one related earlier about who dances on a rope for money] it appears that one should not hold oneself back from the good deed or *miẓvah* which is performed at the counsel of the Evil Urge; for just as the one who walks on the tight-rope, even though he does what he does because of the money he will receive and the honor and the glorious name, in any event he does not have any

An important place in the attempt to provide a spiritualistic interpretation of the *mizvot* is occupied by R. Yitzḥak of Radzivilow, one of the five sons of R. Michel of Zloczow. Like his predecessor, R. Menaḥem Mendel of Vitebsk, he sees in "corporealization" the leading enemy of religious life; for this reason, he does not advocate the path of the Maggid, who recognizes *ᶜavodah be-gashmiyut* as a legitimate form of Divine service bearing a religious stamp, even if only directed towards the spiritualization of the physical.[38] He accepts the relevancy of the *mizvot* only when they are literally performed "for their own sake," without compromise. He interprets the following saying of the Ba'al Shem Tov in a way quite different from its original meaning. According to R. Yitzḥak, "'The Torah of God is perfect' [Ps. 19:8] — that no person has ever touched it," means, "that he has taken nothing from the Torah ... and this [refers to] the one who engages in Torah for its own sake."[39] In his uncompromising manner, he defines Adam's sin as the betrayal of his sublime mission to do everything for God's sake, which is the significance of the freedom of choice given to him. The failure to exploit this intellectual privilege is tantamount to surrender to the snake:

> ... who fooled him [into thinking that] God desires free-choice in the physical sense and that He so-to-speak receives greater pleasure from this, for the essence of the creation of the universe was for free choice, to abominate evil and to choose good, and the more corporeal the free choice, the greater pleasure God thereby receives and the greater his reward.[40]

extraneous thoughts in his mind at the moment that he is walking on the tight-rope, but only [that of] protecting himself against danger. So ought it be when the Urge comes to him to do a *mizvah* or some such thing, or to urge him in a matter of *mizvah* out of self-interest or greatness, that he will be called 'Rabbi' and the like, to listen to his voice, to hasten and arouse his soul to do it. But at the time of the action itself there is no self- interest [present] in his thoughts, but only to protect himself, lest he fall down into the waters of contention, Heaven forbid ..." — *Seder ha-Dorot*, pp. 20–21.

It is interesting to note that Hasidism, which championed the loss of the "I," pursued the ego ruthlessly, and did not give it credence even for a brief moment. This was expressed by the rabbi of Kotsk, "The 'I' is a hidden thief"; see R. Glikson, *Der Kotsker Rebbe* (Warsaw, 1938), p. 32.

38 See, for example, the story concerning his father, who appeared to him in a dream in order to stress the need to distinguish between one kind of service and another; see, *ᵓOr Yizḥaq*, p. 171b. Throughout this book, one finds no positive relation to the question of *ᶜavodah be-gashmiyut* ("service in corporeality") — and not by accident.

39 Ibid., p. 4a. The introduction is by his son-in-law, R. Yeshayahu Muscat of Prague, and is consistent with the spirit of the book as a whole.

40 Ibid., p. 10a. This is clearly an internal Hasidic polemic against *ᶜavodah be-gashmiyut*, understood as the temptation of the Serpent. Moreover, the formula, "that He, so to speak, receives greater pleasure from this" appears in several Hasidic books which speak of the merits of this service. It seems to me that the object of this polemic is the book *ᵓOr ha-Meᵓir*, who was the principal spokesman for this formula.

> ... But in truth, his choice was in the subtle intellective matter, as is written, "and you shall choose life, that you and your seed may live" [Deut. 30:19]. For in the matter of life, which is Torah and *mizvot*, there also exists a choice, that he do everything for the sake of heaven and not in order to receive a reward.[41]

In this first statement, in which he evaluates the [extent of the person's] spiritual ability, R. Yitzḥak of Radzivilow laid the foundation for the second assumption which is important to our subject. Unlike R. Menaḥem Mendel of Vitebsk, one does not find spiritualistic sermons of an explicitly eschatological character in his writings; they are instead filled with a cautious, down-to-earth tendency. He no longer "becomes excited occasionally" as to how it is possible to "corporealize" the *mizvot*, as did his predecessor (even though he certainly thought that one ought to perform every *mizvah* in practice!),[42] but relegates them to a secondary position vis-a-vis spiritual revelation in the present. This does not imply the decorporealization of the *mizvot* in each and every case, but a doctrine of hearing new voices of revelation, predicated upon spiritualist *kavvanah* within the rubric of performance of the *mizvot*.

This doctrine of revelation is accompanied by the theory that an individual who lives a spiritual life within his own soul alone merits hearing within himself the voice of God, God and the soul being in fact synonymous. This "voice" of revelation is none other than the "great voice" heard by Israel at Mt. Sinai, and may even be superior to it in terms of the inward revelation of the Divine will. The status of the individual spirit within this spiritualistic thinker embraces all of the major historio-philosophical approaches found within Jewish mystical thought, which seek the path back to the revelation at Sinai, in which they see the peak of the elevation of the human spirit. In the eyes of R. Yitzḥak of Radzivilow, Sinai is no longer seen as the pinnacle of the revelation of Divine will, for there the Torah was given "dressed" — i.e., in its human interpretation.[43] The pinnacle reached at Sinai can also be attained today, and it is even possible to anticipate in the eschatological period a Torah which will "be more openly manifest than at Mt. Sinai."[44]

R. Yitzḥak ascribes something of the character of the Sinaitic revelation to the Sabbath: following in the Kabbalistic tradition, he speaks of the Divine will as

41 Ibid. On the relationship between the ideas of free-choice, Creation and sin, which influenced Hasidism, see R. Schatz, "Luzzatto's Thought Against the Background of Theodicy Literature" (Heb.), *Divrei ha-ʾAqademyah ha-leʾumit ha-Yisraʾelit le-Madaʿim* 7, no. 12 (1988), pp. 275–291.

42 See R. Yitzḥak's testimony concerning R. Wolf Kitzes of Medzhibozh, who would even take care to purify a needle! — *ʾOr Yiẓḥaq*, p. 188.

43 As a spiritualist, he has numerous complaints against Moses. See, e.g., pp. 160a–b and 197a–b.

44 Ibid., p. 170a–b.

being present in the cosmos to a greater degree on the Sabbath than on week days. While the Kabbalistic tradition not refer to a specific "revelation" granted man in light of this indwelling of the Divine will, it did state that the Divine will in principle "behaved" in a special manner on the Sabbath, marked by harmony and the attributes of mercy and forgiveness. R. Yitzḥak adds to this the spiritualistic doctrine that "on the Holy Sabbath we are able to come to this True Will,"[45] because man goes outside of the aspects of "command" and "necessity" of the Torah in favor of "choice" and spiritual "love."[46] Moreover, the Evil Urge, which obstructs a person's spiritual ascent during the week days, has no dominion over him on the Sabbath, when he is able to attain an unobstructed vision of the Divine will. "For we have the ability that our will may be like the will of the Creator, and we are thereby able to draw down faith in His uniqueness and unity, as it was at Mount Sinai."[47] R. Yitzḥak explains elsewhere that, in the final stage of spiritualization, man discovers that he — that is, his soul — is identical with God's self-knowledge:

> "'And they saw the God of Israel' [Ex. 24:10]. But does it not say, "No man may see me and live' [Ex. 33:20], and, "there is none that know You at all" [*Tiqqunei Zohar* §1]? But His essence knows Himself — and let a hint be enough for a wise man. For indeed, in the corporeality of his body a person is unable to see or to hear the voice of God; but when he casts off the physical body, the holy soul, which is of His own essence, is able to perceive His essence. For this reason, at the Revelation at Sinai, at which only the souls were [present],[48] they themselves saw that they were of the essence of the God of Israel, and this is what they perceived — and let this hint be enough for the wise man ... And they said, "this is my God" [Ex. 15:2] ... that is, that we are ourselves [are] "this my God," as is stated in the Holy *Zohar* [I:94a], "'With my flesh I shall see God' [Job 19:26] — from [within] my flesh, literally." ... Therefore, a person is required to see himself as if he has [himself] come out of Egypt, like our ancestors whose contamination ceased when they left Egypt, and who saw that they were themselves His essence; so ought a person in every generation see himself as if he has left Egypt. And understand that these are very profound matters.[49]

Thus, R. Yitzḥak believes the Sabbath to be the archetype of the eschatological era already in the present, and that it is possible to hear the inner "voice," which is the voice of God, in our present spiritual situation.

45 Ibid., p. 171b.

46 Ibid., p. 15a.

47 Ibid., p. 191b.

48 This view is influenced by that of the *Zohar*. See, for example, several times in *Parashat Shelaḥ Lekha*. It is clear that the *Zohar* does not have the doctrine of identity of man's soul with God, which he teaches further on in its name.

49 ʾ*Or Yizḥaq*, p. 182a–b.

Among the homilies of this type is one involving a biographical motif, homiletically connecting the motif of the Sabbath to that of receiving the face of the Shekhinah, which is viewed as synonymous with the face of the teacher. One may infer from this subtle homily[50] that R. Yitzḥak "preached" his doctrine, and that it was perhaps not accepted. He writes here with a note of chastisement and pain over the fact that the "truth" which he revealed has not yet been accepted. Indeed, it is surprising that this was in fact the case, unless he intended his teachings to go beyond mere "theory." He says the following:

> My brothers and dear ones, hear me well: that which is said, "the glory of the Lord shall be revealed upon you" [Isa. 40:5] refers to you, literally, upon your face [51] — and let a hint suffice [to a wise man]. And [about] that which is written (Rosh Hashanah 16b) that "a person is required to receive [the face of] his teacher on the Sabbath" — why [is this so] specifically on the Sabbath? Because his divinity, may He be blessed, [is revealed] in his teacher, and the indwelling of the Shekhinah occurs on the Sabbath, and the reason why he should receive his teacher on the Sabbath is because of the receiving of the face of the Shekhinah — and let a hint suffice.

> My brothers, they will surely ask you in the World of Truth about a person they had with you in Radzivilow named R. Itsikel Nadvorner, who taught you the true path to the will of the Creator, blessed be He; and you did not wish to go to hear words of truth, which are from Him, may He be blessed, for "who" is "this"? ⟨...⟩ [52] I tell you, that he is I: after [my] death it shall be ⟨...⟩ will speak nought, but so long as the holy soul is within me, that S.... the holy one, of blessed memory, whose soul speaks with you. And the soul is ⟨...⟩ You hear the voice; Woe to us for the great shame ⟨...⟩ [of him] that did not wish to hear the voice of God.[53]

There seems no doubt that the essence of R. Yitzḥak's message revolved around the abnegation of the *mizvot* in practice, something which he would seem to have manifested in practice only on the Sabbath, in a symbolic manner. We find an allusion to his justification for these things in his comment that the laws of *tefillin* and of mourning are not observed on the Sabbath[54] because of their corporeal nature.[55] It seems clear that his views concerning the spiritual Torah to be given

50 Ibid., p. 190b. Several words are missing in these homilies, which are also illegible in the MS.; these lacunae are indicated here by dots placed within pointed brackets.

51 "Your face" clearly refers to the *penei ha-dor* — that is, the leaders, the *zaddiqim*.

52 There is an editor's note here that something of the text is missing in the MS., but the homily is clear enough as is: the identification of he who is called him (*hu*) — that is, God — with the one called "I" (*ani*) — man.

53 *ʾOr Yizhaq*, p. 190b.

54 Ibid.

55 Note the remarks in support of Sabbath observance, and particularly the Sabbath prayers, articulated by R. Meshullam Feibush of Zbarazh — the living conscience of Hasidism — which between the lines

in the future were integrally related to his views on the performance of the *mizvot* in the physical sense, which he saw as a temporal need only; he did not elaborate further upon these matters.

A similar tension is already reflected in the mood of the teachings of his father, R. Mikhel of Zloczow, of whom an unusual story is told in the course of a homily concerning the value of the performance of *mizvot* in a spiritual manner. The account is truncated, and reads as follows:

> I will relate here an incident concerning my father, our master and teacher ... who was in Zloczow together with several other great ones of the land ⟨...⟩.[56] R. Ze'ev Wolf of Dubnow ⟨...⟩ R. Ḥayyim said as follows: "Let the Maggid of Zloczow say his teaching." And he thought in his heart that, because there were prominent *mitnaggedim* [present], it was not fitting that he say Torah in the Hasidic manner concerning some esoteric matter, but he instead asked them to bring a folio of Talmud. And Rabbi Ḥayyim asked him [57] which tractate they ought to bring, and R. Michel answered: "Whatever tractate comes into the hand to the messenger." And the messenger went and brought a copy of Tractate *Yevamot*, and the rabbi took it and opened the book. And the first time he opened it he said to the great ones gathered there, "Hearken and see this matter which came to me when I opened the book," and they all saw. And R. Michel read the section to them in its literal interpretation, and afterwards he read what Rashi said, and afterwards he expounded to them a lengthy *Tosafot* concerning this matter which disagreed with Rashi. And the rabbi began to

contain allusions which appear to be directed against R. Yitzḥak of Radzivilow (R. Meshullam was a disciple of the Maggid of Zloczow, R. Yitzḥak's father!). One senses that he knew something, which he did not wish to state explicitly, concerning the status of the Sabbath day even among the Hasidic "masters of Torah," against which he protests vigorously: "... Therefore one must take very great care concerning the Sabbath prayers, for this is the essence of the Sabbath, and not as the masses think; and even the masters of Torah do not take care for the words of God and have contempt for the prayers of the Sabbath day, there being in their eyes another matter (sic!), I know not what. But the truth is as I have written." — *Liqqutei Yeqarim*, 25c.

56 ⟨...⟩ signifies lacunae in the text.

57 This was perhaps R. Ḥayyim Sanzer, the leading Kabbalist of the Brody *kloiz*, who was a *mitnagged*; see the important note concerning him in G. Scholem, "Two Letters from the Land of Israel from the Years 1760–1764" (Heb.), *Zion* 25 (1956), p. 436, n. 16. The above account may reflect an actual historical confrontation which took place in Brody between the Hasidic group there and the Kabbalists of the *kloiz*, or again it may be no more than a "tradition" of which there are many in Hasidism. See, for example, the account of the author of *Seder ha-Dorot*, pp. 82–83, concerning a kind of "fraternal meeting" of this type between R. Meir of Przemyślany and R. Shlomo Kluger of the Brody *kloiz*. No historical echos of such a "debate" are mentioned by N. M. Gelber, *Toldot Yehudei Brod ⟨1548–1943⟩* [ʿArim ve-ʾImahot be-Yisraʾel. Vol. 6 (Jerusalem, 1955)]; there would seem to be a tendency within Hasidism to generate stories about their receiving the "acknowledgment" of their opponents. A similar well-known story circulated among the Hasidim concerns R. Yehezkel Landau, the *Noda' be-Yehudah*.

engage in *pilpul* with them concerning on what and why the *Tosafot* disagrees with Rashi, and he said a penetrating conjecture concerning this, until they saw and were astonished by his great ⟨. . .⟩ And before this they called him the Maggid of Zloczow, but after they heard him ⟨. . .⟩ Rabbi Ḥayyim called him, "My master R. Michel." ⟨. . .⟩ From your mouth [it follows] that your honor is not a scholar, and now I ⟨. . .⟩ And Rabbi R. Michel [answered] them as follows, ⟨. . .⟩ My intention is the true one in this Torah [i.e. Talmudic passage] ⟨. . .⟩ Certainly I am a greater scholar than you, but concerning this Torah which was given on Mt. Sinai in black fire on white fire, the Baᶜal Shem Tov, may his soul rest in the sublime heights, was a great scholar in his Torah. Now I have great knowledge, but I am not a scholar (*lamdan*), and I speak the truth. From that day on, the elder R. Ḥayyim ceased to be a *mitnaggid*, and called him Rabbi. Now we may infer from all this that we have no portion in hidden things. But this is a faith that we need ⟨. . .⟩ [that as we don't understand what] was in the first tablets [of the Law, which were broken], prior to the sin [i.e., of the Golden Calf], so are we unable to understand what will be — and let a hint suffice to a wise man.[58]

The background to this story is the confrontation between a *mitnaggid* and a *ḥasid*, wherein the former becomes a *ḥasid* once he discovers that Hasidism is not opposed to scholarship and that its ranks include outstanding Talmudic scholars and dialecticians. The essential purpose of the story, though, is that there is an esoteric Torah, both far more difficult and far more important than that concerned with the literal meaning. It is clear that this esoteric Torah involves an attempt to read the Torah in a spiritualistic manner without corporeal *miẓvot*, as given at Sinai.[59] R. Michel tells us that the Baᶜal Shem Tov was a great "scholar" in this sort of reading. We are not concerned here with determining the authenticity of this "tradition" (although we note that other sources also speak of such a reading by the Besht).[60] It is sufficient for our purposes to note the interest of this spiritualist group in attributing special "knowledge" and "learning" to the Baᶜal Shem Tov, suggesting that this question was a central element of their system which they may have experienced in practice.[61] The intensity with which these

58 *ʾOr Yiẓḥaq*, p. 2b–3a.

59 As he interprets the matter on p. 2, preceding the story.

60 See below, at the beginning of Chap. 13, especially the testimony of R. Meir Margaliot.

61 Evidence from another source concerning the pneumatic ability of the Maggid of Zloczow — which was subject to the characteristic criticism of his disciple, R. Meshullam Feibush of Zbarazh — is cited in his name in the course of an extensive discussion of the possibility of arriving at *devequt* via the reading of a Talmudic or halakhic text dealing, for example, with torts. The Maggid of Zloczow states, according to the account of his disciples, that he is entirely indifferent to the nature of the text or its contents, and can arrive at *devequt* taking any text whatsoever as his starting point. R. Meshullam does not doubt the ability of "great ones" to do this, but claims that this is not applicable to every person: "And I heard thus from the holy mouth of the Maggid [of Zloczow] who said that, throughout his whole life, whatever he sees in a book, be it a Talmud folio or Kabbalah, he sees not anything save how to serve God. And in truth it is thus, but it was thus for him, who was a *ẓaddiq* son of a

ideas are expressed by R. Yitzḥak of Radzivilow, even if not different in essence from those of the Maggid of Mezhirech, reminds us of the concrete attempts to nullify the corporeal fulfillment of certain *miẓvot* on certain occasions. Even the comment "let a hint suffice to a wise man," which appears at the end of the section containing this story, does not fully correspond to the spiritual position of the Maggid, which never dared to ignore the concrete which serves as a bridge to the spiritual realm.[62]

I have cited here an additional stage in the teaching of R. Yitzḥak of Radzivilow, which does not represent a departure from the teaching of the Maggid except in the practical sense. This kind of spiritual anarchism is itself rooted in the tradition of the Maggid, even if he warns there that one ought not to take lightly the realm of realization and practical action, as we said. The Maggid even cites a number of homilies in praise of action, such as the ones directed against those who argued their deprecation or unimportance. But the purpose of such homilies must be properly understood: they were intended to emphasize the spiritual element, without which no action has meaning. The following are the Maggid's words:

> It is impossible to cling to the Holy One, blessed be He, save by means of Torah and *miẓvot*; and the *miẓvot* are divided into three aspects: action, speech and thought. For example, [regarding] the commandments of *ẓiẓit* and *tefillin*: the section in the Torah in which they are written is speech, and their intention is thought, while the *miẓvah* itself is an act. Therefore, our Sages said, "Whoever reads *Shema*ᶜ without [wearing] *tefillin* testifies falsely against himself" [Berakhot 14b], for how can thought embody itself in speech [and] upon what can thought and speech dwell, if not upon action? But if he reads *Shema*ᶜ while wearing *tefillin*, the speech becomes a garment of thought, and the action [a garment of] speech. Therefore the Sages instituted the reading of all the sections in their [proper] times, in accordance with the above-mentioned intention. For speech and action are within their [proper] times, but thought is not in time ...[63]

So that we not misconstrue the intention of such passages as the above, and not

ẓaddiq and had other perfections, but not for we who do not know what and how, but only with faith do we believe this and [there are] a few others who take the example from him." — *Liqqutei Yeqarim*, 20d (and also in *Derekh ᵓEmet*).

Note that in R. Meshullam, the term "Maggid" always refers to the Maggid of Zloczow, and not to the Maggid of Mezhirech, as erroneously explained by Horodetsky in his *Toldot ha-Ḥasidim veha-Ḥasidut*, Pt. I, Ch. 5.

62 On the spiritualistic reading of the Torah, see at length in G. Scholem's article, "The Meaning of the Torah in Jewish Mysticism," in his *On the Kabbalah and its Symbolism* (New York, 1965), p. 66 ff. [originally published in German: "Der Sinn der Tora in der Jüdischen Mystik," *Zur Kabbala und ihrer Symbolik* (Zu"rich, 1960), p. 90 ff.]

63 *ᵓOr Torah* on Psalms, p. 114a.

have any ground for argument regarding the role of action in the Maggid's teaching, I shall cite the following:

> Therefore every one must direct [his intention] at the time of the performance of the *mizvah* in speech and action and thought, for he thereby elevates the *mizvot*, strips it of its corporeality, brings it closer to its root, and unifies it in the upper worlds. And the main thing is the pleasure [i.e., which he causes God!] at the time of the performance: and understand this![64]

The anarchistic element is not anchored in the spiritualistic tendency per se, but is rather a result of the thrusting of spirituality upon history, on the one hand, and of the spiritualization of the *mizvah*, on the other. I have already discussed the former subject at the beginning of this chapter in connection with the homilies concerning the patriarchs, who achieved sublime spiritual attainments prior to the Giving of the Torah and before the existence of the very concept of *mizvah*. I shall now address the latter problem.

The Maggid expands the concept of *mizvah* over and beyond the rubric of the six hundred thirteen *mizvot*, thereby allowing room for a non-orthodox understanding of the concept:

> Our Sages said, "the Holy One blessed be He wished to bring merit to Israel, therefore he multiplied for them [Torah and *mizvot*] ..." [Makkot 3:16]. That is, the *mizvot* themselves are six hundred thirteen [in number], but when a person fulfills [the verse], "Know Him in all your ways" [Prov. 3:6], he can fulfill many times more than six hundred thirteen, without limit, for all of his deeds are for the sake of heaven. We thereby find that he fulfills the commandment of his Creator at every hour and every moment, as in the saying concerning Hillel the Elder, who said of his eating, "I am going to perform a kindness to my host [i.e., of my soul]" [Lev. R. 34:3]. Concerning this it is written, "therefore he multiplied for them Torah and *mizvot*," for the term "multiplication" is appropriate to something which is without limit, which would not be the case were there only six hundred thirteen; what sense then would there be to speak of "multiplied"? Would one call them "multiplied" or "many" because they are six hundred thirteen [in number]? But according to the approach that I have mentioned it makes sense, for one who fulfills "Know him in all your ways" performs an infinite number of *mizvot* ...[65]

The neutralization of the concept of *mizvah* implied in the ascription of equal weight to the six hundred thirteen *mizvot* and to all other actions intended for the sake of heaven, through use of the concept "multiplying *mizvot*," opens the way

64 Ibid., p. 48a; on this matter see also ibid., p. 41a and 139b, and the explicit instruction on p. 15a and 138a not to intend the simple meaning of the *mizvot* — that is, their performance alone.

65 ʾ*Or Torah*, p. 147a.

for a certain anarchism. Even the obligation to perform the *miẓvot*, as stated by the Maggid, does not blunt the edge of ideas such as these, and it was impossible to avoid the constant confrontation between act and thought or act and intention inherent in the constant emphasis upon the supremacy of the spirit over the flesh, or intention over action. This confrontation led to the great scandal concerning the postponement of times for prayer, which was a natural consequence of the preference of *devequt* to halakhic rules concerning fixed times for the performance of such-and-such an action as a *miẓvah*. Indeed, R. Ḥayyim of Volozhin opened his anti-Ḥasidic polemic precisely on this point of the demonstrable preference of the Hasidim for intention above action:

> Let not your Urge lead you to say that the essential thing is to be involved all day long only in purifying your thoughts as they should be, and that your attachment (*devequt*) to the Creator be constant, and that you never abandon your purity of thought even for a moment, and that everything be done for the sake of heaven, saying to you that the essence of Torah and *miẓvot* are specifically when they are done with awesome intention and true *devequt*. ... But see his path and get wiser: today, [the Urge] will tell you that all Torah and *miẓvot* [performed] without *devequt* are as nothing, and because of this you will take trouble to direct your thoughts until the time for the *miẓvah* or the prayer shall have passed, and he will show you arguments why any prayer or *miẓvah* which is performed with great *kavvanah*, with holiness and purity, even if not done in its proper time, is more precious than the performance of that *miẓvah* in its proper time without *kavvanah*. And once your Urge shall accustom you [to this], until it is fixed in your heart that you not feel so much the change in the fixed time of that *miẓvah* or prayer, because of the attention of your heart to be pure and to direct your heart first, it will gradually push you from level to level, so that you not feel it at all, until it will seem to you as if it is a permitted thing to transgress the appointed time for prayer, even when you turn your heart in vain for empty things. And he will leave you with neither the act of the *miẓvah* in its proper time, nor with good thoughts. And this is the destruction of the entire Torah altogether, if heaven forbid we consent to turn our ears to his [the Urge's] words. Imagine to yourself that a person would trouble himself on the first night of Passover with the eating of the olive's-size piece of matzah, that the eating be performed with holiness and purity and *devequt*, so that he postponed the time for its eating until after dawn or after sunrise: all the purity of his thought would be unfit and unacceptable [to God] [an allusion to Lev. 19:7] ... And this path leads to him being consumed by the abyss, Heaven forbid, and destroys several principles of our Holy Torah and of the words of the Sages. We have already mentioned that the essential thing in all *miẓvot* is the portion of action, and that purity of thought only adds to the action, as an [additional] *miẓvah*, but does not disqualify it [i.e., by its absence]. For not only is the essential thing in practical *miẓvot* the practical element, but even in the *miẓvah* of prayer, which is called the service of the heart, the main thing is that a person

> pronounce the words with his lips;[66] but if he [merely] thought [the words] he did not fulfill his obligation.[67]

The fact that Hasidism did not take the ultimate step towards spiritualism by removing the soil of practical activity from under its feet entirely is not to be credited to the pressure of its opponents. The degree of self-reflection on the part of Hasidism, and the resultant conservatism, were far greater than its anarchistic longings and propensities would indicate. It did argue in theory on behalf of the supremacy of the "inner" above the "outer" element in religious life, and knew the nature and rationale of such a conflict. Indeed, it created a series of legends and stories concerning hidden pneumatic *ẓaddiqim* who exhibited no external signs of good deeds and whom one might even suspect of disregard for the "external" realm of behavior. At the same time, those strong chords, which still appear in the teaching of the Maggid, in which the inner wages battle with the outer, began to fade:

> One must perform one's deeds in secret, so that people will think that he is not [involved] in pious action. But before he attains this sublime level, he must perform his actions openly, for if he does not behave as the world does, but only wishes to be a *ḥasid* inside himself, it is possible that he may be drawn after the world, and "from doing it for its own sake, he shall do so not-for-its-own-sake" [a satiric inversion of the familiar Rabbinic dicta].[68]

It is clear that the longings for "inner" life in no way replaced the "external" values, although they occasionally appear through struggle and confrontation as principles of Hasidic life, in sources from the school of the Maggid.

This problem, which also entails a major social element, appeared in a concrete way in Kotsk Hasidism. It is stated concerning the circle of Kotsk that they performed *miẓvot* secretly[69] — to which the sceptics of the generation evidently added: "and sinned openly." This is the social aspect of the spiritualistic problem, which constituted a thorn in the side of persecutors of quietists of all types.

While the Christian quietists openly rejected all forms of sacramental activity, Hasidism of course dared not do so. But the formulation of the problem of inten-

66 This is the halakhah. See Maimonides, *Mishneh Torah, Hilkhot Tefillah* 5:9: "How is one to modulate his voice [i.e., during prayer]? He should not raise his voice overly much, nor pray in his heart alone, but he should pronounce the words with his lips, and hear them with his ears quietly." On this subject, see below near the end of Chap. 7 in connection with the problem of prayer.

67 See *Nefesh ha-Ḥayyim*, IV: 4. 5.

68 *Ẓava᾽at ha-Riva"sh*, p. 15. See also below, concerning social spiritualism, at the end of Chap. 11.

69 See Glikson, *Der Kotsker Rebbe*, p. 34. The Kotskers wished it thought that they deviated from Jewish practice, so that people would leave them alone. Things were taken so far!!!

tion and action per se, in the Hasidic sense, or that of "external" and "inward,"
in the social sense, is of considerable significance in the history of religions. The
scholar of religions H. Heppe rightly defined the nature of quietism, in comparison
with the churchly mode, as follows: "Two important concepts changed among the
quietists from those present in the consciousness of the church — that of perfection
and of spirituality."[70] The same distinction holds with regard to Hasidism as
against the prevalent moods within the tradition from which it sprang. All those
values which were accepted as "self-evident" ultimately became problematic, and
what eventually led to the image of a renovated Judaism was the question-mark
which Hasidism posed at every major cross-roads. But even if the conclusions of
Hasidic doctrine are far more moderate than those of the classical quietists and
one does not find there the same appetite for uncompromising iconoclasm,
Hasidism nevertheless confronted anew the entire concept of "perfection,"
whether in great or small measure. It seems to me that we would not be far off the
mark to state that this was the "pulse" of Hasidic literature.

But if Hasidism, like quietism, argued in principle that external and corporeal
elements interfere with spiritual attainments, it did not usually state this explicitly
with regard to the *miẓvot*, and even engaged in explicit apologetics against the
suspicion of such a charge against itself. Even such a radically spiritual figure as
R. Yitzḥak of Radzivilow stated that it is forbidden to ask of God that everything
be on the spiritual level alone.[71] Such an injunction is not a necessary consequence
of the spiritualistic approach, but rather a function of Hasidism's conservative
self-critique.[72]

A commonly-raised argument in Hasidism states that man is specifically lifted
above the level of the service of the ministering angels by the performance of
miẓvot in the corporeal realm; there are clear signs of a lively polemic around this
question within the school of the Maggid. But even if this polemic was only a
theoretical one, it exposes a new weak-point exposed by Hasidism regarding this
problem. In *Tifʾeret ʿUziel* of Uziel Meisels, one of the disciples of the Maggid,
we read:

> At the time of the giving of the Torah, the angels protested, saying, "Your glory is
> placed in the heavens" [Ps. 8:2; see Shabbat 88b]. And this *midrash* is a difficult one:
> for on the face of it they have the Torah, and perhaps they wished that the Torah not

---

70 H. L. J. Heppe. *Geschichte der quietistischen Mystik in der Katholischen Kirche* (Berlin, 1875), pp.
    106–107. One of the innovations of the quietists was the revival of the inner life, rather than the outer.

71 *ʾOr Yiẓḥaq*, p. 33.

72 See J. Katz, *Tradition and Crisis* (New York, 1961). Katz raises the problem of observance of *miẓvot*
    in terms of its social aspect; see pp. 237–238.

> be embodied at all in this garment, as it is at present, to protect [human beings] even within corporeality. But the glory to be in the heavens is in a spiritual garment, and not in a physical garment, and this physical garment was brought about by His mercies, may He be blessed, so that human beings may thereby also be close to Him. For they learn and fulfill the corporeal, and [thereby] merit to enter within the inward, which would not be the case if it had no physical garment at all, for there would then be no way for man to start to merit the Torah at all, as in the homily of the tailor who is somewhat closer to the king than other people, because he comes to make a garment for the king. Therefore, a *ẓaddiq* is superior to an angel, for he also fulfills the Torah corporeally, while the angel only fulfills it spiritually.[73]

One can see here quite clearly that the terms of the debate in the school of the Maggid between spirit and action has changed from the original stand of the master, who stressed the formula that it was "not only in practice," to the dual formula, "both in spirit . . . and in practice." The spiritualists, who were in principle closer to the teaching of the Maggid, found room for justifying praxis "also," while those who argued "also" on behalf of spirit placed the stress upon the importance of praxis. One can already hear in this approach faint echos of an internal hasidic polemic, which developed into an openly anti-Maggidic position in the Habad doctrine of R. Shneur Zalman of Lyady.[74] The spiritual ground was completely eliminated from his thought, while the essence of *miẓvah* was specifically understood as action.

It is clear that one does not find in Hasidism that anti-sacramental, "holy indifference"[75] of which the quietists, such as John of the Cross and Molinos, were accused. It did not challenge the Jewish sacramental tradition in the same manner as that described in one of the Church accounts concerning a certain quietist who tore down the cross because it impeded him from coming close to God.[76] However, Hasidism also needed to give account of its "thinking aloud" to the Mitnaggedim, who accused it of nullifying[77] and showing contempt for the *miẓvot*. The common denominator of the Church's accusations against the quietists and those of the Mitnaggedim against the Hasidim[78] lies in the fact that both groups were aware of the inherent danger to the sacred act of religion posed by the spiritualist idea.

73 Uziel Meisels, *Tif'eret ᶜUziel* (Tel Aviv, 1962), p. 38b.

74 See Chapter 12 below, "*Ḥabad* — Antispiritualism as a Quietistic Value."

75 See Underhill, *Mysticism*, p. 326; by these words she defines the essence of quietism, in a severely critical spirit.

76 See Heppe, *Geschichte*, p. 132.

77 See Underhill, p. 324, for a critique of Molinos, who taught that passivity is a virtue, and the argument of the Mitnaggedim concerning this matter in all of the anti-Hasidic polemical writings. This motif was also popular among the Maskilim, such as Perel and Kalmanson, and this claim was passed on from them to the historians, beginning with Jost.

78 See above, near note 67, concerning R. Ḥayyim of Volozhin.

When Molinos spoke of "breaking the [physical] bonds" in order to receive the divine spirit, the Church accused him of wishing to "break the chains together with Catholic dogma."[79] Similarly, R. Ḥayyim of Volozhin argued that the spiritualist posture of Hasidism constituted a "true danger" to the Torah of Moses.[78] These remarks refer to the idea itself, while the accusations of "contempt" and "making light" of the *miẓvot* refer to the nonchalant spirit betrayed by Hasidism in its everyday path, although it is difficult to know what prohibitions they violated apart from delaying the times for prayer.

One of the figures within the school of the Maggid who displayed a positive leaning towards the concrete realm was R. Levi Yitzḥak of Berdichev who — together with his other views in support of action — understood the *miẓvot* as a psychologically necessary, concrete basis for the love of God, because the structure of the human consciousness requires clearcut definition and limitation. Stripped of all concrete expression, he saw the love and fear of God as too chaotic and too liable to lead a person into inner struggles. On the other hand, when expressions of love and fear are embodied in action and fall upon the soil of praxis, their significance is restricted to the definition given them by praxis. Action thereby becomes a limited tool, but it stabilizes the storm and tempest within the human soul:

> "Lest they break through to God to see" [Ex. 19:21] — this is a negative commandment which God stated at the time of giving the Torah. As Nahmanides expounded the verse, "If you waken or arouse the love until it is satiated" [Song of Songs 2:7] — that when the love of the Creator or fear of the Creator come to a person, he should immediately perform a *miẓvah*, and thereby bring the love and fear of the Creator within limits. For so long as he has not performed a *miẓvah*, he has struggles, but when he performs a *miẓvah* with this love or fear, then he brings it within limits, and all struggles are removed from him, and the *miẓvah* which he performs is like a vessel in which he places the awakening which comes to him from above. And this is, 'until it be satiated' (*ᶜad she-teḥpaẓ* — Songs, op cit.), for the desiring [*ḥefeẓ*] is the vessel; and see there the words of Nahmanides.[80]

The two examples cited — from *Tifᵓeret ᶜUziel* and from *Qedushat Levi* — were

79 See Heppe, *Geschichte*, p. 128, who quotes Molinos concerning the spiritual goal of man: "... die Seelen zuruckzuhalten welche Gott auf geheimen Wegen zum inneren Frieden und zur vollkommenen Seligkeit ruft."

80 *Qedushat Levi ha-Shalem*, Pt. I, p. 132b See a similar homily on p. 141b: "When man achieves connection with these attributes [i.e., fear and love], he must immediately perform some *miẓvah*, and he is like a vessel ... and when he has connection, then he is called a live organ, but if he has not this connection, he is called a dead organ." The phrase *ᵓever ḥai* ("live organ") refers to the *membrum virile*.

a kind of counterbalance to the interpretation found in the Maggid's teaching, in which the main burden is placed upon the spiritual element. In order to demonstrate the clear difference between the way in which the problem of the *miẓvot* is presented in these two branches of the Maggid's school, one must examine the texts in full and compare our understanding of this problem with that of additional problems. *Prima facie*, everyone wanted the same thing — namely, what the Maggid of Mezhirech himself taught. But while some of his students formulated the question in a manner which tended towards spiritualization, others were already seeking a way to retreat from what they saw as excessively daring positions — running forward, so to speak, while looking back at the distance they had already dared to go. The differences among the different approaches are of tone, but in the history of religions the tone often obscures the color.

One ought to note that one senses the same uneasiness and sense of confrontation between the fulfillment of the *miẓvot* and the self-interest involved therein even among the "concretists" among the students of the Maggid — albeit the conclusion reached is often not the same. R. Uziel Meisels, for example, prefers the passive path — "sit and do not perform [i.e., the *miẓvah*]" — to the performance of a *miẓvah* in which there is an element of self-interest, while R. Levi Yitzḥak prefers to announce the act which he has performed as a *miẓvah*, so that his Evil Urge might free him of the pride entailed in its performance.[81] The author of *Tifʾeret ʿUziel* states:

> "And she seized him by his garment, saying" [Gen. 39:12] ... [i.e.,] by his garment, literally. For it is known that the *miẓvah* is [called] a garment for the soul, and the Evil Urge always takes hold of it and also wishes to derive benefit from it, for if a person performs a *miẓvah* with external motivations, it [the Urge] also has an external portion. And this is, "Lie with me" [ibid.] — that is, let us be joined together in performing the *miẓvah*, so that I may also have benefit from it. But what does the righteous man do? "And he abandoned his garment with her" [ibid.] — as he sees that he cannot be saved from the self-interest and the external part at the time of performing the *miẓvah*, he abandons the entire garment — that is, he finds it preferable to sit and do nothing, and not to perform the *miẓvah* at all, rather than to perform it with self-interests, so that "there will be neither for me nor for you [i.e., the Evil Urge]." And this is, "and he abandoned his garment with her" [op cit.] — i.e., that he does not even wish to have the portion of holiness thereof [i.e. of the *miẓvah*], because it is mixed with the evil portion. "And he fled outside" [ibid.] — that it is better for him to engage in a thing which is entirely external, rather than to combine good and evil.[82]

81 Likewise in *Darkhei Ẓedeq.*
82 *Tifʾeret ʿUziel*, p. 24b.

On the other hand, R. Levi Yitzhak prefers to wage battle against ulterior motivations by acknowledging their presence, in order to become liberated of the Evil Urge. In his opinion, the attempt to stand before God from a stance of total negation of all self-interest is futile, being a self-deception from which there is no escape. He states:

> "For when Esau my brother meets you, and asks you, to whom ..." [Gen. 32:17]. For the rule is that when a person begins to draw close to God and the Evil Urge becomes strengthened upon him, he should think that by his service of God he will attain the goods of this world as well — and thereby the Evil Urge is subdued, not to provoke anger against him for his attachment to God. And afterwards, when he is already attached to God, his service is only intended to cause pleasure to his Creator, and not for any benefit in this world. And this is, "When Esau my brother shall meet you, and asks you, to whom ..." — that is, the Evil Urge, which is known by the name Esau, will meet the messengers of Jacob, which are the holy thoughts of Jacob from which the angels are created. And he will challenge these thoughts, "Whence do you go?" "And you shall say, 'from your servant, Jacob ...'" [v. 18] — we are the messengers of Jacob, who were created through the good deeds, but do not provoke anger against Jacob for his good deeds, "for this gift is sent to my master, to Esau" [ibid.] — for the good also pertains to you, for by means of the good deeds he will attain this world's good, there shall come to him this world, for this world is the gift of the Evil Urge.[83]

83 *Qedushat Levi ha-Shalem*, p. 59b.

Chapter Six

Petitionary Prayer and Its Position in Hasidism

It is reasonable to assume that the revolutionary thrust of the quietistic approach found its fullest realization in the question of prayer. Prayer, which is the focal-point of religious activism, was paradoxically transformed — beginning with the earliest quietists of Greek Orthodoxy and ending with the French and Spanish quietists of the seventeenth century — into the sublimest expression of religious quietism. Prayer, which in its very essence is the hour of verbal communion with God, in which man acts deliberately, beseeching and pouring forth his entreaty before the Creator of the Universe, was transformed by the quietists into the time of great resignation, as this was expressed by Molinos.[1] It is difficult to imagine a greater revolution in the history of religion: since the complete eradication of the ego was an essential condition of religious life, prayer came to be thought of as the technique and the road of ascension to total self-abnegation, which prepared the ground for the exclusive presence and dominion of God alone as actor. God's listening and responding to prayer were examined in terms of the new criteria of a reality acting and manifesting itself within man, who nullifies and negates his own existential reality — his feelings, will, and reflective thought — to the extreme limit. If, for the quietists, the sentence "I want" is considered a sin, a person can only pray to God that He assist him to negate his own will, so that he no longer knows whether he ever had any will, or whether such a will was fulfilled.

The perception of human will as the enemy of God completely transforms the meaning of prayer, and nullifies its original meaning as petition. Thus, among the quietists, prayer became a technique for achieving resignation which conditioned God's immanent activity within man. A close reading of the Philokalia literature, specifically that of Gregory of Sinai and his disciple Callistus, leads one to the unavoidable conclusion that prayer is transformed there into a psychological exercise of the maximal concentration of the powers of the soul to the point of their loss and extinction, and that "silent prayer" (*Oratio mentalis*) is paradoxically the highest expression of this concept of prayer. Not only was prayer progressively contracted to the recitation of one short sentence — "Have mercy on me, Lord

1 Prayer and resignation are seen as one. See the article on Molinos in *Dictionnaire Théologique Catholique*, Sect. 24–32.

Jesus" — but this sentence itself was clearly not intended as "prayer," but as a technique of preserving the "equanimity of the soul" (Callistus) in order to prevent it from wandering away from its proper focus upon the inwardness of the "supernal I."

Callistus explicitly defines prayer as "the planting of the remembrance of God within the spirit in an active way,"[2] similar to the "*Shiviti*" placards, bearing the verse, "I have always placed God before me" [Ps. 16:8], found in Jewish synagogues. As such, it is conditioned upon the attainment of a psychological state of total indifference. This form of "continuous prayer," at which the hesychasts were adept, implies the complete abandonment of petitional prayer by stating that, wherever contents and requests are still present, there is no room for the appearance of God; therefore, to petition and to pray became negative concepts in the world of the quietists.

Petitionary prayer is replaced by contemplative-meditative prayer: John of the Cross defined the relation between the two by stating that one neutralizes the other. Contemplative prayer causes man to forget his will, of which God has to remind him; a soul lost in the bosom of God only wishes to enjoy the fulness which God wants to grant him. True, the person who engages in contemplative prayer continues to ask and to petition, but on a new basis: he asks that the will of God be done (*Non mea voluntas sed tua fiat*).[3] St. Francis of Assisi compares petitional prayer to a bride who looks at the wedding ring, rather than at the bridegroom who is giving her this ring.[4] Heppe, the scholar of comparative religions, describes the essence of quietism as the loss of thought and of will. He sees in the sacrifice of petitional prayer and the elimination of the individual will one of the central principles of quietism, which is conditional upon the loss of the very consciousness of prayer. So long as reflection continues to exist, so does the individual will and hope still live, and the spirit has not yet acquired control over nature. He describes the essence of quietism as the loss of thought and of will.[5]

The theoretical basis for the quietistic approach is anchored in the perception of religious life as supranatural life. Prayer as the meeting with God beyond the realm of human nature, and the extinction of the existential element by placing man before God, totally obliterates the literal meaning of prayer, just as it denies the ontic existence of the object of petition and prayer. Thus, Molinos says that one who abandons himself to the Divine will need not request anything of Him,

2 See the chapter on Callistus in *Philokalia*, pp. 271–276.

3 Knox, *Enthusiasm*, p. 254.

4 Ibid., p. 257: "If we neglect this advice [i.e., of indifference] we shall be for ever interrupting our prayer to take stock of the consolations which our prayer gives us..."

5 Heppe, *Geschichte*, pp. 7–8.

as every petition is incomplete, an act of self-will and self-choice. To petition means that the divine will is directed towards our own will, rather than the opposite. The souls who live an interior life reach a state in which they are unable to ask anything of God; just as they are unable to ask anything, so are they unable to thank or to praise Him, both of which are acts of self will. Similarly, one should not seek atonement for one's sins, because it is better to rely upon Divine justice.[6] If feelings of humility, of prayer or of grace are by chance aroused at the time of communion, they ought to be suppressed, as they do not come from divine inspiration, but only from the movements of nature which are not yet entirely dead.[7]

We have described in some detail the reservations of the quietists regarding the recitation of prayer in its ordinary (i.e. petitionary) sense in order to define the proper place for this question in the world of Hasidism. While the importance of this question was emphasized in Christianity due to the struggle between the quietists and the Church, Hasidism conducted an internal debate concerning the proper place of petitionary prayer within its own system of values.

The problem of prayer in Hasidism was unrelated to the historic formulation of the question of whether or not prayer requires intention (*kavvanah*).[8] The need for intention in the classical sense — i.e., "that his mouth and heart be one" — was the self-evident minimal content of prayer. The religious problematic arose against the background of the assumption that "his mouth and his heart are one"; however, the meaning of this "unity" of heart and mouth was understood in a new and revolutionary light which upset the fundamental contents of the literal understanding of prayer.

Hasidism, which in its own way placed itself at the disposal of God, primarily marshalled prayer for such service. The concept of prayer as serving the needs of man, providing him with salvation and hope, was thus subject to severe questioning. In other words, if Hasidism saw prayer as a means of contemplation in order to arrive at *devequt*, it needed to answer the question: what is the religious role of non-contemplative, petitionary prayer? Analysis of the variety of different answers given to this question within Hasidism will help us to understand the nature of the problem.

The question which stands out in the discussions of Hasidic thinkers as to whether or not a person is permitted to utter requests on his own behalf during prayer is itself one which calls for explication. Even among the conflicting

6 See Pourrat, "Quietism," sec. 14–16, and Bossuet, *Ouvrages*, p. 153, sec. 15.

7 Ibid., sec. 32.

8 See TB, Berakhot 13a and Rosh Hashanah 28b.

traditions brought in the name of the Maggid, and especially in the various independent exegeses of this question within the school of the Maggid, we sense a common denominator uniting the flow of Hasidic thought: reservations in principle concerning petitionary prayer. Even if the reason for this reservation differs from one thinker to another, and their arguments stem from different points of view, the reservation itself is indicative of an approach of resignation *ab initio*, albeit the limits of this resignation varies from one thinker to another. There were those who argued on behalf of resignation at any price, while others claimed that theory and practice are two separate matters, and that the limits of resignation depend in the final analysis upon the capacity of the individual. The possibility that resignation might be revealed as feigned, as not standing up before man's existential givens, led several of these thinkers to affirm petitionary prayer as well and to grant it their approval. One should not belittle the significance of the fact that petitionary prayer required such a seal of approval. Even if its conclusions are not in themselves particularly radical, the very existence of such a discussion greatly contributes to understanding the Hasidic mood and to emphasizing its problematic points.

In the theoretical sources of Hasidism, one finds a surprising and understandable combination of humility of spirit and human daring in the presence of God. The element of daring and the sense of spiritual strength felt by man in the presence of God was a motif which evoked jealousy in the eyes of the opponents of Hasidism;[9] on the other hand, the emphasis upon humility is intended to point out man's degree of nothingness as an individual, and not to entirely eliminate the power of the "spirit." One may also properly understand from this the argument that man should not ask anything of his own needs, as he is not worthy enough for God to heed him. Resignation is entirely individual (in most cases), and is not resignation of the spirit. Even the various sorts of quietists placed all their hopes upon the most activist sort of prayer, although they stripped it of all individual elements and personality. After all, *Contemplatio Acquisita* is the archetypal activist act, intended to fill the vacuum of passivity until one attains the stage of *Contemplatio Infusa*. Moreover, the practitioners of *Contemplatio Acquisita* (who infuriated the Church) did not sit with folded hands waiting for the spirit to descend upon them from on high, but engaged in a spiritual leap upwards (or, if one prefers, into their own inner depths) in which they hoped to discover the supernal and interior "I" whose liberation was understood by them as being in itself a divine act. It is thus important to stress that in Hasidism too the ethical "Nothing" was paradoxically transformed into "the ladder of ascent placed on the

9 See *Nefesh ha-Ḥayyim*, IV: 3.

ground, whose head reaches the heavens" [cf. Gen. 28:12]. Individual resignation and activist spiritual daring were here combined with one another.

The Maggid of Mezhirech made some sharp remarks concerning those who ask for their own needs in prayer:

> Let not a person pray concerning matters of his needs, but let him always pray only on behalf of the Shekhinah, that it be redeemed from its exile. The *Zohar* calls those who pray for themselves and not for the Shekhinah, "arrogant dogs who bark, 'Give! Give!'"[10]

One can clearly see here the motif which states that the worshipper must know that he is totally undeserving of praying before God, and that it is best that he know how remote and insignificant he is in light of the greatness of the Holy One blessed be He. This motif appears more emphatically in another source, in which the Maggid explicitly formulates which might be called an anti-existentialist position: man's petty concerns disturb God when the former stands in prayer and asks concerning them. His troubles are not worth disturbing the king, who must "descend" from his supernal spiritual throne in order to listen to trivial matters brought before Him in prayer. Interestingly, the Maggid does not argue that God does not listen to prayer, but rather that it is lacking in true meaning in comparison with the momentous matters involved in the spiritual life. The conclusion is, of course, that man ought not to disturb God concerning his own personal needs. These ideas are expressed in the following rather lengthy parable, which is worth quoting in full:

> ... The matter is comparable to that of a human king who rules over several countries, near and far, all of which are governed by the command of the king, and his fear is upon them and they always listen to his commands, at the will of the king. For this reason, the king also sets his eye and heart upon those countries and protects them in all sorts of ways from all harm and enemies, so that they may be free to do his command. The king therefore turns away from all his concerns and pleasures and joys to do good to these countries, and all the king's thoughts and concerns are constantly involved with the improvement of those countries and their needs and protection, and he constantly thinks about their wise guidance ... One day, a certain poor and oppressed person of little worth came from a far-off land, suffering and striken with leprosy, and cried out behind the king's palace about another one like himself who had robbed him on the highway. When the king heard the cry of that person, it disturbed his clear and pure thought, and the king sent his servant to find what it was all about. But the man paid no attention to the servants of the king, and continued to cry out, "Save me, my Lord the king," so that the king needed to come down

10 *Maggid Devarav le-Yaᶜaqov*, §12, p. 25.

> [himself], to abandon the great and lofty thoughts with which he was constantly engaged at every hour and moment, concerning great and profound improvements without end or limit, to concern himself with the case of this person who was crying out "theft" — when that theft was itself not even worth a penny. But the rule of the kingdom was that all must be heard, great and small, so that they might know that there is a judge in the world. But it was clearly a great descent for the king, to be forced to turn away from the improvement of the country and from his pure and subtle thoughts in order to hear the cry of that fool, which was not worth a penny. Indeed, that leper was not worthy of the king looking him in the face, how much more so to come into the royal palace to present his arguments before the great and noble king — this is certainly called a descent! And the parable is clear: when there is no judgment below, the Holy One, blessed be He, must make judgment above, and He must look down and oversee minor corporeal matters of this lowly world. Even though He oversees with a sharp eye all of the created things and beings and what is done [in the world], nevertheless the providence effectuated [in response to] the cry of the humble man makes it as if he forces Him to oversee them, and it is therefore called a descent ... But when there is judgment below ... He is not required to descend — that is, to look at the small and corporeal matters. Thus we find that the Holy One, blessed be He, may His glory be blessed, is supernal ...[11]

This motif, in which a human being is not deserving that God fulfill his will, is repeated elsewhere:

> ... that he not pray for that which is lacking to his body ... that he should not desire that the part[12] not be lacking so that Your will be done, for this is self-interest, as is well known ...[13]

The latter statement is primarily intended as a warning against transforming the doctrine of non-petition into a purely formal doctrine, which may be used to attain one's ends indirectly. A person may not argue that he is permitted to pray for what is lacking to "the part" of the Shekhinah (i.e., himself), thereby gaining personal benefit from a distorted version of the doctrine of the permissibility of prayer on behalf of the Shekhinah. This motif of prayer on behalf of the Shekhinah requires further discussion and explanation; for the present, let us return to that point in the discussion from which we started — namely, the claim that a person is not allowed to pray for his own needs *per se*.

The negative opinion concerning petitionary prayer held by the Maggid of Mezhirech is quite clear, even though we do not find the same sharpness of expression in all versions of the Maggid's teaching regarding people who engage

11 *Liqqutei Yeqarim*, 7a.

12 This is a specific term, meaning that everyone in Israel is part of the limbs of the Shekhinah, and that Israel together constitute the full stature of the Shekhinah.

13 *ʾOr ha-ʾEmet* (Hussiatin, 1899), p. 1b.

in explicitly petitionary prayer. A more moderate formula concerning this subject appears in *ᵓOr Torah*:

> *Beinonim* [i.e., people of average spiritual attainments] are those people who direct their prayer also [to the aim] that the Holy One, blessed be He, shall fulfill their request concerning their needs in this world [assuming their intention in their worldly petitions is for the sake of Heaven].[14]

It is interesting that we do not find in the writings of the Maggid a certain motif which later appears extensively in his school, and which already existed in his day — namely, that if a person is in a situation of trouble or crisis, he is allowed to explicitly ask God to have mercy on him and to perform his wish.[15] Even those who cite traditions in his name conflicting with those enumerated above, and who argue that the Maggid did as-it-were allow petitionary prayer, do not refer to the restriction which states that it is only permitted in time of dire trouble! This restriction evidently dates back to the time of the Baᶜal Shem Tov and R. Menaḥem Mendel of Bar, and was willingly received by certain circles among the disciples of the Maggid of Mezhirech, even if he himself did not refer to it. He would appear to have rejected any compromises regarding the principle of petitionary prayer, leaving no room at all for the personal element.

As we said, we found nothing in the actual writings attributed to the Maggid in support of petitionary prayer, even in situations of distress. On the other hand, there are different traditions among the writings of his disciples, representing two opposing positions: 1) one arguing that the Maggid prohibited petitionary prayer; 2) one which argues that he permitted it. We shall cite two traditions here for purposes of comparison.

R. Benjamin of Salositz, some of whose teachings were recorded during the Besht's lifetime or shortly after his death,[16] cites the following:

14 *ᵓOr Torah* (Jerusalem, 1956), 161a; cf. MS. Jerusalem 3282, fo. 31b.

15 See, for example, the remark in *Darkhei Ẓedeq* (sec 8), that it is preferable that one pray and beseech, because otherwise he perjures himself. Cf. in the name of Menaḥem Mendel of Bar and in the name of the Besht on the verse "Out of the strait place I called out to God" [Ps. 118:5], cited in *Toldot Yaᶜaqov Yosef, Parshat Beshalaḥ*, p. 47b. R. Moses Ḥayyim Ephraim of Sudylkow, the author of *Degel Maḥaneh ᵓEfrayim* and the grandson of the Baᶜal Shem Tov, states in his name that he opposed petitions in prayer and, on the contrary, asked that his prayer not be fulfilled so that he never need to cease from it and may thus be close to God. Not only does one find here the motif "that all his intentions be concerning the needs of On High," but "that prayer in which his request was not fulfilled brought him great joy and a [cause for] great song" — *Degel Maḥaneh ᵓEfrayim* (Josefov, 1883), 75a. One finds characteristic influences of the Maggid intermingled in many traditions of the *Degel.*

16 "As I heard from our holy rabbi, R. Israel Baᶜal Shem *z"l*" — *Ṭorrei Zahav* (Mohilev, 1816), 6a. When he mentions the teachings of the Baᶜal Shem Tov elsewhere, he always takes care to mention that he heard it in his name only. Several pages after this testimony, he mentions that he is writing these things in 1768.

> In the name of the holy rabbi, our master Dov-Baer *Maggid Mesharim* of Mezhirech: Let it not enter your mind at the time of prayer to pray for yourself or your wife or the people of your household, but pray only for the Shekhinah. Concerning this they said, "Go out of the ark (*tevah*; lit., 'word')" [Gen. 8:16] — i.e., from the word [spoken] in prayer — "you and your wife and your sons ..."[17]

Incidentally, this is a unique variant on the exegesis of this verse, which was given a number of interpretations in Hasidism, all of a strongly spiritualistic character. The main idea here is that the words spoken by man in prayer ought to leave his own individual domain and no longer be "his" in terms of any self-interest he may have in them.

R. Benjamin of Salositz is extremely cautious in the formulation of his teaching regarding petitionary prayer, repeating several times the idea that man is totally undeserving of the kindnesses that he asks God to perform for him. He nevertheless agrees with those who claim that there is special permission for one to do so specifically during times of distress:[18]

> But if he prays for himself, he certainly ought to examine his ledger [i.e. his own deeds] to see if he is deserving of this kindness for which he is praying.[19]
> And our Sages gave us sound advice, [saying] that we should send our prayers forth with tears, for all gates are closed save the gate of tears.[20]

In any event, his formulations, which are more moderate than those of the Maggid of Mezhirech — leaving some sort of allowance for petitionary prayer, even if a person does not know if he is deserving as an individual [21] that his prayer be heard — are not cited in the name of his teacher. His above-cited quotation in the Maggid's name is of quite a different character.

R. Uziel Meisels also cites the Maggid's opinion concerning the idea that there is no explicitly personal element in prayer. However, when he came to formulate his own view on this subject, he also added the motif of the permissibility of praying "for himself," namely, "so that he may be able to serve God without obstacles."[22] He quotes the following in the name of the Maggid:

17 *Ṭorrei Zahav*, p. 5d.

18 The Maggid also spoke positively about the greatness of tears, but of tears reflecting intensity of joy and spiritual elevation, not tears of supplication and entreaty; see the opening page of *Liqqutei Yeqarim*. The same understanding of "sweet tears" also appears in St. Teresa of Avila; see Heppe, *Geschichte*, p. 16.

19 *Ṭorrei Zahav*, p. 63c; cf. the same author's *Ahavat Dodim* (Lemberg, 1796), p. 14d.

20 *Ṭorrei Zahav*, 64a.

21 See the same author's *Amtaḥat Binyamin* (Minkewicz, 1796), p. 48b: "Even when you pray with *kavvanah* of the heart, you should in any event not think that, '[if so] I am deserving that my request be fulfilled.'"

22 *Tifʾeret ʿUziel*, p. 79a. This motif reappears in the name of the Maggid himself in *Dibrat Shlomo*, although R. Shlomo of Lutsk attempts to obscure it somewhat. See below.

> I received the following from my teacher and master, the Gaon, the Holy Kabbalist, R. Dov Baer, *z"l*: "Go out" [i.e. "Go out after the flock" — Songs 1:8] from yourself, and let all of your *kavvanah* be for naught but "for the dwelling places [*mishkenot*] of the shepherd" [ibid.] — i.e., on behalf of the Shekhinah of His Glory, as it were; and this is, "for the dwelling places of the shepherds."[23]

R. Uziel makes some comments of special interest concerning the question of the response to prayer, based upon the words of his teacher, the Maggid. We have already seen, in the previously-quoted passage from *Liqqutei Yeqarim*, the parable of the king who is forced to descend, even against his own will, to answer the plea of the person who cries out for justice; although the plea itself is of no importance in his eyes, he does so because he cannot abandon his creatures. This stance is typical of the Maggid of Mezhirech, who does not deny individual providence, but sees its authentic nature in a spiritual light in which man approaches God insofar as he can, until this proximity itself becomes a kind of providence. That approach which gazes down from on high and which holds in contempt worldly matters and the "troublesome" needs of man, is itself the deepest inner reason for the Maggid's opposition to petitionary prayer. According to this, petition and prayer are themselves identical on the spiritual plane, just as the response to prayer is rooted in the spiritual body of prayer. The petition is itself the reward, and God's response to man. R. Uziel explains his opinion concerning this question by means of a paradox, describing two kinds of worshippers — those who pray for concrete things and are answered immediately, and those who pray in a spiritual manner and are (seemingly) not answered at all, their prayers being answered in a different manner. God desires their prayer, elevating it and drawing it out until they understand the true meaning of this response: namely, to come close to God, so that all other requests are automatically nullified. This answer is a typical expression of the quietistic mentality, which states that, when man attains spiritual heights, he should no longer hope or expect a response of the vulgar type implied in petitionary prayer. R. Uziel writes as follows:

> There are two paths in the matter of the influence of the father upon the son. There is one in which the son wishes to receive from his father and comes before his father like a beggar at the door; immediately, as soon as the father wishes it, he orders that he be given his heart's wish so that he no longer need to approach his table, the father's intention in this being to show that he no longer wishes him to come close, and therefore he hastens to fulfill his wish. One sees from this the great lowliness of the son in his father's eyes, and this is compared to the shape of the letter *vav* [of the Divine Name], which is the drawing down of the divine plenitude, which He draws down immediately so that he [the son] need not approach the inner courtyard. The

23 Ibid., p. 79b.

> second way is that of the son who is pleasing in his father' eyes, and from whom he wishes to take pleasure, and from which it is difficult for him to part. Then he does not give him that which he seeks immediately, so that he may stay with him longer and approach the table of the king. And at times, when the son sees his father's great love for him, he himself takes for himself a portion of the high table, as is written, "in the light of the face of the king is life" [Prov. 16:15]. And we find that there is no difference at all in the portion they each receive, for in either event each one receives his portion: for the former it is given as Bread of Shame (*nahama de-kisufa*), because he sees that his father pushes him away, which is not the case in the latter, who comes very close to the king to receive plenitude from His own hands. And this is like the letter *yod* [of the Divine Name], which does not indicate the drawing down to below, but that he himself ascends on high to receive the plenitude — and this is a very sublime level. This is also alluded to in the verse, "the will of those that fear Him He performs, and he hears their cry and saves them" [Ps. 145:19].
>
> I heard from my teacher and master, the *gaʾon* and *ḥasid* R. Dov Baer, *z"l*, may his soul rest in Eden, that the Holy One, blessed be He, indeed does the will of those who fear Him. And even if at times it seems that this is not so, for he cries out and his words are not heard — i.e., he is not answered — this is only because "he hears their cry"; that is, that He wishes and longs for the prayer of the righteous, and therefore He postpones giving them of His plenitude immediately so that they may stay longer with Him ...[24]

The spiritualistic turn is of course based upon the point at which a person does not expect his prayers to be answered in the mundane realm, but with his own hands takes that which he seeks by the very act of ascent to God; he no longer receives there the aspect of "drawing down," but his approach and being up above are themselves the response to his prayer (this is the difference symbolized by the letters *vav* and *yod* of the Divine Name in this homily). The Maggid of Mezhirech elsewhere explains the meaning of this response to prayer in an explicitly spiritual fashion:

> ... A person needs to uplift the words from below to above, to their root; that is, when a person connects and unites word to word and sound to sound and breath to breath and thought to thought, which are the four letters of the Divine Name, as is known. If a person does so, all his words fly up to their source, and he thereby causes the words to come before Him, and He gazes at them. And by this he is answered in his prayer, for the [divine] gazing is a kind of influx from above to below.[25]

The mechanical perception of the influx of blessing into the world is here understood in an entirely non-literal sense! God engages in a kind of spiritual contem-

24 *Tifʾeret ʿUziel*, p. 134a–b.

25 *ʾOr Torah*, p. 59a.

plation of "prayer," which is itself identical with the elevation to the supernal worlds, and this contemplation by God is the most sublime spiritual activity that is longed for. This function can only be fulfilled through contemplative, not by petitionary prayer.

Another interesting point ought to be noted in this context. Rabbi Levi Yitzḥak of Berdichev also heard words of Torah from the Maggid, just as R. Uziel Meisels did, and he likewise quotes in the name of his master the formula that "the Holy One blessed be He desires the prayers of Israel" — for which reason He does not answer them immediately, so that they might continue to pray (just as is explained in the above-cited passage from R. Uziel in the name of the Maggid). However, R. Levi Yitzḥak interpreted these words in an entirely different way: namely, that God specifically wants His children to pray for mundane material matters, and He is pleased to fulfill their request. R. Levi Yitzḥak is the only one I know who explicitly quotes the Maggid as advocating petitionary prayer. He says the following:

> It is known [what is said] in the name of my master and teacher, R. Dov Baer, *z"l*, concerning the verse, "The will of those that fear Him he shall do" [Ps. 145:19] — that the Holy One does the will of those who fear Him when they ask benefit of Him, and because the Holy One, blessed be He, wishes to bring down good things upon Israel He sends the will [i.e., of the petitioners] so that they may request this. There are thus two aspects here in the granting of the good: first, that the Holy One, blessed be He, sends him his will so that they may ask of him, and second, the [fulfilling of] the request itself. This is alluded to in the Talmud (Yevamot 34a), "A woman does not become pregnant from first intercourse," for "intercourse" (*bi'ah*) means "connection" (*hitḥabrut*), and Israel, who receives plenitude from the Creator, are identified with the attribute of woman. Both of these two attributes are for the good, but the Holy One, blessed be He, wishes the evil decree to be nullified from his people Israel by means of the righteous, and for this [reason] He does not draw the will down directly, so that they may request this, but he only alludes to it ... That is, he does not send the will explicitly concerning this good, but only alludes to it in a hint ...[27]

These remarks are aimed at a specific position. R. Levi Yitzḥak consciously brings about the neutralization of the concept of human will, which is not seen as competing with and being nullified by the Divine will, but receiving positive approval from it: that is, man's own desire to pray or to beseech comes from the

26 The Maggid himself repeatedly emphasizes the formula that, "the Holy One blessed be He desires the prayers of Israel," arguing that otherwise in principle one would be unable to pray altogether! See, for example, *Maggid Devarav le-Ya'aqov*, §161, p. 257.

27 *Qedushat Levi ha-Shalem*, p. 76b–77a.

divine will, so that there is in principle no conflict between these two wills. The human will to pray must therefore be the "hint" or sign from above of the prayer being desired and acceptable. He adds elsewhere in the name of the Maggid of Mezhirech:

> I heard the following in the name of my teacher, Rabbi Dov Baer of Mezhirech, concerning the verse "a wise son shall bring joy to his father" [Prov. 10:1], etc. When a person serves the Creator, the Creator has pleasure from this; therefore, when one attributes merit to Israel, the Creator has joy from this. A person must serve the Creator, not for his own benefit, but only so that the Creator has pleasure, and not for himself. Nevertheless, in the Prayer of Eighteen Benedictions we pray for ourselves, as, "grant us [wisdom]," "return us," "heal us," and the other benedictions. But as the Creator gets pleasure when Israel has goodness and blessing, the petitions on our behalf are therefore also good, for the Creator takes pleasure in our goodness and blessings. And this is what the Sages said, "From whence was the light created? This teaches us that the Holy One, blessed be He, wrapped Himself in light . . ." [Gen. R. 3:4], for light [*orah*] is in the feminine, that is, the receiving of the plenitude. And the Talmud [sic!] asks, "From whence was the light created?" which is the receiving of the plenitude, for does not man need to serve only for the pleasure of the Creator and not in order to receive goodness and blessing? And it answered: "this teaches us that the Holy One, blessed be He, wrapped Himself in light" — that is, since the Holy One has pleasure from the plenitude of goodness to us, the Holy One gives us goodness and blessing even when we pray for ourselves, and He has pleasure from this prayer, for He has pleasure from the plenitude of goodness to us . . .[28]

The Maggid clearly agrees that God also receives pleasure from all of the good deeds of Israel, but these things were nevertheless placed upon another ideational basis, which is less popular and literal. R. Levi Yitzḥak makes use here of his own variation of the doctrine of the Maggid, the two of which are not consistent. He wishes to allow petitionary prayer in the name of the Maggid, so to speak, to which he gives the "approval" of the Divine will.

I do not wish to conclude from what has been said that the entire school of the Maggid of Mezhirech, with the exception of R. Levi Yitzḥak of Berdichev, followed the path of resignation in prayer. This would be incorrect; there were those disciples within this group who did not refer to the question at all in their writings, while there were others who explicitly taught that the main thing is to receive "children, life and sustenance" (*banei ḥayei u-mezonei*) — a kind of concentrated, spiritual prayer whose essence is the achievement of very pragmatic results (namely, the basic needs of every human being). Two outstanding spokesmen of this tendency are R. Elimelekh of Lyzhansk and his disciple, R. Kalonymus

28 Ibid., p. 100a–b.

Kalman,[29] who speak at length about prayers for wealth and offspring, etc. Their teachings on this subject are not brought in the name of the Maggid.

One of the Maggid's closest disciples was R. Shlomo of Lutsk, who also cites his master's teaching in the following question:

> I heard from my master, *z"l*, who asked, "How does the heart of a person who is so lowly and contemptible, formed from a fetid drop, dare so much as to come before the King, the Ruler of the World, three times every day to ask his needs, and to detail healing and sustenance and other things?" And he answered with the parable of a king who hired a worker to care for his pleasure orchard of royal dainties, to plant and to hoe; and that same worker requires sustenance and other things which are required for one who engages in the labor of the king. Would such a worker be embarrassed to come every day to ask his needs of the king, seeing as he deals in his things and performs his labor? On the contrary, the king will have pleasure and great honor from this, and will grant all his requests with joy. But when this same worker is slothful in his work, and takes what he is given from the king's house and eats and drinks with a shameful appetite, how will he dare to return every time to ask his needs? Therefore, let this [thing] be before a person's eyes continually, and let him be as zealous in the labor of the king as he is able and to engage in its different aspects. Up to this point were the gracious words of the wise man [i.e. the Maggid].
>
> And in my opinion, one may understand from this the scripture, "Thrust upon God your burden" [Ps. 55:23] — that is, that you shall be like a faithful servant and act in a righteous and zealous manner in your labor, and then your burden shall be [thrust] upon God. For it is incumbent upon the master of the house to feed his workers, and he will then support them, and you shall see clearly that it is He who gives you strength to do valour, and that all your matters and goings about are under His direct providence.[30]

It is difficult to say that this tradition reflects an attitude of resignation, even though petitionary prayer is limited from the outset to that which is necessary for the service of the king — that is, the avoidance of obstacles to service as the result of external disturbances from his world. R. Shlomo of Lutsk felt that the Maggid departed excessively from his principles (compare the above-cited homily in *Liqqutei Yeqarim*) in this homily, and he attempts to restore him to the familiar path better known to him from his master's teaching. In introducing the more specifically quietistic motif of "thrust upon the Lord your burden," he adds the words, "according to my opinion," interpreting the entire homily in a non-literal

29 See, for example, *Maʾor va-Shemesh* (New York, 1958), p. 29a, and his teacher, the author of *Noʿam ʾElimelekh* (Lemberg, 1874), 7c, 9b, 14c [unpaginated], and elsewhere.

30 *Dibrat Shlomo*, Pt. II, pp. 50b–51a.

sense. But it may be that, while distorting the specific sense of this homily, he was directing it towards the intent of the Maggid's teaching generally.

R. Joseph Bloch quotes the following brief homily in the name of the Maggid:

> I heard it said in the name of Rabbi the *Ḥasid*, the Maggid R. Dov Baer, *z"l*, concerning the verse "God shall fulfill all your requests" [Ps. 20:6]. The Rabbi said this interpretation: "All of man's requests should be only that God's Name be 'completed,' that the Name be made whole ..."[31]

This is a kind of variation upon the motto that a person should always pray only on behalf of the Shekhinah.

Among the traditions recorded in the name of the Maggid, I would like to cite the remarks brought by R. Menaḥem Mendel of Vitebsk in the name of his teacher on the same verse expounded above by R. Levi Yitzḥak: "He shall do the will of them that fear Him" [Ps. 145:19]. R. Menaḥem Mendel heard something entirely different from R. Levi Yitzḥak (Menaḥem Mendel specifically states that he heard this interpretation when he was with the Maggid in Volhynia):

> One who truly serves God ought not to wish or desire any thing, but only to do His will. So whence does he come to pray and to ask mercy from Him for himself or even for others, that He change and turn about His will, so to speak? ... And how is it that one who serves God is not ashamed to pray for a certain thing, even if He took great pity upon him? But the matter is that God desires the prayers of the righteous; therefore He contracts and conceals his compassion, and does the will of the righteous person.[32]

Further on, R. Menaḥem Mendel explains (evidently as his own teaching) that:

> According to the above, this may also be the meaning of "He will perform the will of those that fear Him" [Ps., ibid.], meaning, that upon revealing the will of those that fear Him alone, the Holy One will immediately perform the request of their will in actuality ... And afterwards it says, "and He hearkens to their cry"; but it is understood from this that it is the will and longing of the righteous man to continually remain always be in a state of *devequt* above. [Thus] God acts so as to fulfill his will and desire, so that he may always be in *devequt* above by his will, even if at any event he must descend from this level as stated ... [32]

In any event, these remarks are close in spirit to the commentary on that same verse cited by R. Uziel Meisels in the name of the Maggid. Both versions place the focus upon the spiritual identity of prayer, and argue for the lowliness (in the case

31 *Ginzei Yosef* (Jerusalem, 1960), p. 123a, according to the Midrash, "a full Name in a full world."
32 *Peri ha-ʾAreẓ*, 57–59.

of R. Uziel) or total abolition (according to R. Menaḥem Mendel, who argues that God answers the worshipper before his will even leaves his lips!) of concrete prayer.

R. Menaḥem Mendel of Vitebsk explicitly defined his position regarding the matter of petitionary prayer, seeing the concrete contents of prayer as merely a stimulus for awakening the prayer of attachment and meditation; once this is attained, one may cast away the ladder of ascent, which is no longer of any importance.

> And so he ought to do by way of petition, when he requests and prays for some lack, let it not be except in concern of the arousal of prayer and ascent and *devequt.* But after he is aroused, he should cling to the source, that his desire to attain the lack be nullified, for he too desires naught save that which is necessary [i.e. the basic things needed for existence]. Then, when he approaches his root, the hidden light influences him from within, and the lack is automatically filled.[33]

The most radical position of all was that taken by R. Ḥayyim Ḥaykl of Amdur, whose quietistic tendency was reinforced by the motif implied between the lines of his teacher's writings. In his view, it is utterly absurd to seek mercy from God — God lives a life which is beyond time, and is unable to meet man so long as the latter is within time. He does not deny the fact that God oversees and knows what is good for human beings, but this question is one which need not concern human beings. Man is to serve on behalf of God, and no more! This strict approach, also known to us from R. Ḥayyim Ḥaykl's stance on other questions discussed earlier, is expressed in the following language:

> A homily from the divine Rabbi Dov Baer, *z"l*: it is known that the Holy One, blessed be He, is above time, and that if [the people of] Israel are good, they are also above time, but if not, they are Heaven forbid below time. It follows that, if they are below time, how can the Holy One, blessed be He, who is above time, have mercy upon them? . . .[34]
>
> This is the rule: How dare we ask the Creator to have mercy on us? But because of the love of the father for the son, even when the son grabs the father by the beard, the father has pleasure. For example, when one looks at a certain thing and he completely forgets his own existence before that thing and thinks only of that thing, this looking is called face to face. So when he looks at the Creator and thinks only of that thing, this is called face to face; and this is what is said, "Recite [*Malkhuyot* — i.e., Kingship verses] before Me" [Rosh Hashanah 16a] — that is, by gazing face to face you recite *Malkhuyot.* Also, "Recite before Me *Zikhronot* [verses of

33 Ibid., 84; elsewhere, R. Menaḥem Mendel of Vitebsk says: "He will be seized with shuddering from the truth of his heart if he requests [anything] in prayer" — ibid., p. 95.

34 MS. Jerusalem 3282, fo. 79b.

> remembrance; ibid.]" — that is, that he be in the aspect of the male [*zakhar*, word-play on *zakhor*, "remembrance"], to serve God with the attribute of the male, which is the aspect of fear. For the service of desire is like the female [aspect], for he has pleasure from the service of the Creator, but he must think of nothing but the Creator alone, blessed be He.[35]

Despite the somewhat awkward phrasing of this passage, the general thrust of these remarks is clear enough. R. Ḥayyim Ḥaykl refers to the Maggid's motif of the father who takes pleasure in his son, doing him favors and granting him everything that he lacks, even if the latter grabs him by the beard, in a grasping manner — but this is a side remark, just as the Maggid deals with this subject with good will. The essential Hasidic message, on the other hand, is implied in the statement that a person must be "face to face"[36] with the Holy One, that is, "when one looks upon a certain thing and completely forgets his own existence." It follows that a person is only truly before God through contemplative prayer, in which he negates his own independent identity. Even if one's petitionary prayer is answered, this is unimportant and immature from a religious perspective, like the act of the child who grabs his father's beard.

We must in fact assume that this formula of the father receiving pleasure even from his son who asks him for his needs in a degrading way was a common one in the Maggid's teaching. Although this subject is raised with greater reluctance in the parable brought in *Liqqutei Yeqarim* than it is in other sources brought in the name of the Maggid, it also reappears in the teaching of R. Ḥayyim Ḥaykl of Amdur brought in the name of his teacher:

> "I have always placed God before me" [Ps. 16:8]. In the way that my holy master and teacher said: [We can know that] He is merciful by means of analogy, for one who is merciful infuses his thought within the one upon whom he takes mercy, so that the one having mercy [shares in] his pain and needs. Thus far [the words of the Maggid].[37] But in their ability to lower His thought within our corporeality, and also to ask this from Him, whence is the Fear? For are not all those prayers which descend into our thoughts[38] through love alone "contemptible to him"?[39] . . . As our master and teacher said, when the son grabs his father's beard because of the son's love, not only is it not

35 Ibid., fo. 69b. This formula likewise appears in *Kitvei Qodesh*, 6d: that is, this is literally the Maggid's teaching.

36 A Hasidic variation of the concept of *panim be-panim* ("face to face"), which in Lurianic Kabbalah is attributed to the Godhead alone.

37 Cf. in *Kitvei Qodesh*, 16d: "The thought of one who has mercy descends into the thought of the one upon whom he has mercy, and he is together with [him] in his trouble and wants..."

38 Ibid.: "... that he shall descend into our thoughts only in love."

39 He interprets here the verse, "If a person gives all the wealth of his house for love, they will surely have contempt for him" [Songs 8:7], to mean that the essential thing here is that one combine love with fear as well.

> an insult to the father, but he takes pleasure from the son pulling upon his beard. And love accomplishes this, for God lowers Himself into our thoughts and has compassion upon us — and this is, "I have always placed God before me."[40]

The contradiction between these two motifs is quite transparent, as he simultaneously states that: 1) it is an insult to God for human beings to ask Him to turn His attention toward them; 2) God lovingly accepts the entreaties of human beings.

His approach is essentially directed towards the concept of gazing face to face, so that one "negates oneself" in terms of one's own individual self-interest; however, the doctrine that God retroactively also accepts petitionary prayer because He wishes to bring benefit to His creatures seems to me to be valid only within a narrow context. In his book *Ḥayyim va-Ḥesed*, R. Ḥayyim Ḥaykl states:

> He should take care when he prays that he include his prayer among the prayers of all of Israel and forget all his own needs, for it is certainly clear to the Creator what he needs; and when He wishes to do our will, we must then strengthen ourselves and remove our own needs from our heart, so that we forget ourselves completely because of our attachment to Him.[41]

It is interesting to add to the list of commentaries on the verse, "The will of those that fear Him he performs," the following comments of R. Ḥayyim Ḥaykl, which bear a strikingly quietistic character:

> The Holy One, blessed be He, desires the prayers of the righteous, and this is, "the will of [them that fear Him he will perform]" — that is, the prayer of those that fear Him is performed by the Holy One, who places in their heart that they should pray for a certain thing, for the man who fears [God] will not wish to pray or to ask for anything at all, for one does not need any thing![42]

This implies that the fact that a person utters a petitionary prayer is literally done in opposition to his own human will. It is performed by God's own hand; God Himself prays within us by the power of His will, and we are unable to escape it — but there is in fact no need for a person to pray a petitionary prayer, for "one does not need any thing"! It follows from this that when a person prays a simple prayer, he submits to the Divine will, for were it not for this enforced submission he would be unable to ask for anything. We find here the exact opposite of the conventional line of reasoning: man does not force God to listen to his prayers,

40 MS. Jerusalem 97a; in *Kitvei Qodesh* there appears the sequel: "Whatever He, may He be blessed, placed before his thought always, which is from the power of the right."

41 *Ḥayyim va-Ḥesed*, in the section on letters, p. 9.

42 MS. Jerusalem 160a, and cf. fo. 31b. This is again reminiscent of the formulations found in the Maggid's teaching.

but God forces His own will upon us so that we should pray. Upon closer examination, one sees the distinction in tone between the external motif that God "takes pleasure in the prayers of the righteous," and the quietistic character of the deeper theoretical interpretation.

It is clear that the words of the Maggid himself, in which he speaks about prayer as causing pleasure on High, must be understood in terms of the explicit direction of R. Ḥayyim Ḥaykl: the very inclusion of this motif, and the frequency of its appearance in Hassidic sources, reveals the dissatisfaction felt by the Hasidim concerning petitionary prayer.

R. Yitzḥak of Radzivilow, whom we have already mentioned as an indubitable spiritualist,[43] was also included within that circle which demanded total resignation in prayer. He describes petitionary prayer as diametrically opposed to "simple service":

> My beloved brothers, the revelation of His divinity is through that service of which they spoke in the Talmud concerning the verse, "'And to serve Him with all your hearts' [Deut. 11:13]. What is service of the heart? That is prayer" [Taᶜanit 2a]. We must understand this, for is not prayer [performed] with the mouth!? What then is meant when they speak of prayer as being of the heart? But the truth is this: that when man prays for his needs this is certainly not called service, but [is referred to] by the language of petition. For example, just as a person who asks a human king to grant his wish does not thereby perform a service to the king — and a hint is enough for the wise. But what is that prayer which is called service? This is [when] a person who is whole prays to God, even for his needs, but intends in his heart only that there be wholeness in His kingdom. For when man is lacking in his own concerns, there is no wholeness to His Glory. Therefore, when he prays for healing and livelihood, a person must negate himself completely and not wish for anything, but as the *Ari* [R. Isaac Luria] *z"l* said, let his entire intention be for the sake of the Shekhinah [44] — that is, for the unification of which we spoke — and as we wrote, that when a person is lacking, there is no completeness in His glory. With such an intention, that which seems in his mouth to be petition, is in [the person's] heart pure worship. And this is comparable to one who stands before a human king who abnegates himself entirely, and wishes nothing but to perform the will of the king.[45]

43 He received this tendency from his father, the Maggid of Zloczow, in whose name there are explicit remarks concerning the total contradiction between petitionary prayer and prayer on behalf of the Shekhinah. See *Ṭorrei Zahav*, p. 54c-d, where it states explicitly that the "external," literal sense of prayer does not enter into the palace of the King, nor is the Holy One blessed be He able to listen to it from within His palace. He even interprets the verse, "out of the depths I have cried out" [Ps. 130:1] as meaning, "I cry out to Him because of His pain" (ibid., p. 52b), in the manner to be explained below concerning prayer on behalf of the suffering Shekhinah, and not the suffering human being.

44 In Luria's formula, *Le-shem Yiḥud.*

45 *ʾOr Yizḥaq*, pp. 98b–99a.

Verbal prayer is therefore only seemingly prayer, for by changing its direction (towards the Shekhinah), man takes prayer away from its literal, personal and petitionary sense. It is precisely this which serves as a ground for negating his total personal will.

This passage states explicitly what was implicit in all the other opinions of this kind found among the other Hasidic figures quoted. *Kavvanah* is represented here as diametrically opposed to that which is recited with one's lips, contrary to the classical definition that, "one's lips and heart are one." A person pours out his petitionary prayer before God, while in his heart he ignores and negates the personal moment, the apparent subject of prayer. Prayer acts upon the spiritual worlds according to its inner intention, while the actual content implied in the speech of one's lips is completely negated. In one place, the Maggid of Mezhirech gives a pungent formulation for this phenomenon:

> . . . We find that when man does not rely upon his own merits but makes himself as nothing, then he is attached to the Nothing, which is the attribute of Divine wisdom; and we find that he is attached to life, for "wisdom gives life to those that possess it" [Eccl. 7:12]. This is the meaning of the verse, "From whence (ʾ*ayin*, lit, "Nothing") shall come my help" [Ps. 121:1]? When "I lift up my eyes to the hills" [ibid.][46] — meaning that I rely upon the merits of the patriarchs and not upon my own merits. And when I am attached to the attribute of "Nothing," this is an [even] higher level than the patriarchs;[47] for even though the patriarchs are on a high level, nevertheless the attribute of Nothing is even higher than that of the fathers. And whatever a person may be lacking in his vital needs, [such as] healing or forgiveness, he should pray for this. And He who knows all thoughts shall bear witness for him that he does not wish [anything], but only for [holy] speech [itself], but not the [substance of] the requests. This is "One does not stand up in prayer except out of seriousness (*koved rosh*, lit., 'heaviness of head')" [M Berakhot 4:1]. The prayer is that which is heavy, and the "head" refers to the portion of God within man, which is heavy and lacking, and he should pray concerning this. "Even if the king gives him greeting" [Ibid.] — that is, when speech reaches the supernal realms it brings pleasure to the Holy One, and the Holy One blessed be He is present in all the worlds, and pleasure is brought about in all the worlds, and in man as well excitement is born because of this . . .[48]

I wish to stress two points regarding this passage: 1) that "speech" is a spiritualized concept, and is not entirely identical with the speech of one's lips. One

46 "The mountains" is one of the symbols widely used in the Kabbalah to symbolize the Sefirot of *Ḥesed*, *Gevurah* and *Tifʾeret*, which correspond to the three patriarchs.

47 "Nothing" is generally used by him as a symbol of *Ḥokhmah*, rather than of *Keter*, as is generally done in Kabbalistic teachings.

48 MS. Jerusalem–National Library 1467, containing the version of the Maggid's teaching in the possession of R. Shmelke of Nikolsburg, fo. 22b.

might understand the sentence, "he does not wish [anything], but only the "speech," in two different ways: that he asks that the speech which he utters with his mouth ascend and act in the upper worlds; or that he prays on behalf of the Shekhinah, which is called "Speech" (*dibbur*) in Kabbalah. These two interpretations are ultimately the same, and are both explicitly opposed to the literal understanding of prayer as "request." 2) That this formula — namely, that the Shekhinah on whose behalf we pray is present within us, in a hidden point of our spiritual nature — is extremely uncommon in the other writings of the Maggid; it is viewed as a kind of *apex* which is both identical with and differentiated from us, being a part of God above. We will discuss below in detail the question of how the Shekhinah became transformed from a transcendent, metaphysical concept to an immanent psychological one. This problem relates to an important aspect of our understanding of Hasidic quietism.

In order to sum up the present problem concerning the matter of petitionary prayer, I must emphasize that most Hasidic texts on prayer contain a kind of conventional formula concluding with the words, "that he should pray for the Shekhinah and for all of Israel"[49] — i.e., unlike petitionary prayer. Such formulae already appear in the name of the Baᶜal Shem Tov, and continue through the entire gamut of Hasidic writings down to those of the third generation of disciples of the Maggid. The inclusion in one breath of the two concepts, "Shekhinah" and "all of Israel,"[50] clearly stems from the Kabbalistic tradition wherein the Shekhinah is designated as the supernal, metaphysical Congregation of Israel, which combines with the romantic motif developed in the circle of Safed stressing the sharing of pain by the Shekhinah in all of Israel's troubles.[51] The logical conclusion that follows from this is that, "Israel are the organs of the Shekhinah."[52] If they suffer, the supernal Shekhinah likewise feels this; therefore, in order to diminish its suffering above, we must ask that our troubles be decreased below. I do not know whether this is a sophisticated method of permitting petitionary prayer on behalf of the community of Israel, proscribing only individual petitionary prayer, or whether it is merely a verbal formula.

49 See, e.g., *Liqqutei Yeqarim*, p. 6b.

50 See, e.g., for example, R. Abraham Ḥayyim of Zloczow, *ᵓOraḥ le-Ḥayyim* (Jerusalem, 1960), p. 51b, in the name of the Maggid: "it is also a spark of the Shekhinah, of the totality of Israel."

51 See, e.g., *Ahavat Dodim*, 15a, and *Amtaḥat Binyamin*, 48c, where it states that the Shekhinah suffers on our behalf in order to free us of the birthpangs of the Messiah.

52 In the name of the Baᶜal Shem Tov: "that he also [each one in Israel] is part of the limbs of the Shekhinah, for his dominion rules over all, and there is no place empty of Him" — *Toldot Yaᶜaqov Yosef*, p. 91b. It is interesting that the reason given for the identity between Israel and Shekhinah is in terms of the immanentist understanding of the presence of the Shekhinah in the world and in man. See on this also *ᵓOr ha-Meᵓir*, p. 8d.

Another point must be emphasized here. When Hasidic sources state that we pray for God and not for ourselves, these remarks are directed towards certain distinct and clearly-defined ideas: namely, the unification of the Shekhinah with her Husband, as envisioned throughout the Kabbalistic tradition. Whoever used the concept "to pray for the Shekhinah" in Hasidism intended thereby to exclude the opposite — namely, that a person should not pray for himself, but must use prayer in order to affect the transcendent world.

In the majority of the teachings of the Maggid, the term "Shekhinah" appears as a transcendent concept, although we have already seen (as we shall see further below) that this concept also acquired an immanent psychological meaning. The world of Hasidism in no way nullified the Kabbalistic heritage — and with it the transcendent understanding of the Shekhinah. On the contrary, it appeared there as a very concrete idea, even if the detailed working out of the "what" and "how" within the divine world were neglected in favor of other problems that engaged Hasidism. The Besht and his contemporaries,[53] as well as the Maggid and his circle,[54] remained loyal to the concept of prayer on behalf of the Shekhinah, that she be united wih her Husband and leave her Exile, in both senses of the word. But one cannot ignore the other side of the problem, which is of great importance in clarifying the quietistic motif involved in the immanent perception of the concept of Shekhinah. There seem to be two principal explanations of how a person's prayers are answered, even though he prays only on behalf of the Shekhinah. One explanation is rooted in that tradition which has a transcendent perception of the Shekhinah: namely, that when a person, in the course of prayer,

53 For example, in the name of the Besht: "A person should not pray on behalf of himself, but only on behalf of the Shekhinah, that she unite with her lover, for the righteous are the agents of the Matron [*Metronita*; i.e., the *Sefirah* of *Malkhut*] who prays, 'please, my master'; for the intention of the Shekhinah is not for itself, but only for His Glory, may He be blessed, that Your mastership over the world be made known through me" — *Toldot Yaᶜaqov Yosef*, 32d. Cf. ibid., 38c and 91b, in the name of R. Menaḥem Mendel of Bar. See also A. J. Heschel, "Rabbi Nahman of Kosow," p. 135 and n. 96, who specifically cites R. Naḥman of Kosow, as quoted in the works *Ben Porat Yosef* and *Ẓofnat Paneᶜaḥ*, on those motifs concerning prayer on behalf of the Divine flow of blessing into the world. R. Naḥman sets up a clear social differentiation of tasks: the elect (*anshei ẓurah*) pray only for spiritual matters while the common men (*anshei ha-ḥomer*) pray for material things.

54 In *Liqqutei Yeqarim*, p. 6: "For this is the essential blessing and plenitude which he brings about through his prayer in the upper attributes. And this is what our rabbis said, 'One does not stand up to pray except with seriousness' [*koved rosh*; lit., "heaviness of head" — M Berakhot 5:1]. This alludes to the above, that one does not stand up to pray for one's own needs, for they will not be answered, but on the contrary, they may incite [prosecution] and remind [God of] his sins; but his prayer should be [performed] out of heaviness of head — that is, for the Shekhinah who is called 'the head' ... it being above the head of man."

lifts the Shekhinah to become connected with the upper worlds, the plenitude automatically descends (in accordance with the mechanistic laws governing the upper worlds). The second explanation is closer to an immanent, pantheistic perception of the world, in that it attributes to the Shekhinah the significance of the inner life of the world: when a person prays on its behalf, he quickly comes to realize that all that he is "lacking" and all of his troubles are meaningless, external "garments," and his "lack" and pain are automatically nullified in the encounter with the all-embracing, true, unique reality which is the Shekhinah. According to this perception, prayer is a kind of psychological neutralization, both of the request itself and of the I, even if it directly perceives the Divine reality. This approach is already stated in the name of the Ba^{c}al Shem Tov:

> ... I heard from my master [the Ba^{c}al Shem Tov] an interpretation of the verse, "Then Judah drew near, and said to him, please, my master ..." [Gen. 44:18]. It states in Berakhot [p. 32a] "Let a person always [first] recite the praises of God and thereafter pray." But in ^{c}Avodah Zarah [p. 7b] there are those who state the opposite, and it is explained there that one [authority] said one thing and one said the other, and that they did not disagree. Naḥmanides wrote that the active power immanent within the object [of the action], and the Creation of the world as a whole, are like the locust which is dressed in its own body [cf. Gen. R. 21:5], and in all kinds of pain there is [yet] a holy spark from Him, only it is [concealed] within many garments; and this is the matter of the seven maidens which it is fitting to be given her from the house of the king [Est. 2:9]. For when one sets one's heart to understand that here too He is with him, then the garment is moved aside and revealed and suffering is abolished ... And this is what is said, "he should recite His praises" [Berakhot, op cit.] — for this is His praise, that His Glory fills the entire world [Isa. 6:3], and in all their troubles He is troubled [Isa. 63:9]; then he [the worshipper] will not be anguished [word play on *lw ẓ^{c}r* and *lʾ ẓ^{c}r*] . "... and pray" — for in any event the pain is nullified after he knows how to recite His praises in this matter. ... [I heard elsewhere the same from my master.] And the other sage is of the opinion that, "let him first pray" [Berakhot, op. cit.] — and this, because, as he believes that God is [already] there, it is as if He is actually there, and he is able thereafter to order His praises; and the words of a sage are pleasing.
>
> Through this we may understand, "And Judah drew near" — [i.e.,] thanks [*hodaʾah* — a word play on the name *Yehudah* = Judah] and praise to Him — "and said, please, my master" — for all of the pain is within this name [*ʾadoni* — "my master" — is the Shekhinah], and once he brings to Him thanks and praise, the pain is nullified.[55]

It is not too great a distance from this position to the inclusion of the personal ego within the formula, "the whole world is full of his glory," whereby God merited the title of the only actor within man, whose soul became "an organ of the

55 *Toldot Ya^{c}aqov Yosef, Va-yeḥi*, 34b–c.

Shekhinah." God here speaks within man when a person is willing to make himself "Nothing" and to remove his own presence. Before addressing this question in detail, we must still accompany the Hasidic worshipper a certain distance and describe his struggle for spiritual prayer, which allows for the revelation of God within man.

In concluding the discussion of petitionary prayer, I must make one further comment pertaining to the question of whether one is permitted to utilize prayer in order to force the Redemption — a position for which one could certainly find adequate justification in the argument that one is not praying on one's own behalf, but for the end of the suffering of the Shekhinah! While I have not found this question discussed in many places, I wish to note that it is explicitly stated in the name of the Besht that it is forbidden to do so. He does not mention Sabbatai Ẓevi in this connection, but the legendary Joseph della Reina,[56] who fell prey to this extreme activism.

> As I heard from my teacher ... There is another more sublime aspect in the *tiqqun* of the supernal realms also; [namely,] he should not force himself so that his will necessarily be done, for there is a great danger in this, as is written in the verse, "If you awaken or arouse the love until it is willing" [Songs 2:7, etc.], as proven by the acts of R. Joseph della Reina, Heaven forbid. Therefore, the counsel given to the enlightened man is that he do his part and pray concerning the event, and the Master of Will will act according to His good will. And this is the most sublime aspect of worship, which is not in order to receive a reward.[57]

R. Benjamin of Salositz also warns explicitly against attempting to force the End through prayer, because such prayer is liable to be perceived as prayer on behalf of the welfare of Israel!

> And then he further warned that, when he prays with *kavvanah*, he should not pray too much on behalf of the End, because it is writtten that one of the oaths which the Holy One adjured Israel to swear was that they would not force the End, that they not press overly much concerning the End — and it was for this reason (i.e., that it is only on their behalf!).[58]

We likewise find reference to the idea that it is forbidden for a person to request special spiritual accomplishments, such as clarity of vision or to receive of voices

56 On della Reina, see G. Scholem, *Sabbatai Ṣevi*, pp. 75–76 and n. 110 there.

57 *Toldot Yaᶜaqov Yosef*, p. 134b.

58 *Amtaḥat Binyamin*, 46d, and see also in the name of R. Leib Piestiner, a member of the Besht's circle, as cited in *Toldot Yaᶜaqov Yosef*, p. 164a, that one is to wait until God restores Israel (on Ezekiel's vision of the bones).

from heaven,[59] even though there are accounts of people who attained such things in actual fact.

Among all the Hasidic thinkers during the time of the Maggid, I know of only one *ẓaddiq* who explicitly opposed this mood of resignation, specifically instructing his Hasidim to pray for their livelihood — R. Pinḥas of Korets. This demand logically follows from the thrust of his arguments with the Maggid of Mezhirech; R. Pinḥas objected to contemplative prayer in principle, and saw the Maggid as the representative *par excellence* of the dissemination of the doctrine of contemplation and *devequt* in prayer. There was a controversy between the immediate circle of R. Pinḥas and the *ḥasidim* of the Maggid in Korets concerning this matter, which we shall discuss below [60] in our analysis of the concept of contemplative prayer in Hasidism. At this point, I merely wish to emphasize that R. Pinḥas's repeated statements concerning the matter of prayer for livelihood are to be understood in the context of the larger controversy concerning the theoretical image of Hasidism. For example:

> Several times I heard him adjure us to pray for our livelihood and other needs, and to believe that God would surely fulfill his request! And this is a great *mizvah*, for thereby he lifts up the Shekhinah.[61]

Elsewhere, he says:

> When a person prays for a certain thing many times and is not answered, he should go on praying and not give up, since everything depends upon the hidden light, which is revealed daily in the world.[62]

59 See *Darkhei Ẓedeq*, s.v. *ᶜod hanhagot*, 1.

60 See Chapter 7 below.

61 MS. Jerusalem 3759, in which there is a collection of traditions of several disciples of R. Pinhas in the name of their master (fo. 123a).

62 Ibid., fo. 106a.

Chapter Seven

Contemplative Prayer

Contemplative, meditative prayer constituted the primary message of the spiritual world of Hasidism. If, when the *ḥasid* stood up to pray, he did not do so in order to attain the "casting off of corporeality," the loss of his attachment to this world, so as to ascend above time and nature and to reach the perfect unity, the Divine "Nothing," he felt he had done nothing of any spiritual value or significance at all. The intensive manner in which these teachings are repeated in the world of Hasidism is a reflection of the longing and the true desire implicit in them: prayer serves as a guide for the break-through beyond nature, towards the spirit. In this context, we are speaking of spiritual prayer, its methods being that of meditation and mental concentration upon the spiritual element present within the natural world. The break-through to the spirit is equally appropriate to either one of two theoretical positions: that which argues a transcendent God, whose "Nothing" is man's desire; and that which posits an immanent God, in which the "Nothing" of man himself is the object of this breakthrough. Both positions are entertained alongside one another in Hasidic teaching, their common denominator being the perception of the essence of prayer as a supra-natural act, through which man seeks to break through the limits of his own natural existence in order to reach divinity. It is man's natural existence, subject to his self-interest, pride and desire for personal greatness, which blocks the path towards unity. By the very nature of natural existence, individual life is life in multiplicity; spiritual life can only be that life in which one encounters the one exclusive, authentic reality, which contains the unity of all opposites and the blurring of all the individuals which are paradoxically incorporated in the Divine "Nothing."[1]

Prayer obviously holds a primary role in the religious life within this system of ideas, as the "ladder planted in the ground whose head reaches to the heavens." It is the embodiment of both the letters of the text of prayer and the Divine spirit; it is the symbol of the natural order and of differentiation, being subject to the

1 For an explanation of the various changes in the concept of the "Nothing" (*ʾayin*) in Hasidism, see above, Chapter 2; and see now also Rachel Elior, "'Yesh' and 'ʾAyin': Basic Paradigms in Hasidic Thought," in *Proceedings of the First International Conference on Hasidic Thought, Dedicated to the Memory of Joseph Weiss* (London, 1992).

contours of the letters of the Hebrew alphabet and their forms, but it is beyond nature by virtue of the Divine life which may be activated when man engages in contemplation.

True, Hasidism expanded this principle of seeing to include the entire cosmos, in which there is shell and kernel, so that the individual who contemplates through the shell to the kernel is likely to penetrate to the mystical significance of this principle — but we will need to devote our attention to this question separately when we discuss the question of "service in corporeality."[2] Notwithstanding the overall outlook mentioned above, a special place was reserved for prayer wherein, as in the Jewish tradition generally, it enjoyed a place of honor in the service of God.

The starting point of prayer is a kind of taking hold of its most concrete component, the letters themselves, in order to ascend within them and through them to the spiritual inwardness of the infinite chaotic lights shining there, stripped of all defined contents. This chaos exists within the orderly and stable framework of the revelation of God. Every unambiguous, external "revelation" of Divinity contains within itself the infinity of God, in such a manner that a person who has broken through the barriers of "externality" and entered within it with the maximum degree of spiritual concentration, is able to bring about an encounter between the spiritual element within it and that outside it. Contemplative thought is thus the only means to true prayer, which uncovers God behind the concealment of the concrete. We may understand from this that every prayer in which the spiritual meaning is absent is worthless — it possesses neither power nor essence, but remains within the realm of external wondering, neither penetrating or breaking the chains of nature nor liberating the spirit.

Traditions concerning contemplative prayer within Hasidic literature already appear in the name of the Baᶜal Shem Tov. His disciple, the Maggid of Mezhirech, who devoted himself to the development of these points in the teaching of the Besht, cites its main points in his name:

> I have written in *Parashat Noaḥ*, in the commentary to the verse, "and you shall place the opening of the ark in its side" [Gen. 6:16] — I wrote in the name of the holy rabbi, the holy light, our teacher Dov Baer, *z"l*, who said in the name of the Besht, *z"l*, that that which is written in the *Zohar* [stating] that a person is judged in every palace (*Heikhal*) refers to the words and letters of prayer, which are called "palaces." There a person is judged as to whether he is worthy to enter into the letters of prayer, and if not, he is expelled — that is, they send him an alien thought, and push him away. Thus far his words.[3]

2 On the question of *ᶜavodah be-gashmiyut*, see above, Introduction, Sec. V–VI.

3 Abraham Ḥayyim of Zloczow, *ʾOraḥ le-Ḥayyim*, p. 98a. Many sources cite the Besht on this subject.

The beginning of the meditative path is thus described here as "entering into the letters of prayer." There are times when the way to this gate is blocked to a person, and he is unable to (i.e., "unworthy to") contemplate the object of his meditation, because straightaway the external world (i.e., "the alien thoughts") appears in his way, and does not enable him to concentrate his thought so as to move from palace to palace and from one level of meditation to another. Such a person is "expelled" from the supra-natural world back into the world of nature.

The spiritual perception of the object of contemplation is depicted in Hasidic sources as a transparent vision via the object: during the course of the person's meditation, the letters are gradually disembodied of their concrete form and the Divine spiritual attributes hidden within them are then revealed.[4] The Baᶜal Shem Tov[5] compared this (albeit unsuccessfully) to gazing at the stars through a telescope, which serves as a tool for observing things which cannot be seen by the naked eye. In his view, such a vision is dependent upon the loss of all the powers of the soul and their complete negation until the person is turned into nothing, whereupon the emptiness left by this "nothing" is filled with a new kind of being which rests upon him from above. He is then no longer active and no longer the speaker of the prayer, but directly confronts the Divine reality which acts and speaks within him. The following are the words cited in his name:

> There are two [kinds of] fear: external fear and internal fear. The external fear is simply when, because of fear, all powers and virtues and attributes disappear and become as nothing. But internal fear takes place thereafter, when he becomes as naught and the supernal forces and attributes dwell upon him, and then there rests upon him the [feeling of] shame — and this is the essence of life, when the supernal attributes dwell upon him. But whereby do the supernal attributes dwell upon him? Just as the star-gazers are able to look at the stars by day by means of their [telescopic] lenses, so there are instruments by means of which one may perceive supernal attributes and levels, and these instruments are the letters. For example, if one wishes to perceive the greatness of the Creator when he recites [the word] "the Great" (*ha-Gadol*) [i.e. in the first paragraph of the ᶜ*Amidah*], and he gazes intently upon the letters *gimmel dalet vav lamed* in his mind's eye, and all of his levels and powers are nullified during the time of that gazing, then the [Divine] greatness is revealed in those letters. And likewise in the letters of *ha-Gibbor* (the Mighty) the might of the Creator

4 A good description of the blurring of contours at the height of meditation and the perception of all the words of prayer as one point is found in the book of one of the disciples of the Maggid, R. Asher Ẓevi, *Maᶜayan ha-Ḥokhmah* (Korets, 1816), p. 43d ff.

5 According to the text given in *Shemuᶜah Ṭovah*, edited by R. Levi Yitzḥak of Berdichev, these remarks are attributed to the Besht by the Maggid, appearing in a seemingly "continuous" list of the Besht's words. It seems, however, reasonable to assume that the parable itself is from the Baᶜal Shem, while the literary working of the explanation bears clear stylistic signs of the Maggid himself.

> is revealed, and in the letters of *ha-Nora*ᵓ ("the Awesome") the awesomeness of the Creator — for there is power in these letters to contract the supernal attributes and to draw them into them, and by means of these letters they dwell upon the one who speaks them. Even though it is written in the *Zohar* that His Glory, may He be blessed, is not grasped in the tail of the *yod*, and is not contained in these vessels, but He only contracts Himself within these vessels because of the love of the infant, as is written, "and you shall make two cherubim" [*keruvim*; Ex. 25:18]; as our Sages said, *keravya* [a play on the word *ke-ravya*: "like an infant"]. That is, such is the way of the father who, because of his love for the child, distorts his speech and speaks in the manner of a child, or contracts his intellect into that of the child. We therefore find that the father is on the level of (the intellect of) the son, and that is "and you shall make two cherubim." And this is, "and I shall speak with you from between the two cherubs" [ibid., v. 22] — that is, that you should act through your good deeds so as to cause to draw the love of the Creator down upon you, that he shall contract Himself to your level, so that they shall be as if two cherubs. We find that the level of the Divine essence which cannot even be apprehended through the tail of the *yod* is called the Holy One, blessed be He . . . and when they are contracted within the letters — to each righteous man according to his level, and to every person in Israel, and to all individual providence — this already dwells upon the deeds of the lower beings, and is called Shekhinah — and let [a hint] be enough to one who understands.[6]

That is, it is difficult for man to comprehend "God" — i.e., the Divinity in its full, un-contracted sense — but the Godhead as contracted within the Shekhinah may be encountered through means of meditation. He goes on to say there:

> And this small (contracted) intellect is literally from the great essence (ᶜ*eẓem*), and is renewed by the power of the disciple. Nor is it called renewed, because it was always [there] in potential . . . and all of the attributes are intellective attributes and not ones of limit.[7]

These remarks add two further points: first, that the degree of God's manifestation and appearance to us and in us depends upon the power of renewal of the "disciple," and his own potential for spiritual receptivity. Second, the revealed attributes and levels "and those which rest upon he who speaks them" do not come from the world of Sefirot which is "within limits" — i.e., the lower part of the Sefirot — but from the world of Sefirot which is within "thought" — i.e., the higher part of the Sefirot — as intellective attributes. The path to the infinite God is reopened by the possibility of man's "thought," which becomes progressively greater and greater, and is able to communicate with God's thought. He then goes on to explain[8] that the teacher first shows his pupil the greatness of his intellect

6 *Shemu*ᶜ*ah Ṭovah* (Warsaw, 1938), p. 73b.

7 Ibid., p. 75a.

8 Ibid., p. 75b.

so that he may fear him, and afterwards starts to show him his intellect in limited form, in graduated stages, until he again shows him his intellect in its greatness — "and it is enough that a wise man receives a hint." It would seem that he wished to explain the possibility of man comprehending everything of the way to the Infinite.[9]

The spiritual possibilities opened to a person depend upon the breaking of the bonds of limited matter; in the course of an active effort of spiritual concentration, directed entirely towards thought on God, God Himself comes to man's aid and frees him completely from those bonds.

> The aim sought is that, prior to prayer, he should cast off corporeality, which is of end and limit, and enter into the attribute of Nothing, which is without end. A person ought to direct all of his attention towards the Creator alone, and not to any thing or [even] half a thing of his own being, which is impossible unless he bring himself within the attribute of Nothing — that is, that he does not exist at all, and he then may not turn to any thing of this world, since he does not exist at all, but let man rely only upon his Maker, upon God alone — and understand this. This attribute of casting off corporeality is a redemption of the [vital] soul of man, [and] of his spirit and soul which are redeemed from the corporeality of the body, which is confined and limited and narrow (*meẓarim*), and [they] cling to the Creator, who is Infinite. And this is called the Redemption from Egypt (*Miẓrayim*). And this is the reason for joining Redemption to Prayer [i.e., linking together the end of *Qeriʾat Shemaᶜ* to the *ᶜAmidah* of the Morning Service]. And this is perhaps what the ancient ones meant when they said that one should to recite the verse "O Lord, upon my lips" [Ps. 51:17] prior to the Eighteen Benedictions. The meaning is that we beseech Him — "O Lord" — that "my lips" — when the language of border and limit, like the bank of a river (*sefat ha-nahar*), which is corporeality — "open" — that is, You shall open the fetters and chains of corporeality, to cast them off me, that I may be attached to the Nothing.[10]

Prayer, which begins with man's activity — through means of his speech and his intense effort to concentrate and to focus his mind "upon God alone" and to suppress consciousness of the external world — is ultimately transformed into an act of pure passivity. Instead of man sending the "words" on high, they are placed within his mouth, through a kind of supernal coercion which is no longer voluntary: the mouth continues to speak automatically while the spirit has withdrawn far away to the world of thought. This is the final point of separation between the word and its articulation from the spiritual element rooted therein, a kind of separation of man from his past. The Besht described it as follows:

9 It is clear that thought and apprehension are not to be understood here in the sense of rational apprehension.

10 *Shemuᶜah Ṭovah*, p. 79b–80a.

> R. Israel Ba^cal Shem said: Regarding this act, when I attach my thought to the Creator, blessed be He, I allow my mouth to speak what it wishes, for I connect the words to their supernal root in the Creator, blessed be He, for every word has its root above in the Sefirot.[11]

It is stated elsewhere in his name:

> ... From this power [i.e. which strengthens the attribute of Mercy above that of Judgment] he comes to the gate of the Nothing, and completely forgets his existence; only his thought and his love and all his attributes remain attached to the fear of God and His attributes. We find that all of his speech [consists of] vessels of the supernal speech, as it were — that is, the combinations of the supernal letters.[12] We likewise find that the word leaves the supernal worlds, and is sent into his mouth. Certainly, they are able to awaken the supernal lights by means of speech such as this, and the attributes are likewise able to overcome one another in accordance with the letter combinations and according to the need.[13]

Further on, he continues:

> ... Among the *ẓaddiqim*, who have great souls and who are able to ascend to the highest heights and to achieve such an apprehension, the movement of speech is from Him. Certainly, simple speech among them is not called speech at all, and they [i.e., the words of prayer] do not operate in the simple [meaning] of speech at all ..[14]

We are explicitly told here that a person's speech in prayer does not bring about a theurgic influence upon the Divine world; rather, ordinary human speech becomes silenced, making room for the Divine speech, by means of a transformation described in the doctrine of letter combinations. Under the influence of the new power of the concentrated spirit, the concrete combination of the word within prayer ceases to exist and is transformed into the living speech of God.

The moments of this transformation cannot be comprehended by man, because it takes place at those very moments that man becomes transformed into "Nothing." This psychological nothingness is a kind of break within the continuity of time, by means of which man is plunged into the transnatural atmosphere; at the same time, it is a point of connection between the corporeal and the spiritual form of existence. The neutralization of all contents and activity at the moment of "nothingness" is the guarantee of their persistence beyond the moment of their

11 *Liqqutei Yeqarim*, p. 2b.

12 This refers to spiritual combinations having their own inherent law and significance, and are not similar to the combinations in the concrete word.

13 This is the meaning of the phrase, "if his prayer is fluent in his mouth" — *Shemu^cah Ṭovah*, p. 71b.

14 Ibid., p. 72a. Here too the words seem to me a Maggidic formulation, although I do not deny the fact that the Besht already advocated the doctrine of personal "annihilation," as is shown by the quotation preceding it in several sources in the name of the Besht.

appearance in time — a manifestation of the paradoxical principle that "their breaking is their correction" [cf. Shabbat 16a, used here metaphorically]. In the Maggid, this idea of the Nothing parallels all stages of the cosmos and all areas of existence, including the corporeal world, being subject to the law of the spirit. The transition from the being of the egg to that of the chick is described by him as a continuity within a break, if such a paradox is tolerable. Similarly, the movement from concrete speech to concrete thought is subject to a law which cannot be pinpointed, becuse it is a "trans-temporal" one operating within time. The force of this law also holds true regarding the transition from discursive logical thought to "clinging thought" (*maḥshavah deveqah*); the same holds true also of Divine thought which, even if trans-temporal in terms of its attributes, also contains the attribute of the "Nothing," in which everything is negated and returns to life in a new dimension. "Communication" between the two worlds is allowed for by this parallel between the natural law of the transcendent world and that of the immanent world, and it is also what assures the significance of spiritual prayer. The transformation of man into "Nothing" is indeed the bridge into the world of the spirit, and only here do true spiritual processes commence. On the other hand, man's inability to obliterate his temporal being blocks the way to the breakthrough of the spirit and halts the progress of the law of the spirit. The Maggid of Mezhirech says the following:

> "The Torah and the Holy One blessed be He are One." How is one to explain this, for is not He infinite and the Torah finite? But the matter should be understood, that the power of the subject acting is [manifested] in the object acted upon. For example, when a person speaks a word of wisdom or does a wise thing, the power of the actor is present in everything he did or in the word which he spoke, for the wise man who spoke is able to speak many more wise words. Thus, the Torah is wisdom [coming] from Him, and His power is in the Torah, for the power of the actor is in the object of his act, and this power is indeed infinite. And there are several levels: the Object of Intellection (*maskil*), the Intellect (*sekhel*), and Speech (*dibbur*), and all from each other. And speech is within time, and in thought there is also time — for today he thinks thus and tomorrow thus — and there is an attribute which connects everything, the Object of Intellection to the Intellect, and this attribute is not comprehended, for it is the attribute of the Nothing, which is the "hyle" — as in the parable of the egg from which the chicken is born. There is a [certain] hour when it is neither egg nor chicken, and no man is able to ascertain this exact hour, for then it is in the attribute of Nothing.[15] Thus, when Intellect is made from the Object of Intellection, and speech from thought, we are unable to apprehend the thing connecting them, and it is then called "Mighty" (*eitan*), which in reversed letters is *tânya* ["we studied" — the phrase used in the Talmud to introduce tannaitic teachings], because in the Intellect it is

15 ᵓ*Or ha-*ᵓ*Emet*, p. 9b–10a.

> *tanya* because it studies with the thought, and by itself it is mighty (*eitan*), the language of strength, for it is not apprehended . . .[16]

It is against this background of the law of the "inversion of things" that an individual can meet God. This is the very basis of the common law of spirit, man's soul being a portion of God above.

> "Go, you and all your household into the ark" [word-play on *tevah*, which means both "ark" and "word"; Gen. 7:1] — for the Torah and the Holy One, blessed be He, are all one. But the Holy One, blessed be He, is embodied in the Torah, and if [man] emits the word from His mouth with all his strength, then his strength is likewise embodied in the word, which is Torah. And his strength, which is the soul that spreads all over the body and the soul, is a portion of God above. There is thereby a complete attachment of the portion to the source, for the soul of the righteous are the limbs of the Shekhinah, as it were. And this is the union of the Holy One, blessed be He, and the Shekhinah,[17] and this is "the Lord your God" [Deut. 6:5] — that is, with the Ineffable Name [i.e., the Tetragrammaton], which represents the Holy One, blessed be He, should be your God[18] — that is, your power, which is the Shekhinah.[19]

A variation of the same idea is brought elsewhere in the name of the Maggid:

> When he studies or prays, let the word go out of him with all his power, like the drop of seed which goes out of all his limbs [i.e., with the trembling of all his limbs], and then his strength is embodied in that drop. Thus, within the word is embodied all of his strength, as is written, "Go, you and all your household, into the ark [word]" [Gen. 7:1].[20]

The Maggid of Mezhirech is greatly occupied with the issue of the nullification of the "intellect" and the nature of thought, being subject to time,[21] for so long as

16 The same parable also appears in *Maggid Devarav le-Ya^caqov*, §56, p. 84.

17 The "unification of the Holy One blessed be He and the Shekhinah" is interpreted here in an extremely daring way as the unity between God and man's soul.

18 The God who is within you, i.e., the "Shekhinah," will be united with *YHWH*, which corresponds to the Holy One, blessed be He. The formula, "the unity of the Holy One blessed be He and the Shekhinah," which ordinarily refers to the divine world, is turned about here to refer to the unity between God and man.

19 *ʾOr ha-ʾEmet*, p. 36b.

20 *Shemuʿah Ṭovah*, p. 56b.

21 I rely here upon the assumption that those things which are cited in the lists in *Shemuʿah Ṭovah* were said by the Besht. This question is one that is still open to discussion, into which I cannot enter here. But I will certainly not sin against the truth if I state that these things were said in the name of the Maggid (the entire book having been written as the teachings of the Maggid), as there are more or less exact parallels to most of the teachings brought there in other sources of the Maggid. On the version of the Maggid's teachings found in *Shemuʿah Ṭovah*, see Schatz, "Introduction," p. xix.

self-reflection exists and the human mind is capable of involvement with itself, it is unable to come to the Nothing. The complete extinction of reflective consciousness is therefore a necessary precondition of liberation from the *yesh* [roughly translated as the "Ego" or "Self-Being"], and only then may man acquire a "new intellect," a form of pure spiritual thought which is beyond time.

> And we thus arouse every day the Redemption from Egypt: for by means of these letters we are able to attach our vitality [to God]. And we must first remove the vitality from our corporeal thoughts and from our own being: that is, so that we may enter the gate of the Nothing, and we are then easily able to be attached by our root to the Cause of all Causes. And this is the matter of the redemption from Egypt: while our intellect is still [concerned with] the matter of our selves and is within the gate of being, the intelligibles are contracted and narrowed; but when one comes to the root, they are in [a state of] expansion ...[22]

After withdrawing to the Nothing, the "limited intellect" is transformed into an entity having "Divine capability", turning into broad, expansive intellect capable of absorbing the voices of the spirit, which it could not receive before it had negated itself and been transformed into Nothing. This "expanded intellect" flows from the Divine "nothing" and is embodied in man. The Maggid says:

> Moses is called the Intellect, for man has the power to escape from that intellect to another intellect, and to enter into the realm of the Nothing. And Moses is named for the language of "removal," as in, "from the water he was drawn" [Ex. 2:10]. For he leaves his [own] mind and goes into the border of the Nothing, and this is, "Suffer me a little, and I will tell you" [Job 36:2], for he needs to enter into the limit of the Nothing, to leave the Intellect and Knowledge and go into the limit of the Nothing, and afterwards "and wisdom is found from Nothing" [Job 28:12] [literally: "from whence is found?" — word play on ᵓ*ayin* as "from whence" and "from Nothing"].[23]

The Maggid elsewhere gives a definition of man's presence within the Nothing:

> Also the Rav [this refers to the Besht — editor's note][24] said, "How does man [come into] the attribute of nothing? Only if he does naught but that which pertains to the soul is he in the attribute of nothing, for the soul is a thing which none can apprehend ..."[25]

That is, with the cessation of all activities within man apart from thought, he may become spiritualized and enjoy a new dimension of spiritual existence. The

22 *Shemuᶜah Ṭovah*, p. 70b.

23 Ibid., pp. 49a–b.

24 The disciples of the Maggid referred to their teacher in writing as "the *Rav*," without any adornment, unlike their practice regarding the Besht.

25 ᵓ*Or ha-*ᵓ*Emet*, p. 45b.

Maggid sees the "life of the soul" or of the intellect (in its second stage) as God calling out to man; it is only within such a life that God is likely to be revealed to him, for otherwise man's existence in the world has no justification at all. True, at certain moments the Maggid attacks weakness of mind, as he does when at times he becomes sceptical concerning the true spiritual potential of man, but he nevertheless does not despair of advocating spirituality, and heeds the constant cry for elevation above corporeality, whose final consequence is a lifting up of the spirit in the meeting with the awesome mystery (*mysterium tremendum*, to use Otto's phrase) and the divine grace revealed within man. The Maggid compares man to a bird, who sings his (seemingly) "foolish" songs before the king, which rejoice and attract his heart. The sermon ends with the words, "Happy is the king who is thus praised in his home — thus that the body will be the home of the Holy One, blessed be He."

> "A woman is [created] for naught but beauty." That is, the Holy One created this physical world and created man within it in His image, so that he might reside within it, like the parable of the house of the nobles within the House of the Council, outside of which they write, "this is the home of so-and-so." And why did He do this? Do not the angels make up a third of the world, and [there are also] brilliant lights — that is, [there is] a very beautiful world. But even though this thing is very beautiful, like the parable of the bird who speaks before the king, and even though he speaks words of foolishness, the king has greater pleasure from this than from all of the words of wisdom which are spoken. Similarly about this contemptible matter: when he brings into his thoughts all the world, there descends upon them trembling and fear because of their fear of God, and they see a great shining light, and all this is revealed because of man, who is the lowest thing in the world, and he becomes very proud. And this is, "A woman is [created for naught but beauty]" — that is, the body is called woman, and because of the body there is born great beauty.[26]
>
> "Let us lift up our heart with our hands to God in heaven" [Lam. 3:41]. That is, on behalf of that which this *mizvah* does, we are aroused: if it is for this world, He brings abundance into this world; and if on behalf of the Next World, He brings about abundance in the next world. "Hands" refers to those *mizvot* which cause an abundance of giving, like the hand which he stretches out, and it is fitting that one only do that which brings pleasure to the Holy One, blessed be He, as in the parable of the speaking bird (see above). Thus God puts aside the song of all the worlds without end, and all the angels are silent in order to listen to the speech of man. And he says in His heart, "Who am I, lowly and contemptible [being], that I should bring about such great pleasure to the Holy One blessed be He, in all the worlds?" But he should not say that because of his lowliness the Holy One, blessed be He, does not receive pleasure, for on the contrary, He dwells with the one who is injured and of

26 Ibid.

> lowly spirit. And pleasure is a great thing — "then shall you rejoice in God" [Isa. 58:14] — and one must perform the *mizvot* for this thing. And this is, "Lift up our heart" — that is, our thoughts; "with our hands" — that is, the *mizvot*; that the *mizvot* be "to God in heaven." For David said, "the compassion of God fills the earth" [Ps. 33:5] — [that is,] it is a great compassion that God fills the earth, that in such a gross thing as this there is embodied a spiritual thing such as that. And Moses our teacher said, "who is a God in heaven ... " [Deut. 3:24]. "Who" (*mi*) refers to the non-apprehended Intellect, and this is the meaning of "who" — that is, the attribute of "who" is God (*ʾEl*), using a phrase indicative of compassion (*Ḥesed*).[27] "In the heavens" — this attribute is of such great brilliance that even the heavens could not bear it were it not for the [Divine] compassion. And this is the meaning of, "and the Holy One blessed be He nods with his head" [Berakhot 3a] — as in the analogy of one who shakes his bowl so that he may receive more. And this is what is stated in *Pirqei Heikhalot*: that when the Holy One, blessed be He, is sitting upon the throne, there descends upon the creatures (*ḥayot*) a silent fire; that is, when the Holy One dwells upon the words, there descends upon the vitality (*ḥayut*) of the person a fire of silence,[28] that is, a great fear, as in "the craftsman and the smith" [*he-ḥarash veha-masger*, II K. 24:14; wordplay on *ḥeresh*, "deaf" or "silent"], who become like deaf ones when they begin to say a matter of halakhah, and do not understand what the speaker says. Thus fear falls upon him, and he does not know where he is and does not see and does not hear, for the power of the corporeal is negated. And this is the meaning of "happy is the king who is thus praised in his house" [Berakhot, op. cit.] — that the body becomes the home of the Holy One, blessed be He, for he must pray with all his strength until he bursts out of corporeality and forgets himself, but all things are only the vitality of God, may He be blessed. All the acts of his thoughts will be on Him, and he will not even realize to what extent he prays with *kavvanah*, for if so he remembers himself. And all this comes about in one moment, in a flash, so that we see that he has transcended time.[29]

The poetic power of this passage is characteristic of the expressive force of the Maggid of Mezhirech, and is also typical of his feeling of ambivalence towards Heaven. On the one hand, one experiences great humility, to the point that one calls human prayer "a song of foolishness"; on the other hand, there is a feeling

27 *ʾEl* is a designation for the *Sefirah* of *Ḥesed*, used here symbolically as a literary figure. The sense is that at its height man's prayer is a reflection of the attribute of kindness (i.e. *ḥesed*) which man performs for God.

28 See the term *ʾesh ḥarishit* in *Merkavah Shelemah*, which the Maggid interprets here as applying to deafness (*ḥershut*).

29 *ʾOr ha-ʾEmet*, 2b. The entire passage, beginning with "Let us lift up our hearts with our hands," also appears (with the same wording) in MS. Jerusalem 1467, where it is presented as the teaching of the Maggid as found in the possession of R. Shmelke of Nikolsburg; see the beginning of Gate II, Chapter 7, p. 17b.

of spiritual "greatness" or "highness" in relation to the spirit. The Maggid said that the Holy One, blessed be He, appears to man just as the latter appears to Him; thus, man must come before God with his attribute of "highness," in order for Him to appear to man in turn in the fulness of His greatness.[30]

Let us return to the final section of the above passage: "all this comes about in one moment, in a flash; so that we see that he has transcended time." The state of loss of individual identity and of union with God is like the blink of an eye, being without duration in time. Spiritual apprehension, "which is above time," is depicted elsewhere as the supreme pleasure and as a sudden vision to which there is no comparison.[31]

These remarks apply to the intensity of the mystical experience. We shall return later in greater detail to a discussion of the metaphysical and psychological meaning of the concept of the "Nothing," and learn how human thought can bridge between these two states of existence — if they are indeed two.

Gershom Scholem discovered an important truth about Hasidic doctrine when he made the observation that transcendent concepts from the world of Kabbalah were given psychological embodiment in Hasidism.[32] This point is of great importance in our discussion of the quietistic phenomena within Hasidism, as the identification between Divine dynamism and spiritual activity within man was more than a matter of mere linguistic usage, drawing a parallel between psychological and metaphysical activity. The immanentist axiom in Hasidic doctrine transformed the external parallel between the two — i.e., "this corresponds to that" — into a quietistic doctrine which equated human activity with Divine activity. From this point of view, the complex activity within the world of the Sefirot, one inside the other, was transformed into the multi-layered activity of the Divine world immanent within man: that is to say, man speaks and thinks because "the World of Speech" and "the World of Thought" speak and think within him; man receives intellectual or mystical "flashes" of insight because the world of Divine intellect sends its beams and enlightens him by virtue of the identity between the

30 See *ᵓOr ha-ᵓEmet*, 68b, and *Maggid Devarav le-Yaᶜaqov*, §132, p. 229.

31 "... but the moon has pleasure when the light comes to it, and [this] pleasure is a high level, 'then shall you rejoice upon the Lord' [Isa. 58:14] (but the constant pleasure of the sun is not pleasure)." — *ᵓOr ha-ᵓEmet*, 12b. Cf. ibid., 70a: "He must draw himself towards *devequt* until he reaches pleasure (*taᶜanug*)." This *taᶜanug* is the happiness deriving from the "meeting" between the divine element within man with the Godhead which is outside of him. The idea itself remains problematical, and indeed constituted a problem in the world of Hasidism, in which the motif of the prohibition of the appetite for "mystical drunkenness" emerges from many sources.

32 See the article by G. Scholem, "The Unconscious and the Pre-Existence of the Intellect in Hasidic Literature" (Heb.), in his *Devarim be-go*, pp. 351–360 [originally published in *Hagut; teshurah le-Sh. H. Bergman bi-meloᵓt lo shishim shanah* (Jerusalem, 1944), pp. 141–151].

transcendent and immanent world. In other words, the immanentist outlook which states that "the whole world is full of His glory" served as the revolutionary background for the identification of psychology with metaphysics. Accordingly, human speech and human thought are two stages of the "raiment" of the spirit, the latter being unable to exist in disembodied fashion even in the Divine realm. Even the Godhead itself apprehends itself and is known to itself through a flash of an eye, in which the element of "its thought" and "its speech" return to Nothing. True, it undergoes an eternal and permanent process of transformation into the nothing and in the creation of Being from Nothing, unlike the case with man. Man engages in a prolonged and active battle of negation of the "garments," in the form of speech and thought, in order to receive that same enlightenment and insight from the world of the Divine Nothing, where it is found in an immanent way — but the path to this is difficult and tiring.

Those stages of divine existence which are depicted as Divine speech and thought (or, to use Sefirotic language, *Binah*[33] and *Malkhut*) are nullified before one another when they are elevated to meet their total nullification in the Nothing. In the course of their return to "Being" — in an image which may be compared to spiritual vessels or "letters" of thought and speech — they are likely to be revealed and to pour out their influence upon the person who is ready for this revelation at that moment. One who knows how to "purify" his organs of speech and thought is deserving of and liable to merit that transfer of the divine vessels of speech and thought into his own vessels, which become translucent and open to the divine influx. This is in brief the meaning of true prayer, whose words are merely vehicles which are liable "to shine and to give light," in the words of the Besht.

In light of this situation, we may understand the significance of the repeated comments in the Maggid's teaching that "he should think that the whole world is full of His glory." The quietistic interpretation of this is: the measure of true indifference is to know that God alone acts. We shall return to this question further on in our discussion.

I would like to give some illustrations of the above remarks concerning the stages of the divine worlds of speech and thought, which are nullified in the Divine Nothingness through an endless process.[34] The Maggid states:

33 In the Maggid's teaching, "thought" (*maḥshavah*) is not identical with "wisdom" (*ḥokhmah*), as the latter is designated as "the Nothing" (*ʾayin*); cf. n. 36 below.

34 It is interesting that this parable, intended to depict the metaphysical world, uses terminology which suits the human psychological world. The transition from one world to another is extraordinarily natural, to the extent that the original Kabbalistic approach is obscured.

The Torah came out of wisdom, for there is a written Torah and Oral Torah.[35] The written Torah is called the World of Thought,[36] as in the verse, "write them upon the tablet of your heart" [Prov. 3:3], while the World of Speech is called the Oral Torah, whose master is the mouth, as stated above. And the connection [between the two] is called the Concealed World (*ᶜalma de-itkasya*), for no one knows what is in his neighbor's heart, for only if he enters into the World of Thought is he then able to know what is in the heart and thought of his fellow. And the World of Thought is a unity in all the worlds ... and thought is called the World of Freedom, for Kingship (*Malkhut*) is equated with speech, as in, "Where the word of the king is, there is power, and 'Who' (*mi*) shall tell him what to do" [Eccl. 8:4]. And the speech of the king is like action, for whatever he speaks of doing, his servants do, and "at the word of God the heavens were created" [Ps. 33:6] ... But by means of thought the kingship is negated from existence, for the servant does not know what is in the heart of his master ... Now let us return to the former matter: speech is a garment of thought, for when a person speaks his thoughts are revealed, and even in deeds there is wisdom. For example, when we see the deeds of a craftsman, we understand that the craftsman is wise. We find that there is hidden wisdom in this vessel, so that in thought there must be the pre-existence of the intellect (*qadmut ha-sekhel*), which raises thought [in order] to think. And the [so-called] *Maskil* cannot be apprehended, for it is Wisdom (*Ḥokhmah*), and one understands it with [the attribute] of Understanding (*Binah*) [i.e., which is a lower level]. And thought is [written] in letters, which are vessels, while Wisdom is above the letters, and no vessels are able to contain it. And this is, "and wisdom from whence [*me-ᵓayin*; or, "from Nothing"] shall be found?" [Job 28:12] — this refers to Torah, that is, the intellect [i.e., *Binah*] which emerges from wisdom (*Ḥokhmah*),[37] meaning, from the "enlightened" one (*Maskil*). And He, may He be blessed, contracted Himself in the Torah; therefore, when one speaks words of Torah or of prayer, he should speak them with all his strength, for one thereby brings about unity with Him, may He be blessed, for all of his strength is in the letter, and He, may He be blessed, dwells in the letter. And he should think in this manner: for example, when he says, "Abbaye said," the letters of the name "Abbaye" are his vitality. We find that he connects his own vitality to the vitality of Abbaye, through the words of Abbaye. And the [particular] law which he recites is [the embodiment of] the intellect

35 The "World of Speech" (*ᶜolam ha-dibbur*) is a designation used in Kabbalah for the *Sefirah* of *Malkhut*, which is also known as "the Oral Torah" (*Torah she-beᶜal peh*). On the "World of Speech" in Hasidic thought, see Ch. 9 below.

36 A symbol for the world of *Binah*, not used in Kabbalah. The term used for the Written Torah is the *Sefirah* of *Tifᵓeret*; the heart is *Binah*, represented by the Written Torah, which is different from divine wisdom (*Ḥokhmah*). The latter identification, which more closely fits the Kabbalistic tradition, is impossible here, because for the Maggid *Ḥokhmah* is the divine Nothing, totally undifferentiated, without any "letters" ["signs"] of thought; it is the negation of all thought having any content.

37 Based upon *Zohar*, *Yitro*.

> of Abbaye, so that he connects his intellect to that of Abbaye: for he reflects upon that law in his intellect, and his intellect comes from the World of Intellect, which is a limb of the Shekhinah. And when he speaks with awe and love, he uplifts it and gives life to Abbaye, for he brings the mind of Abbaye into his body. So the person who is a scholar ought to be God-fearing, for he is a limb of the Shekhinah ...[38]

It is astounding to what extent the boundaries between the discussion of Divine thought on the transcendent plane and the psychological discussion are blurred. The first part of this homily begins with the negation of the realm of Divine speech within the realm of thought, from which it is sustained, while the second part discusses the identity of human and divine thought, not only as an expression of parallel action, but as an identity of their essence. Divine thought likewise stems from "the pre-existence of the Intellect" — i.e., from *Ḥokhmah* ("Wisdom") — which does not reach its unified source in terms of its own particularity. Human thought, which likewise derives from the pre-existence of the intellect,[39] achieves its ultimate embodiment in the Infinite, which resides in the letters of prayer and Torah.

Many homilies concerning the nullification of human speech within human thought may be found in the remarks brought in the name of the Maggid of Mezhirech, which repeatedly stress the process whereby a person progresses from speech to thought, in which speech is no longer possible because the particular is absorbed in the "general" during the psychological process of thinking. To this end, man is also expected to make the effort to negate his psychological powers and to concentrate upon "one thought" alone — namely, that "the whole world is full of His glory." The unity of Being — which is the Godhead — can be apprehended by means of the intellectual stage of thinking, when man is able to nullify the other powers of his soul. From this point of view, speech is merely the point of departure for meditative concentration, which is of necessity nullified in the higher stages of meditation. It follows that mental prayer is a necessary stage in the spiritualization of prayer, and that vocal prayer is of secondary significance in the psychological process undergone by man on the way from multiplicity to unity.

The Maggid has the following to say about the relationship between speech and thought:

> "Glorify the Lord with Me ..."[Ps. 34:4]. "Where the word of the king is, is power, and who may say to him, what do you do?" [Eccl. 8:4]. Kingship [*Malkhut*] is speech,[40]

38 *ʾOr ha-ʾEmet*, 15b–16a.

39 This point is discussed at length in the homily in *Maggid Devarav le-Yaʿaqov*, §175, p. 274; cf. the above-cited article by Scholem, "The Unconscious and the Pre-Existence of the Intellect."

40 One again sees here the blurring of the border between metaphysics and psychology. He discusses human speech and must relate to the symbolic system of the Sefirot; but, as we mentioned, this is

> and thought is a higher stage than that of speech, as in "the heart of kings and princes is in the hand of God." And when the World of Speech ascends to be included in the World of Thought, it is not visible at all, but only the World of Thought appears greater, as it were; and this is "Increase (*gadlu*) God ..." Speech says that you should glorify [Him] with me.[41]

Elsewhere, the Maggid preached the identical homily, with a slight variation, in connection with the world of the Sephirot; here, it is said concerning man's psychological world. This describes a kind of "expanded consciousness" of thought, which includes the World of Speech, albeit at the same time the World of Speech is negated in its particularity,[42] so that the enunciation of the letters becomes superfluous. The Maggid speaks elsewhere of the seamless transition between speech and thought,[43] while here he stresses the sharp discontinuity between the two, in which speech prevents the concentration of the spirit, and thus the possibility of true understanding, which he interprets as transcending time, like that intuitive glimpse which is the deepest wish of the man of spirit. The stage of speech remains within the confines of "dissipated intellect," while thought is oriented towards the world of unity which is beyond time. This spiritual motivation seems to me to be the true reason for the pushing of study to the margins of religious life, as the Maggid did not see any reasonable way of reconciling discursive with intuitive thought, which is more easily done with regard to matters of prayer. The following remarks do not seem to support any other interpretation:

> "This is the Torah, when a man dies in a tent" [Numb. 19:14]. Our rabbis taught, "the Torah is only sustained by one who kills himself over it" [Berakhot 43b]. That is, when a person speaks he is unable to understand by himself how and whether he understands a thing clearly; he will then be unable to speak properly and the word will be dead. And, contrariwise, the understanding will be dead, so to speak. For that thing which does not rule because of another is dead ... And *Mi* ("Who") is called *Binah*, because [about] what I understand, I ask "Who is this?" but if he does not understand, it is not relevant for him to ask, "Who?" Therefore, *mi* alludes to [the Supernal] Mother, so that one who wishes to study Torah must do so aloud with his voice and his speech; therefore, he must kill the *mi*, that is, [the Sefirot of] *Neẓaḥ Hod Yesod*, of understanding.[44]

not seen as an analogy, but as actual identity, the Shekhinah itself speaking from his throat. These points will be further clarified below.

41 *ᵓOr ha-ᵓEmet*, 3b.

42 As the "World of Speech" is unable to incorporate the "World of Thought," as in the words of R. Ḥayyim Ḥaykl of Amdur.

43 "From speech he shall proceed to thought, and from thence to nothing..." —*ᵓOr ha-ᵓEmet*, 41b.

44 Dov Baer of Mezhirech, *ᵓOr Torah*, 76a.

The Maggid of Mezhirech also acknowledges the creation of a unique situation in which a person is able to continue to speak words without thereby disturbing the concentration of his thought. This situation creates a kind of automatic speech which no longer has any connection or relation, conscious to man, to his world of thought, as the distance between speech and thought has grown to such an extent that his speech no longer disturbs him: it is therefore not likely to disturb the intensive continuity of his thought. This does not mean that the words spoken in this situation are not rooted in thought, but that they lack any conscious connection with his thought. The Maggid does not believe there to be any activity in the world which is not sustained by an inner spirit, even though it may be that it has not reached man's consciousness, and therefore does not disturb the continuity of his conscious thought. Only the thought concerning "letters" is conscious to man,[45] but there is also a "hidden" form of thought which fructifies automatic speech. He says the following:

> Or he shall say, "How goodly are your tents O Jacob" [Num. 24:5; used as the opening sentence of a section of the Morning Service]. That is, "tent" (*ᵓohel*) is written with the same letters as [the name] Leah [in Hebrew], and there is no break [discontinuity] save in the letters, but not in the [pure] thought, but only in that thought which is needful of letters.[46] Meaning, that everything which is [verbally] articulated, prior to being articulated must first be present in the thought, and it is very hidden, for they are unable to speak save for those letters which are the attribute of [being] in the thought. And we see that he speaks (*medaber*) this, and in his thought there is another thing (*mi-davar*),[47] only that his thought of articulation is very hidden.[48]

It seems to me that the Besht's saying (which I have already mentioned) — "when I attach my thought to the Creator, I allow my mouth to speak whatever it wishes"[49]

45 This distinction between thought which includes "letters" (the letters of thought) and thought without "letters" likewise applies to the transcendent world, as at times he designates thought as *Ḥokhmah*, while thought involving "letters" is called *Binah*. Nor is that thought which is without "letters" able to comprehend the thought which is above it, because the latter is so-to-speak its unconscious counterpart within the Divine world.

46 See also *ᵓOr ha-ᵓEmet*, 12a, in which there is no "break" between the "attached" thought — which is beyond "letters" — and its discursive contents. This is an instantaneous continuity, which arrives at unity, and therefore has no "break."

47 The total split between thought and speech within a certain state indicates another source for that same speech, which is not identical with the source of his thought at that same moment.

48 *ᵓOr Torah*, 78b; cf. *Liqqutei Yeqarim*, 10b, where it is only alluded to with the words, "a hint suffices for the wise."

49 *Maggid Devarav le-Yaᶜaqov*, Introduction, p. 4; cf. the same saying brought in the name of the Besht, *Liqqutei Yeqarim*, 2b.

— may be explained along similar lines. From this stance, it is clear that the text of the prayer is of no importance *per se*. Once he has reached the higher levels of meditation, it does not matter whether the individual is silent or speaks, as what is requisite for the matter is his silence, while his speech may even be automatic speech.[50]

Concerning silence, the Maggid repeatedly emphasized (as the Besht already had done) that:

> ... thus in prayer he is able to engage in the service of prayer to God, so that his service is not visible to people at all. He makes no motion whatever of his limbs, but only within his inward soul it is burning in his heart, and he will cry out in silence because of his excitement in this matter, so that his inner service shall be greater than the service apparent from his limbs.[51]

The process of becoming cut off from speech in prayer is described as follows:

> From the beginning the body of the word shall speak, and afterwards he shall place the soul into the words; and he must initially arouse himself in his body with all his strength, so that the power of the soul may shine within him [in the person himself], as it says in the *Zohar* [III:168a], "If a log does not burn, he shall stir it and then it will [burn] brightly." Thereafter, he may serve through thought alone, without the body. At times, when a person is attached to the supernal world, to the Creator, blessed be He, he must guard himself not to perform any motion, even in his body, so as not to nullify his attachment ...[52]

Service through thought alone, without a body, explicitly implies silence, without any speech at all: "For when he is silent, he is able to attach himself to the world of thought, which is *Ḥokhmah* ..."[53] For the same reason, namely, the need to nullify all of one's senses in order to attain that *devequt* which is "above time," the Maggid recommended that a person close his eyes and remove them from the Siddur when he feels that he is rising above the level of verbal prayer.[54]

The Maggid distinguished two different stances during contemplative prayer. The former is that of total silence, which accompanies the peak of the ecstatic state,

50 For the connection of this matter with "the Shekhinah speaking within him," see below, towards the end of Chap. 8.

51 *Liqqutei Yeqarim*, 14a and ᵓ*Or Torah*, 160b. The limbs of course also include "the speech of the lips."

52 *Liqqutei Yeqarim*, 1d.

53 Ibid., 13a.

54 "When a person is on a low level, it is better that he pray from the Siddur, as by virtue of his seeing the letters, the prayer is recited with greater *kavvanah*. But when he is attached to the upper world, it is better that he close his eyes, so that his seeing not prevent him from becoming attached to the upper world." — *Liqqutei Yeqarim*, 1c.

when he "cries out in silence because of his enthusiasm." The latter is a similar psychological state, but one in which there is still the element of "recitation" of the prayers, which appears to one who sees it from without as a completely automatic recitation without any involvement on the part of the one praying. The two stances described above exemplify our earlier statement that "recitation with one's lips" is in no way an indication that "his mouth and heart are one." On the contrary, he has attained a spiritual level in which "his mouth and his heart" (i.e. his thoughts) are no longer the same. In the one case he no longer speaks at all, while in the other only his mouth speaks.

> At times one must serve God with the soul alone, that is, in his thought, while the body stands in its place, so that it not become ill when he uses it a great deal. And at times a person may recite the prayer with love and fear and great excitement without any motion, and it appears to another person that he recites those words without any *devequt*. And a person can do this when he is very attached to God; then a person can serve Him with his soul alone, with very great love. And this service is better and goes with greater speed and becomes attached to God more so than that prayer which is visible upon the limbs from without, and the *qelippot* have no hold upon this prayer, for it is entirely inward.[55]

The Maggid calls this transition from verbal prayer to prayer within thought alone the state of "forgetting the words" — that is, a kind of nullification of the particular memory within the process of contemplation. He explains in these terms the sound of the shofar, which is a more spiritual expression of prayer than the speech of the lips, because it includes all the meanings and contents of the specific words, and simultaneously is vacant of any contents.

> A parable for before the sounding [of the Shofar]. A great and renowned king sent his sons to trap some game, and the sons lost the way and cried out, so that perhaps their father would hear them, and they were not answered. And they said in their hearts, "Perhaps we have forgotten the language of our father, and therefore he does not hear our cry; so let us cry out in sound without speech." And they took counsel among themselves, to send one person to cry out, and they warned him, "See and understand that all of us are dependent upon you."
>
> And this is the analogy: the Holy One, blessed be He, sent us to raise up the holy sparks, and we have lost the way to our Father. And perhaps we have forgotten the speech of our Father, so we are unable to pray with words; therefore we send you, the shofar-blower, to arouse mercy upon us through sound without speech, and see and be warned that all of us depend on you.[56]

55 *ᵓOr ha-ᵓEmet*, 79b.

56 *ᵓOr ha-ᵓEmet*, 7b; further on in these remarks, the idea is discussed — which I shall expound below — that the one who truly emits the sound from the shofar is the Holy One, blessed be He. This quotation also appears in MS. Jerusalem 1467 (R. Shmelke), fo. 20c, in the words of the Maggid.

Between the lines, one can read here the same stance which the Maggid did not explicitly identify when he spoke about literal, petitionary prayer.[57] It seems to me that his intention here is quite clear: it is only spiritual prayer which has any real meaning, and a person cannot find the way from his own concrete personality to God save by way of the spirit, for it is there that God is revealed to him, and the meaning of "hearing of prayer" has only a spiritual meaning.[58]

One should not infer from the Maggid's remarks that he advocated the abolishing of "speaking with one's lips" during prayer in practice, as he was not one to say anything contrary to the formal halakhah.[59] The Hasidic revolution is not to be measured in terms of struggle against the formal world of the halakhah, but by the power of the spiritualist elements within it to reshape the existing system of values. Nor is it my intention here to suggest a superficial conservative formula for understanding Hasidism, as it is in the nature of such a pneumatic phenomenon to be unsettled to the extent that the objects which it refashions are liable at any moment to be subject to outbursts of the spirit. Hasidism reached a certain cross-roads under its spiritual impulse, from which it continued no further. All of those external outbursts which were demanded by its own logic were restrained by its own hands, and perhaps in no small measure also under the influence of the "cries" of the Mitnaggedim.

To return to our concrete question: the Maggid advocated a spiritual life removed from this world, so that the "utterance of the lips" became transformed for him into lip service. Under the spiritualistic impulse, even such well-known concepts of the world of Judaism as self-sacrifice (*mesirut nefesh*) were transformed into concepts bearing pneumatic contents. Thus, in the case of this concept, it no longer referred to the willingness to engage in a physical sacrifice under the pressure of external circumstances, but of the power of the spirit to negate the feeling of physical existence.[60]

It is clear that the spiritual contribution of Hasidic prayer is not expressed through the abolition, in practice, of the concrete element in Jewish prayer. The same holds true with respect to its relation to the concrete in general, even if on the purely theoretical plane there was a certain break with the concrete framework,

57 See above, Chapter 6.

58 The continuation of the passage which speaks about God as speaking from within the person who spiritualizes himself leaves no doubt that this spiritual interpretation of things is correct. Here, the spiritual motif connects with the quietistic one.

59 See Maimonides, *Mishneh Torah, Hilkhot Tefillah* 5:9.

60 See *Ẓavaʾat ha-Riva"sh*, 10: "Therefore I wish to afflict myself, so as to offer myself as a sacrifice before Him"; cf. *Peri ha-ʾAreẓ*, 88.

in the course of its efforts to bring light into the "dark letter" in prayer. This was the case generally with regard to the negation of the concrete during the course of uplifting the sparks hidden within it. The change which took place in the concept of "prayer with *kavvanah*," in which the intention is directed "above," to strip off the spiritual from the corporeal and to arrive at "pure" Divine thought — this change fixed the stance of the spirit in the Hasidic system, transforming the phrase, "his lips and his heart are one" into empty rhetoric, albeit the Maggid himself did not make use of this formula at all.

Chapter Eight

Divine Immanence and the Question of Prophecy

The question of mental prayer was part of the Hasidic milieu from an early date, and was already discussed favorably by Menaḥem Mendel of Bar, one of the members of the Besht's original circle.[1] This was in fact not a new theory which entirely negated the value of spoken prayer, but a kind of "allowance" thereof — and at that only "for the present" — bearing a quietistic character. R. Jacob Joseph of Polonnoye, the author of *Toldot Yaᶜaqov Yosef*, quotes the following in the name of R. Menaḥem Mendel:

> One may also explain this according to what I heard from the holy Rabbi, the Maggid of the community of Bar, explaining the talmudic passage,[2] "There were four kings: whatever one asked, the other did not ask [(i.e. each did less than his predecessor). They were: David, Assa, Jehosaphat, and Hezekiah] ... [3] Jehoshaphat said, 'I have not the strength either [to kill or to pursue (my enemies), but I] sing songs [(i.e. of praise to God) and You (God) will act] ... [Hezekiah said: I have not strength either to kill or to pursue or to sing songs, but] I sit [sic! sleep] upon my bed and You shall kill them.'" And this is an astonishing matter; but he explained that a person may unify the Holy One blessed be He on all of his levels, whether in act or in speech, such as prayer and study. And when he is unable to unify Him even in speech, then he ought to unite Him in thought, as in the mystery of, "To You silence is praise" [Ps. 65:2]. For even in life and on this level the Shekhinah is [present] there at that time, and he should also accept this joyfully, for it is a unification, as said, and there is no unification through quarreling [4] — and understand.

1 Concerning him, see the article by J. Weiss, "The Beginnings of the Hasidic Path" (Heb.), *Ẓion* 16, nos. 3–4 (1951), pp. 46–105, particularly the second half of the article.

2 The reference is to Lamentations Rabbati, *Petiḥta*, sec. 30.

3 *Toldot Yaᶜaqov Yosef*, beginning of *Parashat Shemot*, p. 36b. The phrase here, "through quarrelling," evidently means without inner harmony between thought and speech. This practice was known as an extremely difficult one according to other sources as well, but in those cases the solution was not always in the direction of [performing] unification of thought, but instead imposed the obligation to struggle as far as the person was able. "And behold, this [i.e. spiritual service] is a very difficult thing; nevertheless every person is obligated to pray in accordance with his ability, in mind and in thought of the greatness of God, be His Name blessed" (without sacrificing, of course, the struggle with speech) — Kalonymus Kalman ha-Levi, *Maᵓor va-Shemesh*, 31a.

4 See above, n. 3 in this chapter.

From the remarks of the *Toldot*, it would seem that such a "question," concerning the need for speech in principle, was known in Hasidic circles. It is clear that the answer to this question was to be self-evident, albeit not at all immanent:

> It seems to me that I heard them asking: As the Holy One blessed be He knows man's thoughts and his needs, why must man utter words while praying? Is it not sufficient to have thought itself?" And R. Nahman of Kosow answered that, by means of speech, vessels are created through which the influx of blessing is brought down, etc. — and see on this in my writings elsewhere. And from this may be understood [the use of the phrase,] "And you shall serve" [*va-ᶜavadtem* — i.e., God; Deut. 11:16] in the plural — that is, through matter and form, so that speech may be by means of the vessels of the body, and thought by means of the form. For it is not enough to have it with only one — [namely,] thought — alone ...[5]

The obligation to engage in verbal prayer — at least at the beginning of one's spiritual path — is based upon two assumptions, according to the Maggid. One is the perception of the entire cosmos as a chain, no one of whose links may be bypassed, from the most corporeal to the most spiritual. Within this system, prayer provides the ideal conditions for the raising of the material to the spiritual, an obligation that is implicit in the concept of a human mission upon the earth. For this reason, no Jewish person is excused from passing through the "letters," either of the spirit or of matter. The Divine spirit is itself present within the overall paradox of individual existence as spirit and matter, seeking its own expression specifically within matter; therefore, "[divine] thought longs to come into the voice and into speech."[6] This "longing," which is fundamentally dialectic (as all physical existence seeks to ascend to the spirit), brings man as well into a dialectical situation, in that it requires "speech" in order to become free of it, in the course of entering it.

The second assumption is based upon the first. This is the unequivocal statement that, during the stage of abandoning conscious speech in which man "is turned into nothing," the Godhead itself acts and speaks from within his throat. Man speaks here against his will — although "he" no longer really speaks at all, as his conscious personal identity is only that of the divine "World of Thought," which is a more sublime and spiritual stage than that of the "World of Speech." He moves from one condition to another via the "Nothing," just as one thing is transformed into another via the simple laws of nature. From the very outset, human speech is a metaphysical act of liberation of the "divine speech" within man, which is acquired

5 *Toldot Yaᶜaqov Yosef*, p. 62b, *Mishpaṭim*.

6 *Maggid Devarav le-Yaᶜaqov*, §105, p. 184, and *ᵓOr ha-ᵓEmet*, 1b.

by means of meditation. The early traditions identifying human with divine speech are cited by the Maggid in the name of the Besht:

> It is fitting that he be shamed before the words that he speaks, for the World of Speech is the World of Fear (*yirʾah*), and the Shekhinah as-it-were contracts itself and resides in the speech, as we saw in *Sefer Yeẓirah*, "he fixed them within [His] mouth." And it says, "O Lord open my mouth" [Ps. 51:17] — that is, so that the Shekhinah should hear, for if the Evil Urge should lead him astray, Heaven forbid ... From whence this interpretation? Has not our teacher Moses, *z"l*, said, "I am the Lord your God" [Num. 15:41]? For certainly the Holy One blessed be He Himself said this, and the word itself requires this, as the Besht said, "send forth your word, and your mission shall be done." He should think that the World of Speech is speaking through him, and that without it it is impossible to speak, as it is written, "O Lord open my mouth" — referring to the Shekhinah. Nor can thought exist except by means of the World of Thought, for it is no more than a shofar: whatever one blows into it, that same sound is emitted, but if the shofar blower removes himself from it, then it no longer brings forth any sound. So with the absence of Him, may He be blessed, he is unable to speak or to think.[7]

On the basis of this passage, one may still entertain some doubt as to whether these remarks concerning the immanent concept of the Shekhinah — "which contracts itself, so to speak," and resides within speech — were made by way of analogy. But the appearance of the Shekhinah as the active "root" of man, when he succeeds in destroying the "powers" which stem from this root, leaves no room for doubt that this is a definite attempt to see the Shekhinah as a dynamic factor within the human soul (and not only metaphorically), which only appears when man is capable of overcoming ("killing") the external personality. These are his words:[8]

> And the second level [the first was called *yirʾah* (fear), which corresponds to the *mysterium tremendum*] is called Shame (*bushah*) — that is, [to know] that his *potentia* and attributes come from the supernal levels and attributes and thereafter dwell in him, and that all his *potentia* are as nothing. And this is the primary source of his vitality: that his levels become as nothing, and his roots dwell upon him.[9] And this is, "He who wishes to live, must put himself to death." And this is the Sabbath, which

7 *ʾOr ha-ʾEmet*, 1b.

8 They are cited in *Shemuʿah Ṭovah* in the name of the Baʿal Shem Tov, but I have already noted that stylistically they seem to me more like the words of the Maggid — but this is not the place to discuss this point. It is not impossible that the theories themselves were already to be found in the Besht's teaching.

9 It would seem that the phrase "his levels" should be interpreted as referring to the human aspect, as from the metaphysical aspect he only begins to live when his "roots" become active.

> is called the Sabbath [because], even though to us it is [perceived as] a supernal level, compared with the supernal levels it is like a lowly level, for it receives influx and dwells upon the lower levels. Therefore it is called Sabbath, for rest is to be found there.[10]

The Maggid elsewhere depicts the psychological condition of "greatness" (*gadlut*) as an expansion of the spark of the Shekhinah present in the human heart, for then the "spark" (*niẓoẓ* — i.e., apex) becomes active and speaks "in place of" man.

> At times there is also smallness (*qatnut*) above, in the Small Face (*Ze*ᶜ*ir* ᵓ*Anpin*), but by virtue of that same smallness one may come to greatness (*gadlut*). Just as, if there is one spark left in the ambers, one may blow upon it greatly until it becomes a great fire, but [in the case] where there is no small spark left he is unable to stir up the fire. Thus, if he does not cling continually to Him, may He be blessed, with a small thought, his soul becomes completely extinguished. Sometimes when the holy spark of the Shekhinah within his soul expands, and it literally speaks the words which are in his mouth, it [then] seems as though he does not speak, for the words emerge from his mouth of themselves — and that is a great level. And we also see the opposite on the Other Side (*Siṭra* ᵓ*Aḥra*) with regard to crazy people.[11]

Such formulae as "your soul is the limbs of the Shekhinah"[12] or "the Shekhinah is embodied in him"[13] (i.e., in man) frequently appear in the teaching of the Maggid. We have already seen that these are not simply figures of speech, but that they reflect an understanding in principle of the pantheistic or immanentist faith. It has long been noted that the pantheistic element provided the ground for the growth of quietistic doctrines.[14] As if to prove this thesis, one finds in the Maggid's remarks concerning "the whole world is full of glory" serving as the basis for the idea of "equanimity" — i.e., knowing that God is the exclusive actor. Such formulae also appear in the writings of the disciples of the Maggid, sometimes in theoretical language and sometimes in the form of a parable, which was the most commmonly accepted form of expression in Hasidic circles. What created the ambivalent ethical relationship was the immanentist element. The feeling of fear and awe of the greatness of the Creator did not derive from his transcendent distance, but precisely from his immanent closeness.

10 *Shemu*ᶜ*ah Ṭovah*, 74a; this clearly implies an identity between the Sabbath and the Shekhinah, which is the "root" of active man and is revealed in the "resting" of the *potentia* of his soul.

11 *Liqqutei Yeqarim*, 12c.

12 ᵓ*Or Torah*, 83a. Cf., on the source of this idea in Kabbalah, G. Scholem, *On the Mystical Shape of the Godhead* (New York, 1991), p. 160ff. [originally in German: *Von der Mystischen Gestalt der Gottheit* (Zürich, 1962), p. 170.]

13 ᵓ*Or Torah*, 159a.

14 See Pourrat, "Quietisme," sec. 9, and Weiss, "Via passiva in early Hasidism," p. 137.

This feeling of closeness opened two paths: one which aroused feelings of nothingness and self-annihilation; the other, in which man is called upon to act and to give account of his spiritual mission in order to become transformed into a vessel fit to incorporate the Divine reality which wishes to act within him. The Mitnaggedim did not understand, or did not want to properly understand, the profundities of this dual approach of Hasidism, and protested superficially against its "arrogance towards heaven."[15] It is true that one cannot reasonably argue that the Hasidic social ethos developed specifically from the immanentist posture. Such a teaching is not reflected in any of the theoretical writings of Hasidic doctrine, and perhaps not only by chance.[16] But if one can test an ethos by the stance taken towards God and the world, the sense of life which flowed from the immanentist outlook was one which implanted a kind of daring within humility towards the Creator, and a sense of strength based upon the stance of abnegation towards the world. The same dual relation towards God is expressed in the following remarks of Issachar Baer of Zloczow:

> "And Judah drew close to him and said, please my master" [Gen. 44:18], etc.[17] To understood this, we shall first explain what is said in the Sabbath prayers: "There is none like You and none apart from You." For it says in the Talmud, "A person cannot pray unless he makes himself like nothing"[18] — that is, that he thinks of the greatness of the Creator and His supremacy, and that no place is empty of Him and everything is His divinity, and apart from Him all is nothingness and vanity. And each person, when he wishes to pray in this aspect, must first think of the greatness of the Creator and [then] begin. But when he begins to think about the greatness of the Creator, a great fear falls upon him, saying, "Who am I, a mere man and contemptible as I am, a putrid drop, to pray before the great, high and exalted King." But afterwards, when he thinks further about the greatness of the Creator and realizes that there is no place empty of Him and that he is himself naught but a portion of the Godhead, then, to the contrary, he will pray with great ardor, wishing to cling to his root, in saying that I myself am also part of the Divinity. And this is the meaning of "there is none like You" — [i.e.] that there is no created being which can compare with Your greatness,

15 This argument was a matter of principle for the Gaon of Vilna. See S. Dubnow, *Toldot ha-Ḥasidut*, p. 247.

16 The quietistic stream was completely contemptuous of ethical teaching, a fact clearly reflected in the Church's arguments against the quietists. See Bossuet, p. 242, sec. iii.

17 This verse was already explained by the Maggid himself as applying to the passive existence of God within man; see *Kitvei Qodesh*, 10a.

18 I have not found this passage in the Talmud, but it may be a paraphrase of Taᶜanit 8b: "A person's prayer is not heard unless he places his soul in his hands," or a conflation of the saying of R. Johanan in Soṭah 21b, "The words of Torah are not preserved except by one who makes himself as if he is not."

> and all the creatures are lowly compared to You, and are unworthy to praise You with praises and hymns. But afterwards he says that, on the contrary, there is nothing apart from You, for there is no place empty of Him, and he himself is also part of the Godhead and is fit to cling to God. And this is the meaning of, "And Judah drew close" — i.e. when the Jewish person [lit., "man of Judah"] draws close to pray before the Holy One, blessed be He; "and says" — that is, thinks in his heart; and he must come in this aspect [to know] that there is no place empty of Him and that "You are in me, my Lord" [*bi Adoni* — usually translated, "O my Lord" or "I pray thee, my Lord"] — that within me there is also a portion of his divinity; and then he can pray — and understand this.[19]

Between the lines of this and similar passages, one can perceive the struggle within Hasidism between a pneumatic, spiritualistic ethics and a traditional ethos which values the performance of the *mizvot* and the avoidance of transgression — even if the boundaries of this confrontation are not always evident. The fact that, from the pantheistic view-point, one could argue the irrelevance of the concept of sin is not unimportant, and again reminds us of the type of argument put forward by classical quietism.

> The essence of the service of the Creator and all acts of *mizvah* are that he come to the attribute of humility — that is, to the attribute of knowledge — to understand that all his *potentia* and intellect and powers are only because of the portion of the divine within him, and that he is naught but a conduit for the attributes of the Holy One blessed be He and for the end which brings about humility — that is, the awe of [His] sublimity. For [if] he understands that there is no place empty of Him, etc., he will then come to the aspect of Nothing, which is the attribute of modesty, as said above ... And this is the meaning of the verse, "I, even I, am He who erases your transgressions for My sake, and I shall not remember your sins" [Isa. 43:25]. For we have already mentioned that there are three levels of repentance: the fear of punishment, and thereafter the love [of God], and thereafter he comes to the awe of [Divine] sublimity. But in these three kinds of repentance mentioned, his knowledge is not yet complete to understand that everything is a part of the Godhead, but [he thinks] nevertheless that he has an independent essence, to which the word "I" is pertinent. But this is not the case of the higher repentance, in which there is no place empty of Him,[20] etc., for then he arrives at the aspect of "He" [as in "I am He" in the above verse], [in which] He is concealed, for he [himself] has no essence, as if he were incorporated within the Creator blessed be He. And by means of that [form of] repentance, there is no longer any place for the accuser to stand against him, and his sins are transformed into virtues ... For in two forms of repentance, his essence has

19 Issachar Baer of Zloczow, *Mevasser Ẓedeq* (Berdichev, 1817), p. 8b–c.

20 The sin was only forgiven him by means of "supernal repentance," which is itself the mixing with the "He" and the unification with God.

> not been negated, but only upon the third level is He called "Him" — i.e., in the third person[21] — and this is by means of the "upper" repentance. And then He erases your transgressions, because I am in every place, and have no place. And then I will not even remember your sins which were done unintentionally ... And this is the meaning of the verse, "And Moses hid his face" [Ex. 3:6], because Moses went from fear of Him to the hiding of his [own] face[22] — that is, that he perceived no [divine] essence, for everything was a part of the Godhead ...[23]

There are not many sources in Hasidism which explicitly teach that the responsibility for "sins" devolves upon God.[24] In his article concerning the "Via passiva" in Hasidism, Joseph Weiss mentions R. Pinḥas of Korets as the sole representative of this viewpoint, following an allusion to this in *Ḥayyei Muhar"an.* R. Pinḥas indeed speaks about God's indirect responsibility for man's sins, although he primarily stresses the positive aspect of the subject — namely, that God also prevents man from sinning. But Weiss quite justifiably felt that R. Pinḥas does not belong among the "metaphysical" thinkers within Hasidism, and that his entire outlook is even explicitly and clearly anti-metaphysical. His approach to the question of sin likewise indicates a more ethical, "popular" understanding of the meaning of such "events."[25] On the other hand, in R. Yeivi we find such explicit statements such as:

21 This term is used in Kabbalah for *Keter*. Here, it seems to allude to *Binah*, the World of Repentance, which in Hasidic teaching is also the World of Thought; when he arrives at that level, he and *Binah* in any event become one, and everything is forgiven him and nullified in its essence.

22 It is interesting to note the use of the metaphor, "hiding of the face," for the negation of autonomous personal existence.

23 *Mevasser Ẓedeq*, p. 9a–b.

24 See Weiss, "Via passiva," p. 143, n. 18. It is worth noting here the proximity of the subject of the immanent existence of God within man to the question of responsibility for the sin performed by man. Reuben ha-Levi Horowitz, the author of *Dudaʾim ba-Sadeh* and a disciple of R. Elimelekh of Lyzhansk, reports a sermon he heard concerning this matter from the *ḥasid* R. Pinḥas of Gniboshov, based upon the verse, "for thou art even as Pharoah" [Gen. 44:18]: "that is, both of them, God and Pharoah, dwell together in an immanent manner within man, so that it is difficult not to fall into sin" — ibid., p. 19a. True, this only implies an indirect recognition of God's responsibility for man's sin.

25 I shall cite here the remarks concerning this matter brought by his disciple, R. Raphael of Bershad, in the name of R. Pinḥas, in MS. Jerusalem 3759, fo. 127b (this MS. seems to be parallel to the one used by Heschel, known as MS. Cincinnatti 62): "Nothing, great and small, could exist were it not for His help. We find that all the obstacles [to observing the] prohibitions, or even thoughts, are from the Almighty alone. And without His 'help,'" he continued, "I would become a *meshumad* [apostate]. But if you ignore this principle you may think that you are 'something' and value yourself as a man of virtue [*a sheiner yid*]. [You say to yourself,] I went away from sin and I am clean of sin. But the result is that God leaves him, for every haughty-hearted person is an abomination to God, and he

> When the evil-doer performs a sin, at the time he commits the sin the Holy One blessed be He also gives him the power to commit this sin. For if not, his soul would depart from him at the first breath prior to committing the sin.[26]

The soul does not "leave" the body at the time of the sin only because it "sees that the whole world is full of His glory, so it returns and says, 'It is sufficient that the servant be like its master.'"[27] In other words, he comes to the conclusion that, if God is able to dwell within the body while man sins, this must be the will of God, and he does it — that is, the sin — by His power; thus, "it is sufficient that the servant be like its master." Even though the tone with which these remarks are made is explicitly one of acceptance of the Divine judgment, which revolves around questions of reward and punishment in this world and not on purely metaphysical questions, it nevertheless draws upon the immanentist presupposition.

The formula which occasionally appears in Hasidic literature — that "God does everything" — is not always to be strictly understood in its naive, literal sense; it is more a figure of speech intended to remind man that he ought not to be haughty about his own acts, because they are performed by God, and not by himself.[28] Even the idea, found in some isolated passages, that God Himself fulfills the *miẓvot* in practice,[29] did not occupy a central place in Hasidic sources and was not a subject of serious discussion. It is worth mentioning in this context an interesting opinion which attempts to grasp both ends of the stick: i.e., to save the idea of the immanence of God operating within man, while avoiding the difficult problem of "reward and punishment" in its traditional formulation. I refer to the following charming parable brought by the author of *Ahavat Dodim*:

and I cannot live [in the same place.] Then he finds himself in the grasp of his Urge and be caught in its trap and do whatever it tempts him to do. And [R. Pinḥas] said that all this is because of the compassion of the Holy One, blessed be He, and His great kindness which is continuously over the soul, he is seduced in order to fail through a [small] thing in order to remind him that without the help of God he is worth nothing. [If] he does not remember through a small thing, he would stumble in a great thing until he comes to ... [unclear] the belief in his own power... Then he must break himself very much, until he knows that he himself becomes nothing and very small, and then he becomes a vessel prepared to accept help and assistance from God, may He be blessed." R. Pinḥas's teachings have been handed down in Yiddish.

26 *Sefer R. Yeivi*, 36c.

27 Ibid.

28 For example, *Darkhei Ẓedeq*, 11, or *Liqqutei Rama"l*, *Va-etḥanan*.

29 See Weiss, "Via passiva," pp. 143–144. which mentions the unique nuance in R. Abraham Ḥayyim of Zloczow of performing the *miẓvot* as the act of God. If so, one already sees this position in principle in relation to prayer and to all the motions of man's limbs in the Maggid of Mezhirech. See, for example, at length in *Kitvei Qodesh*, 39d.

> According to this, when the righteous man is like a steed to the Holy One, blessed be He, who rides upon him,[30] there might be a case for the righteous man to say: If so, I need not guard myself so as not to fall into any sin, for the Holy One, blessed be He, who is the rider, will protect me. Just as, when the horse wishes to go over a ramshackle bridge or through mud and slime, then the rider guards him ... But if this were so, it would negate man's freedom of choice. Therefore, the Holy One blessed be He rides on the righteous man without reins, and the rider does not pull the horse, but the horse pulls the rider. And wherever he goes, there he brings Him. Therefore, the righteous man must watch himself in all his actions to assure that he go in the straight path, and not to rely upon the Holy One blessed be to guard him without watching over himself, for if so, his free choice would be nullified.[31]

This parable is not the only one of its kind in the teaching of R. Benjamin of Salositz, but appears in a number of variations, suggesting that R. Benjamin struggled within himself about the possible quietistic conclusions that might be drawn from the immanentist approach. He therefore limited divine activity to seemingly one-time actions, even with regard to matters of prayer, and not only in such practical matters as *mizvot* and transgressions. True, all Hasidic thinkers, including the Maggid of Mezhirech, advocated intense activism in the life of prayer, with the intention of arriving at a stage wherein the powers of the body and the soul would be extinguished, so that God might then act within man as the exclusive actor. However, in the writings of R. Benjamin one finds a unique idea, in that he recognizes a single, initial act on the part of God leading man to his initial experience of *devequt* and ecstasy, in order to prod him to repeated actions in this direction at his own initative. Paradoxically, this one-time "divine grace" is a stimulus to human activity, a kind of action of the rider without reins. These remarks contain nothing which would weaken the quietistic idea of the exclusive activity of God, but they do imply an emphasis in practice upon the need for human activism. This activism "for its own sake" is rooted in his positive evaluation, which is *sui generis*, of the ideology of the elevation of alien thoughts.[32] He states:

30 The term "riding" is used in Hasidism as a description of an immanent reality, such as "the thought rides upon the speech."

31 Benjamin of Salositz, *Ahavat Dodim*, p. 17a.

32 We cannot discuss this question here, nor the place occupied by R. Benjamin in its development. I only wish to mention an interesting fact, which is that the entire approach expressed in this homily — which renders it relevant to the issue of activism and quietism — involves dressing in dramatic tension a teaching which he quotes frequently in the name of the Besht concerning the deliberate distancing of God from man at the time that he begins to find the path to Him, in the way preached by the Besht: "he will guide us above death (*ᶜal-mut*)" [Ps. 48:15] — substituting the word *ᶜolamit*, eternally.

> "My beloved put his hand by the hole of the door" [Songs 5:4] — we find that the beginning of his repentance did not come from himself, but from His awakening, may He be blessed, that He infused him with His fear ... But behold, such a fear of his which comes from Heaven cannot stay with him permanently, for if so, his entire [Divine] service would not be from himself, but only from God, may He be blessed. He therefore removes this fear which he has infused upon him, so that he may go and strengthen himself towards His love, and his service may be called after his own name ... And it does not come to him easily, but by great force and persistence over a long time; and then, when man seeks to go to this love and does not find it, he prays to the Holy One blessed be He to help him as in the beginning — but he is not answered, for his service must be from himself. For had this great love been with him, it would be impossible for any alien thought to come to him, because of the power of the love and *devequt* which he has for God; but when he does not have that same *devequt*, the *qelippot* may confuse him and stand against him, to steal his prayer.[33]

One may cite another interesting view of R. Benjamin of Salositz which expresses the height of the paradox which sustains a militant social activism with quietistic arguments. He arrives at a kind of self-sacrificing enthusiasm, both religious and social, when he urges ethical preachers to say what they think without fear of their audience or worrying about unpopularity. The inhibitions and hesitancies in their sermons[34] came about, in his opinion, because they think that the sermon is the "creation of their minds," when it is in fact identical to the words of the living God which become embodied in them and which "instruct their heart" as to what they must say. The filling of the preacher's consciousness with this pneumatic feeling serves as the psychological guarantee of the possibility of doing battle "to the end." This phenomenon is in itself interesting: in order to provide a grounding for the unequivocal reliability of the mission of the "preacher." Hasidism no longer argues in terms of the preacher hearing a vision or receiving a prophetic revelation which confirms the truth of his message. This idea is instead

33 *Ahavat Dodim*, p. 61a.

34 For the historical background of these hesitations, see Weiss, "The Beginnings of the Hasidic Path," p. 59. There is no doubt that the remarks of the Maggid also alluded to the contempt shown by society for those who "prophesy." Following a description of "the casting-off of the holy spark of the Shekhinah within man," he adds: "Even though they have contempt for him, he should be silent and not answer those who insult him, so that those who insult him should not cause him to interrupt his service of the Creator, so that by reason of this he will not be important among people and will not be able to achieve his goal. ‹Lacunum›." — *Liqqutei Yeqarim*, 12c. We see here the development of an interesting psychology of pneumatic "chastisers," who see themselves as the victims of a society which does not "understand" them, and who sacrifice themselves on the altar of the spiritual ideal of "prophecy" or "saying of Torah." It is difficult to know whence the end of the passage, which is truncated, was leading.

rooted in the idea of the Divine immanence which "makes its voice heard" through the throat of the preacher, and which transforms him into a social instrument in its hands. The preacher need only be prepared to be "like a vanquished corpse" — that is, to completely abnegate his own individual personality — whereupon he will arrive, via the bridge of quietism, to his social mission. R. Benjamin writes as follows:

> "Cry out with your throat" [Isa. 58:1]. It states in the Midrash, *Parashat Emor* [Lev. R. 29:6], "Thus said the Holy One, blessed be He, to Israel. 'If you have improved your deeds, I shall become for you like this shofar. [Just as the shofar] brings in at this end and emits [its sound] at the other,[35] so do I rise from the Throne of Judgment and sit upon the Throne of Mercy.'" Thus one who chastises [others] for the sake of Heaven must reflect in his mind that his intellect and his sermon are not from himself, but that he has died like a vanquished corpse and that everything is from Him, may His Name be blessed. One therefore ought not to withhold chastisement or fear any person, for he is like a shofar, literally, which takes in at this end and emits it on the other.[36] So does [God] place in his heart the words and the chastisement which he is to say to the public, that each word may be in his heart like a burning fire to bring forth all the words, for otherwise he is like a prophet who suppresses his prophecy.
> So it states in the *Yalkut* [*Shimᶜoni*], *Parashat Shemot*, p. 54a, on the verse, "And I shall teach you (*horetikha*) what you shall speak" [Ex. 4:12]. "I shall teach" is the same [i.e. linguistic root] as "he shall surely shoot through" [*yaroh yiyareh* — Ex. 19:13]; that is, the Holy One blessed be He shoots the prophetic word into his heart, like burning fire. But when he does not think so, but rather thinks in his mind that he is saying Torah and wisdom from himself this is not so, [for then] he will sometimes suppress words of rebuke when he fears some person. And this is what is said, "Call out in your throat" — that which He, may He be blessed, places in his heart — "like a Shofar" — what he places in here comes out there. Likewise, all of the words which He, may He be blessed, places in your mind, you must utter.[37]

R. Kalonymus Kalman, a disciple of R. Elimelekh of Lyzhansk, gives an interesting testimony about the ecstatic states reached by the *ẓaddiqim* when they cast off corporeality. During the ecstatic state, a person utters words of which he is totally unaware after he emerges from that state; these words are interpreted, in

35 Weiss already notes the idea of the sermon which "comes from above" in the teaching of the Maggid himself, particularly according to the testimony of Solomon Maimon. He also discussed at length the motif of passivity found in the homilies connected with the shofar in Hassidic teaching generally. See "Via passiva," pp. 143–144, 149. For Maimon's testimony, see Salomon Maimon, *An Autobiography*, ed. M. Hadas (New York, 1947), pp. 49–51.

36 *Ṭorrei Zahav*, 56d.

37 Ibid. The same idea reappears in *Ahavat Dodim*, 54a–b.

Hasidic circles, as being spoken by the Shekhinah. This phenomenon is described as "prophecy," in which prophetic words are uttered concerning the future. There are not many testimonies concerning this phenomenon within the Hasidic camp (apart from folk tales, in which the psycho-metaphysical element is of course absent) but, from the totality of warnings found in various places, according to which it is forbidden for a person to engage in deliberate efforts "to attain" prophecy or the holy spirit,[38] one may assume that such phenomena did exist. In the account to be brought below, one can clearly see that the Hasidim did not regard this as a particularly unusual event; the testimony refers to "great *ẓaddiqim*," in the plural, who underwent the experience of prophetic ecstasy connected with the technique of casting off of corporeality. It does not explicitly state that prophecy rested upon them at the time of prayer, but this seems to have happened whenever they were able to "separate the soul from the body." The testimony follows immediately upon a discussion of the nature of death, which is understood as the "separation of the hylic soul from the physical body." Prophecy appears in their eyes, to borrow the language of the Midrash, as a kind of "miniature" death. The following is the text:

> And this is known — I have indeed seen some great *ẓaddiqim* who had attached themselves to the upper worlds, and stripped off the garment of their physicality, so that the Shekhinah rested upon them and spoke from within their throats, and their mouths spoke prophecy and future things. And these *ẓaddiqim* themselves did not know afterwards what they spoke, for they were attached to the supernal worlds while the Shekhinah spoke from within their throats.[39]

38 See, for example, *Darkhei Ẓedeq* ("ᶜ*Od Hanhagot*," 1): "Also when he hears about the accounts of what his friends have seen and heard, he should take heed [not to say to himself]: 'I will pray and perform good deeds so that I may be the same way.' This is the temptation of the Evil Urge, for his friends did not do so in order to ascend in level, but they simply did what they did, and they merited this. Therefore, be very careful to serve God with truth, not for any self-interest to ascend in level, but only to bring pleasure to God." There is also an interesting account brought by *ᵓOr ha-Meᵓir* "from the time of the Besht," about how a certain anonymous person wished to attain the Holy Spirit, and the Besht scoffed at him: "For our eyes see a person who performs afflictions and immersions and does much Torah and prayer, and his main aim is to achieve the Holy Spirit or a revelation of Elijah and the like. And I heard that in the days of the Besht *z"l* there was a person like this who performed afflictions and went to the *miqveh* to achieve the Holy Spirit, and the Besht said as follows: 'In the world of transformations [i.e., *qelippot*] they laugh at him, and this is the truth. How can a person pursue this when there is missing in his heart the main thing, attachment to God (*devequt*), which is the goal of service'" — ibid., p. 43d. Cf. on the question of the opposition to illumination in St. John of the Cross in the same spirit in R. J. Zvi Werblowsky, "On the Mystical Rejection of Illumination and Revelation of Secrets" (Heb.), ᶜ*Iyyun* 14 (1964), pp. 205–212.

39 *Maᵓor va-Shemesh*, 51a.

One of the few concrete descriptions of this found in Hasidic theoretical literature is that of R. Uziel Miesels, who describes the ecstatic Hasidic circle as comparable to a band of prophets who are enthralled by the Divine spirit and from whose throats the Shekhinah speaks. Anyone seeing them from outside is unable to enter into their secret and has contempt for them; only those whose ears are attuned to the divine resonance which speaks within them can join the dancers and cause God "to dance" with them. One clearly sees here that the idea of the pneumatic society is based upon the quietistic motif of the divine immanent reality acting within man. As we said, this motif of the pneumatic society is not found extensively in the theoretical literature, but it should not be surprising to find it in a society which tended to apply the finest of its thought and deeds — which by nature belonged *ab initio* to the realm of individual religious life (that is, to prayer) — to the social realm, which in turn became a pneumatic realm. One can therefore clearly understand the sequence of ideas in R. Uziel, who moves from the idea of prayer to the idea of the group which dances in ecstasy:

> It is known of Moses our teacher, *z"l*, that the Shekhinah spoke from his throat; and even though none like Moses has arisen since, in any event there are several on this level who merit that the Shekhinah of His power, may He be blessed, praises [God] from within their throats.[40] And perhaps it was with this intention that our Rabbis said, "From whence [do we know] that the Holy One blessed be He, prays?"[41] And this is called, "the praises of God in their throats" [Ps. 149:6] That is, when the praises of the Shekhinah are in their throats, the Shekhinah of His Glory, so to speak, speaking out of the throat of the righteous, then "a two-edged sword is in their hands" [ibid.] ... And this is, "The praises of God shall my mouth speak ..." [Ps. 145:21] — because my mouth only guides the words of the Shekhinah, as it were, and the God-fearer does naught but the Will, that he wishes to pray, but the praise is not his own, as said. And this is, "the will of them that fear Him he shall do" [ibid., v. 19] — for he does nothing but the will, but "The praise of God ...", etc. And this is, "O Lord open my lips" [Ps. 51:17]; for the one who attains this level is the man who is nothing but a conduit which carries the words from above, and the person only opens

40 This is an interesting side-comment, which attempts to remove pneumatic ability from the exclusive preserve of Moses.

41 The intention here is clearly that God Himself, and not the person, prays within man at the time of prayer. On this, see *Tif᾽eret ᶜUziel*, 53a–b, and MS. Jerusalem 1467 (in the name of the Maggid), 24b, or the interesting image that God is like a high priest who serves Himself by Himself (in man's prayer), *Maggid Devarav le-Yaᶜaqov*, §109, p. 186. There are also such formulae as "to serve God with God," *᾽Oraḥ la-Ḥayyim*, 280a, and many other similar phrases. In Hasidism, the Rabbinic poetic conceit, "From whence do we know that the Holy One blessed be He prays?," becomes a serious theological question.

his mouth ... But the essence of praise [42] is that man be clean of all impurity, so that the supernal voice not be made corporeal by his voice; for it is possible for every person to merit this level, but it is necessary to cease his voice and his deeds because of the grossness of the idolators.[43]

And this, I think [is what is meant by] the Talmudic passage in Rosh Hashanah: "He placed one shofar within another shofar: if the sound of the inner one was audible, he fulfilled his obligation; if the sound of the outer one was heard, he did not fulfill his obligation" [R.H. 27b]. And as it is written in the *Shulḥan ᶜArukh*, "that is, that the inwardness of the sound was not changed from what it was," and see there [*Oraḥ Ḥayyim* 586:20]. This is according to the above intention — that there is a supernal voice within the lower voice: if the inner voice is heard, so that it was not changed by the external voice, then he fulfilled [the *miẓvah*]. And if not, [that is,] that the external voice was strong — because of the corporeality of man, he did not fulfill it. And this is the intention of what is written, "The Song of Songs which is Solomon's" [Songs 1:1] — that this song is holy of holies, which is of Solomon — i.e., to the Holy One blessed be He Himself. That is, that the Shekhinah of His glory itself sings and makes music from the throat of the *ẓaddiq*. In this manner he concludes, "Let him kiss me" [ibid., v, 2] — that is, this is the manner in which the Holy One blessed be He joins Himself to the lower mouth — "from his mouth" [ibid.] — of above, and this is said in the verse, "a two-edged (*pifiyyot*) sword in their hands" [op cit.]. That is, two mouths (*piyot*) — his mouth and the mouth of the Shekhinah, as it were. And this is the prayer which we say and make heard with the voice of the word of the living God — that their voice is the voice of the Shekhinah, so to speak, only they are the conduits.

For this reason, we find in the Scripture and the Talmud that pious people sing and dance with great ecstasy, as that which we found of David king of Israel, *z"l*: "and David was leaping and dancing ..." [II Sam. 6:16]. Likewise in the Rejoicing of the Water Drawing, and likewise what was said, "foolishness gives joy to the old man" [Ketubot 17a]. And this is, that one who stands in the palace of the king, and the king hears the sound of the lyres and harps and the dance and the drums, and he also dances. But if one stands at a distance and does not hear the music of the instruments, and sees that this one dances and sings, it appears to him as if he were a crazy person.[44]

42 This implies that man does not praise God, but that he is only able to prepare the "vessels" and to purify them, and that the reference to prayer applies to God Himself. The Christian quietists spoke in a similar spirit in opposing all praises and psalmody. See on this Pourrat, "Quiétisme; Molinosisme," col. 1567.

43 The ecstatic state does not persist because of external disturbances.

44 This same parable of the person gazing at the members of an ecstatic circle and considering them crazy because he does not hear the sound of the music is already brought in the name of the Besht (see *Degel Maḥaneh ᵓEfraim*, 35b), although there the motif of the Shekhinah activating and causing people to dance does not appear. The change in meaning which takes place here as a result of the pneumatic shift is extremely interesting.

> But the truth is that, to the contrary, he [the observer] is crazy, and if he were to hear the sound of the instruments he would also dance and sing. For this reason we find that they referred to the prophet as a mad-man, for the Divine spirit beats within him like a bell, and he dances and sings because God is within him.[45]

An interesting account of the above type of ecstatic prophecy appears in *ʾOr ha-Meʾir*, where we find an eye-witness account of how the Maggid of Mezhirech exemplified before his disciples how to "say Torah" in this manner of metapsychic hearing:

> Once I heard the Maggid *z"l* tell us explicitly: I will teach you the best way of how to say Torah, it being that he did not feel himself at all, but his ear heard how the World of Speech speaks within him, and he himself does not speak, for as soon as he begins to hear his own words, he stops. And several times I saw with my own eyes, and not those of another, that when he opened his mouth to speak words of Torah, it seemed to the eyes of everyone that he was not in this world at all and that the Shekhinah spoke from within his throat. And at times, even in the midst of a subject or a word, he would stop and wait some time, and it all indicates how the enlightened one (*maskil*) must await the [divine] knowledge, and then the word emerges with that knowledge, as mentioned . . .[46]

I cite these last testimonies in order to demonstrate that the identity between God and man and the quietist conclusions drawn from it were not merely theoretical, but constituted a living doctrine in Hasidic society. There were even those sources in which the "activities" of the *ẓaddiq* were interpreted as total submission to the passive state, by means of which he came to enjoy the direct activity of God. This theory is implied by the author of *Dudaʾim ba-Sadeh*:

> . . . Only when the *ẓaddiq* has the attribute of submission does the portion of divinity within him perform this action. If so, everything is from God, both the evil and its negation, but the *ẓaddiq* is the Throne and the Temple for His Name, may He be blessed. For by virtue of the fact that His glory and His portion are embodied within the *ẓaddiq*, he is able to act and to bind the worlds to their root.[47]

45 *Tifʾeret ʿUziel*, 53b–c.

46 *ʾOr ha-Meʾir*, 95c. There is also an expansion of the theoretical question of the introduction of "knowledge" (*daʿat*) into speech, as well as an important testimony from the Maggid R. Michel of Zloczow concerning this same matter.

47 *Dudaʾim ba-Sadeh*, p. 9b.

Chapter Nine

The World of Speech and The World of Thought

Let us now return to the question of meditative prayer. We discussed above the first stage of meditation, which is a long and extended process involving contemplation of the letters of prayer, their spiritualization through means of speech, and their disappearance from human consciousness when they continue to be enunciated by the unconscious — identified here with the Shekhinah. They continue while man's thoughts ascend to a higher sphere than speech, that of "thought."

The ascent to the "World of Thought" seems to carry a distinct theological connotation: namely, that man ascends from the World of Speech, identified with the lowest of the divine worlds, to a higher sphere known as the World of Thought, identified in Hasidic symbolism with *Binah*. The function of human thought is to bring every particular thought back to its source; that is, to nullify its individuality and incorporate it within its divine source until it is negated. The redemption of the particular thought is synonymous with its immediate destruction. Thought exists in this sense as spiritual energy, emanating endlessly from the source of divine thought in its aspect of "letters" or that of "expansion" (*hitpashṭut*). The expansion of the divine "Nothing" appears to man in the form of "existence" (*yesh*) subject to thought. Expansion is thus existence itself. The dialectical return to the source of all of man's thoughts is simultaneously the return to the "Nothing" and the root.

The same problem which was raised concerning the negation of the World of Speech in the divine World of Thought, in the sense of an infinite dialectical cyclicity within the structure of the Sefirotic system, returns in the question raised here regarding the World of Thought. Dialectical divine thought negates itself in the course of its continuous dynamic flow.

The entire world of the Sefirot is perceived here as a system of divine instruments of thought, in which the dialectical forces of "expansion" and "nothing" (*ʾayin*) act, except that this "game" is infinite and trans-temporal.

Certain concepts which were only used in Lurianic Kabbalah in connection with specific events, were utilized and transformed by Hasidism into a kind of immanent lawfulness within the divine world. I refer to the reworking of that midrash which states: "The world exists for six thousand years and in one [thousand] is destroyed," upon which the Kabbalists developed the doctrine of the "death of the kings," and which received extensive play later on in Lurianic Kabbalah. With all its dialectical inventiveness, Kabbalah did not make room for this midrash in its own dialectic, but connected it to the specific "history" of the one-time Divine catastrophe of the "breaking" (*shevirah*). Hasidism, which was never interested in "events" *per se* but only in their significance for its own psychological homilies, transferred the entire event into the realm of the inner dialectical law of the divine world; it likewise moved the entire "event," including the concepts of *ẓimẓum* and *shevirah*, into the psychological realm — a point which we shall discuss below.

The Maggid of Mezhirech describes the "destruction of the worlds" as a continuous process of "negation from existence," of transformation of the "existing" (*yesh*) or the "expansion" into "nihility" (*ᵓayin*), and vice versa:

> "The redeemed of the Lord shall return" [Isa. 51:11]. Concerning the matter of, "Six thousand years the world exists and in one it is destroyed" [Rosh Hashanah 31a; Sanhedrin 97a]; the meaning of "six" is six stages; "years" (*shanin*) — that they change (*mishtanim*); "shall be the world" — thus is the way of the world; "and in one it is destroyed" — when everything returns to unity, the world is destroyed and negated of its existence.[1]

The destruction of the "world" (i.e. the Godhead) is tantamount to its rebuilding, while its rebuilding is destined to be destroyed once again. Elsewhere, the Maggid describes the same dialectical process in abstract terms — which I used above — as the tension between the "nothing" (*ᵓayin*) and the "expansion" (*hitpashṭut*). One already sees here the first signs of the problem — namely, that one does not know for sure if these words refer to divine or human thought. There would seem to be no difference between the two, just as there was no difference between the divine "World of Speech" and the realm of human speech. He states the following:

> "And you shall honor the face of the elder" [Lev. 19:32]; and our Sages remarked: "['the elder'] refers to one who has acquired wisdom" [Kiddushin 32b]. For it is written, "Suffer me a little, and I will tell thee" [Job 36:2], which is a phrase [indicative] of waiting. For when a person wishes to tell his friend something, he says, "Wait and I shall tell you something" — that is, a person's thought is continuous, without interruption, in expansion. And when he wishes his friend to turn from his own thought in order to hear what he is saying to him and to understand that thing, he wishes his friend to contract his thought from its expansion until he tells him his words. Thus, when we investigate where his thought was at that moment before he told him these things, he knows with certainty that he was at that moment above his place, for at that moment he does not think anything, and it is very contracted above

1 This clearly refers to "negation from existence" within the divine world itself; *ᵓOr ha-ᵓEmet*, 5a.

> in the place called "Nothing" (*efes*) until he says his words, and then it spreads into the letters that he says to him. Similarly, when man[2] wishes to empty his thought which is somewhat in a state of expansion, and wishes to empty it of this thing entirely up to the place called "Nothing," and thereafter there falls into his thought another thing — accordingly there cannot be any change unless it come between one thought and another in that Nothing. But according to the extent of that change, so shall there be the Nothing, for there is a thing which is to some extent a change from the first thing, but on the whole it is truly one with it. And according to this shall be the Nothing, that it shall not be completely withdrawn, for in truth the first thing [together] with this thing in its entirety are one,[3] and there is no need for him to remove himself from the whole. For there is complete change, and it is in its whole a different thing, and so likewise the Nothing shall be an absolute Nothing. And this is what is written here, "Suffer (*kater*) me a little" [ibid.]; from this it is learned that there is one crown [*keter*; a word-play on *kater*] which is greater than Him, in which is included everything from the beginning, and from it he comes to *Ḥokhmah* and *Binah*, as is known . . .[4]

We have already mentioned above that the "letters of thought" come from the source of dynamic unity, known as "the pre-existence of the intellect" (*qadmut ha-sekhel*).[5] These letters, which are in a state of continuous expansion from the divine world, may rest upon a person either in the form of flashes of insight within discursive thought[6] or by means of intuitive thought, through which he attains a glimpse beyond time to the world of unity free of any particular contents. The letters from the World of Thought are no more than a stimulus to the particular thought, and are in no way identical with the actual contents of human thought.[7]

2 The entire passage in its literal sense is addressed to man, although it is clear that the author of this teaching had in mind the divine principle of the activity of thought, which he transferred to the psychological sphere. But the main point here is not the parallel in the laws governing thought, but in the identity of the thinker, which we shall discuss more fully below.

3 The intention is evidently simply to an associative change as such, and not a total transition from one matter to another, which is called here "to remove himself from the generality" or "to arrive at complete nothingness."

4 *Maggid Devarav le-Yaᶜaqov*, §131, pp. 224ff.

5 According to *Maggid Devarav le-Yaᶜaqov*, §175, p. 274, and the article by G. Scholem, "The Unconscious and the Pre-Existence of the Intellect."

6 *Maggid Devarav le-Yaᶜaqov*, §180, p. 281.

7 See, e.g., *ᵓOr ha-ᵓEmet*, 70a: "And this thing is clear and wondrous: that when a person has difficulty with a given thing he begins to think in his thought. And by means of this, there suddenly falls into his thought a kind of spark, which is a sudden flash; likewise, there falls into him a certain invention, and this thing comes to him from the pre-existing intellect, which is Wisdom. But the fact is that this wisdom falls into his mind suddenly, like a flash from the foundation of Wisdom [of the Godhead], which is the foundation of Wisdom. And the wisdom [i.e. the concrete idea] which has fallen into his mind now is not called *Yesod ᵓAbba* ("the foundation of Father"), but the aspect which

Human thought thinks the thought of the divine in a "contracted" mode, in accordance with the greatness of its apprehension.

The Maggid of Mezhirech speaks about *ẓimẓum* as a psychological term applied to human thought, rather than in terms of the Lurianic myth, which sees in *ẓimẓum* the be-all of its theological teaching. To put it more precisely, one might say that in the eyes of the Maggid, so long as a person thinks, God contracts Himself or is contracted within his thought. *Ẓimẓum* is not a single, one-time event within the divine world, but an immanent law of thought. God is held captive by the law of human thought in the sense that, if a person does not think, there is no significance to Divine thought: it is only possible to think within the framework of human intellect; when a person nullifies his thought, he thereby releases the Divine element "contracted" within it and returns it to its source. The chaotic letters of the divine world therefore "expand" within the human intellect; in the course of this expansion, they become contracted, as they become defined in it and by it and then, in the words of the Maggid, "He, may He blessed, thinks what they think." The Godhead does not "think" as a separate persona with its own thoughts, but it manifests itself as the source of thought. More than it thinks itself, it is thought by man or "contracted" within his intellect. The more human thought "wanders," the further away it is from accomplishing that redemption, in which it redeems the divine element within it; the more concentrated and directed towards the goal of self-annihilation, the more it merits to perceive the Godhead stripped of its contraction and to reach the Nothing or the roots of thought which are beyond time.[8] Thus God says: "I have come into [human] thought, and there is nought in thought because his thought rambles about."[9] It follows from this that the Godhead lives a hidden existence within the soul of man, and that man is able to live and to release the divine element within him by virtue of his thought.

In the final analysis, *ẓimẓum* is the way by which the human intellect forces God, by His own laws of existence, to appear within it. The Maggid says the following:

fell suddenly is called *Yesod* (Foundation), which is the mystery of the unification of the pre- existent intellect, which is Wisdom [*Ḥokhmah* is identical with "Father"] with thought, which is [called] *Binah ʾAbba ve-ʾImma* ... because this wisdom which fell upon him is in great contraction, and is naught but simple intellect ..."

8 The Maggid indeed felt the dialectic of the activity of "bringing to *ʾayin*," which is preceded by the activity of Divine "contraction" (*ẓimẓum*). He refers to this dialectic as "two passages which contradict one another," yet nevertheless calls this activity of the return to the Nothing "a great kindness" (in association with the Lurianic idea that all "reflected light" [*ʾor ḥozer*] is a manifestation of the *Sefirah* of *Din*). See *Kitvei Qodesh*, 9b.

9 MS. Jerusalem 1467, of the teaching of the Maggid (17a). One of the hesychasts also expresses this tendency: the spirit has a tendency to dream and to long, memories have the power to change a person into a dreamer instead of a Hesychast! (And further on: God descends and finds man's thought floating about). See the chapter on St. Gregory of Sinai in *Philokalia*.

> And this is the interpretation of: "The eyes of God are upon the righteous" [Ps. 34:16]. Just as the son, when he performs an act of youthful [foolishness], brings the intellect of his father within those deeds, so do they cause the Holy One blessed be He [to enter], so-to-speak, into the image of their intellects, so that He must think what they think. If they think in love, they bring the Holy One, blessed be He, into the world of Love, as is written in the Zohar, "'The King is trapped in the tresses' [Songs 7:6] — in the tresses of the mind."[10] And this is the interpretation of, "He contracted His Shekhinah between the two staves of the Ark" — and that is the meaning of "the lobes [lit., "wings"] of the lungs," which are the Shekhinah. And the Holy One, blessed be He, dwells where he [the human being] thinks, and the intellect is called "the eye [of God]," and it is in the hands of the righteous. But how does one merit to this level? By thinking that they are dust and they are unable to act at all without the power of the Holy One blessed be He. But we find that what he does is, [in fact,] done by the Holy One blessed be He, for were it not for Him, may He be blessed, he would be unable to do anything.[11]

The conclusion of this passage turns the formula on its head, and would seem to refute the possible argument for the autonomy of thought. In principle, there is no autonomy of the spirit in the world of Hasidism, but there is limitless freedom of both action and thought, as the more man is able to experience the dialectical concept of dominance over and submission to the divine element within himself, the more the horizon of his spiritual ability expands — i.e., to think the Godhead in its restricted manifestation within human thought, while freeing it and redeeming it from the imprisonment of its limitation. The man who has contracted God within his own thought (which is the meaning of *ẓimẓum*) frees it from the "tresses of the mind" when he ascends to *devequt*. God so-to-speak "forgives" man for the

10 See the Introduction to the *Zohar* and *Tiqqunei Zohar*, Ch. 6; the reference here is obviously to the supernal *moḥin* ("mind"), and not to the human "mind" (even though in the *Zohar* these things are also connected with *tefillin*). It seems to me that *rehitei moḥin* ought to be translated here as "the rushing of thought" (from the Aramaic *rahit*, to run), i.e., the process of thought.

11 *Maggid Devarav le-Yaᶜaqov*, §1, pp. 11–12. The same idea is alluded to in *ᵓOr ha-ᵓEmet*, 5a — i.e., that the immanent contracted existence of the Godhead within man goes beyond itself to "the great clarity," as follows: "... And this is the meaning of 'wings like eagles.' That the eagle, because of his flying at a very great height, until he reaches the source of the fire, his wings are burnt. Thus the righteous, because of their good deeds [this refers to their mystical attainments] come to great brilliance until they do not apprehend and descend from their level — until they perform other good deeds and again cling to Him, may He be blessed. And this is the meaning of 'and the redeemed of God shall be returned' [Isa. 51:11] — [that] those who repent [through mystical ascent] redeem God. 'And they shall come to Zion in joy' [ibid.] — Zion is that by which the Holy One blessed be He is hidden as it were within the image — in his love for Israel — in their likeness, as is known [the image is a likeness, and is a signpost [*ẓiyyun*; a wordplay on "Zion"], as in, 'To whom did He go? To the souls of the righteous' [Gen. R. 8:7], as is known."

contraction of His Glory within the confines of human thought, requiring Him to "think" in its patterns and form, even though the source of human thought is in truth to be found in the world of Divine letters. Moreover, unlike all of the thought contracted within the human intellect, the roots of that thought are anchored in a kind of "naked" idea, and this idea may be none other than the dynamic source from which human thought flows.[12] What is interesting about all that has been said with regard to our own subject is that, for Hasidism of the school of the Maggid, the gap between the transcendent and the immanent was largely blurred, so that theology became psychology. The description of the processes of human thought and speech becomes an ontic description of the "expansion" (synonymous with the psychological concept of "contraction") and regression to the Divine "nothing" (whereby man arrives through contemplation at psychological nothing). The psychological practice of thought and annihilation took over the role of the dialectical principle of Lurianic Kabbalah in the theosophic realm.[13]

Man's task is to draw himself towards "the active power" (*koaḥ ha-poᶜel*), to use the Maggid's word.[14] This drawing means a gradual negation of the "I" until it "becomes nothing" — and not only until it reaches the nothing — because thinking and experience are unified in Hasidic teaching. The complete negation of the thinking subject is thus the liberation of the thinking element within us — that is, the Godhead.

It seems to me that psychologistic expression reaches its height in the words of R. Ḥayyim Ḥaykl of Amdur, who also interprets the Lurianic concept of "breaking" (*shevirah*) as a psychological concept. He describes the repair of the *shevirah* as a doctrine of remembering and recreating a psychological continuity with those same deep layers in the human soul which have not yet become apprehended and known. He uses the formula that "the breaking was necessary for the repairing"[15] in order to explain the idea that man is able to arrive at *tiqqun* and higher spiritual attainment if he does not surrender to the lawfulness of the world

12 *Maggid Devarav le-Yaᶜaqov*, §125, p. 216: "And it is known that whatever was and is, everything was in the preexistent thought, and it is the woman which is filled from everything; and all the letters and words and thought, it all was there, and what is done at every moment is what is drawn from there. And if a person prays and lifts up the other letters to their root, that is, that these letters which he speaks attach themselves to those letters above ..."

13 On this principle in Lurianic Kabbalah, see G. Scholem, *Major Trends*, p. 263.

14 *Maggid Devarav le-Yaᶜaqov*, §133, p. 233.

15 The Kabbalistic sources know of the formula, "spoiling in order to repair" (*qilqul ᶜal menat le-taqqen*), but they do not stress the explicit formula that the *shevirah* occurred for the sake of the *tiqqun*, even though this is a dominant idea in Lurianic Kabbalah. Of course, in the Kabbalah the *shevirah* is spoken of as a phenomenon in the divine world, and not as a psychological one.

of the psychological "breaking," but is able to lift himself up by means of that same "light" preserved in his soul prior to the crisis of forgetting — the *shevirah*. Even here, he made use of the Lurianic terminology of the "residue" (*reshimu*), which remains in the emptiness following the contraction and removal of the light of the Infinite — albeit this "trace" is a technical term for a half-conscious and unclear psychological state. If a person is able to grasp onto and to ascend the stages of the spirit when the "influx" "spreads out the substance of light," he then frees the memory which is captive in the world of *shevirah*. Here too, as in the Maggid's teaching, one is struck by the tendency to see the acts of man as essentially acts of God because, while it is true that this captive memory may be corrected by means of a human-spiritual effort, this is only the other side of the coin; that intellectual act is itself an act of divine activity. It is interesting to note the ease with which the author moves here from "His" breaking (in the divine world) to "our" breaking and to "our" *tiqqun*, as if it is self-evident that the two are really the same. The following are R. Ḥayyim Ḥaykl's words:

> See that it is written, "we have a little sister and she does not have breasts" [Songs 8:8]. That is, we are unable to apprehend the essence of the Holy One, blessed be He, but only His Wisdom, which is Fear, as it is said, "for the fear of God is wisdom" [Job 28:12]. For [regarding] any thing which is apprehended, he who apprehends that thing is above that thing, but we are unable to apprehend the essence of the Holy One, blessed be He, because He is above us. And it is known that there was a breaking in the worlds, so that there could be a *tiqqun* for us, and this is, "ten *tiqqunim*," etc., which are ten Sefirot. For if there had not been a breaking, we would not have a *tiqqun*; therefore, there was a breaking. And there remains with us a residue, and by means of this residue we are able to apprehend the essence of the pleasure which there was previously, and this is called Discernment (*tevunah*), for thanks to this residue he is able to remind himself of what he had previously had in his apprehension. And this is called "firmament" (*raqi*ᶜ*a*), meaning the spreading out of His self-light, and this is, "and the wise ones shall shine" [Daniel 12:3]. When shall he who receives the intellect shine like the brilliance of the firmament? When the One doing the influxing creates a firmament within his intellect.[16]

In one place, the Maggid describes the highest form of psychological event within man as an occurrence in the divine world. According to this view, *devequt* is a situation of lucid consciousness of what occurs within the Godhead; however, as we have said, to be conscious that something has taken place means that one is identical with the event itself. The Maggid says:

> Know that man is a part of God above, and when he attaches his thought above, he

16 *Ḥayyim va-Ḥesed*, p. 153 (on Daniel).

> can know what is done up above. For all those things which are done above pass through his thought, as R. Simeon bar Yohai said, "I am a sign in the world" — that is, all the *middot* [i.e., Sefirot] which are aroused above are aroused below in the *ẓaddiq* . . .[17]

The "acts" and "deeds" which take place above are thus in fact identical with human "thought," and there is no gap between thought and event, even though one is, so to speak, located up "above," and the other is below. Human thought which reaches up towards true "unity," which glimpses at that which is "beyond time," is in itself an aspect of the divine dynamic which nullifies itself at every moment. It was doubtless thus that the Maggid understood the entire system of symbolic relationships in the divine world, and attempted to interpret this symbolic dynamic according to immanentist directives.

It is never clearly explained in the Kabbalah how man's thought can "make an impression" up above and influence the processes within the divine world. The Maggid was the one who first attempted to identify the psychological processes with the theosophic processes, from an immanentist posture, so that man's activity within his own psyche seems identical with God's activity within the realm of the *Sefirot*. This is not to be confused with a psychologistic understanding of the Sefirotic system; in other words, the stance here is not one which claims that the entire divine structure is no more than a form of human thought and that it does not exist in itself (the Kabbalists themselves make such claims within the context of their own controversies). The position here is an entirely different one: the Maggid, in my humble opinion, teaches that mystical thought (discursive thought is not discussed here) is unificative thought,[18] and as such functions as a manifestation of divine activity both within Himself and within man. This seems to me to be the proper interpretation of the following passage, with which R. Levi Yitzḥak of Berdichev, the editor of the Maggid's teaching, had some difficulty:

> I will write what I heard, even though it is not clear to me,[19] which is the following: Thought is letters; that is, whatever he [a person] may think in any matter, is all in letters,[20] so it is clear, that there cannot be but one thought. That is to say, a person

17 ʾ*Or ha-ʾEmet*, 77b.

18 "And speech and action are within time, but thought is not within time; even though thought is also within time, in all events the supernal world as against the lower world is not within time. For example, when a person has understanding he is able to understand a thing in one moment, but when he needs to recite it [i.e., explain it] he must recite it for an hour or more" — ʾ*Or ha-ʾEmet*, 41b.

19 Today it is clear that these words were formulated by R. Levi Yitzḥak of Berdichev. See Schatz, "Introduction," p. xiv ff.

20 In the letters of the Divine thought which "spread out" unto him.

> is unable to think two thoughts simultaneously, or two thoughts in one. And it is known that Leah is the World of Thought,[21] and therefore she is called Leah [i.e., vocalized with a *qamaẓ*], for Leah is pleasure (*taᶜanug*),[22] for thought is the world of pleasure. But Rachel, who is the World of Speech, is not so. For a person can speak about one matter, and in his thought think about another matter, and speech and thought are not one. But when thought and speech are two, this is the secret of when the two faces,[23] Leah and Rachel, become one, and then they are with the Little Face [*zeᶜir ᵓanpin* — i.e., the masculine configuration of the Godhead in Lurianic theology] face to face. This is what I heard, but it is incomprehensible.[24]

The main thrust of this homily is that the unity in the divine world (between Leah and Rachel, or between divine "speech" and "thought") depends upon the unity of human thought. But in order to create unity in that world, there must be a division here: that is, "when thought and speech are two" — i.e, when a person achieves the maximal stage of concentration, until his speech is no longer of the same kind as the thought (speech then becoming automatic, as I explained above) — only then does he reach the stage in which thought has active power.

To conclude my remarks concerning the importance of the question of immanence in Hasidism, I would like to add that this question should not be understood the same way in Hasidism as it is in Kabbalah: what we are concerned with here is not an additional historical layer which negates or affirms the doctrine of *ẓimẓum*, either in its literal or non-literal sense.[25] Nor are we interested in a speculation or theory whose purpose is to confirm one or another of the existing paths in Kabbalah and determine its historical continuity and survival. Hasidism was not interested in these kinds of questions in a theoretical manner,[26] but simply adopted for itself one of the theoretical positions already widely found in Kabbalistic teaching, which it then used as a basis for its own interests, which were remote from those of the Kabbalists. It sought to arrive at *unio mystica* by means of the doctrine of psychological immanence. To use the language of R. Ḥayyim Ḥaykl: it did not wish to "measure" the mystical body of God, but to become

21 In Kabbalah, Leah is the symbol of *Binah*, which in the Maggid's teaching is identified with the world of Divine thought.

22 He refers to thought as the World of [mystical] Pleasure (*taᶜanug*), identical in Kabbalah with the concept of the World to Come, which was united with *Binah*.

23 There is a division in Lurianic Kabbalah into two faces in the world of the female, which is itself one of the five configurations of the divine world.

24 *ᵓOr ha-ᵓEmet*, 77a.

25 The dispute concerning this matter between Rabbi Joseph Irgas and R. Immanuel Hai Ricchi and others from the 17th century on is well known.

26 Albeit the question arose in a theoretical manner in Habad Hasidism. See the opening chapters of

attached to it.[27] The *Ma^caseh Merkavah* of man became identical with the Divine *Ma^caseh Merkavah*, and in its wake was created the theoretical basis for the teaching of contemplation which leads to union with God. The extinction of all those powers of the soul which do not lead to the moment of *devequt* was a precondition for the liberation of the divine within man by means of God Himself; as such, contemplation is in the final analysis a quietistic phenomenon.

In one place, R. Ḥayyim Ḥaykl makes some unequivocal statements concerning the identity between the human and the divine *pneuma*. The five-fold division of the human soul according to Kabbalistic tradition into *Nefesh* (animative soul), *Ruah* (spirit),The five-fold division of the human soul according to Kabbalistic tradition into *Nefesh* (animative soul), *Ruaḥ* (spirit), *Neshamah* (soul), *Ḥayah* (angelic soul), and *Yeḥidah* (unitive soul) — is an expression of the wandering of the human spirit throughout the entire cosmos, which it fills once it is freed of the body:

> A great rule: God roves about and fills all the worlds, even the world of action (*ᶜAsiyyah*). Thus does man, in his *Nefesh–Ruaḥ–Neshamah–Ḥayah–Yeḥidah* [go up] to the World of Emanation, but his root remains in the World of Action, even after his death, [in] his son and his grandson.[28]

This identity of essence between the spirit of man and the spirit of God — which found expression in the Maggid's parable of the "two horns of brass make thyself,"[29] in which both man and God are each understood as "a half form," as two manifestations of one perfection — was not intended to serve the accepted theory of the elevated origin of the human soul, but primarily to stress the activist motif of God within the spirit of the human being who empties himself of all his substance. Various different formulations which appeared in the Maggid's school, such as "God dwells within you from your head to your ankle"[30] or "man is a nest for the aspect of bird,"[31] or the repeated parables comparing God and man to a

Mordecai Teitelbaum, *Ha-Rav mi-Ladi u-Mifleget Ḥaba"d* (Warsaw, 1913), Pt. II.

27 "'Whoever knows how to depict the *Shiᶜur Qomah* has a portion in the World to Come' (*ʾOtiyot de-Rabbi ᶜAkiva*, §8), meaning, it matters not what he knows in his mind of the thing, rather, whoever attaches himself to the *Shiᶜur Qomah* is the Holy One blessed be he. And this is [Ḥagiggah 13a], 'Come and I will teach you the Works of the Chariot' — that is, by that same chariot of which you are composed [wordplay on *Merkavah* / *murkav*] from God blessed be He in the attributes, in this [same] combination you shall be attached to the Holy One, blessed be He." — *Ḥayyim va-Ḥesed*, *ᶜInyanim Kelalli'im*, sec. 639, p. 210.

28 *Ḥayyim va-Ḥesed*, ibid., sec. 623, p. 207.

29 See above, Chapter 2, quoting *Maggid Devarav le-Yaᶜaqov*, §24, pp. 38–39; and cf., for example, *ʾOr Torah*, p. 73a–b; *ʾOraḥ la-Ḥayyim mi-Shem ha-Maggid*, p. 193b; *Ṭorrei Zahav*, p. 68a.

30 *ʾOr ha-Meʾir*, p. 4d.

31 *Meʾor ᶜEynayim*, p. 15b.

great stringed instrument and a small stringed instrument, in which each contain the same things as the other,[32] were all intended to serve the quietistic idea stating that the ontic identity between God and man allows for the relation between actor and object of action.

32 An analysis of these parables and their passive significance has been made by J. Weiss, "Via passiva," p. 142 ff. There no longer seems to me to be room for Weiss' hesitancy about drawing "far reaching" conclusions concerning the passive outlook to be attributed to these parables. Weiss properly emphasized the ethical meaning which accompanies them, but in the broad context of the theories which are brought here it seems possible to me to understand it as teaching a passive doctrine in practice.

Chapter Ten

The Doctrine of *Kavvanot* and Its Place in Hasidism

We now come to a question which cannot be avoided by any student of Hasidic sources: namely, why did many of the Hasidim reject the Lurianic doctrine of *kavvanot*? What was there about this doctrine which contradicted the very essence of Hasidic teaching and caused it to be excluded from their world, whether directly or obliquely, notwithstanding the fact that the *apologia* for this rejection was accompanied by a certain sense of unease? In the final analysis, as a typological idea, the words of R. Isaac Luria (the "Holy Ari," 1534–72) were placed in the very center of their spiritual world, and they were prepared to insist, with great tenacity and self-sacrifice, upon praying specifically according to the the *nusaḥ* (i.e., specific textual tradition and order of prayer) of the Ari! Yet their attitude toward that specific and unique praxis which served as the foundation and corner-stone in the history of the Lurianic Kabbalah over the course of generations — namely, its doctrine of *kavvanot* — ranged between restraint and open opposition!

It seems to me that elucidation of the various arguments, and especially of the "apologies" implied between the lines of the Hasidic writings concerning this subject (which are not all that numerous!), will contribute to a phenomenological understanding of Hasidism from the quietistic stand-point.

The Maggid of Mezhirech justifiably saw the doctrine of Lurianic *kavvanot* as a technical, magical construction, in which every combination of letters serves as a key for opening one of the secrets of the divine world. "Knowledge" of the *kavvanot* is indeed effective in the supernal world, but it does not accomplish the goal for the sake of which Hasidism came into the world: namely, *devequt*. In his opinion, knowledge of the use of *kavvanot* does not elevate man to that level of integration, beginning with "Speech" and concluding in "Thought," whose ultimate goal is Unio Mystica. The practice of *kavvanot* does not give the necessary "push" to that encounter with the Godhead in which man becomes part of the "divine body," as this was defined by the rabbi of Amdur. In other words: even though he may be expert in all the intricacies of the divine life and know the proper keys by which to draw down influx from above, man remains outside.

More than it wished him to know the Godhead, the Maggidic doctrine wished man to be incorporated within it, and as such it elevated the way towards *devequt* above that of the use of *kavvanot*. While the doctrine of *kavvanot* sought a way to break outwards to the divine world, Hasidism sought a way to delve inside to the human essence, within which it is possible to find the Divine essence. The combinations of *kavvanot*, which were seemingly objective and sure keys to the knowledge of Godhead and to drawing upon its realm, lost their concrete value for the Hasidim when they came to argue on behalf of the spiritual ability of the individual to uncover the divine element in itself, in the course of contemplation and disembodiment.

The words of the Maggid cited below appear to be not without a certain subtle irony, and even strike a certain anarchistic note, when they describe the "householderish" aspect of the practitioner of *kavvanot*, who behaves like one holding the keys to his own home, unlike the *Hasid*, who is compared to a thief boldly breaking through to the king's palace even when he can anticipate the dangers and insecurity awaiting him. In the words of the Maggid himself, we do not yet find that apologetic tone which reverently elevates the "early generations"; this attitude does emerge later, when Hasidism became less spontaneous.[1] The following are the Maggid's remarks:

> ... He who wishes to take shelter under the Holy One blessed be He must place himself within the words of Torah and prayer so that he dwells within the letters, and the Holy One blessed be He is present within the letters — then He is as a shelter to him. And this is the meaning of, "If he is accustomed to studying one page, he should study two pages" — that he should place himself more within the words, and all the workers of iniquity shall be separated [cf. Ps. 92:10]. This is to be compared to a door which one opens with a key, while there are thieves who open it with an object which smashes iron. The earlier ones used to intend the appropriate *kavvanah* for each thing, but today we have no *kavvanah* save for the brokenness of the heart, which opens every thing. And this is the meaning of "Manasseh tunneled underneath the throne of Glory" [Sanhedrin 103a], and of, "Wherefore do you cry out to me? Speak to the children of Israel that they should move!" [Exodus 14:15], which is interpreted in the *Zohar*, "'to me' — specifically." For these things depend upon the Ancient One (*ᶜAtiqa*). For He, may He be blessed, is called the Ancient One, because one cannot apprehend Him, like the parable of the child who does not apprehend the intellect of an adult; and the Holy One blessed be He created the world by speech. And they[2] needed to do something against the [order of the] world — that is, to split the sea — and to do this one needs the intellect which is above the worlds, that is, which the worlds do not apprehend. And this is the meaning of the midrash, "These are

1 See on this especially the quotation from R. Meshullam Feibush of Zbarazh at the end of this chapter.

2 That is, the children of Israel.

idolators, I shall return to my sons" — that is, when you say, "Why should He perform a miracle for us?" I answer, "For them, with the intellect which you do not apprehend, it is fitting that You do a miracle." And this is the meaning of "tunneled underneath" — that he brought himself to the intellect which is above the worlds,[3] where even a great sinner is accepted in repentance. And in every person there is a Manasseh, from the language of forgetting [Aramaic, *yitnashey*], who forgets the Holy One blessed be He and places a graven image in the Tabernacle, for thought is called a Tabernacle (*heikhal*). Speech is the lower *he"h*,[4] and the thought in it also includes the speech,[5] and thought is called *h"y k"l*, because it includes both [letters] *he"h* [6] — that is, speech and thought, the upper *he"h* and the lower *he"h*.[7]

The polemical spirit present in the above remarks is no longer evident in the version brought in the name of the Maggid by R. Benjamin of Salositz. While he does quote the Maggid's opinion against the doctrine of *kavvanot* — specifically based upon a quietistic argument — it is coupled with an apologetic note towards the greatness of the "masters of *kavvanot*." The implication is that it is no longer possible to break the locks with the keys of *kavvanot*, so it is necessary to break the heart; that is, we find an ethical doctrine in place of the doctrine of *kavvanot*. This ethical teaching is founded upon a quietistic base, which sees abnegation as a precondition of attainment; as such, we may assume that the doctrine of *kavvanot* seemed too goal-oriented to Hasidism. R. Benjamin writes:

In the name of the venerable Maggid of the Holy Community of Mezhirech, our Master R. Dov: There is one who opens the lock with a key, and there is one who does not have the key but must break open the door and the lock with a strong object which smashes iron. So the former ones opened all of the gates which were locked following the Destruction with keys — that is, with the known *kavvanot* for each gate.[8] But this is not the case for [we] latter generations, for whom the power of the *kavvanot* is no longer in our hands, so that we must break all the locks without keys, but only

3 The stealing in of the thief is used as a metaphor for man's lifting himself above the worlds. The above passage may perhaps also be intended as an apologetic answer to those who argue against the daring of the Hasidim in their Divine service.

4 Corresponding to the World of Speech, which is the Shekhinah, known in Kabbalah as "the lower *he"h*" of the Divine Name.

5 This is the idea developed above, concerning the integration between speech and thought.

6 The "upper *he"h*" corresponds to *Binah*, which corresponds in the Maggid's teaching to Divine thought.

7 *ʾOr ha-ʾEmet*, 14b. This last phrase is misprinted there as *dalet tataʾah*; the correct reading is *heh tataʾah*, as in MS. Jerusalem 1467, f. 23b. It is clear that the homily as a whole counterposes the doctrine of *devequt* to that of *kavvanot*.

8 This refers to those who pray according to Lurianic *kavvanot*. "There are twelve gates in Heaven corresponding to the twelve tribes" — Ḥayyim Vital, *Shaʿar ha-Kavvanot*.

> by breaking our evil heart, as I interpreted the verse, "God is close to the broken-hearted" [Ps. 34:19] ... But only that it be broken into several broken pieces, so that his heart melt within him like water. Thus it is written, "to the broken hearted" (*nishberei lev*), in the plural ... For [in the case of] an earthenware vessel, its breaking is its repairing [cf. Shabbat 16a]. That is, man, who is an earthenware vessel made of shards of soil, is purified by his breaking — that is, the breaking of his heart; but it must be broken so that it is no longer fit [to reflect upon] its original use.[9]

Elsewhere, the Maggid presents an argument that complements the above remarks against the doctrine of *kavvanot*. He speaks out against the limitations of the system of *kavvanot* because it is inherently impossible to carry them out to their fullest exaction and perfection, because the inner dynamic of the Sephirotic world allows room for an infinitude of possibilities of *kavvanot*, only part of which man is able to "grasp"; by contrast, the doctrine of "connection" or "attachment" [i.e., *devequt* or *hitqashrut*] offers a complete, if one-time solution, of the unification of man with God by means of the spiritualization of the letters. In other words: the technical aspect of the doctrine of *kavvanot* serves as an obstacle in man's path, while unmediated connection or *devequt* achieves true integration between man and God. He says:

> One who intends [meditates] in his prayers all of the *kavvanot* known to him does not concentrate save upon those *kavvanot* which are [in fact] known to him. But when he recites the word with great attachment, there is [then] included in that word all of the *kavvanot* by themselves and from themselves, for each and every letter is a complete world. And when he recites the word with great attachment, he certainly arouses those supernal worlds and performs great actions through this. A person should therefore take care to pray with attachment and with great enthusiasm, and he will certainly bring about great actions in the upper worlds, for every letter arouses up above.[10]

A view which states explicitly that the doctrine of *kavvanot* and the doctrine of *devequt* are two distinct and different paths is implied in the teaching of one of the disciples of the Maggid, R. Shlomo of Lutsk. He makes a claim (unsupported) that there is no one who understands the inner meaning of the doctrine of *kavvanot* as well as the Ari himself understood them, with his holy spirit. As an alternative, he develops the doctrine of "incorporation" within the letters, advocating a pneumatic understanding of the letter as a substitute for the doctrine of *kavvanot*.

9 *Ṭorrei Zahav*, 57c; i.e., they will be unable to take notice of their previous accomplishments in Divine service.

10 *ʾOr ha-ʾEmet*, 77b, and *Liqqutei Yeqarim*, 15a. See also J. G. Weiss, "The Kavvanot of Prayer in Early Hasidism," *Journal of Jewish Studies* 9 (1958), pp. 163–192, esp. p. 178 [in *Studies*: pp. 95–125].

He understands the written letter as the divine pleroma by means of which man ascends to the infinite. The Maggid's teaching is here presented in elaborate homiletic clothing, based upon the famous midrash which tells how Moses saw God placing crowns upon the letters. This midrash is no longer taken literally,[11] but is given a Hasidic significance of mystical walking towards the Infinite (*halikhah*, instead of *halakhah*), alluded to in the "crowns" of letters.

> And so it is in the matter of *kavvanah* of prayer: there are people who in their mind intend *kavvanot*, but to my mind they are small. For one must know that the brilliance of His unity, blessed be He, is present in every letter and point; the Infinite is within it. And even more so when he does not know and cannot understand any *kavvanah* of the Ari with the vitality and clarity of the *kavvanah* as he [i.e., the Ari] of blessed memory, understood it, by his holy spirit, great and very awesome apprehensions. And he must certainly intend all the *kavvanot* going backward and forward to the unity of the Infinite, blessed be He, which is apprehended with great speed, that He is the Infinite, blessed be He.
>
> And the Sages said, "I counted beams,"[12] referring to the beams and pillars which strengthen the house, for the letters and words are like the beams and pillars which sustain the world, and in this way their vitality and abundance are drawn down to all the worlds. And by means of this awe and fear and greater shame fall [upon him] because of the letters and words and vowel-points, until he is unable to direct his mind.[13] And when the Sages said, "Let us be grateful to our heads which bow at *Modim*," they meant to say: Is it possible to intend and to apprehend the greatness of His unity, blessed be He? But in His great kindness and goodness God, blessed be He, contracted His Godhead into the praises and thanks with which we praise Him. And of this it is said, "Come, let us be grateful to our heads" — [that is,] His Godhead — "that it bows at *Modim*" — that it becomes contracted and small, analogous to the matter of bowing, so that we may apprehend Him in our thoughts when we know Him. As is written in the Holy Zohar on the verse "the king is caught in the tresses" [Songs 7:6] — the Holy One, blessed be He, is tied up and bound and contracted in the tresses of the mind, which are our thoughts.[14]

11 See Menaḥot 29b, and the analysis of this midrash by G. Scholem in his article, "Revelation and Tradition as Religious Categories in Judaism," in *The Messianic Idea in Judaism*, pp. 282–303 [German: "Tradition und Commentar als religiöse Kategorien im Judentum", *Eranos Jahrbuch* 31 (1962), 19–48, esp. p. 20ff.]

12 On Rosh Hashanah 16b, Tosafot s. v. *ve-ᶜiyyun tefillah* cites the Jerusalem Talmud, Berakhot 2:4 (5a).

13 It is clear that he grants a superior position to the doctrine of *kavvanot*, which enjoys the status of that which is "above our comprehension," on condition that he is able to preach the Hasidic doctrine of *devequt*. The true reason for the rejection of the system of *kavvanot* is not explicitly explained here, and one can only sense that this rejection was widespread and well-known so that there was no great need to defend it.

14 See above, Chap. 9, for the Maggid's interpretation of "the king is caught in the tresses." This is expanded upon at length in my commentary to *Maggid Devarav le-Yaᶜaqov*, §1, pp. 9– 12.

And he told him concerning that which our rabbis said: "When Moses ascended on high he found the Holy One blessed be He making crowns for the letters, and he asked him: 'Master of the Universe, the world and all that is in it are Yours. Who forces You [to do this]?' He said to him: 'There is a certain man who shall in the future expound mountains upon mountains of *halakhot*.' He said to him: 'Master of the Universe, show him to me.' He replied to him: 'Go back' ... etc." [Menaḥot 29b] They wished to say that he saw that the Holy One blessed be He was making crowns for the letters — that is to say, that the brilliance of the letter is not fine and small, as the image of the letter shows it to be [when it is] contracted, but it has another crown which is drawn through *devequt* from above the letters to within them. And by means of this one may see the greatness of their cleaving on high to the Infinite.[15] And this is "mountains of *halakhot*" — that is, that he ascends stage after stage, and going after going, to the Infinite blessed be He. But the greatest *ẓaddiq*, such as Moses our teacher, may he rest in peace, who was the master of all the prophets, saw and apprehended within the letters themselves — which are the image and contraction of the letter — and in the vitality which is drawn and fills up within the letter, the great brilliance of the Infinite. As is written in the Holy Zohar and in the *Tiqqunim*, "And He fills all the worlds and surrounds all the worlds, and He is within the worlds and in the thickness of the worlds, and in every attribute one may apprehend the great brilliance of the Infinite, blessed be He, that there is nothing which contracts Him. And of this it is said, 'And to whom shall you liken Me, and to whom shall I be compared' [Isa. 40:25]." For after all the images, he is comparable with a complete equanimity and a complete unity. And in [the liturgical poem] *Anᶜim Zemirot*,[16] "You are compared [in metaphors] in many visions, and You are one in all likenesses." How much more so Moses our teacher, whose apprehension was most wondrous in His unity, may He be blessed! And this is what is written, "the world and its fulness are Yours" — that is to say, that every letter is called a world (*ᶜolam*), because it contracts and conceals (*maᶜalim*) the vitality and the light inside it, and the vitality which is within is called "its fulness." And this is what is written, "The world and its fulness are Yours" — in them, too, we can apprehend the greatness of Your unity. Who stops You, that the greatness of Your unity may be apprehended in them by this means! "He said to him [i.e. God to Moses]: 'There is one man who will be in the future, who will not be at your great level, and he will need to expound by means of the crowns of the letters, etc.'[17] He said to Him: 'Show him to me.' He replied: 'Turn back.'" That is, descend

15 These remarks are intended to portray the tremendous power of *devequt*, beginning with the activism of identification with the "contracted" Godhead and concluding with the breaking out of the "limited" framework into the contours of the letters via their crowns through to the Infinite. Man himself ascends by means of the "crowns" which come from above him, meaning: the Godhead goes out to meet man who thinks about It in the aspect of *ẓimẓum*, bringing him out into a broader scope. The quietistic aspect of the concept of *devequt* has already been discussed above.

16 i.e., *Shir ha-Kavod*, "the Hymn of Glory."

17 One can of course present the question here in terms of the possibility that R. Shlomo of Lutsk nevertheless thought that Moses' spontaneous vision of God, and not "by means of" the crowns of

> for some time from the sublimity of your level. And this is the small ᵓ*Aleph* [i.e. at the beginning of the Book of Leviticus], which was [together] with Moses our teacher, the Master [ᵓ*aluf*; wordplay on ᵓ*Alef*], which is the smaller learning and apprehension, because of his great attachment and his great level, as mentioned.[18]

R. Zeᵓev Wolf of Zhitomir makes the explicit claim, based upon a Beshtian tradition, that the doctrine of *kavvanot* is an illusion of the human will, a false obscuring of the religious life. He does not reject the doctrine of *kavvanot* as such, but gives it a new meaning, which completely alters its original intention. R. Zeᵓev Wolf allows for *kavvanot* in preparation for prayer, its purpose being to arouse in the individual who is praying a feeling of awe at God's sublimity and a sense of his own human nothingness. This is doubtless an extremely original reworking of the saying of the Sages that, "The early Hasidim would wait one hour and pray, in order to direct their hearts towards God" [M Berakhot 5:1]. The "*kavvanah*" which devolves upon man in an almost accidental manner serves as the ethical background for the beginning of true prayer. The sharp and ironic parable brought in the name of the Besht is intended to dispel the illusion of the original doctrine of *kavvanot* and to show its absurdity:

> For even when he prays according to the manner described, this is not the purpose of service in the heart; for by rights, before he stands up to pray he should receive into his heart the greatness and sublimity of the Godhead and be aroused inwardly for the service. And whatever he feels in himself as a lack, which he had originally transgressed, he should repair prior to standing up to pray.
>
> And afterwards it is possible for him to intend the *kavvanot* which it is appropriate for him to intend in the holy names, as is said, "The early Hasidim waited one hour before the prayer" [ibid.], in order to take within their hearts the greatness of the Creator and to enwrap themselves in modesty and fear of His greatness — and every evil attribute is automatically negated. And afterwards, when they stand in prayer, they intend the *kavvanot* which one needs to intend in prayer, as known from books, that there is no letter similar to its fellow, which allude to unifications and couplings of the supernal lights.[19] And certainly not every mind is able to undertake this, to know the sublime intention, even if he believes he performed them as they should

the letters, corresponds to the path of apprehension by means of the *kavvanot*. There is at least support for such an interpretation in the connection between the beginning of the homily on the subject of Luria and its conclusion relating to Moses. Interpreted thus, the argument concerning the "superiority" of the doctrine of *kavvanot* and its accompanying line of interpretation were said in complete seriousness, even if motivated by a rejection of the doctrine of *kavvanot* itself.

18 *Dibrat Shlomo*, 6b.

19 The comments I made earlier concerning his opinion refer to the continuation of his remarks (what I have quoted thus far is only the introduction), concerning his reservations about *kavvanot* for the masses.

be according to his understanding; albeit if he himself is remote from the *kavvanah*, its benefit is [in fact] considered as worthless.

And I heard a parable regarding this in the name of the Baᶜal Shem Tov, *z"l*: A person who wishes to eat, and is very desirous of certain kinds of food which are pleasing to him, and afterwards sees that kind of food resting directly before his eyes on a high place where his hand does not reach and he intends [within himself] as if he had eaten — what does his intention help him! The more he intends, the hungrier he is. So is it with those persons who intend awesome and lofty *kavvanot* in the most sublime highest heights of the world, but the span of whose intellect does not reach to there, because they are very far from the *kavvanah*. What does his *kavvanot* help? It would have been better had he not put himself in a place higher than his capability and his grasp, and at least pray in the described manner. But he to whom God has given understanding of the soul knows very well that the main point of the use of *kavvanot* is only that aspect in which he takes upon himself one aspect of the *kavvanot* of this verse, and brings into himself love of the Creator or fear of the Creator, according to the value and essence of the *kavvanah*. And afterwards he intends another intention in a second verse, and takes upon himself another aspect to arouse his heart to utter the words before God with awe and love, so that we find that he prays with Divine awakening and enthusiasm. For from each combination of the words of the prayer he sees and understands how to direct his thoughts to His greatness and loftiness, may He be blessed, and he is enthused as with fire burning inside him at every moment, in different attributes of the value of the *kavvanot*. And this is the purpose of the *kavvanot*: that man should intend in Torah and prayer, save that person who does not understand within himself how to take upon himself different attributes of the *kavvanot* of Torah and prayer and the acts of the *miẓvot*. It were better for him that he henceforth pray as is fit and proper, and that the intention of all his deeds be for the sake of heaven, with simplicity of heart. And he should protect himself, not to utter any letters without pure thought, for then the letters are dry and without the vitality — [lit., wetness] of the influx of supernal light it does not ascend on high, for man must bring the filling of the light into the letters by means of his pure thought. And I have explained elsewhere that therefore the letters are called *ᵓAvnei miluᵓim* ("stones of filling in").[20]

It is clear that the end of this passage contains a description of mystical prayer

20 *ᵓOr ha-Meᵓir*, 14a–b. Joseph Weiss questions the authenticity of the citation of this homily in the name of the Besht; but the parable form in which it is brought actually seems to me quite typical of the Besht's form of expression. Weiss also questions a similar tradition opposed to the doctrine of *kavvanot*, cited in the name of the Besht within the circles of R. Pinḥas of Korets; on this see below. There is inadequate reason to reject the reliability of this tradition, specifically within circles which cite the positive opinion of their master concerning the question of *kavvanot*. See Weiss, "The Kavvanot of Prayer in Early Hasidism," p. 276, n. 36, and his remarks on the Besht pertinent to this matter, p. 168. Weiss's assumption that the doctrine of *kavvanot* was too "aristocratic" for the Besht does not make sense.

in *devequt*, which "fills the letters" with the active presence of God — the alternative to the pretentious and ambitious doctrine of *kavvanot*. To the author of these words, praying with "*kavvanot*" is seen as a kind of fictitious activism, accompanied by desires for the attainment of greatness (in the parable of the Besht), as opposed to the Hasidic religious ethic, which seeks the negation of self rather than "apprehension." Such prayer is prey to an intense desire for combination; R. Zeʾev Wolf advises those who specifically wish to pray while using the system of *kavvanot* to adopt for themselves "one or two" *kavvanot* to serve as stimulus to arousal and enthusiasm — important spiritual values making prayer lead to *devequt*. This Hasidic approach thus shakes itself free of the authentic intellectual constructions of the Lurianic doctrine of *kavvanot*.[21]

R. Ẓevi Aryeh Malik, a disciple of the school of the Maggid, levels criticism against the doctrine of *kavvanot* from another angle. His criticism makes it clear that those who pray according to the system of the "*kavvanot*" are "sunk in the *kavvanah* of the *miẓvot*" rather than being "constantly attached to their Creator." It stresses Hasidism's innermost interest in the teaching of *devequt* — i.e., "to be a chariot for the Shekhinah." The important thing is constant life with God, and not intellectual speculations which cannot be followed through to the end. R. Ẓevi Aryeh enumerates three kinds of worshippers of God, the most sublime of whom are those who choose the way of *devequt*. Here too one can clearly sense the tension which existed within the Hasidic camp over this question.

> The first aspect is that of one who performs the *miẓvah* in order to fulfill what is written in the Torah, which was given by the Creator blessed be His Name, but who

21 The author of *ʾOr ha-Meʾir* discusses this matter extensively elsewhere, on p. 132c: "... For certainly he who has not seriously devoted himself [lit., 'entered with his neck'] into the service [of God] — even if he is a scholar (*talmid ḥakham*), and even if he knows all the *kavvanot* reliably — has not yet tasted the taste of prayer, and it leaves no impression in the supernal worlds, for he knows nothing about the nature of *kavvanah*. And certainly, this was not what the Men of the Great Assembly intended, when he in his slight consciousness and apprehension imagines that in his soul and his intentions he is intending the *kavvanot* of the Ari, *z"l*. And why is this given into the hand of a fool, who has no heart? I am a guarantor for the matter that, if he had even the smallest bit of fear of God, he would certainly fear in his soul to seek and to gaze upon these *kavvanot* which are on the sublimest heights of the world, while he stands with his head and most of his being down below, and does not even know one letter of the *kavvanot* of the Ari." Further on, there is a critical note directed against a specific group of people who dare to pray according to the Lurianic *kavvanot*, "and imagine in their minds that they have a share [lit., 'name and hand'] among the great ones." He argues that they have not learned these *kavvanot* from an authorized teacher of this, even though they are themselves scholars. From the context,it is difficult to know who is authorized, and whether this criticism is directed against those within the Hasidic camp or outside of it (e.g., the Brody *kloiz*, who prayed with the Lurianic *nusaḥ*).

does not know the intention of the *miẓvah*. They are called "masters of knowledge," for those who perform "commandments of men learned by rote" [from Isa. 29:13] are called "lacking in knowledge" ... But those who perform the *miẓvah* in order to fulfill what is written in the Holy Torah draw down knowledge from this *miẓvah*, and they are called masters of Torah. And there is a second aspect, above this one, which is that of those who know the intention of the *miẓvah*, who are called Masters of Understanding (*Baᶜalei Binah*), for he understands one thing from another: that is, he understands the *kavvanah* from the action, and also understands the greatness of the Creator blessed be He from the *kavvanah*. And there is a third aspect, of those who are called Masters of Wisdom (*Baᶜalei Hokhmah*), and who are also called masters of form (*baᶜalei ẓurah*), whose main intention in the performance of the *miẓvah* is to make the form similar to its Creator and to attach and to connect themselves to the Creator blessed be His Name, as is said, "Great are the deeds of the righteous, who make the form to resemble its Creator" [Gen. R. 24:1], for they have no matter, but only the form.[22] And by means of the performance of the *miẓvah* they are always attached to their Creator, and they are not sunk within the *kavvanah* of the *miẓvot*, but the *kavvanah* is performed by itself. And they derive great pleasure from the *miẓvah*, like that of the World to Come, and of them it is said, "the reward of the *miẓvah* is the *miẓvah*" [Avot 4:2], and they constitute a chariot for the Shekhinah — these are the masters of wisdom, which is the third attribute.[23]

Elsewhere in this treatise, R. Ẓevi Aryeh Malik makes some other remarks, unmatched for precision of formulation, concerning the sense in Hasidism of the relationship between the *nusaḥ* of the prayer and the doctrine of *kavvanot*. He is evidently attempting to explain why Hasidism rejected the path of the Lurianic *kavvanot*, while at the same time accepting the Lurianic prayer *nusaḥ* rather than remaining loyal to the Ashkenazic tradition. His explanation seems more intent on explaining the reason why they do not make use of the *kavvanot* of the Ari than it is on defending the use of the Lurianic *nusaḥ* in prayer. In his own way, he follows an approach which draws a distinction in principle between the actual prayer text and the spiritual intention inherent therein, so that alteration in the verbal *nusaḥ* is separated from the issue of the meaning "intended" thereby (in the precise meaning of this term in the doctrine of *kavvanot*). On the other hand, the use of a different prayer text does not separate the one who recites it from the original spiritual *kavvanah* implanted in it by the ancient ones, even if they prayed in a different verbal formulation. In other words, he sees the spiritual continuity between the generations in the inner, overall spiritual intention inherent therein, while the question of alteration of the *nusaḥ* is irrelevant to the claim of those who

22 That is, cast off their corporeality.
23 R. Ẓevi Aryeh [Malik], *ʾOr Ḥakhamim* (Warsaw, 1885), 10a.

denounce this change![24] In response to the dilemma of "loyalty" to the *nusaḥ*, on the one hand, or to the *kavvanah*, on the other, he proposes a third alternative: that of the spiritual value which is subject to neither one nor the other, and is free to choose what its heart feels. To my mind, this response belongs to the anarchistic aspect of the Hasidic mentality which, despite its anarchism, knows how to live at peace within historical and authoritative frameworks. The following are the words of R. Ẓevi Aryeh:

> It is possible that one ought to hint that in truth the prayers, which the Patriarchs and other prophets instituted, were made with great *kavvanot* and great attachment, and they introduced lights into the *nusaḥ* of prayer. So much so, that the prayer itself would make an impression always, [and] even though the generations which came after them would not pray in the *nusaḥ* which they instituted with the same clarity as they instituted it, nevertheless, the prayer itself also leaves an impression. And we

24 It is interesting to note in this connection the remarks cited by the Ḥatam Sofer (R. Moses Sofer) in the name of his Hasidic (!) teachers, R. Nathan Adler and R. Pinḥas b. Ẓevi Hirsch ha-Levi Horowitz, the author of *Sefer Hafla*ᵓ*ah*: "All the prayer rites (*nusaḥ*) are equal to one another, and everything found in one is also in the other, only we do not know in what way [this is so]. And we pray according to the path of those who instituted the prayers and the various rites, for they all intended one thing, just as there is one [sic!] style to several different prophets ... but they all ascend to one place. And once the lamp of God, the Ari, came and balanced and examined and instituted, for he knew the nature of the thing, he placed in his prayer book everything in its place, and revealed hidden things of the Sephardic rite, for he was a Sephardi, but had he been an Ashkenazi, such a person would have done a similar thing with the Ashkenazic rite. And now in our latter generations it is sufficient for those entering into the secret of the Lord to understand the words of the Ari, but there is none who knows how to do a similar thing in the Ashkenazic rite. Therefore, it is good for them to pray out of a Sephardic Siddur, in which are written the location of the various palaces (*heikhalot*) and unifications (*yiḥudim*) according to the Ari. But as for one who prays in the Ashkenazic [rite], even though there too everything is alluded to, one who prays according to the view of those who instituted it [i.e., without conscious meditation upon the *kavvanot* inherent therein, which are nowhere explicated] will rapidly race in it; nevertheless, it is preferable that they pray that which they understand rather than relying upon those who instituted it. Therefore my teacher, the *ga*ᵓ*on* and *ḥasid* among the priests [i.e., he was a *kohen*], Rabbi Nathan Adler, *z"l*, himself led the congregation in prayer in the Sephardic rite, using the Siddur of the Ari *z"l*, and likewise my teacher, the *ga*ᵓ*on*, author of the *Hafla*ᵓ*ah*, *z"l*, for they alone prayed in the rite of the Ari, but none of those who were in the minyan [prayer quorom] prayed anything other than the Ashkenazic rite. And even his [i.e., Horowitz's] son, the *ga*ᵓ*on* author of *Maḥaneh Levi*, *z"l*, did not deviate from the Ashkenazic rite, and immediately following the death of his father, the *ga*ᵓ*on*, *z"l*, nullified his prayer gathering, and prayed in the synagogue of the community of Frankfort-am-Main, as is well-known, and all this because of the reason that one who does not know for what they are [i.e., the *kavvanot*] is not allowed to change the rite that is incumbent upon us." — *Ḥatam Sofer; She*ᵓ*elot u-Teshuvot* ᵓ*Oraḥ Ḥayyim*, Section 15 (Pressburg, 1855).

> pray in the *nusaḥ* of prayer with the *kavvanot*[25] which they intended at the time they instituted it.[26]

A particularly interesting approach to the problem of *kavvanot* was taken by another disciple of the Maggid of Mezhirech — R. Ẓevi Hirsch of Zhidachov, an important figure well known for his Kabbalistic works. He may have tried his hand at a harmonistic interpretation of the question of *kavvanot* due to his own unusual closeness to Kabbalah. In the course of a fictitious debate with the halakhic sources, he attempts to preserve the honor of both the Lurianic *kavvanot* and the Hasidic concept of *devequt* at one and the same time. As a *ḥasid* and disciple of the Maggid, he well understood the fundamental difference between these two approaches, placing the doctrine of *devequt* above that of *kavvanot* in principle, without negating the importance of the latter. It is important to note here that this is not an attempt at apologetics for the Hasidic doctrine of *devequt*, but rather one to "save" the theory of *kavvanot* — a point which clearly indicates misgivings on this question within the Hasidic camp. He sees the doctrine of *kavvanot* itself as a technical means for the beginning of meditation, for which one may substitute concentration upon objects on this world or any other external actions which allow for a similar mental concentration. Thus, in order to compare the subject of

The fundamental argument is the same in both cases — i.e., that of the Hatam Sofer and of R. Ẓevi Aryeh — although the conclusions drawn do not refer to the same subject. Regarding additional customs about which the Ḥatam Sofer differed with the Hasidim, see Louis Jacobs, *Hasidic Prayer* (London, 1972), pp. 154–166.

25 *Kavvanot* is used here in the sense of the inner meaning or significance, and not in the technical sense used in the doctrine of *kavvanot*. It is perhaps worthwhile explaining here in brief how, in my opinion, this passage ought to be understood: "For in truth the prayers which the patriarchs and other prophets instituted were made with great *kavvanot* and with great connection (*hitqashrut*)" — implying that there is a profound spiritual investment in the body of the words of prayer — "and they introduced lights to such an extent in the text (*nusaḥ*) of the prayer until the prayer itself would make a permanent impress" — without being dependent upon the precise *nusaḥ* of the words — "even though the generations which followed them will not pray according to the version which they instituted with such great clarity as they themselves instituted" — as happened to the generation of the author, who prayed according to *Nusah ha-Ar"i*. That is, a small change in the *nusaḥ* does not affect the inner weight of the prayer, for "nevertheless the prayer itself makes an impression always."
"And we pray by the prayer rite" — that is, the renewed Lurianic *nusaḥ*, but — "according to their *kavvanot* which they intended at the time they instituted it" — that is, with what was intended in the original inner investment of those who instituted the prayers. The point here is that one prays, not according to the doctrine of *kavvanot* but, on the contrary, to *kavvanot* in the most general sense of the term, according to the specific matter.

26 It seems to me that the natural conclusion of the sentence should be: "and not on *kavvanot* as in the text before us" — *ʾOr Ḥakhamim*, 14c.

kavvanot to such technical means, R. Ẓevi Hirsch makes use of an example which the Hasidim were particularly fond of using (albeit in another context, to explain the possibility of *devequt* without *miẓvot* prior to the giving of the Torah; see above, Chapter 6, on the *miẓvot*) — namely, that of the "sticks" of the patriarch Jacob. Elsewhere, he also uses the examples of the amora Samuel, "I counted flowers," or of R. Bon bar Ḥiyya, "I counted the beams" (i.e., the beams and rows of his house — Rashi).[27] A comparison of the doctrine of *kavvanot* with these two examples which are themselves problematic removes the *kavvanot* from their primary, true power and their original meaning in the Lurianic Kabbalah. There the *kavvanot*, which also contain an element of spontaneous and magical power, themselves act and not only serve as instruments of meditation! By contrast, R. Ẓevi Hirsch wishes to explain that service by means of *kavvanot*

> ... was not in the aspect of Emanation (*ʾaẓilut*), for at times one needs [to perform] the service of Creation (*beriʾah*) for the sake of creation ... and there are hidden secrets in this for those who are enlightened in the ways of service, concerning which the mouth and the pen cannot elaborate, because it depends upon the wisdom of the heart.[28]

In order to distinguish between the two kinds of service — i.e., "with *kavvanot*" and "without *kavvanot*" — he makes use of a paradoxical dialectic which applies the doctrine of *devequt* to those conditions about which it is said that, "*miẓvot* do not require *kavvanah*" and "one does not need *kavvanah*." This is read as meaning that one does not require the doctrine of *kavvanot*, in the exact and technical meaning of the word, but that one may arrive directly at the Infinite through means of "self-sacrifice." The idea of *devequt* to the Infinite was clearly a formula much beloved of the Hasidim, which R. Ẓevi Hirsch needed to justify in his discussions and to pose in opposition to the doctrine of *kavvanot*, which only deals with the lower realm of the Sefirot. The question of *devequt* to the Infinite remained in his teaching as something permitted to those individuals who were already able to achieve complete identification with the Infinite at the beginning of their prayer and did not require the doctrine of *kavvanot*.

> His acts and his thoughts are one in the path of Emanation, in which He and His life

27 *Peri Qodesh Hilulim* (Arsciva, 1927), 1d, who quotes the "Jerusalem Talmud on Berakhot cited by Tosafot in R. H. 17b" [see above, n. 12], and further on in the discussion, p. 3a, "and also those pious people who counted flowers or boards certainly do not remove it from its literal meaning, and certainly did an act, but they performed great *yiḥudim* with combinations of His Names, blessed be He."

28 Ibid, 3a.

> are one within them and He and His essence are one in them, and the thought and the action come to them as one, after the supernal holy ones have suppressed their corporeality and refined their thoughts, coming into their thoughts in the way of Emanation mentioned. And when he got to *Modim* he bowed from his Self, for he and his Self are one . . . and they did not need to engage in *kavvanot*, for the *kavvanah* indicates that he changes some thing from his own will, and he forces himself to act according to this *kavvanah*, specifically, and not any other.[29]

Further on, he explains that the meaning of the statement, that "*mizvot* do not require *kavvanah*" refers to the case in which

> . . . his will to be attached to His Creator is so great that his thought and his acts become one, and it is as if he had acted without *kavvanah*. And this is the example of Emanation, that when he reaches *Modim* he bows of his own accord.[30]

The path of direct *devequt*, without the intermediacy of the doctrine of *kavvanot*, is referred to by him as "a *mizvah* in Emanation," where "one does not require *kavvanah*."[31]

The non-literal interpretation of the ancient concept of *kavvanah* is not relevant to our discussion here; what is significant was the fact that there was a need to confront this concept within the context of the Lurianic doctrine of *kavvanot* to establish the "legitimacy" of the use of this teaching. At times, it also occurs to me that it was perhaps specifically the doctrine of *devequt* of the intellectual elite (i.e., of those who bow automatically when they come to *Modim*) which was "almost" impossible of realization, and that this represents a renewed attempt to replace it by the doctrine of *kavvanot*, with which other Hasidism disagreed. The attempt to reject the teaching of *devequt* as the exclusive "preferred" doctrine was already present in those days in the teaching of R. Meshullam Feibush of Zbarazh, although the latter also rejected the Lurianic *kavvanot* with the argument that "we are unable to understand it."[32] The equal rejection of both doctrines by R. Meshullam Feibush was intended to leave room for an ethical teaching — which is interesting in itself — while the stance of R. Ẓevi Hirsch seems to me in principle be less extreme and less serious in its rejection of the doctrine of *devequt*, and ought to be seen primarily as a speculative, harmonistic attempt to integrate *devequt* and *kavvanot*.

There seems no doubt that, from the historical point of view, the Lurianic doctrine of *kavvanot* never enjoyed a dominant position within Hasidism, and that

29 Ibid., 1d–2a, which is an interesting argument!

30 Ibid., 2a.

31 Ibid., 2b.

32 See the end of this chapter.

— to quote the words of Gershom Scholem — "it has become again what it was in the beginning: the esoteric wisdom of a small group of men out of touch with life and without any influence on it."[33] The Kabbalists of the 18th century Beth-El circle in Jerusalem likewise attempted, according to Scholem, to remove the magical elements present in this doctrine, albeit it was presented in a more spiritual manner in the center of their world.[34] R. Ẓevi Hirsch of Zhidachov may have functioned as a kind of mediator on this point, in addition to having an independent theological reason for not praying "directly to the Infinite." In his words:

> Behold, my brothers, this is the path in which light shall dwell. Do not make bold to ascend to God immediately, to pray to the Infinite, but as you shall see in the words of this holy one [R. Ḥayyim Vital], one must elevate the Shekhinah with all one's movements — that is, with all of one's human strength — with every motion to shake up the roots and the Sefirot, to uplift the Shekhinah which spreads about in the worlds, the root of the attribute of *Malkhut*, which is the attribute which dwells in the lower realms, to give them life and to separate out ... And in truth our main weapons of war are the names of the Holy One blessed be He, to unite [His Name] with them — they are the life and the souls of all the world ...[35]

It follows from the entire discussion that there is indeed a substantial difference between the goal of the Kabbalist, which is "to unite the world of the Sefirot," and that of the *ḥasid*, which is to nullify his individuality by means of immediate *devequt* with the Infinite. For the latter, the fact that the Sefirotic world is unified at that moment by his mystical activity is only a sort of by-product or after-thought of the system. It is clear that an approach, the main aim of which is the extinction of the ego at the time of prayer, was unable to concern itself with matters of unifications (*yiḥudim*) in the supernal worlds, which prevented the natural development of inner contemplation. We may therefore state that the quietistic interest definitely held the upper hand in Hasidic teaching, and it was this that led to the rejection from its realm of the Lurianic doctrine of *kavvanot*.

In order to complete the historical picture concerning the struggle over this question, I would like to present the unique position of R. Pinḥas of Korets. His uniqueness lies in his opposition in principle to the Maggidic doctrine of *devequt*, from which it would appear that he indirectly supported the doctrine of *kavvanot*. R. Pinḥas, who was an outstanding example of a popular charismatic leader and held a very concrete understanding of the Besht's doctrine, did not view the spiritualistic tendencies of the Maggid in a favorable light, and argued with him

33 See *Major Trends*, p. 34.

34 See ibid., p. 277–78.

35 *Peri Qodesh Hilulim*, 3b.

concerning these questions. It seems clear from his words that he and his school attributed prayer with *devequt* (of the kind which I have described above) to an explicitly Maggidic doctrine, and that he did not consider this to be the proper interpretation of the doctrine of the Besht.

R. Yitzḥak b. R. Shlomo, the Elder of Korets, preserves some important traditions which he himself heard from R. Pinḥas on various occasions, including various matters pertaining to the tension between the Maggid and R. Pinḥas regarding several fundamental aspects of the Hasidic path. He relates, for example, that "also concerning matters of prayer the Rav said:[36] 'the world says that the Maggid lifted up prayer, but I have lifted up prayer.'"[37] R. Pinḥas denies that he disagreed with the Maggid, but does state that his path and that of the Maggid constitute two differing ways of serving the Creator:

> And there stemmed from this a great dispute[38] in the city; and there were people opposed to him because he even sent them away from his household and was unable to tolerate that they performed the gestures of the Maggid[39] and that they called themselves the people of the Maggid. And the rabbi said: "They are the people of the Maggid; do they think that I would dispute with the Maggid?! If I would go in the Maggid's way, or he in mine, we would be burned!"

These remarks have been passed down directly from R. Pinḥas but, according to the testimony of those who were close to him (such as this elder from Korets), there seems to have been tension and competition between the two leaders regarding fundamental questions in Hasidism. It is even clear from the following story that R. Isaiah of Dinowitz was sent (or perhaps went of his own accord?) to Korets regarding these questions. This R. Isaiah is known to us as a loyal disciple of the Maggid, and was perhaps one of the editors of his teachings in the volume, *ᵓOr Torah*.[40] The following is the story, as told by the Elder of Korets:

36 In all writings of the school of Korets, *ha-Rav* ("the rabbi"), without any further adjective, refers to R. Pinḥas himself.

37 "I lifted up the prayer"; many of the sayings of R. Pinḥas are brought in their original Yiddish phrasing. See MS. Jerusalem–National Library 3759, fo. 155b.

38 Concerning the question of the slaughter house in Korets. which is a continuation of the story of the Elder of Korets in the same MS., 155b–156a.

39 See on this the interesting testimony in Menaḥem Mendel Bodek, *Seder ha-Dorot* (n.p., n.d.,), p. 14, concerning R. Pinḥas, who distinguished between two kinds of *devequt*, one of which is performed without any motion whatsoever!

40 It is possible that R. Isaiah of Dinovitz, in whose posssession the MS. of *ᵓOr Torah* was discovered, was also the editor of this manuscript. On the problem of *ᵓOr Torah*, see the Introduction to my edition of *Maggid Devarav le-Yaᶜaqov*, p. x.

Once R. Isaiah of Dinowitz spent the Sabbath with the *Rav* of Korets [i.e., the rabbi of the city of Korets, R. Isak],[41] and that elder [that is: R. Yitzḥak b. Shlomo] heard from him that after the Friday evening meal he complained about the Rav [42] [i.e., R. Pinḥas] and he did not know why, [saying] as follows: "Long life to him — [but] we have also gotten to know God a bit."[43] And after the Third Meal [of the Sabbath] he saw that he was very satisfied with the Rav and he praised him [saying] that there

41 The author of *Seder ha-Dorot he-Ḥadash* says of the community rabbi of Korets: "the great *gaʾon* of the priesthood, the divine Kabbalist, disciple of the holy Maggid of Mezhirech, and the close disciple of the holy Rabbi M. Yeḥiel Mikhal of Zloczow, the author of *Sefer Berit Kehunat ʿOlam*, very profound sermons in Kabbalah."

42 See A. J. Heschel's article, "Rabbi Pinḥas of Korzec," in his *The Circle of the Baal Shem Tov*, pp. 1–43; Hebrew: *ʿAlei ʿAyin* [Schocken Jubilee Volume] (Jerusalem, 1948–52), pp. 213–44. Heschel brings a great deal of material about R. Pinḥas based upon MS. Cincinnatti 62, which is evidently a parallel MS. to the one here, in which the word "complained" in this sentence and "and did not know why" are deleted; it is difficult to imagine that these phrases are missing in that MS. See ibid., p. 32, n. 161; Heb.: p. 242, n. 156.

43 "May God grant him long days, I also have known the Holy One, blessed be He, a little." It is surprising that the Elder of Korets did not know why R. Isaiah complained, for he himself describes the entire controversy; or else perhaps he did not understand exactly why R. Isaiah supported the teaching of the Maggid against that of Rav Pinḥas, or complains against him! It is clear from the story that the controversy also pertained to matters relating to the essence of their paths in the service of God. It is worth noting here the existence of a unique and rather enigmatic letter of R. Pinḥas of Korets addressed to R. Isaiah Dinovitz, which deliberately concealed more than it reveals (see its end). However, its overall testimony is very interesting and transparent enough in its general intention. R. Pinḥas writes that he had succeeded in "meeting" the soul of R. Isaiah in a dream, and saw that the latter was "worried" concerning matters of divine worship, and that his path was not clear to him: "I saw in my contemplation that it was perceived while awake, and he fell into deep confusion, and there still was no healing for the straightness of his path, for he had not yet reached the true form." Further along in these remarks, R. Pinḥas criticizes him for "distorting his path," alluding here to the verse which he (R. Isaiah) saw in a dream, which he did not know how to interpret: "'You are all fair, my love, and there is no blemish (*mum*) in you' [Songs 4:7]. And behold, the honor of his Torah began with this matter, and in the middle you went off on a crooked path, to think in a different way than was conveyed to him ... That is [the meaning of the verse is]: you went in a good way at the beginning, but there is no blemish (*mum*) in you, *Mu"m* being the fullness of *Yah* in gematria [the sense is that there is no God within him, *Elohim* in gematria equalling *mum*, 86]. There is not this intention in you, therefore you were pushed away from understanding it clearly ..." — at the end of R. Abraham ben Dov of Mezhirech (the Malakh), *Ḥesed le-Avraham* (Jerusalem, 1954), pp. 40a–b. Abraham J. Heschel mentions this "meeting" without mentioning the unique note of rebuke which accompanied it. See his article, "Umbekante Dokumenten tsu der Geshikhte fun Hassidus" (Yid.), *YIVO Bletter* 36 (1952), p. 123. This note of complaint against R. Isaiah is also implied (in the MS in my possession, Jerusalem–National Library 3759, fo. 181a) in the words of R. Pinḥas as they were transmitted by his disciples: "And he said in the name of R. Isaiah of Dinovitz, who referred to himself as *tanna u-falig*" [i.e., a teacher of the tradition and one authorized to dispute].

> was none like him. And the elder said that there were several people who left the rabbi puzzled.[44]

We learn of the inner spiritual character of this dispute from another source:

> Since the essence [i.e., purpose] of the Creation of the world was to apprehend his godliness, those worlds which are not apprehended by thought at all belong in the aspect of secret [*sod*], and "He destroys them." For this is not the main intention of the Creation — and understand this.[45]

What is the point of this saying? These remarks are addressed to some very specific things in the teaching of the Maggid, which tirelessly attempt to break through from the world of divine thought into the Infinite. The preacher from the school of R. Pinḥas (or perhaps R. Pinḥas himelf?) accepted another, quieter and more "polite" principle of divine service, according to which those worlds which God does not reveal and which remain hidden away in the attribute of *sod* (in the sense of "he built worlds and destroyed them"), are not subject to human apprehension, and we are not even allowed to inquire into them, "for this is not the main intention of the Creation." He explains that, paradoxically, the "principle" that the Creation of the world was in order to "apprehend" His Godhead only applies insofar as God wished us to apprehend Him, and not regarding those attributes which are hidden from us. In other words: it seems to the author of this statement that the Hasidic breakthrough of the type found in the teaching of the Maggid was not directed towards the correct address — and this was the meaning of the remark, "and understand this."

In several of his sayings, R. Pinḥas touches upon the relationship between intention and deed and does not refrain from himself criticizing the doctrine that the deed in itself was not enough, but wishes the deed to serve as an instrument of *devequt*.[46] But even though he fought for the honor of the act for its own sake, he did not abstain from "adding a few *kavvanot*" at the time of prayer, though he

44 This addition of the "Elder" suggests that the Elder himself was not among the supporters of R. Pinḥas, or perhaps he simply described in all innocence the circumstances surrounding the controversy in the court of Korets.

45 R. Pinḥas of Korets, *Nofet Ẓufim* (Lemberg, 1864). One cannot know whether the quotation is from R. Pinḥas himself or one of his disciples. In any event, it is helpful in explaining the anti-Maggidic atmosphere from a point of view that is extremely important for our understanding of the naturé of spiritualistic prayer.

46 See the version of the Maggid's teaching in *Kitvei Qodesh* (Warsaw 1884), p. 11a: "When a person serves the king, he does not require any intention in his service, for he serves! His thought only need be that he serves the king to make him king, to give the king pleasure, and this is the combination of supernal and lower wisdom through the world of imagery — and understand."

knew full well that the Besht did not agree with the Lurianic doctrine of *kavvanot*. According to one of the traditions of the school of Korets transmitted in the name of the Besht, R. Pinḥas said:

> The main *kavvanah* is that he should think, "I am going to the *miqveh* (ritual bath)." For there are several [different] *kavvanot*: one person intends to act by it in this world, another intends concerning the World to Come, and yet another intends that he will be able to pray with *devequt*; but the best of them all is that he performs it for the sake of that thing itself which is written in the Torah, and this is for its own sake (*le-shem poᶜolan*) — for the sake of the act alone, and not for any other purpose. And this is the rule in all His service: not that he should intend that afterwards he come to *devequt*, but that directly, by this thing [itself], I perform a commandment of God. And this is, "Would that you abandoned me" — that they not intend for *devequt*, "but guarded my Torah" — in its simple meaning, to fulfill the Torah and the *miẓvot* themselves.[47]

A similar tradition is transmitted in the name of R. Shmerl, one of R. Pinḥas's important disciples, stating explicitly that which was only implied in the earlier quotes: namely, that the Koretser path was opposed in essence to the spiritualistic approach of elevation of things from the realm of action to that of thought:

> The path of the Besht was that, when he would intend a *kavvanah*, he would perform an act with the *kavvanah*. And R. Shmerl, *z"l*, said, that they are therefore called *kavvanot*, because one must direct (*kavven*), but it does not state that one must think. For the word *kavvanah* comes from the phrase, "even and directed" (*shavveh u-mekuvvan*) — that is, that the person should be at one with the *kavvanah* — and understand this.[48]

The overall tendency of these remarks is clear enough — namely, to argue against the legitimacy of the Maggid's teaching regarding the manner of *devequt*, according to which one must lift the deed up to the thought and thereby attain *devequt*. In Korets, the Baᶜal Shem Tov's doctrine was not understood as a spiritualistic teaching, so the Maggid was perceived as a dangerous "innovator." Elsewhere, too, it seems to me that R. Pinḥas's sayings are directed against the "innovations" of the Maggid, whether in his customs or in his teachings as such:

> From the Rav [R. Pinḥas], the eyes of the congregation, that is, of those who have eyes to see the hidden light from one end of the world to the other: Therefore, the righteous are able to perform great deeds and new customs, because they see what is pleasing before Him may He be blessed. But for us who do not have eyes, it is for-

47 MS. Jerusalem 3759, 49b–50a and 189b–190a, as well as *Midrash Pinḥas* (Belgoray, 1931), p. 10.

48 *Peᵓer la-Yesharim* [traditions of R. Raphael of Bershad, a disciple of R. Pinḥas] (Jerusalem, 1921), 19b.

> bidden to innovate any thing or custom,[49] but only to follow the way of the *Shulḥan ᶜArukh* and of the righteous of yore.[50]
> Of the Rav: all the new books which have been written within the [last] seventy years are not in accordance with the truth, apart from the books of the rabbi of Polonnoye [Jacob Joseph], of which he [R. Pinḥas] said that there is no author like them in the world except for *Sefer ʾOr ha-Ḥayyim* [by R. Ḥayyim ben Attar] ... And he, may he long live [i.e., this tradition was transmitted during R. Pinḥas's life-time], said that he gave publicity to *ʾOr ha-Ḥayyim* by saying: My words are at times closer to the truth than the *ʾOr ha-Ḥayyim*.[51]

It is quite clear against whom these remarks are directed, for the first book of the teachings of the Maggid of Mezhirech, *Maggid Devarav le-Yaᶜaqov*, was published only one year after the appearance of *Toldot Yaᶜaqov Yosef*, in which R. Pinḥas sees the authentic repository of Hassidic teaching.

There is a certain Beshtian tradition extant from the school of R. Pinḥas himself which, even though it does not explicitly oppose the doctrine of *kavvanot* as such, does (in its extant form) argue on behalf of other values in prayer which counterweigh the doctrine of *kavvanot*:

> In the name of R. Shmerl, he told of R. Naḥman — and he did not know which R. Naḥman [52] — that he used to recite the prayers with the *kavvanot* during every day

49 He may refer here to the renewed practice of postponing the time of prayer, which R. Pinḥas strongly opposed; see the above MS., fo. 56b: "And he spoke a great deal about this matter, not to transgress the time for the reading of *Shemaᶜ*, and I heard from R. Ḥayyim [of Krasina] that he blamed the trouble of the fires, Heaven forbid, on this matter ... And our teacher R. Raphael (of Bershad), although he on occasion would also delay his prayers, said that they should not learn from him concerning this matter, for he was forced to do so because of a *mizvah*, that he needed to speak words of rebuke with many people, which was his craft." This is an extremely peculiar form of "coercion"; it would appear that R. Pinḥas did not completely "succeed" regarding his own disciples. A similar tradition opposed to delaying the time for prayer is given by R. Shmuel Voltzis, another disciple of R. Pinḥas, in the above mentioned MS., fo. 84b. There is no proof of the idea that the Maggid "introduced" this practice, but it is clear that there were many in his school who behaved in this manner, while in the earlier arguments of its opponents against Hasidism, this complaint is not yet found.
The fire mentioned above may refer to the well-known incident in which the writings of R. Levi Yitzḥak of Berdichev, including teachings of the Maggid which he had transcribed, were completely destroyed by a fire in his Bet Midrash, the only thing that was saved being a copy of his writings made by R. Ḥevi of Hannopol, a disciple of R. Ḥayyim of Krasina and of R. Levi Yitzḥak. See the publisher's Introduction to *ʾOr ha-ʾEmet* by the Maggid of Mezhirech, and Schatz, "Introduction," p. xv.

50 MS. ibid., 184b.

51 MS. ibid., 179b, and *Peʾer la-Yesharim*, p. 20b.

52 Either R. Naḥman of Horodenka or R. Naḥman of Kosow. It seems more likely that it was the former, as many traditions in his name are brought by this school, which were greatly valued by R. Pinḥas

> of Elul, until the Besht sent him [a message] that he should cease doing so, for a person must prepare for himself the tools of war for Rosh Hashanah. And even though he does not know if he will pray with those *kavvanot* [53] — for the battle belongs to the Lord — a person must in any event prepare for himself the tools of war, for one does not rely upon a miracle, etc.[54]

The only possible interpretation of the expression "tools of war" here seems to me to be a reference to the doctrine of *devequt*, which is the only effective weapon against the "alien thoughts" which visit man at the time of prayer.[55] This is also a new and interesting aspect, which serves as a reason — and perhaps the primary reason, for the Besht — for the rejection of the doctrine of *kavvanot*.[56] The rejection of *kavvanot* by the Besht, especially during the month of Elul [the month of preparation preceding the Days of Awe] seems reliable from an historical point-of-view, as prayer during the month of Elul constituted a special problem for the early Hasidim. This problem is discussed by the Maggid of Mezhirech in the tractate *Liqqutei Yeqarim*,[57] as well as at greater length and explication by Meshullam Feibush of Zbarazh.[58] In the sources mentioned, the discussion does

according to the testimony of this MS; see there, fo. 107a. It is precisely the lack of certainty here which indicates the reliability of the tradition, as a forger of traditions would not have left this type of uncertainty. Heschel, in his article, "R. Nahman of Kosow, Companion of the Baal Shem," brings this quotation without the addition of the phrase, "and he, may he long live, did not know which R. Nahman was spoken of." He evidently took the entire subject from Matityahu Guttman's edition (op. cit., n. 47), sec. 71, when he evidently had at hand the full account in MS. Cincinnatti! Incidently, Heschel states unequivocally that the one referred to is R. Naḥman of Kosow, a point which is by no means so certain to me.

53 It is difficult to know the tendency of this sentence, as already felt by Weiss in his article on "Kavvanot," p. 176, n. 3. However, I think that the sentence, "we do not know if he will pray with the same *kavvanot*," means that we do not know if he will succeed in praying with *kavvanah* (and not *kavvanot*!, the plural use of the term *kavvanot* among Hasidim frequently being misleading). Heschel, in the above-mentioned article, adds the word *kavvanot* in parentheses, following the words, "tools of war," not realizing that he thereby increased the confusion, ending up with a sentence that was self-contradictory!

54 MS. ibid., 203a.

55 The concept "tools of war" appears in the words of R. Ẓevi Hirsch of Zhidachov: "And in truth our main tools of war are His Names, blessed be He" (*Peri Qodesh Hilulim*, 3b). This seems to refer to the technique of seeing the name in its letters for the sake of concentration and attainment of *devequt*, and not combination of *kavvanot*.

56 Allow me to mention that some of the Sabbatians also rejected the *kavvanot* of the Ari, but for reasons involving metaphysical changes which take place in the messianic age, according to their view. See on this I. Tishby, "Between Sabbatianism and Hasidism," in his *Netivei ʾEmunah u-Minut* (Ramat Gan, 1964), p. 225, n. 171; originally published in *Knesset; Divrei Sofrim le-zekher Ḥ. N. Bialik* 9 (1945), p. 266, and n. 162 there.

57 *Liqqutei Yeqarim*, 8d.

58 *Liqqutei Yeqarim*, in the letters of R. Meshullam Feibush, 26d.

not relate to the question of whether or not to pray with "*kavvanot*," but rather emphasizes the fact that during the month of Elul and on Rosh Hashanah one needs to pray with particularly great *kavvanah* in order to do battle with the alien thoughts and prosecuting angels which are more numerous during the Days of Judgment.[59] In this connection, the Maggid issues an explicit warning to the masses of ordinary people, who do not recite any prayers with much devotion except for the ᶜ*Amidah* (which is precious to them because of its newness on that day), in which they pour out their hearts. He argues that the main thing is "to prune [*zamer*; also 'to sing' — a wordplay on *Pesuqei de-Zimra*] the arrogant" (a euphemism for the *qelippot*) in the Preliminary Psalms (*Pesuqei de-Zimra*), and thereby prepare the way for the ᶜ*Amidah* Prayer. I mention this question here (in an aside) in connection with the unique and important task of the prayers of Rosh Hashanah — namely, to do battle against alien thoughts — which squares well with the Besht's stance concerning the "preparation of tools of war" expounded in this connection. What the tradition of Korets added to the Besht is the claim, relating to our topic, that "prayer with [Lurianic] *kavvanot*" do not help in this matter.

To return to the tradition of the Korets Hasidim: there are remarks concerning *kavvanot* transmitted by R. Raphael of Bershad, through which one can observe the conflict over this question within the school of Korets, even though it is noted there that R. Pinḥas himself actually held a positive stand towards the doctrine of *kavvanot*. These are his remarks:

> On several occasions he adjured us to practice *kavvanot* during the prayer of ᶜ*Asiyyah*,[60] and R. Raphael explained that the essential root of prayer is to correct

59 This point is made in the letters of Meshullam Feibush in a more obscure and hidden manner than in the words of *Liqqutei Yeqarim* of the Maggid's teaching, although here too the remarks are intended "to place his soul in his hands," which is an allusion to the battle with alien thoughts. On the other hand, R. Meshullam stresses the true value of prayer with *kavvanah* in his own formulation, which was not found in the Maggid. In the testimony of these letters, it is mentioned that R. Menaḥem Mendel of Przemyślany (who was Meshullam's teacher) already behaved in the manner required by the Maggid. There is no ground for assuming that the Besht himself did not already behave in this way, and that the Lurianic doctrine of *kavvanot* was also rejected by him because of the doctrine of the lifting up of alien thoughts. However, both R. Israel Ḥarif and R. Shabbetai of Rashkov, as well as the *Toldot*, mention specific *kavvanot* in the name of the Besht, the best known of which is the Besht's "*kavvanah* of the *miqveh*" (ritual bath), testimonies concerning which are doubtless to be accepted as reliable. Here too, there may be various shades of the use of the doctrine of *kavvanot* as a fixed system of prayer, or only on occasion for certain specific things. In any event, even if there is no unequivocal position taken here on the part of the Besht, one may at least acknowledge the hesitancies about this question as they arose from the conflict of various theoretical interests.

60 i.e., a prayer which corresponds to the World of Action (ᶜ*Olam ha-*ᶜ*Asiyyah*) and not the World of Emanation (ᶜ*Olam ha-*ᵓ*Aẓilut*) — and that the address seems to me to be clear. The first sentence seems to refer to R. Pinḥas himself. It is occasionally difficult, in reading these traditions, to know about whom the things are said, as further on the reference is evidently to R. Raphael of Bershad.

> the world of ᶜ*Asiyyah*. And once he dreamed during his life that he told me[61] to practice the *kavvanah* of the Incense, and I said to him, "Why should I engage in *kavvanot*, since I do not know the source of the *kavvanot*?"[62] And he said to me, "What has this to do with you? It is written thus in the Siddur, to intend such-and-such a *kavvanah* at such-and-such a word, so one must intend it thus."[63]

We thus see that, under the influence of R. Pinḥas, they attempted to ignore the basic claim of Hasidism that it is impossible for one to practice *kavvanot* because of the limitations of its potential practitioners. Further on in this same document we read:

> Even though in the Prayer Book of R. Shabbetai [of Rashkov] the *kavvanot* are written in all three [daily] prayers, he [the reference is evidently to R. Raphael] of blessed memory, said that this is only to avoid conflict, and these were his words: "What harm does it do [if I don't know the exact meaning?] [64] The main thing is as above! It is written in the Siddur that one should intend thus!" And he said that elsewhere it is written that this is a charm to remove anger, and it seems to me that this is found in the Siddur of R. Shabbetai.[65]

It is clear from what has been said that this approach is in no sense an attempt at substantive confrontation with the spiritual meaning of *kavvanot* as against the doctrine of *devequt*. It is rather a conservative tendency, not an anti-*devequt* tendency opposed to the teaching of the Maggid.

I will cite two more traditions in the name of R. Shmerl, the disciple of R. Pinḥas, in which one can detect other anti-Maggidic motivations. I refer to the anti-aristocratic tendency of this school. The Maggid of Mezhirech tended to unequivocally emphasize the value of prayer as rooted in its spiritual element, while prayer lacking in *devequt* seemed to him to be totally lacking in significance.[66] This stance

61 This is a conversation between R. Raphael and his disciple, citing the remarks in his name.

62 It is clear that this was a widespread version in the days of Hasidism: "that we no longer know the roots of the *kavvanot*." But it was possible to follow the guidance of Luria himself, who said that one who does not know to which one of the twelve gates — corresponding to the twelve tribes of Israel — he ought to direct his *kavvanot*, should direct his thoughts towards the thirteenth, "general" gate (*shaᶜar ha-kollel*). See R. Ḥayyim Vital, *Shaᶜar ha-Kavvanot*; the Maggid also alludes to this place in *Maggid Devarav le-Yaᶜaqov*.

63 MS. ibid., 57b.

64 That is: what difference is it to us that we do not know the exact contents!

65 MS. ibid., 60a.

66 R. Ḥayyim of Volozhin, the disciple of the Gaon, R. Elijah of Vilna, also protested against this vehemently, seeing in this the Evil Urge of the spiritualist. "Be very careful of this in your soul, that your Urge not lift you up ... telling you that the entire essence of Torah and *mizvot* is specifically that they be with great *kavvanah* and true *devequt*, and that so long as man's heart is not full to perform them with holy *kavvanah* and *devequt* and purity of thought, they are not considered a *mizvah* or

was one which the majority of the community was certainly unable to live up to, so that the formulation of R. Shmerl represents a renewed attempt to fix the value of prayer in terms of the criteria of good will and individual ability. R. Shmerl even cites an early tradition in the name of R. Menaḥem Mendel of Bar, which may be interpreted as intended to protect the ordinary person who is unable to "dance on the rope" of the spiritual meaning required in the doctrine of *devequt*.

> In the name of R. Shmerl: "empty vessels, do not spare" [II K. 4:3]. On the face of it, this is difficult. Why does one pray every day, even though ones mind is not clear and one does not have the heart or desire at all,[67] and what good does it do? But in this [respect] they are called "empty vessels": the words are called vessels, and every prayer, even though it is without the heart, is in any event effective and not in vain. For when man merits to pray once with *kavvanah*, properly, with good thought — for thought is called oil — by means of this all the empty prayers ascend, and all the empty vessels are filled, and at times they even ascend and are grasped in the prayer of another person.[68]
>
> [Further on:] I believe it is said in the name of R. Shmerl in the name of Mendel of Bar that there are things which a person is unable to teach his friend. For example: one who dances on a [tight] rope, when he moves the rope here he must balance his weight over there. But if a certain person should want to learn from him that in this place one leans here and in that place there and he should wish to do likewise, he would certainly fall. Thus, in matters of Divine service, each one must measure himself, etc.[69]

There is no doubt that the practice of *kavvanot* demands intense intellectual discipline, which cannot be expected of every person — even by those who advocated the doctrine of *kavvanot* — whereas *devequt* was the one exclusive demand made of every true worshipper in the school of the Maggid. That same "attention of *kavvanah*," to use the phrase of R. Pinḥas, is by no means a true confrontation of the doctrine of *kavvanot* in its full force with the teaching of *devequt*. R. Pinḥas spoke in its favor only from a stance of "preservation" of this path, as it was clear that as such it was no less aristocratic, and the aristocracy was not particularly beloved by him.

R. Meshullam Feibush of Zbarazh, a third-generation disciple of the Maggid of

divine service at all" — *Nefesh ha-Ḥayyim*, Part III, Chap. 4. Cf. his other arguments in the Introduction to this book.

67 Concerning this, the Maggid said that he must make great efforts until the will comes to him! See *Ẓava*ʾ*at ha-Riva"sh*, p. 21.

68 MS. ibid., 203b.

69 Ibid. However, it is not impossible that this passage is directed against the teaching of *kavvanot*, and not specifically against the doctrine of *devequt*.

Mezhirech, was the only one, as far as I could tell, who equally rejected both of these approaches in practice — the doctrine of *devequt* in its spiritualistic sense, and the Lurianic doctrine of *kavvanot* — from a stance which placed the emphasis upon the ethical motif in the service of God. He confined the Maggidic practice of *devequt* to the chosen few of past generations[70] or to unique figures of the present — among whom he did not count himself — and he held a similar attitude towards the doctrine of *kavvanot*. In a letter to one of his own followers, he wrote:

> Regarding the subject [under discussion] of thought in prayer, do you not know (if you have not already heard) that they all say that the essence of prayer is to accustom himself to pray with *kavvanah* — that is, the [plain] meaning of the words — so that there be nothing in his thought but the letters of the speech which he speaks,[71] and that love and fear are the essential [thing].[72] And not every person merits to this, but only he whom God helps, and as we pray concerning this thing in the blessing ᵓ*Ahavah Rabbah* [73] [in the Daily morning service], "and unify our hearts to love and to fear Your Name."[74]
>
> Concerning the matter of study of the Kabbalah, know with certainty and in truth from the speech of true sages that truly, even regarding the revealed Torah, if there does not come about from it the purpose of the thing, which is to guard and to do and to fulfill, etc., with love, this is certainly not the intention or the will of our Creator, may He be blessed. For whatever He created was all for His glory, and all is by means of man and of the fulfillment of His Torah, to learn in order to attain His service and to cling to Him. And if this is so in the revealed Torah, how much more so with regard to the study of Kabbalah, which requires many conditions, of which it is impossible to fulfill even part of one of them, and without these conditions even one who learns it does not know [anything] at all, but only the parables and [outer] garments found in the books of Kabbalah, but the inner [meaning] is impossible to grasp at all.[75] And what benefit is there from these garments, which are

70 See *Derekh ᵓEmet*, pp. 22–23.

71 This is a precise description of the initial stage of *devequt* to the letters, according to the teaching of the Maggid. And it seems that there is a bit of an argument here against such an exaggeration in the dissemination of the Maggid's teaching.

72 The same is true in the Maggid's teaching, in which love and fear are preconditions of meditative prayer.

73 It may be that, due to his above-mentioned fundamentally ethicist position, he also did not accept the version of the prayers (*nusaḥ*) generally accepted among the Hasidim, in which one recited ᵓ*Ahavat ᶜOlam* rather than ᵓ*Ahavah Rabbah*. On differences in *nusaḥ*, see Aaron Wertheimer, *Halakhot ve-Halikhot ba-Ḥasidut* (Jerusalem, 1960), p. 113.

74 The emphasis there is placed upon the point that we do not even attain to authentic love and fear, let alone *devequt*. For him, love and fear are in truth the primary values.

75 These remarks may also be indirectly directed against the Kabbalists of the Brody *kloiz*, who were not among the Hasidim. His letters as a whole are directed to the center of *ḥasidim* in Brody, from

like a riddle and a parable, without knowledge of that alluded referred to [by the parable]? What will it help and what benefit will be gained? How much more so [i.e. is it pointless] to intend *kavvanot* in the matters of the garments and parables, or to unify unifications in the ways said there in the books of the Kabbalists.

Will the Honor of His Torah believe me in truth, that all of the words said in the books of Kabbalah and all the *kavvanot* and *yiḥudim* (unifications) in their words were written for people like themselves?! That is, each and every one of the Kabbalists had cast off corporeality, as explained in *ᵓOraḥ Ḥayyim*, Sect. 98, in the Laws of Prayer; and they had the Holy Spirit, and they looked upon the [Divine] Chariot and the intelligibles, and they unified and connected world with world and light with light and radiance with radiance and brilliance with brilliance through their clear and pure thought; and all their days they had no alien thought save the love of the Creator and His fear, and even at the time of their eating and coupling everything was the opposite of what it appeared [namely,] that they were indulging in corporeal things, for there were flames of Divine fire burning in their hearts, which are the love and fear [of God] — people such as this are fit to unify and to intend *yihudim*. But let us measure whether we are for even one moment during the entire year on a level such as this, that they were all their days, even when they were performing corporeal actions....

For this [reason], people like us must serve the Creator according to our sense, and each one is only required to act according to his measure, and to go by stages and to pray with *kavvanah* — that is, the meaning of the words[76] — and to study books of *Musar* [ethical exhortation] to know the manners of service and the matters of "depart from evil" [Ps. 34:15] which depend upon the attributes of the heart, from pride and anger and appetites of this world, and jealousy and hatred and avarice ... And his study in books of Mussar shall be directed to understand the things, to guard and to do them ...[77]

To summarize the rejection of the Lurianic doctrine of *kavvanot* in Hasidism, we may assume that the religious interest of the early Hasidim did not square with the intention of this doctrine. The emotional and intellectual spontaneity of the worshipper tended to blur and to reject the limiting constructions of the precise mapping of Divine secrets. The *ḥasid* sought to break down the barriers between himself and God without any fixed "keys," and on the other hand scoffed at any attempted evaluation of religious "attainments" based upon a measured and planned ladder of *kavvanot*. The doctrine of *devequt* advocated the erasure of the

whence questions pertaining to matters of Hasidism emanated. The question of the relation of Hasidism to the study of Lurianic Kabbalah in general, and the preference of the study of Mussar works, still demands extensive study, for which this is not the proper place.

76 This is not similar to "the intention of the words" (*kavvanat ha-milot*), which refers to the doctrine of *kavvanot*. Here he wishes to say: to pray according to the simple meaning of the words.

77 At the end of *Derekh ᵓEmet* (I have copied the text according to the 1933 edition of *Kitvei Qodesh*).

Ego and its nullification in order for one to become repeatedly involved in the infinite reality of the Godhead to the limits of the possible. One might state that the "uncompromising mystic" within the *ḥasid* consciously rejected the doctrine of *kavvanot*.

The spiritual climate of the *ḥasid* — which begins in activistic enthusiasm and ends in the loss of the I and silencing of all the capabilities of the soul, in which the divine element within man ascends in spiritual purity and goes into action — is unable to find authentic expression in the doctrine of *kavvanot*, which was no more than planned meditation. The *ḥasid* not only sought a guide, but life with God in its fullest emotional and intellectual realization to the point of loss and extinction. He sought to be "negated from existence before Him like a candle in front of a torch,"[78] as the doctrine of Hasidism taught that there is nothing within man but God Himself, who reveals Himself upon the extinction of the fleshly garments.

78 *Ḥayyim va-Ḥesed*, p. 162. This is a variation upon the Midrash, which states that the souls before the Shekhinah are like a candle before a torch.

Chapter Eleven

Anarchic Manifestations in Hasidic Life

The innovations of Hasidic thinkers in the realm of prayer were not explicitly articulated. But while they did not define these matters explicitly, they did testify that a change had in fact taken place with the appearance of the Besht. Kalonymus Kalman of Cracow, disciple of R. Elimelekh of Lyzhansk and author of the work *Ma'or va-Shemesh*, states:

> Since the holy Baʿal Shem Tov, *z"l*, came, there has risen in the world the light of the strengthening of holiness of prayer for whoever wishes to approach the service of God, blessed be He. But for this one needs to engage in pure prayer, much service of the wise, and to labour day and night in Torah and in good deeds, until by this means one comes to know in truth how to pray with great fear and love, as is known to those who understand. And behold, through his prayer the true *ẓaddiq* goes through all the worlds, until he reaches the Supreme Mind (*moḥin ʿila'in*), and from there to the Infinite, blessed be He, which is the nullification of apprehension ...[1]

There was indeed a flowering of "the strengthening of the holiness of prayer," all of life being directed towards receiving this light. However, the emphasis on the acquisition of spiritual perfection signified an inner transvaluation within the history of Jewish mysticism in several respects. Mental prayer took the place of vocal prayer; even though the latter was not abolished, it clearly occupied a place close to the bottom rung in the new hierarchy of spiritual values. This tension between speech and thought was created by the pneumatic feeling that speech served to hold back and limit the dominion of the spirit, which wished to surge forward and break out of the written word. The longing for the total negation of the word may be sensed in the sermons of a number of Hasidic thinkers, which I have already discussed in their proper place.[2] The quietists were reproached for

1 *Ma'or va-Shemesh*, p. 576. R. Kalonymus Kalman ha-Levi's book is in fact not a testimony of the quietistic spirit at all, but serves primarily as a valuable source for understanding the social psychology of Hasidism. However, his testimony regarding prayer as the central innovation of Hasidism is doubtless of great interest.

2 See on this also R. Ḥayyim Haykl of Amdur: "Behold, the fact that the intellect is drawn [down] into speech is called 'Egypt' (*Miẓrayim*) with regard to the intellect, for it is in straits (*meẓar*)... And this is, 'All the diseases which I placed upon you in Egypt' [Ex. 15:26] — i.e., that I placed [him] in the

similar views, effectively abnegating verbal prayer,[3] on the grounds that it interferes with the path towards encounter with God and the death of the self.[4] In addition to verbal prayer, they also nullified all of the sacraments.[5] Thus, in the eyes of the quietist Malaval, mental prayer was a means of clinging to God, which meant His active presence within man.[6] Hasidism did not go so far as to negate those acts which preceded the apprehension of the constant presence of God, nor was it satisfied with a single act in which a person thrust himself at the feet of Godhead once during the course of his lifetime; rather, it struggled for a path which would enable man to periodically renew that act which restores him to this presence. R. Jacob Joseph of Polonnoye, the author of *Toldot Yaᶜaqov Yosef*, tells some interesting things concerning R. Naḥman of Kosow in this regard:

> I heard that the *ḥasid*, our teacher R. Naḥman Kosover, gave a fixed amount every week to a certain person, [in order] that he might go among the people to remind them by a hint not to forget [to place] the Divine Name before themselves constantly ...[7]

straits, that he must continue in speech — 'I will not place upon you, for I the Lord... am your healer' — that is, that you be healed from the emptiness and not need to contract yourself in speech." — *Ḥayyim va-Ḥesed* (*Tefillah va-ᶜAvodah*), p. 196. At the end of p. 175: "'My beloved is like a hart' [Songs 2:9], for just as a hart's skin does not contain his flesh [Ketubot 112a], so speech does not contain the thought and the voice. 'Behold, he stands behind our wall' [ibid] — this refers to the appetite of the body, which holds up prayer." For the view among the Christian quietists that verbal prayer is a low level, see Heppe, *Geschichte*, p. 7.

3 See Dudon, *Molinos*, pp. 117–118.

4 See also Heppe, p. 459.

5 Dudon, p. 46. However, the Holy Office declared that the congregation had not banned silent prayer (*oratio mentalis*) as such, but rather the conclusions of those who reject verbal prayer and other sacral acts customary in the Roman Church. It rejects the opinion of those who argue that salvation is guaranteed them as a result of prayer (and not by the Church!) — ibid., p. 47. On January 30, 1682, Cardinal Carraccioli wrote to Pope Innocent XI that the Church's fear of the quietists stems from the fact that the masses practice mental prayer while rejecting vocal prayer and the confession. See the section on Molinos in Pourrat, "Quietisme," col. 1561.

6 In his eyes, every activity is a potential occasion for attachment to God: "Pour le contemplatif, lectures, sermons, pensées, saints, ne doivent être qu'une *occasion de se recueillir*, et non matière à s'occuper. Ils doivent servir à élever l'âme, à l'enflammer; et en cet état, que, *l'âme s'arrête en Dieu seul et se tienne en sa présence.*" Dudon, p. 52.

7 *Toldot Yaᶜaqov Yosef*, *Parashat Shoftim*, p. 186b. This subject serves there as an example of the meaning of the verse, 'I have always set God before me" [Ps. 16:8]. Concerning the Besht's praxis of "seeing" the Divine Name, see J. G. Weiss, "Kavvanot of Prayer," pp. 173–174; the testimony of R. Jacob Joseph of Polonnoye's *Ketonet Passim*; and more recently the article by A. J. Heschel, "Rabbi Naḥman of Kosow: Companion of the Baᶜal Shem." On p. 116–7, n. 31 (in the English version), the author draws our attention to various pre-Hasidic sources in which the above verse is interpreted. Particularly relevant to our subject is the example brought from *Shenei Luḥot ha-Berit* concerning the praxis of seeing the Divine Name while man is engaged in corporeal activity (*ᶜavodah*

This story in particular brings out the difference between Hasidism and classical quietism, in that Hasidism was not only a spiritual phenomenon and way of thinking, but also a social phenomenon, and as such constituted an innovation within the Jewish world. R. Naḥman of Kosow was unable to isolate himself from the everyday framework in order to create more suitable spiritual conditions for the realization of the imperative, "I have always set God before me." The *ẓaddiqim* could not just sit in a monk's cell and contemplate, but were also leaders of congregations and heads of families, and as such they had to learn how to be alone with their Creator while in the midst of the multitude. These psychological difficulties are clearly implied in the Hasidic sermons, and their impact is also visible in the recoiling from extreme quietistic interpretations. Purely mental prayer could not be sustained in a situation in which a new society was coming into being and wished to create social values, of which shared communal prayer was a central pillar. Recitation aloud united the worshippers, even if the actual meaning of prayer, in terms of its contents, gradually disappeared.

The external symptom of this attitude of taking lightly the actual contents of prayer was its "snatching" or "grabbing" (Yiddish: *khapp'n* — i.e., its super-rapid recitation). Paradoxically, this anarchic "grabbing" served a unifying social function; while the "wildness" expressed in the swallowing of the words of prayer upset the sense of proper order which required the articulation of each word with *kavvanah* and seriousness, it also emphasized the collective voice as a cry of yearning leading to the ecstasy felt in the "expiration of the soul." The Maggid of Mezhirech taught that this kind of "grabbing" or "rushing" was permitted, as may well be understood within that theoretical and social atmosphere:

> One must go from level to level in prayer, so as not to exhaust all of his strength at the beginning of the prayer; he should begin moderately, and in the middle of the prayer cling with great *devequt*, and then he will be able to recite it even while racing along the words of prayer. Although at the beginning of the prayer he was unable to pray with *devequt*, he should nevertheless say the words with great *kavvanah* and strengthen himself bit by bit, until God assists him to pray with great attachment.[8]

During the course of the ascent of the spirit, the meditative value of the letters is progressively reduced until they become a factor that disturbs *devequt*. One can then utter them quickly, in order to reach the pinacle of prayer — namely, *devequt*.

be-gashmiyut) — i.e., eating. It is also told of R. Yitzḥak of Drobitch (the father of R. Michel of Zloczow) that whenever he sat down to eat he placed in front of himself a board upon which was written the Divine Name. The account describes the visit of this R. Yitzḥak to the Besht. See *Mifʾalot Ẓaddiqim* (Lemberg, 1865), n. p.

8 *Ẓavaʾat ha-Riva"sh*, p. 8.

R. Moshe of Satanov, the author of *Mishmeret ha-Qodesh*, already noted this phenomenon in his critique of early Hasidism (the book was published in 1746!). In referring to the subject of the Morning Prayer, he says:

> He should recite from *Barukh She-amar* through to the *Shemonah ᶜEsrei* with joy and song, not "grabbing" at all; but in the *Shemonah ᶜEsrei* he should make his prayer [one of] mercy and petition before God ... And I saw many of the devout ones of the generation who had set their heart to pray with attachment to God, with melody and joy and prayer and weeping, who did not take care to read the words correctly. Surely they are close to losing their reward, and shall be punished ... And would that they did not push their prayer toward that of a strange person [*Siṭra ᵓAḥra*; the "Evil Side"].[9]

In *Liqqutei Yeqarim*, the Maggid of Mezhirech unequivocally defends his remarks concerning the merits of recitation of the prayer "quickly," noting that the sense of closeness to *devequt* causes the person to thrust the proper pronunciation of the words behind himself:

> At times the person is as if drunk, because of the joy of the Torah that burns in his heart with great love. And let him know himself: at times he can recite the prayer at very great speed, because the love of God greatly burns in his heart, and the words emerge from his mouth by themselves.[10]

I have already noted in the previous chapter the issue of the postponement of prayer among Hasidim past the proper time, due to their great devotion to preparation prior to prayer. I should like to add that this habit of deliberate denial of the rule of time also contributed to the confusion of the daily schedule of the *ḥasid*, and played no small role in the creation of an anarchistic and nonchalant atmosphere with regard to everything surrounding him.[11]

9 See G. Scholem, "The Two Earliest Testimonies Concerning Hasidic Circles and the Besht" (Heb.), in *Sefer ha-Yovel li-khevod Y. N. Epstein* (Jerusalem, 1950), p. 231 (the above quotation is taken from that article). Scholem interprets this prayer as reflecting the ignorance of those who do not understand the "reason" of the letters but wish to engage in ecstatic prayer. While this idea is legitimate within Hasidic teaching, it seems to me that this passage from R. Moshe of Satanov did not specifically relate to this matter, but to what the Maggid mentions in the *Ẓava'ah*, where it is not necessarily a matter of ignorance, but part of his overall anarchistic-contemplative approach. See Scholem's explanation, ibid., p. 236, at the bottom.

10 *Liqqutei Yeqarim*, 12d–13a.

11 Over the course of time the subject of the time for prayer seems to have become "institutionalized" among the Hasidim, serving as a sign of differentiation between themselves and the Mitnaggedim, thereby losing all of its original value as a symbol of spiritualistic anarchism. R. Ḥayyim of Volozhin depicts Hasidim who considered it clever to deliberately wait until the "time for prayer" had passed until they stood up to pray: "And my eyes saw many who have sought the closeness of God and who stumbled in matters such as these, who told me themselves what was in their hearts. And I myself

This custom, which was opposed from within the Hasidic camp by R. Pinḥas of Korets, is first attested to by the Mitnaggedim only from the early 1780's. R. Abraham Katzenellenbogen of Brisk, in a letter to R. Levi Yitzḥak of Berdichev, accuses the Hasidim as follows:

> When I pondered how I might know this, it was wearisome in my eyes [Ps. 73:16] — that they make the peripheral of essential importance, and the essence peripheral, without the king, the King of the Universe. For it is forbidden [even] to engage in [the study of] those *halakhot* which are not straightforward close to the time for prayer, so that he not draw out his study [i.e., and thereby pray later than the proper time; *O. H.* 93:3, following Berakhot 31a]. And they arrogantly and deliberately violate the time for prayer, [both] for reciting the *Shemaᶜ* and for *Tefillah* [i.e., the *ᶜAmidah*], and they sin and cause the multitude to sin, placing a stumbling block before those who follow them and are together with them, praying in their minyan.[12]

In the same letter, we also find the argument that the Hasidim are proud and aloof, and distain to participate in ordinary prayer with their fellow Jews (a similar claim was addressed by the Church against the separatist quietists[13]):

> "[Divine] service, which is prayer" [Taᶜanit 2a]. They offer their vanity [*tiflah*; double-entendre on *tefillah*, "prayer"] to God in abandoning the stones of the altar like chalkstones beaten in pieces [Isa. 27:9], casting fault and aspersion upon the prayers of our brothers, the children of Israel, who are whole and God-fearing, as if the land were theirs alone. And in truth their way is not seemly, for whoever alters the usual custom bears the burden of proof, and particularly the "crown" [*Keter*; i.e., a reference to the version of the *Kedushah* for *Musaf* used in the Hasidic rite] which they place upon the head of the King of Kings the Holy One blessed be He, outside of the land, like one who offers sacred things outside [of the Temple precincts]...[14]

saw in a certain place how certain people had become accustomed to this for so long a time that they have almost completely forgotten the time for the *Minḥah* [Afternoon] Prayer fixed by our rabbis. On the contrary, through long habit there is fixed in their hearts, as if a law and halakhah, that the proper time for *Minḥah* is after the stars come out. And when one person says to another, 'Let us pray *Minḥah*,' he is answered, 'Let us go and see if one can already see stars in the sky.' May God forgive them, and atone for the mistaken and foolish [people]." — *Nefesh ha-Ḥayyim*, Part III, Chap. 8.

12 See S. Dubnow, "Writings of Opposition to the Hasidic Sect (Chassidiana)" (Heb.), *Devir* Vol. 1 (Berlin, 1923), p. 294.

13 See, for example, Dudon, p. 104.

14 Dubnow, op cit., p. 296. The author criticizes them here for using the *nusaḥ* of the *Qedushat Musaf* prayer which reads *Keter yitnu lekha*. The argument that "the burden of proof is upon whoever changes," which is a relevant argument in halakhah [see, e.g., the argument of R. Moses Sofer who rules against the Gaon of Vilna in a certain matter, and concludes by saying: "and whoever changes bears the burden of proof" — *Teshuvot Ḥatam Sofer*, ᵓ*Oraḥ Ḥayyim*, Sect. 101] did not find a

This argument concerning the separatism and excessive spiritual "haughtiness" of the Hasidim already appears in R. Israel of Zamosc's *Nezed ha-Dema*ᶜ, which was evidently composed in the 1760's:[15]

> They thought to ascend upon the heights of the cloud, to know the thoughts of the Most High and what God who dwells in Zion has wrought, and they speak wonders of God, [bringing] hardship upon hardship. They spread their wings up above, [even] the heavens are not pure in their eyes, and the angels they charge with folly ...[16]

As a result of these spiritualistic motivations, a profound transformation of values took place in Hasidic society, expressed specifically in its paradoxical placing of the spirit beyond the realm of social criticism. Thus, we find clear statements of by R. Meir of Przemyślany and the Maggid of Mezhirech that, "as far as the eye can see," the inner judgment of the spirit cannot be controlled and that, on the contrary, true spiritual activity does not require social authority. Indeed, at times this is embodied in external forms which even seem to contradict this authority and opinion: the appearance of the *ḥasid* belies his inner being, in the sense of being "good within and his garment being bad," to cite a passage from the *Tiqqunei Zohar* which the Sabbatians were fond of quoting. By making the

receptive ear among the Hasidim, just as many of the claims against them did not move them for a long time. But in the final analysis the Hasidim bowed to the pressures of criticism far more than is usually thought.

15 It seems to me that Scholem was correct in choosing this date, as opposed to the assumption that the book was written as early as the 1730's, because to my mind it contains definite ironic allusions, not only to the teachings of the Besht, but also to those of the Maggid of Mezhirech. There is no doubt that this is also an argument against the stance of H. Lieberman, mentioned in G. Scholem, "The Polemic Against Hasidism and its Leaders in the Book *Nezed ha-Dema*ᶜ" (Heb.), *Zion* 20 (1955), pp. 73–81. I refer to the passage which reads: "You generation, who have seen that this man angers the earth with his many songs for those that lie in wait, changing his garment and his language, and has called understanding 'Mother' [i.e., speaking in Kabbalistic language], but speaks to the people in another tongue [i.e., is hypocritical] ..." (ibid., p. 76). This is an attempt to interpret the well-known parable of the Baᶜal Shem Tov, concerning the king who sent a messenger to the other countries and "changed his garment and his language" in order to test the people. The author sarcastically mocks this matter, arguing that the Besht himself was hypocritical! Elsewhere, he refers to the Maggid's teaching: "Today he will not seek gold and his righteousness shall answer for him, [while] yesterday if a person would give all the wealth of his house, he would show contempt for his love [after Songs 8:7]." — ibid., p. 76. This verse is interpreted by the Maggid as referring to the love of God, which is more precious than treasures, which the author of the *Nezed* interprets ironically against him [the Maggid] for receiving *pidyonot* [gifts of money from supplicants].

16 The phrase, "the angels they charge with folly" (after Job 4:18) doubtless refers to the doctrine of the Maggid, which raised the service of Hasidism above that of the ministering angels. See on this above, near the end of Chap. 5. A direct and interesting evocation on behalf of "highness" in the service of God appears, for example, in R. Binyamin of Salositz, *Amtaḥat Binyamin*, p. 2c.

inner values of the spirit absolute, some of the Hasidim were able to propose an attitude of apathy and equanimity towards another person's external assessments of their outer deeds. They did not in fact grant these "spiritualists" full freedom to behave in whatever way they fancied in the sense of violating the halakhic framework, as did the Sabbatian dispensation; however, they did allow themselves the right to "conceal" their piety and their inner *devequt* from the outside world by means of an external appearance of nonchalance towards the *mizvot*.

Alongside the tremendous effort invested by Hasidic thinkers in finding a basis for their collective, social spiritualism and bringing the masses into the covenant of the spirit, they knew how to isolate the inner judgment of the spirit from the criticism of the masses: thus, the ultimate judgment was left to the individual. This self-valuation was understood in terms of a rendering of account between the individual and his Maker, so that in this realm there was no concern with social judgments of the kind of, "what will people say?" One of the most interesting symptoms of the Hasidic religious phenomenon, and one of the innovations of its social psychology, was doubtless this reality of living on two levels, one of which was indifferent to the other. The question which confronts us is not that of external change, if there was such in fact — as there were indeed Hasidim who had contempt for Torah study or engaged in very little study, as emphasized by scholarship on the subject. The problem is rather: what changes in the Hasidic mentality, in the depths of the Hasidic soul, allowed for this external change?

It is not correct, in my opinion, to say that Hasidism belittled the value of Torah study in the sense that this opposition was in itself the mainstay of their revolutionary call. What value and chance of success could there have been in an approach which opposed existing, firmly established values? The conventional wisdom which argues that Hasidism differed from non-Hasidic Judaism on this point is the product of the Mitnaggedic polemic, which began to feel, quite justifiably, that something of their authoritative stability was being pulled out from underneath their very feet. But this upsetting of the basic axioms was caused by an overall transformation of values, in which the authority of the spirit, rather than that of society, was recognized as ultimate. Inevitably, the position of Torah study as the highest value was also shaken, as it was sometimes found that it (i.e., Torah study) did not square well with the supreme goal of *devequt*. It is important to note that there is no support in the Hasidic source themselves for the assumption that the shift in the center of gravity from study to *devequt* was motivated by any "socio-political" considerations, such as that of attracting the ignorant classes (*am-aratzim*). Such a perception is superficial and groundless; this transformation of values had no "populist" polemical aim. The masses did not come to the courts of the *rebbe* because the latter allowed them to be ignorant, or because they found there, so to speak, validation or legitimation for their existence as such. Such a sociological interpretation ignores the inner processes of the spirit and their true center of gravity. Even the activist streams within Hasidism, which sustained its social vision, were not at all populist or interested in "lightening" the religious burden of the simple person; nor did they come to affirm his existence "as he is," as Buber argues in his various essays on Hasidic thought.[17] On the contrary, far more than they required intellectual involvement in the study of Torah, they insisted that man make a spiritual effort to overcome his own self. I am not concerned here with what happened in reality — i.e., how many people there were who in fact "ate with spirituality" in the corporeal world; such a question is irrelevant to the ideological teaching of Hasidism. However, it is clearly impossible to argue in their name that the opposite is the case. The powerful social motifs in the teachings of the Baᶜal Shem Tov and the *Toldot* were of far greater polemical weight than the quietistic, spiritualistic message implied in the teaching of the Maggid of Mezhirech. Nevertheless, the social doctrine was not separate from its spiritual basis, from which it drew sustenance.

The Maggid's comments that a person must see himself as belonging in principle to "the upper world" were revolutionary in terms of the existing values of the period, which were concerned with that which was manifest in behavior and subject to objective measurement and examination. This new dimension of the spirit, which is a rule unto itself, was never so much emphasized in Jewish mysticism as it was in Hasidism, precisely because the latter struggled to manifest the pneumatic within the social realm, and even created a social ideology suitable to this criterion. I will accept that this is a paradox. The history of the evolution of these ideas within the school of the Maggid is indeed proof that there was a time when it was difficult to accept the existence of this paradox of life on two different levels; instead, the *ẓaddiq* was "brought down" to the people, with only a small spark of spiritualistic striving continuing to echo, in a theoretical manner, behind his concrete image.[18] On the other hand, one finds a strengthening of the original Maggidic position among several of his disciples, such as R. Ḥayyim Haykl of Amdur and R. Menaḥem Mendel of Vitebsk, who did not recant the principle that man is first and foremost a denizen of "the supernal world."

I would like to give here some examples of the ideas which I attributed above to the Maggid and to R. Meir of Przemyślany. In *Ẓavaʾat ha-Riva"sh*, we read:

> "I have always placed (*shiviti*) God before me" [Ps. 16:8]. *Shiviti* — in the sense of equanimity. In every thing [the text known used by R. Ḥayyim Ḥaykl adds here the

17 See Introduction, n. 13, for bibliography of Buber's writings on Hasidism; for a critique of Buber's approach, see Section III of the Introduction, and ns. 18, 19 there.

18 See on this, for example, R. Schatz, "The Doctrine of the *ẓaddiq* in R. Elimelekh of Lyzhansk" (Heb.), *Molad* 18, nos. 144–145 (1960), pp. 365–378, esp. pp. 370–372.

> words: "which God sends you"] all is the same to him, whether it be in matters in which man praises him or in which they belittle him.[19]
> Equanimity is a great principle, meaning that it is the same to him whether [people] presume him to be lacking in knowledge or one who knows the entire Torah. And what brings this about is constant attachment to the Creator, for because of the concerns of *devequt* he has no free time to think about these things, because he is always concerned to attach himself above to Him, blessed be He.[20]

It is clear that the latter passage is not to be read as implying contempt for the value of learning as such, but rather as a breaking with accepted social conventions and authority with regard to the determination of the scale of the spirit. We read elsewhere, "He shall make himself as one [who does not] exist in this world; for what benefit is it to me to be important in the eyes of men?"[21] This is indeed the most basic assumption! Its social anarchism is based upon the quietistic conception that one does not "belong" to this world at all in any real way. The Maggid derives his permission to engage in "holy deception" on the basis of this very tendency — namely, that "one must perform one's deeds in hiddenness, so that it seems to other people that he does not engage in pious deeds."[22] That is, the true Hasidic values are to be protected from exposure to external confrontation, for which reason it is better that they be entirely concealed from the eyes of others, so that ones external acts do not reflect the inner process, and at times even contradict it.[23] In fact, the Maggid warns against a dangerous perception of

19 The list of those areas in which he ought to be equanimous is continued there; see *Ẓavaʾat ha-Riva"sh*, p. 1. But a question of considerable importance arises here: is the Maggid referring to "people" outside of Hasidic society, who hold Hasidism in contempt — in which case the discussion has a social-oriented, polemical aim — or is it brought within the overall context of Hasidic theory? Incidentally, the interpretation of this verse as referring to equanimity was generally attributed by Hasidic sources, not to the Besht, but to the Maggid of Mezhirech. The Besht was credited with the authorship of the classical interpretation of "I have always held God before me," as referring either to the visualizing of the letters of the Divine Name, or else as a paraphrase for perpetual meditation about God. See, e.g., Ephraim of Sudylkow, *Degel Maḥaneh ʾEfrayim*, 62d. He cites a similar view on pp. 7d and 12c. The model for the quietistic interpretation of this verse already appears in *Hovot ha-Levavot, Sha'ar Yihud ha-Ma'aseh*, p. 128.

20 *Ẓavaʾat ha-Riva"sh*, pp. 4–5.

21 Ibid., p. 13.

22 Ibid., p. 15. The greatest rebels against social conventions were the Hasidim of Kotsk, who went so far as to commit transgressions in public so as not to be suspected of piety in secret. Their ethical radicalism stemmed from the assumptions described here, which were already present during the early years of Hasidism. On the behavior practiced in Kotsk, see, in Yiddish, A. J. Heschel, *Kotzk; ein gerangl far Emeskeit* (Tel-Aviv, 1937), Vol. I, Chap. 7.

23 The latter motif was primarily developed in a number of theories concerning the *ẓaddiq*, who descends in order to save the sinners, for which reason he as-it-were behaves as they do — but in a general theoretic approach it does not at all apply to the principle of service for all of Israel. Cf. the previous note.

this matter in which the man of spirit allows himself to build a new facade which will, ultimately, trap him in his own paradox: through the attempt at concealing his own inner piety, he will end up with at true love of worldliness! His remarks continue:

> Before he arrives at the supreme level, he must perform his acts openly, for if he does not perform them openly, as the world does them, but only wishes to be a *ḥasid* in his inwardness, he may be drawn after the world, and [instead of] doing it for-its-sake he will end up doing them not-for-its-sake.

Hasidism had a higher degree of reflective consciousness regarding these sorts of questions than did Sabbatianism, perhaps because the two movements were not driven by the same motivations or towards the same goals.[24] Sabbatianism was primarily an ideological movement, which was prepared to sacrifice its mysticism for the sake of its ideology, whereas Hasidism was first and foremost a free and spontaneous growth of mysticism, whose doctrines included certain ideological elements; its self-criticism emerged from its awareness of and alertness to certain possibly dangerous ideas lying on the borders of Hasidism. This sense of historical responsibility towards the Jewish people and towards the halakhah was the pulse which limited its revolutionary line of thought up to a certain point — and no further. We are interested in what happened within the Hasidic consciousness up to that limit, before its anarchistic tendency to create implicit, hidden values came into conflict with the established, accepted values of Jewish society.

Hasidism's call to the individual to be simultaneously within and without society is, in the final analysis, the most interesting one from an ideological point of view, in terms of Hasidism as an historical attempt to cultivate mysticism within the life of society. This attempt was the progenitor of the paradox within the Hasidic phenomenon, and led to a number of important theories within Hasidic thought, such as "service through corporeality" (*ᶜavodah be-gashmiyut*) and "the descent of the *ẓaddiq*." In some Hasidic sources, the balance is weighed in favor of the social pole, and one can begin to sense a far-reaching abandonment of its purely mystical concern. But in several other thinkers, one finds a refusal to compromise or to sacrifice one realm in favor of the other. On the contrary: it was precisely the imperative of contemplation and separation from society which became stronger, as the theories of the descent of the *ẓaddiq* in order to redeem the masses from sin became more sharply stressed. The teaching of R. Benjamin of Salositz, who was not numbered among the close disciples of the Maggid,[25] includes some extreme

24 Concerning these questions of Sabbatianism, see G. Scholem, *Sabbatai Sevi*. I refer here specifically to the "dual" valuation both of the personality of the Messiah and of history. See pp. 793–794.

25 He mentions elsewhere that he heard this from the Maggid himself; see the continuation of this passage: *Ṭorrei Zahav*, 38d.

positions regarding the redemption of society and of the world based upon activist tendencies and the development of explicitly Beshtian motifs, alongside a tendency towards contemplation in isolation, drawn from the words of R. Meir of Przemyślany and the Maggid of Mezhirech. Most important: the external deed receives its force from the inner act, which is not always given to manifestation. These are his words:

> Thus are the righteous (*ẓaddiqim*) that, even if at times they need to reveal their righteousness, in any event they keep watch over themselves. So long as they remain attached to Him, blessed be He, they reveal themselves; but when they understood that, if they reveal their righteousness any more, it will no longer be possible for them to remain attached to Him, blessed be He, but that this [matter] will lead them to some self-interest, Heaven forbid, they then return to their original connection (*hitqashrut*), and no longer reveal their righteousness.[26]

In the name of R. Menaḥem Mendel of Przemyślany, he cites:

> I heard in the name of the renowned *ḥasid*, R. Menaḥem Mendel of Przemyślany, concerning [the verse], "How goodly are your tents, O Jacob, your tabernacles, O Israel" [Num. 24:5]: It is known that there are two kinds of *ẓaddiqim*. [There is] one kind who are the same within and without; that is, just as they are attached to their Creator, blessed be He, from within, so is it visible from without to the eyes of all that they give pleasure to their Creator at every hour and moment, and they are unable to hide their deeds from human beings. And then there are those *ẓaddiqim* who seem from without like ordinary people, while inside them there burns great ardor (*hitlahavut*) and *devequt*, for they hide themselves with all their strength. This level is certainly a greater one than the former, for they do not need to protect themselves from self-interest as do the former.[27]

26 *Ahavat Dodim*, 43a.

27 *Ṭorrei Zahav*, 34a; cf. *Amtaḥat Binyamin*, 78c. It is worth noting here that the dualistic approach to internal and external behavior, due to the fear of distortions, was also subjected to criticism by R. Ḥayyim of Krasni, who was close to the circle of R. Pinḥas of Korets: "In the name of R. Moshe of Krasni, who said in the name of his father, R. Ḥayyim of Krasni, "'Be lowly spirited before every person' [Avot 4:4]. That you not say, I will display the quality of arrogance to the world, but within myself I shall be humble. But be lowly-spirited before every person, so that everyone shall say that you do not posssess this quality ... But in all events, it is forbidden to be haughty before any person within ones heart, as it says, 'that he not lift up his heart above his brethren' [Deut. 17:20]." — MS. Jerusalem–National Library 3759, fo. 205b. The implication is that this dual-valued approach of "within" and "without" allows for the distortion of true qualities, and may harm the value of true humility, as a person is liable to act arrogantly while claiming that within his heart he fulfills the good quality, even though it receives no external manifestation. See the note by G. Scholem in his article, "New Material on R. Israel Löbel and His Anti-Hasidic Polemic" (Heb.), *Ẓion* 20 (1955), p. 156. In note 11, R. Israel's opinion is brought from the period of his book, *ᶜOzer Yisraᵓel*, when he still saw Hasidism in a positive light, and he considered "holy deception" to be a positive value.

Not only is the *ḥasid* expected to be apathetic to the contempt or "non-valuation" of society, but he is asked to be suspicious of the open admiration of society, as the latter — which is superficially a positive value, in that he serves as "a good example" — harms the inner self-valuation of the spirit, which does not relate to any "record" of accomplishment. The Maggid therefore instructs one to be completely "alone" among the throng of worshippers, as if there were no one there at all. As R. Benjamin brings in his name:

> ... I heard from the holy mouth of our teacher Dov Baer that there is "a strange fire which God has not commanded" [Lev. 10:1] — that is, when he combines some interest of his own benefit with his service of *hitlahavut*. Of this it is said, "and the fire of the altar" — which is the supernal fire — "is burned by it" [Lev. 6:2] — that is, that it [should] be for naught but God alone. Also: "and the priest" — that is, the one engaged in service — "shall wear his linen garment," etc. [ibid. v. 3]. For it states in *Ḥovot ha-Levavot* that man must accustom himself to the quality of aloneness, to be separated from other people, until he accustoms himself so that, even if he is among a thousand people, he will also be attached to Him blessed be He, and there will be nothing separating or interrupting him from his attachment to Him blessed be He. And as I explained the verse, "And no person shall be in the Tent of the Meeting when he enters to atone for the holy place until he goes out, and he shall atone for himself and for his household ..." [Lev. 16:17]. For it is known that prior to prayer a person must cast off his corporeality and attach his thoughts to the exaltation of God, as if he is not standing among people, but only among the angels in the upper worlds. Then, when he forgets that he is standing among people, he is able to pray with great *kavvanah* and without self-interest. Of this it is said, "And no man shall be in the Tent of Meeting" — that is, in the synagogue or the House of Study, in the place where people gather to pray. Then, "there shall be no man" in your thoughts — that is, you shall cast off your corporeality so much so that you shall forget that you are standing among people. Then he will surely "atone for the holy place" — that is, at the time of prayer, which is in place of the sacrificial atonement — "until he goes out" — that is, from the beginning of the prayer until its end. And then, surely "he will atone for himself and his household" — for his prayer is certainly pure when it shall be in this fashion. And I have [thus] explained, "In the place where there are no men, try to be a man ..." [Avot 2:5] ...[28]

28 *Ṭorrei Zahav*, pp. 38d–39a. Another, similar version of these ideas, using the identical verses, was given in the name of R. Naḥman of Horodenka by R. Ephraim of Sudylkow in *Degel Maḥaneh ʾEfrayim*, 64d. As against this, R. Uziel Meisels cites this idea several times in the name of R. Meir of Przemyślany: "For the essential fear [of God] is inner fear, so that from without his righteousness will not be perceived at all, but that only within the walls of his heart and his heart it be true with him, like a fire burning for His service, may He be blessed, and this is a very great level" — *Tifʾeret ʿUziel*, p. 191b. Cf. p. 68a and p. 100a on the verse "I am black and comely" — in each case cited in the name of R. Meir of Przemyślany. Gershom Scholem already alludes to the idea of the duality

The essence of the paradoxical nature of Hasidism lies in its stance of being within society only "so-to-speak," thereby establishing a dualistic stance in all realms; of seeing concrete reality as in fact illusory, and the true, hidden reality as one over which one has no visible control. Hasidism thereby succeeded in preserving all of its traditional frameworks, which it only broke out of within the context of "self-evaluation" and not in real terms.[29]

The difference between Hasidism and Sabbatianism in terms of its common spiritualistic outlook lies only in the inversion of the formula. That which Sabbatianism gained through the formula, "he who permits the forbidden," was achieved by Hasidism through that of, "who prohibits the permitted." But in terms of the judgment of history, this reversal is important in principle; Jewish Orthodoxy struggled equally with both of these outlooks and, in terms of the history of the struggle for the preservation of a unified image of Judaism, they were indeed synonymous.

of "inside" and "outside" in "Die 36 farborgenen Gerechten in der jüdischen Tradition," *Judaica I* (Frankfurt am Main, 1963), p. 223.

29 Only one among the many vocal opponents of Hasidism, R. Ḥayyim of Volozhin, understood the quietistic-social nature of Hasidism, polemicizing against it in the name of ethics, which does not tolerate the paradoxicality inherent in this dualism. He well understand that true spiritual interest is the enemy, concealed or open, of social morality, and accused Hasidism of "hypothetical," a-moralistic interests. He went quite far in demonstrating the way in which devotion to the pure ideal of the mystical "fear of Divine sublimity" (*yir'at ha-romemut*) can conflict with the interests of halakhah and of law. Thus *Nefesh ha-Ḥayyim*, Part IV, Chap. 8: "Yet another [i.e., Evil Urge] can seduce you, by bundles of proofs that the aim of man's service is only to achieve fear of sublimity, and that his eyes and heart shall be turned only towards this all the days, and that fear of [Divine] punishment and shame before other people is the worst possible quality, and deserving of being uprooted from your heart ... And it can lead to this: that if a person chastises you and shows that you have violated some law, you will lift up your heart not to separate yourself from this so long as the fear of the chastiser is upon you, saying that this is not for [the sake of] fear of God, but only out of fear of man and external fear."

In my opinion, E. Etkes, in his biography of R. Israel Salañter, did not at all understand the figure of R. Ḥayyim of Volozhin and his stance. For my position on this, see above, Introduction, n. 47.

Chapter Twelve

Ḥabad: Anti-Spiritualism as a Quietistic Value

I

The phenomenon of spiritualism constitutes a part of every movement for religious renewal: renewed attention to the fundamental questions of religion, such as the relationship of man to God and to the world, and the question of religious action, brings in its wake the spiritualistic direction. Spiritualism need not necessarily be of a mystical cast, but may instead have a rationalist bent, as in the case of Maimonides. Its main characteristic is that it gives priority to the spiritual value implied by any given religious act or datum, such as the Torah and its *miẓvot* or sacramental activity in general. This priority may be moderate, allowing those values occupying a lower position on its scale to continue to exist of necessity, while simultaneously developing its eschatological dream of the negation of this realm at the end of days; or it may also be revolutionary and negate these values in the here and now on the basis of cogent inferences.

It is difficult to imagine the latter possibility in the realm of Hasidism, since the movement as a whole bears the character of a conservative renewal. Even such an extreme spiritualist as R. Menaḥem Mendel of Vitebsk did not dare to derive the ultimate conclusions of antinomian spirituality;[1] one need not add that the same was true of the founder of this direction, the Maggid of Mezhirech.

Religious spiritualism is first and foremost a question of religious stance rather than of an abstract philosophical world-view. Adopting a spiritualistic stand in principle does not yet indicate the actual inward features of the path to be followed by the spiritualist, be it activist or quietist. These points need to be made, because

* This chapter originally appeared under the title, "Anti-Spiritualism in Hasidism — Studies in the Teachings of R. Shneur Zalman of Lyady" (Heb.), *Molad* 20, nos. 171–172 (1962), pp. 513–528; it is published here with minor revisions and updated bibliographical references.

1 See Rufus Jones, *Studies in Mystical Religion* (London, 1909). A similar accusation was leveled against Martin Luther's conservatism, in the course of a polemic concerning the sacraments, in which he writes: "God chose not to give any man his [spiritual] gifts unless he receive them via the external things" (ibid., p. 13). Cf. ibid, p. 38, for the arguments of the Anabaptists.

both extremes — those of unrestrained activism and of the tendency to passivity — coexisted within the Hasidic path shaped by the Maggid of Mezhirech, which is in principle a spiritual one by virtue of its very stance as a religious phenomenon. This schematic definition is only intended for purposes of general orientation within the rich and diverse climate of Hasidic thought.

In the present chapter, I wish to describe one branch of Hasidism, that known as *Ḥabad*, and particularly the teaching of its founder, R. Shneur Zalman of Lyady (1745–1813), from a standpoint which is in principle anti-spiritualistic. My primary concern here is to show that the ideational framework of the Ḥabad system is complete and whole within itself, and represents a tendency clearly opposed to that of the Maggid. The removal of the Maggidic elements from the teaching of R. Shneur Zalman may be interpreted as tantamount to the rejection of the spiritual elements therein. With the removal of these elements, one arrives at a Hasidic world-view substantially different from that of all other streams of classical Hasidism. I would like to describe here this unique perspective.

II

One of the better-known controversies within Hasidism was that between R. Abraham of Kalisk (1741–1810) and R. Shneur Zalman of Lyady. R. Abraham of Kalisk, like R. Shneur Zalman himself, was a disciple-colleague of R. Menaḥem Mendel of Vitebsk. Together with R. Menaḥem Mendel, R. Abraham immigrated to the Land of Israel in the *ᶜaliyyah* of 1777, settling in Safed and thereafter in Tiberias, where most of R. Menaḥem Mendel's teachings — both those which were published and those which have remained in manuscript form to the present — were written. Throughout R. Menaḥem Mendel's lifetime, relations between the center in Eretz-Israel and that in White Russia, which R. Shneur Zalman was later to head, were harmonious. Following his death in 1788, however, a fierce controversy broke out within the Hasidic world. Historians have generally[2] seen this controversy as being rooted in disputes over *ḥaluqqah* moneys and questions of prestige and leadership, as confirmed by the extant correspondence between the two centers. However, they tend to overlook a small passage which appears repeatedly in R. Abraham of Kalisk's remarks,[3] which has remained little understood.

2 See Teitelbaum, *ha-Rav mi-Ladi u-Mifleget Ḥaba"d* (Warsaw, 1910), Ch. 15.

3 J. A. Brawer, "On the Quarrel Between R. Shneur Zalman of Lyady and R. Abraham Kalisker (Heb.), *Qiryat Sefer* 1 (1925), pp. 142–150, 226–238, insists that the theoretical background of this debate is actually of great importance. He disputes Horodetzky and Kahana on this point (pp. 143–144), claiming that he saw comments concerning this matter in a manuscript he received from the Rabbi

Some nine years after the death of R. Menaḥem Mendel of Vitebsk, R. Abraham of Kalisk argued that R. Shneur Zalman had departed from the system of his teacher, the Maggid of Mezhirech, and that there were dangers inherent in his teachings.

> For my part, I did not find satisfaction in that the honor of his Torah [i.e., R. Shneur Zalman] "removed the sun from its container" — that is, to embody the words of the [Maggid] of Mezhirech, which are the very words of the Besht, within the holy words of the Ar"i *z"l*. For even though all comes from one place, [nevertheless,] the language of the Torah and the language of the Sages are distinct from one another. [This is so,] particularly because of the danger that, because of our great sins, the rain [*geshem*; word-play on "corporeality"] falls and penetrates, but the generation is not worthy. It would have been preferable had he chosen an allusive language, whereby the ways of the fear of God and of faith would be revealed so as to purify the body and the character for God alone [and not for any mundane interests]. And I have much to wish concerning this, without limit, and the consequence of what may come about because of this — but it cannot be written. And I say what may come about because of this, heaven forbid, according to the nature of those who receive it, for one spark may divide several different ways, and such is the way of Torah. And the increasing of the oil in the lamp may, Heaven forbid, cause it to be extinguished; and man's impulse overcomes him every day, saying: "Come see this new thing, which is in

of Slonim, which presumably contained greater details of the theoretical arguments of R. Abraham of Kalisk against the Ḥabad system (see ibid., p. 227). In this article, Brawer cites remarks which parallel some things found in the letters of R. Abraham Kalisker published in *Ḥibbat ha-ʾAreẓ* (Jerusalem, 1897), pp. 70a–b; 71a–b. One of Brawer's important observations is that in R. Menaḥem Mendel of Vitebsk's *Liqqutei ʾAmarim* (Lemberg, 1911), all of the letters concerning this polemic were deleted, out of respect for the *ẓaddiqim* (ibid., p. 229), a point to be discussed further below.

Naftali Ben-Menaḥem reedited and republished this 1797 letter of R. Abraham of Kalisk in *Areshet* 1 (1960), 405–413. His revised text, based upon a manuscript found in the library of R. Naḥum Dov Baer Friedman of Sadgora, is fuller and contains an explicit argument against the publication and dissemination of the teachings of the *Tanya*. The *Tanya* was first published anonymously in Slavuta, in 1796–97. This text says: "We have seen the *Sefer Beinonim* [i.e., the *Tanya*] published by the honor of His Torah, and I did not find therein much benefit for the saving of souls, for it is very learned in giving many pieces of advice concerning the *miẓvot* performed habitually ... and according to the path of the Kabbalists ... But putting too much oil in the lamp may cause it to be extinguished. For man's Evil Impulse strengthens, every day uttering new words of Wisdom, Understanding and Knowledge (*Ḥokhmah, Binah, Daᶜat* — i.e., *Ḥabad*), but his heart is not with him..." R. Abraham Kalisker argues here against the exaggerated battle against the Evil Urge described in *Tanya*, as well as against the renewal of *Ḥokhmah Binah Daᶜat*, which is too "clever" and "artificial," being closer to Lurianic Kabbalah than to the teaching of the Maggid and the Besht. There are other interesting social elements discussed in this letter, but this is not the place to expand upon them.

Concerning the Kalisker's emphatically ethical approach, see Joseph Weiss, "R. Abraham Kalisker's Concept of Communion with God and Man," *Studies in Eastern European Jewish Mysticism* (London, 1985), pp. 155–169 [originally published in *JJS* 6, no. 2 (1955), pp. 87–99].

> wisdom and understanding and knowledge [i.e., the words initialized as *Ḥaba"d*]." ... And it was the practice of our teachers to take great care concerning their words, that they be not be [uttered in the presence of] most of the Hasidim (i.e., nearly all), and each one delivers his words and enters into the covenant of the faith of the sages, so the word of Torah is pure and clean ... And all the leaders of the generation in our time regretted very much the publicizing [of his thoughts]; and particularly my master, the holy rabbi, R. Menaḥem Mendel, whose soul rests in Eden, was greatly pained before his death over this publicizing, and literally tore the hairs of his head over this.[4]

In a letter from 1788, he says:

> ... I fear that this is the counsel of the Evil One and his trick, to uproot that which is planted and to uproot that root which tends towards grace — the holy rabbi, our master R. Menaḥem Mendel, *z"l.*[5]

The letters of R. Menaḥem Mendel published thus far [6] contain no reference to any such controversy with R. Shneur Zalman, but R. Abraham argues forcefully that the former in fact concurred in this opinion. It is difficult to ascertain at this point whether there is any truth to this matter, and whether things were decreed intentionally or whether these rulings were attributed to him only following his death.[7] In any event, in a letter sent by R. Levi Yitzḥak of Berdichev to R. Abraham of Kalisk concerning the controversy with R. Shneur Zalman, one can see his astonishment at this claim:

> [Concerning] that which you write pertaining to the practice [of the *Rav*], saying that it is not in accordance with the [teaching of] our master and teacher the Maggid, *z"l*:

4 *Ḥibbat ha-ᵓAreẓ*, 70a–b.

5 Ibid., 71a–b.

6 In *Ḥibbat ha-ᵓAreẓ*, in *Peri ᶜEẓ Ḥayyim* and in *Liqqutei ᵓAmarim.* Regarding the latter treatise, it appears to me that only the letters are by the Rabbi of Vitebsk, while the other homilies are by the Maggid of Mezhirech himself.

7 One of the rabbis of Jerusalem, R. Yosef Hoffmann, conveyed to me in the summer of 1962 an explicit testimony from the rabbi of the Old City, R. Orenstein, who owned an extant unpublished manuscript of R. Menaḥem Mendel of Vitebsk consisting of letters in which he wrote explicitly against the theoretical position of R. Shneur Zalman. However, I have been unable to receive details of the character of the arguments. What I was told orally — namely, that Ḥabad Hasidism had as-it-were opened a door for the Haskalah — seems to me to be a late argument, which one cannot assume was already found in these manuscripts; it is unfortunate that these documents are not available. In any event, it seems clear to me that the publication of these manuscripts was suppressed in order to avoid controversy and to silence the differences of opinion.
Years later, I asked permission of the Court of Slonim to allow me to see manuscripts from the Rabbi of Vitebsk which had been preserved among them since the days of his sojourn in Tiberias, but I was denied permission. I was told that the manuscripts were lying somewhere in a cellar in B'nai Berak!

> First of all, you have forgotten a Talmudic passage found in several places, that after the fact [i.e., the death of R. Menaḥem Mendel] one is not reliable to give testimony. And after this, it is astonishing to me how one can even think of complaining about the behavior of the Master, whose entire concern is to teach to his people Torah and *mizvot*, this being the very essence of service, as we have received from our teacher, *z"l*, and whose behavior is also according to this way. To the contrary, whoever does not behave in this way does not follow the way of our teacher, and whoever complains of this way is as if he complains, Heaven forbid, against the honor of our teacher, *z"l*, for his service and behavior are in accordance with this way. And it is astonishing to me regarding one [i.e., such as yourself] who was so faithfully together with him by our teacher, that this should be surprising to you.
> As for what you wrote to me in the name of the late Menaḥem Mendel *z"l* — who was precious in the eyes of our master — I have not heard. But I can bear reliable witness to the following: that the honorable rabbi, the Gaon [i.e. R. Shneur Zalman], was very precious in the eyes of our teacher [the Maggid of Mezhirech], and he constantly praised him, very much, without limit. And as to what you wrote that this was [going on for] about twenty-five years [i.e., R. Menaḥem Mendel's opposition to R. Shneur Zalman] — it is surprising to me that for such a long time, you have not written to me anything about this matter. And if the truth is with you, you should have written to me some sort of explanation as to why you have now spoken to me about this. For in my opinion such was the way of our master the Maggid [of Mezhirech], may he rest in peace, and this is the way by which shall be given the light of God.[8]

Of course, this letter in itself in no way constitutes any evidence as to the truth or falsehood of the claim *per se*, as R. Abraham of Kalisk was closer to R. Menaḥem Mendel than any other person, and might have known things of which R. Levi Yitzḥak was ignorant. We have no way of knowing from the extant material whether R. Menaḥem Mendel in fact saw treatises in the handwriting of R. Shneur Zalman during his lifetime, or heard his teaching.[9] But whether or not this testi-

8 Teitelbaum, p. 144.

9 I do not know which of his writings he could have seen, as the *Tanya*, referred to here, was first published in 1797, nine years after R. Menaḥem Mendel's death. R. Shneur Zalman may have intentionally refrained from publishing this work during the lifetime of his teacher, R. Menaḥem Mendel, as from a theoretical point-of-view he related negatively to his Hasidic approach, even if he did not say so in as many words. As to R. Menaḥem Mendel's reaction to the printed book, see above, n. 3.
Brawer cites an interesting account, cited by R. Ḥayyim Meir Heilman in *Beit Rabbi* (Jerusalem, 1953), Pt. I, p. 84, in which R. Shneur Zalman replies to the criticisms of R. Abraham of Kalisk as follows: "I never requested of him [i.e., R. Abraham] any agreement concerning words of Hasidism, that they be the words of the holy mouth of our teacher [i.e., the Maggid of Mezhirech]." This is an interesting answer.

mony will be confirmed, or whether it remains only as a large question mark, one thing may be said with certainty: that the accusations made against R. Shneur Zalman of Lyady were not made for naught.

III

Chroniclers have always seen Ḥabad as a somewhat "unusual" or "aberrant" school within Hasidism, primarily due to its rationalistic approach,[10] for which reason it enjoyed more serious attention on the part of the Enlightenment historians, whose interest in a given religious phenomenon was in direct relation to its degree of rationalism. This statement, true as it might be in itself, was never explained in the context of Hasidic doctrine: that is to say, they never really understood the significance of this point, either in terms of the Ḥabad approach to life, or even more particularly, in relation to the classical teachings of Hasidism. Hence, the present attempt to compare the teaching of Shneur Zalman of Lyady with that of his teacher, the Maggid of Mezhirech, will hopefully contribute to our understanding of the innermost questionings and issues of Hasidic thought. Moreover, such a comparison will lead us to the true nexus which will enable us to examine Hasidism as a living religious phenomenon with greater clarity. Once one attempts to understand in what sense R. Shneur Zalman differed from the school of the Maggid in Volhynia, the deepest internal conflict within Hasidism, which is obscured by the term "rationalism," emerges with full severity and seriousness. We are amazed at the turnabout represented by his major work, the *Tanya*, as against the background of the teachings of his master.

There were many disciples in Mezhirech, each one of whom clearly derived his own personal message from the teaching of the Maggid, but who nevertheless shared a common ground giving meaning to the concept, "the school of the Maggid." Within the pages of the *Tanya*, one finds a completely different spirit which, more than it seeks to explain the teachings of the Maggid (albeit in a more rationalist manner), seeks to substitute for it another, substantially different teaching. If one dares say such a thing, one might state that, in terms of its inner rhythm, there is no more thoroughly anti-hasidic document than the *Tanya*.

The message of Ḥabad (the name is taken from the initials of the words, *Ḥokhmah, Binah, Daᶜat*, referring to the three highest, "intellectual" Sefirot) was intended more to undercut the central Maggidic elements in Hasidic teaching than it was to build up and to continue Hasidism. The different climate of religious life

10 Graetz, *Geschichte*, XI: 116; Dubnow, *Toldot ha-Ḥasidut*, Chap. 6, esp. the end.

found in Ḥabad, which I shall describe presently, can not only be interpreted on the basis of a different social background or on a type of leader who leaves his own personal imprint upon the religious mood; they were based upon a totally and deliberately different theoretical basis *ab initio.* I do not mean to blindly accept the accusations of R. Abraham of Kalisk, nor is it his testimony alone which draws my attention to the difference between Hasidism and the phenomenon called Ḥabad. The statement that R. Shneur Zalman "went outside of his teacher's system" is interesting in itself, as it implies that the leaders of this generation were attentive to theoretical "changes" of this type. But even if there were no "comments" of this type (and it would have been possible to conceal them, just as the explicit testimonies of R. Menaḥem Mendel of Vitebsk were evidently concealed), in the final analysis anyone who studies Hasidism in an unbiased manner, wishing to understand this phenomenon from within, will reach similar conclusions to those proposed here.

The basic assumptions — cosmological and psychological — upon which R. Shneur Zalman built his Ḥabad system are substantially different from those of the Maggid and his school. These assumptions are not intended to demonstrate that it is possible to remain within the framework of the classical Maggidic teaching of life, even if one here and there changes some theoretical elements. On the contrary: they are meant to provide the basis for an alternative Hasidic outlook, and to lead us step by step to carefully formulated conclusions pertaining to the teaching of everyday action.

Prima facie, the author of the *Tanya* would seem to have been the most legitimate heir of the Maggid's teaching, repeatedly stressing as he did the pantheistic outlook.[11] The acosmic approach, which the Rabbi of Lyady likewise received from the Maggid,[12] is analyzed at great length and emphasis in the *Tanya*, and particularly in his work entitled *Shaᶜar ha-Yiḥud veha-ᵓEmunah.* All of the created beings are:

> . . . [merely] like a diffusing light and effulgence from the flow and spirit of God, which issues forth [from Him] and becomes clothed in them, and brings them from naught to being. Hence, their existence is null and void in relation to their source, just as the light of the sun is nullified and considered naught and utter nothingness, and is not at all referred to as "existing" when it is within its source, but [the term "existence applies to it] only beneath the heavens, where it is not its source. In the same manner,

11 See J. Weiss' article on Ḥabad, "Contemplative Mysticism and 'Faith' in Hasidic Piety," *Studies in Eastern European Jewish Mysticism*, pp. 44–45 [originally published in *JJS* 4, no. 1 (1953), pp. 19–29].

12 Scholem, "Devekut," pp. 224ff. Scholem cites there the acosmic elements already appearing in the parables of the Besht. See also *Liqqutei Yeqarim* (Lemberg, 1865), 12a.

> the term "existence" can be applied to all created things only as they appear to our corporeal eyes, for we do not see nor at all comprehend the source, which is the spirit of God that brings them into existence... But in the following respect, the illustration is apparently not completely identical with the object of comparison. For in the illustration, the source [i.e., the sun] is not present at all in the expanse of the universe and upon the earth, where its light is seen as actually existing. By contrast, all created things are always within their source, and it is only that the source is not visible to our physical eyes.[13]

Two major assumptions are implied by this passage: 1) that creation is a kind of "dissemination of light" from the Divine source — that is, a distant and distorted echo of authentic existence, of true being; 2) that this "light" is imaginary and "non-existent" in relation to its source. The former assumption is, so-to-speak, Neo-Platonic, assuming as it does that our existence is a kind of distortion of the divine reality, and that it is not merely a question of level. The second assumption, which is built upon the feeling of an acosmic world — that is, the consciousness of its non-existence as an independent entity — refutes the seriousness of the Neo-Platonic claim, assuming the world to be no more than an image. The third assumption in this sentence is important: "all created things are always within their source, and it is only that the source is not visible to our physical eyes" — that is, the existence of the world within God is immanent. Up to this point, R. Shneur Zalman has not innovated much in his cosmological directives.

The new motif in the *Tanya*'s system which attracts our attention relates to the repeated, uncompromising emphasis upon the fact that God's manner of existence is the same everywhere, both above or below, only below it is more "hidden" — that is, our own apprehension of His absolute existence is smaller.

> ... But even in the higher, hidden worlds, He is hidden and concealed within them, just as He is hidden and concealed in the lower worlds, for no thought can apprehend Him at all, even in the higher worlds. And ... just as He is found there, so is He to be found in the very lowest [worlds]. The difference between the higher and lower worlds is with regard to the flow of vitality which the blessed ᵓ*Ein Sof* causes to flow and illumine in a manner of "revelation out of concealment." ... For the higher worlds receive [this vitality and light] in a somewhat more revealed form than do the lower ... But the lower [worlds], even the spiritual ones, do not receive [the divine life-force] in quite such a revealed form as it is received in the higher worlds, but only by means of many garments, wherein the blessed ᵓ*Ein Sof* invests the vitality and light ... These

13 *Liqqutei ᵓAmarim: Tanya* (Brooklyn, 1954 [photo copy, Vilna, 1937]), pp. 78a–b (*Shaᶜar ha-Yiḥud veha-ᵓEmunah*, Ch. 3); the English translations of *Tanya* and *Shaᶜar ha-Yiḥud* used in this chapter are taken, with minor changes, from *Lessons in Tanya*, elucidated by Yosef Wineberg, translated by Levy and Shalom B. Wineberg, ed., Uri Kaploun (Brooklyn, 1987–89), 3 v. [Below: *LT*], pp. 855–857.

> garments, wherein the blessed ᵓ*Ein Sof* invests and conceals the light and vitality, are so strong and powerful that He thereby created this world that is verily corporeal and physical ...[14]

It is important to stress here that the use of the active verbs, stating that the Infinite "draws down" and "illuminates" the lower worlds, is no more than a figure of speech. "However, the *ẓimẓum* and concealment is only for the lower worlds, but in relation to the Holy One, blessed be He, 'everything before Him is considered as actually naught' [*Zohar* I:134a]."[15] God is "revealed" or "hides Himself" in keeping with the law of His own existence, which is completely indifferent to the phenomenon known as this world or other worlds. R. Shneur Zalman's attitude to the world of the *Sefirot* likewise follows from this. Further on, we shall see that, not only was the concept of *ẓimẓum* reinterpreted in a non-literal manner by R. Shneur Zalman, but the system of *Sefirot* itself as an autonomous structure of Divinity likewise lost its meaning in his thought, and was transformed into a quasi-"Maimonidean" system of attributes.[16]

The theoretical tension in the teaching of R. Shneur Zalman oscillates between the two poles of divine "existence" and "concealment" or, in other words, between existence and *ẓimẓum* (contraction): *ẓimẓum* is no longer the opposite of immanent existence, but a form of revelation. In a paradoxical way, the act of divine revelation is more likely in the world through His hiddenness and concealment and being embodied therein: i.e., in *ẓimẓum*. That is, the external act of Creation is an aspect of His concealment and hiddenness; the hiddenness and absorption of God within the world is itself the act of creation. In other words: the active aspect of God is His *ẓimẓum*, identified with the creation of an external garment for His immanent existence, which is passive and indifferent to everything that takes place in the world, as "everything before Him is considered as naught" — i.e., is considered as "nothing" and "nullity."

Alongside these purely theoretical considerations, we find in his thought the traditional formulations of Creation as *ex nihilo* and of Creation as taking place

14 *Tanya*, p. 72a (Ch. 51); *LT*, pp. 776–779.

15 Ibid., 81b (*Shaᶜar ha-Yiḥud*, Ch. 6); *LT*, p. 905.

16 Such an approach is in fact typical of nominalistic interpretations of the doctrine of Sefirot, such as those of R. Moses Cordovero or of R. Moses Ḥayyim Luzzatto, who was influenced by him, and was in turn perhaps the major influence upon the doctrine of R. Shneur Zalman of Lyady. See R. Schatz, "R. Moses Cordovero and R. Isaac Luria — Between Nominalism and Realism" (Heb.), *Meḥqerei Yerushalayim be-Maḥshevet Yisraᵓel*, No. 3 (1982), pp. 122–136; idem., "Ramḥal's Metaphysics in its Ethical Context (A Study in *Qel"ḥ Pitḥei Ḥokhmah*)" (Heb.), in *Sefer ha-Yovel li-Shlomo Pines*, Vol. II [*Meḥqerei Yerushalayim be-Maḥshevet Yisraᵓel*. 9] (Jerusalem, 1990), pp. 361–396.

in order "to benefit His creatures," as required by the Lurianic parallel. However, the explanation given in Lurianic Kabbalah — namely, that the world is unable to withstand the great goodness of existence without Divine contraction (*ẓimẓum*) — was transformed into the claim that the world is unable to exist without the external garment in which the immanent existence of God is concealed, whether this is present in the Infinite itself, in the *Sefirot*, or in this world.

The emphasis upon the motif of "equal existence" above and below not only places the existence of the *Sefirot* in question, but also raises the issue of the entire doctrine of emanation in the literal sense; the problem of creation *ex nihilo* likewise becomes far more difficult. A decisive change took place already among the early Kabbalists, for whom creation *ex nihilo* was interpreted as the emanation from *Keter* of the *Sefirah* of *Ḥokhmah*, and not as explained literally in medieval philosophy. Indeed, R. Shneur Zalman, who does not see the *Sefirot* as fixed and permanent entities constituting a Divine structure or "Divine world" in the literal sense, does not need these symbolic concepts, but immediately admits that:

> It is beyond the scope of the mind of any creature to comprehend the essential nature of the *ẓimẓum* and concealment, and [to comprehend] that nonetheless the creature itself be created *ex nihilo*, just as it is not within the capacity of the mind of any creature to comprehend the essential nature of the creation of being out of nothing.[17]

R. Shneur Zalman not only moved the concept of *ẓimẓum* into the immanent realm of the world (as did the Maggid), but the entire complex of concepts surrounding "the Attribute of Judgment" and "the Attribute of Mercy" were also explained in this way.

Lurianic Kabbalah constructed its own theory concerning the midrashic concept of *Middat ha-Din*, upon which the world is built, explaining this concept in terms of the Divine contraction and the attempt of the light which remains within space to return specifically to its own essence. This is the "reflected light" (*ʾor ha-ḥozer*), which is the carrier of the Attribute of Judgment, which is the opposite of Creation outside of the Godhead. On the other hand, the expansion of light into the cosmos is identified with the Attribute of Mercy (*Middat ha-Raḥamim*). Within this internal dialectic,[18] new expression is given to the pair of concepts, *Middat ha-Din* and *Middat ha-Raḥamim*, by which the world was created. R. Shneur Zalman explains that the act of God's "concealment," or the divine hiddenness or contraction within the world, corresponds to the Attribute of Judgment, whereas the Attribute of Mercy represents the potential of uncovering it, inherent in a dialectic manner in the fact of His "hiding" within the world. This is the Attribute of Grace

17 *Tanya*, p. 79b (*Shaʿar ha-Yiḥud*, Ch. 4); *LT*, p. 866.

18 G. Scholem, *Sabbatai Ṣevi*, p. 28 ff.

(*Ḥesed*), upon which the world is constructed, with which God combines the attribute of Mercy (*Raḥamim*): "that is, the revelation [within the world] of Godliness through the *ẓaddiqim*, and through the signs and miracles recorded in the Torah."[19]

The entire question of divine attributes is problematical, as I have already mentioned. The attempt to obscure their uniqueness and their becoming substance well suits R. Shneur Zalman's monistic understanding of Divine reality, in which there is no difference between the upper and lower reality. He paradoxically derives a functional concept of the upper attributes from the fact of their multiplication:

> From the mutual inclusion of the attributes [that is, from the fact that the activity of Judgment always comes together with that of Mercy, and that this is a necessary dialectic], it is evident that "He and His selves" — i.e., His attributes — "are One," for since they are in complete unity with Him, they therefore unite with each other and are comprised of each other.[20]

The most extreme example of this approach appears in his use of the traditional concept of "His unity with the attribute of His kingship." There are two innovations here: the first, that this union is no longer seen as occurring within the world of divine *Sefirot*; second, that His "attribute of kingship" is the attribute of divine existence in its embodied form — that is, the attribute of *ẓimẓum*. He says the following:

19 *Tanya*, p. 79b (*Shaᶜar ha-Yiḥud*, Ch. 5); *LT*, p. 871. This remark is in my opinion directed against the tendency towards miracle working by the *ẓaddiqim*; their real advantage lies in revealing God's hiddenness. This attitude is reminiscent of Ramḥal's rationalistic stand. See my article, "Moses Ḥayyim Luzzatto's Thought Against the Background of Theodicy Literature" (Heb.), *Proceedings of the Israel Academy of Science and Humanities* 7, no. 12 (1988), pp. 275–291, note 10. Cf. Yoram Jacobson, "The Doctrine of Creation in R. Shneur Zalman of Ladi" (Heb.), *ᵓEshel Beᵓer Shevaᶜ* 1 (1976), 307–368. Jacobson discusses Ramḥal's influence on R. Shneur Zalman on pp. 359–368, stressing particularly that, "that which was designated as 'evil' in the thought of Luzzatto becomes 'the existent' in the doctrine of R. Shneur Zalman." While this is indeed true, Jacobson does not refer to the Hasidic orientation of the Maggid's teaching and its influence upon R. Shneur Zalman. His ignoring of this aspect led to an understanding of R. Shneur Zalman in purely Kabbalistic terms, free of all interior Hasidic polemic. Perhaps R. Abraham of Kalisker was correct when he understood this "bypassing" of the Maggid's teaching as a non-Hasidic tendency; see note 3 above. Cf. Isaiah Tishby, s.v. "Hasidism" (Heb.) *Enẓeqlopedyah ha-ᶜIvrit* 17, col. 789–797, where he does not acknowledge the polemical nature of the *Tanya*, claiming it to be a popular work. See also the summary of this dispute in Rachel Elior, *Torat ha-Elohut be-dor Sheni shel Ḥasidut Ḥabad* (Jerusalem, 1982), 121–124. I wish to note here that my own stance concerning the speculative force of Lurianic doctrine within the doctrine of the Maggid, as opposed to that of R. Shneur Zalman, has changed since this chapter was originally published in 1962, and I have omitted those lines in the present version. However, my overall position regarding the nature of the *Tanya* as a whole has not altered.

20 *Tanya*, p. 80b (*Shaᶜar ha-Yiḥud*, Ch. 6); *LT*, p. 897.

> Now, although God transcends space and time, He is nevertheless also found below, within space and time — that is, He unites with His attributes of *Malkhut* (Kingship), from which space and time are derived and come into existence. And this is the "lower-level Unity" (*yiḥuda᾽ tata᾽ah*) . . . i.e., His essence and Being, which is called by the name *᾽Ein Sof* ("the Infinite One"), completely fills the whole earth temporally and spatially. For in the heavens above and on the earth [below] and in the four directions, everything is equally permeated with the *᾽Ein Sof*-light, . . . for everything is within the dimension of space, which is utterly nullified in the *᾽Ein Sof*-light, which clothes itself in it through [God's] attribute of *Malkhut* that is united with Him, albeit His attribute of *Malkhut* is the attribute of *ẓimẓum* and concealment, hiding the *᾽Ein Sof*-light, so that the existence of time and space should not be completely nullified and there will be no dimensions of time and space whatsoever, even for the lower worlds. Now, from the foregoing exposition one will be able to understand the verse, "I, the Lord, have not changed" [Mal. 3:6]. This means: there is no change [in Him] at all; just as He was alone before the creation of the world, so is He alone after it was created . . .[21]

The attribute of kingship is hence transformed from the revelation of God within the world of *Sefirot* to one of the "modes" of God, just as *Middat ha-Din* and *Middat ha-Raḥamim* were likewise seen as aspects of the Divine being. But while the former are aspects of hiddenness and revelation (partly following in the wake of Lurianic Kabbalah), the Aspect of His Kingship is a form of His being in space and time.

Rather free use is made here of Kabbalistic terminology, explained further on in *Sha^car ha-Yiḥud veha-᾽Emunah* as the authentic expression of the idea of Divine hiddenness and revelation. Thus, according to R. Shneur Zalman, the true meaning of the phrase that God wanted "His kingdom to be revealed" is that He specifically wanted to reveal the attribute of His concealment in *ẓimẓum*. This explanation is required by the system, because in principle there always exists a tension between hiddenness and revelation, which constitutes the central pillar of the justification for divine service in Ḥabad Hasidism. We shall enlarge upon the meaning of these things in terms of the doctrine of Hasidic action below.

Close study of the two sources, in *Shaᶜar ha-Yiḥud veha-᾽Emunah* and in *Tanya*, will reveal two different formulations of the subject of God's existence within the world.[22] *Shaᶜar ha-Yiḥud veha-᾽Emunah* is clearly intended for those who understand esoteric teaching, while the formulation in *Tanya* is a more cautious one, intended for the broader public. In *Shaᶜar ha-Yiḥud veha-᾽Emunah*, R. Shneur

21 Ibid., p. 82a–b (*Shaᶜar ha-Yiḥud*, Ch. 7); *LT*, pp. 915 -917.

22 The formulations in *Liqqutei Torah* (Vilna, 1885), match those in *Tanya* for cautiousness. See, i.e., p. 52b.

Zalman stresses the acosmic element, in no way obscuring the seriousness of the problem, while in *Tanya* he makes use of the Kabbalistic concepts of *sovev* (bypassing) and *maqif* (surrounding the cosmos) in order to overcome this difficulty. The following are his remarks in *Shaᶜar ha-Yiḥud*:

> Since this is so, you will consequently know that "in the heaven above and on the earth below, there is nothing else [but God]" [Deut. 4:39]. This means that even the material earth, which appears to everyone's eyes to be actually existing, is naught and utter nothingness in relation to the Holy One, blessed be He ... since He and His Name *ʾElohim* are one. Therefore, even the earth and that which is below it are naught and utter nothingness in relation to the Holy One, blessed be He, and are not called by any name at all, not even by the name "else" [in the verse "nothing else"] ... so that it should not enter your mind that the heavens and all their host, and the earth and all it contains, are separate entities in themselves,[23] and that the Holy One, blessed be He, fills the whole world in the same way as the soul is invested in the body, and that He causes the flow of the "vegetative force" into the earth, and the power of motion into the celestial spheres, and moves them and directs them according to His Will, just as the soul moves the body and directs it according to its will.[24] In truth, however, the analogy bears no similarity whatsoever to the object of comparison, since the soul and the body are actually separate from each other at their sources. The source of the body and its essence comes into being not from the soul, but from the seed of one's father and mother ... This is not so, however, in the case of heaven and earth, for their very being and essence was brought into existence from naught and absolute nothingness, solely through the "word of God" and the "breath of His mouth." And now, too, the word of God still stands forever [i.e., in all created things], and flows into them continuously at every instant, constantly creating them anew from nothing, just as for example, the coming into existence of the light from the sun within the very ... globe of the sun ... Hence, in reality they are completely nullified out of existence in relation to the "word of God" and the "breath of His mouth," which are unified with His Essence and Being.[25]

The unequivocal statement that God does not act in the world in a manner analogous to that of the soul in the body — in which case the world would be understood as a secondary element alongside the divine reality — forces one to the monistic conclusion that the world is the Godhead in contracted form: that is, one of the possible forms of its manifestation.[26] On the other hand, there is an emphasis

23 Compare the treatment of this problem in the thought of R. Moses Hayyim Luzzatto, who particularly stresses the distinction between the appearance of things and what they are "in themselves." See Schatz, "The Ethical Context of Ramḥal's Metaphysics," esp. pp. 366–374.

24 The opposite of these ideas appears in *Liqqutei Torah*; *Sefer Va-yiqraʾ*, p. 41b.

25 *Tanya*, p. 81a-b (*Shaᶜar ha-Yiḥud*, Ch. 6); *LT*, p. 899– 904.

26 As he says in greater detail in *Shaᶜar ha-Yiḥud*, Ch. 7: "... until created beings, by nature finite and limited, as they really are, may be brought into existence from its power and light." — ibid., p. 84a; *LT*, p. 932.

here — as there was among many Kabbalists prior to R. Shneur Zalman — on the assumption of creation *ex nihilo*: God's *nihil* is regarded as the common substance of Creation, and as the source from which the world emanates. The idea of *ex nihilo* is of course not so easily harmonized with that of Divine immanence, but is rather in opposition to the pantheistic view. This seemingly contradictory underlying character, which was maintained by the Kabbalists, was nourished by the positive character of the *nihil* itself as a manifestation (*Sefirah*) of God. Hence, Kabbalah could maintain both at one and the same time: i.e., the formula *ex nihilo* and the monistic, immanentistic outlook. There is no question, despite the historical background, as to R. Shneur Zalman's immanentistic motivation.[27]

An attempt is made in the *Tanya* to distinguish between the Torah and the world as the locus in which God is revealed. This distinction is invoked, not only in order to increase the value of the Torah as a Divine revelation over and above every other thing, but also for another reason, which we shall discuss further below: namely, the refusal to turn toward the world in the course of divine service (i.e., the idea known in Maggidic Hasidism as *ᶜavodah be-gashmiyut*). In any event, the theoretical statement that the Torah is the ideal subject of God's revelation in the world conveys an entirely different status upon the world as such in the *Tanya* than it does in R. Shneur Zalman's other writings, and blunts the sharpness of the question of divine immanence.

> This explains why Torah study is so much loftier than all the other commandments, including even prayer, which effects unity within the supernal worlds. . . . From this the wise man will be able to draw upon himself a sense of great awe as he engages in the study of the Torah, when he considers how his soul and its "garments" [i.e., of thought and speech] that are found in his brain and mouth are truly fused in perfect unity with the Divine Will and the [infinite] light of *ʾEin Sof* that is manifest in them. That all the upper and lower worlds are truly as naught in comparison with it; are in fact as absolutely nothing at all, so that He is not literally clothed within them, but surrounds all the worlds with His attribute of *Maqif*, enlivening them with the essence of their vitality, [so much so that] they can only bear to have a minute glow of it clothed in them without their reverting to nothingness altogether. Their main life-force which they receive from it, however, is not clothed within them, but animates them from the outside, so to speak, in a transcendent, encompassing manner.[28]

Elsewhere in *Tanya*, R. Shneur Zalman engages in a terminological discussion of the concepts of *sovev* and *maqif*, raising the entire subject to the level of a more

27 See, more recently, my analysis of this problem in the thought of M. H. Luzzatto, as reflected in his book *Ql"ḥ Pitḥei Ḥokhmah*, in the Pines Memorial Volume (op. cit., n. 16).

28 Cf. *Tanya*, p. 29a–b (Ch. 23); *LT*, pp. 308–310.

transparent allusion; that is, that even these concepts do not exclude the notion of immanence, but merely allude to the degree of "revelation" of His immanence.[29] But he is also drawn here into a rationalization of the concept of *haqafah*, understood in a Maimonidean sense, stating that the intellect "surrounds" the object of knowledge. This implies that it is possible to understand *haqafah* in such a way that the existence of God in the world is identified with no more than His knowledge of it.

As we stated above, despite such "harmonizing" formulae, it seems to me that the pantheistic, acosmic doctrine of R. Shneur Zalman remains as it was and as he intended it. While it is true that the teaching of the Maggid is also imbued with the feeling that "the whole world is filled with His glory," and he also assumed that *ẓimẓum* is not to be understood in its literal meaning, but refers to God's contraction within the world,[30] it is precisely this seemingly parallel element which brings out the difference between the religious world-views of these two personalities. In the Maggid, the Lurianic doctrine of the uplifting of sparks is the basis for all redemption of the world and of man, while in the doctrine of the *Tanya* these Lurianic motifs are totally absent as a basis of *praxis*. It is no accident that R. Shneur Zalman immersed himself in the purely pantheistic feeling of life, removing all mythical elements from Hasidism. He did not wish these directives, just as he did not wish their religious conclusions; he only drew upon their intellectual implications. The teaching of the spiritualization of the world, so striking in the Maggid's doctrine of lifting up sparks, is transformed into a quiet "revelation" of God, discovered by man when he is involved in the performance of *miẓvot*. We do not find here a struggle with the world for the sake of its redemption; rather, one feels here a quiet, tranquil sense of wholeness and continuity, of "the even-handed presence" of God in all, so that man is not commanded to even set his mind to this at all. R. Shneur Zalman arrives at a further paradox when he explains the need for man to see the world as "a thing in itself," in order for him to serve God truly, even when he knows that "it is not a thing in itself" — a knowledge which *ipso facto* entails uncomfortable spiritualistic assumptions. Man's desire to be at peace with the world is attributed to God Himself; namely, that God wishes to be worshipped specifically through the aspect of His hidden presence in the world, rather than in the attempt to explicitly reveal the Divine element, as implied in the Lurianic idea of "uplifting sparks." Thus, the religious vision of R. Shneur Zalman is strikingly different than that of the Maggid. The following are his remarks:

29 See, e.g., *Tanya*, p. 68a–b (Ch. 48).

30 See the references under the entry *ẓimẓum*, in the index to my edition of *Maggid Devarav le-Yaᶜaqov*.

> The cause and reason for this *ẓimẓum* and concealment with which the Holy One, blessed be He, obscured and hid the life-force of the world, making it appear as an independent existing entity, [is as follows:] It is known to all that the purpose of the creation of the world is the revelation of God's sovereignty, for "there is no king without a nation" [*Pirqei de-Rabbi Eliᶜezer*, Ch. 3]. The word *ᶜam* ("nation") is related etymologically to the word *ᶜamumot* ["dimmed" or "extinguished"], for they are separate entities, distinct and distant from the level of the king ... But only "in a numerous nation is the glory of the king" [Prov. 14:28] ... Thus, it is this attribute [i.e., *Malkhut*] and this Name [i.e., *ᵓAdonay*, the name designating divine lordship] which bring the world into existence and sustain it so that it should be as it is now — a completely independent and separate entity, and not absolutely nullified.[31]

The fact of the existence of the world in appearance alone is an expression of the divine will. Moreover, he asks that this remain so, for "there is no king without a nation" ... But only "in a numerous [i.e., 'dimmed'] nation is the glory of the king." The Maggidic spiritualistic imperative is thus contrary to the divine will, seeking as it does to break the barriers of time and place and to arrive at a situation that is beyond them;[32] R. Shneur Zalman's imperative attempts to explain that God is present within time and place, just as He is beyond them, so that there is no need to seek Him beyond them. In light of this teaching, the transcendent world loses its central significance for man, who is commanded to live joyfully within the world as it is given to him according to the divine will:

> Now when one contemplates deeply and at length on this matter [of God's true unity], his heart will rejoice with this faith; his soul will be gladdened by it to the point of rejoicing and singing with all his heart, soul and might. For this faith is tremendous — it actually constitutes the closeness of God. This [in fact] is the whole [purpose]

31 *Tanya*, pp. 81b–82a (*Shaᶜar ha-Yiḥud*, Ch. 7); *LT*, pp. 909–911.

32 See *Maggid Devarav le-Yaᶜaqov*: "when he connects himself to God, may He be blessed ... not in order to know what is within time, but for God alone." — p. 149.
A reading of the text of *Tanya* as if it refers to a spiritual praxis by the term *ᶜavodah be-biṭṭul* seems to me harmonistic. *Biṭṭul* is not a matter of praxis, but of theory, and does not involve the slightest hint of *hanhagah*. The *Hanhagot* of the Maggid, who prescribes *devequt* and self-abnegation (*ᶜiyyun*), instruct one how to achieve these in practice. The *Tanya* only contains a description of the consciousness of negation of the world in relation to His unity (exactly as in Ramḥal). This consciousness does not create a practical-mystical consciousness, but is a rationalistic utterance — i.e., to be "considered before Him like nothing, literally."
There is a certain contradiction in the remarks of Rachel Elior, "ḤaBaD: The Contemplative Ascent to God," *Jewish Spirituality [II]*, ed. Arthur Green [World Spirituality. 14 (New York, 1985)], pp. 157–205. She acknowledges there that "*Biṭṭul* ... is not to be understood as an everyday practice," but a few lines later she writes, "*biṭṭul* is understood as the spiritual practice derived from the acosmic assumption" (p. 182). There is no place in the *Tanya* which in fact speaks about man's self-negation. This is a false impression one might gain from what she writes on p. 181.

> of man, and the purpose for which he, and all the worlds, both upper and lower, were created; that God should have such a dwelling-place here below ... How great is the joy of a common and lowly person when he is brought close to a king of flesh and blood who lodges and dwells together with him in his home! How much more, infinitely more, [ought one to rejoice] in the nearness of the King of kings, the Holy One, blessed be He, and in His dwelling.[33]

The heritage of the Lurianic Kabbalah is here completely obliterated: the world is no longer perceived as an enemy, overwhelming by its corporeality the divine spark which wishes to be redeemed. The entire teaching of the "revelation" of God within his concealments takes on instead the coloration of clear intellectual apprehension. The intellective soul rejoices in the presence of God, in its dwelling with Him and in the fact that it has conquered the Other Side.[34] R. Shneur Zalman's cosmological assumptions thereby eliminated the possibility of spiritualistic tendencies, which represented the best of religious life in the school of the Maggid. Rationalism is no longer a question of "a little more" or "a little less" of this or another element, but a negation of the religious character of the Maggidic approach *per se*. This stance, expressed in cosmological assumptions, is expressed even more powerfully in the psychological assumptions of Ḥabad teaching.

IV

The fundamental assumption of R. Shneur Zalman's psychological teaching is that the soul of the Jew draws upon two sources: a divine source and a demonic source in the *Siṭra ʾAḥra* (the "Other Side"). In effect, there are thus two different realms, each one of which seeks domination over the human being; his entire doctrine of religious life therefore rests upon the assumption of a permanent struggle between two souls. The battle is heretofore joined in the realm of the psychological life of man, who is commanded to suppress the urges which surge up from the antagonistic realm of the forces of the "other" soul. The spiritual level of the Ḥabad *ḥasid* is determined by the degree of his success in carrying out this suppression: the decisive importance attributed by the author of *Tanya* to the various levels of righteousness derives from this fact.

The Jewish people are divided into *ẓaddiqim* (those who are wholly righteous), *beinonim* ("intermediate ones"), and *reshaᶜim* ("wicked") — all according to the

33 *Tanya*, 42a (Ch. 33); *LT*, pp. 434–435.

34 Ibid.

degree to which they have succeeded in overcoming the evil within themselves. The *ẓaddiqim* are in turn divided into two types: one referred to as the "*ẓaddiq* who has evil," and the other as "the *ẓaddiq* who has good." The former is a righteous man whose own evil has not yet been entirely uprooted (i.e., the evil is still "his" — i.e., *ẓaddiq ve-ra*ᶜ *lo*), but is completely subordinated to him and is not in an active state. The *ẓaddiq* "for whom there is good," on the other hand, is one who no longer has any connection to evil, holding it in contempt to such an extent that he has completely erased its existence from his animal soul. A *rasha*ᶜ "in whom there is evil" is one who never regrets his evil at all. Finally, the *beinoni* — who is the main object of our concern — is one in whom

> ... the three "garments" of the animal soul — namely, thought, speech and action originating in the *qelippah* — do not prevail within him over the divine soul to the extent of clothing themselves in the body — neither in the brain, nor in the mouth, nor in any of the other 248 organs — to cause them to sin and to defile them, God forbid. Only the three garments of the divine soul alone manifest themselves in the body, these being the thought, speech and action related to the 613 commandments of the Torah. The *beinoni* has never committed any transgression, nor will he ever transgress; the name *rasha*ᶜ has never been applied to him, not even for a moment, throughout his life ... After prayer, however, when the intellect of the blessed ᵓ*Ein Sof* is no longer in a state of sublimity (*moḥin de-gadlut*), the evil in the left part of the heart reawakens, and he [i.e., the *beinoni*] once again feels a desire for the lusts of this world and its delights.[35]

But even then,

> It does not enter his mind to transgress in actual practice, God forbid, but thoughts of sin, which are "more heinous than actual sin," can manage to rise to his mind, and to distract him from Torah and divine service.[36]

These distinctions between a *ẓaddiq* and a *beinoni* play an important role in the system of R. Shneur Zalman, implying as they do a covert polemical barb.

Maggidic teaching imposes the obligation to confront evil and the material world of matter upon whoever is called a *ḥasid*. This confrontation is directed towards the "transformation" of evil into good by the spiritualization of evil — be it by separating and uplifting the sparks (*niẓoẓot*) from matter or, at a more abstract level, by uplifting alien thoughts. The metaphysical basis for the doctrine of uplifting is that the entire cosmos stands before man at every moment and seeks its redemption, because the sparks that fell in the primordial shattering (*shevirat ha-kelim*) cannot be redeemed without man. It is therefore man's obligation to

35 Ibid., p. 16b (Ch. 12); *LT*, pp. 170–175.
36 Ibid., p. 17b (Ch. 12); *LT*, p. 181.

accept them even when they are manifested in the corporeal and evil, external garment. This idea of "lifting up," which was particularly developed in the tradition of Lurianic Kabbalah, represented an important innovation in the school of the Maggid. If we briefly examine the formulation of this problem in R. Shneur Zalman, we shall immediately see that the entire problem of evil is displaced from its metaphysical source to the psychological realm. The *ẓaddiq* is no longer one who succeeds in altering the evil which confronts him from without in order to seek its redemption, but he whose *own* evil is already turned to good — meaning, that the evil present within his animal soul no longer exists even in hidden form! The *ẓaddiq* has completely transcended the struggle and is no longer disturbed by any thing, either from within or without: his is the perfect life of the Divine soul alone. Against this, the *beinoni* is the focus of Ḥabad interest, as the one who confronts this struggle on an everyday basis.

R. Shneur Zalman claims that only a very few people may be counted among the *ẓaddiqim*.

> Concerning the rank of the "complete *ẓaddiq*," Rabbi Simeon b. Yohai's statement applies: "I have seen superior men (*benei ᶜaliyyah*) and they are but few" [Sukkah 45b]. The reason that they are called *benei 'aliyyah* is that they convert evil and make it ascend to holiness.[37]

One clearly sees here that the Maggidic concept of "uplifting" has been changed for an empty rhetorical phrase, not only because the entire problem of evil has been transferred to the psychological realm, but primarily because by its very definition the status of the perfect *ẓaddiq* is seen as being beyond evil. This "ascent" after the fact is precisely what the Maggid did not intend; he intended the uplifting of alien thoughts or of *nizozot* to be the main everyday activity in all Divine service. What is left here of the Maggidic doctrine is thus no more than the linguistic formula — a point that is strikingly clear as well in many other places, as we shall observe further on.

Another, perhaps more concealed point relates to the concept of the *ẓaddiq*, and implies a certain anti-*ẓaddiqic* argument — namely, that it is impossible to claim that all those known as *ẓaddiqim* in his generation had in fact attained the level described here as characteristic of *ẓaddiqim*. Indeed, according to his own categories, R. Shneur Zalman saw himself as a *beinoni*. The *beinoni*, as against the *ẓaddiq*, does not have the power to "transform the evil to good" in the Maggidic sense, as all of his strength must be marshalled in every renewed confrontation with evil, so as to reject it:

37 Ibid., p. 15a (Ch. 10); *LT*, p. 155.

> Immediately upon [the thought's] rising to [the mind], he [i.e., the *beinoni*] thrusts it aside with both hands, and averts his mind from it, the instant he realizes that it is an evil thought, and will refuse to accept it willingly.[38]

The psychological explanation of this rejection is that the very appearance of the evil thought at this moment is a sign that the Divine soul has no domination over the animal soul.[39] The obvious conclusion to be drawn from this is that this psychology was intended to have the Maggidic doctrine of "uplifting" emptied entirely of content, changing it into an utter fiction by means of the two above-mentioned definitions: the first removed the metaphysical basis of evil into the psychological realm, while the other stated that, from a psychological viewpoint, this "uplifting" implies either the complete erasure of evil from the soul of the complete *ẓaddiq* (in which case the problem no longer exists), or a self-removal from evil with all the divine powers available to the *beinoni* (in which case "uplifting" in the Maggidic sense is no longer possible). Of course, a different conception of evil emerges here in contrast to that which appears in the Maggid, since the entire demonic character of the *Siṭra ᵓAḥra*, which is an integral part of the Maggid's dialectical teaching, is completely eliminated.

Another important passage casting barbs against the Maggidic doctrine refers to those *ẓaddiqim* who are known as *benei ᶜaliyyah*:

> Even their divine service in the area of "doing good" [Ps. 34:15], in their fulfillment of Torah and its *miẓvot*, is for the sake of the Above, and [toward] a most high level, toward the loftiest heights. It is not [intended] merely to attach themselves to God, so as to quench the thirst of their soul which thirsts for God, as it is written, "Ho, all who are thirsty go to the waters" [Isa. 55:1] ... Rather, as the *Tiqqunei Zohar* explains [Introduction, p. 1b], "Who is a pious one (*ḥasid*)? One who is benevolent with his Creator (*qono*) — with his nest (*qen*) — uniting the Holy One, blessed be He, with his *Shekhinah* in the lower worlds." ...[40]

We shall see below that the Maggidic interpretation of *devequt*, in terms of those who seek "to quench the thirst of their soul in God alone," does not square well with the use of the verse concerning "all who are thirsty go to the water," referring to Torah study in the literal sense, uniting God with His Shekhinah in the lower realms.

The true subject of religious life is the *beinoni* — which, as we have mentioned, is the main subject of the *Tanya* — because we are no longer dealing here with a small handful of mystical adepts (*benei ᶜaliyyah*). R. Shneur Zalman does not

38 Ibid., p. 17b (Ch. 12); *LT*, p. 182.
39 Ibid., p. 18b (Ch. 13).
40 Ibid., p. 15b (Ch. 10); *LT*, p. 156–157.

address himself to those who seek to achieve the level of *ẓaddiqim* — which hardly exists at all, according to his theory. In reality, every person can attain the level of the *beinoni*, provided he says to himself that,

> "I do not wish to be a *rasha*ᶜ even for a moment ... I desire, instead, to unite my *Nefesh*, *Ruaḥ* and *Neshamah* with God, through investing them in 'His' three garments, namely, action, speech and thought ... Even the simplest person is capable of sacrificing his life for the sanctity of God [should he be forced to deny Him]. Surely I am not inferior to him. It is only that a spirit of folly has overcome him; he imagines that committing this sin will not affect his Jewishness, and that his soul will not be thereby severed from the God of Israel ... But as for me — I have no desire to be such a fool as he, to deny the truth!"[41]

The Ḥabad program is here quite transparent. The *ḥasid* sacrifices himself for the Sanctification of the Name by means of *devequt*, whereby he embodies himself within the divine soul, composed of thought, speech, and action — an act which even "the simplest person" can do. Indeed, at one stroke the entire Maggidic problematic regarding the possible unification of act, speech and thought is here dismissed.[42]

Two motifs determine the inner tension concerning this question within the Maggid's teaching. The first is the assumption that the transitions from action to speech, and thereafter to thought, correspond to three stages of spiritual action found in the fulfillment of every *miẓvah* or prayer. Were this not the case, the act would be of no mystical value at all, and one would be unable to lift it to the level of its true significance. The other motif stems from the first, and concerns the difficulties lying in the way of any spiritual action of this kind when a person's world of thought is troubled by alien or external thoughts or impressions. This latter motif is deliberately omitted in the above-quoted passage from R. Shneur Zalman, as one who imagines that, "by committing this sin I will not affect my Jewishness!" (i.e., one who thinks that he cannot so easily unite speech and action!) is one "who has been overcome by a spirit of folly." It is clear that, according to the *Tanya*, this preoccupation with the troubling idea of "evil thoughts" is in no way the issue in the service of God, so that there is nothing simpler than to connect one's thoughts with God through intellectual involvement with matters of Torah. We arrive here at the very opposite of the former Maggidic motif, as R. Shneur Zalman does not see the spiritualization of action as concerned specifically with the realm of thought, and finds no substantive or significant connection between

41 Ibid., p. 19b (Ch. 14); *LT*, pp. 204–207.

42 See above, Ch. 9, "'The World of Speech' and 'The World of Thought,'" on this theme in the Maggid's teaching.

thought and action. Rather, these are simply three realms required in the service of God: one performs *mizvot*, first, through action; second, through speech and recitation; and third, through thought. In this way, it becomes clear how R. Shneur Zalman returns to the classical doctrine of *kavvanot*:

> When he ponders this subject in the recess of his heart's and mind's understanding, and his mouth and heart are in accord, in that he fulfills with his mouth the resolve of his mind's and heart's understanding.[43]

In contradistinction to this, Maggidic *kavvanah* fundamentally negates the real contents of prayer and of action, and concentrates upon their spiritual significance. The removal of the problem of alien thoughts and the pursuit of the harmonious life is summarized as follows:

> This matter is very easy and very near to every man who has a brain in his head. For his mind is under his control [sic!], and with it he can meditate as he pleases, on any subject. If, then, he will contemplate with it the greatness of the Almighty, he will inevitably generate — in his mind, at least — a love of God, to cleave to Him through the performance of His commandments and the study of His Torah. This constitutes "the whole purpose of man" [Eccles. 12:13], for it is written, "that you do them this day" [Deut. 7:11] — "this day" referring specifically to this world of physical action.[44]

Below, we shall specifically note the value of action in this context; at this point, I wish to observe that statements such as this aim at a very specific point, and are not inconsequential matters in a religious phenomenon. Even the triad of "thought, speech and action" used by the Maggid — which in his teaching is pregnant with spiritual content — is in principle voided by R Shneur Zalman, because they are dispossessed of their spiritual background and ultimate aim, which is true *devequt* and not intellectual comprehension.[45]

The true task of the *beinoni* is described in the *Tanya* as follows:

> Let us also understand [at least] in a very small measure, the purpose in creating *beinonim*; also, [the purpose of] their soul's descent to this world, being clothed within an animal soul deriving from the *qelippah* and *Sitra ᵓAḥra* [the very antithesis of the divine soul]. Since they will not be able to banish [the animal soul] throughout their lives, nor [even] dislodge it from its place in the left part of the heart, so that no [evil] imaginings rise from it to the brain.... Why then did their souls descend to this world, to strive in vain, God forbid; waging war all their lives against their evil inclination, yet never being able to vanquish it? Let this be their solace, to comfort them in a

43 *Tanya*, p. 22a (Ch. 16); *LT*, p. 229.
44 Ibid., p. 23a (Ch. 17); *LT*, p. 240.
45 Cf. *Tanya*, p. 64b (Ch. 45).

> double measure of aid, and to gladden their hearts in God Who dwells amongst them in their Torah and [divine] service.[46]

Elsewhere, he says the following:

> Even if lustful imaginings or other extraneous thoughts occur to him during his service of God — in Torah or in prayer with *kavvanah* — he should pay them no attention, but avert his mind from them immediately. Nor should he be so foolish as to engage in "sublimation of the *middot*" of the extraneous thought, as is known. For such things were intended only for *ẓaddiqim*,[47] in whom there do not occur any evil thoughts of their own [evil *middot*], but only [from the *middot*] of others. But as for one [i.e., a *beinoni*] to whom there occurs an evil thought of his own, from the evil that is lodged in the left part of his heart, how can he raise it up [to the spiritual realm] when he himself is bound below? ... This refutes a common error. When a foreign thought occurs to some people during prayer, they mistakenly conclude that their prayer is worthless, for if one prayed properly and correctly, [so they mistakenly believe,] no foreign thoughts would arise in his mind. They would be correct if there were but one soul [within a person,] the same soul that prays being also the one that thinks and ponders on the foreign thoughts. But in fact there are two souls, each waging war against the other in the person's mind. ... for he who wrestles with a filthy person is bound to become spoiled himself. Instead, he should pretend not to know nor hear [sic!] the foreign thoughts.[48]

The basic line of thought underlying the theory of the double soul clearly follows from this. Were there only one soul, whose source is holy, we would need to think more seriously about the ontological problem of evil and its metaphysical foundation. The doctrine of the double soul facilitates the pushing of this problem onto the realm of man's battle with his Urge, which has no relevance to the question of intellectual apprehension. The *beinoni* only needs to have contempt for the *Siṭra ᵓAḥra* and to abhor evil to thereby reduce its arrogance and vulgar spirit.[49]

> The reason is that in truth there is no substance whatever in the *Siṭra ᵓAḥra*. That is why it is compared to darkness, which has no substance whatsoever, and is automatically banished by the presence of light ... Only in regard to the holiness of man's divine soul, God has given it permission and ability to raise itself against it, in order that man should be roused to overpower it and to humble it ...[50]

46 Ibid., p. 44a (Ch. 35); *LT*, pp. 452–454.

47 See Chapter 10 of this book, near the end, on the similar approach of R. Meshullam Feibush of Zbrarazh, who attempts to limit divine service through spirituality to singular individuals.

48 Ibid., p. 35a–b (Ch. 28); *LT*, pp. 366–372.

49 Ibid., p. 36a (Ch. 29).

50 Ibid., p. 37b (Ch. 29); *LT*, pp. 387–88.

Not only is the metaphysical problem of evil obscured here, but its existential aspect is further weakened. While in the Maggid's teaching the existential edge is also removed from this question for reasons of theodicy,[51] in the teaching of R. Shneur Zalman evil is only left with its traditional instrumental task.

The *Tanya* continues:

> If sadness occurs to him ... from sinful thoughts not during his service of God ... he should be happy in his lot; for although these sinful thoughts enter his mind, he averts his attention from them ... and when he averts his mind from them, he fulfills this injunction [i.e., "you shall not go astray after your hearts and after your eyes"]. Our Sages have said: "When one passively abstains from sin, he is rewarded as though he had actively performed a *miẓvah*." Consequently, he should rejoice in his compliance with the injunction just as he does when performing an actual positive precept. On the contrary, such sadness is due to conceit. For he does not know his place, and that is why he is distressed because he has not attained the level of a *ẓaddiq*, to whom such foolish thoughts surely do not occur. ... Therefore one should not feel depressed or very troubled at heart, even if he be engaged all his days in this conflict, for perhaps this is what he was created for, and this is the service demanded of him — to subdue the *Siṭra ʾAḥra* constantly.[52]

There are a number of significant points that may be inferred from these passages:

a) The distinction drawn here between the time of "service" and a time which is not one of "service" is fundamentally anti-Beshtian and anti-Maggidic. One of the more important innovations of Hasidism was precisely the fact that it expanded the boundaries of the service of God to encompass "know Him in all Thy ways."

b) The removal of one's mind from bad thoughts is understood here in halakhic terms, as the fulfillment of the passive imperative implied by a negative commandment. Consequently, a person who refrained from performing a transgression is considered as if he had performed a *miẓvah*. The Besht disagreed with this viewpoint, as he recognized only two essential states: action and failure to act. Failure to act is itself treated as a kind of sin; he left no room for the neutral category of "non-action."[53]

c) R. Shneur Zalman polemicizes against those who claim that service which is disturbed by evil thoughts is not considered as divine service. While it is true that such an approach does appear in the Maggid and his school generally, the con-

51 *Liqqutei Yeqarim* (Lemberg, 1865), p. 12b.

52 *Tanya*, p. 33b–34a (Ch. 27); *LT*, pp. 353–357.

53 See *Ẓavaʾat ha-Riva"sh* (Jerusalem,. 1948), p. 18. I also explain this subject in my article, "Man Facing God and the World in Buber's Interpretation of Hasidism."

clusions drawn in the two places are very different. In the Maggid's teaching, a person is required to break through the wall of evil thoughts in order to arrive at pure holiness [54] as a positively ordained action (*qum ᶜaseh*), while in *Tanya* this is regarded as a passive, negative act of abstinence — "sit and do not act" (*shev ve-ʾal taᶜaseh*). The interesting point here lies in the implied claim that the attempt to deal with evil thoughts will, in the final analysis, not be a profitable one from a religious point of view. This is so because, since it is beyond the powers of the *beinoni* to overcome these thoughts, he arrives at a state of sadness, which makes his entire service spiritually unfit. It is clear that the Maggid also saw this danger as one that was present within man's unsuccessful efforts, and warned against the harsh consequences of sadness;[55] however, he did not understand this "daring" as implying arrogance towards Heaven. One of the leading signs of the Maggid's teaching is its spiritual audacity, while the opposite is true of R. Shneur Zalman.

One should not conclude from this that Ḥabad prayer is a calm and serene type of service lacking in emotional turmoil; on the contrary, the battle was simply transferred to the attack upon the Evil Urge, which prevents concentration during the time of prayer. Man is no longer asked here to break through his way to the supernal spiritual worlds, but battles for the minimal accomplishment of reciting the prayer in its simple sense, while his heart and mouth are at one. The sharpness is removed here from the doctrine of spiritual prayer. The author of *Tanya* says the following:

> Therefore, every person ought to weigh and examine his own position, according to the standards of his place and rank in divine service, as to whether he serves God in a manner commensurate with the dimensions of such a fierce battle and test. In the realm of "do good" [Ps. 34:15] — in the service of prayer with devotion (*kavvanah*), for example, to pour out his soul before God with his entire strength, to the extent of exhausting [all the powers of] his soul. He must wage a great and intense war against his body and the animal soul within it, which impede *kavvanah*, crushing and grinding them like dust every single day, before the morning and evening prayers. Also during prayer he must exert himself with an exertion of the spirit.[56]

From what has been said above, it also follows that an individual whose urges and lusts are by nature weak may find his service easier and simpler, so long as he succeeds in attaining mastery over his appetite by means of rational life. According to this, the domination of the mind over the "left part of the heart" is a sufficient manifestation of hasidic service.[57]

54 *Ẓavaʾat ha-Riva"sh*, p. 16.
55 See above, Chap. 4, on dejection, regret, etc.
56 *Tanya*, p. 38b (Ch. 30); *LT*, pp. 397–398.
57 See Ibid., 21a–b (Ch. 15).

V

Just as R. Shneur Zalman's anti-spiritualistic tendency clearly followed from his view of the world and of the structure of the soul, so is it reflected in his meditations upon the Torah and upon the nature of the *mizvot* and of the value of religious action. R. Shneur Zalman is extremely artful in his use of traditional formulations, particularly Kabbalistic ones, which he directs towards his own system. The *Zohar* formula, "The Torah and the Holy One blessed be He are wholly one,"[58] originally intended to refer to their symbolic identity, was used in Hasidism to refer to the presence of the Divine substance *per se* in the letters of the Torah. This assumption constituted the theoretical basis for Hasidic exegesis of Scripture, which stripped away the concrete character of the texts in order to encounter the divine element hidden within them. Such an understanding is essentially spiritual,[59] differing in this respect from that of R. Shneur Zalman, who does not wish to uncover the divine element, but to "know" it in a rational manner beyond its "garments" — i.e., the concrete contents of the Torah. An interesting analogy is drawn between the person who embraces the Torah and one who embraces He who is embodied therein, because:

> ... There is no difference in the degree of his closeness and attachment to the king whether he embraces him when the king is wearing one robe or many robes, since the king's body is in them ... [by knowing and understanding the Torah,] he then actually comprehends and grasps the Will and wisdom of God, whom no thought can grasp, nor [can any thought grasp] His will and wisdom, except when they clothe themselves in the *halakhot* set before us. His intellect is also clothed within them. Now this is a most wonderful unity; in the physical realm there is no unity similar or parallel to it, that they should actually become one and united from every side and angle.[60]

In the previous passage, he spoke about the true unification, meaning the identity among the intellect, the intellectually perceiving subject, and the intellectually perceived object, which become one through reflection upon and study of words of Torah. It is clear that, for the *Tanya*, that unity "like which there is no other unity" was the Maimonidean intellectual unification, which substituted for the Maggidic idea of *devequt*.

58 On the history of the use of this saying in Hasidism, see G. Scholem, "The Historical Image of R. Israel Ba^cal Shem Tov," p. 321ff. On its use in the Kabbalistic tradition generally, see I. Tishby, "'The Holy One, blessed be He, Torah and Israel are all one' — The Source of this Aphorism in Ramḥal's Commentary to the ᵓ*Idra Rabba*" (Heb.), *Qiryat Sefer* 50 (1975), pp. 480–492.

59 See the Maggid's ᵓ*Or ha-ᵓEmet* (1899): "And afterwards he shall come to the letters of thought, and will not hear what he speaks, and thereafter he comes to the level of nihility (ᵓ*ayin*), in which all his physical powers are nullified" — p. 10a.

60 *Tanya* p. 9a–b (Ch. 4, 5); *LT*, p. 87, 92–93.

From his approach to the value of the halakhah as the innermost manifestation of the divine will, we now turn to the clarification of the place of the *miẓvot* in R. Shneur Zalman's teaching. The *miẓvot* may be performed by means of the three garments in which the divine soul within man is embodied — thought, speech and action.

> But thought and meditation on the words of Torah, which is accomplished in the brain, and the power of speech engaged in the words of Torah, which is in the mouth — these being the innermost garments of the divine soul — and surely the divine soul itself which is clothed in them: all of them are fused in perfect unity with the Divine Will, and are not merely a vehicle, a "chariot" for it [as are the commandments involving acts]. For the Divine Will is identical with the halakhic subject of which one thinks and speaks, inasmuch as all the laws of the *Halakhah* are particular expressions of the innermost Divine Will itself; for God willed it thus — that a particular thing be deemed permissible or kosher, or that [a person] be found exempt or innocent, or the reverse ... Now, since the Divine Will, which is in perfect unity within ᵓ*Ein Sof*, blessed be He, stands completely revealed and not at all concealed in the divine soul and in its inner garments — i.e., its thought and speech — while a person occupies himself with words of Torah ... It follows [that at that time] the soul and these garments [of thought and speech] are also truly united with ᵓ*Ein Sof*, blessed be He, with a unity comparable to that of God's speech and thought with His essence and being, as explained above ... Moreover, their unity is even more exalted and more powerful than the unity of God's infinite light with the upper [spiritual] worlds. For the Divine Will is actually manifest in the soul and its garments that are engaged in Torah study, since His Will proper is identical with the Torah itself...[61]

The question of man's standing before God as a personality possessing an independent will, which does not necessarily correspond to the divine will, was always one of the central problems in all religions, and not only Judaism. Maggidic Hasidism also recognized the problem of the duality of the wills, and sought a means to unite them in the course of its struggle concerning the negation of the human will and the abandoning of personal interest. In such doctrines, in which man was confronted at every moment by the challenge of self-conquest and self-abnegation, both the divine and the human will were understood in a dynamic manner. R. Shneur Zalman, by contrast, understood the divine will in a static manner, as one which was embodied in the fixed halakhah; it is sufficient for man to reflect upon it, and it alone, in order to find himself in total unity with this will. The entire conflict around the subject of human will is no longer the subject of discussion; the intellectual unity with the Godhead which comes about as the result of Torah study is "even more exalted and more powerful than the unity of God's

61 Ibid., p. 69a (Ch. 23); *LT*, 303–306.

infinite light with the upper [spiritual] worlds" (sic!). The divine will revealed in the Torah relieves man of the need to exhaust himself with excessive exegeses, so as to reach beyond its simple understanding to the spiritual plane. Likewise, the reading based upon the doctrine of combinations, which is the decisive expression of the dissatisfaction with the *peshaṭ* alone, seems pointless. The attempts towards spiritual penetration of Scripture assume a dynamic, multi-faceted divine will which pneumatic man seeks to reveal. The same is likewise true of the Maggid's teaching, unlike that of R. Shneur Zalman. The unequivocal rationalism found here shuts the door against the true mystical attempt.

From his position on the value of Torah study and the performance of the *miẓvot*, he comes to an open polemic with the Maggid's teaching:

> In the upper spheres, this union [i.e., between the soul and God] is eternal ... Here below, however, it is only while it is engaged in Torah study or in the performance of a *miẓvah*. For if he engages afterwards in anything else, he becomes separated, here below, from this supernal union — that is, if he occupies himself with entirely useless matters (*devarim beṭṭeillim*) that are in no way useful in the service of God — nevertheless, when he repents and resumes his service of God through Torah study or prayer, and he asks forgiveness of God for not having studied Torah when he could have done so, God forgives him.[!] ... For this reason, the Sages ordained that the blessing beginning, "Forgive us ..." for the sin of neglecting the study of the Torah, be recited three times daily, for no one avoids this sin even a single day.[62]

What are those things which "are in no way useful in the service of God" — a statement directly opposed to the statement in *Ẓava'at ha-Riva"sh*, in which everything is useful in the service of the Creator? Indeed, it is specifically stated there that God wishes to be served thus, in all the ways[63] — implying that the divine will is not necessarily revealed in Torah and prayers, but at times even in "negligent matters" which can be turned into divine worship. This is so, because in the Maggid's doctrine the realm of service is not conditional upon the contents of the action, but upon the intention of the actor. R. Shneur Zalman again limited the realm of holy action, returning to the older formulae in Judaism, in which holy action is based upon the doctrine of the divine will. This second point, in which he polemicizes with the anti-scholastic tendency which dominated Hasidism, cannot be emphasized too much.[64]

R. Shneur Zalman discusses the difference in principle between positive commandments and negative commandments. Positive commandments are rooted in the divine will, so that one who performs them thereby fulfills this will.

62 Ibid., p. 32a (Ch. 25); *LT*, pp. 337–339.

63 *Ẓava'at ha-Riva"sh*, p. 2.

64 See below, Chapter 14, on Torah study in Hasidism.

The negative commandments, by contrast, are rooted in the *Siṭra ʾAḥra*, the "reverse side" of the Godhead (according to the picture of *Adam Qadmon* — "Primal Man" — given in Lurianic Kabbalah). According to his teaching, the *Siṭra ʾAḥra* is, generally speaking, a passive factor in the world, which may be described in terms of the non-performance of the divine will. The *Siṭra ʾAḥra* is not active and does not rebel, but is awakened to activity when a person performs a transgression. That which, in the case of the positive *miẓvah*, is regarded as a manifestation of godliness, is seen in the case of the prohibitions as concealing the Divine face.[65] Hasidism does not generally engage overly much in the question of the substantive difference between the *miẓvot*; however, R. Shneur Zalman has a particular interest in repeatedly stressing the severe sanction that applies specifically to the prohibitions, because his Hasidic ideal is based upon overcoming the Evil Urge and the perfection of the soul on the part of the *beinoni* who, by very definition, is one who does not sin in actuality. The Maggid, on the other hand, seeks to perfect the individual who seeks spiritual attainments, which can be specifically achieved through means of the actions entailed in the positive *miẓvot*. His stress upon the negative commandments as sin and "the absolute separation" of man from God through their violation somewhat "softens" the seriousness of the demands of classical Hasidism. For them, failure to perform a positive *miẓvah* in its full weightiness — that is, with true *devequt* — is sufficient cause for complete "separation" from God; even more so the violation of a prohibition of the Torah. By contrast, in the teaching of the *Tanya* a person may be considered a *beinoni* (i.e., a good *ḥasid*) so long as he has not sinned in practice and not violated any prohibitions of the Torah. It follows that only if a person engages in Torah or performs any *miẓvot* "not for their own sake," literally, do they lose their religious validity. Ḥabad Hasidism is satisfied with religious action in which there is no sin in the simple sense.[66]

The heavy religious burden of divine service taken upon itself by Hasidism, seeking the maximal realization of encounter with God in the transcendent world at every possible moment, is expressed in the school of Ḥabad in the form of a simple joy over the act in its simplest sense:

> As our Sages say: "Even [if he studies] one chapter in the morning and one at night ..." [Menaḥot 99b]. Thereby, his heart shall rejoice; he shall be glad and offer joyous thanks for his fortune in meriting to be the Almighty's "host" [i.e., through Torah study] twice each day, according to the extent of his available time, and according to the capacity which God has granted him. If God grants him a greater abundance [of time], then "He whose hands are pure will increase his effort" [Job 17:9] ... Even

---

65 *Tanya*, p. 29b (Ch. 24).
66 Ibid., p. 53b (Ch. 39).

> during the remainder of the day, when he is engaged in business, he will be an abode for God by giving charity out of the proceeds of his labor; charity being one of God's attributes.[67]

The rule, "according to the extent of his available time," is a doctrine calling for the performance of *mizvot* with generosity and full-hearted willingness, but under no circumstances does it require the Hasidic strictures of *devequt* sought within everyday activity, and especially in Torah and prayer. The joy described in the above passage could as well be a strictly Mitnaggedic joy: for what in truth is the difference between it and the Hasidism of R. Shneur Zalman?[68]

Moreover: one of the most striking characteristics of Hasidic service consists in the struggle to free the individual of ulterior motivations during prayer, Torah study, or other *mizvot*, since the "motive" at the time of actual performance, whatever it may be, utterly negates even the highest spiritual attainment and the sublimest *devequt*.[69] R. Shneur Zalman, by contrast, has a more moderate understanding of the question of "motives." He only pays lip service to the Maggid's doctrine, saying that, if a person has "motives" of this type, he may repent for them and everything will be fine. The deep significance of action "for its own sake" is not thereby negated, nor need one be broken-hearted because of it.[70]

He goes on from here to an explicit polemic with the Maggid's doctrine, saying:

> He, however, who has not attained to this level of savoring a foretaste of the World to Come [in his simple service], but whose soul yet yearns and thirsts for God and goes out to Him all day long, and he does not quench his thirst [for godliness] with the "water" of Torah that is in front of him — such a person is comparable to one who stands in a river and cries: "Water, water to drink!"[71]

Is there not more than a little irony here? Further on, he writes:

> Then the Torah he studies or the commandment he performs because of his submission [to the heavenly yoke] and because of the fear that he has drawn into his mind, are termed "complete service," like all service [performed] by a slave for his master or king. On the other hand, if one studies [Torah] and performs a commandment with love alone, in order to cleave to him through His Torah and His

67 Ibid., p. 43b (Ch. 34); *LT*, pp. 445–457.

68 In general, there is a remarkable and interesting similarity between R. Shneur Zalman's teaching and that of R. Ḥayyim of Volozhin, the leading disciple of the Gaon of Vilna. See his *Nefesh ha-Ḥayyim*, Pt. 3, and above, in my introduction to this volume. The latter's struggle is directed entirely against the teaching of the Maggid and authentic Hasidism, and agrees with the doctrine of R. Shneur Zalman.

69 *Zavaʾat ha-Riva"sh*, p. 5–6.

70 *Tanya*, p. 53b (Ch. 39).

71 Ibid., p. 56a (Ch. 40); *LT*, pp. 576–577.

> commandments, then this is not termed the "service of a servant," of which the Torah has declared, "You shall serve the Lord your God" [Ex. 23:25]. [72]

R. Shneur Zalman sees the desire to attain *devequt* through the service of God as the very opposite of religious interest, because of the danger that the spiritual interest would become an "interest" in itself. This problem was one already clearly noted in the school of the Maggid itself, which struggled with the problem of mystical "intoxication" which was liable to displace the value of authentic *devequt*.[73] But R. Shneur Zalman goes further, seeing the concept of *devequt* itself, even within the limits established for it by the Maggidic school, in a negative light. For him, *devequt* corresponds only to the concept of the integration of man's soul — that is, the domination over the animal soul — and there is no "service for its own sake" (*ᶜavodah li-shemah*) apart from absolutely simple service, without any spiritual venture:

> This should be his intent when occupying himself with the Torah, or with the particular commandment: that his divine soul as well as his vital soul, together with their "garments," shall cleave to Him, as has been explained above ... And although in order that this intent should be sincere in his heart, so that his heart should truly desire this Higher Union, his heart must harbor a great love for God alone, to do what is gratifying to Him alone, and not for the purpose of quenching his soul's thirst for God ... And this union is His true desire — namely, the Supernal Union in the World of *ᵓAẓilut*, which is produced by an arousal from below, through the divine soul's union and absorption in God's light that is clothed in the Torah and the commandments in which it is engaged, so that they [the divine soul and God] become One in reality.[74]

From the fact of the devolution of the worlds by the will of the Creator, R. Shneur Zalman infers that man is to serve God specifically in the lower world rather than to strive for mystical unity with the supernal worlds; that he should not attempt to break through the circle of creation and of nature in order to reach God, but instead discover Him in this world, by performing *miẓvot* and studying Torah. The Maggidic longings for transcendent mysticism are here transferred to the inner realm of the world.

> The purpose of the *hishtalshelut* [chain-like, graded, downward devolution] of the worlds, and of their descent from level to level, is not for the sake of the higher worlds, since for this they constitute a descent from the light of his countenance. Rather, the

72 Ibid., p. 56b–57a (Ch. 41); *LT*, pp. 587–588.

73 R. Menaḥem Mendel of Vitebsk likewise stressed the need for the love utilized in the service of God to be accompanied by fear, out of his suspicion of extreme spiritualism.

74 *Tanya*, 57b–58a (Ch. 41); *LT*, p. 594, 598–600.

> purpose of *hishtalshelut* is this lowest world, for such was His will — that He finds it pleasurable when the *Sitra ᵓAḥra* is subjugated [to holiness], and the darkness is transformed into light, so that in place of the darkness and *Siṭra ᵓAḥra* [prevailing] throughout this world, the *ᵓEin Sof* light of God will shine forth with greater strength and intensity, and with the superior quality of light that emerges from the darkness than its radiance in the higher worlds. There [i.e., in the higher worlds] it shines through garments and [through] concealment of the Countenance, which conceal and screen the *ᵓEin Sof* light, so that [the worlds] do not dissolve out of existence ... Now this ultimate perfection of the Messianic era and [the time of] the resurrection of the dead, meaning the revelation of *ᵓEin Sof* light in this physical world, is dependent on our actions and [divine] service throughout the period of exile. For it is the *miẓvah* itself that causes [i.e., creates] its reward. For by performing [the *miẓvah*] man draws the revelation of the blessed *ᵓEin Sof* light from above downwards, to be clothed in the physicality of this world — i.e., in an object which has heretofore been under the dominion of *qelippat nogah* ...[75]

According to this, the Jewish people is not destined to enter the eschaton by virtue of their uplifting sparks and redeeming the broken remnants of the Godhead in the world, thereby restoring them to the divine world, but rather because of the fact that each Jew "suppresses the Other Side" (*ᵓitkafya le-Siṭra ᵓAḥra*) — that is, by bringing about the integration of the soul in this world. By making everything dependent upon the performance of the *miẓvot*, R. Shneur Zalman left the realm of "service" open to an optimistic, pantheistic rationalism. The joy of one who serves God is based upon the fact that he strengthens holiness within the world by suppressing his own impulses. It is interesting that this selfsame motif is that which, according to R. Shneur Zalman, places the greatest stress on "action," as opposed to speech and thought. By means of "action," which, of all the ways of divine service, is the closest to the corporeal world, a person is able to more easily suppress the power of his Urge. In Ḥabad, we find an inverted scale of values from that found in the spiritualistic tendency. The Maggid's aim was to bring about an integration of action, speech, and thought, in which pure spiritual service stood at the top of the scale — an approach that is particularly strongly felt in the teaching of R. Menaḥem Mendel of Vitebsk. R. Shneur Zalman advocates the reverse approach: the very act of turning towards the body in the observance of *miẓvot* is sufficient to essentially break the power of the Other Side. Close examination of this point will reveal that, whereas the Maggid emphasized the turning towards the corporeal world, as a requirement of service, as the locus at which the mundane is turned into the sacred, R. Shneur Zalman stressed the animal soul as the locus for the breaking of the powers of impurity. By means of this religious obligation,

75 Ibid., p. 45b–46b, (Ch. 36, 37); *LT*, pp. 474–476, 483– 484. *Nogah* is the name of the highest *qelippah*, closest to the world of holiness.

he arrives at the anti-spiritualistic conclusion that, if one were forced to choose between "thought" (*maḥshavah*) and "action" in the service of God, there is no doubt as to which of the two paths is the preferable one. He returns several times to the problematics involved in the halakhic principle that, "we hold that thought is not equivalent to action" — that is, that action is preferable to thought — in order to provide a basis for his anti-Maggidic position.

> In light of all that has been said above [i.e., concerning the value of *miẓvot* performed in action and speech], one will clearly understand the halakhic decision expressly stated in the Talmud and the Codes that meditation is not valued in lieu of verbal articulation (*hirhur lav ke-dibbur dami*). Thus, if one recited the *Shema*ᶜ in his thought and heart alone, even if he did so with the full power of his concentration, he has not fulfilled his obligation; he must repeat it [verbally].... If, on the other hand, one spoke the words but did not concentrate his thought, he has, *post facto*, fulfilled his obligation, ... This is so because the [divine] soul does not need to perfect itself through *miẓvot*; rather, [the goal of *miẓvot*] is to draw down [divine] light to perfect the vital soul and the body, by means of the letters of speech, which the soul utters by means of the five organs of verbal articulation ...[76]

Further on, he states explicitly that "thought" enjoys no inner advantage of any spiritual significance over "action." In his opinion, the combination of intention and thought with action comes about for entirely non-immanent reasons — namely, that God wished it so. These remarks are diametrically opposed to those of the Maggid, who explains that "action" is the non-immanent element of divine service, and is required as such because that is the divine will.[77] According to R. Shneur Zalman, true *devequt* consists in the simple performance of the *miẓvot*; he thereby departed drastically from the accepted, literal meaning of *devequt* in Hasidism. He writes as follows:

> Likewise regarding *miẓvot* performed through speech and verbal articulation — which is regarded as actual action, as mentioned above — when performed without *kavvanah*, [the resultant illumination] bears no comparison] with the [superior] illumination and flow of the blessed ᵓ*Ein Sof* light radiating and clothed in the *kavvanah* of the *miẓvot* of action, meaning man's intention to attach himself to God by fulfilling His Will, since He and His Will are one. Similarly with regard to *kavvanah* in prayer, the recital of *Shema*ᶜ and its blessings, and in other blessings, where, through one's *kavvanah* in them, he attaches his thought and intellect to God. It is not that attachment of man's thought and intellect to God is intrinsically superior to

76 Ibid., p. 49b–50a (Ch. 38); *LT*, pp. 513–516.

77 See *Keter Shem Tov* (Benai Berak, 1957), pp. 35–39, and *Maggid Devarav le-Yaᶜaqov*, §90, p. 156: "that the act of the *miẓvah* does not reach to there." The same problem likewise arose in *Toldot Yaᶜaqov Yosef*, *Parashat Mishpaṭim*, p. 62b.

attachment through the actual, practical fulfillment of the *miẓvot* dependent on action
— as will be explained further on. Rather, [*kavvanah* is superior] because this, too,
is God's will — that one attach himself to Him by intellect and thought, and by the
kavvanah of the active *miẓvot*, and by one's *kavvanah* during the recital of *Shema*ᶜ,
and in prayer and other blessings; and the illumination of the Supernal Will that
radiates and is clothed in this *kavvanah* is infinitely greater and loftier than the
illumination of the Supernal Will that radiates and is clothed in the performance of
the *miẓvot* themselves, in action and speech, without *kavvanah*.[78]

At the end of the passage, R. Shneur Zalman somewhat retracts the sharpness of
his formulation concerning the status of action as against *kavvanah*. One can nevertheless clearly see in this passage the polemic against spiritualistic *devequt* as
opposed to "practical *devequt*."

One can also understand from this his attitude towards the *miẓvah* of *ẓedaqah*
— i.e., giving charity — which he values above all other *miẓvot*.

> ... because [charity] is the core of all the *miẓvot* of action and surpasses them all. For
> the purpose of all these *miẓvot* is only to elevate one's animal soul to God. ... Now,
> you will find no other *miẓvah* in which the vital soul is clothed to the same extent
> as in the *miẓvah* of charity.[79]

Because it bears such an explicitly practical character, this *miẓvah* is one which is
most capable of suppressing the *Siṭra ʾAḥra* within man's vital soul. R. Shneur
Zalman closed the transcendent world off to the human being; with boundless
intellectual enthusiasm, he stated that,

> The intellect of a created being delights and derives pleasure only in that which it
> conceives, understands, knows and grasps with its intellect and understanding, as
> much as it can grasp of the Blessed ʾ*Ein Sof* light, through His wisdom and His
> understanding which radiate there. These souls [i.e. who serve God with natural love
> and fear] are privileged to rise [occasionally] higher than angels [i.e., to *Beriʾah* rather
> than *Yeẓirah*], although they [too] served God only with natural fear and love.[80]

According to R. Shneur Zalman, this intellectual contemplation, which represents the highest level of human comprehension, is available to every person,
provided that he overcome his impulses which prevent him from contemplating
intellectual objects.

> The essential thing is to immerse one's own mind deeply into [those things which
> explain] the greatness of God, and to fix one's thoughts on God with strength and
> vigor of the heart and mind, until his thought shall be bound to God [as against

78 *Tanya*, p. 50b (Ch. 38); *LT*, pp. 523–525.
79 Ibid., 48b (Ch. 37); *LT*, p. 501.
80 Ibid., p. 52a (Ch. 39); *LT*, p. 540.

> *devequt*!] with a strong and mighty bond, as it is bound to a material thing which he sees with his physical eyes and upon which he concentrates his thought. For it is known that *daᶜat* [knowledge] connotes union, as in the verse, "And Adam knew Eve ..." [Gen. 4:1] This capacity and this quality of attaching one's *Daᶜat* to God, is present in every soul of the House of Israel, by virtue of its nurture [*yeniqah*, literally, "suckling"] from the soul of our teacher Moses, peace unto him. Only, since the soul has clothed itself in the body, it needs a great and mighty exertion, doubled and redoubled [i.e., in order to feel and be attached to God].[81]

This is the world of Hasidic "minimalism," in which the "intermediate" man, the *beinoni*, reigns supreme. True, the ecstatic joy of the encounter with God in the world is preserved, but without the path of suffering which brings man to God: that path filled with the force of its inner dialectic, in which man alternately rises to the heights and falls down, in which he "erases" his individuality in order to arrive at the true "I," in which "self-interests" can nullify spiritual attainments completely, and in which man tirelessly gathers the remnants of the cosmic "rupture" on behalf of God, undertaking this mission with a combination of pride and lowness of spirit.

81 Ibid., p. 59b (Ch. 42); *LT*, pp. 613–614.

Chapter Thirteen

Diary of an Agnostic: "I Know Not" as a Quietistic Value

A little-known Hasidic document from the early 19th century presents another face of Hasidic quietism — the agnostic position of "I know not," which might be described as a kind of intellectual quietism. The author of the document discussed here, R. Israel Dov of Stepan, was the second son of R. David ha-Levi of Stepan, born from his second marriage, to Yentl, daughter of R. Yeḥiel Michel of Zloczow, known for her spiritual gifts of "the Holy Spirit." Her oldest son, R. Yeḥiel Michel Pechenik,[1] was the founder of the Hasidic dynasty of Berezno in Volhynia, adjacent to Rovno (the home of the Great Maggid prior to his move to Mezhirech). Following his father's death, R. Israel inherited his position as *Maggid* (official community preacher) in Stepan. His father, who was a descendant of R. David ben Samuel ha-Levi, better known as the *Ṭa"z* (1586–1667; author of *Ṭurrei Zahav*, one of the most prominent commentaries on the *Shulḥan ᶜArukh*), after whom he was named, was well-known in his day as one of the disciples of the Maggid of Mezhirech. In M. Bodek's *Seder ha-Dorot* (p. 55), we read of him the following:

> Son-in-law of the holy rabbi, R. Yeḥiel Michel of Zloczow, *z"l*, one who was holy like the angels of God: Rabbi David ha-Levi, a righteous man, pillar of the world in his generation, *Maggid Mesharim* of the holy community of Stepan — this is printed from the listing of *Seder Hanhagat ha-ᵓAdam*. And he was filled with asceticism and holiness and purity, may his merit protect us.

I have found only one direct reference to his son, R. Israel Dov, appearing in an approbation to the book *ᵓOr ha-Meᵓir* by R. Ze'ev Wolf of Zhitomir, Periczec

* This chapter was originally published under the title, "Notes of an Agnostic Hasid" (Heb.), *Molad* 5, nos. 25–26 (235–236) (1972), pp. 135–145. Some minor changes have been introduced in this version.

1 See the note concerning the geneology of the family in: Aaron ha-Levi Pechenik, "Chronicle of one Hasidic Dynasty" (Heb.), *Mi-shanah le-shanah* (Jerusalem, 1967). R. David ha-Levi's geneology is also mentioned in the chronicle of Radzyn and Chernobyl published by Aaron David Twersky, in connection with the dynasty of Brezhno, which was related by marriage to R. Aaron of Chernobyl; but again, there is no information about the second son, R. Israel Dov of Stepan, beyond his name.

edition, dated 8 Elul 5575 (1815), when he lived in Rovno. His father, R. David, died in Tishrei 5570 or 5571 (i.e., 1809 or 1810); it is not clear whether R. Israel moved from Rovno to Stepan only after 1815, in order to inherit his father's position.

The "notes" or "diary" discussed below are bound together with another collection, a manuscript containing teachings of R. Israel of Rizhin.[2] The document under consideration here is a copy made following the author's death, and not an autograph. The colophon reads: "Hidden things from his honor, the rabbi, the holy and pure Maggid, of blessed memory, the holiness of his Torah, our teacher Rabbi Israel Dov ha-Levi of Stepan, may his merit protect us." The text includes more than twenty rather crowded pages, which seem to be part of a larger personal diary, based upon an allusion found at the end of one of the sections: "This was written as a reminder, according to what was revealed to me at times, in the manner described above." We find no mention in the extant portion of the fact that these thoughts are the product of "revelations" received by the author at times. Reference is made only to the appearance of the *Ba^cal Davar* (i.e., the Intruder; literally, "the Master of the Thing"), who disturbs his thoughts and speculations concerning various sublime matters, particularly the question of how one is to realize Hasidism in everyday life.

The phrase "hidden things," used at the beginning of the colophon introducing these notes, is hardly surprising, as this is not the accepted manner of writing Hasidic teachings; the notes were not written as a tractate intended for publication and in order to clarify such questions for the outside world, such as we find in Meshullam Feibush of Zbarazh's *Derekh ᵓEmet*, or even in the *Tanya*. R. Israel Dov of Stepan's treatise is unusual both from the literary viewpoint, and in terms of its treatment of theoretical problems. It is constructed as a series of notes (nineteen in all), each one beginning with the words, "I have come to clarify ..." or "I weighed in my mind the matter of ..." Each section consists of a brief and clear discussion of the views and reflections of a person who ponders his sufferings and his thoughts, seeking peace with himself and with a clear and radical world-view. His style is learned and clear, and he records what comes from his heart. There is a sense in his words of intellectual enthusiasm and of the certainty of one who has arrived at his conclusions via personal experience. No particular individuals are mentioned in the tractate apart from his father, and that only once, while on one occasion a certain saying is also quoted in the name of the Besht. The basic assumptions guiding his world-view are those of the Maggid of Mezhirech — a point to which I shall return in greater detail further on in this analysis.

I do not know which Hasidic court (if any) he was accustomed to attend, but

2 Jerusalem–National Library 8° 5301, fos. 30–53.

it seems clear that he did not have any "local patriotism"; he expected all of the *ẓaddiqim* to bow to the authority of the man of spirit. His own position in the covert polemic within the Hasidic world concerning the question of who was to be the authoritative figure in Hasidic society was quite clear:[3] namely, that the *ẓaddiq* who corresponds to the aspect of *nefesh*, and hence more revealed in the eyes of the masses, must submit to the authority of the one who corresponds to *ruaḥ* (corresponding to the various levels in the psychological scheme, going from the lower to the higher), who is "more hidden and concealed." The function of the "revealed" *ẓaddiq* is to "make known" the existence of the hidden *ẓaddiq*: "and I and you are obligated to honor and fear him ... and when the leadership is thus, then the kingdom of Heaven is magnified and increased, according to His will, may He be blessed." If the lower *ẓaddiq* is glorified in the eyes of the world and takes honor upon himself, then the divine influx upon him ought to be diminished.

This discussion is the only "concrete" allusion contained in these writings; the rest is divided into two subject areas which are intermingled with one another in terms of their order: 1) the individual reflections and trials of Hasidism; 2) views on various essential theoretical questions in Hasidic thought.

I

The former category includes all those problems which relate to the root of the individual's soul, its ability to apprehend divine knowledge, the means of its apprehensions, as well as confrontation with the views generally found in the Jewish tradition concerning the scale of values and of obligations. The decisive point of departure for the author's decisions is the knowledge of the root of one's soul, its attributes and its mystical longings. His behavior in this matter is dictated by independent "judgment." The position opposed to this tendency, and which corresponds remarkably to the excessive pettiness of a spiritual *Shulḥan ᶜArukh*, is represented by the Intruder, who confuses him and induces him to accept a mistaken position of "judgment." The personification of the Intruder, with whom he enters into conversation, is highly unusual in Hasidic thought, although it does appear here and there in the Hasidic narrative.

3 See R. Schatz, "R. Elimelekh of Lyzhansk's Doctrine of the *Ẓaddiq*" (Heb.), *Molad* 144–45 (Aug.–Sept. 1960). R. Elimelekh had a different criterion regarding the leader. It may be that R. Israel Dov preferred the model of the man of spirit and the Kabbalist, such as R. Ẓevi Hirsch of Zhidachov, to the *ẓaddiqism* of the Chernobyl dynasty, to which his family was connected by marriage. On the question of the *ẓaddiqim*, see the recent article by Arthur Green, "Typologies of Leadership and the Hasidic Zaddiq," *Jewish Spirituality [II]* (op. cit., Ch. 12), pp. 127–156.

The first point considered by the author is his wish "in the matter of *devequt*, to connect himself to God without any garments." The "garment" corresponds to the attribute of *Pardes* (i.e., the various exegetical paths) by means of which a person seeks to "know" God more and more. By contrast, R. Israel Dov wishes more and more to "know not," even though the Intruder tries to confuse him by saying that "this is not as it needs to be for the behavior in the world." If he does receive any sort of insight through the path of *Pardes*, he makes no attempt to clarify it thoroughly, but merely accepts it "as it flowered in my mind." The Intruder argues against him that this is not true apprehension, "since it does not achieve thorough clarification," while the goal of knowledge of the Torah is specifically to arrive at the knowledge of *Pardes*. The Intruder's arguments are, according to the author, "lies and error," which do not at all square with "my own knowledge of my attributes and the root of my soul."

The author has two basic criteria for attaining wholeness: the Hasidic principle of *devequt*, with all the severity of this concept, and his own awareness of the root of his soul.

There is no equivalent anywhere else in Hasidic literature to the extreme individualism which guides R. Israel's decisions — certainly not in the "normative" Jewish approach, which stresses the value of intellectual "clarification" and "study." R. Israel Dov argues that he is unable to accept such pre-determined "rules of behavior," as they contradict the root of his soul and the immanent rules of his attachment to God: as soon as he fully clarifies an "apprehension," he feels himself falling from his level of "attachment and connection to His Name," and is therefore literally performing a sin! The author's remarks here undoubtedly allude to and are based upon an extreme reading of the Besht's saying concerning the verse "and you shall go astray and worship other gods" (Deut. 11:16): If a person goes astray one moment from his attachment, he thereby worships idols! Thus, R. Israel concludes, one who can himself maintain a state of *devequt* — in accordance with the root of his soul — but forces himself to engage in intellectual reflection, thereby deliberately distancing himself from God — "What greater sin than this can there be?" He explains the statement that a person should study Torah even not-for-its-own-sake, so that he will eventually do so for-its-own-sake, as referring to one who in any event is lacking in the element of *li-shemah*, which refers to *devequt*.

The Intruder asks him: "What have you 'apprehended'?" He answers him with the argument:

> On the contrary, this is the essence of my knowledge and apprehension, in accordance with my knowledge and understanding of my own attribute. As I am unable to attach myself to God with *hitqashrut* [attachment] and *devequt* except through this manner, this is for me the essential element in apprehension and knowledge of the Torah,

> according to the will of He who Commands, may He be blessed . . . and it is forbidden for us to violate this in any manner whatsoever, so that we do not become distanced from the source of life.

The use of the term *meqor ha-ḥayyim* ("the Source of Life") appears in nearly all of the sections of this work, instead of the terms ᵓ*Ein Sof* or ᵓ*Ayin* ("the Infinite" or "the Nothing"), which are more commonly used among Hasidim. The author of this treatise considers "apprehensions" and "intellectual perceptions" as essentially secular matters, in contrast with *devequt* and *hitqashrut* to God.

The casting aside of "apprehensions" and attachment to the Source "without any garment" — that is, without any separation — is symbolized by the Sabbath. For R. Israel Dov, the concept "seventh" reflects the aspect of all-inclusiveness, and "thought" (as against "speech" and "action") is identified with the Sabbath — distinctions which are also accepted as symbols in Kabbalistic and Hasidic teaching. The attributes of the "mundane," as opposed to the "Sabbath," which represents the peak of its potential or, as he calls it, its "point" (*nequddah*), may also exist within thought itself. The "point" represents the boundary of the mystically possible, so that were he to attempt a level of "apprehension" beyond what his own "point" is able to incorporate — in terms of connection and *devequt* "without any garment of apprehension" — he would be leaving his place (cf. the verse, "let no man leave his place" (Ex. 16:29)!, i.e., the "Sabbath" of thought), according to his particular level, and he thereby enters into the aspect of the mundane. Therefore,

> There seems no better way before me but to strengthen myself, so that I not leave my place. That is: to the extent that my point, which is called the Sabbath, is able to include it in a way such as not to be distanced from its root, and that I be attached to its source and root, and thereby be attached to His Name, may He be blessed, which is the root of life. . . .

The author disagrees with the widespread view that a person must engage in intensive effort and preparations in order to achieve "apprehension"; in truth, this matter seems to him to be misleading, for: "If God, be He blessed, wishes, He may open the gates of understanding and knowledge, so that in one hour he may apprehend that which, in the way of nature, requires a great deal of time." The issue of study and intellectual speculation provides a fruitful source for R. Israel's struggles, regarding both the times for study, the material to be studied, and the method of study. In each of these subjects, he is reluctant to surrender to pre-conceived norms, which disturb him and make him a slave of the Intruder. In his view, the very act of "opening the book" has an arousing effect, "for at times when the soul is on a certain level, it then gains benefit even from opening the book and seeing the letters." The example brought here states that, just as the powers of the body are aroused to ejaculate seed by "the sight of the eyes," so do the letters arouse holy thoughts and spiritual worlds.

> By this means, the image activates his thought, and it emerges from a concealed to a revealed state, casting off the knowledge and arousal of the heart with greater clinging to God, with longing and desire and will ... And this is also seed.

The activation of the powers of the soul and their similarity to the process of procreation — as stated explicitly in the simile used here — is a common motif in the teaching of the Maggid of Mezhirech; as we shall see below, many of R. Israel's formulations originate in the Maggid's teaching. However, the posture of personal confrontation in practice is unknown in the Maggid's teaching. In fact, the entire dimension of Hasidic praxis is hidden in the Maggid's works.[4]

In another stage of study, the "Intruder" again enters — this time, when the author is engaged "in some subject which he does not wish to examine in the course of this study." There is a special *tiqqun*, whose character he does not explain, so that the "undesirable" thing does not impose itself upon his mind to disturb him. The Intruder confuses him by pressing him to perform this *tiqqun* immediately, "even though the hour is not fitting for it." He in turn struggles with the "Confuser," arguing that the performance of the *tiqqun* may be postponed to a time when the matter again comes to heart, and that if it does not rise, this is a sign that the *tiqqun* was unnecessary. It is clear that he is speaking here of an experience in which one attempts to concentrate upon a particular matter, while the abundance of subjects surrounding a person and occuring to him at that moment disturb him from his concentration. These misgivings are known from Hasidic teachings concerning prayer, which direct man to *devequt*, but we have not found it characteristic with regard to study.

In another related discussion, the author describes another kind of "confusion" brought about by the Intruder. When a person wishes to learn a new subject and begins to study it in a book, the Intruder appears and tells him that it is not suitable for him to begin now. Making use of an "intricate" exegesis, the author argues that all times are equally appropriate for study, the concept of "beginning" not applying at all to matters of learning and speculation. The same is true with regard to another situation, regarding which he had "considerations and thoughts of the mind regarding the fit time, according to his path, to examine some book and some

4 This was also the claim of R. Shlomo of Lutsk, when the Maggid of Mezhirech asked him to record the teachings which he had heard from him. R. Shlomo said that, as in any event this cannot express the hidden plane of these teachings, he could not fulfill his master's request. See his remarks on this in his Introduction to *Maggid Devarav le-Yaᶜaqov*, published in my critical edition, p. 3.

matter of study." But several different wishes may present themselves to him at one and the same time. He may decide to study a certain subject, but when he opens the book he feels a "desire" in his heart to turn to the book which he has rejected. In his words, it seems that "love is more easily found in the remote than in the nearby." But the Evil Urge is fickle, so that when he picks up the second book, to which he was drawn after pushing aside the first one, he is again attracted to the former, and so on and on. One way or another, he is unable to advance in reading. R. Israel's conclusion is that he needs to hold fast to his initial decision. On second thought, he attempts to understand the reason for the attraction of that which is "remote"; it seems to him that,

> [The reason that] his heart desires another matter is the feeling that he will lack the innerness, the *devequt* and the sweetness of the other matter, while engaged in study of the former! Therefore his soul specifically desires those matters from which he has withdrawn his hand, because of the pleasantness of a distant love over one close by.

The ability to decide, in order to nullify the feeling of oscillation and longing for a thing which is not readily available to him, is accompanied by an act of self-conviction, based upon Hasidic logic. R. Israel invokes here a Hasidic rule:

> Following profound examination, according to that which has been handed over to us by people of truth, this is not so, for there is a well-known saying of the Besht, z"l, that whoever apprehends a bit of unity is as if he apprehends it all. Therefore, one who has inner attachment regarding one thing is automatically attached to it all, in truth.

According to the author, rationalization neutralizes the longing for specific things, as well as clearing their overall significance. The author concludes that eagerness and longing are manifestations of the intense desire for *devequt*. This being the case, it is possible to utilize this longing for the sake of the holy goal itself by becoming attached to some object or another without it serving as a source of attraction and stimulation in itself. This is only possible if man is capable of negating his personal relation to the object.

This is the classical reasoning underlying the famous Hasidic idea of *ᶜavodah be-gashmiyut*, the sophisticated interpretation of which derives from the formulations of the Maggid's teaching. Another basic principle in the thought of R. Israel Dov relates to the psychological explanation and analyses the psychological aspects of the relationship to "specific things" in terms of "the revelation of feeling": he says of the moment of *devequt* which comes in wake of the "attraction" of things that, "*Devequt* is manifested feeling in this aspect. In other aspects, it is concealed from the point of view of the incorporated unity." Indeed, this stance corresponds to the monistic approach of the Maggid of

Mezhirech, who saw in the totality of phenomena a revelation of the unity of the spirit, which *ipso facto* leads each "part" of being to this unity. What is unique in the remarks of our author is the sharpening of the existential moment and the confrontation with a concrete situation which directs the ethos, the decision. The paradox which emerges from this ethos says that, if one's "desire is for but one thing," and one finds oneself on a limited and unequivocal path — in which one is not torn by uncertainty to choose one way or another — one is enslaved to that "one thing," without sufficient objective reason. Inasmuch as this impairs the equal right of all of existence to be the point of choice of your involvement and your *devequt*, this conflicts with the Hasidic ethos. The legitimation of the "lack of decision" is thereby by its very nature rooted in the monistic world-view; on the other hand, one is called upon to decide and to be at peace with ones first decision, precisely because there is no objective significance to the object of ones choice. All times and all objects are equal in terms of their capability of leading one toward *devequt*, but falling in love with a particular mode or a particular object as the path to *devequt* is the enemy of Hasidism (!), according to R. Israel Dov.

R. Israel hereby only confirms what we have already seen to be the correct interpretation of the tendency of Hasidic thought: an a-personal and a-dialogic mysticism. The question of *ᶜavodah be-gashmiyut* likewise relates to R. Israel Dov's view that one ought not to completely reject the appetites, but lift up the "spark" from their midst, as "there is nothing in the world which is not subject to the rules of its existence and unity." "At times," states R. Israel Dov, "one wishes to go to a great country and an expansive hall which are in the hands of another kingdom" — and one need not be afraid of crossing such a kingdom! On more than one occasion one is astonished: to what extent did Hasidism set this position before itself as a reminder, and what is the living spirit underlying this activist principle? Is it only the attraction of the great hall? This overall "attraction" to mundane experience is justified by two contradictory factors: namely, the objective reduction of "all things," and the opposite human factor which says "I know not" why I should prefer one thing to the other.

II

More than half of R. Israel Dov's treatise is devoted to reflections upon various different matters, such as the problem of evil, the concept of unity, the World to Come, the survival of the soul, asceticism, etc. Throughout his reflections, one finds a well-formulated and in principle agnostic position: a stance that denies the mind's ability to completely understand that which can be apprehended and lived in this world. The mystical approach is turned around: one can live the unity and break through all the boundaries of existence, but one must leave the understanding of these situations for the end of days. Eschatology is transformed into the best hope of reason, while any such effort in this world is in vain, harming the fulness of the perception of unity.

Once Hasidism began, in the Maggid's teaching, to follow its new exegesis of the Lurianic doctrine of *ẓimẓum*, which clearly stressed that Creation is no more than a progressive expansion and revelation, corresponding to the progressive contraction and concealment of the light of the Infinite, its stance towards the realm of Hasidic ethos was defined in terms of a new inspiration. Not only did it no longer trouble with thoughts based upon Gnostic dualism, but Hasidic thought failed to be satisfied even by the (Maimonidean) position, which defined evil as the absence of good and was satisfied with monistic thought. The "equanimity" of God — that is, of the spirit in its pure form — towards the problem itself not only dictated the ideal of the Hasidic ethos and required it to lift itself to a similar plane of vision, but this "equanimity" operated by virtue of the philosophic recognition that things were "equal to one another" — i.e., that the entire cosmos is merely the play of a system of more or less expanded and contracted lights, and that there is no greater difference between good and evil than there is between a point and a line. One can describe the line as an extension of the point, or the point as a contraction of the line.

R. Israel Dov discusses the entire problem of good and evil on this basis. Good and evil are the same in God's eyes, both of them being mentioned in the Torah: the blessing and the curse. The only difference between them is the following: that the good is "good in itself," while evil is only the "lack" of the factor making for the good, but not good in itself — "but in truth they must be literally the same." "And the entire Torah is a divine revelation and influx of vitality and goodness, and in their spiritual matter they are absolutely and completely equal — the letters of the blessing and the letters of the curse." The difference between them is only that one is an "expansive" principle, while the other is a principle of contraction of the divine lights themselves. Indeed, this is also an understanding of evil as "lack," but one that is necessary for the dialectic definition of the perfection of absolute good. We shall return to this point later.

The sense of "good" within man comes about as a result of the expansion of the divine lights into all realms of reality, to "all the pleasures and delights of this world." In spiritual matters there is only a very slight expansion of the lights, implying that the degree of *ẓimẓum* increases, the closer we come to the ever growing unified sphere, which is the greatest contraction of this expansion — until we reach the point where the Infinite becomes only one point. This means that the most infinite and complete is also defined by the growing "lack" of expansion. It follows from this that, the more a person is capable of ascending to the realm of the spirit, the more he is able to feel the good in an increasingly "contracted" manner, and not to feel the "evil," which is the lack of that good which resides in a lower sphere in the material world — the feeling of evil thereby automatically becoming negated. It is self-evident that evil does not exist at all with regard to the ontic question; man need only work on himself in order to feel the sensation of good on the highest level where, paradoxically, the divine expansion which causes the feeling of material good is contracted. On the other hand, the feeling of spiritual pleasure of unity with the spirit grows in inverse relation to its dependence on enjoying physical pleasures. The distinction is [only] in the matter of the one receiving, for in matters of godliness

> there is no distinction, for all is from the essence of His godliness and spirituality . . . Only that the one is in an expanded state and can also expand somewhat to external realms, while the latter is very much protected from external things, to an extreme, and is not allowed to expand even to a hair's breadth. And the person who is very much refined, and not "caught" by the external, so that even if he sinned, he does not feel any of the pain of the *ẓimẓum*, but only great pleasure and satisfaction and spiritual pleasantness — it is the same to him whether the light and vitality flow to him in their expansion [or the opposite], for he should not mind because he tastes the pleasantness of the supernal light and vitality in one as in the other. And all is of the essence of His divinity, "For I, the Lord, have not changed" [Mal. 3:6].

The difference between the two situations therefore consists in the following: "that a man who has a bit of grasp in external things" feels the pleasure which comes in wake of the expansion of the lights into the material world, but is denied the light which is "in a state of contraction," which does not expand outwards into the external world — and thereby he experiences suffering! Suffering is thus not the withholding of the good of the pleasures of this world, but specifically the residual effects of the lack of the contracted light.

Particularly interesting is R. Israel Dov of Stepan's application of the Cordoverian theory of "essence and vessels" (*ʿaẓmut ve-kelim*) into the new arena of the existential understanding of good and evil. R. Moses Cordovero makes the substantive changes between various phenomena dependent upon the differing essences of the divine "vessels"; the manner of reflection of the divine essence is understood as a new and different form of existence. Our author understands man as a "refined" vessel, on various different levels:

> For in truth, one who is properly refined does not at all feel any pain or deprivation in the revelation of the lights from the side of *Gevurah* [i.e., Divine Rigor], for the feeling of pain is brought about only because there grows within them the holy spark which is within him [in his soul] by virtue of the lights of *Gevurot*, and are revealed

> upon him from the side of his [soul's] evil. They overcome the holy spark and imprison it. Therefore [the spark] destroys and makes desolate his [soul's] evil: if he himself is rooted in the side of his [own] evil, he feels pain together with him. But when he is refined and is rooted in the side of his [soul's] holiness, then in accordance with the strengthening of the holy spark within him and its ascent, so does he ascend and overcome the side of evil within him, and he does not feel any suffering or pain. On the contrary, he has satisfaction with the great feeling — all in accordance with his refinement.

This sort of struggle in the innermost recesses of one's soul is highly reminiscent of Ḥabad's manifestation of Hasidism, which is in any case more aware of the psychological aspect of God's worship. The other characteristic of R. Israel Dov's thinking mentioned above, his anti-Zaddikism, also brings him closer to Habad.

As an implication of the principal of contraction and expansion, the author notes the two ways of Israel's service: by pain and suffering, and through a mood of expansiveness and complacency. Pain tempers their sins, they serve Him "according to their ability," even if not with complacency. It makes no difference to God out of what situation people serve Him. Sin and punishment, abundance and goodness, all arrange themselves according to an inner logic dependent on a conscious human effort. But the author does take the trouble to note that even service through constraint and suffering brings about "the good results in essence." This being so, "the feeling of constraint and pain is the essence of the good, to the same extent that it comes about from the aspect of His will, which is the quintessential good; even if it is embodied in the feeling of constraint, there is no fault in that." In order to illustrate the paradox[5] that sufferings are an inseparable part of the good, he cites the parable of the fruit whose taste is good, while its "flesh," which constitutes part of it, is not necessarily good. However, we are unable to separate between the good taste and the not-good "flesh," because the taste and the "flesh" are literally one essence; it is therefore entirely good in its essence! The point of the comparison is that the Supreme Will cannot act save through its embodiment in pain! The "embodiment" and the will are one, and are the very essence of the good; therefore, in the final analysis, there is no difference between the good and the evil felt by man, both being equally "complete" units of the manifestation of absolute good.

At times, the pleasure of good found within constraint may be more pleasing than the pleasure of the good brought about in the state of "expansion of the good," because the latter is constant, while the former is not constant. (The saying of the

5 This was of course the position developed by Moses Ḥayyim Luzzatto under the impact of his own theodistic outlook. There is a line leading directly from him, via the author of the *Tanya*, to R. Israel Dov of Stepan. See my article, "The Thought of Ramḥal" (op. cit.).

Besht that constant pleasure is no pleasure is well known!) "Pleasure" and "delight" which come about through constraint and pain enjoy the merit that, by their means, the lights of His will are more clearly revealed, because the one who is suffering discovers that, in His eyes, there is no difference. Regarding the manner of embodiment whereby the Supreme Will is revealed,

> . . . as he does not feel himself, and he is as if he does not exist, the more the pleasantness and friendship increase from his attaching himself to His will, which dwells in this embodiment. To him this seems the essence of the good — this embodiment is literally equivalent to the embodiment of the good in this world — and all according to his refinement and self-negation to His will, may He be blessed.

We have already seen that the stance of indifference towards pain and suffering is a fundamental principle of Hasidic thought,[6] but we have not found in Hasidism itself the agnostic stance typical of R. Israel Dov throughout his discussions — i.e., the position that one must accept the paradox that the absolute good is embodied in want and suffering, and is not subject to our understanding. This point is explicitly stated in the writings of Moses Ḥayyim Luzzatto (Ramḥal). But were we to understand this paradox, suffering would no longer exist and God's will would no longer be activated! Could we overcome this contradiction, we would already be in the eschatological aeon. Therefore, the pursuit of such a solution is not legitimate, because this contradiction is rooted in the very existence of the duality of right and left within the divine world, of the sweetening of *gevurot* with *hasadim* (i.e., of "rigor" with "mercy"), so that "everything is *hasadim.*"

> Because this matter is done in the embodiment of constraint, and it is itself mercy and goodness, it follows that all sides are equally for the good, and the very good which is in a contracted embodiment is needed for the completion of the stature, as the essence of good *per se* is [intrinsic] in the embodiment of revealed good. For just as in its absence, there would be no perfection in [that] stature, there is likewise no perfection in the absence of the essence of the good which is in *ẓimẓum*, not even in the essence of the good which is embodied in a revealed manner.

This approach, through its definition of evil as "lack," implies a certain lack in the expansion of the divine light; however, its innovativeness does not only lie in the use of the philosophical idea of lack in a new Kabbalistic system, but rather in the shaping of a dialectical system in which "lack" is a requirement of perfection not subject to understanding. The same holds good for any dialectic which represents unity in its purity; it is not subject to understanding, but is an eschatological matter. One must also not forget a certain point stressed a number of times in the

6 See above, Chapter 3.

remarks of the author, which calls our attention to the ethical mood that follows from his philosophy: namely, the irrelevance of good and evil with regard to the Godhead, because they are relative criteria, so that the struggle for the transformation of "evil" into "good" is left entirely in the hands of man, as his path towards unity. The sufferings of Israel are either incomprehensible from the divine point of view, or else are seen as an unavoidable battleground, subject to the divine will. While there will be no change in the laws governing divine activiy in the messianic future, so that its embodiment in *Ḥesed* and in *Gevurah* will persist forever, the ability of man's vessels to receive pleasure will thereby prevent the sense of evil and suffering. Hence, Rabbi Akiva's sufferings in having his flesh lacerated will be perceived as a spiritual pleasure (!). At one stage of his thought, R. Israel Dov explains his position on behalf of the pleasure which man feels in divine service. *Prima facie*, one might think that corporeal pleasure contradicts the Hasidic axiom that man must serve God alone, so that the feeling of pleasure derived therefrom is inconsistent with love of the Creator. But in truth — thus argues the author — the contradiction is only an apparent one, for there is no continuity in this matter between spirit and matter, and it is impossible for us to understand how physical pleasure can combine with spiritual service of God and *devequt* to "the source of life."

Yet it is not only in the world of suffering that we are sentenced to not-knowing, but in the world of pleasures as well. One must therefore accept contradiction and duality in every realm, with an equal measure of sobriety and standing firm. In the end, one is always left with the imperative of the need for "refinement." The agnostic statement opens the way for liberation from dependence upon conventions, since by means of the dialectical approach well-established positions in historical Jewish thought are refuted. One strides beyond things and does not worry about them:

> For in truth one need not worry [that one has pleasure and satisfaction], for the essential intent of one who engages in service is to cause pleasure to God alone, and not to any other thing apart from Him. But because of the corporeality of the world, and because true and clear awareness and knowledge of faith is gone for this reason, it seems from what is revealed as if the body and its pleasures and delights are separate from the delights of the soul and opposed to it. Furthermore, so long as true knowledge is hidden — and this is so because the body is insufficiently refined — and so long as it is truly in physicality, its pleasures are opposed to the soul because it is separated from it. For the soul is the divine portion and the body is separate [from it]; hence, when the body receives pleasure, it is not in accordance with the intention of the one serving. But in the future, when it becomes clear that everything is one devolution from Him, may He be blessed, and that the soul is literally a manifestation of the divine, and the body is a manifestation of the soul, and there is no curtain dividing

> them, for the body is extremely refined — then the body will receive pleasure and joy from the reward of its service, and there will be no lack [in the fact that it receives pleasure] from its service, and we shall be attached in complete unity: on that day God shall be one and His Name one [cf. Zech. 14:9]. What shall man do that he may live? He shall kill himself, that he will refine the body until he no longer feels any separate existence and standing by himself, but negates everything to *devequt* to God, and feels only His life: then shall he be attached to the Source of Life!

R. Israel Dov feels the burden imposed upon man by the ethic of asceticism, and asks the question: what is the end of this burden, and why are we commanded to sanctify ourselves by refraining from those things that are permitted? His thoughts here follow the classical lines of Hasidic thought, which require turning towards the physical world, on the one hand, and caution regarding it, on the other. However, he stresses the inner necessity of the relation to the world as a necessity of cause and effect. According to this theory, the desire for physical things comes:

> . . . from the inwardness of the life-force which is in every mineral, vegetable or animal thing, so that every attribute of cause and effect may desire one another, in order to connect spiritual with physical, and to the attribute of supernal man who is above all. And all of them devolve from the root of his soul, and he is literally a portion of God, as it were . . .

Man clings to God, just as an effect clings to that which causes it. Indeed, according to this theory — in which man is a kind of "Primal Man" in the sense used in Lurianic Kabbalah, the roots of all things being dependent upon his limbs, while he himself is a proto-type of all existence — the author adds that, "it would be fitting that we not separate ourselves from longings of this world, as is the way of nature for the cause to be attached to that effected by it." It would be fitting for us to attach ourselves to nature and act as a part thereof, and give up our dream of transcendence! The author asks: Why should we break our natural tendencies? And why should our reward and punishment depend upon our ability to break our nature? His answer is interesting: we only seemingly break our nature and act as-it-were with the power of the divine command, but in fact the law of nature itself demands that we elevate it, for it is the nature of things that they wish to be elevated to their source. Man is no more than a link in this chain, who is able to activate that which is given in nature. In principle, nature acts according to the longing of effect to cause, and the shared root of existence, within which man serves as a focal point, requires him to uplift the material to the spiritual, through which he merits the supreme delight anticipated from this activity. Were it not for this natural imperative of "the pleasure of cause to effect," man would be left with only the physical pleasure from his contact with the world, and "the wise man would have no pleasure from this." It is true that, were our bodies sufficiently refined and spiritual, there would be no need for the "embodiment of His will" in physical being, but as this is not the case, we are still required to,

> ... use some of the matters of this world, including the fulfillment of our marital duty and that food which is necessary and commanded — but all this with great caution and holiness and inner *devequt* to His Name, may He be blessed. And all this, so as not to separate ourselves from attachment to Him ... so that we may be attached to the Source of Life.

There is thus a paradox in things, which requires us to relate to the physical in order not to lose the spiritual; we must however add that there remains here nevertheless, as in other Hasidic thinkers, an apologetic tone towards the material world.

This tendency towards limited asceticism overrides "natural philosophy." The troubles of man, who finds himself within a system of coordinates between matter and spirit, may stem from two different points of view: from the fact that he is required to relate to matter, or that he must withhold himself from contact with matter. The author also presents the second question — namely, whether one who seeks out this world is considered to be distancing himself from God, or whether his path is not in fact the proper one:

> ... for in our hearts there is the faith that all of existence confirms the truth of His existence and unity. If so, matters of this world are also included in His unity. Why, therefore, should one who deals with matters of this world be considered to be "distancing himself"?

Our author felt that the Hasidic ethos is only one available option or choice flowing from the philosophy of "the world as a unity"; one could easily construct a univalent ethos in which spirit and matter — which are no more than two sides of the same reality — would also be considered of equal value in terms of our ethical relation thereto. At this point there is another saying of R. Israel Dov, leaving no doubt as to the value of the material: the physical world is but a parable of the world of spirit which, although needed for understanding the object of its comparison, has no separate existence as such. Thus, the ethos cannot be directed towards life in the parable, except for those for whom the referent of the simile is beyond their comprehension. In principle, man is given the ability to comprehend the object of the parable, while for the Godhead the object of the parable precedes the parable itself — i.e., the principle of the Absolute is prior to Creation, Creation being a development of the Absolute and compared thereto; therefore, "matters of this world are included within His unity." The author stresses that our need to reconcile ourselves with the fact that we in principle live within the parable, and that the object of the parable only springs into our consciousness at times by virtue of its being an *a priori* given of our own spiritual foundation, is the result of the "darkness of the intellect," an absence of knowledge which has no solution within our present existence. According to this view, the self-removal from the world demanded of the *hasid* is not because the world is an "enemy" of the spiritual element, but because it is only its shadow or parable; the world is not hostile or demonic, but is an element which removes one from the truth and from the absolute. This aspect of his approach is what determines the Hasidic ethos as one that is directed towards the mystical issue without being nevertheless hysterical concerning mundane problems.

The question of unity occupies an important place in these notes: the main goal seems to be the longing to apprehend unity.[7] The author states that we acquire awareness of the possibility of the existence of a unified cosmos through intellectual knowledge alone, but not "with clear consciousness and natural knowledge." Such a recognition is only possible when we become purified of the body: "then we will fully acquire in the ultimate degree how the world emerges from the truth of unity, literally." In a paradoxical way, the perfection of divinity and of the world is only understood through means of attachment to the corporeal.

It would seem that not only the principle of unity is concealed from us by that self-same "natural knowledge," but that the principle of the unbroken continuity and constant influx of the divine world into the physical world is insufficiently clear to us altogether, so that it appears to us that the connection between the two was broken following the Creation — just as the fetus is cut off from its very source in the drop of the father's seed — and the world is apparently conducted by itself. This perception is a "lack in the human law." The author brings an interesting example for the "lack of communication" with the element of the absolute within creation — i.e., with unity — by pointing out that it is precisely this "lack," connected with man's physicality, which necessitates our turning towards the physical. This argument is based on the assumption that every physical act is in fact a unitive act, even though this matter is "not naturally clear to us." R. Israel Dov makes use of the metaphor of union between a man and his wife. He states that the body is the foundation for the dwelling of the different parts of the soul (*nefesh-ruaḥ-neshamah*), but that the body is "the completion of their revelation." Through this illustration, he of course stresses the continuity between spirit and matter, based upon the definition of matter as the "contraction" of the light of the Infinite, which is a condition of the revelation of all being. It is hence clear that the body is likewise "the completion of revelation" — i.e., revelation in its fullness and its perfection. The author admits that it is true that the various parts of the soul have no need for "physical connection," as it is

> ... clear to them in a natural way that both husband and wife are presently connected [that is: through their physical union] in His unity as well, and that by this means his

7 Exactly as it was for Ramḥal. See note 5.

> *nefesh ruah neshamah* is able to cleave to hers in the place of the root of their soul, because the [divine] unity includes them. But because the lower [physical] level of their life is unable to be connected in such a manner, because it is not included within the unity through natural knowledge — it is therefore lacking in completion, and because of the absence of completion it is not completely whole.

According to this, there is therefore a lack of correspondence between the legitimate natural "completion" within the divine law, which is the law of the existence of bodies, and the legitimacy of the possibility enabling man to live the "fullness" of this realm within the physical plane. This is so because man is unable to know it in a "natural" way: it is not transparent to him, and its continuity with the spirit is not self-evident to us. It follows from this that we do not hold it in contempt or reduce its status in our consciousness, but neither is there any possibility of our living it "naturally," so that we need as well to know the limitations of our ability to manage it.

The sharp note woven here into Hasidic thought, the like of which I have not found elsewhere, is not found in the author's ethical position, which corresponds to the classical position in Hasidism, but in the deepening of the consciousness of man's relationship to the world. In a paradoxical manner, we might say that, because there is no possibility of living with the material "in its wholeness," it can function for us as a trap. Herein lies the struggle between affirmation and negation, between the positive imperative in the turn towards the physical, and the commandment "to lift it up" and to connect it with the chain of spiritual experience. It is clear to the author that,

> ... everything which comes to completion returns to its source, to the place of its origin. The source is thereby greatly opened to the [divine] flow and vitality; the source of the unity is opened up, which is the attribute of the Infinite, of flow and light which is the desired end and happiness destined for us. Because of the lack of the completion, there is lacking the opening of the source. This is certainly an inestimable lack, for this is considered a lack of all.
>
> At first, at the beginning of Creation, when man was created upright, the revelation of knowledge was natural with regard to the body, which is included in His unity. And even after the Creation and the existence of the world, he is connected to the unity, like a flame to the coal. For when a person blows upon the coal, a flame springs up; and [if] the contrary, the flame withdraws and is included in the coal.

The classical analogy, dominant in mysticism, which infers the existence of transcendental truth by means of comparison to the processes of the soul, is also implied in the following remarks of R. Israel Dov:

> Just as in the spreading out of knowledge from the source of the mind, even though it is revealed in speech, nevertheless it is utterly connected to the source of the mind

> without any separation at all. And since at the time he was born he was whole on his mind, according to the [divine] will, he was not necessarily attached to physicality. For even if he was far away [from the physical element]. the attachment to the spiritual one was not prevented from him, in terms of the unity and the way of completion and opening of the source, as above.

He concludes from this that, in terms of the conditions of our present existence, "one specifically needs physical connection." The "natural consciousness" of Adam, which had the attribute of the "supernal glow" (*zihara᾽ ᶜila᾽ah*; i.e., the highest portion of the soul, which was removed from him following the sin!) was what gave him the ability to understand the constant processes of becoming *ex nihilo*, and the continuity of becoming essence from naught, its ranking and vitality. This is a point — says the author — which cannot be comprehended today, but which he anticipates in the World to Come.

What troubles our author in all these discussions is the fact that we do not apprehend the "light" of things, but operate with absolute confidence in their truth without the same "natural" perfection. The same is true with regard to the study of Torah and the performance of *mizvot*. It is true — our author says — "that there is within Torah study an inner pleasure of pride and greatness that one is teaching Torah to the people; but the main thing is not in the greatness and honor and financial benefit, but in terms of the unity." In this way, the law governing common existence brings about pleasure in which, not only is there no negation, but is a guarantee of the act being correct. The same is true regarding the relation of the teacher to his disciples, or of a generation and its leaders. The relation based upon pleasure, even if this entails certain beneficial aspects, such as the acquisition of honor or money, is in the nature of things. The sureties given to us about "the lifting up of one's head to the next world" — he says — is the reward of knowledge of "the light" of things, the light of the *mizvot*, and the natural taste of every act which is hidden from our understanding.

It is man's destiny to live to the End of Days without a clear, "natural" knowledge, according to R. Israel Dov. However, this approach does not lead to uncertainty; on the contrary, he attempts to support the certainty of the values of the spirit and faith in the eternity of the soul over his agnostic approach. In his view, faith in the eternity of the soul is connected with the theory — which the Maggid of Mezhirech introduced within Hasidism — that all of existence is the result of prior non-existence, and that the continuity of existence also implies a continuity of nothingness. This is the great "darkness," which is the father of all light. We cannot isolate the precise moment of transition from a given situation to a new situation, just as one cannot know the exact moment at which the egg is transformed into a chick. Death is understood by R. Israel Dov as one of these "moments" of nullification of one form of being and its embodiment in another form. In man's eyes, the nullification of consciousness, which is the moment of darkness, is equivalent to non-existence.

> Man does not fully know what will become of him after his departure from this world, even though we believe in the survival of the soul in Paradise, and its embodiment in a spiritual body, made of Torah and prayer.

Nor do we have,

> ... natural, independent, sensory knowledge. Just as a man knows when he goes to sleep that this is not a complete nullification of his powers, and that after he sleeps he will wake up the same person that he was, and he knows that this is not his destruction, but another garment — and it is all clear knowledge.

Were the soul to possess this kind of clear knowledge regarding death, it would not experience the pain of separation. The author refers again to Kabbalistic concepts in order to explain the processes of the activity of the soul. The law which operates in the upper world states that the aspects of *ᶜatiq ve-ᵓarikh*, "Ancient" and "Long" (according to Lurianic Kabbalah, these are the highest "faces" or configurations within the Godhead: *ᶜatiq* symbolizes the stages of transition from world to world, and is the dialectic principle connecting the end of one world with the beginning of the next, while *ᵓarikh-ᵓanpin* is that face which is crystallized in an unequivocal way), are present in every thing, and are also attributes of the soul. Similarly,

> ... prior to the coming about of the *Yesh* [a term used for *Ḥokhmah* in Kabbalah], there is no apprehension thereof, it being called "nothing and nihility," *ᵓayin va-ᵓefes* [a designation for the *Sefirah* of *Keter*], even though everything is present therein [in *Keter*] in the manner of God's knowledge, not as knowledge *per se*. And it is called darkness because of the concealment of the things there, and also because it is the intermediate world [i.e., between lack and existence] between one world and another, and there also exist *in potentia* the attributes of the world which is beyond it, and the entire world is considered darkness in relation to the world which is higher than it; and every thing which needs to come into being and into an embodiment which is different than previously, must come to negation [beforehand].

In this passage, the law of "darkness" and of "nullification" is explained as the necessary progenitor of all new birth, even though this law is not made known to man by means of natural, clear, primary self-knowledge. Man knows only one direction of the process through clear knowledge — namely, the negation of certain states, such as death with regard to life, but he does not have knowledge of the actual process of transition from one state to another. In his consciousness, the "jump" is lacking in continuity, but this law also operates with regard to the soul, as we have said:

> and for this [reason] the soul, which leaves this world of physical embodiment to enter

> into spiritual embodiment, is regarded as returning to the state of negation of the senses, which is the state of ᶜ*atiq* and ᵓ*arikh* within it, and in this it seems to be negated and unable to know what will be following it, for the comprehension of the mind does not reach to there.

This concludes a series of "non-knowledges" of man; every attempt to transcend beyond the things is a kind of "forcing of the end" — i.e., of knowledge which will be revealed at the time of the End. No refinement of the body is capable of taking man beyond his natural boundary, "and one ought not to force oneself specifically to the realm of the hidden, for this is not His [i.e., God's] will." "Complete natural knowledge" is a matter for eschatology. While attachment to and unity with God are matters which can be attained even in the present age, "the spirit of Messiah" and the "kingdom of Heaven" are the perfect states, the state of clear knowledge and the refutation of all contradictions. This is not a longing for the Eschaton, seeking a substantive alteration in the structure of being or longing for an extravagant change in which the lower things are above and the upper worlds below. Rather, the Eschaton is intended to change being into transparent and "comprehensible."[8] R. Israel Dov's declaration that he wishes "not to know" is therefore the logical conclusion of the "human condition," for which there is no correction prior to the end of time. With his agnostic chisel, our author forces the ideological assumptions of Hasidic thought to their logical conclusion, defining their limits and sharply stressing the weight of *devequt* as a path towards life with the absolute. A confrontation of this sort between the boundaries of the rational and of the mystical are his contribution to the understanding of Hasidism.

8 This "rational" messianism is likewise characteristic of the teaching of Rav Kook. There seems to me to be a line of rational utopianism related to this understanding of "unity," going from Ramḥal, via Ḥabad, and through R. Israel Dov of Stepan, the Hasidism of Isbitza and Radzyn, and R. Ẓaddok ha-Cohen of Lublin, down to Rav Kook. See my article, "Utopia and Messianism in the Thought of Rabbi Kook" (Heb.), *Kivvunim* 1 (1979), pp. 15–27.

Chapter Fourteen

The Problem of Torah Study in Hasidism

Any school of spirituality, however conservative it may be, constitutes a danger to the tranquility and order of society; the emergence of any new values shakes up the entire community and upsets its orderly hierarchy. Thus, there arose an outcry against the neglect by Hasidism of Torah study. This accusation, directed against the earliest Hasidic groups of the period of the Baᶜal Shem Tov, preceded the Maggidic theory that study and *devequt* are in conflict with one another; in this early polemic, we hear nothing apart from the claim that the Hasidim did not study Torah because of their tendency towards laziness, and that they spent their leisure time reading Musar (i.e., ethical-homiletical works), because they claimed that they already knew all the laws from the *Shulḥan ᶜArukh* (so that Talmud study, which formed the heart of traditional Torah study, was therefore superfluous), and there was no need to delve into *pilpul* (Talmudic dialectics), which is of no value in itself. It is difficult to know whether this was in fact the opinion of the Hasidim of the circle of the Besht concerning Torah study, or whether the confrontation was formulated in these terms by the opponents of Hasidism simply because the former spent a good deal of time engaged in the study of Musar works.

The responses of the Hasidim to these accusations come relatively late; nor do we hear in them any discussion of the question, "what is the essential thing in Judaism," as the problem was formulated by the author of *Mishmeret ha-Qodesh*. It is certainly not impossible that only later was the fact they engaged relatively little in Torah study, together with their devotion to Musar literature, interpreted in terms of the confrontation between study and *devequt* — primarily by the Maggid of Mezhirech, who emphasized the superiority of *devequt*. R. Moshe of Satanow, author of *Mishmeret ha-Qodesh*, writes as follows:

> I have seen those who serve God with all their hearts in their prayer, who think nothing of wasting two or three hours in idle conversation, or at times in [studying] words of Musar. And they drink buckets-full of wine, saying that it was not for the wicked that pleasures were created, and dust into their mouths [a Talmudic curse] ... And their punishment is very severe, particularly concerning their neglect of Torah, for they cause others to sin as well, to adhere to ways of laziness and to pursue things which are not thus. Nor is it correct to devote too much [time] to Musar and to neglect Torah on account of it, for from Musar he will be drawn towards vain

> things; [indeed,] the essence of Torah is not Musar itself... [but rather] the laws, and their details and precise formulations. And in engaging overly much in Musar, he will spend less time in Scripture and Mishnah and *halakhah*... And in the end they will rise up like thistles to permit that which is forbidden, stumbling at noon-time and descending to the Pit, filled with the anger of the Lord... And they and their disciples will fall down, particularly because of the "burning wine" [i.e. hard liquor] which literally burns the soul; for he who permits it [i.e. liquor] is like one who denies the entire Torah.[1]

Similarly, R. Shlomo of Helma, author of *Mirkevet Mishneh*, writes that:

> There are those among them whose heart is drawn towards words of *aggadah*... And its words are on their tongues, they call out with their throat and do not spare [after Isa. 58:1] in the book of [R. Moses] Alshech — the living words of God, which are more precious than pearls, and is one of the forty-nine faces [by which one may expound the Torah] ... and he has a name and share in the book *Shenei Luḥot ha-Berit*. But he who dwells in the depths of halakhah is in his eyes an object of scorn and contempt, and he hates the masters of reflection [i.e. analytic study of *halakhah*], and he is accustomed to saying, "why do you exhaust yourselves for naught, for so long a time, and the table is spread before you [a pun on the title of the *Shulḥan ᶜArukh*], and the cloth [i.e., R. Moses Isserles' glosses] is upon it, to know the deed and the quintessence of study." ... And his soul eats him, "What is there for me and for you in *pilpul* and sharpness of vanity?"[2]

An interesting account relating to the Besht's path in Torah study is brought in the name of his friend and disciple, R. Meir Margalioth, which may have been an indirect answer to the claims of the Mitnaggedim, as may be seen from the passage brought below. He cites various remarks in the name of the Besht concerning the need to engage in Torah study for its own sake: that is, that one ought not to have any alien intention accompanying the act of study. In other words, an attempt is made here to explain the position of the Besht, post mortem, in terms of the social debate and criticism aimed against those who do not study "for its own sake," as well to forestall any debate concerning the position of study within Hasidic thought as such. In Margalioth's remarks, one can also sense an attempt to understand the "additional" spirit with which the Besht (that is: Hasidism, as opposed to the Mitnaggedim!) was graced, as a unique form of pneumatic vision derived from the light inherent in the words of Torah and their study.[3] This ability gave a kind of

1 *Mishmeret ha-Qodesh*, Vol. I, p. 2a (*Dinei Birkat ha-Nehenin*). The above quotation is taken from G. Scholem, "The Two Earliest Testimonies," pp. 231–232.

2 Ibid., pp. 232–233.

3 A similar tradition appears in the account of R. Zeᵓev Wolf of Zhitomir, who was an eye-witness to it. See *ᵓOr ha-Meᵓir*, 84c–d.

oracular character to the text studied, through which the Besht was able to tell the future. This latter account may be authentic, but clearly the initial section is intended to emphasize, first and foremost, that words of Torah must be studied as they always have been, and that when one learns the simple meaning, one does so for its own sake. The following are his remarks:

> ...One's principal study of Torah must be for its own sake, to learn in order to observe and to do and to fulfill, and the things go after the intention of the heart, and this is the perfection of the *mizvot*. And this is alluded to in the language of preparation,[4] "that they should prepare that which they are to bring" [Ex. 16:5] — that, prior to [beginning] to study in proper and pure thought, he should contemplate that he is preparing himself to study for its own sake, without any alien intention. And as has been warned concerning this by our great teachers in Torah and Hasidism, among them my dear friend, the rabbi and *ḥasid*, wonder of the generation, R. Israel Baᶜal Shem Tov, *z"l*: that the preferable intention in learning for its own sake is to connect oneself in holiness and purity to the letters, in potential and actuality, with speech and thought; to connect a portion of his *nefesh-ruaḥ-neshamah-ḥayah-yeḥidah* [i.e., the five levels of the soul] to the holiness of the lamp of mitzvah and the light of Torah, [to] the letters which give wisdom and bring down abundance of light and true eternal life. And when he has merited to understand and to attach himself to the holy letters, he is even able to understand the future from the letters themselves; therefore the Torah is called "illuminating the eyes" [Ps. 19:9], because it enlightens the eyes of those who attach themselves to it with holiness and purity, like the letters of the Urim and Tummim [i.e., the jewels in the breastplate of the High Priest, which had oracular powers]. And from my childhood, from the day that I came to know the *devequt* of love from my teacher, R. Israel, *z"l*, mentioned above, I have faithfully known that such was his custom, in holiness and purity, with great piety and separation. And by the wisdom of the righteous he shall live by his faith [Hab. 2:4], for secret things are revealed to him, and the honor of God is in the hiding of the thing [Prov. 25:2].[5]

This account makes no mention of the fact that Hasidim devoted little time to

4 An allusion to prayer.

5 *Sod Yakhin u-Boᶜaz* (Satmare, n.d.), p. 4a. On p. 4b there is an interesting example, describing how King David, by means of the light within the letters (like that of the Urim and Tummim) perceived that which was said in the saying of the Sages: "Bathsheba was destined for David from the Six Days of Creation," and he was satisfied with it [Sanhedrin 107a]. Perhaps through this same approach one may also explain the words alluded to in *Ẓavaʾat ha-Riva"sh*: "Through the power of the Torah that he learned that day and thereafter, [if] a certain thing comes before him to do and he does not know whether to do it or not, he may understand what to do by virtue of that thing which he learned, [provided] but that he be in constant *devequt* to God..." — *Ẓavaʾat ha-Riva"sh*, p. 8. One can see that R. Ephraim of Sudylkow also knew something of the interpretation of "reading in the Urim and Tummim": see *Degel Maḥaneh ʾEfrayim*, p. 37c–d.

study, nor to any belittling of Torah study on the part of the Besht. On the face of it, the Hasidim only augmented the understanding of the concept of Torah study for its own sake.

The Besht's grandson, R. Moses Ḥayyim Ephraim of Sudylkow, quotes some remarks in the name of the Besht concerning study from which one can sense a certain social criticism directed against the "scholars" [*lamdanim*], but not against study itself. According to these accounts, the change brought about by Hasidism involved an added element of enthusiasm during the time of study, which stressed bringing God back into a world which had been made barren by *pilpul*:

> It is in this way that one is to interpret, "And it was that which stood for our fathers and for us, for not only did one stand against us to destroy us [. . .] and the Holy One blessed be He saves us from their hand" [Passover Haggadah]. That is, must study Torah for its own sake, that is, for the Name of God; and the Name of God has three combinations, which is "it" (*hiᵓ*).[6] And this is what is said, "and it was that" (*ve-hiᵓ she-ᶜamdah*) — that is, the study of Torah for its own sake, which is for the sake of God and His three combinations — "stood for our fathers and for us." "For not one alone" — that is, because there is not the One, who is the Master of the World, [present] in the Torah which he studies — "they stand against us to destroy us. But the Holy One, blessed be He" — that is, when the Holy One blessed be He is there — "saves us from their hand." As I heard from my master, my grandfather, may his memory be a blessing for eternal life, concerning, "One who repeats his lesson one hundred times is not similar to one who repeats his lesson one hundred and one times" [Ḥagiggah 9b]. That is, there is present within it [i.e., his learning] the One, who is the Master of the World.[7]

R. Ephraim likewise cites remarks in the name of the *Toldot* which have a clear polemical background:

> Furthermore, the small ᵓ*aleph* [i.e., in the traditional orthography of Lev. 1:1] alludes to what I heard said in the name of R. Joseph, the righteous preacher of the community of Polonnoye, *z"l*, who stated, regarding what the world says, that the *lomdim* [i.e., the scholarly class] learn and the Hasidim do not learn:[8] "The truth is, the more the *lomdim* learn, the greater they are in their own eyes, and they think in their own eyes that they have already learned a great deal, as much as is needed; while the Hasidim, the more they learn, the smaller they are in themselves. And this is their entire aim, that they teach themselves to be small [humble] and lowly in themselves.

6 That is, *h"y h"h h"ᵓ*: the final letters of which combine into *hyᵓ* — the feminine pronoun.

7 *Degel Maḥaneh* ᵓ*Efrayim*, 45c.

8 The social terminology used here is itself interesting: the two extremes are designated as *lomdim* (scholars) and *Ḥasidim*, the term *Mitnaggedim* not being used.

> And this is what is alluded to by the small ʾ*aleph*: ʾ*aluf* — learning; *zeʿira* (small) — to make themselves small." And understand this.[9]

It is clear from this that, in these responses, the Hasidim avoided any discussion of the true value of study and did not respond to the question which was really posed to them by the Mitnaggedim, namely: why did they learn less and neglect the Torah?

Discussion of the subject itself is first alluded to only in the teaching of the Maggid of Mezhirech, who reflected upon the problem from the internal point of view of Hasidic values. In this discussion, the value of study is indeed defined as secondary to that of *devequt*, as we stated above. The formulation of the Maggid's teaching by R. Mendel of Przemyślany states:

> A further general rule: that one ought not to engage overly much in study. For in the former generations, when their intellects were strong and they learned with great holiness and greatness, they did not need to trouble themselves concerning fear of God, for as fear was always present before them, they were able to learn a lot. But we, whose intellects are limited, if we remove our thoughts from *devequt* to God, may He be blessed, and study too much, we may, Heaven forfend, forget the fear of God, which is the essence of "the fear of God, which is His storehouse" [Isa. 33:6], as is written in *Reshit Ḥokhmah* [by R. Elijah de Vidas].[10] Therefore, he must engage less in study and think continuously upon the greatness of the Creator, may He be blessed, in order to love Him and fear Him, and not to keep thinking many thoughts, but only one thought [i.e., *devequt* to Him], as I wrote above.[11]

The first problem which confronts the reader is the new claim that intellectual involvement is incompatible with *devéqut*, which is a contemplative rather than a discursive activity. "To learn with *devequt*" is, according to the strict understanding of the formula — although not according to the enthusiastic interpretation — self-contradictory. True contemplation is intended to obliterate all intellectual activity and therefore cannot coexist with it. Thus, the conflict between the demand for contemplative-*devequt* and for Torah study is an extremely serious one. This is also the significance of the Maggidic sentence: "Even though at the time of study it is impossible to attach himself to the Creator, may He be blessed ..." [12] Even though the above-cited sentence concerning the

9 *Degel Maḥaneh* ʾ*Efrayim*, 44b–c.

10 Elijah de Vidas, *Reshit Ḥokhmah*: *Shaʿar ha-Teshuvah*, Ch. 2.

11 *Darkhei Yesharim* [*Hanhagot Yesharot*] (Lemberg, 1865), p. 2.

12 Ibid. It is worth noting here that only R. Ḥayyim of Volozhin fully realized the serious implications of the Maggidic theory and took a position which was in principle correct, in presenting Hasidic doctrine as systematically denying the value of "learning" in the literal sense. See *Nefesh ha-Ḥayyim*, Pt. IV, Ch 2: "... For how many laws there are in the Talmud upon which, while a person is involved in their study, he must reflect and involve his mind and intellect deeply in the physical matters [which

limitation of Torah study has been entirely removed from the printed editions of *Ẓavaʾat ha-Riva"sh*, evidently out of fear of the Mitnaggedim,[13] I must add here that even this version of the Maggid's words is fragmentary and does not faithfully reflect his stance concerning this question. It seems to me that the so-called "Maggidic revolution" which strikes one here is not even supportive of a true revolution, but in fact the opposite. It represents a certain restrained, compromise formula within the context of the Hasidic milieu: the claim that one must "minimize" Torah study, so to speak, is not intended to belittle it, but rather to stress that one must engage in that "little."

In the full version of the remarks of the Maggid which I shall bring below, one may detect the fear of a total and revolutionary reliance upon the idea of *devequt*, lest one's gain be lost in the loss of the *devequt* itself. This restriction of the teaching of meditation to a small number of adepts, implied in the manuscript containing the teachings of the Maggid owned by R. Shmelke of Nikolsburg, reminds us of the interpretations of the teaching of the Maggid by R. Meshullam Feibush of Zbarazh, and adds weight to the authenticity of his interpretation.[14] The Maggid's essential position is formulated roughly as follows: among the early Hasidim the gap between contemplation and study did not exist at all, because their *devequt* was so great that the act of discursive learning was an integral part of the "Stature of the Creator" without disturbing their *devequt*: they were in practice indifferent to the question of "study" as an independent value, since in any event they attained *devequt* as a supreme value in another manner. Study motivated by such a psychological state did not lead to disintegration — to the contrary! In the days of the Maggid himself the problem of the *ḥasid* is a different one: he has to struggle to attain *devequt* at every moment, and there are no longer living people like the

they involve], such as *qinim* [the laws of groupings of birds for sacrificial purposes] or discharges of menstruants, which are basic *halakhot*, or the discussions within the Talmud and the rules concerning the premises used in [cases of] deception, that the liar could argue thus and such. For it is nearly impossible that he should at that point be in the proper state of *devequt*!" He claims that there is an essential difference between the psychological state of *devequt* and that involved in discursive activity, which is precisely the argument of the Maggid of Mezhirech, only they reach opposite conclusions: R. Ḥayyim tends towards a simple explanation of the concept of *devequt* in the Jewish tradition, as many of the Hasidim themselves did later on, as we shall see below. See also R. Ḥayyim's remarks in ibid., Pt. IV, Chap. 6. Zweifel, *Shalom ʿal Yisraʾel*, Pt. II, also cites the remarks of R. Pinḥas of Polotsk ("who was among those who saw the face of the king, Elijah of Vilna") in his book, *Keter Torah*, where he makes similar statements to those of R. Ḥayyim.

13 *Darkhei Yesharim*, first published in 1805, in Zhitomir.

14 I refer, not to the actual interpretation of the practice of *devequt*, which was certainly quite different in the thought of R. Meshullam Feibush, but to the fact of the restraint and the use of certain techniques by an intellectual elite alone.

Hasidim of old who were in a constant state of *devequt*. Therefore, the introduction of study into the daily routine of the *ḥasid* creates tension, it clearly being assumed that there is no direct path from study to *devequt*. The solution of "engaging little in study" therefore accented the fear that, as a result of the inability to perform such an integration, the Hasidim would abandon study completely and end up with "the worst of both worlds": i.e., they would cease to learn because of the effort put into contemplation, in which they would in any event not succeed at attaining *devequt* due to their spiritual inadequacies. The Maggid found an appropriate compromise solution by engaging in study without forgetting the main thing, which is that one must pause periodically during the course of one's study in order to "attach oneself."

These remarks seem to me to be addressed to a very definite element in society, and there were specific circles of Hasidim who neglected study because of the claims of *devequt*. It may be that this was the same group against which the Mitnaggedim raised an outcry; however, the Maggid's remarks were not intended to encourage this posture of popular spirituality, but to restrain it. It may be that the decision of the editors to eliminate this passage from the *Ẓavaʾah* was prompted by the manner in which R. Menahem Mendel of Przemyślany edited the Maggid's teaching, which is fragmentary (or perhaps someone else "gathered" it after him) and does not provide a true and accurate picture of the position of the Maggid. I shall quote the passage as it appears in the above-mentioned manuscript:

> And when he learns, he should rest a bit every hour, in order to attach himself to Him, may He be blessed. And during the time of study [itself], even though it is impossible to attach himself to Him, because the mind does not allow it — for only unique individuals like R. Simeon bar Yohai and his companions [could] learn with fear and love — he must nevertheless learn continually, for the Torah purifies the soul, and it is a tree of life to those who hold fast to it. But if he does not learn, he will not have the intellect to attach himself to Him, may he be blessed; as our rabbis wrote, "A boor cannot be God-fearing, nor can an ignoramous be pious (*ḥasid*)" [Avot 2:5]. And how much more if he is already a scholar, the time for study will not be inferior to the [periods of] "falling of the *moḥin*" [i.e., of lower spiritual consciousness] or the time of sleep, for then too he is unable to attach himself to the Creator, blessed be He. And if he sits idle, the [Evil] Urge will cause him to have alien thoughts and lust and vain things, and [to sap] the remnants of his strength and powers. For thought is constantly in motion, and does not rest at all. And certainly, if he would be able to contemplate the wisdom of the Torah of the Creator in all the creations, and recognize that the kindness of the Creator and His abundance are constant and never cease, and attach himself to Him with complete love and longing for His will and His service, to sacrifice his self and spirit and soul [*nefesh-ruaḥ-neshamah*] for the sanctification of His Name, and unite his acts for His name alone, without any combination, as did the early Hasidim, whose thoughts were attached to naught save to Him, may He be

> blessed — it would be as good as study, and perhaps more so. And as the author of *Ḥovot ha-Levavot* wrote, and the *Shenei Luḥot ha-Berit*, as follows, "*devequt* is seven times better than study." But in our generation, it is sufficient to attach ourselves to the Creator, blessed be He, in our three daily prayers and in the blessings over food, but if we abandon learning we will find ourselves losing on all counts. In any event, he should not learn continuously and with unflagging diligence without any interruption whatsoever.[15] For if it were in the early generations, when their intellects were very strong, and their characters were proper and God-fearing, they were attached to Him constantly without any interruption, and they did not need to trouble themselves at all about this, for the fear of God was always upon their faces, and they learned with supreme sanctity and with love, and they were engaged in the Mystery of the Stature of the Creator even in their [study of] revealed Torah, for the Torah and the Holy One blessed be He are one, and they made a throne for the Shekhinah, and they were able to learn a great deal. But we, whose intellect is weak and with our poor characters, if we learn continuously without interruption, we will forget the fear of God and the [need to] correct our qualities and the unification of our qualities to His Name, may He be blessed. And this is the important thing, as is written, "the beginning of wisdom is the fear of God" [Ps. 111:10]. And the *ḥasid*, author of *Ḥovot ha-Levavot* [wrote] at length to chastise and to shame one who asked an improper question regarding matters of divorce — see there. And the Ari *z"l* wrote: "He who is sharp and expert will learn for one or two hours"... Therefore, one needs to set aside a bit of one's study-time to think about the greatness of the Creator, may He be blessed, in order to love Him and to fear Him, and to be shamed before Him and to long for His *mizṿot*, and not to think many thoughts, but only the one thought as written above ...[16]

As we said, to date only the second half of the Maggid's teaching in the above-cited text was printed in *Darkhei Yesharim*, edited by Mendel of Przemyślany; the first half of the text passage found in the manuscript[17] contains, in my opinion, material which balances the Maggid's remarks, and places the problem in correct proportions.

The Maggid's cautious and conformist position only applies, as we said, with regard to practical life; the theory of the opposition between *devequt* and study remains as it was, and is formulated more clearly in the Maggid's interpretation of the verse "and He gave to Moses when he finished speaking with him" [Ex. 31:18]:

> ...But the Torah [i.e., in contradistinction to all of man's other activities], even though while he is engaged in it his fear of God drops somewhat, they [i.e. the statutes]

15 A formulation in the same spirit appears in *Liqqutei Yeqarim* (Lemberg, 1865), p. 1c.

16 MS Jerusalem–National Library 1467 (*Torat ha-Maggid*, edited by R. Shmelke of Nikolsburg), Pt. III, Ch. 2, p. 12bff.

17 Only isolated and non-consecutive sections of this passage appear in the *Ẓavaʾah*.

> are nevertheless upright. And whenever he separates himself from them, he comes to the Creator blessed be He. And this is, "The statutes of God are upright" [Ps. 19:9] — that even though because of them he is absent from God, in any event they are upright, for this is their uprightness, that he come [i.e., because of them] before the Master of All.[18] "Rejoicing the heart" — for when he engages in fear and is in the Nothing and is unable to bring abundance into his soul, the Torah which comes into his intellect[19] brings flour [i.e., material wealth]. And this is, "if there is no Torah, there is no flour" [Avot 3:17]. Indeed, the Torah guides man, guiding him in all of His service, may He be blessed, on the wayside, to the bird's nest [an allusion to Deut. 22:6–7], and in the field, to the commandments pertaining to the field; therefore, when he separates himself from them, he comes [straight] to the service of his Creator.[20] Therefore Moses our teacher, of blessed memory, when he was in Heaven in the Nothing, even though they told him on the way to attach himself (*devequt*) to his Creator, in the bird's nest, was unable to attach himself with his intellect, for he was [already] attached to the Creator, but only when he finished speaking with him he came to the place called *Matanah* (i.e., "gift").[21]

Let us return to the problem of the polemic surrounding the question of Torah study. Although the outcry raised against the Hasidim — i.e., that they neglect Torah study and have contempt for the *Shulḥan ᶜArukh* — might not have been fabricated out of whole cloth, the sources from which the Mitnaggedim drew this information are not entirely clear. The claims brought in the name of the *Toldot* are a vicious forgery, as the words ascribed to him simply do not appear there.[22]

18 The sentence is somewhat convoluted, its sense being paradoxical and rather interesting: namely, that the statutes of God — i.e., the commandment of the Torah itself — require that one leave one's study in order to come before the Master of All in *devequt*!!

19 Because when he is in the "Nothing" he leaves his "intellect" and the realm of the rational.

20 Again, a paradoxical interpretation, which attempts to base the abandonment of study upon the supreme *mizvah* of Torah.

21 *Kitvei Qodesh*, p. 9d. This alludes to the Midrash: "that Moses learned and forgot throughout the forty days, until they were given to him as a gift." The entire homily is extremely interesting, explaining that even Moses was unable to receive the Torah during the time that he was in *devequt* to the Nothing, and only when he descended and returned to the life of reason did he merit to receive it.

22 In the MS. of *Shever Poshᶜim*, f. 55b, reprinted by M. Wilensky in *Ḥasidim u-Mitnaggedim* (Jerusalem, 1970), vol. II: 155: "It is his tendency to incite and to lead all Israel astray, to walk in [these] ways, and to no longer go in the way of the holy Torah and the path of our forebears, *z"l*, whose essence is based upon the abolition of the constant study of the Torah, both revealed and hidden [Torah]." The spurious quotation from the *Toldot* is as follows: "He should not be habituated to study constantly, but he should be among people and not study at all, for study brings about haughtiness." Wilensky was correct in noting there that this was a distortion of the matter! The quotation actually reads: "(in the name of Moharan [R. Nahman of Horodenka]). He should not be accustomed to always be constantly studying, but he should also be among people, and there too let the fear of God be upon his face, to fulfill [the verse], 'I have always placed God before me.' Even though it is its opposite, being the negation of Torah learning or of prayer, he should nevertheless take heart that there too is Musar and the service of God..." — *Toldot Yaᶜaqov Yosef*, 24d.

As for the arguments advanced in the name of R. Moshe ha-Melamed of Brody, whose "notes" to the *Ṭur* and *Bet Yosef* aroused great controversy in 1787:[23] there is no proof that this individual was in fact a devotee of Beshtian–Maggidic Hasidism (assuming that we reject the possibility that the whole incident was no more than the vicious joke of a *mitnagged*!). It is nevertheless possible, in principle, that there were Hasidic thinkers — at present difficult to identify — against whom the remarks of *Mishmeret ha-Qodesh* and *Merkevet Mishneh* were originally directed, and from whose position the Maggid of Mezhirech also took exception in certain matters. In the heat of the anti-Hasidic polemic, they may have all been lumped together in one category.

But the source for the Mitnaggedic argument that the Hasidim were contemptuous towards the *miẓvot* cannot be understood in terms of their having read Hasidic manuscripts or a deep, serious examination of their thought. It seems to me that the Mitnaggedim were justifiably suspect of the nonchalant atmosphere which hovered over Hasidism, and its exaggerated inner confrontation with the accepted scale of Jewish values; nevertheless, the Mitnaggedim seemed to have given the Hasidim too much credit for "anti-nomian" daring. If we wish to risk a guess, one can even state that Hasidism placed limits upon itself in reaction to the Mitnaggedic "outcry," and not only due to its own inner sense of historical responsibility.

As much as Hasidism was marked by spiritual daring, it also perceived the chasm which lay before unadulterated spirituality. This tension seems apparent in the descriptions cited in the previous chapters; the easy-going attitude towards the *miẓvot*, which resulted from the confrontation between the value of the *miẓvah* and that of *devequt*, was accompanied by considerable reflection and hesitation, at least in Hasidic theory. It is also worth noting here that the formulation brought in *Darkhei Yesharim* in the name of the Besht himself, concerning the question of observing "stringent rulings" in the fulfillment of the *miẓvot*, is considerably softened in the manuscript of R. Shmelke of Nikolsburg by the addition of an interesting final section to the passage. Moreover, whoever judges the teaching of the Besht and the Maggid from the viewpoint of the formulation in *Darkhei Yesharim* sees only half the truth. The following is the text brought in *Darkhei Yesharim*:

> The Ba^c^al Shem Tov said that if a person does not have any self-interest, but everything is the same for him, he will certainly receive the [supernal] levels, of which the greatest is humility. And even humility which is not for-its-own-sake is greater than chastisement for-its-sake, as stated in ^c^Eruvin [15b]. But because we do not have

23 See Dubnow, "*Ḥasidim* as Law-Breakers" (Heb.), *ha-Shiloah* 7 (1901), p. 315, p. 317ff.

> a strong intellect like the former [generations], we cannot strictly observe all the "stringencies," for *devequt* may [then] cease because of our weak intellect; and this was not the case of the former ones, whose intellect was very strong and who were able to observe all the stringencies.[24]

In R. Shmelke's manuscript, we read:

> The Besht *z"l* said that if a person has no self-interests, but everything is the same to him, he will certainly merit all the levels, of which humility is the greatest of all. And even humility which is not for-its-own-sake is greater than Torah [25] for-its-own-sake, as stated in ᶜEruvin 15b.[26] But because our intellects are not strong like the former [generations], we are unable to strictly observe all the "stringencies" as is proper, for the *devequt* would be negated because of our weak intellect, unlike the former ones, whose intellects were very strong. But we must in any event take very great care of this [thing], and weigh the deed in the balance of the intellect; if it is renounced because of that stringency between himself and his Creator, it is better not to be overly strict. But this is specifically so concerning those excessive "stringencies" that a person takes upon himself; but [as for] those things which are explicitly stated in the *Shulḥan ᶜArukh*, he must be strict, even if to his mind his *devequt* would be abnegated, for this is surely an error. For the Torah as a whole, with all its details and restrictions and precise regulations, from the Faithful Shepherd [i.e., Moses] through to the *Shulḥan ᶜArukh*, was only given to us that we may be attached to His Great Name, by means of the deeds which are performed, including their restrictions. As the world says, "Even that which a venerable student is to expound in the future [is Halakhah given to Moses on Sinai] . . ."[27]

In the formulation found in the *Hanhagot* [Regimen Vitae] of R. Ḥayyim Ḥaykl of Amdur, these things are interpreted in much the same spirit:

> Every day he should set himself [a period of time] during which he studies Bible and Mishnah, and the rest of the free time he has, he should engage in inner [teaching; i.e., Kabbalah and Hasidism]. And he ought not speak much with people who do not have *devequt* with the Creator, blessed be He. And when he learns, he should rest a little bit and remember the Creator, blessed be He.[28]

24 *Darkhei Yesharim*, p. 6.

25 This word is correctly printed in *Darkhei Yesharim* as *tokhehah* ("rebuke"), rather than as "Torah."

26 The correct reference should read: Arakhin 16b.

27 MS. Jerusalem–National Library 1467, fo. 13d–14a. This formulation seems close to the words of the Maggid, and not necessarily to the Besht, unless we assume that the final section in the MS. is a Maggidic interpretation of the Besht's teaching, which did not have the same reflective note of self-examination and restraint. The language also sounds like that of the Maggid of Mezhirech.

28 *Hanhagot*, Sect. 5, at the beginning of *Ḥayyim va-Ḥesed* (p. 9). The accusations of the Mitnaggedim against R. Ḥayyim Ḥaykl — namely, that he preached contempt of study — are patently absurd. On the dispute concerning this, see Zeᵓev Rabinowitz, *Ha-Ḥasidut ha-Litaᵓit me-reshitah ᶜad Yameinu* (Jerusalem, 1961). Rabinowitz claims that the only full Mitnaggedic text of *Maḥshavot Kesilim* is

The theory that there was in fact a specific Hasidic group to whom the remarks of the Maggid and of his disciple R. Ḥayyim Ḥaykl were addressed may perhaps be given a sounder basis by a letter written by R. Ḥayyim Ḥaykl to his fellow Hasidim (*anshei shelomo*). In this letter, he warns against their attachment to the path of certain specific Hasidim, whom he does not identify by name but whom he describes with a number of distinctive features, reminiscent of the accusations found in the broadsides of the Mitnaggedim. The "circle" which calls itself "Hasidim," against whom R. Ḥayyim Ḥaykl's remarks are directed, is depicted as a group of hedonistic ignoramuses (*am-aratzim*), who place the emphasis upon social relationships and ignore the true Hasidic teaching of ethics and of abstinence from things of this world and the goal of striving to meet God in a spiritual manner.[29] They see themselves as a pneumatic circle, which evidently also has a

that cited by Zweifel in *Shalom ᶜal Yisraᵓel*, Pt. III, p. 37, which explicitly mentions the struggle of the Mitnaggedim against R. Ḥayyim Ḥaykl of Amdur (i.e., the ban which originated in Grodna Province, to which Amdur belonged), because of his being as-it-were opposed to Talmudic scholarship. In his view, the version given by Dubnow (*Devir*, vol. 1, p. 303) is "corrected" (see Rabinowitz, p. 95). He claims (p. 100) to have at hand the full text of *Shever Poshᶜim* by R. David of Makov in the MS of the YIVO Research Institute in New York, which quotes R. Ḥayyim Ḥaykl as saying (in Yiddish): "Let my tongue cleave to the roof of my mouth; fools and apostates are those who learn Talmud rather than the writings of the Ari!" These accusations of the Mitnaggedim seem to me to be baseless exaggerations.

29 A definite criticism of this type also appears in R. Joseph Bloch, containing clearer allusions to the sexual sins of this hedonistic circle. They interpreted the Hasidic concept of joy — according to him — as this-worldly joy, and spoke in affirmation of lusts. See *Ginzei Yosef* (Eretz Yisraᵓel, 1960), Pt. I, pp. 79–80. An allusion to the same group also seems to appear in the remarks of the Maggid himself, *ᵓOr Torah*, p. 35a: "And he thinks that he loves God, and this is naught but joy of frivolity," while in *Liqqutei Yeqarim*, 2a, reservations are expressed concerning the service out of "love" alone without "fear," which can lead to frivolity. An allusion to this (albeit only theoretical) also appears in *Maᵓor va-Shemesh*, 39b. *Degel Maḥaneh ᵓEfrayim* contains clearer allusions to an historical split which occurred within the Hasidic movement, which was originally united. He blames the faction of "the sect of liars" for inciting "strife and contention." He seems to have thought that, were it not for them, the Mitnaggedim would not have lifted their voices against Hasidism at all. This point also accentuates the conformist nature of classical Hasidism in the area of behavior. The following are the remarks of the *Degel*: "'And the whole earth was of one language and one speech' [Gen. 11:1]. This may be interpreted metaphorically, along with the previous [sic! should read 'following'] matter, 'And as they journeyed east, they found a valley' [ibid., v. 2]. 'Let us burn them thoroughly ... and make us a name' [v. 3, 4]. The Torah alludes here to the class of liars, who imitate those who are whole in the faith of Israel, who in the end have no existence but disappear of themselves, for lies cannot be sustained. And this is alluded to in the verse that, at the beginning, 'And the whole earth was one language' — that is, clinging to the Shekhinah, which in *gematria* is *safah* (language), 'and one speech' — that is, because they were clinging to God, there was among them great unity, and they did not speak one way with their mouth and another in their heart, but their mouth and heart were one. But when 'they were journeying to the east' (*qedem*) — that is, [away] from the Primeval One of the World [*qadmono shel ᶜolam*; i.e. God], as the rabbis say, 'and they found a valley,' etc.

special technique of meditation in isolation (*hitbodedut*), as well as certain ideas which R. Ḥayyim Ḥaykl deemed heretical ("their corrupt thoughts").

> ... like those who isolate themselves in their homes, making themselves a special room where they sit with their corrupt thoughts, and cover their eyes from seeing the greatness of their Creator, but only [doing so] that their name be spread as Hasidim and withdrawn from the world (*perushim*), and in truth they are withdrawn, for they have separated themselves from the Life of Life, the shadow of whose Shekhinah hovers over us.[30]

There is no way at present of knowing whether the circles against whom these remarks were directed were also attached to the Besht, or if it was only the Mitnaggedim who made that association. At the same time, I do not wish to assume that there was on the one hand a vulgar "Hasidism" and on the other a pure, idealistic variety. What is significant to us at present is to acknowledge two primary facts: 1) that Hasidism, in all of its manifestations, had within itself an anarchistic core, which endangered several of the basic values of Judaism; 2) that the Maggid of Mezhirech and a number of his disciples were aware of this fact, and labored to isolate this anarchistic element, leaving it in the spiritual realm alone, while conforming to accepted norms in the practical realm. In terms of classical Hasidism — if one may speak of such a thing — this approach was the victorious one. Regarding Torah study and the observance of the *mizvot*, Hasidism did not play a double role; moreover, subsequent to the teaching of the Maggid himself, we hardly hear anything about the existence of a basic problem of Hasidism pertaining to the Maggid's teaching of the conflict between the status of contemplation within everyday life as against the value of Torah and mitzvot. The formula, "it is impossible to study with *devequt*," was entirely forgotten. In its place, there came a formula which obscured the true problem by claiming that one

— that is, they erred and fell into a deep and dark pit. Moreover, they made themselves appear righteous, and of this it is said, 'let us make bricks (*leveinim*)' [v. 3] — that is, we shall wear white (*lavan*) clothing, like the image of the pure *zaddiqim*, 'and burn it thoroughly' — to clap hand against hand in ardor (*hitlahavut* — lit., 'fiery ecstasy'). And all this, in order 'to make us a name there' — literally — 'and build us a city' — to conquer cities beneath our hand. But in the end, 'they had brick for stone' [v. 3] — that is, the white clothes they wore were as a stumbling block, and an obstacle; 'and slime (*ḥomer*) [for mortar]' — the initials of 'extraordinary sage and rabbi of rabbis' — as they held him to be and showed themselves — 'was slime' — literally, to sink and fall therein. 'So scattered them abroad from there ... because he confounded there [the language]' [v. 8] — that is, by their great sins they aroused strife and contention and vain hatred. 'And their languages were confused' [v. 9] — that no one knows what the other speaks. And understand this." — *Degel Maḥaneh ʾEfrayim*, 6a.

30 See this interesting letter in its entirety, which bears neither address nor date — *Ḥayyim va-Ḥesed*, pp. 10–17. I tend to think that this letter is fragmented in several places. The quotation brought here is on p. 17.

must "learn with *devequt*," implying that *devequt* was conceptualized as a certain emotional value connected with study, and not a pure contemplative value.[31]

I raise this question here only in order to point out that such a conflict, which bears major significance regarding its quietistic character, did exist within Hasidism. Analogous arguments were brought against the quietistic streams in Christianity: namely, that they have contempt for study because they are constantly engaged in contemplation, which is their major concern. In Hasidism, one may see this point as indicative of the existence of the problem and of the change of values which it precipitated in Hasidic life.

One is struck in Hasidism by the attempt to create a homogenous society, in which nobody is "outside of the system," and everyone is subject to the strict discipline of an order — a discipline which was organized along extremely conservative lines with regard to all practical questions. This attempt did not always bear actual fruit, and there is a certain wild or bohemian spirit which is very characteristic of it,[32] although not specifically with regard to matters of the *Shulḥan ᶜArukh*. The *Shulḥan ᶜArukh*, R. Joseph Caro's code of Jewish law, together with the glosses of R. Moses Isserles, remained as authoritative as they always had been for pious Jews. R. Ephraim of Sudylkow relates that, "we did not allow anyone to separate himself, Heaven forbid, and to go outside of the system, but all of us remained attached to one another up to the very highest one."[33] Even those sayings which have in them something of the provocative spirit, such as, "he should not be saddened when he neglects Torah or prayer" [34] are expressions, not of an anti-scholarly note, but of the new attitude towards the concept of sin, as I explained in the chapter devoted to this subject.[35] The Maggidic problematic became blurred in the later traditions of his school, as I have already noted, as the concept of *devequt* came to be used in what was a more liberal way from the point of view of mysticism. The concept acquired more of an emotional value, and was incorporated in an immanent manner within the realm of ethical teaching, so that

31 This approach is perhaps more reminiscent of the view of R. Ḥayyim of Volozhin than it is of the original doctrine of the Maggid. See, for example, R. Meshullam Feibush, who defines *devequt* at the time of study and during prayer in the same way: "that soul is attached to and comes close to God, may He be blessed." It is clear that we find here a deliberate obscuring of the Maggidic problematic (*Liqqutei Yeqarim*, p. 23d); see below.

32 See Scholem's description of R. Israel of Ruzhin, the so-called rabbi of Sadagora, "the greatest and most impressive figure of classical Zaddikism," who was "nothing but another Jacob Frank who has achieved the miracle of remaining an orthodox Jew." — *Major Trends*, p. 337.

33 *Degel Maḥaneh ᵓEfrayim*, 65b. The sense here is that one does not allow another person to commit a transgression.

34 *Ẓavaᵓat ha-Riva"sh*, 30b.

35 See Chapter 4.

only the conservative Maggidic formulation relating to the *mizvah* of study remained. One of the leading disciples of R. Meshullam Feibush of Zbarazh, R. Eliezer ha-Levi Horowitz, author of *Noᶜam Meggadim*, repeatedly tells us how much care the Baᶜal Shem Tov and the Maggid of Mezhirech took over Torah study:

> It is known from the holy one, Israel Besht, *z"l*, that thought is called "the father of speech," and speech "son," as is written concerning the verse, "And his father watched the matter" [Gen. 37:11]. And it may also be called "the first-born," it being the origin [lit., "first"] of speech and the preferred one, for following the intention of the heart [are the things]. And through this one may explain the verse, "and he shall assure your fulness and outflow" [sic! a corruption of Ex. 22:28] — that is, the aspects of expertise and dialectics (*beqiᵓut* and *pilpul*), Sinai [and uprooter of mountains]. "You shall not delay" — you shall not need to delay or to be late because of this, as in "and I have delayed until now" [Gen. 32:4], if you take care of the intention of your heart and of pure intention in prayer.[36] And this is what is said, "the first born of your sons give to me" [Ex. 22:28], as above, to interpret the [entire] verse in one way as concerning involvement in the Torah, as we have explained.[37]

Particularly interesting is the tone of his words when he attributes to the Maggid of Mezhirech an explicit warning to R. Yeḥiel Michel of Zloczow (one of the author's teachers) concerning the subject of study:

> He then alluded to their [i.e. the Sages] saying, "He should borrow by day and pay back by night." The Maggid warned our teacher, the light of Israel,[38] Rabbi Yeḥiel *z"l*, to complete his [daily] quotas [of study] at night before eating, even on a fast day. Examine there and see this as in our words.[39] And this is "your fulness" — to complete your set portion in Torah, which you did not complete during the day because of confusion; and "your outflow" take care "not to delay" — during the first free time that comes to you. Also, "the first born of your sons give to Me" — that is, the fast day; as we have expounded at length, and understand it. And the warning of the Maggid is alluded to in this Holy Scripture, as we have interpreted it.[40]

In my opinion, it is not at all impossible that these traditions cited in the name of the Maggid (and perhaps also in the name of the Besht) may contain a grain of

36 The implication is that he need not abandon study of Torah because of his lengthy prayer with *devequt*.

37 *Noᶜam Megaddim* (Lemberg, 1859), 18c. See also R. Meshullam Feibush, who warned strongly about the unconditional nature of study. See *Liqqutei Yeqarim*, 23d.

38 He regularly refers to R. Yeḥiel Michel of Zloczow by the title, "the light of Israel" (*ᵓOr Yisraᵓel*); see, e.g., *Liqqutei Yeqarim*, 19c.

39 I did not find this source.

40 *Noᶜam Megaddim*, p. 19a.

truth. However, there is an additional reason for the emphasis given to them in the school of the Maggid, or among the third generation of his disciples: namely, to completely nullify the fundamental conflict which the Maggid of Mezhirech knew and about which he took a firm stand: the conflict between study and *devequt*, or study with *devequt*. R. Meshullam explained his own path in Hasidism regarding this question as follows:

> ...but the essence of study of Torah for-its-own-sake must be to attach oneself to God, may He be blessed, and to humble and make oneself lowly before Him and before all. And the more Torah he studies, the more he will attach himself to God, may He be blessed, and come close to Him and be more humble of spirit.[41]

While the controversy with the scholars of the Mitnaggedic camp is continued here, it is no longer couched in terms of the confrontation [of values] formulated by the the Maggid, but in terms of the perception that study for the sake of acquiring social standing is invalid *per se*. This likewise corresponds to the traditions cited earlier in the name of R. Jacob Joseph of Polonnoye, and in that of the Ba^cal Shem Tov's grandson, R. Ephraim of Sudylkow. Only for a brief moment — in the Maggid's teaching — does the true controversy, with all of its spiritualistic dangers, rear its head, only to be immediately concealed once more, thanks to the self-censorship of Hasidism.

41 See Dubnow, *Toldot ha-Ḥasidut* p. 34, 62, 329–330, 401.

Chapter Fifteen

History and National Redemption

One of the problems concerning Hasidism which has aroused particular scholarly interest is that of the status of Messianism within the complex of ideas of Hasidic thinkers. Simon Dubnow[1] argues that the concept of redemption within history was blurred, claiming that the essential element in the Hasidic doctrine of redemption was personal rather than collective, and spiritual rather than historical. Gershom Scholem developed this approach further, describing it by the term, "the neutralization of the messianic idea."[2] On the other hand, Ben-Zion Dinur[3] stressed the specifically messianic motifs which are, as-it-were, found within Hasidic sources, his main evidence for this being the Hasidic ᶜ*aliyyot* (waves of immigration to the Land of Israel). I will not address myself here to the status of these ᶜ*aliyyot* in Hasidic ideology, as they are unrelated to the theoretical world of Hasidism and are not even associated with those formulae which occasionally mention the coming of the Messiah. I would accept Gershom Scholem's anti-messianic interpretation of the famous passage in the letter of the Ba'al Shem Tov to his brother-in-law, R. Gershon Kutover.[4]

I do not intend to give here a comprehensive presentation of the understanding of Exile (*Galut*), Redemption and the messianic idea within Hasidic thought, which is still a *desideratum*. I shall rather sketch a number of features of the Hasidic mood in relation to the immanent theoretical foundations of Hasidism, which clearly point towards the interiorization of the messianic interest, as expressed in the climate of intensive life between the *ẓaddiq* and his congregation and between man and himself. The historical realm almost completely lost the intense

1 See Dubnow, *Toldot ha-Ḥasidut*, pp. 34, 62, 329–330. 401.

2 See G. Scholem, "The Neutralization of the Messianic Idea in Hasidism," in his *The Messianic Idea in Judaism*, pp. 176–202 [originally published in *JJS* 20 (1970), 25–55]; *Major Trends*, p. 325 and also p. 330.

3 See Dinur, "The Beginnings of Hasidism" (see Introduction, n. 7), pp. 88–89.

4 Assuming that this is to be seen at all as an authentic letter. See Scholem's remarks in "The Historical Image of R. Israel Baal Shem Tov," p. 309. The letter is published at the end of R. Jacob Joseph of Polonnoye's *Ben Porat Yosef* (New York, 1954); from what is said there, this would seem to be a "reconstructed" version, and not the original version, which he never had; see *ad loc.*.

eschatological coloration which it had in Lurianic Kabbalah, and even more so in the Sabbatian movement. On the contrary: the "betrayal" of the Jewish people by history, so to speak, was interpreted by a number of major Hasidic thinkers as a kindness which God did to His people, which facilitated the possibility of communication between God and Israel in their common exile. This religious intimacy was acquired at the expense of historical life, which was not very highly viewed in the eyes of Hasidism. Spiritual life was understood in terms of an awakening from the Exile — which is no more than a concrete metaphor — to the true meaning of life. For the first time in the history of Jewish mysticism, we find here a mature mood among mystics who reveal a sense of self-awareness, consciously confronting the historical approaches within the Jewish tradition, and stating unequivocally that in Exile itself they have found the way to God. The Exile is no longer an obstacle to the attainment of spirituality; on the contrary, there is even a kind of happiness in sharing their lot with the cosmos as a whole, and with the Godhead therein. This sense of intimacy, experienced in the connection and attachment to the Absolute, pushed the historical messianic ideology to the margins of life. Behind the sayings of these Hasidic thinkers, one hears echoes of passivity with regard to history and external events; echoes, not of disappointment, but of inner spiritual strengthening which takes little notice of external reality. The vision which revealed itself to the eyes of the Hasidim was a kind of awakening and shaking off of the Exile, which was transformed into a symbol of imaginary life. As this was well expressed by R. Ephraim of Sudylkow:

> "And Jacob awoke from his sleep and said, 'Indeed, there is God in this place, and I did not know it'" [Gen. 28:16]. One may interpret this, that it is known that the Exile is called by the name "sleep" — that is, the removal and hiding of the Name, Heaven forbid — as is written, "And I will hide my face" [Deut. 31:18], etc.[5] And the redemption is when the Name reveals itself through the light of the Torah, as in, "Awake, awake, for your light is come" [conflation of Isa. 51:17 and 60:1] — that is, he shall awake from his sleep, for the light of the Torah and of the revelation of God may He be blessed has come, so to speak. And this is, "I will surely hide my face" [Deut., ibid.] — that is, I will conceal the Torah and its light, which is included in "I" (*anokhi*), and there will *ipso facto* result the hiddenness of My face, heaven forbid, for it is the revealing of His face, as-it-were, by the light of Torah which sheds light to those who exert themselves in it. And this is, "I am the Lord your God" [Ex. 20:2]; that is, "I" — which is the entirety of the entire Torah — am the Name *HVYH* blessed be He, which is the revelation of the Name by the light of the Torah, for the entire

5 The traditional interpretation clearly identifies the hiding of the Face with the historical Galut, while R. Ephraim attempts to remove the discussion from the historical plane and state that the "revelation of the face" is a spiritual change within the Exile itself.

Torah is composed of the names of the Holy One, blessed be He. This is alluded to in the verse, "And Jacob awoke from his sleep" [Gen., ibid.] — that is, from the Exile, [which is] compared to study [*shoneh* — a play on *shenah*, "sleep"], as in "we were as dreamers" [Ps. 126:1], and the Name *HVYH*, blessed be He, was revealed. Then he said, "Indeed, there is God in this place, and I did not know it" [Gen., ibid.]: "I" — that is, the light of the Torah included in *Anokhi* — "did not know" — that I am able to unify, which is knowledge by means of the Torah; because until then His face was hidden, but now the light of His face has been revealed by the light of the Torah; and understand.

Or one may say as is stated in the *Tiqqunim* [i.e., *Tiqqunei Zohar*]: "And the angel of God was seen by him from the heart of the fire" [Ex. 3:2] of prophecy. This was the first redemption, but the latter redemption will be through the heart of the fire of Torah, and this will be the complete redemption, after which there shall be no [more] Exile. And this is alluded to in, "And Jacob rose from his sleep" [Gen., ibid.] — from his studying [again, pun on *shenato*, "his sleep"/*mishnato*, "his studying"]: that is, that the latter redemption will take place in the heart of the flame of Torah. And this is, "and I did not know" [ibid.] — that is, until now I did not know [that this is] from the Torah, which is "I," for the former redemption was through the heart of the flame of prophecy. And the wise one shall understand; "give to a wise man, and he shall become wiser" [Prov. 9:9].

Or one may say, "And Jacob awoke from his sleep and said, 'Indeed, there is God in this place and I did not know it'" [Gen., ibid.]. And Rashi commented, "had I known, I would not have slept," as in the above saying, for the Exile is compared to a dream, as is said [above], "We were as sleepers." The matter being, that during the time of sleep a person sees in his dream imaginary things which are false, for the nature of a dream is an imaginary thing which is not true; similarly, the matter of the Exile as a whole is similar to sleep[6] and to a dream, for he does not know what is the true matter and the true purpose, but only imaginary things, which seem to each person to be true, and that thus it is fitting to serve Him, blessed be His Name. And the Redemption is that He enlightens their eyes, so that everyone sees the absolute truth and they leave Exile, which is falsehood. And thus it is with the individual in each person, in the mystery of "draw close to my soul, redeem it" [Ps. 69:19]. As in the image of a dream, when he heaven forbid sinks down into falseness, he is in Exile, which is compared to sleep and to a dream. And when God, blessed be He, helps him, to refine his mind and his thoughts with holiness and purity, so that his thought not wander about in any thing save to God alone and he enters into the limit of truth, then he merits the aspect of *HVYH*, blessed be He, which is [like] a brilliant crystal, [which casts] a pure and shining light without any admixture. And all his dreams are

6 A variation of the Rabbinic dictum based on Songs 5:2, "'I am asleep and my heart is awake': I am asleep in the Exile and my heart is awake for the time of redemption." However, this variation carries a spiritual rather than an historical message.

> true, and everything he sees is true, and everything that is true — he sees. And this, because he has left the Exile and the falsehood ...[7]

Just as the concepts of Exile and Redemption acquired spiritual meanings, so did the concepts of "the Land of Israel" and "outside of the Land" become, for R. Elimelekh of Lyzhansk, symbols of one's spiritual status:

> For it states in the Talmud, "One who stands outside of the Land and prays, shall direct his heart towards the Land of Israel [...]; one who is in the Land of Israel shall direct his heart toward Jerusalem [...]; one [in Jerusalem] should direct his heart towards the Temple [...]; one [who stands within the Temple] shall direct his heart towards the Holy of Holies" [Berakhot 30a]. Yet it would seem that, if it depends upon *kavvanah*, then even one standing outside of the Land should direct his heart toward the Holy of Holies ... But it is certainly impossible that a person may grasp the greatest, supreme holiness all at once, but he must go from stage to stage. And our rabbis said that one who is still outside of the Land should make an effort and sanctify himself with the extra holiness of the sanctity of the Land of Israel ... And when a person behaves thus, then in whatever attribute he may be, his prayer is acceptable before Him, may He be blessed and praised. But as for one who stands outside of the Land — that is, who has not yet sanctified himself and is full of alien thoughts and fleshly appetites — it is impossible for his prayer to ascend before Him, may He be blessed ...[8]

This homily implies that the directing of oneself towards the Land of Israel is neither a geographical nor a symbolic concept (as the Kabbalists interpreted it), but a value concept. R. Elimelekh interprets another Rabbinic saying likewise:

> "He who dwells in the Land of Israel is as if he has a God" [Ketubot 110b] — it only seems that he has one, but he has not one in truth ... "He who dwells outside of the Land, is as if he has no God" — he too seems as if, but he has one in truth.[9]

In this way, spiritual dependency is completely separated from real historical factors.

The idea that the historical redemption of Israel is tied to its spiritual renewal is already found in the Biblical understanding, and is a fixed element in the unfolding of the various different streams of Jewish historical-philosophic thought. The significant change in the Hasidic climate of thought lies in the effective weakening of the tension of anticipating the Redemption, and in the internalization of the renewal in a spiritual direction. Such sayings as that of the author

7 *Degel Maḥaneh ᵓEfrayim*, 14d–15a.

8 *Noᶜam Elimelekh, Parashat Shemot*, 19a.

9 Ibid., *Parashat Lekh Lekha*, 4b.

of the *Tiqqunim* that, "through this work [i.e., the *Zohar*] one goes out of Exile" — which motivated R. Isaac de Lattes to enter into a polemic permitting the publication of *Sefer ha-Zohar*[10] — or of R. Ḥayyim Vital's struggle to clear the way for Lurianic Kabbalah in the name of the messianic idea,[11] are no longer common coin in Hasidic thought. They do not do things "for the sake of" hastening the Messiah or the redemption of Israel; rather, whatever innovations take place are performed for the sake of the action itself and carry their own value. The one who is addressed regarding action is the individual person, who becomes his own messiah by redeeming himself from the spiritual imprisonment in which he finds himself, i.e., the imprisonment of the spirit within the flesh. The individual expands his knowledge of Torah together with the expansion of his consciousness of the spiritual element within himself, and he does not anticipate a Messiah who will bring a new Torah — neither one of "Creation" nor of "Emanation," as the Sabbatians had it. Moreover: this expansion of consciousness is depicted at times as a teaching of remembering,[12] as redemption from the bonds of matter which stifle the revealing of the elements of the spirit hidden between the lines of the Torah and in the depths of human consciousness: destruction of the Exile of the spirit by the expansion of the "I." From this, one may also understand the fundamental difference between two basic approaches: that which reveals the Torah as a spiritual body which encompasses the path towards a messianic age; and the Hasidic emphasis upon its revelation in the individual realm, as obligating each and every Jew. According to Hasidism, so long as every Jew is not personally redeemed, there is no room for talk about the perfection of the spiritual reading of the Torah. The appearance of a Messiah who will "give" such a Torah is irrelevant, or more correctly no longer possible, as the important thing is that man should "discover" it for himself through his own "labor" of refining his own intellectual reading. Otherwise, some of the Hasidim argue, this mitigates against the idea of free choice! This interesting nuance, which I have not encountered in any earlier source in the Jewish tradition, is indicative of the individualistic direction of the messianic idea, just as it is of the pushing aside of the national messianic tension. Man is required to "arrive at" the Torah and its new reading through his own powers, in order to find the relation of the Divine name to the root of his own soul by means of the unique combination which relates to himself.

10 See his Introduction to the Mantua edition of the *Zohar*, and see also the discussion of the problem by I. Tishby, "The Controversy Concerning *Sefer ha-Zohar* in 16th Century Italy" (Heb.), in his *Ḥiqrei Qabbalah u-sheluḥoteha*, I (Jerusalem, 1982), 79–130.

11 See the Introduction to *ᶜEẓ Ḥayyim*.

12 Particularly in *ʾOr ha-Meʾir*, 48c–d, by R. Naḥum of Chernobyl, where we find an idea reminiscent of the psychological-mystical context used in the explanation of the remarks of R. Ḥayyim of Amdur; see above, Chap. 9.

No redeemer can know the secret of the combination of the root of the individual soul, and it is only by means of the spiritual realization of all "six hundred thousand" souls of Israel, which correspond to the number of the letters in the Torah, that the true redemption may come about. The enslavement of the Exile is understood as a metaphysical bondage, and Hasidism's primary effort is directed towards its understanding within this situation, and not in historical speculations. I shall cite some remarks of R. Ze᾿ev Wolf of Zhitomir, who developed this problem quite thoroughly:

> "And God said to Moses, write for yourself these things ..." [Ex. 34:27]. Rashi explained: "[These] you may write for yourself, but you are not allowed to write down words of Oral Torah."... For the contents of the things, which are Written Torah, are the letters of thought, and the Oral Torah is the letters of the five organs of speech, and it is already known that the aspect of thought is the general rule, which requires detailing.[13] And He, may He be blessed, does not receive such an increment of pleasure from us, the children of Israel, in general, but from each one of us as an individual, each one of Israel ... For God is desirous of us, to receive an addition of pleasure from our separated parts, in distinct bodies; and the more the multiplication of souls is increased and added to, and [the more] they leave the aspect of generality for particularity, so are increased and multiplied the interpretations of the Torah and its combinations, to the number of the portions of the souls and their fastening onto the letters of the Torah. And we have already hinted above that it is incumbent upon every person in Israel to come from his own attribute, with the combination which is incumbent upon him, to perform, by means of the fittingness of his actions, that combination of the Torah made and combined by the value of its letters, in which he has a hold in the Torah; and they wait until his coming through, in the preparation of his actions and his good works, and he makes of the Torah a fixed combination. And these combinations, which depend upon the individual acts, the portions of his soul, are called the Oral Torah, which are the aspect of the individual, as against the letters of thought, that is, the Written Torah, which are the totality of the combinations which the Holy One blessed be He gave to Moses at Sinai. For the giving of the Written Torah by Moses our teacher was only in a general way, the generality of the sixty myriad souls of Israel; and from this totality thereafter, throughout the generations, they expounded the details of their individuality, in their aspects and combinations ...[14] And what follows from all of the above is that even Moses did not

13 Meaning that the Torah as "thought" is undifferentiated.

14 Here he quotes Jacob Ẓemah, author of *Naggid u-Meẓaveh*, on the aggadah in Menaḥot 29b concerning what happened when Moses went on high, and what transpired between him and R. Akiva. See on this G. Scholem's article, "Revelation and Tradition as Religious Categories in Judaism", p. 283. One sees here, particularly, the fundamental difference between the approach of R. Ze᾿ev Wolf and that of *Naggid u-Meẓaveh*, as R. Ze᾿ev Wolf does not at all refer to Oral Torah in the historical meaning of the term, but only as a spiritual teaching which may be derived through

> know the aspect of the Oral Torah in all of its details, according to the number of the generations that were to come after him, but they must arrive by themselves at their own individual combinations, corresponding to their actions and their connection to the Torah and Divine service, upon which their [free] choice depends ... And from this you may understand what is before you: The Holy One blessed be He said, "Write for yourself these things," specifically. And Rashi explained, "You are not allowed to write the Oral Torah": that is, the Written Torah, to be the generality of the Oral Torah, is fitting to be written only by you for yourself, because of your being the general mind of the sixty myriad souls. And in accordance with the attribute of his mind he was able to serve the Creator, blessed be He, and to expound to subsequent generations, in the attribute of "branches of Him"; and they were also called "the generation of knowledge," in the general aspect of the Written Torah. But not so the Oral Torah, which is the aspect of the combinations of the alphabet of the individual souls of Israel from the day it was given until the future, when the Torah will be revealed in the quintessence of clarity ... Therefore, you are not allowed to write the Oral Torah, because upon this depends the essence of the choice to be free, in the hands of man, and they must themselves come to the aspect of their individual combination, according to their consciousness and the fitness of their actions ... "For according to (*ᶜal pi*) these things I have made a covenant with you and with Israel" [Ex., ibid.]. The intention is that, when those things, which at the beginning were in the secret of thought — [that is] Written Torah — come orally (*ᶜal peh*) ... then "I have made a covenant," which touches the value of the power of your consciousness at the end of the generations ... And certainly, the covenant I made with you which pertains to your value is not similar to the covenant I made with you and also with all Israel, in which each and every person must attain by himself the attribute of the combination of the letters of the Torah which await for him, and you are not allowed to reveal [it], so that the choice may be free in the hand of all. Now examine the matter and you will understand wonders.[15]

The author of *ʾOr ha-Meʾir* poses the hypothetical practical question of what would happen were an all-inclusive "general sage" to come and discover all of the soul combinations in one fell swoop, thereby exempting the Jews from the labor involved in discovering a spiritual direction. The negative answer given clearly indicates that the Hasidim were more intent upon directing themselves toward the redeeming path than they were in Messianic results.

> ... And we find regarding the words said in truth that, should there come a great

"combination" from the undifferentiated mystical body called the Written Torah. This is generally speaking the stand of the Kabbalists, who see Kabbalah as an Oral Torah, given at Sinai alongside the Written Torah.

15 *ʾOr ha-Meʾir*, 82a–c.

> general sage and herald good tidings, to teach and instruct each person in Israel, telling him, "Do thus," and revealing those combinations incumbent upon us to do, each and every one in terms of his choice and apprehension. And this righteous teacher would reveal them immediately, saying from the beginning of a thing its end, what will be thereafter at the end of days. Who would not follow his discipline, to do those things by reason of which he will cause the combinations of the future (so that redemption will soon prevail)? But in so doing, the choice is [no longer] free, because it was given over into the hands of the people of Israel that each one according to his awareness and his apprehension and effort in the service of his Creator would come himself to these self-same combinations which he has in the letters of the Torah. And if not, he has affected nothing by his having been created in this world, and what does it benefit him[16] that the general sage, who orders for his good, brought this about and told him what is fitting for him to do, in combinations, when the choice is in his hand. And if so, his choice is nullified![17]

The opposition between free choice and "knowledge" of the spiritual Torah, and the clear position that one should not acquire redemption at the price of reneging on the mystical effort, is a nuance which, as we noted, arouses particular interest in the context of our discussion, and brings out the nature of the Hasidic phenomenon: we find that the value of effort and of individual attainment compete on the national level with that of the "last hour." R. Zeʾev Wolf states this explicitly:

> Just as, when the redemption of the Exodus from Egypt began, Moses took the children of Israel out of their straitness, so today, in every generation until the final Redemption, the aspect of the knowledge [18] of the enlightened person is what takes him out of his own personal straitness.[19]

A homily in a similar spirit, interpreting the "Day of the Lord" as a day of personal tidings, a kind of "revelation of Elijah" to each individual within Israel, appears in R. Naḥum of Chernobyl's *Meʾor ʿEynayim*. The allegorical use of the concept of the "Day of the Lord" as a time of expansion of individual consciousness is significant for its shift of terminology associated with historical concepts to the sphere of values:

16 The answer to the question, "what benefit is it to God...?", lies in the Redemption, which will take place when all of the correct combinations are fulfilled. The author therefore prefers free choice above Redemption.

17 *ʾOr ha-Meʾir*, 39a–b.

18 Moses is called *Daʿat* in Kabbalah, while here Moses is transformed into a symbol of the individual's "*Daʿat*."

19 *ʾOr ha-Meʾir*, 46c. This idea is also expounded by R. Elimelekh of Lyzhansk, *Noʿam Elimelekh*, 24a, and is quoted in the Besht's name in *Degel Maḥaneh ʾEfrayim*, 63c: "And one may explain also, in a particular way, as I received from my grandfather, *z"l*, that every person is required to redeem his own soul, in the manner of, 'Draw close to my soul, redeem it' [Ps. 69:19]."

> Behold, if a person receives some good news, or even if during the time of study, when he has difficulty [understanding] some subject before the knowledge comes to him, there enters into him something like a tiding, that he feels that a certain point has entered into his mind[20] — this is called the aspect of Elijah. And afterwards the earth is filled with knowledge, that his mind is expanded and filled with vitality, and it is then easy for him to unite [all] his parts, including the aspect of his legs, to the good. For in truth, a person who bears a good tiding has embodied in himself a spark of Elijah, literally, for it is he who brings all the good tidings in the world, only it is embodied in the one who tells, for the aspect of Elijah is from the six days of Creation. ... Therefore, when one has the opportunity to tell some good tiding, each one girds himself to run and to tell it, for his soul feels the aspect of Elijah and wants to bring it inside himself; even though people do not feel this [i.e. consciously],[21] nevertheless their "sign" (*mazal*) is deserving of it. And if he were to have awareness (*daᶜat*), he would be able to begin to serve God with the attribute of Elijah embodied within him, and then he would go with it from [one] level to a greater level. And for the person who receives the tiding, a spark of Elijah also enters within him, and his awareness is expanded[22] and he is also able to attach himself easily to the Creator, blessed be He, [through] the portion called "his legs."[23] And this is then called "the coming of the great Day of the Lord" [Mal. 3:23] — that by reason of this he has brought God within himself, and this is, "Behold I send you [Elijah the prophet]" [ibid.]. For "send" is in the present tense, for it is always thus, in every person and at every time, that the aspect of Elijah is sent to the Jewish person, "before the coming of the day of the Lord" [ibid.], as explained ...[24]

Another interesting point, which certainly played a role in the neutralization of the messianic idea, is manifested in the development of the institution of the *ẓaddiq*. In Hasidism, the *ẓaddiq*[25] does not fulfill any function as national redeem-

20 He does not view the understanding of the subject itself, in the discursive sense, as a "revelation of Elijah," but rather identifies it with the meta-intellectual process which precedes the concrete contents, which is also referred to here as "one point." This question is reminiscent of the Maggid's doctrine concerning the knowledge which comes to a person from "the pre-existent intellect" (*qadmut ha-sekhel*), although there the messianic-individual connotation is not stressed.

21 Implying that this "attribute" is not known to everyone, but is nevertheless present in everyone.

22 The "spark" may be lit in the heart of the other, to "expand his knowledge." This point is particularly interesting for an understanding of the group mysticism connected with meta- psychological elements in Hasidic teaching.

23 The "feet" are used here as a euphemism for the lowly matters of everyday life which need to be brought into holiness; as such, it is peripheral to our present discussion.

24 *Meʾor ᶜEynayim*, 69a–b.

25 One must not forget that we are concerned here only with Hasidism through the end of the 18th century; we do not discuss here, for example, Braslav Hasidism, which was a unique phenomenon which does not enter into our historical framework. Concerning Braslav's approach to this matter, for example, see J. G. Weiss, "Studies in R. Naḥman of Braslav's Self-Understanding" (Heb.), *Sefer*

er, but purely that of individual redeemer. By this, we refer not to his teaching of a spiritual path, but to the actual involvement of the *ẓaddiq*'s consciousness with that of each individual in his flock.[26] This is not the place to discuss the nature of Hasidism's intense involvement with the "descent" of the *ẓaddiq* to redeem man from sin, although this in itself is evidence of the non-urgent sense of time, the feeling of leisure implied by the postponement of questions of national redemption and of the End. The atmosphere is no longer like that of the *tiqqunei teshuvah* (theurgic acts of repentance) of Nathan of Gaza,[27] which were a kind of "recipe" for the eve of redemption by which to hasten the final hour. Here, the *ẓaddiq* works to build a society of individuals who seek to pave the way towards spiritual perfection in the here and now. True, there do occasionally appear messianic formulae, such as that "our righteous Messiah" will be revealed "quickly in our day" in wake of this perfection, just as many other traditional formulae appear in sources such as this. However, not only is there a difference between the atmosphere present in Hasidism with regard to these questions and those present in Sabbatianism, but it even differs from the more long-term theology of Lurianic Kabbalah in terms of its inner interest. Whereas the Lurianic doctrine of *kavvanot* sought to repair the stature of the Godhead conceived of as "the stature of Primeval Adam," Hasidism sought first and foremost to correct the stature of the lower Adam [i.e., earthly man]; in Hasidic sources, one clearly feels a kind of love and attention of man to spiritual matters for their own sake. The intimate tone with which these individual questions are treated, and the theories of the congregation and the *ẓaddiq*, bear testimony to a new spirit within Jewish mysticism, and of a satisfaction with an interiorization going beyond history, and not necessarily concerned with meeting it. The *ẓaddiq* is a kind of messianic age writ small, with which one may be satisfied for the present; he quenches the thirst for redemption at the historical cross-roads. True, he serves as a kind of "little temple" in the eyes of the Hasidim, but this "little" is sufficient to serve as a long-term temporary substitute, and in particular is able to bring about a profound psychological transformation in which the attitude towards the immediate question of concrete historical redemption is a passive one.

It would be misleading were we to speak about a deliberate silence concerning

ha-Yovel li-khevod Gershom Scholem bi-meʾot lo shishim shanah (Jerusalem, 1958), pp. 232–245; I. Tishby and J. Dan, "Ḥasidism," *Enẓeqlopedyah ha-ʿIvrit*, Vol., 17 (Jerusalem–Tel Aviv, 1964–65), col. 772; Arthur Green, *Tormented Master* (University, Ala., 1976), pp. 182–220.

26 See on this J. G. Weiss, "The Beginnings of the Hasidic Path"; R. Schatz, "The Doctrine of the Ẓaddik," pp. 370–371.

27 See I. Tishby, "The *Tiqqunei Teshuvah* of R. Nathan of Gaza" (Heb.), in his *Netivei ʾEmunah u-Minut*, pp. 30–51 [originally published in *Tarbiẓ* 15 (1944), pp. 161–180].

the question of Messiah and the historical redemption; on the contrary, the traditional formulae accompany the sources from time to time as self-evident. But that is in itself the strongest proof: they are echos of a historical consciousness which has no internal continuity with the aim of the homilies in whose context they appear, being used by their authors almost unconsciously without forming an integral part of the spiritual renewal. It is true that popular Hasidic folk-legend places more stress upon the concrete messianic element, but even so we find the Kotsker Hasidim singing: "To Kotsk one does not travel, to Kotsk one walks on foot [as on a pilgrimage]; Kotsk is like the Temple." This ditty was a spontaneous expression of the feeling of the existence of a Temple within Exile. The nostalgia for finding God and for closeness to God are so overpowering in Hasidism as to nullify the feeling of Exile. Its thinkers waged war against the "feeling of Exile," in which they saw the stumbling block to true redemption; many of them saw the Exile as providing the ideal conditions for man's communion with God, a communion of destiny between the exiled Divinity and the people of Israel in Exile — as if both needed to be exiled from their rightful place in order to revivify the true connection between them. R. Uziel Meisels states in the name of the Maggid:

> By way of parable, my master and teacher, the *Gaʾon* and *ḥasid*, R. Dov Baer, *z"l*, may his soul be in Eden, said: [This is compared to] a king who, when he is in his home and his palace, not everyone is allowed to come to him; but when he is travelling on the way, at that time whosoever wishes to come close is allowed to do so.[28]

According to these sources, the historical Exile is no longer an obstacle to the true meeting with God. On the contrary, the renewal of true "knowledge of God" in Exile overcomes the traditional ideologies which state that one cannot "apprehend" in Exile that which can be apprehended in the Land of Israel. For example, R. Abraham Ḥayyim of Zloczow quotes the Maggid:

> In Egypt there was exile of knowledge (or "consciousness" — *daʿat*), so that even Israel did not clearly know the aspect of knowledge, as was said by the Holy Rabbi, the holy lamp, R. Dov Baer, *z"l*: "In the beginning our ancestors were worshippers of idols" [Passover Haggadah]. "Our ancestors" are called Wisdom, Understanding and Knowledge (*Ḥokhmah–Binah–Daʿat*). And Knowledge [is the attribute] that discriminated between the light of the deeds of the righteous and the darkness of the deeds of the wicked. But since Knowledge was in Exile, they worshipped God for their own pleasure as well,[29] and this was idolatry. "And now the Place [i.e. God] has brought

28 *Tifʾeret ʿUziel*, 137a and, in greater detail, in *ʾOr Torah*, 11a.

29 The distinction between Divine service which entails self-benefit and that which does not is a quietistic distinction *par excellence*. The Christian quietists protested against pleasure derived from mystical drunkenness. Hasidism was also opposed to mystical hedonism.

> us close to His worship" [ibid.] — that the attribute of knowledge has been revealed, and they worship God alone. Thus far his words.[30]

In Hasidic teaching, the common destiny of Israel and God became an existential religious problem for the first time. The ancient Midrash, according to which the Shekhinah went into exile wherever Israel was exiled,[31] itself has a history as long as the Exile. The myth concerning the sharing and mourning of the Shekhinah for the pain of Israel remains alive and vibrant alongside other interpretations within Jewish mysticism, in which the Shekhinah acquired the symbolic image of a Divine hypostasis. The symbolic level in Kabbalah did not negate the weight of myth, which reflects the bitter lot and sense of participation of God with Israel in which God descends to "the marketplace of the tanners"[32] in order to court a part of His own Self — the Shekhinah. It is difficult to know whether Jewish mysticism paid more attention to the satisfaction felt in this intimacy with God in Galut, or to the pain that it was thus. The mystics and religious poets of sixteenth century Safed wove their finest expressions of lyricism and of nostalgic national romanticism around the figure of the Shekhinah. One of them, while visiting the Wailing Wall, even had a vision of the Shekhinah in the form of a woman filled with anguish[33] — not to mention the personal erotic motifs with which Sabbatianism clothed the description of the relations between the Messiah and the Shekhinah.[34] Hasidism retained these mythical motifs as they were, but gave them a meta-psychological interpretation. In its homilies, which have a definite theoretical aim, the shared destiny of the people and of the Godhead which went into Exile with them was removed from the mythical realm and became a sharing by virtue of a meta-psychological law. For the first time, this was understood as a shared destiny of inner essence, taking place by virtue of the law of Divine immanence. The Shekhinah here becomes a part of Jewish mysticism,[35] whose redemption from Exile depends upon the redemption of the soul of each individual. The redemption is no longer a matter of a metaphorical use of language (which is perhaps the way one ought to understand the original intention of the Midrash), nor is it thought of as a matter of the wholeness of the processes within the theosophical life, a maturing process by which the divine elements living within it in latent form are developed. This aspect of "Revelation of the Shekhinah" is the freeing of the

30 Abraham Ḥayyim of Zloczow, *ʾOraḥ le-Ḥayyim*, 127b.

31 Megillah 29a.

32 See *Zohar* III: 115b.

33 See on this Scholem, *Sabbatai Ṣevi*, p. 61, n. 83.

34 See ibid., p. 802, and also pp. 870–71.

35 On the details of the doctrine of the Shekhinah, see above, Chap. 8.

Shekhinah from the inner bondage of the soul, an active revelation of the spirit and of self-messianism. The Hasidim are no longer particularly interested in the metaphor of the "tanner's market," but in emptying this inner "place" called the soul of man, so that God may find it clean and pure and worthy of dwelling therein. The paradoxical romanticism of the Midrash, which knows how to bring God within the boundaries of the filthy "marketplace" and to expose His love to the test, is a far cry from the spiritual interest in the purification of the character and the heart to welcome the appearance of the redeeemer from within. In Hasidism, myth was transformed into mysticism.

In this mood, the historical exile does not stand in the way of the encounter between God and the Jew, for it is precisely His presence in Exile which is the guarantee of His communion: He is able to speak to us out of our own consciousness and within the framework of this consciousness itself. He may lose something of the glory and awe of His transcendence, but He is far closer to man in his immanent presence (that is: the presence of the Shekhinah in Exile, within the soul of man), and the Shekhinah goes into Exile in order to meet man.[36] In the following sermon of R. Elimelekh of Lyzhansk, all of the motifs thus far mentioned are combined, and there is no doubt in my mind as to their tendency. These are his words:

> As I heard, a sweet parable from the mouth of our master, the Rabbi, the Maggid of Rovno [i.e., the Maggid of Mezhirech], *z"l* ... We see that at present, while we are in this bitter Exile, there are people who enjoy the holy spirit more easily than in the days of the prophets, who required oaths and much isolation, as is known, in order to acquire prophecy and the holy spirit. And he said a marvelous, sweet parable of this: it is like a king who is in the place of his glory in his house, in his court and palace, whom a certain friend of the king wished to invite to his home to a banquet. The king will then certainly be angry with him, for it is not suitable to the honor of the king to leave his palace for the home of others, even if the banquet be very elaborate. And it is impossible to invite the king to one's home until he has made many preparations, and placed there advisors and nobles who will find favor in the eyes of the king, that he should come to the banquet. But when the king is travelling on the way and wishes to lodge on the way, then when he finds a clean place in an inn, even if this inn be in a village, it is a fitting resting place for him to lodge, so long as it is clean. And the [meaning of the] parable is understood: When the Temple was standing, and the Shekhinah of His glory was in the Holy of Holies, then if a person would wish to draw down the Holy Spirit or prophecy, he needed to perform great labors, as we find in the Rejoicing of the Water-Drawing [*Simḥat Beit ha-Shoʾevah* — a celebration held in the Temple during the nights of the festival of Sukkot], where they drew down the

36 See the story related in *Seder ha-Dorot he-Ḥadash*, p. 30, concerning the rabbi of Sadagora who was "exiled" to the Czarist state, where he attained a sublime level of living as a transient.

> Holy Spirit. But now in our bitter exile, when His holy Shekhinah has been exiled with us, and because of our great sins It wanders about the land, and Its great longing is to find a dwelling place in which to lodge: then if It finds a lodge and a clean place — that is, a person who is clean of sin and transgression — there shall be His dwelling.[37]

If the highest expression of the doctrine of the Exile of the Godhead in Lurianic theosophy is found in the idea of God's withdrawal (*ẓimẓum*) into the recesses of His own self,[38] in Hasidism a fundamental change has come about — namely, the perception of the metaphysical Exile in terms of the psychic realm of man. Regarding the question under discussion here, the cutting edge of this transition was that the inner process of individual liberation and redemption functions, at least for the present, as a replacement for the historical redemption. Put otherwise, Hasidic spirituality is clearly non-Messianic in the national sense.

37 *Noᶜam Elimelekh*, *Parashat Va-yeshev*, 12c.

38 See on this Scholem, *Major Trends*, p. 261.

Afterword

In the present work, I have attempted to present one of the central view points within Hasidism during the period of its splendor. Through analysis of its theoretical sources, based upon philological examination, I have tried to clarify those problems which arise from a consistent, close reading of its sermons and homilies, in which one seemingly finds only intellectual chaos. Such a reading, with the aim of understanding specific problems, is not to be understood as an attempt to impose the problems of the scholar upon irrelevant texts, but rather as an attempt to understand those problems of which the author himself was conscious and translate them into the language of the reader, if need be. The term quietism, which I have used in reference to the phenomenon I have attempted to describe, was not necessarily known to the authors of these Hasidic teachings; nevertheless, the use of such a term is valid for purposes of communication among all those interested in Hasidism as a phenomenon within the history of religion, provided that its connotations are consistent with its own spiritual contents. This work is thus an attempt to identify the quietistic elements within Hasidic thought, to isolate them through analysis, and to demonstrate that these elements, as they may be distinguished from the many subjects which I have treated, combine into a coherent pattern of thought which supports a religious phenomenology. I have also discussed the nature of Hasidic quietism as compared with Christian quietism, and the points with which it differs. My intention in this was not to engage in a full-scale comparative study, but merely to define the problematics involved in tracing the parameters of Hasidic quietism, and to clarify the matter by means of comparison with a similar phenomenon, at least in its general outlines.

The common denominator of the principal questions discussed — such as the problem of the *miẓvot*, of prayer, and of man's relation to his personal and his national-social destiny — is concern with the praxis of man: that is, the question of the meaningfulness of activity. I have shown that, even where all of the normative obligations of the tradition regarding action remained in force, and perhaps specifically through them, the problem of the value of action arose. The quietistic element was manifested in a different way with regard to each of the problems we have mentioned, but the totality of these elements supports the conclusion that what we find here is a strikingly clear example of a fundamentally quietistic phenomenon. To my mind, the religious problematics implied in the presentation of these problems by the various Hasidic thinkers cannot be read differently. Even though there are numerous sources in which these same questions are dealt with without entering into the problematics of quietism and activism, this does not free us from relating to those sources which do explicitly relate to the *ḥasid* as such, as one who creates something new in his innermost world. I am aware that there were many innovations created in the Hasidic world, but I believe that the problem of quietism is deserving of special attention as the decisive *novellum* of Hasidism as a phenomenon, as we are here no longer dealing with isolated elements, but with a broad, overall conception, a fundamental tendency of a religious movement, and the way in which this tendency is expressed.

It is not the intention of this book to represent Hasidism as identical with quietism, but rather to point towards quietistic elements which were dominant within the religious life of Hasidism. The accepted pattern of discussion regarding Hasidism, which primarily focused upon the active element therein — which is what is most strikes in terms of external practices — in my opinion both required and justified the treatment of the inner theoretical aspect of Hasidism, which perhaps led us towards a deeper understanding of what is taking place between the lines of this complex world. The history of Hasidic speculation during the eighteenth century is largely marked by this question, as illustrated by the struggles within the school of the Maggid of Mezhirech described in this volume.

We are not concerned here with those aspects of Hasidism which can be expressed as a new *credo*. The confrontation of its ideas with those of traditional Judaism was not one which destroyed the values of the past in an unequivocal manner, nor does it enter into conflict with specific dogmas as was the case with Christian quietism. Nevertheless, there is a kind of border line "discomfort": a sense of walking a tightrope, on which it is difficult to know at exactly which point one would find oneself endangering the basic heritage of Jewish tradition. Hasidism did not always publicly walk this tightrope, and at times even refrained from doing so as a matter of principle. But here we are already leaving the realm of our discussion, whose purpose has been to describe the nature and meaning of this tightrope walking, to the point that it did go.

Appendix

The Baᶜal Shem Tov's Commentary to Psalm 107: Myth and Ritual of the Descent to Sheᵓol

I

The commentary to Psalm 107, popularly known as the *Commentary to Hodu* (after the first word of that psalm), was attributed to the Baᶜal Shem Tov from the time of its first appearance under the title *Sefer Qatan* (Zhitomir, 1805),[1] based upon the text in the possession of R. Shmelke of Nikolsburg. It was printed a second time in Lestzov in 1816, and has since then been reprinted numerous times and corrected on the basis of the conjectures of the various printers.

In the first collection of the writings of the "early masters" of Hasidism — *Keter Shem Tov* (Zolkiew, 1784) — mention is made of the Besht's Commentary to Psalm 107, and his comment on v. 5, "hungry and thirsty ..." — a section which appears in all the printed versions — is quoted. This section is also brought in R. Levi Yitzḥak of Berdichev's *Shemuᶜah Ṭovah* (Warsaw, 1938).[2] In Prayer Books of the Lurianic rite from the eighteenth and nineteenth century, Psalm 107 is printed immediately prior to the *Minḥah* service for Friday afternoon; in most of

* This Appendix was originally published in Hebrew, in *Tarbiẓ* 42 (1973), pp. 154–184.

1 On the editions of this tractate, see A. M. Haberman, "*Sefer Ẓavaᵓat ha-Riva"sh* and Other Early Collections of the Besht's Words: A Bibliographical Listing" (Heb.), in *Sefer ha-Besh"t*, ed. Y. L. Maimon (Jerusalem, 1960), pp. 48–49.

2 This is a collection of the teachings of R. Levi Yitzḥak of Berdichev, recorded mostly during the late 1760's and early '70's. The manuscripts from which the book was prepared belonged to the Maggid of Kosnitz and to R. Judah Aryeh Leib Alter of Gur (the author of *Sefat ᵓEmet*); there is no way of knowing in which of the two manuscripts the above-mentioned passage in the name of the Besht was found. One should note that, at the end of this passage, the printed edition states: "examine his [i.e., the Besht's] commentary elsewhere." If this is not the editor's addition, then R. Levi Yitzḥak must have known of the existence of an entire commentary to the psalm, of which he only cited a brief passage. To strengthen my argument, see below, note 14. Meanwhile, it has become clear to me that R. Levi Yitzḥak of Berdichev is the author of the main body of traditions of the writings of the Maggid of Mezhirech, and he was also the (first?) one to transmit the tradition that the *Commentary to Hodu* was from the Besht. See Schatz, "Introduction," *Maggid Devarav le-Yaᶜaqov*, p. 14 ff.

these *siddurim*, this custom is not specifically identified as an innovation of the Besht. The only exception to this is *Sod ᶜAvodah u-Moreh Ẓedeq* (Slavita, 1821), which states on p. 128b:

> A person [should feel] an awakening during the Afternoon Prayer of the Eve of the Sabbath. And it was instituted by the Besht, *z"l*, whose soul is in the supernal hidden place, that one should recite Psalm 107 every Sabbath eve, because he needs to refine himself more and more at that time. And there are mentioned there the four who need to give thanks.[3] And the first of these [i.e. those who were lost in the desert] uses the language of speech [a pun on *midbar* (desert) / *dibbur* (speech)], for when he comes to pray, he is lost in the speech, and is unable to bring all of his attributes into the speech.

At the bottom of the page it states: "This psalm speaks of those four who are required to give thanks to God, who has released them from trouble to relief, etc."

The *Commentary* to Psalm 107 was not printed in even one of the above-mentioned Prayer Books of *Nusaḥ ha-Ari*, nor does it appear in any manuscripts of this rite.[4] Only one among all these manuscripts, Jerusalem–National Library 8° 1392, is deserving of special mention, in that on page 4b (unnumbered), Psalm 107 is brought without any commentary, while on p. 67b it states with regard to the phrase *Hodu* in Psalm 105: "*Hodu* is also numerically equal to 'I shall be' (*ᵓehyeh*), alluding to the [*Sefirah* of] *Keter* of *ᶜAsiyyah* ... Therefore we recite the psalm *Hodu* prior to *Qabbalat Shabbat* (the prayer for Inaugurating the Sabbath), and such was the custom of our master."[5] From what is said there, it follows that special ritual practices were connected in the Lurianic Kabbalah in Safed with the recitation of Psalm 105 prior to *Minḥah*, but this does not refer to Psalm 107, which is our present concern.

On the other hand, examination of the prayer books reveals a widespread custom

3 A reference to the Talmudic exegesis of this psalm as the basis for the public recitation of a special blessing, *Birkat ha-Gomel*, by those who have been saved from serious danger: "Said Rab Judah in the name of Rab: Four need to give thanks — those who go down to the sea, those who traverse deserts, those who were ill and became healed, and those who were imprisoned and were released" — Berakhot 54b.

4 The title page of *Sefer Tehillot Shabbat* (Pyetrikow, 1911), specifically states: "This commentary was copied from the manuscript of the *Siddur* of the Ari *z"l*, for the commentary which has been printed thus far is very confused, and this commentary, based upon the manuscript, is correct, as one can clearly see." It is unfortunate that this manuscript is no longer extant. I wish to thank Dr. Zeᵓev Gries, who kindly checked various printed and manucript editions in the National and University Library in Jerusalem on my behalf.

5 In R. Ḥayyim Vital, *Shaᶜar ha-Kavvanot* (on the subject of *Qabbalat Shabbat*), no mention is made of Psalm 105 being recited at the *Minḥah* Prayer of Sabbath Eve; instead, there are extensive *kavvanot* connected with Psalm 29.

to recite Psalm 107 on Passover evenings or during the Morning Service of Passover, as well as in the Morning Service of other festivals.

Explicit evidence that the Besht was accustomed to reciting Psalm 107 at *Minḥah* of Friday afternoons appears in *Sefer Me᾽or ᶜEynayim* by R. Menaḥem Naḥum of Chernobyl, who was a disciple of the Besht. In *Parashat Beshalaḥ* there, it states: "And it was instituted by the Besht, *z"l*, may he rest in Paradise, to recite Psalm 107 every Sabbath Eve, because one needs to purify himself more and more at that time. And there are mentioned there four who need to give thanksgiving." This account also relates something of the contents of the interpretation given to this psalm, and not just the fact of its recital.[6] Even though the contents given there involves a different subject than that found in the extant commentary, it does include one reference[7] indicating that he knew the commentary in the form that we have it.

Hasidic tradition relates that the Maggid of Zloczow preached on the 107th Psalm. However, the lengthy commentary brought in his name is quite different from that attributed to the Besht.[8] On the other hand, R. Reuben Horowitz, author of *Duda᾽im ba-Sadeh* (Lemberg, 1859), *Va-yaqhel*, states the following:

> At the Afternoon Prayer of the Sabbath Eve all prayers and all sparks ascend, and for this reason they instituted the recitation of the Psalm *Hodu* . . . "The redeemed of the Lord say" [v. 2] — these are the sparks which have been redeemed; "whom He has redeemed from the hand of adversity," as has been said by the Baᶜal Shem Tov *z"l* — p. 40b.

Here, one can clearly see that this is a quotation from the Besht's commentary to Psalm 107.

An extremely interesting account pertaining to the struggle over the establishment — or revival — of ritual in general, which is connected to the recital of *Hodu*, appears in *Sefer Shivḥei ha-Besht*. It is related, in an aside, that the Besht recited *Hodu* in the Morning Service (Horodetski ed., p. 81). It is also related that, on a certain occasion when the author of the *Toldot* was also present, R. Naḥman of Kosow recited *Hodu* following *Qaddish de-Rabanan* prior to *Barukh She-᾽amar* (i.e., the proper beginning of the section of Psalms of Praise in the daily Morning

6 It is clear that the wording in the above Sluvita edition of the *Siddur* is taken from *Sefer Me᾽or ᶜEynayim*, even though it does not mention that work's testimony that the Besht was accustomed to reciting this psalm.

7 "'Their souls abhorred all food' — at times he does not feel the taste and joy of his service, like a sick person who eats and does not taste the food." Compare the text of the commentary on this verse below.

8 See *Mayim Rabbim* (Jerusalem, 1964), p. 60b [end]. This comment is related to a polemic with the Mitnaggedim.

Service), and that all those present were furious and wanted to bodily remove him from the Reader's Stand, arguing that it was arrogant of him to dare to change the accepted practice. In any event, even though the *Hodu* under question in this case was not "our" *Hodu* (but rather I Chronicles 16:8–36; etc.), the excitement generated by questions of establishing ritual and liturgy and changes therein is pertinent to our question.

Another account which, while not mentioning *Hodu*, does speak about the ritual of "elevating the souls" on the Eve of the Sabbath (which is the main subject of the present *Commentary to Hodu*) appears in *Shivḥei ha-Besht*, and is very close to our subject. It relates how the Besht continued praying *Minḥah* on Friday afternoon until nightfall, and when he came to the phrase *Meḥayeh ha-Metim* ("who quickens the dead"), drew out the "*kavvanah* of unifications" for a long time in order "to bring up the souls." His brother-in-law, R. Gershon Kutover, laughed at him and said that, while he also prays from the Siddur of the Ari, he does not wait until all the souls have come up![9] This testimony is particularly important for understanding the assimilation of rituals within Hasidic society in its early days. There seems to be no doubt that the Besht's *Commentary to Hodu* was part of the struggle for the renewal of ritual, as I shall attempt to demonstrate below. He would seem to have had in mind the circle of Safed at the time of R. Isaac Luria, according to which he tried to model his own circle. I might mention here at the outset what became clear in the course of my research — namely, that this ritual may be defined as a *tiqqun* for involuntary seminal emissions, which is associated here with the recital of the psalm on the Sabbath Eve.[10]

9 "And Rabbi Gershon said about him, in jest, 'Why do they not come to me?' And he answered him: 'Let him be here until next Sabbath, and I will give him the *kavvanot* written down on paper, and they will also come to him.' And thus he did!!" (pp. 104–105). Further on, there is a description of a frightening situation experienced by R. Gershon when he attempted to act in a similar manner.

10 This *tiqqun* was one of the major subjects with which Kabbalistic books of *tiqqunim* written at the end of the 17th and beginning of the 18th century were preoccupied. See, for example, the works of R. Menaḥem Mendel of Prague, author of *Va-yaqhel Moshe*, especially *Zera*ᶜ *Qodesh Maẓavtah*, which was already printed at the beginning of the 18th century (prior to the 1893 Munkasc edition). The connection between the doctrine of the early Hasidic thinkers and this pre-Hasidic literature still requires investigation, and it is worth noting the similar concentration of literary motifs between both.

It is worth mentioning that Psalm 107 was considered the prayer by which Sabbatai Ẓevi saved the world from destruction; this was reported by R. Yaakov Sorogon, one of the earliest Sabbatian apostates, in his account of a dream he had on Tuesday night, 5 Shevat 5428 (1668). See R. Schatz, "Visions of 'The Secret of the King Messiah' — An Early Source from a Sabbatian Apostate" (Heb.), *Sefunot* 12 [*Sefer Yavan*. 2] (Jerusalem, 1971–78), p. 240.

On Sabbatian and Hasidic use of *tiqqunim* based upon the recitation of psalms generally, see Y. Liebes, "R. Naḥman of Braslav's *Tiqqun ha-Kelalli* and its Relation to Sabbatianism" (Heb.), *Ẓion* 45 (1980), pp. 201–245.

I have thus far brought references to this *Commentary*. We now encounter a surprising phenomenon, in that we encounter some remarks of the disciples of the Besht relating to the interpretation of this psalm — portions of which they even quote — without mentioning it in the name of their teacher. I refer to remarks brought by the Maggid of Mezhirech and R. Jacob Joseph of Polonoyye. In his sermons, the Maggid of Mezhirech mentions certain things which are without doubt paraphrases of the above *Commentary*[11] without, as a rule, citing them in the name of the Besht. But he behaved the same way also with regard to many of the teachings of the Besht which bear no connection to this psalm.

I recently came across a manuscript[12] containing many teachings of the Maggid of Mezhirech (some of which have never been published in any of the printed

11 For example, in *Maggid Devarav le-Ya^caqov*, §179, po. 278:

> He [R. Pinhas b. Yair] went to redeem captives, to lift up holy sparks. He said: "Divide your waters." "Many waters cannot extinquish love" [Songs 8:7] — these are the alien thoughts which are called many waters; they are those who descend in boats, who have descended to lower levels, descending fom their own level in order to thereafter lift up the holy sparks. For the descent is needed for the ascent, as is written elsewhere, "Those who labor on deep waters, they saw the deeds of God" [Ps. 107:23-24] — that even in these acts there is God.

See the commentary to those verses in this text, and with minor variations in *Maggid Devarav le-Yaᶜaqov*, §8, p. 22; and cf. §55, p. 80: "'And she sat in Petaḥ-Enayim, and Judah saw her, and thought her to be a harlot because she covered her face.' [Gen. 38:14-15]. The meaning of the letters of *Tamar* is *Tam Mar* ('simple'–'bitterness') — the alien thought is bitter, but in truth it is simple [*tam*]. As in, 'I saw servants riding on horses' [Eccles. 10:7]." See there also §62, p. 100: "And in truth the Besht *z"l* said, 'and the priests the Levites' [Ezek. 44:15] — that all of the influx which comes is from those two aspects." Cf. §31, p. 50. See also the connection drawn between the notion of the "four who are required to give thanks" (explicitly associated by the Sages with Psalm 107) and the Afternoon prayer of the Sabbath Eve, in §50, pp. 71-72; for the secret of the proselytes who cry out "give" from within the *qelippot*, see the present text, on v. 20. The latter remarks do not come from an explicitly Lurianic source!

I have at hand an interesting tradition from a MS. of R. Menaḥem Mendel of Vitebsk which relates, among other things, the following incident involving the recitation of *Hodu* by the Maggid of Mezhirech:

> An incident involving Dr. Gordon, one of the disciples of our Master the Maggid, *z"l.* On the Sabbath Eve he once stood next to him, and the Maggid was in his old age and was very weak, and prayed in his bed. And the said doctor saw that he was suspended in the air, four hand-breadths above his bed, and was saying *Hodu*. And it was difficult for him to stand it [because of his great fear] until the Rabbi, the Maggid, said [the verse], "all food their souls abhorred... and they cried out," etc. — and he fled. And the doctor said that from the moment he heard our Master the Maggid say, "all food," etc., the appetite for food left him and was completely nullified.

12 See below; I have also used it for purposes of comparison with the commentary brought in Section III. The teachings cited here from the manucript of the Maggid have recently been published, for the first time, in the second edition of my *Maggid Devarav le-Yaᶜaqov* (Jerusalem, 1990).

collections). Among these teachings, we find the explicit testimony: "This Psalm, 107, was instituted by the *ḥasid*, our teacher R. Israel Baᶜal Shem[13] *z"l*, to be recited every Sabbath Eve before the Afternoon Prayer, for the lifting up of the sparks which fell into the shell all the days of the week." At this point, the commentary is brought in the version known to us. While it does not explicitly state there that the Maggid's own testimony applies to this commentary, it is possible to infer this from the overall context.[14] The commentary to this psalm was therefore known among both Hasidim and Kabbalists during the generations following the Besht, even before it was published, and it served as source of inspiration for various paraphrases, whether they mentioned their source or not.

I will mention here some things which I found in wake of this *Commentary*. An indirect and very significant testimony is the commentary of R. Isaiah Jacob ha-Levi from Alesk, one of the sages from the pre-Hasidic circle of the *kloiz* of Brody who, in his book *Bet Ḥokhmah* (Podgorzo, 1898), cites a commentary on Psalm 107, entitled *Maᶜalei Shabbata* ("the Eve of the Sabbath"),[15] consisting entirely of Kabbalistic, and not Hasidic, ideas. Yet in reading this commentary one can clearly see that he has read the Besht's *Commentary to Hodu*, even though he does not mention it by name. From his phrasing one can even surmise that he refers to its contents, as on p. 38a: "therefore he explained how far their punishment goes." From the nature of his commentary, one can even detect a covert polemic against the "Hasidic" interpretation of the psalm, in which the *ẓaddiq* is commanded to descend on the Sabbath Eve to redeem the sparks / souls which are in the deepest pit. The following remarks likewise seem to relate to the Besht's *Commentary*:

> "They stumble and there is none to help" [v. 12]. That is as we have written — that for the attribute of the above, when the sparks fall in the attribute of 'desert' (*midbar*), then they are unable to save themselves at all. But these sparks do not need help save from the Holy One, blessed be He, because by means of repentance they are able to get out. — p. 37a

However, the entire central motif for the sake of which this *Commentary* was written[16] is deliberately omitted; instead, it is transformed into a Kabbalistic commentary which suited this Kabbalist from the *kloiz*.

13 In manuscripts from the 1770's, the Besht is generally designated as "R. Israel Baᶜal Shem" (and not "the Ba'al Shem Tov").

14 The only possible alternative is that this is the testimony of R. Levi Yitzḥak of Berdichev (see above, n. 2).

15 I am grateful to the late Gershom Scholem for calling my attention to this source.

16 See section IV, below, for an analysis of the Besht's *Commentary* on this psalm.

A later account, that of R. Yehudah Ẓevi, rabbi of Razdil,[17] in his work *Daᶜat Qedoshim*, (Lemberg, 1848), is interested in connecting the Lurianic ritual of the Sabbath eve with the Besht's innovation of reciting Psalm 107. From the details which he brings following the testimony itself, one can see that he also relates to our *Commentary*, although here too the uniquely Hasidic element is neutralized: it is as if this were no more than an extension of the Lurianic ritual. Despite the fact that he is himself a *ḥasid*, he cites this commentary in a purely Kabbalistic paraphrase. At the beginning, he notes:

> ... Indeed, by our words it will all be understood according to what is known from the *kavvanot* of the Ari, *z"l*, [concerning] the great holiness of the Afternoon Prayer of the Sabbath Eve, and the ascent of the life-souls, spirits and souls (*nefesh, ruaḥ, neshamah*). And for this [reason] the holy Besht and his disciples came and instituted that one should recite *Hodu* at its beginning, in the sense of a thanksgiving offering. Four are required to give thanks for all the souls which are swallowed up during all the days of the week in the depths of the abyss, and wish to emerge and connect their souls with its source, with all the sparks of their portion. For thus established the king, the king of the world, that this is the time for the water-drawers to go by, to draw water with joy from the wells of salvation. [cf. Isa. 12:3]

His teacher and father-in-law, R. Ẓevi Hirsch of Zhidachov, a Kabbalist who was well-known among the Hasidim, writes the following in his book, *ᶜAṭeret Ẓevi* (Jerusalem, 1966; offset edition: Lvov, 1872), p. 54c:

> Regarding what we have said at length about this: understand that the disciples of the Besht introduced, in the name of the Besht, that one ought to recite Psalm 107 — in which there is *hodu* and *yodu*, as mentioned above — on the Eve of the Holy Sabbath, prior to the Afternoon Prayer. For the essence of the Sabbath is to thank God and to sing to Your Name, Most High [Ps. 92:1]. For the ascent of the worlds takes place on the Sabbath, and we need to prune the arrogant ones [a reference to the powers of the *qelippah*], so that the external forces [*ḥizonim*] not be united, by flashes of fire of the fire of the Lord [cf. Song of Songs 8:6], etc. For we begin to lift up our souls to God through the four worlds, which are incorporated to ascend, and through this no sustenance [is given] to the external things. And we prune [i.e., cut off] through the secret of "the sweet singer of Israel" [a double-entendre on *zamir*, "to sing" and "to prune"], to be victorious for the house of the Lord, etc. ...

This account contains a number of interesting points:

1) The allusion to the Kabbalistic understanding of the commentary to the psalm, based upon the *gematriot* of the words *hodu* and *yodu* ("give thanks" and "they shall give thanks") found in this psalm.

17 The son of R. Moshe of Sambor, and the son-in-law and disciple of his brother, R. Ẓevi Hirsch of Zhidachov.

2) The ritual portrayal of the "pruning of the arrogant" on the Sabbath eve by means of the "flames of the fire of the Lord," which sounds like an ecstatic description of the activity of destroying the forces of the *qelippah* and the *ḥizonim*.

3) The end of the passage refers to the "sweet singer of Israel." Already during the time of the Maggid this verse was interpreted as applying to the Besht, in the context of his struggle with the *ḥizonim* to uplift the soul (see *Maggid Devarav le-Yaᶜaqov*).

4) The testimony given here states that it was the disciples of the Besht — and not he himself — who introduced the recitation this psalm, in his name. His disciple, Yehudah Ẓevi Margaliot of Razdil, reads here, "the holy Besht and his disciples."

Two other references to the *Commentary* of the Besht bear a definite Hasidic tendency, but deliberately remove its ideas from their original context and expound them as general Hasidic ideas. The first of these is that of R. Menaḥem Mendel of Lubavitch, cited in *Ẓeror ha-Ḥayyim* (Belgoray, 1913):

> And this is, "Four need to give thanks" [Berakhot 54b]: [those who are saved from] desert, prison, illness, sea. "And they cried out" [*va-yizᶜaqu, va-yiẓᶜaqu* — v. 6, 13, 19, 28]. It is explained in the name of the Besht *z"l* that the four attributes of *va-yizᶜaqu va-yiẓᶜaqu* are the [sparks] separated out of chaos,[18] which fell in the breaking of the vessels. And this is, "From the desert a present" [Num. 21:18]; and from that gift one must cry out to God when one comes out of prison, which is called the alien thoughts ... For the holy Besht said — may his merit protect us — that the main thing is to cling to the vitality of the letters in holiness and purity. — p. 42b

According to this, for the Besht the "main thing" is the raising of the sparks which fell into the abyss — i.e., the souls — as the Besht in fact explains in his *Commentary*, but the avoidance of ordinary alien thoughts, and one's connection in "holiness and purity" to the letters of prayer.

Another reference is that of R. Ẓaddok ha-Cohen of Lublin, in his book *Peri Ẓaddiq*:[19]

> That the Besht introduced the recitation of the psalm, *Hodu la-Shem*, in which are mentioned the four who need to give thanks, at the incoming of every Sabbath: the reason is that on every Sabbath holiness appears from its root to repair all the faults and harms [resulting] from man's acts. And concerning this it is said, "whom he has redeemed from the hand of the enemy, and ingathered from the lands" [v. 2] — that

18 That is: the sparks which have been separated from the world of chaos which, according to Lurianic Kabbalah, is the world of "breaking."

19 Reprinted in Israel, 1965; *Parashat Masᶜei*, p. 111a. Mr. Moshe Kleinerman pointed this source out to me, for which I thank him.

> is, the sparks of holiness are ingathered from the four corners of the world, from all kinds of earthliness and descents and falls. . . . But when the time comes for *tiqqun*, all the holy sparks are gathered from all the places where they are scattered in the four corners of the world. And after that, there are mentioned in particular all the kinds of descent and falling which are found in every soul by means of its acts during the days of the week, and for all of them there is *tiqqun* by means of the holiness of Sabbath, from the appearance of the root, as said, etc.

His remarks there are extensive and interesting in themselves; however, it is difficult not to sense the transition between the original deliberate "descent" into the *qelippot* on Sabbath Eve, for the purpose of their ascent — as described by the Besht[20] — and "all kinds of descent and fallings which are found in every soul" during the week days, in R. Ẓaddok.

One of the last figures to mention the *Commentary* of the Besht does so in a rather odd way. I refer to R. Aharon Marcus, in his book *Qeset ha-Sofer* (Cracow, 1912), which is a commentary on the Bible:

> However, in the last generation the prophecy of the *Zohar*, *Parashat Va-ʾra*, was fulfilled: namely, that during the sixth millennium, kingship — which is the lower Wisdom, the Wisdom of Solomon[21] — will ascend every sixty years, from level to level, until in the year 5600 [i.e., 1840], there will be fulfilled the verse, "In the sixth hundred year of the life of Noah" [Gen. 7:11], there will be opened the floods of wisdom, above and below. And this was the prophecy of our teacher, Rabbi Israel Baʿal Shem Tov, in the little book[22] containing the intentions of *Hodu*, Psalm 107, and *Lekhu Neranenah* [i.e., the Sabbath Eve psalms beginning with Psalm 95],[23] which he wrote upon his return from his trip to Istanbul, en route to the Land of Israel, when he was forced to return because his ship was wrecked and he was taken into captivity and saved, and he instituted that one should say this psalm upon the incoming of the Sabbath with awesome *kavvanot*. And he wrote there on the verse, "in whose hands are the depths of the earth" [Ps. 95:4] — do not read *meḥqerei* but *meḥaqrei* ("the searchers-out"), and "hand" refers to the final level of kingship, which is now governing . . . — p. 8a.

I do not know from whence R. Aharon Marcus took his story, in wake of which, as it were, the *Commentary* was written by the Besht.[24] What is interesting, for our

20 See the analysis of this subject below, Sect. IV.

21 According to Kabbalistic sources, this is the final *Sefirah*, known as *Malkhut*.

22 This was the name of the *Commentary* in the first edition.

23 We have no extant information concerning this subject.

24 In *Toldot Yaʿaqov Yosef*, *Parashat Shelaḥ lekha*, pp. 128d– 129a, and in MS. Jerusalem–National Library 5298, fo. 11b, mention is made of the well-known "great journey" on which "his ship was broken up and he was in great sadness, and his teacher [Ahiyah the Shilonite] came, and he was surprised at him, and showed him in what worlds he is now." The whole subject is connected with the messianic problem, which it is not in place to discuss here.

subject, is the exegetical metamorphosis which the literal meaning of the Besht's *Commentary* underwent in the hands of Marcus, who was both a scholar and a *ḥasid*, who wished to see in this work a prophecy concerning the beginning of a new era, which he considered as messianic, in 1840[25] — which would also correspond with the opinion of the "searchers-out."

Finally, and more recently, in the Introduction to his book *Maʾamar Tefillat Pataḥ ʾEliyahu* (Jerusalem, 1964), R. Isaiah Asher Zelig Margaliot has written the following:

> I heard it said among elderly Hasidim that — following the well-known great miracle accorded to the Besht, may his merit protect us, upon returning from his trip to the Land of Israel — the holy Besht, as a sign of thanksgiving to God, may He be blessed, for the great miracle which happened to him, introduced in the order of service for the Afternoon Prayer of the holy Sabbath eve that one should recite Psalm 107 at the beginning of Minḥah for the Sabbath eve, which is like a thanksgiving offering, of the four who need to give thanksgiving to God, for all of the souls who are swallowed up all the days of the week in the deepest depths . . . And all the disciples of the holy Besht, may his merit protect us, also took it upon themselves, together with all the *ḥasidim* who walk in their light, to recite Psalm 107 at the beginning of the Afternoon Prayer for the holy Sabbath Eve. And there is also a printed commentary on this psalm by the Holy Besht, and from his commentary one may understand his awesome holy intention in this.

II

I have at hand MS. 5198 from the Jewish National Library in Jerusalem,[26] which consists of 98 pages: part of them contain a collection of teachings of the Besht, according to the tradition of R. Jacob Joseph of Polonnoye, corresponding to what has been printed, while part contain teachings of the Maggid of Mezhirech, nearly all of which appear in the printed editions of *Maggid Devarav le-Yaʿaqov* or other published collections. The manuscript gives the impression of being a deliberate

25 On the vision of redemption held by the Isbicza Hasidim for that year, see R. Schatz, "Autonomy of the Spirit and the Teaching of Moses: Studies in the Teaching of R. Mordecai of Izbica" (Heb.), *Molad* 21, no. 183–184 (1963), pp. 554–561. The formulation cited there concerning "wisdom of nature" reminds one of the position of the rabbi of Kotsk on the question under discussion. On the position of Hasidism with regard to the year 5600 (i.e., 1840), see R. Mahler, *Hasidism and the Jewish Enlightenment*, p. 279. On the "Maskilic" background of Aaron Marcus and his connection to Beshtian Hasidism, see R. Schatz, "Between Metaphysics and Ethics."

26 I wish to thank Dr. Mordecai Nadav, former head of the Institute for Hebrew Manuscripts at the Jewish National and University Library, for making this text available to me.

compilation of "early teachings" as, in the tradition of R. Jacob Joseph of Polonnoye quoted in this manuscript, the Besht's teachings appear without his comments, whereas in his published writings he generally expands upon his words at length and adds to his master's teachings. The tradition of R. Jacob Joseph is brought on fol. 1–12b, 71a–72b, 77b–79a. In my opinion, the lack of continuity is to be attributed to the copyist rather than to the editor. The first page begins simply: "I heard from my teacher an explanation." The heading on p. 2 reads: "Writings from the Besht, *z"l*," and there immediately follows the *Commentary to Hodu* attributed to the Besht. Following the *Commentary to Hodu*, there appear in sequence of all the teachings beginning with, "I heard from my teacher," as in the style of the Besht's disciple, R. Jaco Joseph of Polonnoye, in his *Toldot Yaᶜaqov Yosef*, the earliest published collection of Hasidic teachings. It is therefore clear that the "collector" of these teachings thought that the *Commentary to Hodu* was that of the Besht, as transmitted by the *Toldot*, just as he transmitted other teachings in the name of his master. But nowhere in his printed works does R. Jacob Joseph explicitly state that the Besht expounded *Hodu*, even though extensive portions of this *Commentary* do appear in his printed works.[27] We must also not forget that there are parallels to the teachings said to be part of the *Commentary to Hodu* in the citations from the Besht's words brought by R. Jacob Joseph in various places in his writings.

MS. Jerusalem 5198 is early, as the colophon testifies:

> These holy writings have the source of life in them, and from a holy place they come, and from the hidden holy spring they flow, and they belong to the scholarly, outstanding, fearing and trembling the word of the Lord, his honorable and pure name, Rabbi Jonah, son of the scholarly leader, R. Menaḥem Mendel of Przemyślany. And that this testimony may be reliable, I have signed today, Wednesday of *Parshat Va-ʾera*, 23 Tevet, 5549, here, by the river Waroshei. Signed, Yitzḥak Isaac b. Ḥayyim, may God shelter and redeem him.

We thus have testimony that in Tevet 5549 (i.e., early 1789) this manuscript belonged to R. Jonah, son of R. Menaḥem Mendel of Przemyślany.[28] It was no doubt written prior to the publication of *Toldot Yaᶜaqov Yosef* in 1780, because subsequent to the publication of that work, it was universally cited by those who quoted its teaching.

Some scholars are of the opinion that the *Commentary to Hodu* was written by

27 See the discussion of this problem below, Sect. V.

28 It is perhaps not accidental that the commentary to this psalm was published a number of times together with R. Menaḥem Mendel of Przemyślany's *Sefer Darkhei Yesharim*.

R. Menaḥem Mendel of Bar, from the words of the Besht. In his book, *R. Yisrael Baᶜal Shem Tov* (Yasi, 1922),[29] Matityahu Guttman writes:

> This commentary was printed several times and known throughout the Jewish diaspora. And even among the hidden archives of my grandfather, Rabbi Yisrael *z"l*, there were found various writings of Rabbi Menaḥem Mendel of Baslivo, the father of the Gaon of Lotin (the father-in-law of said grandfather), and I found there the *Commentary to Hodu*, like that which is printed, except for minor changes in the formulation of language and in the order of the words ...

At the end of the *Commentary* in the above-mentioned manuscript, it states: "Finished and completed is the *Commentary to Hodu* from my grandfather, R. Menaḥem Mendel *z"l*" (p. 50). Matitayahu Guttman adds here the comment that the "Menaḥem Mendel" referred to is R. Menaḥem Mendel of Bar, who was a distinguished figure within the circle of the Besht.

There is no unambiguous meaning for the formula cited by Guttman — *Mᵓᵓ"Z* (*me-adoni avi zeqeni*: i.e., from my grandfather) — neither with regard to the author of the commentary nor the ownership of the manuscript. This does not mean that R. Menaḥem Mendel of Bar could not have owned such a copy, but that this is not necessarily stated in the manuscript upon which Guttman relies. There is indeed indirect evidence that R. Menaḥem Mendel of Bar knew of the essential teachings brought in the *Commentary*, without the psalm itself being mentioned. R. Pinḥas of Korets states, in *Peᵓer La-yesharim*: "And this thing the Besht revealed [to Menaḥem Mendel of Bar], that one must descend to Gehinnom on behalf of God, may He be blessed, and this is alluded to in the Talmud, 'Great is a sin for its own sake. ...'"[30]

I would therefore argue the following: 1) There is no proof connecting R. Menaḥem Mendel of Bar to the *Commentary to Hodu*; on the contrary, there is evidence that he heard this teaching from the Baᶜal Shem Tov; 2) There is good reason to assume that R. Jacob Joseph of Polonnoye also heard the *Commentary to Hodu* from the Besht, and that he recorded it just as he recorded his other teachings; 3) The extant manuscript was found in the home of the son of R. Menaḥem Mendel of Przemyślany, a colleague and disciple of the Besht, who considered the *Commentary* to be the authentic teaching of the Besht. This is what is meant by the phrase in the colophon: "from a holy place they come, and from the hidden holy spring they flow."

29 See also G. Scholem's remarks on this problem in "The Neutralization of the Messianic Idea in Hasidism," pp. 189–190.

30 Jerusalem, 1921, p. 21b. However, from the context it would seem that the primary implication of the saying was the social one. The Besht taught both the theological and the social aspects together, while the *Commentary* stresses the former alone.

To summarize: in the generation of the disciples of the Besht, our *Commentary to Hodu* was cited by the Maggid of Mezhirech, Jacob Joseph of Polonnoye, R. Levi Yitzḥak of Berdichev, R. Naḥum of Chernobyl, and R. Shmelke of Nikolsburg. Its existence and attribution to the Besht is likewise attested by various circles from the nineteenth century, following its publication at the beginning of that century.

III

The following is a translation of the Commentary to Psalm 107, taken from MS. Jerusalem 5198. We will refer to this text in our analysis of its subject matter below (Section IV) [the asterisks refer to terms explained in the Glossary, below].[31]

> Writings from the Besht, may his memory be a blessing.
>
> "O give thanks unto the Lord, for He is good; for His mercy endureth for ever" [Ps. 107:1]. It is already known that there is nothing in the world in which there were not holy sparks (*niẓoẓot*),* only that they are embodied there in the secret of transmigration (*gilgul*),* and they themselves are in the secret of the life of the seven kings who died [i.e., the kings of Edom, mentioned in Gen. 36:31 ff.], which require a great *tiqqun* by means of the deeds of the lower [creatures — i.e., man]. And on the eve of the holy Sabbath they ascend from their embodiment in the shells (*qelippot*)* to the realm of holiness, to the supernal Sabbath, which is [the *Sefirah* of] *Binah*,* as it is known that there are three sabbaths: *Malkhut*, *Tifᵓeret* and *Binah*. And this is what is said, "O give thanks unto the Lord" — that he does a great kindness with you by the power of the time of grace which is in the holy Sabbath, that they return to their original strength — that is, to holiness. For on the Sabbath there is rest for all, and *Binah* and *Tifᵓeret* come from the space of the Father* to the Orchard,* which is the secret of Sabbath night. And this is what is written, *Hodu* ("give thanks"), which in *gematria* equals *ᵓEhyeh* ("I shall be"; cf. Ex. 3:14); and every *ehyeh* is an attribute of *Keter*,* and this is the secret of why we recite on Sabbath "*Keter*" [i.e., "a crown shall be given to You . . ." — recited in the Musaf Service of the Sephardic rite]. And all this is in *Binah*, which is a tower suspended in air. "For He is good" — refers to the Sephirah of *Yesod*,* which is called "good," for it draws down the drop [i.e. of male seed] to *Malkhut*,* which is called "world," from *Tifᵓeret*,* her husband. And this is what is said, "His mercy (*ḥasdo*) endureth forever" — that is, *Ḥesed vav* — [*Ḥesed*] in *gematria* is seventy-two, which is the drop [of seed] that descended via the seventy-two* *vav*, which refers to *Tifᵓeret* — and understand.

31 The critical edition of this text is based upon MS. Jerusalem 5198, fos. 1a–2b, with an apparatus containing variant readings from the Zhitomir 1805 edition, and from a private manuscript of R. Levi Yitzḥak of Berdichev (see *Maggid Devarav le-Yaᶜaqov*, Introduction, on the MS. identified as A), fos. 136a–139a. The Hebrew text appears in the 3rd edition of the Hebrew version of the present work: R. Schatz Uffenheimer, *Ha-ḥasidut ke-Mystiqah* (Jerusalem, 1988), pp. 202–208.

"So let the redeemed of the Lord say" [v. 2]. That is, these are the souls which transmigrate, etc., which were in Exile during the six days of Creation, as mentioned above, in the secret of death. And there is no death, save through the secret of Exile, in the Sephirah of the shell. And know that redemption comes to them, and this is the secret of, "whom He hath redeemed from the hand of the adversary" [ibid.], which is the shell. And it is called "the hand of the adversary," in the secret of, "because of the hand which was sent [against Your sanctuary]." "Those he redeemed" (*asher ge'alam*), equals in *gematria* seventy-four (*ᶜD*), in the secret of "Trust in the Lord forever" [*ᶜadei ᶜad*—Isa. 26:4]. "Redeemed" (*ge'alam*)—which is the name *ᶜ"M G"L*, and this is from the shell, which is called "the hand of the adversary" (*yad ẓar*)—in *gematria, Š"D* (demon), without the letter *yod*.

"And gathered them out of the lands" [v. 3], etc. That is, now, on the eve of the holy Sabbath, there is ingathering from the four corners of the land, by the power of the four names, *ᶜ"B S"G M"H B"N*, which are the four winds: East, "Father," *ᶜ"B*; West, *B"N* ("son"), which is the daughter *Malkhut*; South, *Tif'eret, M"H*; North, *Binah, S"G*. And this is the secret of "gathered them" (*qibzam*) — which is the *gematria* of those four names, which are the four directions [i.e. of the compass]. And [on] Sabbath they have redemption — and understand.

"They wandered in the wilderness" [v. 4], etc. This refers to the sparks, which all [during] the week wandered away from the good path, which is [that of] holiness, and went by the way of the wilderness, which is barren, in the shell. And [the word] "in the wilderness" (*ba-midbar*) alludes to the *gematria* of Abraham, which is the attribute of *Ḥesed*, corresponding to the first day of the week [i.e. Sunday]. For when Sunday comes, immediately the shell has the power to rule, and this is the secret of the [torture of] the Hollow of the Sling (*kaf ha-qelaᶜ*).* But when the Sabbath comes, there comes rest to the dispersed of Israel, who are the holy sparks that are called the dispersed ones of Israel have rest; and they are the secret of "drop of seed [spilled] in vain" — *nidḥei* equalling in *gematria* seventy-two — and understand; such is not the case all during the week. "They found no city of habitation" [ibid.], but they are only the secret of the World of Destruction, and on the Sabbath they go up to a settled place — and this is easily understood.

"Hungry [and thirsty]," etc. [v. 5]. A great secret is here expounded, namely: Why has the Holy One, blessed be He, created things of food and drink, which man desires? Because there were holy sparks which were embodied in the mineral, vegetable, animal and human, and they have a longing to cling to holiness, and they are awakened through the secret of Female Waters (*mayim nuqvin*),* and in the secret of, "A drop does not descend from above without two drops ascending to meet it." And all of man's eating and drinking contains a portion of that spark, which he must repair. And this is the secret of "hungry" — that is, Why is it that man is hungry and thirsty? It says: "their soul fainted in them [*titᶜaṭef*; literally, "was enwrapped"]" — in the secret of exile in garments of strangers, [as in] "And he thought her to be a harlot, for she had covered her face" [Gen. 38:15]. And all those things which serve man are literally in the secret of his sons whom he engendered — and understand.

"Then they cried [unto the Lord]," etc. [v. 6]. These sparks cried out to the Lord, because they have great trouble and fear in the Shell, and when the Holy Sabbath comes, their mourning is changed to festivity, from darkness to a great light, and from pain to joy, which is Compassion (*Raḥamim*) — and understand. And this is what is said, "[He delivered them] out of their distresses" — literally, [from their troubles themselves] were made their deliverance. And this is the secret of, "It is a time of trouble unto Jacob, [but out of it he shall be saved]" [Jer. 30:7] — out of it, literally, is made their salvation. And this is the secret of "[transgressions] are made as merits" [Yoma 86b].

"He led them," etc. [v. 7]. This alludes to *Binah*, which is called "a city of habitation" — that the righteous, by power of their prayers, combine the holy sparks, which all during the week were very weak and do not have strength to walk by themselves, but must be brought. And this is the secret of, "that they might go to a city of habitation" — which alludes to *Binah*, which is called "they found no city of habitation" [v. 4] — and understand.

"Let them give thanks unto the Lord for His mercy", etc. [v. 8]. These are the sparks, which one tells to praise the Lord for the mercy He has done them, for they are among the dwellers of darkness. For Adam begat spirits and demons during [his first] one hundred and thirty years, and we must repair them and lift them higher and higher to the Infinite, as is known of the ascents of the Sabbath Eve which we draw down through the Afternoon Prayer: from the Emanator to [the World of] Emanation, and from Emanation to Creation, etc., and afterwards we lift up from [the World of] Action to Formation, etc., up to the Infinite. [This is] alluded to in, "Let them give thanks" [*YWDW*] — which equals in *gematria*, *HVYH** [a permutation of the Ineffable Name of God], corresponding to Emanation, which ascends to the Emanator; and ᶜ"*B*, which is Wisdom, ascends to *S"G*, which is *Binah*. And this is the secret of the eight verses from "Give thanks to the Lord" to here, which correspond to *Binah* [*Ḥesed Gevurah Tif*ᵓ*eret*] *Neẓaḥ Hod Yesod Malkhut* — and understand.

And he once said here, "Let them give thanks" [v. 8], corresponding to the first [Divine] name, which is ᶜ"*B*, and the verse "Give thanks" [v. 1] in *gematria* equals ᵓ*Ehyeh*, corresponding to *Binah*, and this is the [Divine] Name of ᵓ*Ehyeh*. "Say" [v. 2], corresponding to *Ḥesed*; "out of the lands" [v. 3], corresponding to *Gevurah*; "wandered" [v. 4], corresponding to *Tif*ᵓ*eret*; "Hungry" [v. 5], corresponding to *Neẓaḥ*, for there is no sustenance there for the Shell, and he is hungry, in the secret of, "the Eternal One (*Neẓaḥ*) of Israel shall not lie" [I Sam. 15:29], for it [falsehood] has no feet, but only one foot. *Hod* can be inverted — i.e., "They cried out," corresponding to *Hod*, which is wretched [*daveh* — i.e., *hod* spelled backwards: *DWH*/*HWD*], and there is the main crying out. "He led them" [v. 7] — corresponding to *Yesod*, which brings the drop for *Malkhut*; "Let them give thanks" [v. 8], corresponding to *Malkhut* — and understand. Thus far.

"For He hath satisfied [the longing soul]" [v. 9]. Now the Holy One, blessed be He, has satisfied *Malkhut*, which is called "soul," whose feet go down to death [cf. Prov. 5:5] all the days of the week to gather the holy sparks, and it is hungry for them. And now it descends in the attribute of *Ḥesed*, which is the secret of the priest, alluded to in the first letters of this verse. And by this all the shells disperse, which are the secret of the informers upon the children of Adam, in the secret of "For the informers let there be no hope" [Weekday Amidah], as is known from the *kavvanot*. And this word [i.e., *tiqvah*: "hope"] alludes to the five hundred organs of male and female. For the male 248, and for the female 252, and they are themselves *va"v he"h*. And this is "longing" (*shoqeqah*), which in *gematria* equals "hope" (*tiqvah*). "And the soul" — which is *Malkhut* — "[which is] hungry" — that is, the light of the holy seed, when it descends thereto — *gematria* of "hungry" (*reᶜevah*) — from *Yesod*, which is called "good." And this is what is said, "hath filled with good" [op. cit.] — and understand. Now on the Sabbath night, which is the principal [thing], as is known, there is the secret of "and they shall rest in her" and in the secret of "you have sanctified."

"Such as sat in darkness" [v. 10]. This refers to the holy sparks, which she gathers all the days of the week — and understand. "Because they rebelled ..." [v. 11], refers to Adam and Eve, whom the Holy One, blessed be He, commanded not to eat of the tree of knowledge. And this is the secret of "the words of God" [ibid.], which are the letters of "no" [*lo'*; as inversion of *'el*: *L*ᵓ/ᵓ*L*]. "And contemned the counsel of the Most High" [ibid.] — that they caused the destruction of worlds, as is known. And because of this,

"Therefore He humbled [their heart]" [v. 12] — that is, he is *Malkhut* [which is called humble], and stumbled in distress, which is the Shell, "and there was none to help," all the days of the week.

"They cried unto the Lord" [v. 13]. By the power of regret which they have, for evil-doers are always filled with regret, and God saves them from their sufferings, in the secret of "from Job was made an enemy" [inversion of ᵓ*Iyov* to ᵓ*oyev* — Baba Batra 16b] — that is, from holiness is made the secret of the Shell. And on the Sabbath they are repaired, as is alluded [i.e., in the first four words of this verse] in the initial letters of Job (ᵓ*Iyov*) — and understand. "And broke their bonds in sunder" [v. 14]. These are the bonds of the shells which He will break. And here he said seven verses, corresponding to *Ḥesed Gevurah Tif*ᵓ*eret Neẓaḥ Hod Yesod Malkhut*: "For he hath satisfied" [v. 9], corresponding to *Ḥesed*; "sat in darkness" [v. 10], corresponding to *Gevurah*; "because they rebelled" [v. 11], corresponding to *Tif*ᵓ*eret* — for this was the sin of Adam, that he denied *Tif*ᵓ*eret* [i.e., the Tree of Life in the garden of Eden]; "He humbled" [v. 12], corresponding to *Neẓaḥ* — for the shells are humbled when they have no sustenance; "They cried" [v. 13], corresponding to *Hod*, from whence is their sustenance; "He brought them out" [v. 14], corresponding to *Yesod*; "Let them give thanks" [v. 15], corresponding to *Malkhut*. And he mentioned a second time the word "He praised." "For he hath broken" [v. 16], etc. — that is, *Yesod* of the female of Shell. Broken wells and two doors and a hinge from the *Yesod* of the female, which is called "brass and iron He broke." And why of this does it say, "and cut the bars of iron in sunder" [ibid.]? It means that the "other god" was castrated, and it has not the attribute of Knowledge, which is the secret of the bar connecting between *ḥet*/*bet* [*Ḥokhmah* and *Binah*?]. And the Holy One, blessed be He, castrates him, so as not to confuse the world, and for this the Holy One, blessed be He, who did this kindness, is praised — and understand.

"Crazed," etc. [v. 17] — these are the sparks, which are the secret of the evil-doers who transgress from the good way, which is the Torah, whose ways are ways of pleasantness [cf. Prov. 3:17]. And Adam denied the Torah, as our rabbis, of blessed memory, said. "And afflicted because of their iniquities" [op cit.] — all kinds of illnesses which they have during the days of the week, come literally through the secret of the Torah, in the secret of, "If he merited, it is a potion of life for him" — and this is literally "the way of their transgression," for "the viper does not kill, but sin [kills]." And in truth God is good to all, and it is only the one who receives it who is evil, for whom it is transformed to a potion of death.

"Their soul abhorred all manner of food" [v. 18]. This refers to the Torah, which is called food, as in "Come, eat of my bread" [Prov. 9:5], and it is itself abhorrent to their souls, like an ill person, that whatever one gives him is bitter to him. Also, because a person leans towards the Shell, the sweetness of the Torah becomes bitter to him, like the potion of death. "They drew near unto the gates of death" [op cit.], as above. But only on the Sabbath, "He sent His word" [v. 20], which is the potion of life, "and healed them." And because they are regretful there in the Shell, the Holy One, blessed be He, opened their eyes, in the secret of "One who comes to be purified [is assisted]." And then he sees that the Torah is true, and there is naught that is crooked there, but only for the wicked is it changed — and understand. For in truth, "I the Lord have not changed" [Mal. 3:6]; and this is what is said, "and delivered them from their graves" [op cit.] — literally. There is made a birth [*hamlaṭah*; pun on "delivered," *va-yimaleṭ*], that deliberate transgressions are made into merits [Yoma 86b], and He rolled light for them from the dark pit, literally. And this is the secret of, "and the souls which they made in Haran" [Gen. 12:5] — that is, that they proselytized, who were made from evil into good. Thus these sparks are proselytes, and they have been healed from their illness, and "their graves" are made, in the secret of destroying seed for naught. And this is, that a deliverance is made for them, and they are made the children of the living God.

And he recited here six verses, corresponding to *Gevurah Tif᾽eret Neẓaḥ Hod Yesod Malkhut*. "For he hath broken" [v. 16], corresponding to *Gevurah*, for that is the main breaking; "Crazed" [v. 17], corresponding to *Tif᾽eret* — for because of his crazedness he denied *Tif᾽eret*; "All manner of food" [v. 18], corresponding to *Neẓaḥ*; "They cried unto the Lord" [v. 19], corresponding to *Hod*; "He sent" [v. 20], corresponding to *Yesod*; "Let them give thanks" [v. 21], corresponding to *Malkhut*. And he said here for a third time, "Let them praise," equalling in *gematria* the *HVYH* of *mem he* [i.e., one of the kinds of *milu᾽im* of the Divine Name], the six "extremities" [i.e., the six *Sefirot* surrounding *Tif᾽eret*] — and understand.

"And let them offer [the sacrifices of thanksgiving]" [v. 22] — for being restored to their original strength. "And His wonderful works" of the Holy One, blessed be He, "with singing" — that they merited *tiqqun*, as it is known that the Shell is within range of the holiness, and one must repair them.

"They that go down to the sea" [v. 23] — that is, at times the souls descend from a high place to the shells, and the shells rejoice in the joy of the souls who have descended among them, and this is "they that go down to the sea in ships" — referring to the souls who descended to the shells, but the shells do not know that their labor is in deep waters — that is, the activity of the holy souls in descending to the deep waters and bringing up the souls from the Shell, and that from there they ascend to their place. And this is the secret of, "He sends down to Sheol and brings up" [I Sam. 2:6], meaning that He brings the souls down to Sheol and lifts them up, when they act in their labor. And this is alluded to in the initials of "doing labor" (*ᶜoseh melakhah*), whose initials are *ᶜ"M*, in the secret of, "For the portion of the Lord is His people (*ᶜamo*)" [Deut. 32:9] — Do not read *ᶜamo* (His people) but *ᶜimo* (with Him). But if a soul is not upright, there will fall upon it terror and dread [cf. Ex. 15:16] in descending to the shells, which is not the case of a high soul, upon whose head no fear shall come [a play on Num. 6:5: *morah*–"razor"; *moraʾ*– "fear"]. And all this in its descent, but in ascent, in the secret of descent for the purpose of ascent, in the secret of Reflected Light (*ʾor ḥozer*),* it lifts up many sparks, in the secret of "a great nation went out of Egypt." And this is alluded to in the inverted initials of "great waters" (*mayim rabim*, whose inverted initials are *R"B* --"great"). "These saw the works of the Lord" [v. 24] — that is, that by their falling into the depths, they recognize His wonders — and understand.

"For He commanded" [v. 25] — these are the souls which descended there, they saw and they shall make stand the other souls which were taken captive. "Which lifted up the waves thereof" [ibid.] — these are the souls which are exiled there in the Shell. And this is what is said, "They mounted up to the heaven, they went down into the deep" [v. 26] — that they wish to ascend to a high place, to the heavens, which is in holiness. By virtue of this, "they went down into the deep" — to the Shell, and they descended for the sake of the ascent, to repair their root. And this is what is written, "their soul melted away because of trouble" [ibid.] — melting because of the greatness of the evil of their fear. And this is the secret of the exile of the Shekhinah all six days of the week; and this is the secret of the heels of the Messiah, for when [the Shekhinah] finishes gathering all these souls, in the heels of that Impure [Side] which is the end of the impure body, then the Messiah shall come, and death will be swallowed up forever [Isa. 25:8], and all the *Qelippot* which were emptied of holiness will be nullified. Then, "they reeled to and fro and staggered" [v. 27] — that is to say, the Shell acknowledges that it has no reality, for "their wisdom was swallowed up" [v. 27], in the language of "to swallow" — and understand. And this is what is said, "they reeled to and fro," etc, "They cried [unto the Lord]" [v. 28] — that is, that all the strength which is in the Impure Chariot* will be negated.

"Then they were glad" [v. 30] — these are the holy sparks, when the shells are silenced. "And he led them" [ibid.] — the holy souls who merited, and whose desire and request is completed, to ascend to "their desired haven," which [refers to] the place and boundary of the holiness — and understand this.

And he recited here ten verses, corresponding to the ten *Sefirot* of the son [i.e., of *bet nun*, one of the *milu'im* of *YHVH*], and said here for the fourth time, "Let them give thanks [unto the Lord]" [v. 31], which is *gematria* of *HVYH* of *B"N*, which is "each pan [weighing] ten [shekels]" [Num. 7:14, etc.; i.e. corresponding to *malkhut*, which is the tenth].

"Let them exalt Him" [v. 32] — these sparks are required to thank the Lord in the congregation of the people, and it is ten people who are called a congregation, corresponding to the above-mentioned ten *Sefirot*, which is *qahal*. "In the seat of the elders" [ibid.] — Father and Mother, who are called "the elders," "Praise Him" — and understand.

(And they say) — these are the sparks, [speaking to] the Holy One, blessed be He. "He turneth" — now, on the holy Sabbath, "rivers" of the Shell "into a wilderness" [v. 33] — that has no sustenance from the vitality, because the Shell of Nogah* ascends now to holiness, for it gives them life all the days of the week with mercies (*Ḥasadim*), which are stolen up above, in the secret of "stolen waters are sweet" [Prov. 9:17]. It is sweetened from all these mercies which the Bright Shell [*Nogah*] steals, and all the shells have life and sweetening. But now that *Nogah* ascends to holiness, all of the shells remain without illumination. And this is what is said, "watersprings into a thirsty ground" [op. cit.] — that is to say, the shells thirst for lack of water — and understand.

"A [fruitful] land [into a salt waste]" [v. 34] — refers to *Malkhut*. The Shell, which all week brings forth fruits, holy sparks, now has no holy spark, like land from which one digs salt, for even the evil-doers in Gehinnom rest. And this is the secret of "on all your offerings [thou shalt offer salt]" [Lev. 2:13] — in order to weaken the power of the Shell and to blind it, with the secret of the salt of Sodom — and understand. And this is the secret of, "for the wickedness of them that dwell therein" [op. cit.]. That is, that all the week there were sparks there in the secret of *ra*ᶜ ("evil"), and the initials of darkness (*ʾefel*) are inverted into the *ʾalef* of holiness [*ʾFL/ʾLF*] — and understand. "He turneth a wilderness into a pool," etc. [v. 35] — the Holy One, blessed be He, has the power to make a place which is barren and dry, which are the shells, like a barren desert, into pools of water and rivers, by force of the soul which descends to there. And this is the secret of "a dry land into watersprings" [ibid.] — that is, that thereafter there go out of there all of the holiness, which is called water. It also alludes here to the initials of the word *ẓelem* ("image"), because then the image of God ascends to holiness — and understand.

"There he maketh to dwell [the hungry]" [v. 36] — that is, these holy sparks which were hungry without holiness. And thereafter, "and they establish [a city of habitation]" [ibid] — this city, literally, that it be an inhabitation with all the good of their ascent, and on the Sabbath they are sweetened, as is known. "He blesseth them" [v. 38] — these are the sparks. "that they are multiplied" — that is, that which was previously in the secret of death, called "very [good]" [*meʾod* — an allusion to the Rabbinic homily on Gen. 1:31, "'and it was very good' — this is death"; Gen. R. 9:5], which is hidden, and on Sabbath is corrected, as said above. "That they are multiplied greatly, and suffereth not their cattle to decrease" — this refers to the attribute of *Malkhut* of [the World of] Action, for then its feet go down to death [Ps. 5:5]; there is no bereaver at all, in the secret of, "And the Nephilim ..." [Gen. 6:4] — for all has been corrected in holiness.

"Again they are diminished" [v. 39] — that is, to the Shell, which are "dwindled" to the dust. "He poureth contempt upon princes" [v. 40], as known from the verse, "princes pursued me for naught" [Ps. 119:61], which are the initials of *ḥarash* ("silence"). That is, all of the shells are made [as if] deaf at the time that the abundance descends, which is the secret of water, alluded to in the final letters [of this verse]. And the mnemonic is: *ḤR"Š*, third, fourth, fifth. And there are left the second, sixth and seventh, whose sign is *BW"Z* ["contempt", spelt by the second, sixth and seventh letters of the alphabet], and which in *a"t b"sh* is permutated into *shefa*ᶜ ("abundance"). And this is what is said, "poureth contempt upon princes" [op cit.] — when the abundance descends, the princes are made there into silent shells, and the initials are *sheva*ᶜ ("seven"), which is the Sabbath, in the secret of "seven times the righteous falleth" [Prov. 24:16], which is *Yesod.* And the word "falleth" (*yipol*) is an expression of ease, as in, "there shall fall by your side a thousand" [Ps. 91:6]; also the secret of, "I have established my covenant" [Ex. 6:4]. And in the fulfillment of this covenant of holiness, the one which is *Yesod* of the Shell falls. "Falls," in the secret of a "dead" member [i.e., *membrum virile*].

"And causeth them to wander" [ibid.] — this also refers to the shells, which God misleads, and they leave the secret of holiness, where their grasp had been, in the secret of, "Many rise against me" [Ps. 3:3], and "there was a great stone upon the mouth of the well" [Gen. 29:2], and this is what is written, "the waste, where there is no way" — for on the Sabbath he does not stand upon *Yesod*, which is called, "the way of a young man with a maid" [Prov. 30:19] [double entendre on Hebrew ᶜ*almah* / maid and Aramaic ᶜ*alma* / world]. "Yet setteth He the needy on high from affliction" [v. 41], which is *Yesod* of holiness. "and maketh his families like a flock" [ibid.] — that is, those which are behind the flock [the word *ẓon*] are switched and become "new" [*ḥadash* — by taking the letters following *Ẓ*ᵓ*N*, i.e., *QB"S*, and inverting them through the method of *a"t b"sh*]. And understand the secret of the ascents, the initials of "after the word *rosh* [head]," which are the letters of Sabbath [composed of the letters following *rosh*] — and understand. "The upright see it and are glad" [v. 42] — these are the holy sparks. "And are glad" upon seeing their ascent to holiness. "And all iniquity" [ibid.], etc. And the rest is understood, and this is enough for one who understands.

IV

Let us now turn to an analysis of the contents and aim of this commentary.

The *Commentary* opens with the assumptions of Lurianic cosmology, according to which all of existence — that is: the World of Action (ᶜ*olam ha-*ᶜ*asiyyah*) — is filled with holy sparks, which fell there on the occasion of the "Shattering" (*shevirah*) of the seven "kings" (who are, by way of analogy, the seven lower Sefirot), who died before the Divine world entered the stage of *tiqqun*. These sparks are of three kinds: 1) the lights of the Sefirot; 2) the lights of the souls which were uprooted from their source in the original structure of Primeval Adam, which included all human souls; 3) the lights of the Shekhinah, whose sparks were also dispersed.

Thus, the cosmological approach was already combined with the psychological approach in Lurianic Kabbalah, and the doctrine of the sparks with that of transmigration (*gilgul neshamot*). The repairing of the Divine world was a function of the perfection of the soul and the return of its lost parts to their source. Lurianic Kabbalah argues that, in this world, only transmigrated souls are to be found, as only a small part of the roots of the souls remained whole and did not undergo this "Shattering." The souls of the sons of Adam who fell into the "great deep" ascend therefrom, and are embodied in the human body in order to seek their redemption: this redemption takes place by means of those *mizvot* which a person merits to fulfill. The perfection which a person may acquire by the redemption of all the parts of his soul (*nefesh*, *ruaḥ*, *neshamah*, etc.) is not only the redemption of his own soul, but a process within the redemption of the configuration of Primeval Man, and is thus a precondition for historical redemption.

These theoretical assumptions, based upon the myth of the "Shattering," led to the creation in the Safed circle of fixed rituals connected with the Sabbath. The special place held by the Sabbath within the cycle of the days of the week was interpreted to mean that on the Sabbath the souls ascend from the "shells" (*qelippot*) and abandoned their imperfect garments, enjoying a kind of redemption in miniature by means of their restoration to holiness. But this time of opportunity, connected with the cosmic structure and situation of the world unique to the Sabbath day, depends upon the souls incarnated in bodies — i.e., living human beings. By means of special *kavvanot* designed for that purpose, a person can elevate the oppressed souls which are in the *qelippot*, and assist them in this temporal redemption. Indeed, the Ari's famous ritual of Receiving the Sabbath in the field, together with the accompanying dramatic descriptions about the souls which found their way to him from the birds and shrubs of the field beseeching him to redeem them, was devised in order to do so. A description of this ceremony is brought in *Sefer Shaᶜar ha-Kavvanot*, under the heading of *ᶜInyan Qabbalat Shabbat*. The new motif found in the *Commentary* to this psalm is based upon the assumption that the souls which a person lifts up on the Eve of the Sabbath are the disembodied souls of the sons born from his spilling his seed, who descended to Gehinnom in the absence of a body.

In the *Commentary to Hodu*, this fundamental assumption is followed by a description of how and what happens in the upper world that conveys upon the

Sabbath a special status: namely, that at that time *Keter* of *Binah* — refered to in Kabbalistic symbolism as *ᵓEhyeh* — pours out its influx into the lower Sefirot through a close connection, *Binah* and *Tifᵓeret* go into *Ḥaqal Tapuḥin* [i.e., *Malkhut*], which is "the *Tifᵓeret* of her husband," leading the drop of seed, which originated in "the hollow of the father," i.e., *Ḥokhmah*, into it via *Yesod.*[32] At this point, it is explicitly stated that the reason why Hasidim recite the phrase *Keter* ("a crown shall be given to You") in their rite of the Sabbath *Qedushah* is connected with the reference to the attribute of *Keter* of *Binah*, which is that attribute which becomes operative upon the entrance of the Sabbath. *Keter* is symbolized by *ᵓEhyeh*, which is numerically equivalent to *Hodu*.

A description of the hardships endured by the sparks — which are the souls that dwell in Sheol and wait for Sabbath Eve in order to ascend for one day — opens with the passage beginning, "Let those who are redeemed of the Lord say." The entire psalm is interpreted as being uttered by those souls, who praise and thank God for the redemption of the Sabbath day. In brief, this is seen as an impressive and moving hymn of thanksgiving of the souls that dwell in Sheol, and the entire *Commentary* is filled with the pathos of this thirst for redemption.

On the Sabbath Eve, the ingathering of souls goes into the world of the Sefirot ("and from nations has ingathered them") and merit to ascend to their source as they were at the beginning. Indeed, throughout the weekdays they wander about the wilderness of the world of *qelippot*, and the Shell has power over them; they are within the *Kaf ha-Qelaᶜ*, a Kabbalistic term used as a synonym for transmigration. This netherworld is also known as "the World of Destruction" (*ᶜalma de-ḥaruv*), as the world of *qelippot* is designated in Kabbalah, while the souls or sparks are called "the dispersed ones of Israel" — that is, those souls of Israel which were exiled to the world of destruction because of their being "the seed spilled in vain."[33]

In various places, the passage beginning with the words, "hungry and thirsty," is quoted as a classical example of the Besht's *Commentary to Hodu*; in fact, within the context of the *Commentary* as a whole, it is an exception. This is the only passage in the entire *Commentary* that deals with a different problem — namely, the lifting up of sparks from within corporeality by *ᶜavodah be-gashmiyut*, rather

32 The entire function of *Keter* is associated with man's ineffectual attempts to repair *Keter* with *moḥin* of the Divine world. For an extensive discussion of this problem, and its connection with the matter of sin and the *Siṭra ᵓAḥra*, see I. Tishby, *Torat ha-Raᶜ veha-qelippah be-Qabbalat ha-Ar"i* (Jerusalem, 1942), pp. 134–143.

33 In Safedian Kabbalah, this motif is not specifically connected with the uplifting of souls on the Sabbath Eve; this is the Besht's interpretation — namely, that the souls which are in Sheol are also part of the process of divine catharsis. For the question of catharsis in general, see Tishby, ibid., p. 40.

than with the problem of the delivery of the souls from Sheol. The one who recorded this writes: "he expounded here a great secret," as if he is transcribing directly from things he has heard in an oral sermon (if they were not copied from things that were already written down). The passage relates to the question of why man desires food and drink, explaining this appetite as a function of the relation and dependence between the spark within his own soul and that found in the physical world that surrounds him: the lattter wishes to be redeemed and to "ascend" by means of the former. According to this, the appetite is a stimulus of the world: "the desire of the sparks" to be attached to holiness and to ascend from their "impure" embodiment in the mineral, vegetable, animal, or human world — i.e., the four worlds of nature in which they are embodied in a foreign dress, seemingly a dress of whoredom. In fact, all of these sparks participate in the secret of "his children," the root of his soul and body which became enwrapped in "alien clothing" while exiled in the corporeal world. In other words: a person ingathers the source of his soul, not only through the soul-connection between himself and the oppressed souls in Sheol, but from everything that surrounds him. This assumption is not connected with any special act of the Sabbath Eve, but is an everyday act.[34] From this point of view, this section differs from the main body of the systematic commentary to Psalm 107.

The passage beginning, "and they cried out," contains a description of the dread and terror felt by the souls dwelling in Sheol during the weekdays, and the release which they feel on the Eve of the Sabbath when they are redeemed from the obscurity of Sheol into a great light — in the sense of salvation.

A new element is brought to the commentary with the passage beginning, "and he led them": the participation of the *ẓaddiqim* in the process of redemption of the souls "by the power of their prayers." The prayers of the *ẓaddiqim* encourage the sparks — those souls which all week long were greatly weakened and did not have the strength to go by themselves. This implies that they cannot ascend without a connection to the souls of the living *ẓaddiqim.*

The passage which opens, "Let them give thanks," refers to the praise which the souls render to God for the mercy He has shown them by transforming them from "dwellers in darkness" to those who dwell in light. "Dwellers in darkness" refers to the denuded souls which — according to the Midrash — Adam begat before he married Eve; they are demonic souls seeking to find *tiqqun* within a body. Mention is made here only of their being lifted up to the upper worlds by the *ẓaddiqim,* which is their legitimate redemption. Particularly interesting is the note in this

34 On the relationship between man and his periphery in the lifting up of sparks, see Scholem (op. cit., n. 29), pp. 39–42.

passage, "as is known of the ascents of the holy Sabbath, which we draw down in the *Minḥah* Prayer." The writer mentions the special ritual of "ascents" of the souls connected with the Friday Afternoon Prayer as accepted and self-evident: "as is known." At this point, we find a ritual repetition opening with the words, "and he said here." This implies that the Besht was accustomed, not to recite Psalm 107 in a straightforward manner, but to divide the reading into various sections, corresponding to the names of the *miluʾim* (i.e., the computations of the *gematria* of a given word based upon the spelling out of the names of each letter, rather than the letter itself) of the Name *HVYH*, known from Lurianic Kabbalah.[35] In a special *kavvanah*, he stressed the leit-motif, "Let them give thanks unto the Lord," repeated four times during the course of the psalm. Each time he read this leit-motif as directed towards a different one of the *miluʾim* of the name *YHVH*: "And he said here once *Yodu* directed towards the first name, which is *ᶜ"H*." According to Lurianic Kabbalah, the seventy-two letter name is one of the *miluiʾim* of *HVYH* related to the *Sefirah* of *Ḥokhmah*. It would appear that the Besht was accustomed to stress that the first cycle of this reading was directed towards the entire Sefirotic world (*yodu* = *HVYH*): the first eight verses, up to and including "Let them praise," were interpreted as one unit, representing the eight Sefirot from *Binah* down to *Malkhut*, albeit he gave special importance to the word *Yodu*, which he saw as directed towards *Ḥokhmah*.

In the passage beginning, "he has satisfied," yet another motif is introduced — namely, the idea that the Shekhinah, called *Malkhut* in Kabbalah, descends during the course of the week to gather the souls with great appetite, as the sparks which were scattered from her during the Shattering also descended to the realm of *qelippot*. Moreover, all of the sparks which ascend on high on the Sabbath Eve pass via her, as she is the gate to the world of the Sefirot. Here, the verse "her feet go down to death," which is expounded in the Kabbalah as pertaining to the Shekhinah — or to *Malkhut* — is explained as referring to that part of her being connected with the lower worlds, insofar as she reaches Sheol, the powers of the *qelippah*.[36] Hence, all the days of the week she acts in the world of the *qelippot* and is unable to lift anything, while on the Sabbath Eve she descends with the attribute of the *kohen*[37] (from the initials of the verse, "for he has filled the soul . . ."), who

35 The reading of psalms during *Qabbalat Shabbat*, with special *kavvanot*, is mentioned in Ḥayyim Vital's *Shaᶜar ha-Kavvanot*, but Psalm 107 is not mentioned there.

36 This motif was already reworked in this way in Lurianic Kabbalah.

37 The relationship between the priesthood and this "redemption" is not clear to me. Is there some memory of the Priest-Messiah figure preserved here? See on this E. E. Urbach, *Ḥaza"l*, p. 596 [English: p. 662]. Cf. below, n. 58, for the remarks of R. Ephraim of Sudylkow, author of *Degel Maḥaneh ʾEfrayim*, who compares the *ẓaddiq* to the High Priest Aaron, both of whom come from the side of *Ḥesed*.

is filled with mercy to assist in the redemption of the souls which were taken captive there because of the calumny of the *qelippot*. She does this with a "longing soul," described here as a soul filled with hope, because then, when she raises the souls, she becomes filled with influx from the *Sefirah* that is above her — the *Sefirah* of *Yesod*, designated as "good" (*ṭov*). The writer adds here: "now on the Sabbath night, which is the principal thing, as is known,[38] there is the secret of 'they shall rest in her,' and the secret of, 'you have sanctified.'" This clearly refers to a ritual practiced in Safed involving the Shekhinah, in which the "Sabbath queen" played a central role, around which there was woven a romantic and highly poetic system, to which Luria himself contributed by the *piyyutim* which he composed for the Sabbath.[39]

In the section beginning, "and they cried out," there is again a summation of seven verses (from v. 9 to v. 15 — "for he has filled" until "for he broke"): "And here he recited seven verses corresponding to *Ḥesed Gevurah Tifʾeret Neẓaḥ Hod Yesod Malkhut*." In other words, these verses were said in reference to the seven lower Sefirot, with the exception of *Binah*, upon which the first eight verses were expounded. The writer adds: "and he said a second time" — that is, in the verse the word *Yodu* is mentioned a second time, which the Besht stressed, as he did at the end of each cycle of verses.

The next section, "for he has broken," describes the breaking of the world of the *qelippah*, which is built up of male and female, similar to the world of holiness. The *qelippah* has been transformed into the attribute of "broken wells," which cannot contain the holiness in its prison. The term, "doors and a brass bar," is used to refer to the female aspect of *qelippah*, while the male is called "the other god," who was castrated, according to the Midrash (Baba Batra 74b) which explains that God killed the female and castrated the male. The Kabbalah saw this Leviathan as a symbol of the male, corresponding to *Da'at* in the world of Holiness, of which it says that it connects and "bars" from one end to the other. The emphasis here is placed upon the "barring" — i.e., the connection between *Ḥokhmah* and *Binah*[40] — of the impure *Sefirot*; from the moment that this "god" lost "Knowledge" (*Daᶜat*), the whole situation became unravelled.

38 The Sabbath night is the time for the feast of the "Holy Apple Orchard" (*ḥaqal tapuḥin qadishin*), which corresponds to the Shekhinah. And perhaps this is an allusion to Friday night as the night for conjugal union, which may explain the particular emphasis upon the eve of the Sabbath as the time set aside for *tiqqun* of the sin of "spilling of seed in vain."

39 See the critical edition of these *piyyutim*: Y. Liebes, "The Sabbath *Zemirot* of the Holy Ari" (Heb.), *Molad* ns 4, no. 23 [27, no. 223] (1972), pp. 540–555.

40 On the nature of this subject and its connection to the problem of sin, see Tishby, *Torat ha-Raᶜ*, p. 96.

A third kind of soul who has transmigrated and descended to Sheol is dealt with in the section beginning "crazed." These are the souls of the wicked, who violated their Creator's commandments and whose eyes have now been opened, so that they do repentance and regret their deeds. They are also called proselytes,[41] who have so to speak converted and changed from evil to good. This passage concludes with, "and he recited here six verses, corresponding to *Gevurah* ... *Malkhut* (v. 16–22); and he said here a third time that *yodu* is the *gematria* of *HVYH*, of *me"m he"h*, the six extremities." That is, the *milui* of *HVYH*, which yields *M"H*, corresponding to the *Sefirah* of *Tif*ʾ*eret*, in which are included all the six lower Sefirot.

The short section beginning with "and they they sacrificed" speaks about the praises uttered by the sparks or souls which have undergone *tiqqun*. From the verse, "they who go down to the sea" and onward, a new problem is discussed: the involvement of the souls of the living in the process of emptying of the *qelippah*, and the lifting of the imprisoned souls who live therein. In principle, this problem is based upon sources in Lurianic Kabbalah; one finds there a ritual of reciting psalms with the intention of assisting in the uplifting of souls, although this theory does not find its deepest expression there: there is neither a descent into Sheol nor a descent involving any particular danger to life. The problematics of endangering oneself and of deliberately falling down appears in Lurianic Kabbalah only with regard to the ritual of "falling upon one's face" during *Taḥanun*,[42] which is perceived as a kind of symbolic descent into Sheol in order to bring up sparks. In this Hasidic interpretation, the adventure of descent into Sheol is combined with the recitation of Psalm 107 as a dangerous ritual, which only select individuals are allowed to risk.[43] There then follows a description of the great joy in Sheol when

41 They are only called proselytes by way of analogy, and are not identical with the souls of proselytes, about whom there is another theory in Lurianic Kabbalah, which also relies upon the verse, "and the souls which they made in Haran" (Gen. 12:3). It is worth mentioning here that the concept of "transmigration of souls" also has a well-known meaning in Lurianic Kabbalah. In *Shaʿar ha-Kavvanot: Mizmor Shir le-yom ha-Shabbat*, we read:

> "When the wicked spring up as grass" [Ps. 92:8] — it will be understood what is written in *Sefer ha-Zohar, Parashat Terumah*, that the Sabbath day is the day of transmigration of souls. The matter is that, on the Sabbath Eve, even those souls which are sunk in the depths of the *qelippah* ascend to the holy, to be included there up above, but not all souls are able to ascend... Whoever is deserving to ascend ascends, and whoever is deserving to descend descends. And this is the secret of it being called "the Day of Transmigration of Souls," for these transmigrate here, and these transmigrate there.

42 See *Shaʿar ha-Kavvanot*: *Nefillat* ʾ*Appayim*.

43 Joseph Weiss describes the "descent" of the *ẓaddiq* as "an adventurous descent of a religious leader to the depths of sin, in which the sinners are found," thereby giving the entire subject an explicitly psychological meaning, alongside its social interpretation. "The difference in the understanding of the idea of the *Zohar* (III: 220b) in its psychological significance, is that the descent to Gehinnom is transformed into an act of everyday psychology." See his "The Beginnings of the Hasidic Path,"

the souls enjoy the "visit" of a lofty soul, because of its obligation to wage war with the *qelippot* and to repair the oppressed souls. The high souls are called "those who descend to the sea in ships" to perform "labor in deep waters." An element of deception also enters here, as the shells do not know that these souls "descend for the sake of ascent" or, more accurately, in order to lift others. Further on, it says: "If a soul is not so upright, there will fall upon it terror and dread in descending to the shells, which is not the case of a high soul, upon whose head no fear[44] shall come." Via this descent into the depths, a brave soul coming from a sublime source — i.e., from "the straight line" of the world of Emanation — comes to know the great wonders of the Creator. In other words: the endangering is a supreme test in order to see His miracles. Further on, the struggling of the souls is depicted in terms of the verse, "They went up to heaven, descended to the depths." That is, in order to rise to heaven, they must first descend to the depths, "by strength of this they descended to the depths of the *qelippah*." These souls' experience is primarily one of dread, which would seem to have consisted of the fear of remaining below without having the means to ascend again — an idea also expressed in the Lurianic teaching concerning *Nefillat ʾApayim*. The text then summarizes: "and this is the secret of the exile of the Shekhinah, all six days of the week; and this is the secret of the "heels" of the Messiah [*ʿiqvot Mashiḥa*; i.e., the birthpangs of the Messiah]: for when [the Shekhinah] finishes ingathering these souls, in the heels of that Impure [Side], which is the end of the impure body, then the Messiah shall come; and then death will be swallowed up forever, and all the *qelippot* which were emptied of holiness will be nullified." The formula concerning the coming of the Messiah is a Lurianic one, which states that when all the souls shall ascend, even the souls of "the heels of Primeval Man," which are those souls most deeply sunken into impurity — and according to this formulation it would seem that these are sunken within the heels of the Other Side (*Siṭra ʾAḥra*), or in

esp. pp. 69, 74–75 (Weiss does not mention the existence of the *Commentary to Hodu* at all, but attributes all of the teachings concerning the "descent" of the *ẓaddiq* to Menaḥem Mendel of Bar, albeit without adequate proof). In fact, the present *Commentary* was influenced by a number of motifs from that *Zohar* passage. However, the main change which took place in Hasidism was not only the transfer of the scene to this world, as justifiably emphasized by Weiss, but primarily that the subject became connected with a fixed ritual to be performed, and not a "psychological" process of struggle with "moods." The form of action is very similar to that of *Nefillat ʾAppayim*, which I have already mentioned, and which was influenced by Lurianic Kabbalah. The Sabbatian motifs of "descent" also lead us to these very same Lurianic sources, even though there is no doubt that the motif of the Sabbatian "sin" which accompanies this "descent" was decisively influenced by the same theological basis as was Beshtian thought.

44 The allusion is to "fear" [i.e., based upon a word-play of *morah* and *moraʾ*), as many of the Hasidim used this idiom.

its male organ, which in Kabbalah is called "the end of the body" — the stature of Primeval Adam will be built anew, and the Messiah will come. We once again find the summation of the section, "And he recited here ten verses, corresponding to *Y"H* of *bet-nun*, and said here for the fourth time, 'Let them give thanks' — which is the *gematria* of *YHVH* of *B"N*, which is 'each pan ten [i.e., *Malkhut*].'" The name *HVYH*, whose number is *ben*, corresponds to the *Sefirah* of *Malkhut*; it thus concludes a full cycle of *kavvanot* corresponding to all the Sefirot.

In the passage beginning, "and they shall extol Him," the words of the souls after they have already ascended to their source is described; on the one hand, they praise God, while on the other, they seek the destruction of the *qelippot*. They tell their tale of woe to the supernal "congregation" and the aged "Father and Mother" — who are *Ḥokhmah* and *Binah* — and ask that God turn "the rivers of the shells into a wilderness" on the Sabbath, as on the Sabbath the *qelippot* receive no sustenance from *Ḥesed*. The "Bright Shell" (*qelippat nogah*) — the closest *qelippah* to the world of holiness and to the source of sustenance of the *qelippot* — itself ascends to holiness on Sabbath Eve and gives no sustenance to its *qelippot*; therefore they are "thirsty" and are compared to salty land. Three related matters are explained here in an aside: 1) the secret of the rest of the wicked in Gehinnom on the Sabbath, because of the failure of the strength of the *qelippah*; 2) the secret of salt, which is efficacious for sacrifices, its task being to blind the eyes of the *qelippah*; 3) the secret of Sodomite salt, which is connected with the ritual washing of the hands in *Mayim Aḥaronim*, which is already explained in the *Zohar* as "throwing flesh to the Other Side."

The interpretation offered in the passage beginning, "and this is the secret of, 'Because of the wickedness of those who dwelt there,'" is somewhat difficult to understand, as the verse, "He makes a desert into pools of water and dry land into watersprings," is interpreted here in terms of the transformation of the dwelling place of the *qelippot* into a wilderness through the removal of water, and not its transformation into a place flowing with water. This is concluded with a homily concerning the "image" (*ẓelem*), read as an acronym for, "dry (land) to pools of water." According to Lurianic Kabbalah, the "image" is the special mind (*moḥin*) received by the *Zeᶜir ᵓAnpin* ("Little Face") on the Sabbath Eve from the upper *Sefirot*,[45] when one recites, "Come O Bride, Come O Bride."

Another new motif is introduced in the final passage, "and the hungry ones dwelled there": namely, the quasi-sexual connection between the world of the *qelippot* and the Shekhinah during the week-days. On the Sabbath, when *Yesod* of holiness arises, the *Yesod* of *qelippah* — symbolized by the male organ — called "many rise against me," feels that he does not stand up as "the way of a man with

45 See *Shaᶜar ha-Kavvanot*, *Qabbalat Shabbat*.

a maid," but falls impotent. This motif is also reminiscent of the *piyyut* written by R. Isaac Luria to be recited on the Sabbath Eve, entitled *Azamer be-Shevaḥin*, in which it states, "Her husband shall embrace her in her female organ (*Yesod*)" — i.e., as opposed to the *qelippot*, which embrace her on week-days. Incidentally, it is worth mentioning here that R. Jacob Joseph of Polonnoye quotes the Besht[46] on this matter: "I heard in the name of my master, 'Her husband shall embrace her in her *Yesod*,' to ascend the small step,[47] which is *Yesod* of *Malkhut*, and this is more important to God, may He be blessed — and the words of a sage are seemly."

V

Having examined the theoretical approach and ritual basis of the *Commentary to Hodu*, and having noted the Lurianic structure of the Safedian ritual of Receiving the Sabbath, which served as a model for both imitation and renewal, it is worthwhile turning our attention to another problem: namely, what impression was made by the teaching and ritual upon the writings of the disciples or transmitters of the Besht's teaching?

At the beginning of this article,[48] I mentioned the argument of those who found it difficult to identify the Besht as the authentic author of the *Commentary on Hodu*. The fact that R. Jacob Joseph of Polonnoye, a disciple of the Besht and the leading transmitter of his teaching, cites entire sections which, if not precise quotations, are certainly more or less accurate paraphrases of passages from the *Commentary to Hodu*, yet does not cite these things in the name of his teacher but as his own interpretation, is puzzling![49] I must admit that this fact does cause some difficulty for the historical examination of the composition of the *Commentary*, but under no circumstances is it sufficient to refute the claim that these teachings are from the Besht.[50] On the contrary, the author of this testimony himself confirms

46 *Ẓofnat Paneᶜaḥ*, beginning of *Parshat Shemot*; R. Yitzḥak Yehudah Yeḥiel Safrin of Komarno, the author of *Netiv Miẓvotekha* (Lemberg, 1858), cites this source, enlarging at greater length upon the sexual motif of the significance of intercourse with a menstruant woman as a symbol of the place where the *qelippot* had been; see *Netiv ᵓEmunah*, 1. vi.

47 Perhaps in accordance with the use of *ᵓeẓbaᶜ qetanah* (lit., "small finger") as a euphemism for the male organ.

48 See above, Section I.

49 These remarks primarily refer to the Introduction to his book, *Toldot Yaᶜaqov Yosef.*

50 In his article, "Devekut, or Communion with God," (*The Messianic Idea in Judaism*, New York, 1971, pp. 203–227), Gershom Scholem argues that he does not think one should attribute these doctrines — especially those concerning the "descent for the sake of ascent" — to the Baal Shem Tov

two points: 1) that the central teachings brought by the *Toldot* in the name of the Besht appear in the present work; 2) that among those teachings brought in the name of the Besht, some relate explicitly to the ritual of Kabbalat Shabbat and the descent of the *ẓaddiq* to Sheol in order to raise up souls, while others even relate to specific interpretations of verses or homilies which appear in the above *Commentary*. The reader should pay attention to the fact that many of these quotations allude to the fact that one is not allowed to enlarge upon the interpretation, "may God protect," and the like.

The secrecy surrounding these traditions does not seem to me to be related to the theories brought therein — in any event, not to the essential theories — but to the ritual connected with them, which was accompanied by elements not interpreted in exactly the same way as in Lurianic Kabbalah. In the final analysis, most of the teachings concerning this matter were explicitly Lurianic, so what could there be to hide?

In the Introduction to *Toldot Yaᶜaqov Yosef*, R. Jacob Joseph brings the following comment:

> "And he lay with her on that night" [Gen. 30:16] — There was performed a unification of the Holy One, blessed be He, and he lifted up the lower levels which lay on the ground, up to the heavens. And it is written, "and a ladder standing upon the ground" [Gen. 28:12]. And it is written in the Talmud that he was imprisoned, "and he went out" [ibid., v. 10] — that is, the secret of the prison (*ha-ᵓasurim*) in *gematria* is "lay"

himself (p. 221–222; cf. the Hebrew version of this article, *Devarim be-go*, p. 444). In his view, there is only one place in *Toldot Yaᶜaqov Yosef* which allows of this interpretation (*Parashat Lekh Lekha*, p. 15a–b): "In every descent there must be some warning as to how he may again ascend, so that he not remain [below], Heaven forbid. And I heard from my teacher that there were some who remained." I am not at all convinced by his argument here, and have already shown, in my analysis of Scholem's approach to Hasidism, that he erred in his understanding of the Besht — and not only regarding this doctrine. (See the Introduction to the present work, Pt. iii–iv, esp. Pt. iv). In a conversation with Scholem concerning the *Commentary* to Psalm 107, he argued that he did not believe that the Besht knew Kabbalah, and therefore did not agree that one could ascribe the authorship of this text to him. This argument, in my opinion, is not supported by the words of the Besht's disciple, R. Jacob Joseph of Polonnoye. Similarly, the testimony of other close contemporaries does not support this reading of Scholem's. See, e.g., the remarks of R. Israel Ḥarif, a friend of the Baᶜal Shem, concerning the latter's *praxis* and his love for rituals of the sort mentioned in the tractate on Psalm 107. Isaiah Tishby states that the "things which I received from my teacher, the holy rabbi, R. Israel Baᶜal Shem Tov, his soul in the secret high places" (mentioned by Ḥarif) does not refer to matters of "Hasidism," but to magical actions — "the reciting of psalms with *kavvanot* and *yiḥudim* and combinations of Holy Names while performing [circular] processions 'to remove the judgments.'" See I. Tishby, "The Messianic Idea and Messianic Tendencies in the Growth of Hasidism" (Heb.), *Ẓion* 32 (1967), p. 14. In my interpretation here of *Perush le-Hodu*, I have cited an abundance of parallels which correspond to the position of the Besht.

> (*shakhav* = 322). For the Shekhinah is [present] in the secret of, "and she lay against his feet" [Ruth 3:7], and after he repented she was made alive [i.e., gave birth]; ... and understand this. And it is hinted in the verse, "those who dwell in darkness and shadow, chained in iron" [Ps. 107:10] ... And this is what is written, "and he took them out" — that is, by means of *Yesod* of *Zeᶜir ᵓAnpin*, which contains the letter *vav*, there is brought about the unity of male and female, which in *gematria* equals "go out" [*ẓei*; i.e., from this verse, *va-yoẓiᵓem*], and also the unity of Father and Mother ... Then, "he takes them out of darkness and shadow, and breaks their chains asunder" [ibid., v. 14], and God, may He be blessed, shall atone. One may also interpret one who was in prison and came out as alluding to the secret of the six days of the week and the Sabbath ... [and the sermon continues on verse 20, "He sent His word and healed them," concerning the Sabbath]. — p. 2a–b.

The two principle motifs — the combination and mating of the Shekhinah and *Zeᶜir ᵓAnpin*, and the release of the sparks from the prison of the *qelippah* — combined with the use of verses from Psalm 107 concerning this subject, leave no doubt as to the identity of this passage with the above *Commentary*. However, *Toldot Yaᶜaqov Yosef* does not cite these things here in the name of the Besht, and his citation suggests great caution — "God, may He be blessed, shall atone."

Elsewhere in the *Toldot*, it states the following:

> Were it not that I hesitated to set down in writing what I heard from my teacher, [relating] awesome things concerning the sweetening of the judgments of *Š"K* and *P"R*[51] and the sweetening of [licentious] thoughts by means of the Name *Shaddai* and its inverse, *K"T* [*Š=T*; *D=H*; *Y=K*], and also the name *YHVH* in exchange. I have set down the chapter headings on a separate paper, and through this there will also be understood the verse ["and I will remember my covenant (or 'circumcision')" — Ex. 6:5], and understand. And God, may He be blessed, will atone. — *Parashat Shemot*, p. 36b.

I do not know whether a copy of that "separate paper" which he wrote down and did not want to publish is still extant, but a homily concerning the subject of *Š"K* and *P"R* and of "sweetening" appears in the remarks of R. Jacob Joseph in MS. 5198, which I have in my possession, in which he states the following:

> I heard from my teacher, *z"l*, an explanation of the secret of *ᵓalef bet*,[52] about how

51 According to Lurianic Kabbalah; see *Shaᶜar ha-Kavvanot*, *ᶜInyan Qeriᵓat Shemaᶜ*, which speaks of 320 and 280 sparks of "judgment" that ought to be uplifted.

52 The grandson of the Besht, R. Ephraim of Sudylkow, also mentions the secret of the *ᵓAleph-Bet*; he relates that the Besht appeared to him after his death and said that "he would learn with him the letters of the *ᵓAleph-Bet*" (*Sefer Degel Maḥaneh ᵓEfrayim*, Josefov, 1883, p. 89b). It is clear that this refers to a technique of letter-combination. The grandson mentions elsewhere that the Besht "redeemed the letters by [the technique of] change" (p. 54c), which seems like an explicitly technical expression.

> one needs to make in every word submission, separation, and sweetening.[53] For there are *Š"K* and *P"R* alluded to in the word *ᵓAdonay*, in the section of the Eighteen Benedictions. All the *kavvanot* there must be sweetened in every word and speech, and to sweeten the judgments. For the letter *ᵓaleph* is the secret of *peleᵓ* ("wonder" or "marvel"),[54] and is embodied in the letter *bet*, which is two *ᵓaleph*s, and so on with the letter *gimel*, etc., through the letter *tav*. And when one turns his heart to the Exile of the Shekhinah, which is the holy spark of the Shekhinah embodied within the *qelippah*, he should greatly fear, and then all the evil-doers will be separated, and there is a unification of *yirᵓah* with *noraᵓ*, and the holy spark above is united with the vitality [a word play on *ḥayot*–"creatures," and *ḥiyyut* –"vitality"], as in the secret of, "and the creatures run back and forth" [Ezek. 1:14] — and that is their redemption from captivity. And this submission is as if he does not speak,[55] but only the Shekhinah. And separation — to separate from the *qelippot*. And sweetening — to lift them up and sweeten them in their source; and the words of the wise are pleasant. And keep this great principle, and understand it. — p. 7a.

Through means of this example, I have attempted to demonstrate that there are clear parallels to the *Commentary to Hodu* — both in terms of terminology and atmosphere — in certain teachings of the Besht brought in his name by R. Jacob Joseph, even though they do not explicitly refer to the exegesis of verses from this psalm nor to the Sabbath Eve ritual, but only to the technique of "raising up" in general.

I would like to further strengthen the relevant references to the teachings of the Besht, both those which explicitly mention the *Commentary to Hodu* and those which only bear a theoretical connection to this commentary. The overall picture received will possibly broaden our understanding, both of the significance of the *Commentary* to the psalm and of the problem discussed there. In *Toldot Yaᶜaqov Yosef*, it states:

> "And Judah came close to him" [Gen. 44:18]. This is the secret of prayer, to bind and to draw close the *Malkhut* of the lower world, called *yeridah*, with the supernal world, which is *Binah*, by means of the *ẓaddiq*, who is called Joseph.[56] And there are three

53 This formula is also brought numerous times in the name of the Besht in the *Toldot*, but it is never explicit, and has thus far not been understood. Nor is its connection to the lifting up of the sparks of the Shekhinah and "the redemption from its cąptivity," to use the formula of our subject, clear. It seems that the "technical formula" for the the ascent "from its captivity" was considered among those things to be studied secretly, as an esoteric teaching.

54 In the Commentary to Psalm 107, Besht expounds the permutation *ᵓalef* (i.e., the Hebrew letter) — *ᵓafel* (darkness); see above, Sect. III, on v. 35. The secret of the *ᵓalef* recurs in many of his teachings in different variations.

55 During the *ᶜAmidah* prayer, he nullifies himself to the Shekhinah, and she speaks through his throat (see above, Chap. 8, on this phenomenon).

56 Above, on. v. 7.

> kinds of drawing close: [the first being to draw close] for war with the alien thoughts — to shatter the *qelippot* and to lift the inner [portion] to sanctity, as I heard concerning this from my teacher. And one may not write this, albeit I wrote of this elsewhere[57] with extreme brevity. — *Parashat Va-yigash*, p. 32d.

One may perhaps understand this as an allusion to one of the three ways, namely, the uplifting of alien thoughts, while the two remaining paths deal with the lifting up of other things: Perhaps the Shekhinah? Or the souls? Does the uplifting of these two involve a more esoteric teaching than the uplifting of alien thoughts? Or is it perhaps a more adventurous and dangerous kind of uplifting? This may in fact be the case, as nowhere else does the *Toldot* surround a teaching of the Besht with such demonstrative secrecy as he does here with the doctrine of the uplifting of souls from Sheol.

The motif of the fear of descending to Sheol because of the danger that one may be unable to reascend thereafter is repeated in the *Commentary to Hodu*. However, the principle motif is not explained there sufficiently, or is even completely obscured there: namely, the connection between the soul performing the descent and the Shekhinah, represented in explicitly sexual terms.[58] In the Kabbalah of Safed, in which the Sabbath queen was already identified with the Shekhinah,[59] the ritual element had not yet been transformed into an adventure of mating, even

57 Read: "in this book", i. e., in *Toldot Yaᶜaqov Yosef*; perhaps he in fact referred to the introduction to the book, where these things are not brought explicitly in the name of his teacher.

58 The *ẓaddiq* helps to "establish the covenant" (or "the sexual organ" — *berit*) of holiness and to kill the "covenant" of the *Siṭra ᵓAḥra*. He changes the "sons", who were considered "seed in vain," to "sons of the living God," and alludes in the *Commentary* to the psalm that they are "his sons." See above, v. 5. In *Degel Maḥaneh ᵓEfrayim*, it states: "I heard from my grandfather, concerning the verse, 'I shall descend with you to Egypt' [Gen. 46:4] — I, who am the Shekhinah, which is a ladder placed upon the ground... that your ascent shall be subordinate to your lifting up so and so many oppressed souls... And he shall connect himself to God" (p. 20c). He states elsewhere: "It is incumbent upon the *ẓaddiq* to unify, so that there not be separation above. For if not so, he has alien thoughts concerning sexual matters" (this is quoted in the name of the Besht; ibid., p. 19c and 20a). Another matter mentioned in the *Commentary* to the psalm, v. 7 and v. 9: "The conclusion which follows is that there is no correction to the exploited souls in the *qelippot* — that is, only by means of the *ẓaddiq* who lifts them up. And this is alluded to in the verse concerning Aaron the priest, who is the righteous who serves God, who is from the side of mercy" (in the name of the Besht, p. 48c). In the manuscript, p. 76, there is another testimony which I have found neither in R. Jacob Joseph of Polonnoye nor in the *Degel*: "The explanation of the Besht to the hymn sung on the Sabbath night, 'Pass over to those who rest on the seventh day'; for the initials of *ḥara"sh* spell Thursday, Wednesday, Friday (i.e., *ḥamishi, reviᶜi, shishi*), an allusion to the three meals of the Sabbath." These initials are also found in the *Commentary to Hodu*; see above, on v. 39.

59 See G. Scholem, "Tradition and New Creation in the Ritual of the Kabbalists," in his *On the Kabbalah and Its Symbolism* (New York, 1969), pp. 140–146.

though there was no lack of erotic elements or of erotic atmosphere surrounding this ritual. Unlike the case in the ritual of the Besht, everything there remained on the level of a symbol for the relationship between the Shekhinah and the *Zeʿir ʾAnpin* as a supernal mating. It states in the *Toldot*:

> "I have removed my cloak; how can I put it on." [Songs 5:3]. For whenever the *ẓaddiq* has ascended above, he returns and descends to go up another level, in the mystery of "seven times the righteous shall fall and rise" [Prov. 24:16], as stated in the *Tiqqunim* concerning the secret of "the souls which they made in Haran" [Gen. 12:5].[60]
> It follows from this attribute, whether in this world or in the next world, that he returns in transmigration to lift up the levels of the people who are sparks of his branches, to repair them all. But when he descends to repair others, he does not wish to descend, because of the fear that he will not return and come to sin, heaven forbid, until he is promised that he will not come to sin. And it seems to me that this is [mentioned] in *Sefer ha-Gilgulim* ... — *Parashat Ḥayyei Sarah*, p. 18c–d.[61]

The *Toldot* cites the following explanation in the name of the Besht: sexual sin applies only in this world, but when one speaks of the redemption of the Shekhinah by means of mating, things are sweetened in their root and such a suspicion no longer holds:

> "When Pharoah sent the people ... and [God] did not let them go by the way of the land of the Philistines" [Ex. 13:17] ... The fault and sin of lowly human beings does not reach to there [i.e., "the way," which is the supernal worlds] ... and therefore repentance is efficacious ... So if he sinned through harlotry, this arouses naught there but the attribute of love, for it is only below that bad traces are left by means of his sin; but when he repents, he leaves good traces, and all is repaired, for he lifted up the levels to *Binah*, which is *ʾEhyeh*, etc. And he said that there is in this depth marvelous things, and the wise man will understand. — *Parashat Beshalaḥ*, p. 47c.

The *Toldot* contains a number of allusions to the hidden taste connected with the joy of the Sabbath, known to only a select few, such as: "it seems to me that one should understand the reason for feasting and joy on Sabbath and festivals, apart from the reason explained there,[62] but it seems to me ..., etc."[63] However, R. Ephraim of Sudylkow, the Besht's grandson and author of *Degel Maḥaneh ʾEfrayim*, knows something of the secret of "those who enter into the counsel of

60 See above, v. 20.

61 This entire problem is not discussed in *Sefer ha-Gilgulim* (a work of Lurianic Kabbalah), but the things are stated explicitly in the *Commentary to Hodu*; see above, vs. 23–24.

62 In the Lurianic Kabbalah?

63 There appears here an interpretation of the relationship of the body and the soul, which was not considered as esoteric teaching within the context of this circle.

the Lord," and he describes the raising up of the Shekhinah from the dust as an act which brings an enormous illumination to the soul, as if one were born anew:

> And he becomes as a new creature and a new-born infant, who is given new light in his soul which he did not have previously. And when he lifts up the Shekhinah, so to speak, there are lifted [with it] all of the lower levels and holy sparks with the Shekhinah, so to speak, which cling to it, as is known. Thus he becomes a passage-way for all those souls and holy sparks which require repair, so that by his means they receive *tiqqun* and have an ascent, and he is father of them all, and they are called his descendants ... And understand all this, for in it there are hidden things. — pp. 5d–6a.

Further on, he relates an oral tradition of the Besht, passed on to him through his father:

> "And God said to Abraham, Go you forth to the land which I will show you" [Gen. 12:1] ... [This refers to] the unification of *Qeri*ᵓ*at Shema*ᶜ, which he relates to you, as above ... "You" — that is, for the sake of building your soul; see that you give your soul for the sanctity of God, may He be blessed, etc.[64]

Indeed, the descent for the sake of lifting up the Shekhinah participates in this attribute of self-sacrifice for the sake of sanctifying God's Name! This is also a sublime level, particularly as not everyone knows its secret. The *Degel* issues the heartfelt call: "would that one could come to this level in truth," alluding to the sweetening of the judgments in their root. "And 'with this shall the maiden come to the king' [Est. 2:13] — and the enlightened one shall understand all this." (Ibid., p. 19c.) Elsewhere: "As my grandfather [i.e., the Besht] explained, 'And he shall remove her dress of captivity from off her' [Deut. 21:13]" (ibid., p. 25a). This passage in fact begins with a discussion of those alien thoughts which are "combinations" of evil letters, which must be changed into good combinations, but concludes, "that is, that he should see to it to smash and shatter and remove from her the dust and waste, to beautify her[65] and lift her up to her root — and understand." The *Degel* also refers to the secret of the relation of the *ẓaddiqim* to Matronita [i.e., the Shekhinah], whose messengers they are, in connection with the interpretation of the verse, "they shall surely come in joy" [Ps. 126:6], which also

64 *Degel Maḥaneh* ᵓ*Efrayim, Parashat Lekh Lekha,* p. 6a. See also p. 12d: "All things come from the Shekhinah... and are united in a complete unity... for all the matings are through *Da*ᶜ*at*. And this is [the phrase], 'Where [is the place of his glory'] in the *Qedushah* recited in the *Musaf* Prayer for the Sabbath. See there in the *kavvanot* of the Ari. And when unification is performed, birth is brought about — and understand."

65 This refers to Shekhinah and *devequt*.

relates to the secret of the combination of line and point[66] associated with Manasseh and Ephraim. It is unfortunate that the whole matter is not explained at greater length, even though the general intention is clear.[67] The presence of the erotic experience in divine worship is one of the distinctive signs of the Besht's teaching,[68] through which the doctrine of holiness is reflected as a transformation of evil through means of action. These are so to speak the birth-pangs of the Shekhinah,[69] which cannot "give birth to" good without the participation of evil. Likewise, the *ẓaddiq* is unable to reach the heights of *devequt* and purity without seriously entering into the realm of the *qelippah*, or without struggle with the world of Gehinnom and "the valley of weeping."[70] The ritual of descent into Sheol is only one symptom of this mood within the world of the Besht; a profound examination of all the parables and other teachings brought in his name will serve to clarify the new integration concerning the questions of God, the world, man and society, to be found in his teaching. This mood is built entirely upon the consciousness that evil has no independent existence; it only exists so long as one is unable to deal with it.[71] Victory over it lies in the awareness that, after thorough contemplation, one sees that everything is pure Divinity, pure good. This struggling contemplation uncovers that which is beyond the curtain of "Sheol," and forms the ideational background to the many parables brought in the name of the Besht, all of which are subject to the same interpretation — namely, the riddle of external phenomena — as well as the same solution — that the truth always shatters the illusion of the seemingly real world. The famous parable of the king who sent his servant to other countries to see whether they would rebel against him is the classical example of the Besht's approach to this matter; the wise ones among them said that, if it is the king's wish, they will accept it. They symbolize those who understood the law of the existence of the cosmos as a temptation behind which there stands the king himself, and no other element. The *Toldot* connects this parable with "the subject

66 Symbols borrowed from Lurianic Kabbalah, which were doubtless changed to sexual symbols. The secret of Manasseh and Ephraim refers to the verse, "he switched his hands" [Gen. 48:14], which evidently also alludes to a sexual matter.

67 The image of sexual union for the time of prayer appears several times in *Toldot* in the name of the Besht, and not only when referring to the act of descent in order to gather sparks: see *Parashat ʾAḥarei Mot*, p. 88c. In *Parashat Shelaḥ*, p. 131a–b: "... with casting off of the garment, and naked and with true union." Ibid., p. 139a–b: "I heard in the name of my teacher concerning the matter of the adornment of the bride, [a halakhah] that one must remove them in preparation for intercourse." All this is expounded in relation to the verse, "from my flesh I see God" [Job 19:26]!

68 See also *Ẓavaʾat ha-Riva"sh* (Jerusalem, 1948), p. 16: "Prayer is intercourse with the Shekhinah ..."

69 *Toldot Yaʿaqov Yosef, Parashat Naso*, p. 124b ff.

70 A concept used by the *Toldot*: "In the secret of 'those who pass through the vale of weeping.'" — MS. 5198, p. 10a. Used also by Menaḥem Mendel of Bar; see *Toldot Yaʿaqov Yosef, Parashat Ẓav*, p. 87b.

71 On early parallels to this stance, see Urbach, *Ḥazal*, pp. 143–144.

of the Evil Urge, which is compared in the *Zohar* to a harlot whom the king has commanded to seduce his son." He adds:

> But there is also in this an inner matter, as I heard from my teacher, concerning the subject of the Confession [beginning] ᵓ*Ashamnu* ("we have been guilty"), [namely,] that the king himself changed his garment and his speech and came to seduce the queen, etc. — and this is enough for one who understands. And this is a great thing, as I heard from my teacher ... And when this was made known to him, he removed the clothing and nullified the pain and all evil decrees. And he expanded upon this ... And this is the essence of the praise and song, which during the Exile of Egypt they thought to be the enemy, and now they feel to be the essence of Him, may He be blessed, that the enemy became their friend.[72] And this is the essence of the redemption, which is present in every person and at every time ... — *Parashat Va-yaqhel*, p. 67c–d.

Further on, it says:

> And when it becomes known that He Himself is there, the garment is put aside. And this is the matter of the Evil Urge, which will in the future become a holy angel, through the removal of the garment. And the entire matter of [the verse in] *Ḥad Gadya*, "Then the Holy One, blessed be He, came and slaughtered the angel of death," is to be understood in this way. — ibid., 67d.

On the face of it, this is an eschatological comment concerning what will take place at the End of Days; in fact, all these teachings involve an existential statement of opinion. There is an activist sense of breaking through the barriers of illusory reality, and the joy of discovering that everything is no more than "a change of clothing and language" of the king himself. Existence is, so to speak, a change of garment and a change of language: an enormous structure of misleading combinations of language which, when reversed and recombined through knowledge of this technique, will reveal the monistic world in which everything is divinity and everything within it is only good. To use the language of another parable:[73] he who dares to break through the endless walls surrounding the "palace

72 See an allusion to this homily above, Sect. III, on v. 13, where it is connected with a Rabbinic aphorism concerning Job.

73 See R. Jacob Joseph of Polonnoye, *Ben Porat Yosef*, p. 55a. This parable depicts man's attempt to break through the walls surrounding the king's palace in order to get to him, while once he gets there it becomes clear that they were not true walls at all, but that the king himself is present with him. Joseph Weiss's method of interpreting this homily seems to me close to the truth: "The alien thoughts and corporeality are only barriers to one who has not yet come into the secret of the doctrine of lifting up" — "The Beginning of the Hasidic Path," p. 99. R. Ephraim of Sudylkow also understood the interpretation of the matter in this way: see *Degel Maḥaneh ᵓEfrayim*, p. 77c–78. However, it seems to me that Weiss's view — namely, that the Besht did not innovate much concerning the question of the "descent," leaving room for R. Menaḥem Mendel of Bar to innovate — is mistaken. In my

of the King" will come to the knowledge that, in the final analysis, there were never really such walls at all.[74] The universe is an imaginary fortress of obstacles which are progressively nullified by the process of imaginary conquest; but one who is not ready for this quixotic war will never see the king beyond the ramparts of his fortifications. This is the price of the terrible paradox, around which the Hasidim felt, with more than a little justice, that one must spread a curtain of secrecy. The Besht's teaching on this critical point may be formulated by saying: this is a teaching of "the world as experience," but the nullification of the world as personal experience is here a mystical one, and not a cynical test. The truth is that it is no simple matter to represent the knowledge of the Creator as an experience which goes through the "vale of tears" or Sheol or Gehinnom — all depending upon the formula used — but neither is there any naivete here. Even if there were those who opposed it, the external rhythm for the realization of this consciousness is set by the ritual connected with it. Indeed, one can read between the lines[75] certain notes of opposition to the path of the Besht which arose within Hasidic society. At the beginning of this article,[76] I mentioned the testimony of *Shivḥei ha-Besht* concerning R. Gershon Kutover's opposition, or at least contempt, for the ritual of raising up the souls. *Toldot Yaᶜaqov Yosef* cites Menahem Mendel of Bar's protest against those people who do not support the *ẓaddiqim* who are capable of "descending to Gehinnom" in order to lift up the souls of the wicked. He adds his agreement in principle to the position of the Maggid of Bar, as follows:

> It is said, "Whoever exhibits contempt for a scholar, there is no healing for his injury." As I wrote in the name of the Maggid of Bar, our teacher Mendel, that this is according to what is said, "those who pass through the vale of tears,"[77] etc. — and the words of a sage are pleasant. Here too, it follows that, if one is prideful against a scholar who has descended to the level of Gehinnom in order to raise up the souls of the evil-doers from there, and is contemptuous of him and does not wish to cling to him, there is

opinion, R. Menaḥem Mendel of Bar grasped the social interpretation of this matter, leaving the ritual aspect and the mystical technique to the Besht.

74 E. E. Urbach pointed out to me that this seems to be the opposite of the stance expressed in the words of R. Judah b. Ilai, according to which the righteous says concerning the Evil Urge that is to be slaughtered in the future: "How were we able to conquer a mighty mountain such as this?" Sukkah 52a; cf. Urbach, *Ḥazal*, p. 620.

75 On the opposition to the creation of new rituals in all societies, see Scholem, "Tradition and New Creation" (op cit., n. 59). The above-mentioned "pure" interpretations which were given to the Besht's *Commentary* in the history of Hasidism (above, Section I, near the end), are typical of the spiritualization of ritual, while the explicit testimonies concerning the opposition to "acts of lifting up" against the actual social background are brought as testimony above by the author of the *Toldot*.

76 See above, Sect. I.

77 A technical term for the descent to Gehinnom.

> certainly no healing for this injury, for he is judged in the fire of Gehinnom, as is said, "on the pyre, on the fire, which does not swell up" [conflation of Lev. 6:2 and Job 20:26], etc. — *Parashat Ẓav*, p. 78c–d.

Elsewhere, he mentions the reason why many people do not wish to attach themselves to a *ẓaddiq* of the type who practices the descent into Gehinnom, but one can sense a certain confusion about the boundaries between the substantive and the social reason — i.e., this "descent" had a very specific social connotation, which continued to be expressed by the verbal formula of descent into Gehinnom. Between the lines, it seems to be that there were those whose opposition to the Baᶜal Shem's path of "descending to Gehinnom" was combined with their opposition to his descent to the "lowly" members of society, dressing like them so as to be equal to them and to be able to lift them up.[78]

In this context, it is worth noting an interesting literary phenomenon connected with the form of expression used by the Besht, which reveals the psychology of the consciousness of the abyss, of the caution demanded by this dangerous "game," and of the conscious "distance" between man and his environment. We find a play between total involvement and dedication, such as is found both in the ritual of the "abyss" and in the *kavvanot* of the *miqveh* (ritual bath), on the one hand, and between a clear-sighted sense of mastery over the world, on the other. Hence, there are parables concerning the lost son who disappeared somewhere into the world of impurity, carrying with him the secret of his mission, as well as the story of the two people who walked in a forest, one as drunk as Lot and the other sober, both of whom were beaten up by bandits: the drunk one did not even feel the bruises upon his body, whereas the sober one taught others how to be properly armed to protect themselves.[79]

Such parables always bear a rationalist message, albeit it is not always a rationality that says: do not go into the forest because there are bandits. An interesting biographical incident is mentioned by the *Toldot* in the name of the Besht, relating the secret of his mission to see "the suffering of those judged" in Sheol. This story carries a great deal of the power of standing in the gateway, whether one is speaking of the gate to Gehinnom or of the social implications of this stance:

> I heard a parable, in the name of my master, concerning a king who appointed four officials over his treasure house, who stole the treasure and fled. One changed his mind and came back; the second took counsel with a certain wise man who spoke to

78 See also ibid., p. 162b, in the name of R. Menaḥem Mendel of Bar: "... [those] who do not wish to descend to Gehinnom to raise up the evil-doers, do so because they are fond of the evil-doers"(!)

79 *Toldot*, *Parashat Ki Tavo*ᵓ, p. 194c–d.

his heart, [asking him] why he thought to do such a thing, and he also returned. The third came to a place where they judge people for such things, and came back out of fear. And the fourth did not return at all. The king gave the greatest honor to the one who repented by himself, since he decided by his own good sense to return. This was not the case of the second, of whom he said, that had he not found a wise man to counsel him thus, he would not have returned [at all]. The third, who came back because he saw how other people were judged, was appointed to be in charge there, so that he would see this pain. And our teacher said this concerning himself, etc., and understand this. — *Parashat Ẓav*, p. 75bff.

The Besht saw himself punished by needing to stand at the gate of Gehinnom, specifically because of the great pain and fear involved in it. There is perhaps more than a measure of sober humor in this story.

Glossary to the Text of the Besht's *Commentary to Hodu*

Niẓoẓot — Sparks. The lights which, according to Lurianic Kabbalah, were scattered in the world at the time of the primordial break (*Shevirah*).

Gilgul — Transmigration. This refers to sparks of the souls which fell into the abyss because of the sin of Adam and undergo a "refinement."

Tiqqun — Repair, Correction of the cosmic order.

Qelippot — Shells. Those souls which fell into the domain of the "remnants" after the *Shevirah* and were held captive there.

Sefirah, Ten Sefirot — The ten manifestations of the Godhead crystallizing within a given framework.

Binah. (Literally, "Intelligence). The name of the third *Sefirah* — i.e., *Keter*, *Ḥokhmah*, *Binah*.

ʾAbba ve-ʾImma — [The Supernal] Father and Mother, used to refer to the *Sefirot* of *Ḥokhmah* and *Binah*.

Ḥaqal, *Ḥaqal Tapuḥin* — "Apple orchard." A symbolic term designating the last *Sefirah*, *Malkhut*.

Keter — "Crown." Keter is the highest sefirah, also designated by the divine name *ʾEhyeh* ("I Am" — cf. Ex. 3:14].

Yesod — "Foundation." The ninth *Sefirah*, symbolizing the male organ within the divine world.

Malkhut — Kingship. The tenth and last *Sefirah*, symbolizing the feminine.

Tifʾeret — The sixth Sefirah, located at the center of the configuration of the six lower Sefirot, and symbolizes both the male and *Ḥesed*, as opposed to *Malkhut*, which is an attribute of *Din*.

Seventy-two letter Name. The 72 letter name corresponds to *Ḥokhmah*, from which was formed the "drop" to *vav*, which is *Tifʾeret*.

Kaf ha-Qela[c] — Palm of the Sling. A designation for the *qelippot*, in which the souls roll about as punishment after death.

HVYH — The Ineffable Divine Name, written in a different order, as it is forbidden to utter it as written.

Mayim Nuqvin — lit. "female waters." The waters emitted by the female in order to arouse the male. This alludes to the [religious] arousal which comes from *Malkhut*, towards *Tif'eret.*

Maḥshavot Zarot — Alien thoughts. Thoughts which are not related to the prayer upon which man is concentrating.

Nefesh–Ruaḥ–Neshamah. Parts of the soul.

'Or Ḥozer — Reflected light. According to Lurianic Kabbalah, the emanated light makes its way from the Infinite to within a vacuum, and returns to its source in a dialectic way.

Merkavah Ṭeme'ah — "Impure Chariot" — The domain of the *qelippot*, in contrast to the Holy Chariot, which is the world of the Sefirot.

Qelippat Nogah — The "Shell of Brightness" — the name of that *qelippah* which is closest to the world of holiness and which draws from it, thereby bringing light to the *qelippot*.

Bibliography

I. Hasidic Sources

Abraham ben Dov of Mezhirech (the "Malakh"), *Ḥesed le-ʾAvraham.* Jerusalem, 1954.

Abraham Ḥayyim of Zloczow, *ʾOraḥ la-Ḥayyim*, Jerusalem, 1960.

Asher Ẓevi, *Maʿayan ha-Ḥokhmah.* Korets, 1816.

Benjamin of Salositz, *Ahavat Dodim.* Lemberg, 1797.

——, *Amtaḥat Binyamin.* Minkewicz, 1796.

——, *Ṭorrei Zahav.* Mohilev, 1816.

Dov Baer of Mezhirech, *Maggid Devarav le-Yaʿaqov.* Critical edition, with Introduction, Commentary, Notes and Index by R. Schatz Uffenheimer. Jerusalem, 1976; Second, enlarged edition, 1990.

——, *Liqqutei Yeqarim.* Lemberg, 1865.

——, *ʾOr ha-ʾEmet.* Brooklyn, 1960. Photo ed. of Hussiatin, 1899.

——, *ʾOr Torah*, Jerusalem, 1956.

——, *Shemuʿah Ṭovah.* Warsaw, 1938.

Dov Baer b. Shneur Zalmam, *Tract on Ecstasy* [translation of his *Kuntres ha-Hitpaʿalut*], trans., L. Jacobs. London, 1963.

Elimelekh of Lyzhansk, *Noʿam ʾElimelekh.* Lemberg, 1874.

Eliezer ha-Levi Horwitz, *Noʿam Meggadim.* Lemberg, 1859.

Ḥayyim Ḥaykl of Amdur, *Ḥayyim va-Ḥesed.* Jerusalem, 1953.

Horowitz, Reuben, *Dudaʾim ba-Sadeh.* Lemberg, 1859.

Israel b. Eliezer, Baʿal Shem Tov, *Keter Shem Tov.* Zolkiew, 1784.

——, *Sefer Qatan.* Zhitomir, 1805.

——, *Ẓavaʾat ha-Riva"sh.* Jerusalem, 1948.

Issachar Baer of Zloczow, *Mevaser Ẓedeq.* Berdichev, 1817.

Jacob Ẓemah, *Naggid u-Meẓaveh.* n. p., n. d.

Jacob Joseph of Polonnoye, *Toldot Yaʿaqov Yosef.* Jerusalem, 1966. Photo edition of Korets, 1780.

——, *Ben Porat Yosef.* New York, 1954.

——, *Ketonet Passim*, ed. G. Nigal. Jerusalem, 1985.

——, *Ẓofnat Paneʿaḥ*, ed. G. Nigal. Jerusalem, 1989.

Jacob Joseph b. Judah of Ostrog, *Sefer Rav Yeivi.* New York, 1954.

Jeḥiel Michel of Zloczow, *Mayim Rabbim.* Jerusalem, 1964.

Joseph Bloch, *Ginzei Yosef.* 2 pts. Jerusalem, 1960.

Kalisker, Abraham, "Letters" (Heb.), *Ḥibbat ha-ʾAreẓ* (Jerusalem, 1897), pp. 70a–71b.

Kalonymus Kalman ha-Levi Epstein, *Maʾor va-Shemesh.* New York, 1958.

Kitvei Qodesh me-Ḥakhmei ʾEmet (contains works of R. Israel Baʿal Shem Tov, R. Dov Baer of Mezhirech, R. Levi Yitzḥak of Berdichev, and R. Israel of Kosnitz). Warsaw, 1884.

Leiberson, Ḥayyim b. Isaiah, *Ẓeror ha-Ḥayyim.* Belgoray, 1913.
Levi Yitzḥak of Berdichev, *Qedushat Levi ha-Shalem.* 2 pts. Jerusalem, 1958.
Margalioth, Meir, *Sod Yakhin u-Boᶜaz.* Satomare, n.d.
Menaḥem Mendel of Vitebsk, *Liqqutei ᵓAmarim.* Lemberg, 1911.
——, *Peri ha-ᵓAreẓ, ᶜim ᶜEẓ Peri.* Jerusalem, 1953.
Menaḥem Mendel of Przemyślany, *Darkhei Yesharim* (or *Hanhagot Yesharot*). Lemberg, 1865.
Mendele of Lesdka, *Darkhei Ẓedeq.* Lemberg, 1865.
Meshullam Feibush Heller of Zbarazh, *Derekh ᵓEmet.* Jerusalem, n.d.
——, *Yosher Divrei ᵓEmet.* Munkacs, 1905.
Mifᶜalot Ẓaddiqim. Lemberg, 1865.
Moses Ḥayyim Ephraim of Sudylkow, *Degel Maḥaneh ᵓEfrayim.* Josepof, 1883.
Moses Leib of Sasov, *Liqqutei Rama"l,* Lemberg, 1865.
Naḥum of Chernobyl, *Meᵓor ᶜEynayim.* Jerusalem, 1960.
Pinḥas of Korets, *Midrash Pinḥas.* Belgoray, 1931.
——, *Nofet Ẓufim.* Lemberg, 1864.
——, *Peᵓer la-Yesharim* (based upon the traditions of Raphael of Bershad). Jerusalem, 1921.
Reuben ha-Levi Horowitz, *Dudaᵓim ba-Sadeh.* Eretz-Yisrael, n.d.
Shivḥei ha-Besht. Ed., S. A. Horodetzki. Tel-Aviv, 1947.
Shmelke of Nikolsburg, *Divrei Shmuᵓel.* Jerusalem, n.d.
Shlomo of Lutsk, *Dibrat Shlomoh.* Jerusalem, 1955.
Shneur Zalman of Lyady, *Liqqutei ᵓAmarim: Tanya.* Brooklyn, 1954 (photo copy: Vilna, 1937. First published: Slavuta, 1796– 97). [English: *Lessons in Tanya,* elucidated by Y. Wineberg, trans., L. and S. B. Wineberg, ed., U. Kaploun. 3 vol. Brooklyn, 1987–1989.]
——, *Liqqutei Torah.* Vilna, 1885.
——, *Shaᶜar ha-Yiḥud veha-ᵓEmunah* [in all standard editions of *Tanya,* as above.]
Uziel Meisles, *Tifᵓeret ᶜUziel.* Tel-Aviv, 1962.
Yeḥiel Safrin of Komarno, *Netiv Miẓvotekha.* Lemberg, 1858.
Yehudah Ẓevi of Razdil, *Daᶜat Qedoshim.* Lemberg, 1848.
Yitzḥak of Radzivilow, *ᵓOr Yiẓḥaq.* Jerusalem, 1961. (first published edition, based upon MSS.)
Ẓaddok ha-Cohen of Lublin, *Peri Ẓaddiq.* 5 vol. repr. Jerusalem, 1965.
Zeᵓev Wolf of Zhitomir, *ᵓOr ha-Meᵓir.* New York, 1954.
Ẓevi Aryeh [Malik], *ᵓOr Ḥakhamim.* Warsaw, 1885.
Ẓevi Hirsch of Zhidachov, *ᶜAṭeret Ẓevi.* Jerusalem, 1966 [offset of ed. Lvov, 1872].
——, *Peri Qodesh Hilulim.* Arsciva, 1927.

II. Other Primary Sources

Baḥya ibn Paquda, *Ḥovot ha-Levavot.* Leipzig, 1846.
Delmedigo, Joseph Solomon, of Candia (*Yashar*), *Maẓref la-Ḥokhmah.* Jerusalem, n. d.
Gottlober, Abraham Baer, *Abraham Baer Gottlober un Zayn Epokhe.* Vilna, 1828.

Ḥayyim of Volozhin, *Nefesh ha-Ḥayyim.* Vilna, 1824 (rep., Benei-Berak, 1958).
Heller, Abraham, *Zerizuta de-ʾAvraham.* New York, 1952.
Horowitz, Isaiah, *Shenei Luḥot ha-Berit.* Amsterdam, 1695.
Israel of Zamosc, *Nezed ha-Demaᶜ.* Dyhrenfurth, 1773.
Israel Loebel, *ʾOzer Yisraʾel.* Shklov, 1786.
——, *Sefer ha-Vikuaḥ.* Warsaw, 1798.
Joseph Perl of Tarnopol, *Ueber des Wesen der Sekte Chassidim aus ihren Schriften gezogen im Jahre 1816.* Jerusalem–National Library, MS. Var. 293.
Maᶜalei Shabbata, in Isaiah Jacob ha-Levi of Alesk, *Bet Ḥokhmah* (Podgrozo, 1898).
Marcus, Aharon, *Qeset ha-Sofer.* Cracow, 1912.
Margaliot, Asher Zelig, *Maʾamar Tefillat Pataḥ ʾEliyahu.* Jerusalem, 1964.
Menaḥem Mendel of Prague, *Zeraᶜ Qodesh Maẓavtah.* Munkasc, 1893.
Moses b. Jacob of Satanov, *Mishmeret ha-Qodesh.* Zolkiew, 1746.
Mises, Judah Leib, *Qinʾat ha-ʾEmet.* Vienna, 1828.
Sefer Tehillot Shabbat. Pyetrikow, 1911.
Sod ᶜAvodah u-Moreh Ẓedeq. Slavita, 121.
Sofer, Moses, *Sheʾelot u-Teshuvot Ḥatam Sofer; ʾOraḥ Ḥayyim.* Pressburg, 1855.
Vidas, Elijah de, *Reshit Ḥokhmah.*
Vital, Ḥayyim, *Sefer ha-Gilgulim.*
——, *Shaᶜar ha-Kavvanot.*
Zweifel, Eliezer Zeʾev, *Shalom ᶜal Yisraʾel.* Zhitomir, 1868.

III. Manuscripts from the Institute for Hebrew Manuscripts and Microfilms, Jewish National Library, Jerusalem.

MS. 1467. Includes the version of the Maggid's teaching maintained by Shmelke of Nikolsburg.
MS. 3282. Contains, among other items, writings of the Maggid as maintained by Ḥayyim Ḥaykl of Amdur and his disciples.
MS. 3759. Collection of traditions from the disciples of R. Pinḥas of Korets.
MS. 4088. From fo. 139 on, there are recorded teachings of R. Ḥayyim Ḥaykl, and again a version of the Maggid's teaching.
MS. 5198. Teachings of the Besht, according to the traditions of R. Jacob Joseph of Polonnoye; includes the text of the *Commentary to Hodu.*
MS. 5301 (8°). Fos. 30–53 contain the diary of R. Israel Dov ha-Levi of Stepan.
Private photocopy of MS. Commentary to the Torah and to the Hagiographa in 3 volumes, (I have thus far seen only the second part), of R. Ẓevi Hirsch Yoles, author of *Qehillat Yaᶜaqov,* and a disciple of the Ḥozeh of Lublin, R. Menaḥem Mendel of Rimanov, and R. Elimelekh of Lyzhansk, containing many important traditions transmitted in the name of the Maggid.
Private photocopy of MS. of the teachings of the Maggid of Mezhirech, as transmitted by R. Levi Yitzḥak of Berdichev. This manuscript is extremely similar to large sections of

Maggid Devarav le-Ya^caqov, and seems to have served as one of the major sources from which that work was compiled. The present author's critical edition of that work draws extensively upon this MS.

IV. Secondary Literature

Aescoly–Weintraub, Aaron Ze^ɔev, *Le Hassidisme*. Paris, 1928.

Balaban, Meir, *Toldot ha-Tenu^cah ha-Franqit*. Tel-Aviv, 1934.

Ben-Menaḥem, Naftali, "Manuscripts from the Library of Rabbi Naḥum Dov-Bar Friedman of Sadigorai. Appendix: Letter from the Holy Rabbi Abraham Kalisker to the Holy Rabbi Shneur Zalman of Lyady" (Heb.), *Areshet* 1 (1960), pp. 405–413.

Ben-Shlomo, Yosef, "Gershom Scholem's Study of Pantheism in Kabbalah" (Heb.), in *Gershom Scholem; ^cal ha-^ɔIsh u-Fo^colo* (Jerusalem, 1983), pp. 17–31.

Bodek, Mendel, *Seder ha-Dorot he-Ḥadash*. n.p., n.d.

Bossuet, J. B., *Ouvrages sur le quiétisme* (Oueuvres completes. 10.) Besoncan, 1863.

Brawer, J. A., "On the Quarrel Between R. Shneur Zalman of Lyady and R. Abraham Kalisker" (Heb.), *Qiryat Sefer* 1 (1925), pp. 142– 150, 226–238.

Buber, Martin, *Be-Pardes ha-Ḥasidut*. Tel Aviv, 1945.

——, *Hasidism and Modern Man*. New York, 1958.

——, *The Legend of the Baal-Shem*. New York, 1955. [German original: *Die Legende des Baalschem*. Frankfurt, 1908.

——, *The Origin and Meaning of Hasidism*. New York, 1960.

——, *Tales of Rabbi Nachman*. New York, 1962. [*Die Geschichten des Rabbi Nachman*. Frankfurt, 1906.]

——, *Tales of the Hasidim*. New York, 1947–48. 2 vol. [*Erzählungen der Chassidim*. Zürich, 1949.]

——, "Antwort zum Dorstellung des Chassidismus," in *Martin Buber* [Philosophen des 20. Jahrhunderts. (Stuttgart, 1963)], pp. 626–635.

——, "Interpreting Hasidism," *Commentary* 36 (1963), 218–225.

Dinur, Ben-Zion, "The Origin of Hasidism and its Social and Messianic Foundations" (Heb.), in his *Be-mifneh ha-dorot* (Jerusalem, 1955), pp. 83–227 [English translation: *Essential Papers on Hasidism*, ed. G. Hundert (New York–London, 1991), pp. 86–208].

Dubnow, Simon, *Toldot ha-Ḥasidut ^cal yesod Meqorot rishonim*. 2 vol. Berlin, 1930–32.

——, "Hasidim as Law Breakers (An Episode from the Period of the Split between Hasidim and Mitnaggedim)" (Heb.), *ha-Shiloaḥ* 7 (1901), pp. 314–320.

——, "Writings of Opposition to the Hasidic Sect (Chassidiana)" (Heb.), *Devir* 1 (Berlin, 1923), pp. 289–305.

Dudon, P. *Molinos*. Paris, 1921.

Early Fathers from the Philokalia. Selected and translated from the Russian text *Dobrotolubiye* by E. Kadloubovsky and G. E. H. Palmer. London, 1954.

Eckhardt, Johannes. *Meister Eckhardt: an introduction to the Study of his Works with an anthology of his Sermons*, selected and translated, J. M. Clark. London, 1957.

Elior, Rachel, *Torat ha-Elohut be-dor sheni shel Ḥasidut Ḥabad*. Jerusalem, 1982.
——, "ḤaBaD: The Contemplative Ascent to God," *Jewish Spirituality [II]*, ed. A. Green. [World Spirituality. 14. (New York, 1985)], pp. 157–205.
——, "'Yesh' and 'Ayin': Basic Paradigms in Hasidic Thought," in *Proceedings of the First International Conference on Hasidic Thought, Dedicated to the Memory of Joseph Weiss*. (London, 1992).
Etkes, Emanuel, *R. Yisraʾel Salanter ve-reshitah shel Tenuʿat ha-Musar*. Jerusalem, 1984.
——, "R. Ḥayyim of Volozhin's System and Activity as the Reaction of Mitnaggedic Society to Hasidism" (Heb.), *PAAJS* 38–39 (1972), pp. 1–45.
Federbush, Simon, ed., *Ha-Ḥasidut ve-Ẓion*. Jerusalem, New York, 1963.
Friedman, Maurice, "Interpreting Hasidism: The Buber-Scholem Controversy," *Yearbook of the Leo Baeck Institute* 33 (1988), pp. 449–467.
Gelber, N. M., *Toldot Yehudei Brod, HShM"D–TSh"G ⟨1584–1943⟩* (ʿArim ve-ʾImahot be-Yisraʾel. 6.). Jerusalem, 1955.
Glikson, R., *Der Kotsker Rebbe*. Warsaw, 1938.
Graetz, Heinrich, *History of the Jews*. 6 vol. Philadelphia, 1956. [Originally published in German: *Geschichte der Juden*. 11 bd. Leipzig, 1900.]
Green, Arthur, *Devotion and Commandment; The Faith of Abraham in the Hasidic Imagination*. Cincinnatti, 1989.
——, *Tormented Master; A Life of Rabbi Nahman of Bratslav*. University, Ala., 1976.
——, "Typologies of Leadership and the Hasidic Ẓaddiq," *Jewish Spirituality [II]*. [World Spirituality. 14. (New York, 1985)], pp. 127–156.
Guttman, Matityahu, *R. Yisraʾel Baʿal Shem Tov*. Yasi, 1922.
Haberman, A. M., "Sefer *Ẓavaʾat ha-Riva"sh* and Other Early Collections of the Besht's Words; A Bibliographical Listing" (Heb.), *Sefer ha-Besh"t*, ed. J. L. Maimon (Jerusalem, 1960), pp. 48–49.
Heilman, Ḥayyim Meir, *Bet Rabbi*. Jerusalem, 1953.
Heppe, H. L. J., *Geschichte der quietistischen Mystik in der Katholischen Kirche*. Berlin, 1875.
Heschel, Abraham Joshua, *The Circle of the Baal Shem Tov: Studies in Hasidism*, translated and edited by Samuel B. Dresner. Chicago–London, 1985.
——, *Kotzk; ein gerangl far Emeskeit* (Yiddish). 2 vol. Tel-Aviv, 1937.
——, "Rabbi Naḥman of Kosow: Companion of the Baal Shem" (Heb.), *Sefer ha-Yovel li-khevod Ẓevi Wolfson* (New York, 1965), pp. 113–141. [English: *Circle of the Baal Shem Tov*, pp. 113–151.]
——, "Rabbi Pinḥas of Korzec" (Heb.), in *ʿAlei ʿAyin* [Schocken Jubilee Volume] (Jerusalem, 1948–52), pp. 213–44; English: *The Circle of the Baal Shem Tov*, pp. 1–43.
——, "Umbekante Dokumenten tsu der Geshikhte fun Hassidus" (Yiddish), *YIVO Bletter*, 36 (1952), pp. 113–135.
Hoffmann, N., Introduction to Madam Guyon, *Zwölf geistliche Gespräche*. Jena, 1911.
Horodetsky , S. A., *Ha-Ḥasidim veha-Ḥasidut*. 4 vol. in 2. Tel-Aviv, 1953.
Idel, Moshe, *Kabbalah; New Perspectives*. New Haven–London, 1988.
Ish-Horowitz, S. J., *Ha-Ḥasidut veha-Haskalah; Maḥsahvot ʿal devar ha-Ḥasidut ha-Yeshanah (ha-Beshtit) veha-Ḥadashah*. Berlin, 1911.

Jacobs, Louis, *Hasidic Prayer*. London, 1972.

—, *Seeker of Unity*. New York, 1966.

Jacobson, Yoram, "The Doctrine of Creation in R. Shneur Zalman of Ladi" (Heb.), *ᵓEshel Beᵓer Shevaᶜ* 1 (1976), pp. 307–368.

Jones, Rufus, *Studies in Mystical Religion*. London, 1909.

Kahana, David, *Toldot ha-Mequbalim ha-Shabbetaᵓim veha-Ḥasidim*. Odessa, 1913–14.

Katz, Jacob, *Masoret u-Mashber*. Jerusalem, 1958. English: *Tradition and Crisis*. New York, 1961.

Knox, Ronald A., *Enthusiasm; a Chapter in the History of Religion*. Oxford, 1951.

Liebes, Yehudah, "R. Naḥman of Braslav's *Tiqqun ha-Kelalli* and its Relation to Sabbatianism" (Heb.), *Ẓion* 45 (1980), pp. 201–245.

—, "The Sabbath *Zemirot* of the Holy Ari" (Heb.), *Molad* ns 4, no. 23 [27, no. 223] (1972), pp. 540–555.

Mahler, Raphael, *Hasidism and the Jewish Enlightenment*. Philadelphia, 1985. [Originally published in Yiddish and in Hebrew: *Ḥasidut ve-Haskalah*. Merhavyah, 1961.]

Maimon, Salomon, *Solomon Maimon: An Autobiography*, ed., M. Hadas. New York, 1947.

Pechenik, Aaron ha-Levi, "Chronicle of One Hasidic Dynasty" (Heb.), *Shanah be-shanah; TShK"Z* (Jerusalem, 1967), pp. 379–396.

Philokalia. See: *Early Fathers from the Philokalia*.

Pourrat, P., "Molinos." *Dictionnaire de théologie catholique*. Paris, 1899–1950. Vol. X: 2187–2192.

—, "Quiétisme," ibid., Vol. XIII: 1537–1581.

Rabinowitz, Zvi Wolf, *Ha-Ḥasidut ha-Litaᵓit me-reshitah ᶜad Yameinu*. Jerusalem, 1961.

Schatz, Rivka, "Anti-spiritualism in Hasidism — Studies in the teaching of R. Shneur Zalman of Lyady" (Heb.), *Molad*, 20, nos. 171–72 (1963), pp. 513–528. [English: in this volume, Chapter 12]

—, "Autonomy of the Spirit and the Teaching of Moses: Studies in the Teaching of R. Mordecai of Izbica" (Heb.), *Molad* 21, no. 183–184 (1963), pp. 554–561.

—, "The Besht's Commentary to Psalm 107 — Myth and Ritual" (Heb.), *Tarbiẓ* 42 (1973), pp. 154–184. [English: in this volume, Appendix].

—, "Diary of an Agnostic Hasid" (Heb.), *Molad* ns 5, nos. 25 -26 [nos. 235–36] (1972), pp. 135–145. [English: in this volume, Chapter 13]

—, "The Doctrine of the *Ẓaddiq* in R. Elimelekh of Lyzhansk" (Heb.), *Molad* 18: 144, no. 45 (1960), pp. 365–378.

—, "'Freedom on the Stones' — Theology under the sign of a Crisis of Authority" (Heb.), *Yediᶜot Aḥaronot*, December 3, 1977 [Scholem Eightieth Birthday Supplement].

—, "Hasidism," *Encyclopaedia Judaica* (Jerusalem, 1971), VII: 1407–1420. [passim reprinted in this volume, Introduction, Sect. ii and v]

—, "Hillel Zeitlin's Path to Jewish Mysticism" (Heb.), *Kivvunim* 3 (1979), pp. 81–91.

—, "The Influence of Gnostic Literature on R. Shlomo Molcho's *Sefer ha-Mefoᵓar* (Heb.), in *ha-Mistiqah ha-Yehudit ha-Qedumah*, ed., J. Dan [*Meḥqerei Yerushalayim be-Maḥshevet Yisraᵓel.* 6, nos. 1–2] (Jerusalem, 1987), pp. 235–267.

—, "The Interpretation of Hasidism as an Expression of Scholem's Idealistic Outlook"

(Heb.), in *Gershom Scholem; ʿal ha-ʿIsh u-Foʿolo*, pp. 48–62. [Englisn: in this volume, Introduction, iii–iv]
——, "Introduction" (Heb.), *Maggid Devarav le-Yaʿaqov*, ed., R. Schatz, pp. ix–xxiii.
——, "Kabbalah — Tradition or Innovation (An Historical Perspective)" (Heb.), in the *Memorial Volume for Ephraim Gottleib*, ed. A. Goldreich and M. Oron (forthcoming).
——, "Maharal's Conception of Law — Antithesis to Natural Law Theory," *The Jewish Law Annual* 6 (1987), pp. 109–125.
——, "Man Facing God and the World in Buber's Interpretation of Hasidism" (Heb.), *Molad* 18: 149–150 (1960), pp. 596–609.
——, "Moses Ḥayyim Luzzatto's Thought Against the Background of Theodicy Literature" (Heb.), *Proceedings of the Israel Academy of Science and Humanities* 7, no. 12 (1988), pp. 275–291.
——, "Professor Raphael Mahler, Militant Historian" (Heb.), *Kivvunim* 33 (1986), pp. 197–199.
——, "R. Moses Cordovero and R. Isaac Luria — Between Nominalism and Realism" (Heb.), *Meḥqerei Yerushalayim be-Maḥshevet Yisraʾel*, No. 3 (1982), pp. 122–136.
——, "Ramḥal's Metaphysics in Their Ethical Context (A Study in *Qela"ḥ Pitḥei Ḥokhmah*)" (Heb.), *Sefer ha-Yovel le-Shlomo Pines, II* [*Meḥqerei Yerushalayim be-Maḥshevet Yisraʾel*. 9] (Jerusalem, 1990), pp. 361–396.
——, "Utopia and Messianism in the Thought of Rabbi Kook" (Heb.), *Kivvunim* 1 (1979), pp. 15–27.
——, "Visions of 'The Secret of the King Messiah' — An Early Source from a Sabbatian Apostate" (Heb.), *Sefunot* 12 [*Sefer Yavan*. 2] (Jerusalem, 1978), pp. 217–252.
Scholem, Gershom, *Devarim be-go*. 2 vol. Tel Aviv, 1976.
——, *Major Trends in Jewish Mysticism*. New York, 1945.
——, *The Messianic Idea in Judaism and other essays on Jewish Spirituality*. New York, 1971.
——, *On Jews and Judaism in Crisis; Selected Essays*. New York, 1976.
——, *On the Kabbalah and Its Symbolism*. New York, 1965. [German: *Zur Kabbala und ihrer Symbolik*. Zurich, 1960.]
——, *Origins of the Kabbalah*. Trans., A. Arkush. Philadelphia -Princeton, 1987. Originally published in German: *Ursprünge und Anfänge der Kabbala*. Berlin, 1962.
——, *Reshit ha-Qabbalah, 1150–1250*. Jerusalem, 1948.
——, *Sabbatai Ṣevi; The Mystical Messiah, 1626–1676*, trans., R. J. Z. Werblowsky (Bollingen Series. 93.) Princeton, 1973; originally published in Hebrew: *Shabbatai Ẓevi veha-Tenuʿah ha-meshiḥit be-yemei ḥayyav* 2 vol. Tel-Aviv, 1957.
——, *Von der Mystischen Gestalt der Gottheit*. Zurich, 1962. [English: *On the Mystical Shape of the Godhead; Basic Concepts in the Kabbalah*. New York, 1991.]
——, "Devekut, or Communion with God," in *The Messianic Idea in Judaism*, pp. 203–227; originally published in *Review of Religion* 14 (1949–50), pp. 115–139.
——, "The Historical Image of R. Israel Baʿal Shem Tov" (Heb.), *Devarim be-go*, pp. 287–324; originally published in *Molad*, 18, nos. 144–45 (1960), pp. 335–356.
——, "Martin Buber's Interpretation of Hasidism," in *The Messianic Idea in Judaism*, pp.

227–250. [Originally published: *Commentary* 32 (1961), pp. 305–316].
——, "The Meaning of the Torah in Jewish Mysticism," in *On the Kabbalah and its Symbolism*, pp. 32–86; German: "Der Sinn der Tora in der jüdischen Mystik," in *Zur Kabbala und ihrer Symbolik*, pp. 49–116.
——, "The Neutralization of the Messianic Idea in Hasidism," in *The Messianic Idea in Judaism*, pp. 176–202; originally published in *JJS* 20 (1970), pp. 25–55.
——, "New Material on R. Israel Löbel and his anti-Hasidic Polemic" (Heb.), *Ẓion* 20 (1955), pp. 153–162.
——, "The Polemic Against Hasidism and Its Leaders in the Book *Nezed ha-Dema*ᶜ" (Heb.), *Ẓion*, 20 (1955), pp. 73–81.
——, "Redemption Through Sin," in *The Messianic Idea in Judaism*, pp. 78–141; [Hebrew: *Kenesset* 2 (1937), pp. 347–392.]
——, "Reflections on Jewish Theology," in *On Jews and Judaism in Crisis*, pp. 261–297.
——, "Revelation and Tradition as Religious Categories in Judaism," in *The Messianic Idea in Judaism*, pp. 282–303; German: "Tradition und Commentar als religiöse Kategorien im Judentum," *Eranos Jahrbuch* 31 (1962), pp. 19–48.
——, "The Science of Judaism — Then and Now," in *The Messianic Idea in Judaism*, pp. 304–313. [Originally published in German: "Wissenschaft vom Judentum einst und jetzt," *Judaica [I]*. [Bibliothek Suhrkamp. 106. (Frankfort am Main, 1963)], pp. 147–164.
——, "Die 36 verborgengen Gerechten von der jüdischen Tradition," *Judaica [I]* (Frankfort am Main, 1963), pp. 216–235.
——, "Tradition and New Creation in the Ritual of the Kabbalists" in *On the Kabbalah and Its Symbolism*, pp. 118–157; German: "Tradition und Neuschöpfung Riten der Kabbalisten," in *Zur Kabbala und inhrer Symbolik*, pp. 159–207.
——, "The Two Earliest Testimonies Concerning Hasidic Circles and the Besht" (Heb.), *Sefer ha-Yovel le-R. Naḥum Epstein* (Jerusalem, 1950), pp. 228–240.
——, "Two Letters from the Land of Israel from the Years 1760–1764" (Heb.), *Tarbiẓ* 25 (1956), pp. 429–440.
——, "The Unconscious and the Pre-Existence of the Intellect in Hasidic Literature" (Heb.), *Devarim be-go*, pp. 351–360; originally published in: *Hagut; teshurah le-Sh. H. Bergman bi-meloᵓt lo shishim shanah* (Jerusalem, 1944), pp. 145–151.
Shochat, A., "On Joy in Hasidism" (Heb.), *Ẓion* 16 (1951), pp. 30–43.
Teitelbaum, Mordecai, *ha-Rav mi-Ladi u-Mifleget Ḥaba"d*. Warsaw, 1913.
Tishby, Isaiah, *Torat ha-Ra*ᶜ *veha-Qelippah be-Qabbalat ha-Ar"i*. Jerusalem, 1942.
——, "Between Sabbatianism and Hasidism" (Heb.), in his *Netivei ᵓEmunah u-Minut* (Ramat Gan, 1964), pp. 204–226; originally published in *Knesset; Divrei Sofrim le-zekher Ḥ. N. Bialik* 9 (1945), pp. 238–268.
——, "The Controversy Concerning *Sefer ha-Zohar* in 16th Century Italy" (Heb.), *Ḥiqrei Qabbalah u-sheluḥoteha, I* (Jerusalem, 1982), pp. 79–130.
——, (with Joseph Dan), "Hasidism" (Heb.), in *Enẓeqlopedyah ha-ᶜIvrit*. Vol. 17 (Jerusalem–Tel-Aviv, 1964–65), pp. 769–821.
——, "'The Holy One, blessed be He, Torah and Israel are all One' — The Source of this Aphorism in Ramḥal's Commentary to the *ᵓIdra Rabba*" (Heb.), *Qiryat Sefer* 50 (1975), pp. 480–492.

——, "The Messianic Idea and Messianic Tendencies in the Growth of Hasidism" (Heb.), *Ẓion* 32 (1967), pp. 1–45.
——, "The *Tiqqunei Teshuvah* of R. Nathan of Gaza" (Heb.), in his *Netivei ᵓEmunah u-Minut*, 30–51; originally published in *Tarbiẓ* 15 (1944), pp. 161–180.
Underhill, Evelyn, *Mysticism; a Study in the Nature and Development of Man's Spiritual Consciousness*. New York, 1955.
Verses, Samuel, "Hasidism in the World of Berdychewski" (Heb.), *Molad* ns 1, no. 24 (1968), pp. 465–475.
Weiss, Joseph G., *Meḥqarim be-Ḥasidut Braslav*. Jerusalem, 1974.
——, *Studies in Eastern European Mysticism*, ed. D. Goldstein. London, 1985. [below: *Studies*]
——, "R. Abraham Kalisker's Concept of Communion with God and Man," *JJS* 6, no. 2 (1955), pp. 87–99 [reprinted in *Studies*, pp. 155–169].
——, "The Beginnings of the Hasidic Path" (Heb.), *Ẓion* 16: 3–4 (1951), pp. 46–105.
——, "Contemplative Mysticism and 'Faith' in Hasidic Piety," *JJS* 4, no. 1 (1953), pp. 19–29 [reprinted in *Studies*, 44ff.]
——, "The Kavvanot of Prayer in Early Hasidism," *JJS*, 9 (1958), pp. 163–192 [reprinted in *Studies*, pp. 95–125].
——, "Studies in R. Nahman of Braslav's Self-Understanding" (Heb.), *Meḥqarim be-Ḥasidut Braslav*, pp. 150–171 [originally published in *Sefer ha-Yovel li-khivod Gershom Scholem bi-meloᵓt lo shishim shanah* (Jerusalem, 1958), pp. 232–245].
——, "Via passiva in early Hasidism," *Journal of Jewish Studies* 11: 3–4 (1960), pp. 137–155 [reprinted in *Studies*, pp. 69–83].
Werblowsky, R. J. Zvi, "Faith, Hope and Trust: a Study in the Concept of Bittahon," *Papers of the Institute of Jewish Studies, London* (Jerusalem, 1964), pp. 95–139.
——, "On the Mystical Rejection of Illumination and Revelation of Secrets" (Heb.), *ᶜIyyun* 14 (1964), pp. 205–212.
Wertheimer, *Halakhot ve-Halikhot ba-Ḥasidut*. Jerusalem, 1960.
Wilensky, Mordecai, *Ḥasidim u-Mitnaggedim; le-toldot ha-pulmus she-beineihem be-shanim tq"l–tqᶜ"h [1772–1815]*. 2 vol. Jerusalem, 1970.
——, "A Criticism of *Sefer Toldot Yaᶜaqov Yosef* (A Document from the Period of Hasidic-Mitnaggedic Polemics)" (Heb.), *The Joshua Starr Memorial Volume. Studies in History and Philology* (New York, 1953), pp. 183–189. [the text from *Shever Posh'im* is reprinted in his *Ḥasidim u-Mitnaggedim* II: 144–150.]
Zeitlin, *ᶜAl Gevul Shenei ᶜOlamot*. Tel-Aviv, 1976.
——, *Be-Pardes ha-Ḥasidut veha-Qabbalah*. Tel-Aviv, 1965.

Index of Names

Index of Subjects